Yes to Europe!

On 5 June 1975, voters went to the polls in Britain's first national referendum to decide whether the UK should remain in the European Community. As in 2016, the campaign shattered old political allegiances and triggered a far-reaching debate on Britain's place in the world. The campaign to stay in stretched from the Conservative Party – under its new leader, Margaret Thatcher – to the Labour government, the farming unions and the Confederation of British Industry. Those fighting to 'Get Britain Out' ranged from Enoch Powell and Tony Benn to Scottish and Welsh nationalists. Footballers, actors and celebrities joined the campaign trail, as did clergymen, students, women's groups and paramilitaries. In a panoramic survey of 1970s Britain, Robert Saunders reveals the full history of the referendum for the first time, asking why voters said 'Yes to Europe' and why the result did not, as some hoped, bring the European debate in Britain to a close.

Robert Saunders is a Senior Lecturer at Queen Mary University of London. He is the author of *Democracy and the Vote in British Politics, 1848–1867* (2011) and co-editor (with Ben Jackson) of *Making Thatcher's Britain* (Cambridge, 2012). He appeared in the BBC TV series *The Victorian Slum* (2016) and has given interviews and commentary on the BBC, CNN and a wide range of media outlets.

Yes to Europe!

The 1975 Referendum and Seventies Britain

Robert Saunders
Queen Mary University of London

CAMBRIDGE
UNIVERSITY PRESS

University Printing House, Cambridge CB2 8BS, United Kingdom

One Liberty Plaza, 20th Floor, New York, NY 10006, USA

477 Williamstown Road, Port Melbourne, VIC 3207, Australia

314–321, 3rd Floor, Plot 3, Splendor Forum, Jasola District Centre,
New Delhi – 110025, India

79 Anson Road, #06-04/06, Singapore 079906

Cambridge University Press is part of the University of Cambridge.

It furthers the University's mission by disseminating knowledge in the pursuit of
education, learning, and research at the highest international levels of excellence.

www.cambridge.org
Information on this title: www.cambridge.org/9781108425353
DOI: 10.1017/9781108340915

First published 2018
First paperback edition 2019

Printed in the United Kingdom by TJ International Ltd. Padstow Cornwall

A catalogue record for this publication is available from the British Library.

Library of Congress Cataloging-in-Publication Data

Names: Saunders, Robert, 1978- author.
Title: Yes to Europe! : the 1975 referendum and seventies Britain / Robert
    Saunders.
Description: New York, NY : Cambridge University Press, 2018. | Includes
    bibliographical references and index.
Identifiers: LCCN 2017059348| ISBN 9781108425353 (hardback) | ISBN
    9781108442244 (paperback)
Subjects: LCSH: Referendum—Great Britain. | Europe—Economic integration. |
    Great Britain—History. | BISAC: HISTORY / Europe / Great Britain.
Classification: LCC JF497.G7 S258 2018 | DDC 341.2420941/09047—dc23 LC
record available at https://lccn.loc.gov/2017059348

ISBN 978-1-108-42535-3 Hardback

ISBN 978-1-108-44224-4 Paperback

Contents

List of Figures   *page* vii
Acknowledgements   xi

Introduction: 'A Fanfare for Europe'   1

Part One: Europe or Bust?   27

1   Opportunity and Illusion: The Road to 1975   29

2   'A Device of Dictators and Demagogues':
    Renegotiation to Referendum   63

3   'Support Your Local Continent!' Britain in Europe   99

4   'Better Out Than In': The National Referendum
    Campaign   130

Part Two: Themes and Issues   153

5   'The Boardroom Must Lead!' Employers, Unions
    and the Economy   155

6   'Women and Children First!'   183

7   'Come to Pray on Referendum Day'   210

8 'No Good Talking About Sovereignty'   231

9 'The New British Empire'   254

10 'Think of It as the Common Supermarket'   278

Part Three: The Unravelling of Britain?   297

11 'Ulster Says Yes!'   299

12 Cymru yn Ewrop: Wales in Europe   324

13 'The Scottish Time-Bomb'   345

Epilogue: 'We Are All Europeans Now'   365

Appendix 1: The Referendum Result, 5 June 1975   383
Appendix 2: Note on Prices   387
Notes   389
Select Bibliography   469
Index   489

Figures

I.1 Edward Heath signs the Treaty of Accession in 1972. The ceremony was delayed by 55 minutes when a protestor threw a bottle of ink over Heath. Source: Hulton Deutsch, Corbis Historical: www.gettyimages.co.uk/license/613503132 5

I.2 Steeleye Span outside the Royal Albert Hall, 15 January 1973: Frank Barratt/Stringer, Hulton. Source: Archive: www.gettyimages.co.uk/license/3281658 6

I.3 Margaret Thatcher in her 'Yes to Europe' jumper, 4 June 1975. Source: P. Floyd/Stringer, Hulton Archive: www.gettyimages.co.uk/license/641305251 9

I.4 Workers in Bond Street wear duvets to keep warm during power cuts, in the winter of 1973–4. Source: Evening Standard, Hulton Archive: www.gettyimages.co.uk/license/2669881 19

1.1 'The baroque courtesy of two men with murder in their eyes'. Cabinet colleagues Tony Benn and Roy Jenkins debate membership on BBC *Panorama*, 2 June 1975. David Dimbleby holds the ring. Source: Chris Djukanovic, Hulton Archive: www.gettyimages.co.uk/license/451356139 30

1.2 Enoch Powell in full rhetorical flame, at a Get Britain Out meeting in 1974. Source: Wesley, Hulton Archive: www.gettyimages.co.uk/license/508726306 54

2.1 *Sunday Express*, 23 March 1975. Cummings/Express Newspapers/N&S Syndication 67

2.2 Jim Callaghan had castigated the 'Tory terms' in Opposition, but as foreign secretary led the Labour renegotiations. Source: Rolls Press/Popperfoto: www.gettyimages.co.uk/license/80751192 82

2.3 Roy Jenkins faces a hostile audience at the Labour
Party special conference in April 1975. The banner behind him
reads 'Conference will advise. The People will decide'. Source:
Graham Wood, Hulton Archive: www.gettyimages.co.uk/
license/451329611   95

2.4 Every household was sent three pamphlets: one by each of
the campaign vehicles and a third – controversially – by the
government, advocating the renegotiated terms. Source:
Keystone France. www.gettyimages.co.uk/license/107415730   95

2.5 The ballot paper used in the referendum, referring
both to 'the European Community' and 'the Common
Market'   97

3.1 'The most powerful all-party coalition since the War'.
Jeremy Thorpe, Edward Heath and Roy Jenkins team up to
'Keep Britain in Europe'. Source: Keystone, Hulton Archive.
www.gettyimages.co.uk/license/451329613   100

3.2 'It is with some temerity that the pupil speaks before the
master.' Thatcher tries, unsuccessfully, to butter up her
predecessor as they launch the Conservative Yes campaign,
17 May 1975. Source: Central Press, Hulton Archive:
www.gettyimages.co.uk/license/118582787   111

3.3 Harold Wilson at an eve-of-poll rally in Sophia Gardens,
Cardiff. Source: Media Wales. www.walesonline.co.uk/
news/politics/15-photos-show-how-life-11389370   116

3.4 Margaret Thatcher lights a torch for Europe at a youth
rally in Parliament Square, beneath the statue of Churchill.
Source: P. Floyd, Hulton Archive: www.gettyimages.co.uk/
license/641305205   122

4.1 Protestors set sail for France, 17 April 1972. Police
boarded the vessel, prompting the so-called 'Battle of
Calais'. Source: Keystone-France. www.gettyimages.co.uk/
license/107421744   133

4.2 'Out of Europe – and into the World'. Eric Deakins,
Bob Harrison and Peter Shore at a press conference.
Source: J. Wilds, Hulton Archive: www.gettyimages.co.uk/
license/3298518   135

4.3 The *Sun* cartoonist Franklin declines to abandon ship
with Tony Benn, Barbara Castle, Michael Foot, Enoch

Powell and Peter Shore. 2 June 1975. The Sun/News
Syndication 147

4.4 Tony Benn makes a pitch for the No vote at a rally in
Cardiff. Source: Media Wales 150

5.1 'Impact Europe'. The Confederation of British Industry's
mobile conference centre, which criss-crossed the country
in 1972 helping business prepare for entry to the Common
Market. Source: CBI Archive 160

6.1 Lady Avebury, the Liberal who ran Britain in Europe's
Women's Office with the Conservative Ann Money-Coutts.
Source: Frank Barratt, Hulton Archive: www.gettyimages
.co.uk/license/3265968 187

6.2 'I will always say YES to Europe'. Racing cars and racy
slogans in South Glamorgan. Source: Media Wales 189

6.3 Barbara Castle, her great-niece Rachel Hinton and Joan
Marten show off the results of their shopping trip to Brussels.
Source: Keystone, Hulton Archive: www.gettyimages.co.uk/
license/3260793 200

6.4 The 'blond and vivacious' Vicki Crankshaw shows off
the results of her own shopping trip to Oslo. Source:
Evening Standard, Hulton Archive. www.gettyimages.co.uk/
license/2638474 201

6.5 Roy Jenkins radiates enthusiasm. Source: Rolls Press/
Popperfoto: www.gettyimages.co.uk/license/80751456 202

10.1 People queue for bread in London, during a bakers'
strike in 1974. Source: Evening Standard, Hulton Archive:
www.gettyimages.co.uk/license/3273301 293

11.1 An armed soldier on patrol passes anti-Market graffiti
in Northern Ireland. Source: With permission of Victor
Patterson 303

12.1 Mrs Anna Williams, aged 102, delivers her ballot to the
Swansea Guildhall. Source: Media Wales 325

12.2 Women in traditional Welsh costume rally for Europe
in Cardiff. Source: Media Wales 336

13.1 An SNP view: Scotland as the reluctant bridegroom in
a marriage of English convenience. *Scots Independent*,
May 1975, p. 6. Source: © Scots Independent
Newspapers Ltd 355

E.1 Harold Wilson waits to discover the results of the
     referendum. *The Sun*, 6 June 1975. The Sun/News
     Syndication   367
E.2 'Caesar's Triumph', *Daily Express*, 7 June 1975.
     Cummings/Express Newspapers/N&S Syndication   368

Acknowledgements

This book could never have been written without the kindness and generosity of other scholars. I am especially grateful to all those who gave up their time to advise on reading, share their research or comment on draft chapters. My particular thanks to Sam Brewitt-Taylor, Jo Byrne, Saul Dubow, James Ellison, Martyn Frampton, Matthew Grimley, Ben Jackson, Martin Johnes, Helen McCarthy, Alex Middleton, Richard Moore-Colyer, Marc Mulholland, Glen O'Hara, Barbara Taylor, David Torrance and Martin Wilcox, all of whom read and commented upon sections of the text. They are, of course, not responsible for the hash I may have made of their advice. I am also enormously grateful to Alwyn Turner and Philip Williamson, who generously shared their own research on changes in prices and incomes and on days of prayer.

The unsung heroes of any research project are the librarians and archivists without whom researchers would peer gibbering into the void. I am especially grateful to the staff of the Bodleian Library; the British Library; Cardiff University Library; the Church of England Record Office; Churchill Archives Centre; the Conservative Party Archive; the John Sainsbury Archive; the Labour History Archive and Study Centre at the People's History Museum, Manchester; Lambeth Palace Library; the London School of Economics (LSE); the Linen Hall Library, Belfast; the Museum of London Docklands; the National Archives; the National Library of Scotland; the Parliamentary Archive; the Women's Library at the LSE; and the Modern Records Centre, University of Warwick. My thanks to all those who gave permission to reproduce material, including the Confederation of British Industry; the Literary Executors of Roy Jenkins; the Trustees of the Literary Estate of the late J. Enoch Powell; the Conservative Party;

the Labour History Archive; the Parliamentary Archive; and the John Sainsbury Archive.

A number of those who were involved in the campaigns in 1975 gave generously of their time to answer my questions, including Lady Kina Avebury, Sir Tony Baldry, Baroness Betty Boothroyd, Gyles Brandreth, Lord Deben (John Selwyn Gummer), Donald Hardie, Erskine Holmes, Sir John Mills, Berrie O'Neill, David Peter, Fiona Ross-Farrow, Jim Sillars, Diana Villiers Negroponte and Gordon Wilson. I would like to pay special tribute to Lady Avebury and Gordon Wilson, who died before the completion of this book. They were among the most generous and helpful of my interviewees, and it was a privilege to be able to draw on their expertise.

This book was begun at Oxford University, researched and largely written at Queen Mary University of London, and completed back at Oxford as a Visiting Researcher. I am grateful to both institutions for keeping the wolf from the door and for asking only the right number of times when the book was likely to be finished. I have been exceptionally fortunate with my colleagues in both universities, and am thankful to Tim Bale, Saul Dubow, Alex Gajda, Peter Ghosh, Sara Hobolt, Ben Jackson, Reuben Loffman, Helen McCarthy, Alex Middleton, Grant Tapsell and many others for expressing enthusiasm for the book at times when my own was running low. I am particularly grateful to my three Heads of School at Queen Mary – Miri Rubin, Colin Jones and Julian Jackson – for their support throughout the writing of this book. My thanks, too, to Ross McKibbin, William Whyte and St John's College, Oxford, and to the Oxford Centre for European History, for hosting me as a Visiting Researcher.

The key to any book lies in the support of friends and family. I am more grateful than I can say to my parents, Andrew and Penny Saunders, for all their love and support, and to my siblings, Patrick, Timothy and Sara. My warmest thanks are also due to Patrick Porter and Jane Rogers for their friendship, fine cooking and long hours gassing away about the state of the world. Will Thomas showed extraordinary patience in enduring me as a flatmate for three years, even as the tide of books on British and European politics surged inexorably across the communal areas of the flat. Special thanks go to my friend and colleague James Ellison, who read a substantial chunk of the manuscript and provided invaluable feedback. His generosity, encouragement and unflagging enthusiasm for the book contributed enormously both to its (sometimes glacial) progress and to the pleasure I had in writing it.

Finally, I would like to dedicate this book to my godson, William Smith. He will be relieved to discover that there is a cricket match towards the end.

INTRODUCTION: 'A FANFARE FOR EUROPE'

At the bar a florid man in a black suit was predicting the imminent collapse of the nation. He gave us three months, he said, then curtains.

John Le Carré, *Tinker, Tailor, Soldier, Spy* (1974)[1]

In effect, what they were saying was that the final collapse of capitalism might be a matter of weeks away.

Tony Benn, 5 December 1974[2]

This year's referendum is more than a hands up for or against Europe. It is one aspect of a disintegrating political order.

The Guardian, 21 May 1975[3]

On 23 June 2016, the United Kingdom voted to leave the European Union. That verdict, in only the third UK-wide referendum in its history, struck British politics like an earthquake at sea. Within hours a tidal wave had built up that would sweep through Westminster and Whitehall, demolishing a political order established just a year earlier at the general election. Over the days that followed, the prime minister announced his resignation, Labour MPs declared war on their leader and the Scottish government began preparations for a second independence vote. Global financial markets, which had surged in the expectation of a vote to stay in, lost more than $2 trillion in a single day of trading, while the pound dropped to its lowest level for thirty years.[4]

For good or for ill, the vote in 2016 overturned the central pillar of British economic and diplomatic policy since the 1960s. Scrabbling for a precedent, commentators likened what had happened to the break-up of Yugoslavia, the fall of the Berlin Wall and the collapse of the British Empire.[5] For those who had campaigned to leave, 23 June marked Britain's 'Independence Day', when voters 'took back control' of their destiny.[6] For their opponents in the Remain camp, defeat was like a bereavement, stirring feelings of loss, anger and disbelief. A study by the London School of Economics claimed that more than half of Remain voters wept or felt close to tears on learning of the result.[7]

It had all been so different four decades earlier. On 5 June 1975, just two years after joining what was then the European Community (or 'Common Market'), voters had gone to the polls in the UK's first referendum on membership. The result was a landslide, with a majority of more than two-to-one for staying in. Voters endorsed membership by 67.2 per cent to 32.8 per cent, the biggest mandate ever achieved in a national election, almost exactly reversing the state of the polls the previous autumn. The Labour prime minister, Harold Wilson, told reporters that the European debate was now closed. 'Fourteen years of national argument', he proclaimed, 'are over.'[8]

The parallels between the two votes are intriguing. Harold Wilson, like David Cameron, was a reluctant European, convinced with his head rather than his heart of the case for membership. Like his successor, he led a divided party with a tiny majority in Parliament, at a time of rising hostility to membership among the public. Both deployed the referendum as an instrument of domestic political management, calling in the electorate as a political bomb-disposal unit to deal with an explosive issue on their own backbenches. It was Wilson who pioneered the offer to renegotiate the terms of membership and put them to the public in a referendum, which Cameron would repeat in his Bloomberg Speech of January 2013. Cameron followed the Wilson playbook almost to the letter; yet when he sought to replicate his predecessor's success, the device blew up in his hands.[9]

Writing shortly after the 1975 referendum, the political commentator Anthony King called it 'one of the half-dozen most important events in post-war British history'. It ranked, in his view, alongside the Attlee governments, the Suez crisis and the fall of the British Empire in scale and significance.[10] Yet it has attracted none of the attention lavished on those other historical milestones. Dominic Sandbrook, in his popular history of the 1970s, calls it 'The Referendum Sideshow', while *The Official History of Britain and the European Community*, a multi-volume project sponsored by the Foreign Office, dedicates just twelve pages to the referendum campaign.[11] Neglected by historians and political scientists, 1975 has become the property more of myth than of history.

This can be explained partly by what did *not* happen. The electorate did not, as in 2016, overturn the decision of Parliament or reverse the settled policy of successive governments. Its actions did not spark a political crisis, nor end the career of a prime minister. Voters in 1975 did not compel politicians to enact measures they had previously described as disastrous, nor challenge the authority of the political establishment. It was this, thought the *Daily Express*, that constituted the real significance of the vote. 'We are still a United Kingdom,' it exulted. 'We are still a sensible kingdom.' 'The most encouraging lesson of the referendum is that the centre held.'[12]

Yet the importance of what happened in 1975 is not simply negative. This was the first national referendum in British history: the first time that a front-rank political question had been taken out of the hands of Westminster and passed directly to the electorate. That marked a major constitutional innovation, at a time when there was widespread talk of a 'crisis of government'. The referendum challenged the right and even the capacity of MPs to embody the will of their constituents, striking a lasting blow against the sovereignty of Parliament.

The referendum took the European question out of Whitehall and into the country, triggering the only really sustained debate the British had ever had on their role in the world. Businesses produced newsletters, advising customers and employees how to vote. Shops issued carrier bags saying 'Yes to Europe', while Sainsbury's backed membership in its customer magazine. Bishops preached sermons on the blessings of integration, while a quarter of churches held services and days of prayer. In Northern Ireland, experiencing one of the bloodiest years of 'the Troubles', Republican and Loyalist paramilitaries formed an uneasy alliance against membership. The future Speaker of the House of Commons, Betty Boothroyd, held discussions in factory canteens, while the Women's Institutes, the Townswomen's Guilds and the Rotary Club all hosted meetings. Campaign literature was distributed in Gujarati, Hindi, Punjabi and Welsh, and when the BBC screened a live debate from the Oxford Union, in the week before the poll, nearly 11 million people tuned in to watch.[13]

The result was the most full-throated endorsement the public have ever given of membership of the European project. Every part of the United Kingdom voted to stay in, with the exception only of Shetland and the Western Isles. Industrial towns and agricultural districts, Labour heartlands and Tory citadels, all said 'Yes' to Europe. As the *Daily Express* put it, in a jubilant editorial: 'Britain's Yes to Europe' had rung 'louder, clearer and more unanimous than any decision in peacetime history'. The result had shown 'decisively' and 'irrevocably' that 'Britain belongs to Europe'.[14]

This was to prove unduly optimistic; yet the *Express* was right about the significance of what had happened. The decision to remain in the European Community set the course of British history for a generation. Membership would reshape how Britain was governed, who it traded with and who had the right to live or work in the country. Its consequences would be felt in every area of national life: from trade policy and employment law to the criminal justice system and the peace process in Northern Ireland. Over the decades that followed, the European question would pulse like an electric charge through British politics, splitting the Labour Party in the 1980s, the Conservative Party in the 1990s and fracturing the political landscape again in 2016. It drove the two most successful challenger parties of modern times – the Social Democratic Party and the UK Independence Party – and has brought the future of the United Kingdom itself into question. As the dust settles on a second referendum, its capacity to inflame political passions has lost none of its explosive potential.

'A FANFARE FOR EUROPE'

The United Kingdom had joined the European Community on 1 January 1973: sixteen years after the Treaty of Rome and twelve years after its first abortive application. Entry marked an epoch in national history; perhaps 'the most profound revolution in British foreign policy in the twentieth century'.[15] For the first time in the modern era, the UK had pooled its sovereignty with an alliance of Continental states. For the first time since the Reformation, its courts would be subject to an authority outside the British Isles, interpreting laws drawn up not just in Westminster but in Brussels and Strasbourg. In return, it was hoped, Britain would 'be able once again to play a worthy role in the world', gaining a voice in the destinies of a continent.[16]

For Edward Heath, the Conservative prime minister who had negotiated membership, entry was a turning point in British history.

FIGURE I.1   Edward Heath signs the Treaty of Accession in 1972. The ceremony was delayed by 55 minutes when a protestor threw a bottle of ink over Heath. Source: Hulton Deutsch, Corbis Historical: www.gettyimages.co.uk/license/613503132

Heath had come to power in 1970 promising 'nothing less' than 'to change the course of history of this nation', through 'a change so radical, a revolution so quiet and yet so total, that it will go far beyond the programme for a Parliament'.[17] Joining the European Community was fundamental to that ambition. Heath's politics had been forged in the decade before 1945, when war in Europe had brought the continent to the brink of destruction. As a student in the 1930s, he had travelled through Germany and witnessed a Nazi rally at Nuremberg. He had visited Spain during the Civil War, witnessing at close hand the bombing of Barcelona. During the Second World War he had fought in France and Belgium, before ending the conflict in the shattered city of Hanover. European unity, he believed, was not only an economic necessity but a moral imperative. 'Only by working together', he wrote later, could nations 'uphold the true values of European civilization'.[18]

    It had taken three attempts to secure membership, and ministers celebrated with a two-week festival of culture: a 'Fanfare for Europe', showcasing more than 300 different events. The Queen attended a gala opening at the Royal Opera House, conducted by Benjamin Britten and Colin Davis, with performances by Janet Baker, Judi Dench, Laurence Olivier and Elisabeth Schwarzkopf. Europe's most celebrated conductor, Herbert von Karajan, brought the Berlin Philharmonic to the Royal Albert Hall, while Bernard Haitink led the London Philharmonic in Vaughan Williams' Fourth Symphony. There was a televised service of thanksgiving at Coventry Cathedral, famously rebuilt out of the rubble of the Blitz, while a Festival of European Art gathered treasures from across the Continent. Ministers had hoped to borrow the Bayeux Tapestry for display in Westminster Hall, but it was felt that the subject matter – involving the invasion, conquest and butchery of the native population – struck an unduly sanguinary note.[19]

The Fanfare offered something for all tastes. There was a vintage car rally from London to Brussels; a special episode of the talent show, *Opportunity Knocks*; and a beauty contest won by the Dutch model Sylvia Kristel (soon to find fame in the erotic movie franchise, *Emmanuelle*). Slade rocked the London Palladium, the Kinks played at Drury Lane, and there were performances by the Chieftains and Steeleye Span. At Wembley Stadium, a football match pitted the three new member states – Denmark, Ireland and the United Kingdom – against the six founder members. Bobby Charlton captained the home team, Bobby Moore renewed his rivalry with Franz Beckenbauer and 'the Three' won comfortably by two goals to nil.[20]

FIGURE I.2   Steeleye Span outside the Royal Albert Hall, 15 January 1973: Frank Barratt/Stringer, Hulton.
Source: Archive: www.gettyimages.co.uk/license/3281658

Sitting in the Royal Opera House on 3 January, Heath was in buoyant mood: 'my heart', he recalled later, 'was full of joy that night'.[21] Yet the fat lady was singing for Heath in more senses than one. The Fanfare was a flop: Wembley Stadium was half empty, events were sparsely attended and the government was accused of squandering £350,000 of public money. Opinion polls, which had shown a slender majority for entry in January, quickly turned sour. By August, more than half of respondents thought Britain had been 'wrong' to join the Common Market; by Christmas, opponents of membership enjoyed a fourteen-point lead. By March 1974, just 12 per cent of the electorate 'believed that we had obtained any benefit as a result of membership'.[22] An official at the Department of Trade and Industry likened the public to 'a crowd of holidaymakers who, after much doubt and expense, have made a dangerous journey only to find the climate chilly, the hotel not what it was cracked up to be and the food too expensive'. Ominously for the government, he concluded, 'bloodthirsty feelings are mounting, not only towards the other nationalities in the hotel but to the courier who got them there'.[23]

The mood in Whitehall was similarly grim. When John Hunt became Cabinet secretary in November, he was struck by the 'smell of death hanging over the government'.[24] With his premiership disintegrating under the pressure of a miners' strike, Heath was driven into an early election in February 1974. Defeat brought to power a Labour government under Harold Wilson, who shared none of Heath's fervour for the Community. The Labour manifesto promised 'a fundamental renegotiation of the terms of entry', to be followed by a referendum or a general election. It ended with a stark warning: if new, more satisfactory terms could not be agreed, Labour would seek a mandate from the public for 'our withdrawal from the Communities'.[25]

'A DEVICE OF DICTATORS AND DEMAGOGUES'

The decision to hold a referendum was highly controversial. The *Sun* called it a 'constitutional monstrosity': a 'rotten', 'silly', 'alien' and 'unconstitutional' device that menaced the very survival of democracy.[26] Margaret Thatcher, in her first major speech as Leader of the Opposition, labelled it 'a device of dictators and demagogues' and refused to confirm that her party would be bound by the result.[27] For its supporters, by contrast, the referendum promised a rare injection of democracy into a system that seemed more often to frustrate the popular will than to express it. Tony Benn, the paladin of the Labour Left, had been arguing since the 1960s that a mature, educated electorate could no longer be satisfied with 'the five-yearly cross on the ballot paper'. Always an enthusiast for new technology, he predicted that there would soon be an electronic button in every household, making possible 'a new popular democracy' in place of 'parliamentary democracy as we know it'. Regular plebiscites, he hoped, would make governments truly accountable to the public, while enlarging both 'the responsibility and understanding of ordinary people'.[28]

What followed was the first national election of the modern era to be fought outside the conventional party system, a fact that posed real challenges to all involved. The national co-ordinating groups, many of whose activists had little experience of electoral politics, struggled to police the legal guidelines on 'treating' and fundraising. Broadcasters, likewise, found it difficult to apply rules of impartiality and fair coverage to an electoral landscape whose contours were so unfamiliar. New alliances had to be constructed, often along the most unlikely lines. The campaign to get Britain out brought together left-wingers such as Tony Benn and Michael Foot; the right-wing populist Enoch Powell; Ulster Protestants such as Ian Paisley and James Molyneaux; and groups ranging from the National Front to the Communist Party of Great Britain. The 'In' campaign was led by a Labour home secretary, Roy Jenkins, and counted among its vice-presidents a former Conservative prime minister, the president of the National Farmers' Union and the former general secretary of the Trades Union Congress. In the constituencies, party activists found themselves working cheerfully with sworn political enemies, in a festive atmosphere that reminded some of the Christmas truce.[29]

The suspension – or, more accurately, the confusion – of party allegiances opened a space for an unusual array of campaigning forces. Voluntary organisations and ad hoc alliances played a larger role than was conventional in UK elections, while the faces that looked down from posters were those not of politicians or diplomats but of sportsmen, actors and public intellectuals. Star recruits for the Yes campaign included the boxer Henry Cooper, the Olympic gold medallist Mary Peters, and the captain of the British and Irish Lions, Willie John McBride; the No campaign claimed the support of the footballing superstar George Best, memorably described as 'the Enoch Powell of British football'.[30] Women's voices were especially prominent, and close attention was paid to the votes of immigrant communities.

THROUGH THE LOOKING GLASS

Attitudes to the European question have changed significantly over time, both within and between parties. In 1975 it was the Conservative Party that was most enthusiastically European. Margaret Thatcher, newly elected as party leader, stumped the country demanding 'a massive Yes' to Europe, resplendent in a woolly jumper knitted from the flags of the member states.[31] The Labour Party was much more hostile, with a majority of its MPs, activists and some of the biggest names in Cabinet fighting to get Britain out. Newspapers that would later become fiercely critical of the EU – including the *Sun*, the *Daily Mail* and the *Daily Express* – campaigned fervently to stay in. Of the national press, only the *Spectator* and the Communist *Morning Star* backed withdrawal.

The geography of the European debate was also very different. Support for membership was strongest in England, especially in counties with a strong Tory vote such as Buckinghamshire, Surrey, West Sussex and North Yorkshire. Lincolnshire and Essex, which produced the four highest votes to leave in 2016, backed membership in 1975 by 74.7 per cent and 67.6 per cent respectively.[32] Scotland, Wales and Northern Ireland were more hostile, with Plaid Cymru, the Scottish National Party, Sinn Féin and the Democratic Unionist Party all campaigning for a No vote.[33] In 1975, as in 2016, it was feared that the referendum might tear the United Kingdom apart; but in the 1970s, the

FIGURE I.3   Margaret Thatcher in her 'Yes to Europe' jumper, 4 June 1975.
Source: P. Floyd/Stringer, Hulton Archive: www.gettyimages.co.uk/license/641305251

nightmare was that England would vote to *stay in*, while the rest of the UK voted to leave. The future leader of the SNP, Alex Salmond, was just one who campaigned for a No vote, telling reporters that 'Scotland knows from bitter experience what treatment is in store for a powerless region of a Common Market.'[34]

This was reflected in the spread of issues. Immigration, which dominated the campaign in 2016, was barely mentioned in 1975. The number of EEC nationals applying for settlement in the UK actually *dropped* after British entry, as deteriorating economic conditions made the country ever less attractive as a destination for migrant workers.[35] Outside Northern Ireland, where there was some concern about Catholic migration from the South, there was more concern about the *outward* movement of people, with anti-Marketeers warning that the unemployed would be 'forced to leave Britain to find jobs' on the Continent.[36] Conversely, issues like food prices, fishing and the Common Agricultural Policy consumed large amounts of airtime in the 1970s, yet were almost invisible forty years later.

A referendum is nominally a single-issue campaign, yet in practice the debate is rarely restricted to the question on the ballot paper. This was exacerbated in 1975 by the form of campaigning. 'Britain in Europe', the wealthier of the two co-ordinating groups, conducted extensive polling, which it used to target particular cohorts of the electorate. Dedicated campaign vehicles were created for every conceivable constituency: 'Actors for Europe', 'Christians for Europe', 'Communists for Europe', even – for one glorious moment before the leadership intervened – 'Wombles for Europe'.[37] High-level organisers were assigned to work with trade unionists, women, immigrants and professional groups, crafting messages that were tailored to the concerns of each cohort. The result was not simply to carry the European debate into unlikely places (though articles addressed to single parents, Commonwealth citizens and paramilitaries did precisely that). Just as importantly, the effect was to bring the referendum into contact with a much wider range of issues and concerns, so that what had begun as a vote on the European Community became a larger debate about the 'state of the nation'.

What bound all this together was a series of core questions and concerns. Elections do not take place in a vacuum: they respond to the context and climate in which the vote is held. Four themes were especially prominent in 1975: the memory of war; the ongoing struggle between East and West; the search for a new world role; and, above all, a powerful sense of domestic crisis.

'NATIONALISM KILLS'

For the generation that voted in 1975, war in Europe was not an abstract concept. It was only thirty years since the end of World War II; indeed, voters in 1975 were closer to the end of the *First* World War than voters in 2016 were to the *Second*. The campaign was punctuated by the chronologies of war, for the thirtieth anniversary of Victory in Europe fell a month before the vote, while the results were announced on the thirty-first anniversary of D-Day. For many who took part in the campaign, these were personal, not simply public, anniversaries. Tony Benn had served with the Royal Air Force; Denis Healey had fought with the Royal Engineers; while Willie Whitelaw won the Military Cross as a tank commander. Enoch Powell had served in military intelligence, while Roy Jenkins was a code-breaker at Bletchley Park. Neil Marten, the Conservative MP who ran the 'Out' campaign, had been parachuted behind enemy lines to fight with the Resistance; his opposite number in the European Movement, Ernest Wistrich, had escaped from Poland before the Nazi invasion. Wistrich subsequently fought for both his old country and his new, taking to the skies with the Polish division of the RAF.[38]

The memory of war was not restricted to those who had lived through it. As the historian Geoff Eley has written, '"remembering" World War Two requires no immediate experience of those years', for subsequent generations 'grew up suffused in the effects of the war'. Whether in the form of the ration book, national service or the bomb damage that still scarred Britain's towns and cities, the legacies of war were concrete and tangible, and they were bound together by the stories (and silences) of parents, teachers and public figures.[39] Popular culture, too, was pervaded by memories of conflict. The war movie had been a staple of British cinema during the 1950s and '60s, while TV shows such as *Dad's Army* (1968–77) and *It Ain't Half Hot Mum* (1974–81) used the war as a comic backdrop. ITV's monumental, 26-part series *The World at War* ran weekly from October 1973 to May 1974, ending with the single word 'remember' projected onto the television screen. Just months after the referendum, in October 1975, John Cleese would goose-step through one of the most famous episodes of *Fawlty Towers*, shrieking 'Don't mention the War!' at his horrified guests.[40]

Memories of war saturated the referendum campaign, though their significance was fiercely contested. For some, the surrender of national sovereignty to the EEC was a betrayal of all those who had fought and died 'to deliver Europe from Nazi dictatorship'.[41] As a woman from Bournemouth wrote to Barbara Castle, 'I ... did not fight and suffer a war for six years to be dictated to by the Germans.' Anti-German sentiment was rarely expressed in public – and was openly mocked in programmes like *Fawlty Towers* – but it loomed large in MPs' postbags. 'Hitler's ghost', wrote another correspondent to Castle, 'must be shaking with laughter at Roy Jenkins, Hattersley & the rest of the traitor crew.' Such letters often emphasised the price that had been paid for freedom, either personally ('I lost the boy I was engaged to') or in the nation's continuing economic problems ('Saving France and all the other countries has cost us dear'). Some viewed the Community as a new power-grab by Germany, a country which 'on two occasions ... has failed to conquer the British militarily'. The conviction that Britain had been 'sold up the river with the French & two war Germans' caused real anger, with pro-Marketeers likened to the 'Quislings' who would have surrendered to the Nazis in 1940. The notion 'that the GERMANS love us any more today than they did in 1914 & 1939' was dismissed with contempt. 'The leopard does not easily change its spots.'[42]

Campaign officials rarely endorsed such sentiments, but anti-Marketeers did very consciously evoke the language of wartime resistance. The Common Market Safeguards Campaign published a newspaper called *Resistance News*, and the group of MPs around Neil Marten was known as the 'R' Group for the same reason. Such language evoked the war as a struggle for national independence, with the Battle of Britain and the Blitz as its exemplary conflicts. 1940 loomed large in such retellings, recalling a time when Britain had 'stood alone' against overwhelming odds. Only by voting for independence could the living 'honour the memory of the dead', who had 'made the supreme sacrifice in order to maintain our freedom'.[43]

This was linked to a memory of appeasement. Anti-Marketeers likened the Treaty of Accession to the Munich Agreement of 1938, remembered as a craven act of surrender by the 'guilty men' of British politics. Christopher Frere-Smith, who ran the Get Britain Out campaign, warned repeatedly that accession to the Common Market marked a 'new Munich', with Heath and Jenkins playing the roles of

Chamberlain and Halifax.[44] Voters should not be 'fooled by the press bosses and the establishment politicians. They were wrong about Hitler and they're wrong again.'[45]

Pro-Marketeers also invoked the war years, though they drew a different moral. Here the emphasis was on the horror of war, which had devoured millions of lives in the prosecution of national rivalries. Britain in Europe used the poppy, the flower of remembrance, in its literature, while its logo was a dove of peace. 'Nationalism kills', warned a poster. 'No more Civil Wars'. Another, published for the anniversary of victory in Europe, noted that 'On VE Day we celebrated the beginnings of peace. Vote Yes to make sure we keep it.' In perhaps the most powerful slogan of the campaign, a third poster read simply: 'Forty million people died in two European wars this century. Better lose a little sovereignty than a son or daughter.'[46]

For many in the Yes campaign, the war remained the central reference of their politics. The Conservative MP Sir Anthony Meyer, who would later challenge Margaret Thatcher for the Tory leadership, recalled how 'virtually all my friends were killed' during the Second World War. It was the 'senseless waste of human life', he wrote, and 'the absolute conviction that untrammelled national sovereignty is *the* cause of war ... [that] made me enthusiastic about a united Europe'.[47] Heath, likewise, appealed explicitly to the war in an emotional radio broadcast in 1971:

> Many of you have fought in Europe, as I did, or have lost fathers, or brothers, or husbands who fell fighting in Europe. I say to you now, with that experience in my memory, that joining the Community, working together with them for our joint security and prosperity, is the best guarantee we can give ourselves of a lasting peace in Europe.[48]

For the advocates of membership, their opponents had misread the experience of the 1930s. For Roy Jenkins, the most important lesson of this period was 'the sheer impossibility of opting out of events across the Channel'. The British had 'shouted plenty of words of warning and encouragement from the touchline; but until it was far too late we pretended we were not needed on the field of play. Tens of millions of people paid for that mistake with their lives.'

Jenkins also challenged the romantic image of Britain in 1940, 'standing alone' against the continental dictators. Between the fall of

France and the declaration of war by the United States and the Soviet Union, he argued, Britain had been *compelled* to stand alone; but the central focus of its diplomacy had been to find new allies and to return to the Continent in arms. There was 'the world of difference', he noted tartly, 'between standing alone because others have succumbed and you have survived, and standing alone because others are successfully co-operating and you are sulking in a corner'.[49]

COLD WAR AND COMMON MARKET

It was not just past conflicts that loomed over the campaign. The referendum came at a moment of particular anxiety in the Cold War, that great ideological struggle that framed so much of British history after 1945. The same newspapers that were reporting the referendum debate also brought news of the fall of Saigon, the defeat of American forces in Vietnam and the seizure of a US merchant ship, the *Mayaguez*, by the Khmer Rouge. There were fears that Portugal, which had overthrown the authoritarian regime of the *Estado Novo* the previous year, might fall under Communist influence, giving the Soviets a foothold on Europe's western seaboard. If Portugal became 'Europe's Cuba', other countries might soon be drawn into its orbit.[50] The governor of California and Republican presidential hopeful, Ronald Reagan, told a dinner in London that Russia possessed 'all the important elements to substantially alter the political map of Europe'. The *Spectator* agreed: 'The world balance of power is undergoing a major shift and ... the shift is all in favour of the Communists.'[51]

As Reagan was aware, European vulnerabilities fed off concerns about American strength and resolve. The United States was undergoing its own internal convulsions in the wake of Watergate, the civil rights movement and the impeachment of Richard Nixon. With the collapse of the Bretton Woods system, it seemed that America might be entering a period of protectionism, introspection and even isolationism, preoccupied by internal violence, the 'culture wars' ignited by Vietnam and the faltering of the US economy. 'The Pax Americana', thought the *Guardian*, was 'eroding', and Europe could no longer rely upon its protection.[52]

Such fears were widely ventilated during the referendum. Harold Wilson told the Cabinet at the end of 1974 that 'American leadership had gone,' while Roy Jenkins claimed that the capacity of the United States to protect its allies – 'the dominant feature of the 20 years from 1948 to 1968' – had 'declined substantially'.[53] Others predicted that Washington would reduce its military commitments in Europe, or that 'the loss of face in south-east Asia' would see America return to 'isolationism'. A correspondent to the *Scotsman* warned that the peoples of Europe 'no longer have around them a shield of invincible American power … They must stand as a united Europe, or fall.'[54]

The European Community did not, of course, have a direct military function, though the idea had been under discussion since the 1940s. It did, however, fortify the economies of western Europe, binding its members into a prosperous, free market bloc that was resistant to Soviet influence. Speaking at the NATO Council a week before the referendum, Harold Wilson told the assembled ministers that 'it is no good having a credible external defence if our economies collapse'.[55] The existence of the EEC, as the shadow defence secretary, George Younger, put it, provided NATO with 'a firm economic base', giving potentially unstable countries a stake in the prosperity of the West.[56] Heath urged the public to remember the fate of 'the weak and divided nations of Eastern Europe after 1945', now reduced to the status of 'Soviet satellites'. 'British withdrawal', he warned, would constitute 'the biggest blow to the defence of the West in the past 20 years'.[57]

If, as even right-wing newspapers believed, American influence was now in retreat, it was more important than ever that Europe should find 'a common purpose against Communist ambitions and subversions'.[58] This gained urgency as countries like Greece, Portugal and Spain began to emerge from decades of authoritarian rule. Shirley Williams told supporters that, if Britain withdrew, the Community 'would be subjected to powerful strains which might even break it up'. Without that support network, 'the emerging democracies of Greece and Portugal would be damaged, perhaps fatally'.[59] Roy Jenkins warned that withdrawal would put the security of western Europe 'more heavily at risk than at any time since the Marshall Plan and the foundation of NATO'.[60]

The Communist threat was a particular feature of Heath's rhetoric. In a series of apocalyptic speeches, he claimed that a 'vote against the Market could lead to a Soviet invasion of Europe'. Isolationist tendencies in the US, he believed, would be exacerbated by the spectacle of a continent quarrelling among itself. Divided at home and friendless abroad, western Europe would become 'a sitting target for a Soviet

Union with an insatiable appetite'.[61] Some feared that Britain itself, outside the shelter of the Community, could fall victim to Communist penetration. It was enough for some on the Right that the USSR and the Communist Party of Great Britain wanted the UK to leave (though Communist China wanted Britain to remain in), or that a No vote was the outcome favoured by the Labour Left.[62] A vote to leave, warned Tory literature, would give 'Bennery' the biggest electoral endorsement it had ever received, heralding a 'siege economy' and the return of rationing.[63]

Anti-Communist rhetoric could reach levels that would have embarrassed Senator McCarthy. The *Daily Express* likened anti-Marketeers to those Nazi sympathisers who would have welcomed a German invasion in 1940, and wondered which side Tony Benn would be on if the Soviets threatened Britain.[64] A Scottish industrialist told a meeting in Glasgow that the only alternative to the Common Market was 'to draw close to, or perhaps even become a member of the Communist bloc'.[65] In similar vein, the Conservative MP for Bournemouth East, John Cordle, told constituents that Britain 'would become a communist state if we were to leave the market'. 'Each one of us, if we really wanted to do something to help Britain, would be knocking on the doors of everyone in sight and saying: "For God's sake, it's a question of communism".'[66]

At a time when ministers felt the need to ask voters 'Who Governs Britain?' even some on the Left feared for the survival of democratic politics. George Brown, a former foreign secretary, stressed 'the narrowness of the margin ... between maintaining present democratic institutions and losing them, perhaps for ever'. Unless Europe stood together, a 'concerted effort at a Communist takeover could swamp the democratic heritage of Western Europe'.[67]

For a Conservative anti-Marketeer like Neil Marten, who had never so much as waved a red flag, the idea that a No vote would sweep in the Communist millennium was absurd and offensive. In a brave stab at humour, he accused his opponents of introducing 'RED herrings' into the debate, and of whipping up a McCarthyite frenzy to disguise the fragility of their case. At the most recent national elections in each country, Communist parties had won 17,000 votes in Britain, 5 million in France and 9 million in Italy. 'Surely,' he concluded, 'if Communism is the main enemy, the Conservatives should be saying "keep away from the Common Market – it's loaded with Communists".'[68]

Marten blamed 'American public relations people' for the anti-Communist flavour of the Yes campaign, and accused Tory pro-Marketeers of lacking faith in their ability to defeat socialism at the ballot box.[69] Yet this oversimplified the pro-Market case, which emphasised both the economic dangers of withdrawal and the need for solidarity against the Soviet threat. It did not help that anti-Marketeers on the Left tended to play down the issue, viewing the Community as a relic of a conflict that was now drawing to a close. Judith Hart, for example, dismissed it as 'a product of the cold war atmosphere of the 1950s' that was 'totally irrelevant to the needs of contemporary Britain'.[70] Michael Foot, likewise, insisted that Cold War tensions had been 'relaxing' for years.[71] In this respect, the timing of the referendum was unfortunate for the Antis, coming as it did at a moment of rising international anxiety.[72] Polling companies warned the 'Out' campaign that it would have to tackle the fears associated with communism, but this was something it never successfully achieved.[73]

FINDING A ROLE?

Cold War tensions fed off wider anxieties about Britain's place in the world. It was only ten years since a Labour prime minister, Harold Wilson, had boasted that Britain's 'frontiers are in the Himalayas'; yet by 1975, that vision felt as remote as the days of Pitt and Palmerston.[74] In a famous speech at West Point in 1962, former US secretary of state Dean Acheson claimed that Britain had 'lost an empire', but 'not yet found a role'.[75] The question was not only whether it could find that role in the Community, but whether doing so was compatible with what it meant to be 'British'.

Questions of national identity had always been bound up with Britain's role in the wider world. In becoming an empire, Britain could be seen as having burst the confines of western Europe, extending its trade, its military power and even its national sports across the globe. The Victorian statesman Benjamin Disraeli had boasted in 1866 that Britain was no longer 'a mere European power'. As 'the metropolis of a great maritime empire', she had 'outgrown the Continent of Europe'; 'she is really more an Asiatic power than a European'.[76] From that perspective, the attempt to recalibrate Britain as a European power could be seen not simply as a recasting of British policy – perhaps 'the most decisive moment in British history since the Norman conquest or the loss of America' – but as a shrivelling of status; a retreat to parochial irrelevance by an exhausted and diminished power.[77]

That sense of defeat could carry overtones of cultural, as well as political, surrender. In everyday language, 'Europe' tended to mean 'the Continent', understood as 'a geographical area which does not include the British Isles'. Britons talked of 'going to Europe' on holiday; universities taught 'British' and 'European' history in separate courses; and both sides in the accession debate spoke of 'joining' or 'leaving Europe'. In consequence, talk of 'becoming European' could easily conjure fears of 'ceasing to be British'.[78] Asked in the summer of 1971 whether Britain would lose some of its national identity within the Community, 62 per cent of those polled thought that it would. Only 27 per cent thought that it would not.[79] This was not simply a post-imperial nostalgia on the part of metropolitan elites. In Scotland and Wales, as we shall see, nationalist parties were deeply suspicious of the cultural homogenisation they associated with membership, while the Somerset band the Wurzels had a minor hit in 1967 with the song 'When the Common Market Comes to Stanton Drew', a rumination on how farmers would adapt to a world of spaghetti, flamenco and late-night drinking.[80]

The mood in Whitehall was more optimistic. The government's Referendum Information Unit, which took calls from members of the public, told enquirers that 'Britain needs new ways of exerting influence'; 'we have to find a role to replace the one we played up to and immediately after the last war'.[81] The *Sun* put it more bluntly. 'After years of drift and failure', it told readers, 'the Common Market offers an unrepeatable opportunity for a nation that lost an empire to gain a continent.'[82] Pro-Marketeers projected their opponents as isolationists turning their backs on the world and on Britain's role within it. Roy Jenkins mocked the Antis for seeking 'a return to the womb', adding (rather incongruously) that withdrawal would condemn Britain to 'an old people's home for faded nations'.[83] Yet anti-Marketeers insisted that it was the EEC – a group of white, post-imperial states, huddled behind a tariff barrier – that was insular and parochial. The slogan 'Out of Europe and into the World' was blazoned across press conferences, in a rebuke to what the Scottish Nationalist Winifred Ewing called the 'narrow European "regionalism"' of the Market. E.P. Thompson, the celebrated socialist historian, dismissed the Community as 'a group of fat, rich nations feeding each other goodies', united by nothing more elevated than an 'introversial white bourgeois nationalism'.[84]

CRISIS BRITAIN?

All this fed into a wider atmosphere of domestic crisis, which was both economic and political in character. The referendum came at an exceptionally difficult period for the economy. Oil prices had quadrupled as a result of war in the Middle East, triggering power cuts across industry. The balance of payments collapsed from a £1 billion surplus in 1971 to a £3.3 billion deficit in 1974, comfortably the worst since the industrial era began.[85] The same year also witnessed one of the great stock market crashes of the twentieth century – a slump which, according to the City editor of the *Daily Telegraph*, made 'the inter-war crash look like a dent on the bumper'. At one stage in 1974 the stock exchange had lost 73 per cent of its value. 'Hardly a week goes by', one journal complained, 'without another large stockbroking firm putting up the shutters.'[86]

When Labour returned to government in March, the new Chancellor, Denis Healey, told ministers that the 'economic situation ... might well be the worst which had ever been faced in peacetime'.[87] Wilson thought it 'the gravest crisis we have faced since 1931'.[88] Within a year inflation was running at close to 25 per cent, fuelling a wave of strikes as workers fought to protect the purchasing power of their wages. No democracy had ever survived a sustained period of inflation at this level, fuelling predictions that spiralling prices might destroy British democracy in the 1970s as surely as in Germany in the 1930s. Writing in *The Times*, Peter Jay warned that if Britain could not tame inflation, democracy might 'pass away within the life-time of people

FIGURE I.4   Workers in Bond Street wear duvets to keep warm during power cuts, in the winter of 1973–74.

Source: Evening Standard, Hulton Archive: www.gettyimages.co.uk/license/2669881

now adult', while an NOP poll in 1974 found that 65 per cent of those questioned thought that there was either a 'serious threat' or 'some threat' to the survival of democracy.[89] The collapse of parliamentary government in Northern Ireland offered a grim reminder of the fragility of democratic institutions, and of the human cost of their collapse.

Throughout the referendum period, the strapline in the *Sun* read simply: 'Crisis Britain'. This was part of a wider genre of journalism, affectionately nicknamed 'Doomwatch', which charted with sadistic relish the evidence of impending disaster.[90] It was a mood that was echoed at the highest levels of government. The foreign secretary, Jim Callaghan, told the Cabinet in 1974 that 'every morning when he shaved he thought that he should emigrate, but by the time he had eaten breakfast, he realised there was nowhere else to go'. 'There was no solution that he could see to our problems.'[91]

The same grim mood was evident in business. The supermarket magnate John Davan Sainsbury warned of 'the most serious decline in business confidence' for a quarter of a century, while Marks & Spencer breezily told customers that the days were gone 'when we can take for granted hot radiators, endless supplies of hot water from the tap' and 'even electric lights'.[92] A volume of essays published by the Institute of Economic Affairs, entitled simply *Crisis '75 ... ?*, warned that the economy required 'new thought and unpalatable action if it is not to collapse or disintegrate'. As a trading nation that imported most of its food, Britain's ability to feed itself depended upon the export of goods and services to the rest of the world. What was at stake was not simply prosperity or the rate of economic growth; it was the UK's survival as a first world economy.[93]

Both sides in the referendum campaign invoked this apocalyptic spirit, though they shaped it to different ends.[94] 'In' campaigners warned that withdrawal would trigger the collapse of the currency, a public spending crisis and massive job losses. Heath predicted food shortages and a return to the ration book, while a Tory MP in Scotland claimed that 'a No vote would ... mean the closing of schools and hospitals and the stopping of roads, railways and mines'. 'Out' campaigners replied that it was membership that was draining the lifeblood from the economy. Tony Benn claimed that 500,000 jobs had been lost in the first two years of membership. Staying in, he predicted, would mean 'total disaster' for manufacturing and mass unemployment across the country.[95]

The result was what one commentator called an 'auction of fear, a competition to make your flesh creep'.[96] Another called it 'a spine-chilling horror epic', with 'the defenceless voter' trapped 'in the middle of a nightmarish duel between Dracula and Frankenstein'.[97] The apocalyptic tone of the debate seems to have resonated with voters, because it tapped into their personal experience. For a generation that had lived through rationing, seen oil prices quadruple in 1973 and queued for sugar in 1974, the prospect of economic catastrophe was not something abstract. Private polling in May found that more than half of voters expected 'an immediate economic and political crisis' in the event of a decision to withdraw, a conviction that hung like a storm cloud over the campaign.[98]

Some welcomed the evidence that an old order was passing away. Tony Benn, who was on the front line of the economic battle as secretary of state for industry, wrote in his diary in December 1974 that 'the final collapse of capitalism might be a matter of weeks away'. The country, he believed, faced a historic moment of decision: 'whether to adopt Tory measures' (such as EEC membership) 'in order to prop up the old system or to go forward with something else'.[99] From this perspective, the referendum signalled a parting of the ways. The word 'crisis' comes from the Greek word for a 'judgement': it is a moment of decision, not a moment of panic. The conviction that Britain faced a choice of direction loomed large over the referendum debate, and extended far beyond its relationship with the EEC. Should the UK bind itself into an expanded market capitalism, or explore new forms of socialist planning? Did its future lie in Europe or on the open seas? Was democracy enhanced or diminished by pooling sovereignty with others?

'COMMON MARKET OR BUST?'

Such questions provide the starting point for the current book. What follows is not a study of diplomacy, of summit meetings or even, for the most part, of politicians and governments. Instead, it follows the referendum debate out of Parliament and into the country: to the churches, women's organisations, paramilitary groups and business meetings at which the European question was being thrashed out. It shows how attitudes to European integration were shaped by the other great issues and controversies of the 1970s: such as the women's liberation movement; secularisation; the 'Troubles' in Northern Ireland; the rise of nationalism in Scotland and Wales; the Cold War; and the end of empire. In so doing, it seeks to break down the divide between 'British history' and 'the history of Britain in Europe', two fields that have rarely embraced free movement.

The result is as much a social history of the 1970s as a political history of European integration. Despite the strength of feeling among activists, polls suggested that the EEC was a low-salience issue for most of the public. It rarely featured when voters were asked to name 'the most serious issues facing Britain today', coming far behind concerns about employment, inflation and trade union power. Campaigners (and voters themselves) constantly lamented the ignorance and incuriosity of the public about how the EEC worked, what it did and why it mattered.[100] Yet precisely for this reason, voters projected onto the European debate the things that they *did* know and care about. Released from conventional party allegiances, and deprived of many of the cues by which they commonly cast their ballots, voters made the referendum an arena for a much wider set of debates and controversies. In consequence, what might have been a dry, technocratic campaign was liberated into something bigger, becoming a debate about the direction of British politics and society, who to trust in public life and Britain's sense of its own identity.

It is this that distinguishes the book from previous accounts of the referendum. The years immediately following the vote produced three excellent studies, to which the current volume owes a substantial debt. In 1976 David Butler and Uwe Kitzinger co-authored a study of *The 1975 Referendum*, based on interviews with many of the protagonists and extensive access to the papers of the two campaigns. Part of a series covering every general election since the Second World War, it charted the decision to hold a referendum, the renegotiations, the formation and activities of the two campaigns, and the roles played by the press, the television companies and the polling organisations. That same year, the Conservative MP Philip Goodhart published *Full-Hearted Consent*, a lively account that focused particularly on the campaign to procure a referendum. These two volumes were joined, in 1977, by Anthony King's *Britain Says Yes*, which set the referendum within the longer history of the European debate and paid special attention to party opinion.[101]

All three volumes had strong credentials. David Butler was – and remains – the doyen of electoral analysts, and he brought to

the referendum thirty years' experience as Britain's leading psephol-
ogist. Anthony King, likewise, had published extensively on electoral
politics, including studies of the 1964 and 1966 elections, and had a
special expertise in the study of public opinion. Uwe Kitzinger had
worked as an economist at the Council of Europe, as a political advisor in the European Commission, and was one of the founders of the
Journal of Common Market Studies. His 1973 study of *Diplomacy
and Persuasion: How Britain Joined the Common Market* was
praised even by those who did not share his enthusiasm for entry;
and it remains one of the most elegant and perceptive studies of its
subject.[102] Philip Goodhart was one of those who had fought to
secure a referendum, and he brought to the subject a ready wit and an
insider's perspective.

The current book draws on all three volumes, but the questions
it seeks to answer are different. It uses the referendum as a window
into the political and social history of the 1970s, exploring how the
European debate intersected with – and was shaped by – other issues
and controversies in the period. Voters did not shed their wider identities on entering the polling booths: they brought to the European question their beliefs and experiences as men and women; employers and
workers; Catholics and Protestants; consumers and producers; trade
unionists, nationalists and immigrants. For some, the central issue of
the campaign was the economy and the challenge of post-war decline.
For others, it was nationhood and the campaign for self-government.
In Northern Ireland the campaign focused intensively on the border,
the defence of Protestantism and the future of Partition. Depending on
one's perspective, the EEC could be a bulwark against communism, a
site of religious awakening, the spawn of empire or a vehicle for wom-
en's rights. In this respect, the ballot paper functioned as a political
Rorschach test, with responses ranging from nightmare to nirvana.

For this reason, the book ranges more widely than is normal
in books on 'Britain and Europe', both in its subject matter and in its
source material. Parish newsletters, fashion magazines, farming journals and paramilitary writings all feature, as do pop songs, tabloid
newspapers and interviews with some of those who participated in the
campaign. Such material allows us not only to explore public attitudes
towards membership, at a time of unusual voter salience; it also shines
a light on the hopes, fears and world-views of the electorate in one of
Britain's most troubled decades.

The book is divided into three main sections. Part one charts the road to the referendum, showing how this alien form of decision-making burst out of the stomach of Britain's parliamentary democracy. It explores why it was so difficult to contain the European question within conventional party lines, and why the issue proved especially disruptive for the Labour Party. It also introduces the main campaign vehicles on either side, exploring the role of the media and assessing how the pro-Marketeers outgunned, out-generalled and outclassed their opposite numbers.

A second part focuses on key issues and themes in the campaign, ranging from specific cohorts (such as women, business and the churches) to topics of special interest (such as food, sovereignty and the end of empire). Here, in particular, it seeks to reconnect the European debate to the wider history of Britain in the period leading up to the referendum.

The final section explores the territorial dimensions of the referendum. The period leading up to the vote had seen significant electoral breakthroughs for Plaid Cymru and the Scottish National Party, as well as the disintegration of the Northern Ireland Parliament under the pressure of sectarian conflict. Scotland, Wales and Northern Ireland all acquired their own campaign vehicles (England, significantly, did not), and separate chapters explore the debate in each. A closing chapter explores the lessons of the campaign and draws some comparisons with 2016.

Throughout the book, I use the contemporary terms 'pro-' and 'anti-Marketeer' (or the 'Pros' and the 'Antis') to identify the two sides. These terms are not wholly satisfactory, for they derive from a nickname, 'the Common Market', which was itself not strictly accurate. Such labels are preferable, however, to most of the alternatives. 'Eurosceptic' was a word that only entered common usage in the 1980s and was never a very helpful descriptor. If 'scepticism' suggests a doubting, questioning mindset, it is more accurately applied to a reluctant *pro*-Marketeer, such as Harold Wilson, than to a confirmed Anti such as Enoch Powell. Except in quotation, I have avoided terms such as 'anti-European'. The EEC (or even the EU) is not coterminous with 'Europe', and it is possible to oppose political integration without being hostile to European culture, trade or other forms of co-operation.

The organisation itself bore a number of different labels. Strictly speaking, there was no such thing as 'the European Community'. Rather, there were three 'European Communities', which were brought under a common set of institutions in 1967: the European Coal and

Steel Community (ECSC); the European Atomic Energy Community (Euratom); and the European Economic Community (EEC).[103] In practice, it was common to talk of 'the European Community', and I have followed that usage here. 'The Common Market' was a nickname for the EEC that was mostly favoured by its opponents; it was placed on the ballot paper in 1975 at the insistence of the Antis, who wanted to remind Labour voters of its association with market capitalism. Those who favoured membership often cavilled at the term: Heath told the Commons in 1966 that 'the phrase "Common Market" under-estimates and undervalues the Community, and, for this reason, tends to mislead those who have to deal with it'. Like most enthusiasts for membership, he preferred to talk of 'the Community', suggesting partnership and fraternity between countries who were 'living and working together'.[104] I use both labels interchangeably in the chapters that follow.

Problems of nomenclature go deeper still. Well into the twentieth century, it was common to talk of 'England' and 'the English' when referring to any of the peoples and regions of the United Kingdom. Today, 'Britain' and 'the British' are used in the same way, though neither is satisfactory for Northern Ireland. It would be more accurate to talk of the United Kingdom but, as late as 1975, ministers were concerned that this would be 'an unfamiliar term to some voters' if it was included on the ballot paper.[105] Since it is a cumbersome term when used to excess, and has no convenient adjective, it is used here interchangeably with 'Britain', despite the formal inaccuracy.

This book takes no position on membership of the European project, either in 1975 or in 2016. Instead, it seeks to understand why voters in 1975 took the positions that they did – and to do so in the context of their own times. The past is a foreign country, which maintains its independence with the same fierce determination as any 'Brexiteer'. In revisiting the decisions and dilemmas of those who lived there, it is not necessary to conclude either that one referendum or the other produced the 'correct' result. In understanding their decision, however, we may gain fresh perspectives on why the UK joined when it did, why opposition was so durable, and why the vote to stay in did not, as Harold Wilson had expected, bring fourteen years of debate to a close.

PART ONE

EUROPE OR BUST?

1 OPPORTUNITY AND ILLUSION: THE ROAD TO 1975

For too long we have walked in the shadows. It is time for us now to walk out into the light to find a new place, a new Britain in this new world. ... Let history record that when we were shown the way we took the way and walked out to meet our destiny.

Edward Heath, 16 October 1971[1]

I have never been emotionally European. I don't stand on the South Coast, look towards the Continent, and say 'There's a new Jerusalem'.

Harold Wilson, 15 May 1975[2]

You do not haggle over the subscription when you are invited to climb into a lifeboat. You scramble aboard while there is still a seat for you.

Lord Crowther, 27 July 1971[3]

On 4 June 1975, just hours before the polls opened in Britain's first national referendum, two men in top hats and tails fought a duel in St James's Park. They were fighting for the honour of the Eldon League, a student dining club whose motto was '*forwards into the past*', to determine its position on the European Community. Before a hushed and anxious crowd, the two champions paced out the ground, turned and opened fire – not with pistols, but with champagne bottles handed to them by their seconds. As the heavens thundered to the roar of champagne corks, a lucky shot blew one man's top hat clean from his shoulders. His opponent, the future MP Neil Hamilton, was declared victorious, and it was agreed that the League would oppose British membership.

With combat operations at an end, the victory parade began. The combatants, 'monocled and bespatted', mounted a horse-drawn carriage and rode in triumph down Constitution Hill, the Mall and Trafalgar Square. Speaking as imperial grand prior of the League, Hamilton reportedly told journalists that the organisation 'views with unabashed antipathy all forms of democracy, especially the referendum'. 'We oppose anything that is common, whether it be consultation of the common people or the Common Market.'[4]

Two days earlier, a duel of a very different kind had been fought out on the BBC. In a special edition of *Panorama*, the home secretary, Roy Jenkins, went head-to-head with the secretary of state for industry, Tony Benn, on the case for membership. Not since the 1930s had Cabinet ministers argued publicly against one another on a major national question, and the baroque courtesy of two men with murder in their eyes provided one of the most remarkable spectacles of the campaign. Within six years Benn and Jenkins would be in different parties, engaged in a struggle not only for the future of Britain in Europe but for the whole direction of national politics.

St James's Park and the BBC studios were just two of the battlefields in a struggle that had been raging since the 1950s, but which was now spilling over into the public arena. For most of the post-war era, the European debate had taken place chiefly behind closed doors: in the Treasury, the Foreign Office and the Board of Trade. The question had never loomed large in an election and never drew widespread public interest. Polls suggested that the issue was of low salience to voters, though bands of enthusiasts occasionally made the newspapers.[5]

FIGURE 1.1 'The baroque courtesy of two men with murder in their eyes'. Cabinet colleagues Tony Benn and Roy Jenkins debate membership on BBC *Panorama*, 2 June 1975. David Dimbleby holds the ring.
Source: Chris Djukanovic, Hulton Archive: www.gettyimages.co.uk/license/451356139

How, then, did a subject that for decades had trickled through the established channels of British politics come suddenly to burst its banks, flooding out of Westminster and into a national election? To address that question, this chapter provides a brief survey of the European debate from 1945 to 1974. The literature on this subject is large and complex, so the following pages focus on three core questions. Why did the United Kingdom not join the European Community at the outset? Why did its position change in the 1960s? And why did pressure build for a referendum thereafter?

'THE PRICE OF VICTORY'

The story of 'Britain and Europe' has often seemed better suited to the psychiatrist than the historian. For early writers, in particular, it was the story of how Britain 'missed the bus': a tale of 'miscalculations and missed opportunities', at a time 'when Britain could have had the leadership of Europe for the asking'.[6] The UK stands accused of 'hesitation, irresolution and indecision'; of taking an 'intransigent' and 'negative' attitude to the new institutions taking shape on the Continent; and of fighting a 'rearguard action' against its 'inexorable return to a former constituency among the small and medium-sized states of the European peninsula'.[7] The idea that successive governments had failed 'to read the lessons of history' sank deep roots in British politics, especially among the advocates of a more dynamic relationship with the Continent.[8] In a speech at the opening of the European Research Institute in 2001, Tony Blair summarised 'the history of our engagement with Europe' as 'one of opportunities missed in the name of illusions – and Britain suffering as a result'.[9]

In such accounts, Britain features less as a rational actor on the world stage than as a trauma victim, strapped to the analyst's couch. Michael Charlton, for example, diagnosed a pernicious 'national attitude of mind', in a country whose victory in war had led it 'to misinterpret and to misjudge' its strength and interests.[10] Hugo Young described his classic account of the subject as 'the story of fifty years in which Britain struggled to reconcile the past she could not forget with the future she could not avoid'. 'It was a record', he concluded, 'not of triumph, but rather of bewilderment', as successive governments failed to 'truly accept that [Britain's] modern destiny was to be a European country'.[11]

Such accounts tended to assume, first, that Britain *should* have joined at the outset; second, that there was no viable alternative to membership; and third, that its reluctance to bow to the inevitable was a pathology in need of diagnosis. The historian, wrote Young, was entitled to 'cast a jaundiced eye' on those who resisted membership, or who 'pretended to themselves and the country that alternative destinies' were possible.[12] Anthony King took a similar view, asserting that the 'anti-Europeans resisted the modern world; the pro-Europeans, by contrast, accepted it'.[13] Even Sean Greenwood, in a notably even-handed account, wrote of Britain's 'reluctance to accept that her former place in the world had vanished forever'.[14] In such accounts, the British mind takes on a certain prophylactic quality, through which nothing creative was permitted to pass. Jean Monnet, one of the architects of the new Europe, told an interviewer that Britain had paid '*the price of victory* – the illusion that you could maintain what you had, without change'.[15]

As national archives began to open, a seam of revisionist writing emerged that challenged these assumptions. Scholars sought to understand the actions of governments on their own terms, analysing the real dilemmas faced by ministers who were responding not to an abstract ideal of 'Europe', but to specific choices at particular moments in time. Yet the implication – more sympathetically couched – that Britain's relationship with the European project was in some way pathological still sometimes peeps through the arras. Introducing a collection of essays in 2001, Roger Broad warned readers to expect 'an indictment of the British political system', whose governing class, 'blinded by pride', had 'failed to understand the consequences' of what was happening in Europe. Other contributors suggested that Britain had proven 'incapable of thinking strategically', leaving her 'out of sync with the direction of history'.[16] To quote the titles of three (justly) celebrated volumes, Britain was *An Awkward Partner, A Stranger in Europe*, governed and inhabited by *Reluctant Europeans*.[17]

This drew a rebuke from the first official historian of Britain and the European Community, Alan Milward, who argued that 'the national strategy' pursued by post-war governments 'was a rational way in which the United Kingdom might adjust to the post-war world'. In Milward's view, it was striking just 'how little insularity, blinkered devotion to an English-speaking world, or arrogance arising from having won the war had to do with the decisions that were made'. Nonetheless, he concluded, the attempt to find a destiny outside the

Community 'did not succeed, and some of the reasons for its failure are to be found in the strategy itself'.[18]

The account that follows starts from two basic principles. The first is that Britain did not, on any plausible reading, turn its back on 'Europe' after 1945. On the contrary, it was more closely involved with the Continent, through a wider range of commitments, than at any previous point in its modern history. Britain took a leading role in the organisation of the European Recovery Programme ('Marshall Aid') and was an active participant in the formation of the Organisation for European Economic Cooperation (OEEC) and the Council of Europe. In the 1947 Treaty of Dunkirk, Britain agreed an unprecedented fifty-year military alliance with France, a commitment that was expanded across western Europe through the Treaty of Brussels. The formation of NATO ('the most momentous act of British foreign policy for a century or more') involved Britain in a security guarantee to the whole of western Europe, 'an awesome commitment' of a kind that dwarfed anything in its peacetime history.[19] It was the UK government, in 1954–5, that led the creation of a European defence organisation, the Western European Union, as part of which it took the unprecedented step of maintaining a standing army on the Rhine numbering almost 80,000 troops at its peak.[20] The United Kingdom was the first country, in 1951, to ratify the European Convention on Human Rights, something that France did not do until 1974.

When one adds to this the UK's proposal to create an industrial Free Trade Area (FTA) across western Europe, and the creation in 1960 of a European Free Trade Association (EFTA) outside the Six, it is difficult to sustain the notion that it turned its back on the Continent.[21] The foreign secretary, Herbert Morrison, told Konrad Adenauer in 1951 that Britain was undergoing a revolution in its policy towards Europe that was comparable to the abandonment of isolationism by the United States.[22] As Elisabeth Barker has written, British governments were determined not to repeat the neglect of the interwar years; instead, they 'were launching new policies and methods', which included 'permanent involvement in European affairs, binding long-term commitments, full-scale military alliances going as far as military integration in peacetime, [and] economic cooperation'.[23]

The UK's commitment to Europe cannot be measured simply by its relationship with the EEC. When the Treaty of Rome was signed in 1957, the 'Six' founder countries – Belgium, France, Italy, Luxembourg, the Netherlands and West Germany – constituted barely a third of the countries of non-Communist Europe and just over half its population.[24] Despite remaining outside the Community, the UK maintained closer links with the Six than any other non-member state. It was the first outside the founder countries to apply for membership, and it pursued a series of association agreements and partnerships. What needs explaining, then, is not Britain's refusal to engage with 'Europe', but its (temporary) reluctance to participate in *one particular form* of European co-operation: a customs union based on the pooling of key economic resources, under the authority of supranational institutions. This brings us to a second core principle: that, in explaining why the UK did not join at the outset, it is necessary to look beyond stereotypes of national difference or dreams of departed glory to the specific character of the emergent Community.

IDEALISM AND INTEREST: FOUNDING THE EEC

The European Community was born out of a heady brew of idealism, self-interest and fear. The boundaries between them were not always precise: appeals to 'the European idea' could be a useful mask for considerations of national interest, especially where powerful domestic lobbies like French farmers were concerned. Each country (and each government) had its own complex motives, the balance of which changed according to the particular time and issue.

Visions of a united Europe stretched back across time, but it was the apocalypse that was visited upon the continent in the first half of the twentieth century that made it a reality. In the three decades between 1914 and 1945, more than 40 million people were killed in European wars. Millions more were wounded, widowed, orphaned or displaced. The economic damage alone would take decades to repair, with lasting consequences for agriculture and heavy industry. The challenge was moral, as well as material, for the devastation wrought by war – and the mechanised slaughter of Belsen and Birkenau – shattered lazy assumptions about the supremacy of European civilisation. As Winston Churchill put it in a radio broadcast in 1943:

> In Europe lie most of the causes which have led to these two world wars. In Europe dwell the historic parent races from whom our Western civilisation has been so largely derived. I believe myself to be what is called 'a good European' and I should deem it a noble task to take part in reviving the fertile genius and in restoring the true greatness of Europe.[25]

As they began the task of reconstruction after 1945, the architects of the new European order had three principal goals: to eliminate the scourge of war from the continent; to rebuild economies shattered by conflict; and to solve forever the so-called 'German problem' – the destabilising effect of a financial, military and industrial powerhouse that dwarfed its continental neighbours. The three goals were inherently interrelated, for one of the lessons of the interwar period was that visionary commitments to international brotherhood were too flimsy a foundation for peace. To become potent, they had to be annexed to the material interests of individual states, through a process of mutual reconstruction. That would only be possible by rekindling the furnaces of German industry, which would in turn only be acceptable to her neighbours within a new framework of inter-state relations.

The first fruit of this project was the European Coal and Steel Community (ECSC), the vision for which was set out in the Schuman Declaration of May 1950. Under the Treaty of Paris, signed in April 1951, the Six established a common market in coal and steel, under the direction of a supranational 'High Authority'. The choice of coal and steel was no accident: these were natural resources that crossed state boundaries; they were the essential instruments of reconstruction; and they would be indispensable for any programme of rearmament. Pooling these resources across borders, it was hoped, would drive prosperity by promoting efficiency and economies of scale. Just as importantly, it would cut out from national control the sinews of war, making armed conflict 'not merely unthinkable, but materially impossible'. This was a beating of swords into ploughshares on a continental scale, a 'fusion of interests' from which might grow 'a wider and deeper community between countries long opposed to one another by sanguinary divisions'.[26]

The ECSC was followed, in 1957, by the Treaty of Rome, which created the European Economic Community. The EEC sought to abolish trade barriers between its members, on the principle that 'if goods do not cross borders, armies will'. The idea was not simply that increased trade would enrich all its members, though this was a crucial aspiration. More importantly, it was hoped that Europe's economies would become so interdependent as to make war between states an absurdity, because it would destroy the foundations of their own prosperity.

For some of the architects of the new Europe, the goal was an explicitly post-national enterprise, with local allegiances transcended by a new European identity. In the words of the Schuman Declaration, the Community was to be 'a first step in the federation of Europe', a project that was 'indispensable to the preservation of peace'. This reflected, in some instances, a fluid conception of national identity, born of a complex relationship with the nation state. Robert Schuman, for example, had been born in Luxembourg, though his family hailed originally from Alsace-Lorraine. Once a French province, Lorraine had been annexed by the German Empire in 1871, at which point Robert's father had become a German citizen. Robert himself was called up to the German army in 1914, but when Lorraine was returned to France in 1918 he gained French nationality and later served as prime minister of France. A similar story could be told of Alcide De Gasperi, prime minister of Italy from 1945 to 1953. De Gasperi was born in 1881 in the Tyrol, which was then part of the Austro-Hungarian Empire. He served in the Austrian Parliament during the First World War, but took Italian citizenship when South Tyrol was transferred to Italy in 1919.[27] Others, like the Belgian statesman Paul-Henri Spaak, spent the war years in exile in London, where (according to his son) he 'lost faith in the nation state because it had failed'.[28]

Yet the 'post-national' ambitions of the new Community should not be exaggerated. The European Community was fundamentally a creation of national governments. Every step was the work of national politicians, engaged in a process of national reconstruction, for which they were responsible to their own domestic constituencies. As Alan Milward has noted, integration was 'an act of national will'; when it did not serve national interests, it either did not go ahead, was altered so that it did, or formed part of some larger bargain that compensated offended interests.[29] Plans for a European Defence Community disintegrated in 1954, as did the idea of a European Political Community, while the 'Coal Crisis' of 1959 – in which members of the ECSC imposed tariffs in defiance of the High Authority – showed that states would readily defy even those institutions that already existed where domestic interests dictated. It was the Council of Ministers – composed of representatives of national governments – and not the supranational Commission that became the driving force of the new Community. France, in particular, proved at least as 'awkward' a partner as Britain when the national interest required. In the 'empty chair' crisis of 1965–6 it brought the business of the Community to a standstill for six months, rather than give ground on reform of the Common Agricultural Policy.[30]

The genius of the European project, expressed first in the ECSC and subsequently in the EEC, was that it harnessed cross-border integration to the pursuit of national self-interest, rather than setting these forces against one another. After 1945, states that had been impoverished by war, humiliated by occupation or discredited by collaboration now faced the colossal task of national reconstruction. Governments were expected to procure rising living standards, security for their citizens and higher rates of economic growth, as well as social services and welfare provision on an unprecedented scale. For European statesmen, many of whom had spent the war years either in resistance movements or in governments-in-exile, the case for integration rested chiefly on its transactional benefits for the domestic economy, even if their rhetoric spoke also of higher purposes. In this respect, as Milward comments, the European Community 'was not the supersession of the nation-state by another form of governance'. Rather, it marked a 'reassertion of the nation-state as an organizational concept'.[31]

Security, as well as prosperity, loomed large in this calculation. For states that had suffered conquest and occupation, integration offered the prospect of a new relationship with West Germany, in which its political and industrial power could be harnessed to the wider economic good. Fear of Germany was soon augmented by anxiety about the Soviet Union, which had subjugated much of eastern Europe. Konrad Adenauer told Churchill in 1951 that 'No one outside Germany could imagine how the Soviet Union was attempting to undermine the Federal Republic.' The Soviet 'fifth column', he warned, was well funded, organised and confident of success. Integration offered solidarity against the menace from the East, while reinforcing states against internal subversion.[32]

Out of this combination of fear, hope and hard bargaining – promoted, for its own purposes, by the United States – emerged the three founding treaties of the new European order: the 1951 Treaty of Paris, creating the ECSC; the 1957 Euratom Treaty, establishing the European Atomic Energy Community; and the 1957 Treaty of Rome, which founded the European Economic Community. In explaining why the UK was not a signatory to these agreements, the question is not why it turned its back on Europe, but why Britain's own combination of idealism, fear and self-interest produced a different policy calculation – and why that changed in the years that followed.

MISSING THE BUS?

British policymakers were under no illusions about the scale of the challenge in 1945. The long struggle with Nazism had pushed the United Kingdom to the brink of bankruptcy. The UK had liquidated more than £1 billion of overseas assets, lost two-thirds of its export trade and exhausted a quarter of its national wealth. Britain was heavily in debt, not only to the United States but to its own colonies. When the US terminated the 'lend-lease' agreement at the end of the war, triggering what John Maynard Keynes called a 'financial Dunkirk', disaster was averted only by further loans that would take sixty years to pay off. Rationing continued until 1954 and was even extended to new items such as bread. On leaving office in 1945, Churchill is said to have issued a grim warning to his successors. The new government, he rumbled, would face 'terrible tasks. Terrible tasks.'[33]

The challenges were not solely economic. In an age defined by air power and the atomic bomb, the principles that had long governed British defence policy were now in question. At home, the Channel could offer no defence against long-range bombers or intercontinental missiles; abroad, as Clement Attlee observed in 1945, the conditions 'which made it possible to defend a string of possessions scattered over five continents by means of a fleet based on island fortresses have gone'.[34] In 1946 the government was forced to inform the United States that it could no longer protect Greece against Communist insurgents, a recognition that its power to act independently in the world was drawing to a close. A year later India gained its independence from the Empire, beginning the slow disintegration of the British world system. Underpinning all this was a fear that economic collapse might disable British power altogether. As the Chancellor, Hugh Dalton, warned Attlee in 1947, the chief menace to national security was no longer 'armed aggression' but 'financial overstrain and collapse'.[35]

In this context, it was not complacency or a bovine resistance to change that shaped Britain's European policy. Post-war governments engaged in radical new policies both at home and abroad, from the creation of the welfare state and the liquidation of the Empire to the founding of NATO and the building of the nuclear bomb. Nor were the British immune to the appeal of European unity. In the period between the Munich Agreement and the fall of France in 1940, there had been a surge of interest in federal ideas in Britain: W.B. Curry's book

The Case for Federal Union, sold 100,000 copies within six months of its publication in 1939, while Federal Union, a ginger group of enthusiasts for integration, recruited 10,000 British members in 1939–40.[36] During the war years, London had served as the capital of free Europe; it was there that resistance movements and governments-in-exile planned the post-war order, and it was from London that some of the most trenchant appeals for unity were sounded. In the early years of the peace, no one articulated more powerfully than Churchill the cry for 'a kind of United States of Europe … which could give a sense of enlarged patriotism and common citizenship to the distracted peoples of this turbulent and mighty continent'.[37]

Churchill tended to view Britain as a *patron* of a federal Europe, rather than as a participant. As he had put it long before the war, in 1930, 'We have our own dream and our own task. We are *with* Europe, but not *of* it.'[38] Yet policymakers were conscious, in an age of superpowers, of the added weight Britain would carry on the world stage as the head of a regional grouping. A memorandum written by the incoming permanent under-secretary at the Foreign Office, Orme Sargent, in July 1945, argued that Britain should make itself the leading force both in the Commonwealth and in western Europe; only then could she 'compel our two big partners to treat us as an equal'.[39] As foreign secretary, Ernest Bevin took a strong interest in the idea of a European 'third force', led by the United Kingdom, which could act as a balance between the United States and the Soviet Union.[40]

Nonetheless, Britain approached the movement towards European unity from a very different starting point to the Six. Unlike France, Germany or the other founder states, Britain had not suffered occupation or defeat in war; its population had not had to grapple with the painful dilemmas bound up in collaboration or resistance. The British did not have to rebuild their institutions at the war's end, or their sense of their own identity; indeed, the British state and its parliamentary institutions emerged from the conflict with their prestige and legitimacy enhanced. There was even a new national myth in the memory of 1940, when Britain had stood 'alone' against Nazi tyranny. (The omission of the Empire from this story is a curious point, to which we shall return.)

The war also bolstered Britain's sense of itself as a global power. During six years of total war, she had mobilised men, money and armaments from across the world; by the time the war ended, Britain had more than 5 million men-at-arms spread out across the planet. In a military sense, Britain was never more truly an imperial power than in the years after 1945. The alliance with the United States, sacralised by Churchill as the 'Special Relationship', pointed to another possible destiny, in the union of 'the English-Speaking Peoples' across the globe.

This reinforced a sense, derived from history, geography and personal experience, that Britain was '*with*' Europe but not '*of*' it. Churchill had spoken of 'a special relationship' between Britain and Europe – the same language, interestingly, that he applied to the United States – but the sense that Europe was a *partner* for Britain, rather than an element in its own identity, was not uniquely Churchillian.[41] Labour foreign secretary Herbert Morrison, told Adenauer in 1951 that 'it was a fact that Britain was an island and that was not the fault of the British; that was the way God had arranged things and the British had to make the best of it'.[42] His Conservative successor, Anthony Eden, described participation in a federal Europe as 'something which we know in our bones we cannot do'. '[O]ur thoughts', he continued grandly, 'move across the seas to the many communities in which our people play their part, in every corner of the world. These are our family ties. That is our life.'[43] These relationships were personal, not simply political or diplomatic. 'What you've got to remember', Eden commented, 'is that, if you looked at the postbag of any English village and examined the letters coming in from abroad to the whole population, ninety per cent of them would come from way beyond Europe ... Ten per cent only would come from Europe.'[44]

The impact of these cultural and psychological factors is difficult to measure, though it doubtless existed. As we have seen, however, the question facing British policymakers was not whether they were feeling European. Like any other country, Britain had to weigh up the costs and benefits of participation in the particular form of co-operation to which the Six were increasingly committed. The idea that Britain could have led integration in a wholly different direction, had it only shown the imagination, grossly exaggerates Britain's influence, not to mention its ability to override the national interests of other member states. From the Schuman Declaration onwards, the Six were committed to the integration of core industries, a customs union protected by common external tariffs, and common institutions based upon the pooling of economic sovereignty. It was this model, and not some ideal alternative, against which the national interest had to be measured.[45]

The economic climate of the post-war years left little room for sentiment, whether Atlantic, European or imperial. The UK had emerged from the war with foreign debts of £4.7 billion, of which £3.7 billion were held by countries in the sterling area. Export markets had been lost to the United States while production was diverted towards the war effort. In this climate, there were three essential tests against which any economic strategy had to be measured: that it restore exports, so that Britain could rebuild its national wealth and finance its overseas commitments; secure cheap food and raw materials for the work of reconstruction; and husband Britain's scarce supply of dollars, by trading so far as possible in sterling. In the decade after the war, all three considerations pointed towards the Commonwealth, not the Continent, as the focus of its international trade.

It was not a misty-eyed fascination with the days of red-coats and native bearers that inclined policymakers towards the Commonwealth. On the contrary, the practical, economic contribution of the former Empire was probably more tangible after 1945 than it had been in the past.[46] In 1951, Australia alone – with a population barely larger than Greater London – took 12 per cent of British exports, more than the economies of the Six combined. From 1952 to 1954, the Commonwealth accounted for nearly half of British imports (47 per cent) and exports (48 per cent). The equivalent figures for the Six were 12.6 per cent and 19.6 per cent respectively. Whole industries were oriented almost entirely towards Commonwealth markets. In 1954, the Commonwealth took 95 per cent of British car exports, 61 per cent of iron and steel exports, 52 per cent of engineering exports (excluding cars) and 49 per cent of chemicals exports. Just as importantly, the Commonwealth supplied the things that Britain most needed for post-war reconstruction: food, raw materials and commodities. In 1955 Australia and Canada supplied 61 per cent of British wheat imports, while Australia and New Zealand contributed 60 per cent of its meat imports. By contrast, the Six remained a net *importer* of food until 1958.[47] As late as 1960, two-thirds of British exports and perhaps 90 per cent of capital investment went outside Europe.[48]

In this context, to look beyond Europe was not insular or parochial. Rather, it reflected a sober – though perhaps short-sighted – appraisal of Europe's economic and political strength. The ascendancy of Europe had been drawing to a close long before 1939, with the rise of the superpowers, the shifting pattern of world trade and the emergence of colonial nationalist movements. Two world wars had dramatically accelerated that movement, leaving behind a Continent that seemed shattered almost beyond recovery. In 1947, Britain exported five times as much as France and as much as all the future 'Six' combined. As late as 1951, British industrial production was still roughly equivalent to that of France and West Germany put together. Continental agriculture and manufacturing had been devastated by bombing, its empires were disintegrating and the stability of its new political structures was still unproven. Germany was engaged in the painful process of de-Nazification, while Communist parties were in the ascendant in France and Italy. In 1946, the French Communist Party became the largest single party in the Constituent Assembly, triggering a power struggle that culminated in the resignation of Charles de Gaulle. The British foreign secretary, Ernest Bevin, wrote grimly of 'civil war within a year'; 'de Gaulle will fail', he predicted, 'the Channel ports will be virtually in Russian hands and this is a great worry'.[49]

It was the weakness of the Continent that explains, in part, the determination of successive American governments to push Britain into the leadership of a continental federation. This would certainly have suited US interests, allowing it to take over Britain's world role (and trade) while passing on an expensive and potentially hazardous engagement in western and central Europe. The benefits for Britain were less clear, for it risked being sucked into a defensive commitment that was beyond its capacity to manage, while weakening ties with its most important markets. The Foreign Office warned in 1948 'that a federated Western Europe is becoming the battle cry of a new [American] isolationism', in which the costs of reconstruction and defence would be offloaded onto the UK.[50]

Supranationalism also sat uneasily with one of the great achievements of the Attlee government: the taking into public ownership of the 'commanding heights' of the economy. The idea that concentrations of economic power should be under the direction of a democratic Parliament was central to post-war social democracy in Britain, whose national institutions had not been tarnished by the experience of totalitarianism. A Labour Party document in 1950 concluded that the party 'could never accept any commitments which limited its own or others' freedom to pursue democratic socialism'.[51] Morrison put it more bluntly, telling Kenneth Younger that 'It's no good – the Durham miners won't wear it.'[52]

In the long run, Commonwealth trade would prove a diminishing asset, while the threat to public ownership from the EEC proved something of a chimaera. American pressure, global trade agreements and the diversification of the Commonwealth's own trading patterns would all erode Britain's share of these markets, while the economies of the Six embarked on a sustained boom. Yet governments operate in the present tense, and the decision to prioritise Commonwealth trade was born not of nostalgia for imperial glories but of the evidence available at the time. In the 1950s, a decision to prioritise the Continent would have involved a significant gamble on the future, at a moment when Britain could ill afford further economic disruption. Unlike the Six, who traded primarily with one another, Britain did most of its trade outside Europe. In this respect, it was being invited to dislocate existing markets for gains that were purely speculative. The costs of entry would have been high, while the benefits were doubtful and prospective. For this reason, the dilemmas bound up in entry were more acute for the British than for the Six. Even if one accepted the argument that the future of British trade lay with the Six, the immediate costs of reorienting its economy would have been severe. This, as Bernard Porter has commented, was the crux of the British dilemma: 'in order to adjust to the EEC', Britain 'had to uproot and replant, while her neighbours cultivated the fields they already had'.[53]

DEFYING GRAVITY?

Over the 1950s and '60s, those voices calling for a more active engagement with the Community grew in influence, as Britain's economic and diplomatic position deteriorated and the recovery of the Six gathered pace. Policymakers had always known that a prosperous Common Market, over which the UK exerted no influence, could endanger British interests. As a Cabinet committee concluded in 1961, 'the strongest argument for joining the Six was based on the potential dangers of staying outside; as the Six consolidated, we would inevitably enter into a period of relative decline'.[54] There were also concerns for the 'special relationship' if the US came to believe 'that our influence was less than that of the European Community'.[55] Harold Macmillan feared that Britain might 'be caught between a hostile (or at least less and less friendly) America and a boastful, powerful Europe of Charlemagne – now under French control but later bound to come under German control'.

As British power and prosperity diminished, the 'grim choice' he identified would grow ever more pressing.[56]

This was married to changes in Britain's own international position. As a commercial and maritime state, Britain had traditionally found it easier to project power across the oceans than in mainland Europe. In the absence of a large standing army, 'fighting on the beaches' was what the British did best. Yet in the decades after 1945, it became increasingly difficult for Britain to exert independent power overseas. Its inability to defend Greece and Turkey against Communist subversion could perhaps have been attributed to the exhaustion of war, but evidence of a more permanent change came with the Suez Crisis of 1956. In the biggest humiliation of British power since the fall of Singapore, US financial pressure forced French and British troops out of Egypt without firing a shot. This was followed, in 1960, by the cancellation of Britain's domestic nuclear missile programme, Blue Streak. This 'heart-breaking' decision, as Macmillan described it, marked the end of Britain's status as a truly independent nuclear power, leaving it dependent on delivery systems from the United States.[57] The same year saw the collapse of an international summit in Paris at which Macmillan had hoped to play the role of honest broker, following the shooting down of an American spy plane over the Soviet Union. Nominally a meeting of the 'Big Four' – Britain, France, the USA and the USSR – it served as a reminder that the future of the world, and even the survival of western Europe, was now in the hands of two superpowers over whom medium-sized states exerted little leverage.

Macmillan's sorrows came not in single spies but in battalions. In 1961 the Commonwealth, in which such tremendous hopes had once been invested, veered close to disintegration over the position of apartheid South Africa, which withdrew from the organisation following a stormy heads of government meeting in London. It had been clear for some time that the 'new', multiracial Commonwealth would not be the docile instrument of British policy for which some had hoped. As the 'Anglosphere' fractured around him, Macmillan confessed to 'a sense of despair', 'weighed down by a sense of grief and foreboding'.[58]

By the early 1960s, the unravelling of Britain's global position was attracting international comment. In December 1962, the former US secretary of state Dean Acheson delivered a famous speech at the military academy at West Point. 'Great Britain', he declared, 'has lost an Empire and has not yet found a role.' What followed was a brutal critique of British strategy since 1945:

> The attempt to play a separate power role – that is, a role apart from Europe, a role based on a 'special relationship' with the United States, a role based on being the head of a 'commonwealth' which has no political structure, or unity, or strength, and enjoys a fragile and precarious economic relationship by means of the Sterling area and preferences in the British market – this role is about played out.

In attempting 'to work alone and to be a broker between the United States and Russia', he concluded, Britain had found its diplomatic influence to be 'as weak as its military power'.[59]

Acheson drew the moral that Britain should seek a new role in Europe, but there were still those who hoped to reactivate a global strategy. The Labour government that came to power in 1964 was determined to restore Britain as a power with extended military reach. The prime minister, Harold Wilson, boasted in 1965 that 'our frontiers are in the Himalayas', and he informed the US government the same year that 'if the choice had to be made he would rather pull half our troops out of Germany than move any from the Far East'.[60] That vision disintegrated under the weight of a crisis in the public finances and the relentless pressure on sterling. In 1967 the Cabinet finally agreed – in the teeth of strong American opposition – to liquidate Britain's military commitments 'East of Suez'. In a sombre statement to the House, Wilson announced that from 1971, Britain would no longer maintain military bases outside Europe and the Mediterranean. This, he acknowledged, 'means reassessing our role in the world', 'limiting our commitments and outgoings to our true capacities'.[61]

On one level, the withdrawal from 'East of Suez' was merely a long overdue recalibration of Britain's military commitments. Yet in other respects, the decision to axe the UK's South Asian commitments rather than the British Army of the Rhine marked a rupture in national policy. For the first time in its modern history, Britain had chosen to concentrate its military forces on the Continent, rather than at the end of sea-lanes policed by the Royal Navy. Historians have rightly argued that withdrawal encouraged Wilson's turn to the EEC by reducing British influence elsewhere. In so far as it represented a choice, however, the decision to withdraw from Singapore and Malaysia rather than from Germany was a symptom, as well as a cause, of the European turn in British policy.[62]

In this context, membership of the European Community offered a new field for British influence, at a time when its old estates were falling into disrepair. The ambition to exert leadership had not changed (as Wilson commented privately, 'If we couldn't dominate that lot, there wasn't much to be said for us'), but western Europe would take the part previously played by the Commonwealth and Empire.[63] Ministers were finally embracing the role that American governments had envisaged for them since the war, as the leader of a western European bloc that might otherwise fall prey to anti-Americanism in France or neutralism in West Germany. For Macmillan and Wilson alike, entry into the European Community was not an alternative to the 'special relationship'; rather, it was intended to restore Britain's utility to the United States by anchoring western Europe in the Atlantic alliance.[64]

For this reason, de Gaulle's decision to veto British entry – first in 1963, then again in 1967 – came as a bitter blow to British strategy. Macmillan was said to have been close to tears when he told embassy staff that the first application had failed; 'all our policies at home and abroad', he lamented, 'are in ruins'.[65] Wilson insisted, valiantly, that he would not take '*non*' for an answer; the application would remain on the table until de Gaulle was either converted or carried off in a fiery chariot. Yet this was making a virtue out of necessity. Unable to maintain its old position 'East of Suez' and barred from a new position 'East of Calais', the painful truth was that Britain lacked either a coherent foreign policy or any clear role in the global order.

AFFLUENCE AND DECLINE

It was these strategic, rather than economic, considerations that first pushed governments towards membership. As the Chancellor of the Exchequer, Derick Heathcoat-Amory, noted in 1960, entry was 'a political act with economic consequences', rather than the reverse.[66] Yet those economic consequences could hardly be ignored, if only because Britain's economic weakness was the most visible constraint upon its capacity to act overseas. Here, too, the balance of argument shifted over the 1950s and '60s. If the conversion of the Treasury to membership was less swift and less full-hearted than that of the Foreign Office, it was an essential precondition for a successful application.

Assessed on its own terms, the economic record of the post-war years was not to be sneezed at. The real value of exports grew by more than three-quarters from 1946 to 1950, and the ending of rationing in the early fifties triggered an explosion in consumer goods such as cars, washing machines and television sets.[67] Borrowing a term from the United States, academics and sociologists began to talk of 'the affluent society'. The Chancellor of the Exchequer, 'Rab' Butler, spoke of 'doubling our standard of living' by 1970, while Harold Macmillan told voters that Britain was enjoying 'a state of prosperity such as we have never had in my lifetime – nor indeed in the history of this country'. 'Let us be frank about it,' he proclaimed; 'most of our people have never had it so good.'[68]

This was true; yet the suspicion was growing that others were having it better. If 'affluence' was one of the key preoccupations of the post-war era, its vengeful twin was the notion of 'decline'. As Jim Tomlinson has argued, 'declinism' was an 'ideology', not a straightforward description of reality.[69] It drew force, ironically, from one of the accidental by-products of European integration: the emergence of comparative economic statistics. For the first time, opposition parties looking for a stick with which to beat the government had ready access to authoritative international data, measuring growth rates, productivity, industrial output and foreign trade. The lessons drawn from those figures were in some respects misleading – growth rates, for example, took little account of 'catch-up' by smaller economies – but they introduced a new and powerful weapon into domestic political warfare.

On almost every measure, the comparison made gloomy reading for the UK. From 1961 to 1974, gross domestic product (GDP) per capita rose by 215 per cent in the EEC but just 88 per cent in Britain; labour productivity increased by 243 per cent in the Six and 94 per cent in the UK. The EEC enjoyed an average growth rate of 4.5 per cent between 1963 and 1972, more than 50 per cent higher than in Britain (2.9 per cent).[70] West Germany had overtaken Britain as an exporter of manufactured goods as early as 1958, and it stretched its lead over the decade that followed. In 1950 West Germany had accounted for just 7.3 per cent of the value of world exports, compared to 25.5 per cent for Britain. By 1960, the figures were 19.3 per cent and 16.5 per cent in favour of West Germany. By 1970, Britain's share had dropped to 10.8 per cent – a fall from more than a quarter to just over a tenth in twenty years.[71] As early as 1954, a committee of inquiry concluded that, if current trends continued, 'the relegation of the UK to the 2nd division in the industrial league would not be far off. At the moment there is not much visible reason for optimism.'[72]

While continental economies were booming, trade with the Commonwealth was declining in importance. By 1960 the sterling area took just 30 per cent of British exports, down from 48 per cent a decade earlier. Other powers (notably the United States and Japan) were eating into colonial markets, while the liberalisation of global trade rules eroded the value of Britain's imperial preferences.[73] With manufactured goods, not commodities, emerging as the drivers of global trade, there was a growing sense that Britain had backed the wrong horse in prioritising its Commonwealth markets. In 1962, for the first time, Britain traded more with the Six than with the Commonwealth. The UK was being drawn into the gravitational field of the Six, without exerting any influence over its policy.

As its economic performance deteriorated, the mismatch between Britain's global commitments and its capacity to bear them became increasingly obvious. The result was a succession of sterling crises, with governments oscillating between expansionary policies to grow the domestic economy and deflationary budgets to protect the pound. As Labour discovered, on returning to power in 1964, the problem could not simply be chalked up to Tory mismanagement. Britain's problems, it appeared, were structural, requiring more than a change of leadership to address them. It was no coincidence that Labour's application to the EEC, in 1967, came shortly after the collapse of its 'National Plan' a year earlier, which had promised growth of 4 per cent per annum, and amidst the humiliating sequence of events that culminated in the devaluation of the currency in 1967.

As governments tugged ineffectually on the economic levers at home, the more alluring became the success of their continental neighbours. Yet membership, as the Treasury's own studies made clear, would not be a magic bullet. There was no guarantee that entry would transfer to the UK the high growth rates achieved by the Six, and there would be risks in exposing a weakened British economy to the full force of continental competition. Even Roy Jenkins, an enthusiast for membership, believed that 'in the first three or four years we shall lose but not gain'.[74] The danger was that, rather than stimulating British industry to more efficient production, competition from France and West Germany would overpower its domestic rivals. This would be especially true if entry drove up food prices, imposing an inflationary pressure on wages. In the worst case, entry might increase labour costs while exposing British industry to a level of competition that it was no longer able to bear.[75]

The result was a paradox that haunted British thinking on membership. On the one hand, the more Britain was outperformed by its continental neighbours, the more it could be said to have missed out by rejecting membership. Yet the weaker the economy became as a consequence, the more risky it was to dismantle tariff barriers against the Six. To put it differently: the longer Britain shut itself off from European competition, the more uncompetitive its industries would become; yet the more uncompetitive it became, the less it could benefit from the 'bracing' effects of competition.

With the results so uncertain, the arguments deployed in economic debate were often philosophical in character, linked to particular analyses of decline. For those who blamed a reactionary governing class or an atmosphere of conservatism in industry, entry represented 'modernisation' and a willingness to face the future. Those who blamed trade unions or restrictive practices looked to membership to provide a stirring blast of competition, while taking trade policy out of the hands of left-wing politicians. For those who favoured a psychological explanation, or who took the view that Britain was 'dying by the mind', entry offered precisely the kind of new adventure that could rekindle the national spirit.[76] In some quarters it became fashionable to talk about the 'dynamic' or 'bracing' effects of membership, reminiscent of the cold showers and floggings enjoyed by so many politicians at boarding school. Heath told voters in 1971 that 'For twenty-five years we've been looking for something to get us going again. Now here it is.'[77] The *Evening Standard* put it more bluntly: the 1967 application was 'a desperate "try anything" move to jolt the economy into active life'.[78]

Just as importantly, economic decline diminished some of the concerns that had previously impeded entry. As trade with the Commonwealth became a smaller portion of the whole, it became less of a wrench to reorient Britain's trade preferences towards the Continent. (The exception here was food, discussed in Chapter 10.) From 1962, entering the Common Market no longer meant sacrificing a larger trading partner to a smaller; the gamble on the future that would have been necessary in 1957 was now simply an accommodation to reality. In this respect, while the economic benefits of membership remained unproven, there was no longer an overpowering economic case *against* joining if that seemed desirable on political or diplomatic grounds.

This was the conclusion reached by every government from Macmillan's onwards. It fuelled the doomed Conservative application of 1961–3, the Labour application of 1967 and the successful Conservative approach of 1970–2. Yet the case for entry had a curiously schizophrenic character. On the one hand, the assumptions on which it was based were almost brashly optimistic: it was never doubted that Britain's destiny was to *lead* the Continent, establishing a new base from which to exert its global influence. In a tub-thumping performance at the Conservative Party conference in 1971, Geoffrey Rippon claimed that 'the armoured brigade of our language, our technology and our way of life would be thrusting across Europe once Britain joined'.[79] Yet the case for leading in Europe was founded on the disintegration of Britain's position outside the Community. The 1971 White Paper warned that a decision to stay out would mark a dead end for British strategy. 'In a single generation', it intoned, 'we would have renounced an imperial past and rejected a European future.'[80] In this respect, Britain resembled the shipwrecked children in a Victorian adventure story, who crawl ashore onto a tropical island and promptly declare themselves king and queen. The former German Chancellor, Konrad Adenauer, once likened Britain to 'a rich man who had lost all his property but does not realise it', an attitude that was to persist long after entry.[81]

'A CITY AT UNITY IN ITSELF'

Before 1970, there was little to suggest that the European issue would have quite so explosive an effect on British politics. The key debates had taken place far from the public eye, and the conclusions reached within the Cabinet, the Treasury and the Foreign Office had proven remarkably durable across administrations. The first application was made by a Conservative government, the second by Labour, and when the latter application was put to a vote in May 1967, cross-party support produced one of the largest parliamentary majorities in peacetime history. Wilson was preparing to reactivate the application when he was rudely interrupted by the electorate in 1970, but Britain's seat at the negotiations was occupied seamlessly by the incoming Conservative administration under Heath. Neither public opinion nor party differences had featured prominently, nor was the issue much discussed in the 1970 election.

Yet the drumbeat of opposition to membership had been muted, rather than stilled. So long as the negotiations were ongoing, politicians could reserve judgement on the principle of membership, pending a decision on the 'terms of entry'. After 1963, the likelihood that de Gaulle would veto any application also gave the debate an air of unreality. The conviction that 'the General will save us from our folly' undoubtedly helped to preserve Labour unity during the second application, and one (pro-Market) minister recalled 'an overwhelming sigh of relief' in Cabinet when the veto was announced.[82]

De Gaulle's resignation in 1969 – and his death a year later – transformed the situation. In May 1971, Heath held talks with President Pompidou in an atmosphere that was closer to a tryst than a summit. As the two leaders billed and cooed at one another during a press conference, Pompidou expressly disavowed the Gaullist view that 'Great Britain was not and did not wish to become European.'[83] While the negotiations that followed were complex and sometimes difficult, the removal of French opposition meant that a deal was always likely. In consequence, the point of decision moved for the first time from Paris to Westminster. The decisive battles for Heath would be fought, not in the Palais d'Elysée or the Council of Ministers, but on the floor of the House of Commons.

Heath was not, like Macmillan or Wilson, a reluctant convert to membership. In his maiden speech in Parliament, as far back as 1950, he had urged the government to join the negotiations on the Schuman Plan, and entry to the European Community had become 'the main theme and justification of his whole political career'.[84] As the government's chief negotiator during the first application, Heath was said to have flown more than 10,000 miles in an attempt to build consensus. The War was a constant reference point (by a strange quirk of fate, he had first met the French foreign minister, Maurice Schumann, on the beaches of Normandy in 1944) and he set the negotiations explicitly in the context of Europe's century of war.[85] As he put it in a radio broadcast in the summer of 1971:

> When we achieve our ambitions then history will indeed know
> that that spirit of man has at last triumphed over the divisions and
> dissensions, the hatred and the strife that plagued our continent
> for a thousand years. Humanity will be grateful that our European
> civilization, to which it already owes so much, will be able to flower
> afresh in unity and concord.[86]

Heath had a genuine admiration for the cultural life of Europe, though his strangled attempts at French were reminiscent less of the Rive Gauche than of the English policeman in 'Allo 'Allo.[87] He admired what he saw as the more open, unstuffy character of continental Europe and, as a keen musician, felt a special affinity with its musical life. In a speech to the Royal Academy in 1971, he invoked a vision of Europe 'as a city at unity in itself, that had peace within its walls and plenteousness within its palaces ... a place where the arts flourished and were honoured, a place where artists could live and work, a place where men could sing the merry songs of peace to all their neighbours'. When the decisive vote was passed in the Commons, he retired to his private sitting room to play Bach on his clavichord, and it was no coincidence that he chose to mark entry with a festival of art and culture.[88]

By contrast, no prime minister took a more jaundiced view of the 'special relationship' with the United States. Britain, he thought, should aspire to more than 'to nestle on the shoulders of an American President'.[89] When he visited Washington in 1973, reporters were told 'time and again that the phrase "Anglo-American Special Relationship" is not part of his own vocabulary'. The most he was prepared to acknowledge was a '*natural* relationship', which should now be seen in the framework of the US–European exchange.[90]

Anti-Marketeers reserved a special place in their bowels for Heath, whose patriotism, they suspected, began on the wrong side of the English Channel. In this, they underestimated what his biographer, John Campbell, calls Heath's 'sturdy English patriotism, pride in the uniqueness of Britain's history' and 'ardent desire to reassert British leadership in the world'. Heath believed as staunchly as the most tub-thumping patriot in the greatness of his country and in its destiny to global leadership. Membership of the European Community 'was not, in his view, a substitute for a role in the wider world'; rather, it offered 'a broader platform, a wider economic base, from which British influence could be exercised and amplified'.[91] In economic terms, he looked to membership to provide a competitive shock to British industry that would force it to modernise. With a leaner, more efficient industrial base, Britain could play its proper role in the struggle against the Soviet Union, a contest to which Heath was also very powerfully committed.[92]

'FULL-HEARTED CONSENT'

Returning from the negotiations in 1971, Heath found himself under fire from both sides of the House. Opposition within the Conservative Party was led by the maverick figure of Enoch Powell. From his resignation from the Treasury in 1958, through the notorious 'Rivers of Blood' speech in 1968, to his reinvention as a prophet of Thatcherism, Powell was a political meteor, who blazed across the firmament of British politics in a spectacular and sustained act of self-immolation. He combined a formidable intellect, which had once made him the youngest professor in the British Empire, with devastating rhetorical powers, for which he was feared, adored and despised in equal measure. Heath had sacked him from the Shadow Cabinet in 1968, following the 'Rivers of Blood' speech, and since then Powell had positioned himself as a prophet-in-exile, calling down vengeance from the heavens on his former leader. Powell's contempt for Heath was not the cause of his opposition to the EEC, but he made no secret of his desire for revenge on a man whom he viewed as a traitor to his country.

Powell's thought was complex and mystical, but its atomic core was a burning, quasi-religious commitment to the idea of nationhood. The nation, he believed, was the fundamental principle of politics: 'the thing for which men, if necessary, fight and, if necessary, die, and to preserve which men think no sacrifice too great'. For Powell, the fundamental task of politics was the defence of the realm, understood not simply as its physical integrity but as its sense of its own identity. It was the principle for which, in 1940, young men had taken to the skies in defiance of the Nazi war machine; it was the principle that animated those colonial resistance movements so applauded by the Left. 'There is not a state in Africa or Asia,' Powell claimed, 'hewn out of some administrative unit of Western colonial rule, which would not scorn to bargain away its independence.' Britain, he told a rally in Montgomeryshire, was engaged in 'a life and death struggle':

> with other weapons and in other ways, the contention is as surely about the future of Britain's nationhood as were the combats which raged in the skies over southern England in the autumn of 1940. The gladiators were few; their weapons are but words; and yet their fight is everyman's.[93]

FIGURE 1.2   Enoch Powell in full rhetorical flame, at a Get Britain Out meeting in 1974.
Source: Wesley, Hulton Archive: www.gettyimages.co.uk/license/508726306

As Powell freely acknowledged, there was 'no rational basis for nationhood'. A nation was a spiritual entity, defined only as 'what it feels itself to be, instinctively and emotionally'. For Powell, it was precisely this imaginative and emotional conception of nationhood that made the Community such a danger. The EEC would not invade Britain's territory, as the Nazis had attempted, but it would erode a sense of nationhood forged not simply in *isolation* from the Continent but in active *opposition* to it:

> In our history, both recent and earlier, the principal events which have placed their stamp upon our consciousness of who we are, were the very moments in which we have been alone, confronting a Europe which was lost or hostile. That is the picture, that is the folk memory, by which our nation has been formed.[94]

Becoming 'European', Powell believed, would mark a psychological rupture for the British amounting almost to self-harm. Whatever treaties Heath signed, it was psychologically impossible for Britain to be 'European'. 'The relevant fact about the history of the British Isles', he declared, 'and above all of England is its separateness in a political sense from the history of continental Europe. The English have never belonged, and they have always known that they did not belong.'[95]

From the conclusion of the negotiations to the passing of the European Communities Act, Powell stumped the country like an itinerant preacher. His speeches were a call to faith, often couched in the language of national awakening. A former critic, the Labour peer Lord

Wigg, compared him admiringly to de Gaulle, the man who had lit 'the flame of French resistance' in 1940.[96] Powell himself, who had likened the struggle against the bill to the Battle of Britain, had no hesitation in comparing the pro-Marketeers to the men of Munich. As he commented before the referendum in 1975, 'if referendum day is not September, 1939, at any rate it is September, 1938'.[97]

Powell's sacral idea of nationhood was probably a minority taste, but he coupled it with two more specific allegations that ministers found harder to dismiss. The first was that membership struck a decisive blow against the sovereignty of Parliament, a charge made manifest by the process of British entry. As a late arrival to the Community, Parliament was required to adopt wholesale entire volumes of pre-existing European legislation, which it was permitted neither to reject nor to amend. In the words of the European Communities Act, which provided the legal basis for membership, 'All such rights, powers, liabilities, obligations and restrictions' arising from the Treaties of the Community were, 'without further enactment', to take legal effect in the United Kingdom.[98] The Act itself had just 12 clauses, and could not be amended without reopening the entire deal negotiated with the other members. Never before, on a major constitutional question, had the role of Parliament been reduced to a simple Yes/No proposition.

This was annexed to an argument that became central to the anti-Market cause: that ministers had not been honest with the public in the previous general election. The Conservative manifesto in 1970 had been distinctly reticent on the EEC, placing special emphasis on the obstacles and drawbacks to membership. It had taken twenty-eight pages even to broach the topic, and the tone thereafter was notably tepid:

> If we can negotiate the right terms, we believe that it would be in the long-term interest of the British people for Britain to join the European Economic Community ... But we must also recognise the obstacles. There would be short-term disadvantages in Britain going into the European Economic Community which must be weighed against the long term benefits. Obviously there is a price we would not be prepared to pay. Only when we negotiate will it be possible to determine whether the balance is a fair one.

It concluded by sitting squarely on the political fence. 'Our sole commitment', it declared, 'is to negotiate; no more, no less.' 'A Conservative

Government would not be prepared to recommend to Parliament, nor would Members of Parliament approve, a settlement which was unequal or unfair.'[99]

If the manifesto suggested only a willingness to dip its collective toes in the water, the party's candidates were no more forthcoming. A contemporary study of the 1970 election found that 62 per cent of Conservative candidates made no reference to the subject at all, while a further 15 per cent did so without any particular commitment either way. Only 12 per cent expressed support for membership. 77 per cent of Labour candidates were silent on the issue, while just 6 per cent spoke in favour of entry.[100] This was not, in itself, surprising. Election campaigns inevitably focus on those areas where parties disagree (or where they wish to persuade voters that they disagree). In 1970, by contrast, all parties were assumed to favour entry. Yet this, in itself, pointed to a problem of consent. With all three parties backing membership, there was no opportunity for the electorate to register its assent or opposition to the process. Under these conditions, it was difficult to claim a decisive mandate. As the columnist Anthony Sampson noted, 'It is an embarrassing reflection on democracy that, ten days after an election in which the Common Market was scarcely mentioned, it should emerge as the central political issue.'[101]

To make matters worse, Heath had given a speech in France in May 1970, in which he suggested that enlargement could only take place with 'the full-hearted consent of the peoples and parliaments' of each country. Yet a private poll for the Conservative Party, taken shortly before the 1970 election, found only 18 per cent of the public in favour of entry. Heath insisted subsequently that he had never intended any kind of direct mandate; rather, the 'voice of the people would speak *through* their elected Parliament'.[102] Even at Westminster, however, the scale of opposition was becoming a concern. With Labour and a section of the Conservative Party increasingly hostile, it was difficult to argue that support was 'full-hearted', even if a bare majority could be put together. The crucial vote on the second reading of the European Communities Bill was carried by a majority of just eight, falling as low as four in the Committee stage that followed. The bill was finally carried by a majority of seventeen. The 'full-hearted consent of the House of Commons', Powell claimed, 'can be given only by a House of Commons overwhelmingly united'. Ministers could not 'without indelible breach of honour, purport to accede to the Treaty of Rome if Her Majesty's Opposition were against'.[103]

For the Conservative leadership, the first priority was to keep the rebellion among their own supporters within manageable proportions. That meant appealing to party loyalties and emphasising the 'Conservative' dimensions of membership: notably the increased access to markets; the spur to competition; and the potential of the Community as an anti-Communist bloc. The problem, of course, was that the more the government tailored its arguments to the views of Conservative waverers, the more hostility it could expect from Labour. Opposition within Labour had been building rapidly since 1970, and would plunge both British membership and the party itself into an enduring crisis.

'A COMPETITIVE JUNGLE'

Had Labour won the general election in 1970, it would swiftly have reactivated the 1967 application for membership. Talks were scheduled to begin on 30 June – just twelve days after the election.[104] Where the Conservative manifesto had hedged its bets on the subject, Labour promised that its application would be 'pressed with determination', so that the British could 'play our full part in creating a more secure, prosperous and united Europe'.[105]

That mood did not long survive election defeat. At the party conference in October 1970, the leadership only narrowly beat off a motion opposing membership on principle. In January 1971, 119 Labour MPs signed an Early Day Motion opposing entry 'on terms so far envisaged', and the following month Jim Callaghan made the first in a series of speeches attacking the Community. Over the summer, a number of trade unions passed votes condemning the application – in the case of the National Union of Mineworkers, following a discussion that lasted just thirteen minutes.[106] When the Commons debated the terms in October, Labour Members queued up to denounce entry.

For Conservative Marketeers, who had trooped loyally through the lobbies in support of the Labour application in 1967, the willingness of their opponents simply to dump their own policy embodied everything they despised about Wilson's unprincipled political style. As one minister commented, 'a single journey to Damascus is respectable, but when a whole party goes in for a package tour the gullibility of onlookers is strained beyond endurance'.[107] Yet the Wilson application had concealed, rather than abolished, Labour's doubts about membership. When the Commons had debated the application in May 1967, 86 Labour MPs – almost a quarter of the parliamentary party – had defied a three-line whip, with 36 voting against the government and 50 abstaining, despite the widespread expectation that de Gaulle would veto the application. Once it became clear, after de Gaulle's resignation in 1969, that the application would be renewed – and still more, as it became clear that a Tory government would lead the negotiations – Labour opposition became positively raucous.

Labour attacks focused principally on the capitalist credentials of the Community, as a body 'run by businessmen in the interests of businessmen'; the 'real purpose' of which was 'to strengthen and extend monopoly capitalism in Europe'.[108] MPs condemned a Community that 'enshrines the profit motive and worships competition', 'a competitive jungle ... in which all lame ducks go to the wall, in which the trade unions are forced to face the facts of life, and in which a few years of misery will produce a Conservative heaven'. It was widely believed that multinational companies were seeking to liberate themselves from oversight by national electorates, with 'large firms moving around like prehistoric animals eating each other up'. Others feared the consequences for peripheral regions, given 'the gravitational pull of industry towards the South-East of Britain, which is nearest to the Continental "golden triangle"'. There was also suspicion from those with an interest in Third World aid and development, who feared that the purpose of the Community was 'to protect and defend the rich European nations' against 'the smaller, developing and weak nations of the world'.[109]

Running alongside all this was a defence of parliamentary sovereignty. This provided a point of contact with the Tory Marketeers; indeed, Powell claimed that Michael Foot's speeches against the bill entitled him to a place among 'the great figures of parliamentary history'.[110] Yet Labour thinking on sovereignty had a specifically socialist hue. The idea that animated public ownership and state planning was not simply that the state could organise the economy more intelligently than the blind forces of market competition, though this was an important element of the case. More fundamental was the belief that those economic forces which shaped the lives of workers and citizens should themselves be subject to democratic control. If the great battle of the nineteenth century had been to subject political authority to the judgement of the people, the struggle of the twentieth had been to apply the same process to the equally powerful, but less tangible forces of market capitalism. It was on this basis that Foot traced back his socialism to John Milton, the Levellers and the constitutional struggles of the sixteenth century. The charge against the European Community was that it sought to release the market from the control of democratic governments. As Foot told the Commons in 1971:

> Many of us on this side of the House ... have argued for most of our political lives that what we wish to secure is that the great economic decisions shall be made in a way that is responsible to this elected House of Commons. We believe if we go into Europe on the terms which have been arranged under the provisions that have been made there will be some derogation from the sovereignty of this House in dealing with such matters as taxation, coal, steel, the levels of unemployment, and regional policy.[111]

Another MP warned that 'unless we control the commanding heights of the economy we cannot control our own destiny', and 'we shall not be able to do it if we go into Europe'.[112] Foot placed special emphasis on Value Added Tax (VAT), which would be raised to pay for Britain's budget contribution. Once established as part of the UK's financial contribution, 'the British people will have less power to protest against the value-added tax than John Hampden had to protest about ship money. If we go into the Community, that will be settled away from this House.'[113]

'FISH AND CHIPS AND HP SAUCE'

This posed considerable difficulties for the Labour leader, Harold Wilson. Unlike Heath, Wilson was not 'emotionally a Europe man'; on the contrary, as he repeatedly made clear, he was 'fundamentally a Commonwealth man', whose emotional ties lay across the seas in Australia and New Zealand.[114] Bernard Donoughue, who ran the Number 10 Policy Unit, thought that Wilson was 'mildly anti-European, in the sense that *personally* he doesn't like Europeans, their style of life or their politics'.[115] Wilson, wrote one observer, inhabited 'a world of fish and chips and HP sauce – a world that still regarded everything beyond the English Channel as foreign and "other"'.[116] Yet he had applied for membership in 1967 and had been preparing a further application before the election in 1970.

Penetrating Wilson's motives is a notoriously baffling enterprise.[117] It is generally agreed, however, that he had come to the conclusion at some point in 1966 that the global influence to which Britain was entitled could only be exercised through leadership of the Common Market. He was also excited by the possibilities of technological co-operation, in the belief that 'the white heat of technology' required a larger furnace in order to compete with American and Soviet activity.[118] As Donoughue notes, however, Wilson saw the issue not primarily as 'one of principle, but as a question of political party management'.[119] After 1970, in particular, the central object of his European policy was to limit its emetic effect on the Labour Party, while rebuilding a personal authority that had been badly damaged by election defeat.

Wilson faced a party in 1970 that was tearing itself apart over the European issue, at a time when his own standing was at a low ebb. The party had swung sharply to the left since the elections, and grass-roots opinion was increasingly hostile to membership. His long-standing rival, Jim Callaghan, burnished his own leadership ambitions with a series of tub-thumping speeches to party audiences, warning that 'the language of Chaucer, Shakespeare and Milton' was in peril from 'Continental claustrophobia'.[120] Furthermore, a party at war with the Conservatives over trade union reform, local government, the Shrewsbury pickets and Rhodesia could hardly ignore the opportunity to exploit Tory difficulties over Europe. Labour's chief whip, Robert Mellish, was generally thought to favour membership, but he announced in February 1972 that 'I would do anything short of anarchy to bring this government down.'[121]

In this climate, Wilson came under severe pressure to commit the party against membership. Yet quite apart from his own record, a wing of the party was as passionately determined to support the government on this issue as Mellish was to oppose it. This group included senior figures like Roy Jenkins and Shirley Williams, as well as much of the party's younger talent. A hundred Labour MPs signed an advertisement in the *Guardian* in May 1971, urging membership in the interests of 'social democracy, world peace and economic advance'.[122] The Labour Committee for Europe was well organised, well funded and maintained close relations with the government whips, to ensure that its European legislation was never likely to fail. In the crucial debate in October 1971, on the principle of membership, 69 Labour MPs defied the party whip and voted with the government. A further 20 abstained, helping to secure a majority of 112 for ministers.[123]

It was not Wilson's style to align himself decisively with one faction or the other (he once told the Cabinet 'I'm at my best in a messy middle-of-the-road muddle').[124] Instead, his priority was to stop the party breaking up altogether. The spectre haunting the Labour Party was 1931, when a breach between the Cabinet and the party membership had almost destroyed the party under Ramsay MacDonald.[125] As he repeatedly made clear to the Cabinet, Wilson was determined not to preside over a second split, while preserving his freedom to act in what he considered the national interest.[126] His strategy was to avoid any commitment on the *principle* of membership (what he contemptuously described as 'the theology' of the question) by launching an all-out assault on the *terms* negotiated by Heath. In the short term, this meant giving the Antis their head, concentrating on ministers the fury that might otherwise have rained down on Wilson. Yet it also prevented the party from ruling out membership in principle, the position favoured by a majority of trade unions and activists. Just as importantly, it left open the possibility that a Labour government might support membership in future, once the 'Tory terms' had been amended. It was not a heroic stance – Wilson raged that he had 'waded through shit, so that others could indulge their consciences' – but it averted a full-blown civil war.[127]

This emphasis on the terms was tactically useful, but it also reflected Wilson's own intellectual preferences. As Barbara Castle once said of Callaghan, Wilson was 'constitutionally incapable of being stirred by great issues of principle'.[128] Unlike Heath or Jenkins, he was unmoved by the romantic ideal of European unity; but nor did he share the reverence of Michael Foot or Tony Benn for Britain's ancient institutions. Even in 1961, when 'virulently' opposed to membership, Wilson had dismissed concerns about sovereignty as 'out of harmony with this modern age'. 'The question', he continued, was 'not whether sovereignty remains absolute or not, but in what way one is prepared to sacrifice sovereignty, to whom and for what purpose'.[129] Always less interested in the wood than the trees, an emphasis on the *terms* of membership suited Wilson intellectually as well as strategically.

SCHRÖDINGER'S CABINET

Heath won the parliamentary battle, and on 1 January 1973 the United Kingdom became a member of the European Community. But it was Wilson who won the war. By 1974, he had thrashed out an uneasy compromise within his party, by which it reserved judgement on the principle of membership until new terms could be negotiated and put to the public. As he put it in 1975, Labour was 'neither in favour of being in Europe on principle, or being out of the Common Market on principle'.[130] Unable to commit either to membership or to withdrawal, Labour had contained its contradictions within what might be termed 'Schrödinger's Cabinet': a body that was simultaneously pro-Market and anti-Market, until such time as the wave function of Wilsonian ambiguity was collapsed.

That moment came in 1974, with the fall of the Heath government. The Fanfare for Europe had quickly turned into a requiem for Heath, whose dreams of a 'quiet revolution' had disintegrated under a succession of economic shocks. The European Communities Act came to stand almost as the solitary achievement of his premiership, something that probably strengthened the attachment of the Conservative Party to membership. The departure of Enoch Powell from the party also weakened the Tory Antis. Powell stood down from Parliament in February 1974, telling his supporters, in a final act of vengeance, to vote Labour in the election. That act of betrayal deprived Conservative anti-Marketeers of their most eloquent champion, for party members could more easily forgive entry to the Common Market than a decision to back the Opposition. Powell returned to the Commons in October as an Ulster Unionist, but he would never again sit as a Conservative.

Heath's defeat was a triumph for Wilson, but it opened the lid on Labour's internal divisions. As prime minister and foreign secretary, Wilson and Callaghan had now to decide the terms of the renegotiation and make a formal recommendation. Securing a new deal in Europe, while holding his party together and keeping Britain in the EEC, would test to the limit even Wilson's powers of political prestidigitation.

2 'A DEVICE OF DICTATORS AND DEMAGOGUES': RENEGOTIATION TO REFERENDUM

The referendum is a constitutional monstrosity. Heaven only knows how much harm it will do to our Parliamentary birthright.

The Sun, 5 June 1975[1]

the country which has the greatest number of referenda is Switzerland. If anybody can tell me where the dictator or demagogue is in Switzerland, I shall be glad to meet him when I am next over there skiing.

Neil Marten, 18 April 1972[2]

Beneath the still-moving rubble of Her Majesty's Government, the British Constitution lies bleeding.

Daily Mail, 20 March 1975[3]

For Harold Wilson, who returned to Downing Street in February 1974, ambiguity was a political art form. No prime minister of the modern era so baffled and bewildered his contemporaries, or found such a happy home in the fog of political warfare. In Wilson's capable hands, tedium and obscurity became potent tools of party management. He excelled at asphyxiating contentious topics, delivering 'rambling résumés' in Cabinet that left colleagues too bored and exhausted to fight. Ministers could be astonished at what slipped past their defences while minds were wandering. As Barbara Castle confided to her diary, 'when Harold reduces everything to a boring, and almost bored, low key, I reach for my critical faculties'.[4]

There was one subject, however, on which the prime minister could hardly have been more explicit. Wilson's hostility to the referendum was clear, direct and long-standing; as a contemporary wryly observed, 'on this issue, and on this issue alone, Harold Wilson nailed his colours to the mast'.[5] Asked in 1969 whether he would permit a referendum on the European question, Wilson dismissed the idea as 'contrary to our traditions' and 'not a way in which we can do business'. A referendum, he scoffed, would probably 'give 100 per cent support for abolishing income tax'.[6] When the question was posed again, during an election broadcast in 1970, Wilson delivered a gift-wrapped hostage to fortune: 'I have given my answer many times', he announced, 'and I don't change it because the polls go either up or down.' 'I am not going to trim to win votes on a question like that.' The following year, as Leader of the Opposition, he took the unusual step of interrupting the prime minister to assure him of his support on the question. 'I oppose a referendum ... I have always done so, as he has.'[7]

Wilson's animus towards the referendum drew on a deep seam in British political thought. The UK had no national tradition of direct democracy, and the practice was widely associated with despots such as Napoleon III, Hitler and Mussolini. In 1945, when Churchill suggested a referendum to extend the duration of Parliament, he received a thunderous rebuke from Clement Attlee:

> I could not consent to the introduction into our national life of a device so alien to all our traditions as the referendum, which has only too often been the instrument of Nazism and Fascism. Hitler's practices in the field of referenda and plebiscites can hardly have endeared these expedients to the British heart.[8]

The left-wing *New Statesman* claimed in 1970 that, if the UK had been governed by referendum, it 'would still exercise the death penalty, flog young criminals, forbid abortion, repatriate immigrants, punish homosexuals, ban strikes and abolish aid to poorer countries'.[9] Margaret Thatcher (who might have applauded some of this list) used her maiden speech as party leader to denounce the referendum, calling it 'a device of dictators and demagogues'.[10]

It was not simply politicians or dusty constitutionalists who took this view. The *Sun* called the referendum a 'constitutional monstrosity', while the *Daily Mirror* thought it 'a thoroughly bad innovation', which 'MUST NEVER HAPPEN AGAIN'.[11] There was also hostility from religious leaders, with bishops warning that Britain could not be 'godly and quietly governed by opinion poll'.[12] Mocking the kind of voters that would have to decide the question, the *Mirror* published a spoof interview with eighty-four-year-old Mrs Emily Goodweather, who lived at '142 Blackpudding Cottages' with 'her three cats, her two budgerigars, and her potted aspidistra'. 'I don't know a lot about Europe,' she confessed, 'although I did once go to Bournemouth for my holidays.'[13]

The decision to hold a referendum thus constituted a threefold revolution. It changed fundamentally the practice of the British constitution; it overturned some of the most basic assumptions of British political thought; and it marked a 180-degree reversal in Wilson's own position. This spoke volumes for the disruptive potential of the European question and its capacity to rewrite the constitutional practice of member states. It is indicative, too, of the peculiar character of the European debate, both in the gravity of the constitutional issues it raised and in the difficulty of containing the subject within conventional electoral politics.

To win the referendum, Wilson needed to deliver on the second part of the package that was put to voters in February 1974: the promise to renegotiate the terms of membership. After years of denouncing Heath's 'Tory terms', Wilson had to offer at least the pretence of a new deal. Yet there was no guarantee that he would be successful, either in the negotiations themselves or in selling them to his party. Wilson later recalled the 'miserably unhappy period' from October 1974 to the summer of 1975 as 'the most hectic and demanding' of his premiership. He was struggling to juggle the referendum campaign and the diplomatic exercise in Europe with an increasingly dangerous economic crisis, while also suffering from heart problems. 'In all my thirteen years as Leader of the Party', he wrote later, 'I had no more difficult task than keeping the Party together on this issue.'[14]

This chapter is divided into two parts. The first focuses on the referendum, showing how this 'constitutional monstrosity' came to be an accepted tool of government. Wilson's decision to hold a referendum is usually viewed as a tactical device, evidence of his unprincipled political style and preference for short-term fixes over long-term consistency. This chapter takes a different view, arguing that the intellectual case for a referendum was stronger and more influential than is commonly acknowledged. While it is true that Wilson seized on the referendum as an instrument of party management, this was only viable because such a powerful case could be articulated in its support. The existence of a strong constitutional argument for the referendum was not *sufficient* to make it a reality; but it was a *necessary condition* for it to enter the armoury of domestic political conflict.

The second part of the chapter focuses on the renegotiations. Like the referendum itself, the package brought back by Wilson and Callaghan has not been kindly treated by historians. Sean Greenwood dismissed it as 'a sham', perpetrated by a government whose intention was only ever 'to tinker'. Anthony King called the relevant chapter of his book 'The So-Called Renegotiations', while David Sanders dismissed the gains as 'marginal'.[15] Yet the diplomatic exercise conducted from 1974 to 1975 had a precise purpose. The object was not a fundamental overhaul of the Community – which could only have been achieved through a multilateral process of treaty amendment – but a deal that would give Labour voters permission to change their minds. If those who had previously opposed membership were to vote to stay in, it was essential that they felt themselves to be backing a new kind of Europe – a *Labour* Europe – rather than confessing that they had been wrong to oppose membership under the Conservatives. With this in mind, the manifesto targeted with some precision the concerns of Labour supporters, whose votes would be crucial to the outcome of the referendum.

For this reason, the importance of the package agreed in 1975 lay as much in the message it communicated as in its formal content. By the summer of 1975, it was plausible to believe that a new Europe was emerging, that was more Atlanticist, more intergovernmental and more outward-looking to the poorer countries of the world. In this respect, the deal crystallised what appeared to be a wider reconfiguration of the Community, along lines that were more palatable to British tastes. At the same time, the willingness of other member states to engage in the renegotiation process put flesh on an idea that was to become central to the pro-Market case: that British leadership, inspired by Labour values, could steer the Community in a more progressive direction. Both ideas would be central to the Labour message in the campaign.

'THE PEOPLE'S VETO'

Historically, the British constitution reacts to new ideas like a cat presented with an unfamiliar dish. Having stalked the offering for a

"I've produced another rabbit out of the hat—but it's got myxomatosis..."

FIGURE 2.1 *Sunday Express*, 23 March 1975. Cummings/Express Newspapers/ N&S Syndication.

period, the wise cat proceeds to sniff the dish warily before retreating to a safe distance for a wash. In much the same way, politicians had circled the referendum for almost a century before risking the endeavour in 1975.

The referendum first entered mainstream debate in the late nineteenth century.[16] It was both a product of and a reaction against the rise of a new democratic politics, as the electorate swelled in size and understandings of sovereignty and legitimacy changed accordingly.[17] On the one hand, the referendum encapsulated a radical democratic principle: that the laws by which a country was governed should have the direct consent of the people. At the same time, it fed off a growing suspicion of the House of Commons and of the radical politics of its representatives. That tension between its conservative and democratic impulses would mark the referendum debate throughout the modern era.

It was Gladstone's attempts, in 1886 and 1893, to introduce 'Home Rule for Ireland' that popularised the idea. Home Rule meant restoring the Irish Parliament in Dublin, a proposal that electrified British politics and roused furious opposition in both Ulster and the British mainland. In most states, a constitutional change of such magnitude would have required some special legislative process; but the British constitution recognised no fundamental laws, no limits on the authority of Parliament and no special procedures for institutional reform. In theory, if not in practice, a government could abolish the monarchy, repeal the Union or revise the electoral system by the same procedure as the introduction of dog licences or reform of the drink laws.

For Unionists, aghast at the prospect of Irish self-government, the referendum offered the best prospect of stopping Gladstone in his tracks. A.V. Dicey, the great constitutionalist of the age, called it 'the People's Veto'; a chance for the electorate to rein in a Parliament that might be corrupt, misguided or detached from public opinion. When the House of Lords was stripped of its veto in 1911, removing the last institutional barrier against Home Rule, Conservatives urged that the referendum take over its functions. The referendum had the peculiar advantage, unlike the second chamber, that it could be defended on democratic principles, serving not as a frustration of the popular will, but as its most real and true expression.[18]

It was partly for this reason that the Left was so suspicious of the referendum, for it had entered the bloodstream of British politics as a conservative measure that was expressly designed to frustrate radical legislation. Not surprisingly, when the idea re-emerged in the context of the European debate, it was on the Conservative benches that it first found favour. In December 1969, the Conservative MP Bruce Campbell introduced a Ten Minute Bill demanding a referendum, winning fifty-five mostly Conservative supporters.[19] In 1972, during the passage of the European Communities Bill, it was again a Conservative MP, Neil Marten, who raised the question, tabling an amendment requiring a consultative referendum before the bill became law.[20]

Yet the 1970s saw a new factor in the referendum debate, which was the emergence of serious Labour support. One of the first to take up the idea was Douglas Jay, a veteran of the Attlee governments who had been president of the Board of Trade under Wilson. (A long-standing anti-Marketeer, he was rumoured, when travelling overseas, to fill his luggage with home-made sandwiches, rather than subject his digestive system to the hazards of continental food.)[21] In an article for *The Times* in 1970, Jay argued that entry to the EEC would involve the most 'drastic change in our constitution' since the 1830s. In previous changes of this magnitude, such as the Great Reform Act in 1832 or the People's Budget of 1909, consent had been tested at a general election, in which the main parties stood on opposite sides of the debate. In 1970, however, all three parties were committed to entry, making it impossible for voters to intervene. The only alternative, Jay concluded, was a referendum. If that marked a departure from customary practice, it did less violence to constitutional tradition than the proposal to 'hand over the rights of the British electorate to an untried outside body'.[22]

A second Labour advocate of the referendum was Tony Benn, who published an open letter to his constituents in November 1970. Unlike Jay, Benn was still nominally a pro-Marketeer in 1970; but he insisted that a decision of such magnitude could not be made by Parliament alone. 'The whole history of British democracy', he told his constituents, 'has been about how *you* take decisions, and this has always been seen to be more important than what the decisions were.' To drive through membership over the heads of the public would not just be *contrary* to democracy; it would endanger the very survival of popular government. 'If the people are not to participate in this decision, no one will ever take participation seriously again.'[23]

As the tide of support for a referendum began to swell, three main streams of thought emerged. The first stressed the sheer scale of the change in prospect. European membership, it was argued, would change fundamentally how Britain was governed, with consequences that could not be reversed at a single election. The issue was not simply that the treaty obligations bound up in membership would restrict the freedom of Parliament, for the same could be said of NATO, the United Nations and many other organisations. The difference, Jay argued, was that the obligations involved in those bodies had been clearly defined in advance. The EEC, by contrast, required an open-ended surrender of sovereignty: its members committed themselves to obey future laws made outside the country, the scope and content of which could not be foreseen. This had been acknowledged in the White Paper on membership, published by the Labour government in 1967:

> The constitutional innovation would lie in the acceptance *in advance* as part of the law of the United Kingdom of provisions to be made in the future by instruments issued by the Community institutions – a situation for which there is no precedent in this country.[24]

This, Jay suggested, marked a fundamental change in the rights not only of Parliament but of the electorate. The transfer would be 'irrevocable', for the Treaties contained 'no legal or constitutional method of secession'.

This fed into a second argument, which was that MPs were exceeding their powers by voting for membership. On this view, MPs were trustees for the democratic rights of the electorate; sovereignty was *loaned* to them for the duration of the Parliament, but must be returned at each general election. In carrying through a permanent transfer of sovereignty, MPs would be making a gift of that which was not theirs to trade. Only a direct vote by the electorate could authorise such an infringement of their democratic rights; and since the parties were themselves divided on the question, that could only be done through a referendum. A general election would bundle together too many different issues: voters would cast their ballots, not just on Europe, but on subjects like nationalisation, the cost of living and the funding of public services. The argument was summed up by the Labour MP Roderick MacFarquhar, a leading constitutionalist who later taught at Harvard:

> While the people elect their representatives to exercise supreme powers on their behalf, they do not elect them to concede some of those powers in perpetuity to a superior outside body. Therefore, if those powers are to be diminished by entry into the Common Market, the British people must give their consent, and that consent can be given only in a referendum, because only through a referendum can the issue be isolated.[25]

For Benn, such arguments went to the core of British democracy. There was no provision in the constitution, he told MPs, 'for Parliament to surrender part of its sovereignty to an international federation'. Invoking the collapse of parliamentary government in Northern Ireland, he reminded the House what happened when a section of the population felt that they had been subordinated to a foreign government against their will. Democracy was 'a very fragile thing'. 'If ever this House were to create a situation in which people thought that it no longer reflected their power ultimately to decide, I believe that parliamentary democracy, which hangs by a gossamer thread, could easily fall to the ground.'[26]

A third stream of argument was more ambitious, as it ranged beyond the specific issue of membership. This view looked to the referendum for a wider reinvigoration of British democracy, and was most clearly articulated by Tony Benn. In a speech at Llandudno in 1968, Benn had called for an overhaul of the relationship between Parliament and people. It was 'foolish' to believe that a modern, educated electorate would be satisfied 'with a system which confines their national political role to the marking of a ballot paper with a single cross once every five years'. With new technology, Benn predicted, citizens would be able to interact with government from the comfort of their homes, facilitating 'a new popular democracy' in place of 'parliamentary democracy as we know it'. The result, he hoped, would be 'a considerable uprating of the responsibility and understanding of ordinary people'.[27]

It was not necessary to be a Bennite to feel that something was moving in the waters of British democracy. The *Guardian* columnist Peter Jenkins located the enthusiasm for the referendum in the slow collapse of the party system. Labour, he noted, had won just 37.1 per cent of the vote in the election of February 1974, while the Conservatives had sunk to 36.7 per cent in October. In a single year, both parties had recorded their lowest share of the vote since the war. Taken together, they had lost more than a fifth of their vote share since 1951, dropping from 97 per cent of the vote to just 75 per cent. Tapping into an argument with wider application, Jenkins argued that Britain was experiencing a crisis of trust in its democratic institutions. The task of a representative system was to give expression to the popular will in all its moods and currents; if that was no longer possible through a party democracy, then new forms of expression must be developed. The approaching referendum, he concluded, was 'more than a hands up for or against Europe. It is one aspect of a disintegrating political order.'[28]

The argument that there was no precedent for a referendum lost much of its force if, as Jenkins argued, the old order was already broken beyond repair. In any case, it was not true that there were no recent precedents. Parliament had legislated for referendums in numerous former colonies and territories, most of which had subsequently institutionalised the mechanism as part of their own constitutions. A referendum had been held in Gibraltar in 1967 to decide whether it should remain a British Overseas Territory or revert to Spanish control. In March 1972, Heath announced that a plebiscite would be held in Northern Ireland, to determine its place within the UK. This was intended to be the first in 'a system of regular plebiscites', though no further polls were in fact held until the Good Friday Agreement. Successive governments, it appeared, had tacitly accepted that referendums were appropriate when determining the constitutional unit of which a territory should form part. It was not difficult to see how that might be applied to the European question.

Supporters denied that the referendum was incompatible with parliamentary government or the traditions of British politics. As Neil Marten noted in 1972, the referendum was used in half the countries of the Commonwealth, 'all of whose parliamentary traditions have grown out of this country's'. Marten mocked the fashionable argument that referendums were inherently authoritarian, pointing to their widespread use in Switzerland. 'If anybody can tell me where the dictator or demagogue is in Switzerland, I shall be glad to meet him when I am next over there skiing.'[29]

With Heath resolutely opposed to a referendum, enthusiasts took matters into their own hands. Between July and October 1971, activists (mostly from the organisation 'Keep Britain Out') ran sixteen unofficial constituency referendums. Almost a quarter of a million voters took part, with turnout as high as 50 per cent in Gloucester, 48 per cent in Wellingborough and 47 per cent in Middlesbrough. The result, on average, was a two-to-one majority against membership. Fifteen of the votes were held in Tory seats, including those of Ted Heath, Geoffrey Rippon and Jim Prior. Only Beckenham produced a majority in favour of entry; this was the constituency of Philip Goodhart, a pro-Marketeer who had helped to organise the vote, and was the only constituency actively contested by the European Movement.[30]

'A DEVICE OF DICTATORS AND DEMAGOGUES'

The proponents of a referendum had assembled a formidable case, but an equally powerful argument could be assembled on the other side. Responding to Douglas Jay in 1970, *The Times* challenged the argument for a referendum point by point. First, on the peculiar importance of the European question, it noted that many decisions of comparable scale could never be subjected to such a vote. Jay himself had served in government when India was granted independence, a decision that transformed British policy and set off the long process of post-war decolonisation; yet it would plainly have been absurd to hold a referendum in the UK. Nor would it normally be possible to hold a referendum before a declaration of war. The paper denied, in any case, that the European question involved a unique transfer of sovereignty. Over the post-war era, a weakened British economy had come more and more under the control of the International Monetary Fund (IMF) and Britain's creditors overseas. 'We may have been sovereign, but we were not our own masters. Entering the EEC is likely to increase rather than reduce the ability of British government to protect the interests of Britain.'

Second, the paper stressed the constitutional dangers. The referendum, it warned, was 'open to manipulation', 'favourable to autocracy' and 'conservative in its effect'. In the absence of a written constitution, there could be no clear rules on when a referendum should be deployed. Britain had no special category of 'constitutional legislation' and no constitutional court to arbitrate on disputes. On a common-sense view, Heath's reorganisation of local government might count as 'constitutional' legislation, while the decision to allow US military bases on British soil might not. Yet the latter transgressed what Max Weber had given as the essential definition of a state: 'the monopoly of the legitimate use of physical force within a given territory'.[31]

Without clear rules, the power to hold a referendum would devolve into the hands of ministers, enabling them to appeal over the heads of MPs as party advantage dictated. The timing of the referendum and the phrasing of the question would both be important, especially if complex political decisions were reduced to a 'Yes' or 'No' format. Under the parliamentary system, bills could be scrutinised and amended line by line; by contrast, the referendum required a simple proposition to which voters could give or deny assent. The result would be a new weapon in the hands of the executive, allowing it to bypass the scrutiny of Parliament. It was no coincidence, the paper noted, that 'the referendum has been used as a means of pseudo-democratic dialogue by dictators'.

Third, the paper warned of the damage to coherent policymaking. 'Parliamentary government', it argued, 'implies that the government is charged with the whole responsibility for advancing and protecting the welfare of the nation.' Decisions about taxation, expenditure, foreign policy and trade could not be viewed in isolation. 'All these decisions have to be fitted together so that a coherent strategy can be constructed for the nation's future.' Yet it was 'not possible to construct a coherent strategy when three out of four decisions are left to the competence of Parliament and the fourth decision is held to be outside its competence'.[32]

In this respect, the referendum challenged two of the most basic principles of British constitutionalism. The first was the sovereignty of Parliament. The referendum not only established a tribunal for policymaking that was superior to that of Parliament; it also questioned the basis on which all Parliamentary authority was founded – its claim to represent 'the people'. The only rationale for holding a referendum retrospectively was the belief that Parliament, when it voted for the European Communities Bill, had *not* correctly interpreted the will of the people, or that it had exceeded the powers given to it by the electorate. For Tony Benn, this was part of the attraction of the referendum: it exploded the constitutional fiction that a majority of MPs, elected years previously on a different manifesto, spoke the will of the people. Yet the implications for Britain's constitutional practice would reverberate far beyond the European debate.

The second was the principle of 'responsible government'. The British constitution did not, like the American, diffuse power between competing institutions as a safeguard against tyranny. Instead, power was concentrated in the hands of the executive, so long as it commanded a majority in the House of Commons. The proviso was that ministers could not slough off responsibility for what had been done during their tenure; instead, they would be held accountable for the entire conduct of policy. As Peregrine Worsthorne argued in the *Sunday Telegraph*, British democracy did not require governments always to do what the people wanted; it simply required them to face the judgement of the people for the decisions they had made. This, he argued, not only promoted more considered government – for ministers would take the blame for failed policies at an election, however popular they might have been at the time; it also protected democracy itself from opprobrium. Had Neville Chamberlain won a referendum on the Munich Agreement in 1938, it would have been 'the idea of democracy itself that was damaged'. Instead, the responsibility fell on Chamberlain and his ministers, who carried away the blame with them when they resigned.[33]

The danger was that referendums might promote *irresponsible* government, in which ministers promised referendums for party purposes while disclaiming responsibility for the results. 'The new doctrine', Thatcher complained, was 'to pass the buck to the people'.[34] As Enoch Powell put it, a government that was defeated in the country could continue cheerfully in office, enacting policies it did not believe in, while saying to voters: 'don't blame us, it is no fault of ours; we wanted to do one thing, but you decided to do the other; so, ladies and gentlemen, you have only yourselves to blame'.[35]

In addition to these constitutional objections, it was widely believed that referendums were inherently conservative. For some on the Right, this was part of their attraction; but for self-styled 'progressives', such as Roy Jenkins, it was a major concern. 'Progressive' legislation, it was argued, came about in most instances through a gradual process of coalition-building, in which groups undertook to support one another's struggles. By contrast, the referendum promoted a crude majoritarianism, exposing individual policies to a majority opinion to which they would inevitably appear strange and perhaps alarming. The perpetuation of injustice, by contrast, or a conservative policy that protected vested interests, would never face such a challenge, for it did not constitute 'change'. This was not to say, as some Conservatives were beginning to suggest, that progressive politics involved a conspiracy against the public, for progressive parties would still face judgement on their stewardship of power. But it was no coincidence, sceptics argued, that the referendum had historically found favour on the Right. Roy Jenkins warned in 1972 that the referendum 'held back progress and attracted coalitions of reaction'.[36] When he resigned over the party's adoption of the policy, he told Wilson that 'we have forged a more powerful continuing weapon against progressive legislation than anything we have known in this country since the curbing of the absolute powers of the old House of Lords'. Not just the abolition of capital punishment, but 'measures to improve race relations, or to extend public ownership, or to advance the right of individual dissent' would all risk defeat.[37]

This was not an argument *against* democracy, but an argument about *how* democracy should be exercised. For the Conservative MP Norman St John-Stevas, who edited the works of the Victorian constitutionalist Walter Bagehot, parliamentary institutions had developed not only as 'a means for the expression of the will of the people' but as a way 'to moderate its naked exercise'. Through discussion in Parliament, temporary gales of public feeling could be tempered and moderated, upholding the rights of minorities and ensuring that

Parliament legislated on the settled will of the people, rather than on passing spasms of anger or excitement. Handing decisions directly to the voters 'would not consolidate government by discussion but destroy it'. This was also the view of the *New Statesman*, which argued for a 'theory of delegated democracy, according to which only a measure which has run the gauntlet of party approval and parliamentary routine really deserves to be called the people's will'.[38] John Pinder, director of the research institute Political and Economic Planning, argued that a representative democracy acted as 'a buffer for short-term fluctuations of chauvinist or isolationist sentiment, while reflecting those trends that are more durable'.[39]

WILSON'S SOMERSAULT

At the start of the 1970s, support for the referendum was still a minority taste. When Tony Benn brought the idea to Labour's National Executive Committee (NEC) at the end of 1970, he could not even find a seconder. In private, however, some were already weighing up the pneumatic potential of the referendum, as a device that could prevent Labour sinking under its internal divisions. As Callaghan commented, in one of those nautical analogies he so favoured: 'Tony may be launching a little rubber life raft which we will all be glad of in a year's time.'[40] It was a prophetic remark, for while the intellectual case for a referendum had put it on the agenda, it was the needs of party unity that would make it a reality.

The tipping point came in the spring of 1972, as the European Communities Bill made its exhausting passage through Parliament. On 14 March the Conservative anti-Marketeer Neil Marten tabled an amendment, demanding a consultative referendum before entry. A similar amendment in December 1969 had attracted fifty-five votes, mostly from Tory anti-Marketeers, and Marten had probably anticipated an equivalent number on this occasion. Yet the argument had been strengthened by the decision of the other three applicants – Denmark, Norway and the Republic of Ireland – to hold their own referendums on entry, and Benn saw an opportunity to reactivate the question. He submitted a paper to the Shadow Cabinet warning that the reputation of Parliament would be damaged if it did not allow a public vote. Backing a referendum, he suggested, would take the

European question out of the next election, allowing the party to reunite around its opposition to the Tories. It would also distance Labour from Enoch Powell, who Benn feared would tarnish the anti-Market cause by association.[41]

When the Shadow Cabinet met on 15 March, there was 'a substantial majority' against the proposal. Labour's NEC also rejected the move. The following afternoon, however, news broke from Paris: President Pompidou had announced that *France* would hold a referendum on the proposed enlargement. The French, it appeared, were to exercise a right denied to the British public of giving their verdict on the UK's accession. Benn told a meeting in London that it 'would be an outrage if the French people are allowed to decide whether they want Britain in the Common Market, and the British people are denied the right'.[42] As a waspish letter in *The Times* observed, 'All is now clear. When Mr Heath, a man of undoubted integrity, said that he would not take us into the Common Market without the wholehearted support of Parliament and people, he forgot to mention that he meant the *French* Parliament and *French* people.'[43]

This was followed, on 24 March, by news that a 'Border Poll' – a referendum in all but name – would be held in Northern Ireland. The intellectual defences were crumbling, and so, more importantly, was the resolve of the Labour leadership. Benn accused Heath of perpetrating a *coup d'état* on the British people: 'a conspiracy to destroy 700 years of Parliamentary democratic self-government by stealth'.[44] He brought the issue back to the NEC on 22 March, at a meeting from which Wilson, Callaghan and Jenkins were all absent, and this time the vote was narrowly in favour. A week later, the Shadow Cabinet also reversed its decision, agreeing by just eight votes to six to recommend Benn's proposal to the parliamentary party. A stormy meeting of MPs split 129 votes to 96 in favour of Marten's amendment, which was defeated in the House by just 284 votes to 235.[45]

The decisive consideration was less the constitutional argument than the possibility of overturning the government. Callaghan told the Shadow Cabinet bluntly that 'getting rid of the Government was more important than the question of the Common Market'. Peter Shore warned that MPs would not be forgiven by the membership if they did not take this opportunity to defeat the Conservatives. Bringing down Heath, he added darkly, 'is what it is all about'. Pro-Marketeers pointed out in vain that the amendment, even if successful, was unlikely to trigger an election; the government would simply call a vote of confidence, which it would be sure to win. But the scent of blood was in the party's nostrils, and the charge that pro-Marketeers actively *wanted* Heath to stay in office, at least until entry was secure, was uncomfortably close to the mark.[46]

The volte-face on the referendum finally snapped the patience of Labour pro-Marketeers. Roy Jenkins, George Thomson and Harold Lever resigned from the Shadow Cabinet, while Bill Rodgers, Dick Taverne, Dickson Mabon and David Owen resigned or were dismissed from more junior positons. For Jenkins, the decision to 'turn a somersault' on a major constitutional question was as repulsive as the party's increasingly anti-Market tone. Bill Rodgers later spoke of his 'moral repugnance' at the manoeuvre: 'I had joined the Labour Party because I thought it was a principled party,' he recalled. The issue was not one of everyday politics or short-term political advantage. It 'was something great and majestic'; 'history would change as a result of one's vote'.[47]

In theory, Labour continued to favour a general election over a referendum. But as the two parties were not clearly divided on the principle of membership – not least because Labour's emphasis on the terms was designed to *avoid* taking a position on the principle – a referendum was always more likely. As Benn pointed out to the Shadow Cabinet, one of the advantages of a referendum was precisely that it would eliminate the European question as an election issue. Instead of tearing itself apart over the EEC, Labour would be able to refocus its attentions on less divisive questions.[48]

Despite his distaste for the referendum, the strategy suited Wilson admirably. The decision absolved Labour from the impossible task of agreeing a policy on membership, which would otherwise have driven one wing or other of the party into rebellion. Instead, Labour maintained an uneasy truce while attacking the government on its weakest point: its apparent reluctance to consult the people. The drawback was that a Labour government would now have to deliver on the referendum. If the split in the party was not simply to be postponed, it would have to secure new terms that could be sold both to the electorate and to a substantial body of the party. It was this task that would consume the energies of the government in the year after returning to power in February 1974.

'TORY TERMS'

The Labour manifesto had been scathing about the 'Tory terms', which it blamed for soaring food prices, a 'crippling' balance of payments deficit and 'a draconian curtailment of the power of the British Parliament'. Its conclusion was uncompromising: 'The Labour Party *opposes* British membership of the European Communities on the terms negotiated by the Conservative Government.' The manifesto promised 'a fundamental re-negotiation of the terms of entry', with membership contingent on the outcome. If satisfactory terms could be agreed, Labour would put them to the people for their decision. If the negotiations failed, Labour would 'not regard the Treaty obligations as binding', but would seek a mandate for 'our withdrawal from the Communities'.[49]

Attacks on the 'Tory terms' infuriated Heath – and not solely because Labour's own negotiating team had accepted similar arrangements in 1967. Heath had never pretended that the terms of membership were ideal, for the United Kingdom was a late entrant to a club designed by and for the interests of its existing members. The Common Agricultural Policy (CAP) had been settled in the 1960s, under the shelter of the French veto, as had a budget mechanism that would weigh disproportionately on the UK. In Heath's view, it was simply not realistic to think that Britain could rewrite these arrangements from the outside; the priority was to get a seat at the table, so that it could influence the Community from within. Privately, Heath had come to the conclusion that it was now or never for the British application; a third failure would prove terminal to its prospects of membership. Ministers should pursue the best bargain possible, but the stakes were too high to risk a breakdown. As Lord Crowther told the House of Lords, 'you do not haggle over the subscription when you are invited to climb into a lifeboat. You scramble aboard while there is still a seat for you.'[50]

For Heath, membership was a process, not a static position; but as he told the party conference in 1973, the direction of travel could only be influenced from the inside. 'Of course we are not satisfied with the European Community as it stands today,' he declared; but 'the whole nature of the Community is that it should constantly change and develop according to the needs of its peoples':

> Should there be changes in the common agricultural policy?
> Certainly. And it is precisely because we are now members of the
> Community that it has been agreed that plans for change should be

> set in hand … Should there be changes in the way the Community spends its money and in its control over it? Most certainly. And it is precisely because we are now members of the Community that we have already reached agreement on the setting up of the Regional Development Fund.[51]

The government's chief negotiator, Con O'Neill, took a similar view. The UK, he argued, had tested to destruction the idea that it could reshape the European Community from the outside. In the meantime, other states had got on with building a Community that served their own national interests. When disagreements arose, even the smallest found that their 'power to protect their own interests from within the Community is sufficient'.[52]

In this sense, both parties went to the country in 1974 promising to change the deal agreed in 1971. The difference was that the Conservatives anticipated an evolutionary process, as the UK made its presence felt in European institutions, while Labour favoured a set-piece renegotiation, with withdrawal as the nuclear option.

The Labour manifesto identified seven key areas for reform. It demanded: (i) 'major changes in the Common Agricultural Policy', to guarantee access to the British market for 'low-cost producers outside Europe'; (ii) 'new and fairer methods of financing the Community budget'; (iii) securities for the right of Parliament 'to pursue effective regional, industrial and fiscal policies'; (iv) access to the British market (and more generous aid policies) for the Commonwealth; (v) safeguards against any form of Economic and Monetary Union (EMU) that might hamper a government's ability to tackle unemployment; (vi) the right to restrict capital movements when the balance of payments or full employment was in jeopardy; and (vii) guarantees that Britain would not be required to impose VAT on food or other necessities.[53]

This was a less ambitious list than at first appeared; indeed, the West German Chancellor, Helmut Schmidt, concluded cheerfully that 'Renegotiation had proved a misleading term.'[54] Of the seven demands, items (v) to (vii) quickly proved redundant. The Community had no plans to harmonise VAT, there was no realistic threat to the zero-rating on food and its rules already permitted intervention in capital movements to protect the balance of trade. EMU, though nominally a target for 1980, had long disappeared from the realms of practical politics, and its return in the future would be subject to the UK's own power of veto. That left just four areas for meaningful negotiation: the CAP; regional policy; Commonwealth trade; and the budget. Significantly, the manifesto did not spell out precisely *what* was to change.[55] As an analysis by the Trades Union Congress (TUC) drily observed, the document had been 'couched in rather general terms'; its demands 'lacked detail and they lacked precision'.[56] Like most such documents, the manifesto was designed as a political Mirror of Erised, allowing all those who looked into it to find their heart's desire.

Ministers agreed at an early stage that they would not seek changes to the founding treaties, unless all other routes to reform had been exhausted. This made a deal easier to achieve, but it tacitly surrendered any prospect of reforming the supremacy of European law, the ban on policies that might 'distort competition' or the commitment to 'ever-closer union'. On one level, this was merely an accommodation with reality: renegotiating the terms of entry was a very different enterprise to a restructuring of the Community itself. Yet it left anti-Marketeers in Cabinet vulnerable to the charge of bad faith, for it locked them into a negotiating process that could not possibly meet their demands.[57]

With Wilson in Downing Street and Callaghan at the Foreign Office, the renegotiations were in the hands of two men who had no strong emotional commitments on the subject, but who cared profoundly about its consequences for the Labour Party. Neither would have described themselves instinctively as 'European'. Wilson had a romantic attachment to the Commonwealth, while Callaghan was an Atlanticist with an enthusiasm for the open seas, begotten of his time in the Royal Navy. Nor, however, were they stirred by appeals to parliamentary sovereignty or the rights of the freeborn Englishman. Callaghan called himself an 'agnostic' on the European question, while Wilson insisted that membership was 'an important policy issue, not an article of faith'.[58] Both found the willingness of Benn and Jenkins to split the party over the issue utterly mystifying. For Callaghan and Wilson alike, the challenge was to secure a deal with the Community that they could live with and that would enable the Labour Party to get past the issue. If that proved impossible, neither would fight for membership against the odds. But from the outset, the goal was to find a deal that would anaesthetise the question as a disruptive force in the Labour Party.

FIGURE 2.2　Jim Callaghan had castigated the 'Tory terms' in Opposition, but as foreign secretary led the Labour renegotiations.
Source: Rolls Press/Popperfoto: www.gettyimages.co.uk/license/80751192

Shortly after taking office, Callaghan had met with Michael Butler, the senior official at the Foreign Office with responsibility for Community matters. 'They tell me', said Callaghan, 'that you really care about Europe. Well, that's all right as long as you remember that I really care about the Labour Party.' The domestic implications were also the focus of an address to a gathering of the diplomatic corps in March. The government, he told the assembled ambassadors, 'would not be brought down while the anti-Marketeers in the Conservative Party thought that it was set on a really fundamental renegotiation'; so this must be the focus of diplomatic activity.[59]

For Wilson, too, the renegotiations were chiefly an exercise in domestic politics. In a revealing discussion towards the end of 1974, the prime minister told officials that it had been a mistake to focus so much attention on Britain's budget contribution, as no plausible outcome 'would be of any use in winning votes'. By contrast, he thought that New Zealand and Australia 'were of great importance to the British people'. No one cavilled when his press secretary, Joe Haines, said that bringing down prices for the British housewife 'was what the public minded about'. The task, Wilson stressed, was fundamentally political: he must 'be able to show the British people that he had got better terms than the Tories had done'.[60]

The chances of achieving this improved significantly over the course of 1974. The death of President Pompidou in April removed a close ally of the Heath government, while bringing to power a new president, Valéry Giscard d'Estaing (known as Giscard), who shared the Atlanticist instincts of both Callaghan and Wilson. Unlike President Nixon, the British government did not hail Pompidou's funeral as 'a great day for France', but the change in management was undoubtedly welcome.[61] A month later, Helmut Schmidt replaced Willy Brandt as Chancellor of West Germany. As a social democrat, Schmidt had close links to the British Labour Party, and he shared Giscard's determination to co-operate closely with the United States. With Atlanticists installed in Paris, Bonn and London, the Gaullist vision of Europe as a counterweight to American influence had never been further from reality. Schmidt's old friend Henry Kissinger was so excited that he indulged in a rare moment of gangsta: 'it's sick', he told President Ford in 1975. 'There has been a revolution in our relations with France ... our relations with Europe have never been better.'[62]

Schmidt swiftly became the UK's favourite European, for he articulated a very British vision of what the Community should be. Mocking what he called the 'European cloud-cuckoo land' inhabited by the Commission, he demanded an end to the habit of 'pontificating and proclaiming the European targets for the day after tomorrow'.[63] At a heads of government meeting in September 1974, he blocked an increase in meat prices, demanded comprehensive reform of the CAP and launched an assault on the bureaucracy and inefficiency of the Commission that would have warmed the cockles of the most fervent anti-Marketeer.[64] Schmidt wooed Wilson with the vision of a new intergovernmental axis between London, Paris and Bonn – the three governments 'who really mattered' – that could take over the running of the Community and sideline the Commission.[65]

The oil shock and the economic slump of the 1970s encouraged a tendency, on the part of all governments, to focus on internal problems, while accelerating a change in management at the domestic level. By the time the negotiations began in earnest, only one of the nine heads of government (Gaston Thorn, of Luxembourg) had been involved in the original accession talks.[66] With the Italian government at odds with the Ortoli Commission over its right to impose an import deposit scheme, the new generation seemed readier to challenge the Commission's authority. The perception that national governments were reasserting themselves was reinforced at the Paris Summit in 1974, where it was agreed to hold regular meetings of heads of government in what became known as the European Council. The direction of travel, it appeared, was intergovernmental rather than supranational, with states co-operating in their national interest over the heads of the Commission.

At a meeting of foreign ministers in April 1974, Callaghan asked what had been meant by the commitment, announced after the Paris Summit in 1972, to achieve 'a European Union' by the start of the next decade. It was swiftly apparent that no one had the faintest idea. Eight different ministers gave eight different responses, while the French foreign minister, Michel Jobert, claimed disarmingly that the phrase had been invented by Pompidou 'as a term of hope', the vagueness of which might 'paper over' differences. Part of the attraction of the term 'Union' was that it required no commitment on the *form* of co-operation, which might be federal, confederal or intergovernmental according to taste. The Belgian prime minister, Leo Tindemans, was asked to write a report on the subject, which, as everyone recognised, was a useful way of kicking it into touch. Back in London, the Cabinet quickly agreed that the commitment to European Union 'was of such a general nature' as to pose 'no threat to British independence'.[67]

The same applied to Economic and Monetary Union, which was nominally to be achieved by 1980. At a heads of government dinner in September 1974, the target was 'discussed and largely written off'.[68] Schmidt dismissed it as 'an illusion fostered by idealists who did not understand the problem', while Wilson told the Cabinet that EMU was as 'dead as mutton'. 'The Emu', he added, 'had long lost the ability to fly and was not likely to recover it.'[69] In the House of Commons, he compared monetary union to global nuclear disarmament: 'I am all for it. But I do not expect it by 1980.' There was 'not a hope in hell – I mean in the Common Market – ... of EMU taking place in the near future'.[70]

Before the negotiations had even begun, the Community seemed to be reorienting itself in a way that was more palatable to the British. The ghosts of EMU and European Union had been exorcised; it would be years before the ectoplasm of 'ever closer union' began once more to drip from the ceiling of the Cabinet Room. At the same time, changing economic conditions were altering the cost–benefit analysis of membership. In particular, the global economic crisis precipitated by the oil shock increased the risks of leaving while diminishing some of the drawbacks of membership. World food prices rose dramatically, with the result that prices within the Community were no longer significantly higher. As the price gap closed, there was less need either to

limit imports or to withdraw surplus production. It also shifted attention from the price of food to the security of supply.[71]

Just as importantly, a new generation of leaders seemed to
be guiding Europe in a new direction, which emphasised practical
co-operation between governments over dreams of federal union.
That spirit also seemed to be affecting the Commission. Labour had
come to power with ambitious plans for state intervention in industry,
to which the Community was expected to prove a barrier. Yet, as Callaghan
noted in March 1975, 'we have not met with any serious difficulties from
the EEC in the conduct of industrial policy'. Anti-Marketeers were not
reassured: as Benn pointed out, the issue was not how the Commission
chose to exercise its powers, but where the power of decision was ultimately located – and what use might be made of that power once the
referendum was over.[72] Benn triggered a 'prodigious' row in Cabinet
when he leaked documents from the Foreign Office, showing that Roy
Hattersley, the minister of state, had asked the Commission to 'exercise caution in the exercise of its functions during the period before
the referendum, and not act in such a way as to lose favourable votes
in the referendum'. (The German foreign minister assured Hattersley
that the Commission 'fully understood Britain's situation and would
behave accordingly'.) This followed reports in *The Economist* that
ministers were asking the commissioner for industry and entrepreneur-
ship, Altiero Spinelli, to keep a low profile during the passage of the
Industry Bill. The so-called 'Dissenting Ministers' were furious: Castle
demanded to know why caution was necessary if the functions of the
Commission were 'innocuous', while Benn accused the Foreign Office
of conspiring 'to conceal from the British people the extent of the
power the Commission has over our Regional Policy until after the voting was over'. Callaghan insisted that no deception had been intended:
Hattersley had simply wished to avoid giving ill-intentioned critics 'any
pretext to parody the Commission's actions'.[73] It was not a convincing
explanation, but after more than a year of Labour government it was
harder to argue that the Commission posed an existential threat to a
socialist industrial policy.

All this contributed to a more positive atmosphere around the
negotiations than ministers had expected. Callaghan, who had been
'blunt to the point of rudeness' at his first meeting with the Council
of Ministers, confessed in June 1974 that 'the most rewarding aspect
of Community work' had been the 'political cooperation' with other

governments.[74] Bernard Donoughue thought that the prime minister had become 'fascinated by the Market problem', which he saw as exactly the kind of juggling act he most relished. 'He sees it as a challenge', Donoughue noted shrewdly: 'to stay in, get the terms and hold the Labour Party together. He never talks of actually pulling out.'[75]

BIRTHDAY PRESENTS

The renegotiations operated at three distinct levels: contacts between civil servants and diplomats; meetings between ministers; and two high-level summits at which Callaghan and Wilson took the lead. The final package was hammered out over two days of talks at Dublin Castle in March 1975, once the seat of British government in Ireland. It was the first time a British prime minister had returned to the building since independence, a symbolic moment that was not lost on any of the participants. Discussions on the first evening lasted well into the night, culminating in a strategy meeting of the British delegation held in one of the castle's capacious toilets. Emerging shortly after midnight on what was now 11 March – Wilson's fifty-ninth birthday – the prime minister was touched to be greeted with a cake and a chorus of 'Happy Birthday'.[76]

The detail of the negotiations has been exhaustively treated in the official history by Stephen Wall, and does not need repetition. As Wall wryly observes: 'If you are a negotiator, the process is fascinating. If you are not, it can be deadly.'[77] For the purposes of the referendum, what mattered was the package presented to the public at the close of the talks. Its main features can be summarised as follows.

The Common Agricultural Policy, expected to be the fulcrum of the negotiations, proved relatively straightforward. As early as November 1974, Wilson had confessed that this section of the manifesto seemed 'a little outdated'; as a later chapter demonstrates, rising world food costs had closed the gap with European prices, meaning that 'there is less need for, even practical hope of, reaching objectives which were related to longer term, hopefully more normal situations'.[78] Callaghan, likewise, concluded 'that the overall level of world prices will in future lie in much the same area as EEC prices'. In an increasingly volatile global market, the Community 'will offer us greater stability of prices at reasonable levels, and security of supply in times of shortage'.[79]

This eased some of the other objectionable features of the CAP. As the gap with world prices narrowed, it was no longer so important to buy up stocks in order to inflate domestic prices – the 'wine lakes' and 'butter mountains' of popular legend. With world food prices rising dramatically, complaints that the CAP barred cheap food from overseas lost much of their salience. By March 1975, Callaghan could boast of three consecutive price settlements at levels below the rate of inflation. On beef, which had a special importance as a national dish, an agreement was reached that made cheap supplies available to pensioners, rather than locking them away in intervention stocks.

There was also progress on Commonwealth concerns. Wilson took a personal interest in this area, claiming no fewer than forty-four relatives in Australia and New Zealand, and the charge that Heath had betrayed the Commonwealth loomed large in Labour rhetoric. Yet, here, too, the context had changed. Commonwealth economies had diversified since the 1950s and were no longer so dependent on the UK market. Even in agricultural products, which remained the most closely bound to the British economy, global food shortages had increased demand from other markets. Callaghan told the Cabinet in July 1974 that 'Commonwealth apprehensions about our membership of the Community had diminished over the last 18 months and (partly because of high commodity prices) there was no desire to return to traditional trading patterns.' Instead, the Commonwealth looked to Britain to act 'as a friendly spokesman' for their interests within the Community.[80]

There had been evidence of that changing mood in August 1974, when the trade secretary, Peter Shore, toured Australia and New Zealand. Shore used the opportunity to deliver a series of barnstorming speeches in opposition to membership, but was dismayed to find his hosts entirely relaxed about the issue. 'For the most part,' he told the Cabinet, 'Australian Ministers appeared not to care strongly one way or the other.' In New Zealand, he found opinion 'frankly very concerned' about the CAP, but even here 'they did not press their views too hard'.[81] New Zealand's economy was less diversified than Australia's and still relied more heavily on British markets; nonetheless, diplomatic attention had shifted to securing favourable access to the Community as a whole. The Labour prime minister, Wallace Rowling, paid a successful visit to Paris in 1975, at which he dismissed the idea that it would be in New Zealand's interest for the UK to withdraw. The Community had already, in November 1974, agreed an 18 per cent rise in the price paid for New Zealand dairy produce, and it was agreed that transitional arrangements on the volume of imports would be extended for a further five years. Prices would be reviewed regularly to ensure a fair return for New Zealand farmers.

Wilson later concluded that the gains for New Zealand had been 'illusory', but the mood at the time was celebratory. The New Zealand trade minister, Joe Walding, issued a press release thanking the Commission and paying special tribute to 'the positive and sympathetic attitude adopted by the British Government'. At the close of the Dublin summit in March 1975, Rowling released a statement praising the 'goodwill' shown to New Zealand and thanking the UK government for its efforts.[82]

There were also gains for the 'new' Commonwealth – those non-white former colonies in Africa, Asia and the Pacific. Following a shortage of sugar in 1974, the Community agreed to import an additional 1.4 million tons of sugar from developing countries, while improved access was also agreed for tropical oils, soluble coffee and lard.[83] Most importantly, the conclusion of the Lomé Convention in February 1975 secured a new trade deal for seventy-one countries from Africa, the Pacific and the Caribbean. The deal provided tariff-free access for most agricultural products and raw materials; preferential access for commodities, like sugar and beef, which were in competition with the Community's own production; and a commitment to 3 billion Ecus in aid. Lomé was not strictly a part of the renegotiations, though Wilson claimed that it had been 'accelerated and intensified' by their progress.[84] Nonetheless, it put flesh on the idea that the Commonwealth was better served by British advocacy *within* the Community than by preferential treatment outside it. In a coup for Harold Wilson, the renegotiations were formally endorsed at the Commonwealth summit in May 1975, when thirty-two heads of government signed a note expressing support for British membership.[85]

That left only 'the most difficult problem' outstanding, which was the UK's disproportionate contribution to the budget.[86] The problem, from a British perspective, was clear: relative to its size and economic strength, the UK paid too much in and got too little out. This was disguised, in the short term, by transitional arrangements that staggered the British contribution; but those arrangements would cease by the end of the decade. Without them, according to the Commission's own figures, Britain would have contributed 22 per cent of the EEC budget in 1974, despite accounting for just 15.9 per cent of its GDP. By 1980, the UK was forecasted to contribute 24 per cent of the budget on just 14 per cent of GDP. Britain would be the second highest contributor after West Germany, despite having the second lowest GDP per capita.[87]

The problem was one both of revenue and expenditure. Under funding arrangements agreed before British entry, the EEC raised revenue by claiming 1 per cent of receipts from VAT and most of the revenues from levies on imported food and industrial goods.[88] As Britain traded more than most other members with countries outside the EEC – and was positioning itself as an entrepôt for access to the Continent – its contribution would be inflated far beyond its relative economic strength. At the same time, it would benefit less than other states from Community expenditure. Two-thirds of the EEC budget was devoured by the CAP, which funnelled expenditure towards countries, like France, with large farming populations. At a time when just 3 per cent of the UK workforce was employed in agriculture, Britain could expect to get back just 8 per cent of Community expenditure while contributing – once transitional arrangements had ended – roughly a quarter of the budget; a net outflow of £700 million a year.[89]

To the UK, the injustice was obvious; yet finding a solution taxed the ingenuity of all parties. The difficulty was that the Community did not formally recognise the principle of national contributions and receipts. Revenues were claimed, not as contributions from national governments, but as the Community's 'own resources', which it then spent on programmes, like the CAP, that applied to farmers across the Continent. Acknowledging the British case meant recognising a form of national accounting to which most states were averse – not least, because most were net beneficiaries.

Barring a major reform of the funding system or a total overhaul of the CAP, there were two ways in which the problem could be addressed. The first was to increase the EEC's spending in other areas, expanding the pie so that the UK could take a larger slice. Heath had hoped to achieve this through a new Regional Development Fund, from which Britain could expect to be a major beneficiary. Little progress had been made, however, because Germany was reluctant to foot the bill without movement on Economic and Monetary Union. Labour was also less enthusiastic about the issue, since it was keen to keep regional policy under national control. A relatively modest package was concluded which allocated around $1,300 million to a regional fund, with the UK receiving 28 per cent of the total.[90]

A second approach was to offer a partial refund for any state that found itself in a particular imbalance. The advantage of this remedy was that it did not challenge the principle of the Community's 'own resources' – it was theoretically a grant available to any member state that met the criteria – and that it could be justified by the commitment of the Rome Treaties to promote economic convergence between member states.[91] At the Dublin Summit in March, a formula was agreed by which the UK could reclaim part of its deficit, up to a ceiling of £125 million a year. This was less generous than British negotiators had hoped, and was almost certainly less than the German government (which would have to finance the scheme) would have accepted if pushed. But Schmidt was growing tired of the renegotiations and was facing criticism at home. Despite advice from his officials that the German offer was simply a negotiating position, from which they expected to bargain upwards, Wilson closed the deal. Unlike the Commonwealth issue, with which he was closely involved, the budget debate seemed to bore him. As long as he had something to report to the voters, which could be presented as 'a concrete improvement in the terms of British membership', he took little interest in the mechanics of the settlement.[92] The particular number, he believed, would have less influence on opinion than the fact that a refund had been agreed at all. In this respect, the decision of the Dublin Summit was less important than the statement of principle agreed the previous December in Paris, that 'a correcting mechanism' should be established to prevent 'the possible development of situations unacceptable for a Member State and incompatible with the smooth working of the Community'.[93]

SELLING THE DEAL

Addressing MPs on 18 March, a week after the Dublin summit, Wilson acknowledged that the government 'cannot claim to have achieved in full all the objectives that were set in the manifesto'. It could, however, claim improvements on Commonwealth trade, aid and development, the Common Agricultural Policy and the budget. On this basis, Wilson concluded that the government's objectives had been 'substantially, though not completely, achieved'.[94] Measuring the outcome against the manifesto, Callaghan marked his own scorecard at five out of seven. Wilson was more generous, claiming 'five out of seven, and the guts of what we wanted on the other two'.[95]

What had not been achieved – or even attempted – was the 'fundamental renegotiation' promised at the election. The package put together at Dublin fell far short of the list drawn up by the Labour Party conference in 1972, which had demanded, among other things, 'the right of the British Parliament to reject any European Economic Community legislation, directives or orders, when they are issued, or at any time after they are issued'.[96] While paying tribute to Labour's negotiating team, the Dissenting Ministers dismissed what had been achieved as an irrelevance. 'In spite of the exertions of our negotiators, the results have fallen far short of our minimum aims.'[97]

Nonetheless, it was true that the EEC appeared to have changed significantly between 1972 and 1975. For reasons that were only partly connected to the renegotiations, the EEC of 1975 seemed more inter-governmental, more pragmatic, more Atlanticist, and more accommo-dating to national differences. Thanks to the Lomé Convention and the reforms to Commonwealth trade, it also appeared more outward-looking and compassionate. In all these respects, it was plausible to suggest that a more 'British' Europe had emerged, one that had tacitly abandoned the federal ideals of the 'founding fathers'.[98] Wilson harped continually on the changed character of the Community and its greater recognition of national interests, the result of 'changes which had begun before our renegotiations, but which were powerfully accelerated by them'.[99] The success of the renegotiations was as much an expression of this changed environment as its cause, but it was the renegotiations that stood as the symbol of this new, more palatable EEC.

The effects of the renegotiations were real and tangible, espe-cially for New Zealand farmers and the beneficiaries of the Lomé Convention. Nonetheless, their chief significance was always political. The fundamental task was to give Labour voters – not to mention MPs and ministers – who had denounced entry under the Conservatives per-mission to change their minds. After years of castigating Heath for, in Wilson's words, rolling 'on his back like a spaniel', it was essential to prove that a Labour government, fighting for the national interest, could get a better deal.[100] For Wilson to win the referendum, Labour voters had to feel that they were engaging in 'a different argument', rather than coming round belatedly to their opponents' position.[101]

To achieve this, the renegotiations targeted the specific concerns of Labour voters. For those who viewed the Common Market as an insular capitalist club, there was the Lomé Convention, the new regional fund and guarantees that nationalisation would not be prevented. (It helped, in this respect, that British Leyland was part-nationalised – without interference – during the referendum campaign.) Commonwealth enthusiasts could also point to Lomé, as well as to the improved trade deal for New Zealand and for sugar producers in the Caribbean. Those who feared the emergence of a federal Europe could find comfort in what appeared to be a new, more intergovernmental entity evolving, made manifest in the European Council and the British refund.

The renegotiations also played a role in the outmanoeuvring of the Antis. They had endorsed the strategy of renegotiation because they were confident (rightly) that the fundamental changes they thought necessary could not be achieved. However, unless they were to be convicted of entering the process in bad faith, this tacitly surrendered the *principle* of membership and reduced the question to a haggle about the terms. This allowed Wilson to project himself as the faithful exponent of party policy since the early 1960s, not – like Ramsay MacDonald – as a traitor at war with his party. In the run-up to the vote, he quoted extensively from a resolution passed by the Labour conference in 1962, which hailed the Community as 'a great and imaginative conception' but declined to take a fixed position on membership. 'What we then decided', he insisted, 'has been the basis of our approach since.'[102] Addressing the special conference in April 1975, Wilson acknowledged that the principles of the Community could never be acceptable to some; but 'I must remind Conference that the legalism was there, the theology was there, the theoretical limitation upon our sovereignty was there, throughout the 1960s, when Conference endorsed our application for entry.'[103]

Wilson's hand was strengthened by favourable press coverage. The *Daily Mail* led with 'Wilson's £100m Market triumph', crediting the prime minister with a deal 'which even the anti-Marketeers in the Cabinet may find difficult to fault'.[104] More importantly for the prime minister, the best-selling Labour newspaper, the *Daily Mirror*, hailed 'Harold's Birthday Spectacular', with 'two days of tough bargaining' producing 'a splendid present for Britain'. 'The Common Market countries have gone almost all the way towards meeting Britain's claims for a better deal inside the Market. They have shown that they WANT Britain to remain a member.'[105]

That sense of goodwill was as important as any of the specifics of the Dublin settlement. As the *New Statesman* commented, it was debatable whether the Community had become 'a better place for Britain to live in' as a result of the renegotiations; 'but there is no denying that it is different'. The Community, it appeared, had taken a 'more pragmatic approach' on issues such as 'agriculture, ties with the developing world, economic and monetary union and all our other old friends', and it had done so under 'British influence'.[106] The Labour Committee for Europe, similarly, argued that the renegotiations had 'revealed a degree of flexibility in the way the Community actually operates which was not expected by many people on either side of the EEC debate'.[107]

For this reason, complaints that the renegotiations could all have been achieved in the normal course of business missed the point. The significance of a set-piece renegotiation was precisely that it focused attention upon the ability of the Community to respond pragmatically to the concerns of member states. From this perspective, the Dublin summit offered a powerful demonstration effect. For the *Guardian*,

> What Mr Wilson's renegotiation has proved is that the EEC is not an inflexible bureaucratic instrument and that where a member has national interests which, rightly or wrongly, it considers to be important these can be accommodated. It is not the budgetary parings or the name of the subsidy that matter in Mr Wilson's renegotiated terms but the discovery, which may be new to some MPs, that the Community exists for the benefit of its members and not the other way round.[108]

As *The Economist* put it, the 'concessions which Mr Harold Wilson "won" at his rather remarkable birthday party are not in themselves significant. But the winning them, and the manner of winning them, were.'[109]

The effect of all this was substantial. Unlike in 2016, the conclusion of the renegotiations produced a significant and enduring shift in the polls. In October 1974, an Opinion Research Corporation (ORC) poll found that only 6 per cent of respondents favoured remaining in the EEC 'on the present terms of entry'; yet 53 per cent thought that

'We should stay in but try to renegotiate the terms of entry.' A further 15 per cent favoured pulling out, but thought that renegotiation should be attempted first.[110] In January 1975, a poll for the *Daily Telegraph* caused a sensation when it showed that 57 per cent of those who had made up their minds favoured withdrawal. Less attention was paid to the second question, which asked how respondents would vote 'If the Government were to renegotiate the terms, and strongly urge that Britain stay in'. That question found 71 per cent in favour of continued membership, suggesting that a substantial cohort of voters were almost anxious for an excuse to switch.[111] In the week after the new terms were announced, Gallup reported a 29-point lead for the Yes campaign, up from 16 points on 3 March and just 8 points on 27 February.[112] Right up until polling day, Wilson's speeches focused squarely on the renegotiated terms, insisting that the question had changed fundamentally since the days of the Heath government.[113] As Anthony King commented, the electorate responded 'decisively' to the combination of the renegotiated terms and the government's endorsement. 'Between early 1973 and late February 1975, the balance of public opinion was never in favour of Britain's EEC membership; from early March 1975 onwards, it was never against it.'[114]

'CONFERENCE WILL ADVISE. THE PEOPLE WILL DECIDE'

Labour's special conference in April voted down the renegotiated terms, as Wilson had always anticipated. Yet the decision to hold a referendum meant that this no longer mattered. Benn had used the party conference to push Labour policy to the left, but his own determination to extract a referendum lifted the question out of the control of party members. The conference platform was adorned with a giant banner, positioned to gain maximum exposure on television, emblazoned with the slogan 'Conference will advise. The People will decide'.[115] It was the wider democracy of the country, not the internal democracy of the Labour Party, that would determine Wilson's success.

   All that remained was to set the terms of the referendum. With no domestic experience of direct democracy, ministers sought to model the campaign as closely as possible on a general election. It was agreed at the outset that two 'umbrella groups' would be created, which would mimic the functions of conventional parties. This would not, of course, preclude other groups from campaigning, but the lead organisations

FIGURE 2.3 Roy Jenkins faces a hostile audience at the Labour Party special conference in April 1975. The banner behind him reads 'Conference will advise. The People will decide'.
Source: Graham Wood, Hulton Archive: www.gettyimages.co.uk/license/451329611

FIGURE 2.4 Every household was sent three pamphlets: one by each of the campaign vehicles and a third – controversially – by the government, advocating the renegotiated terms.
Source: Keystone France: www.gettyimages.co.uk/license/107415730

would be responsible for co-ordinating with the government and the broadcasters. They would be bound by the usual electoral laws and would have to submit accounts at the end of the campaign. In return, they would each receive £125,000 of public funding and would have access to four TV broadcasts and five radio slots. Each side could draw up an official pamphlet, to be delivered free to every household in the country. Controversially, the government would issue a third pamphlet of its own, setting out the case for the renegotiated terms.

The creation of these groups, recognised and funded by government, caused some unease. The Liberal leader, Jeremy Thorpe, warned that 'We are shovelling money and a considerable amount of political power to the umbrella organizations, one of which is headed by a retired diplomat and the other by an obscure lawyer.' (Rather ungallantly, Marten pointed out that the obscure lawyer, Christopher Frere-Smith, merely ran one of the groups affiliated to the official No campaign.) The Labour MP Paul Rose asked 'who elected the umbrella organisations? To whom are they responsible?' There was no precedent for giving public money to bodies 'which are not elected, which did not seek election at the last General Election, and which have no mandate'. Rose, like many others, disliked being forced into cross-party organisations that expected a Labour pro-Marketeer to align with Mrs Thatcher or a Tory Anti to work with Benn. Others feared that the money would find its way into the pockets of extremist parties like the National Front, or to separatist parties in Scotland and Wales.[116]

Wilson also confirmed what had long been predicted: that collective responsibility – the doctrine that all ministers must publicly support government policy – would be suspended for the duration of the campaign. For the first time since 1931, Cabinet ministers would be permitted to campaign against the official policy of the government, though not to speak against it in Parliament. Margaret Thatcher denounced the decision, warning that 'the whole relationship of government with Parliament depends on that principle'. Yet the whole purpose of the referendum was to contain Cabinet divisions. Driving Benn, Foot and their allies into resignation would have defeated the object of the exercise.[117]

Another potential minefield was the wording of the question. Ted Short, who was responsible for steering the bill through Parliament, complained that every word was potentially open to misconstruction. Even a simple word like 'we' could be ambiguous ('Like the French,' interjected a helpful MP).[118] Ministers were concerned that the term 'United Kingdom' might be unfamiliar to some voters, yet the more familiar label – 'Great Britain' – was technically incorrect because it excluded Northern Ireland.[119] The name of the European entity was also problematic. The government favoured 'European Community', but no such entity existed in law: 'the European Economic Community' or 'European Communities' would have been more accurate, but also less familiar. Antis suspected that the government had deliberately dropped 'Economic' to avoid scaring left-wing voters, while opting for 'Community' as 'a very cosy term'. They demanded instead the label

Referendum Act 1975   c. 33

SCHEDULE

FORM OF BALLOT PAPER

The Government have announced the results of the renegotiation of the United Kingdom's terms of membership of the European Community.

DO YOU THINK THAT THE UNITED KINGDOM SHOULD STAY IN THE EUROPEAN COMMUNITY (THE COMMON MARKET)?

YES ☐

NO ☐

PRINTED IN ENGLAND BY HAROLD GLOVER
Controller of Her Majesty's Stationery Office and Queen's Printer of Acts of Parliament

FIGURE 2.5 The ballot paper used in the referendum, referring both to 'the European Community' and 'the Common Market'.

'Common Market', which was more likely to remind Labour voters of the market principles that underpinned it. Douglas Hurd pointed out that Common Market was itself 'a piece of inaccurate journalese', but the government wearily agreed to include both on the ballot.[120]

There were quarrels, too, over the preamble, which explicitly reminded voters of the renegotiation. Yet the fiercest battle came over the appropriate verb: should voters be asked to 'stay' or 'be' in the Community? The former was more accurate, in that Britain had been a member since 1973, but it also established membership as the status quo, which was expected to carry weight with undecided voters. James Molyneaux, the Ulster Unionist leader, argued for 'be', on the grounds that 'the original decision to enter was taken without the authority of the British people'.[121] The government stuck with 'stay', perhaps – as a columnist suggested – because it reminded voters of other activities enjoyed by the 'timid, idle and listless British public (*c.f.* "stay in bed", "stay indoors", "stay at home")'.[122]

Finally, Parliament had to decide how to count the votes. If the referendum was to mimic an election, the simplest practice would be to declare results at a constituency level. This was the solution favoured by the TUC and the Left.[123] Yet voters were not choosing a local MP; they were casting a Yes/No ballot in a nationwide decision. A constituency count risked setting MPs at odds with their constituents, which might damage the legitimacy of Parliament. Instead, the government proposed a single, national count in London, with ballot papers brought to Earl's Court from across the UK. This was rational in one sense: as Ted Short argued, the purpose was 'to find out what the people of the United Kingdom think and not what any area or region thinks'. Yet it was also wildly impractical: the count would take at least five days, even if none of the boxes went missing en route. There were also (justified) suspicions that the government was hoping to suppress evidence of different outcomes in England, Scotland, Wales and Northern Ireland. Winifred Ewing, of the SNP, threatened to sit on the boxes as they were carried down from Scotland and then to stand over the officials at the count, so that she could report the tally. Others warned that unofficial exit polls would be conducted, feeding rumours of divergences which might not in fact be real. Ultimately the government compromised. To protect individual MPs without centralising the count in Westminster, the votes were to be tallied by counties (except for Northern Ireland, which formed a single voting district).[124]

The Referendum Act passed into law on 8 May 1975, by which time both campaigns were up and running. For the first time in modern British history, the decision of a great national question now moved out of Parliament and into the country. While the vote was technically advisory – there was no mechanism by which it could be given formal precedence over Parliament – it was unlikely that MPs would overrule the verdict. The result would depend, not just on the voters, but on the campaigns that sought their support. Never before had two such important campaign vehicles had to be constructed from scratch. The following chapters explore the tactics, personnel and messages that they sought to deploy.

3 'SUPPORT YOUR LOCAL CONTINENT!': BRITAIN IN EUROPE

> *The Common Market is not an ogre, anxious to gobble up unwary Britons or turn every member nation into an identical garlic sausage.*
>
> The How and Why Wonder Book of the Common Market (1974)[1]

> *I distrust those people who proclaim their love for humanity but illustrate it by being unable to get on with those who live around them.*
>
> Roy Jenkins, 26 April 1975[2]

> *Perhaps I am being unfair. I may well be attributing to wickedness on the part of the advocates of British membership what is really only the effect of stupidity.*
>
> Enoch Powell, 31 May 1975[3]

On 26 March 1975, journalists gathered in the ballroom of a luxury hotel in Westminster for the launch of what the *Sun* called 'the most powerful all-party coalition since the war'.[4] 'Britain in Europe' (BIE), which would lead the campaign for a Yes vote, offered a spectacle for which there was little precedent in peacetime history. Its president, Roy Jenkins, was a Labour home secretary and former Chancellor of the Exchequer, who had made his reputation with the permissive reforms of the 1960s. His vice-presidents included a Conservative prime minister (Ted Heath), Chancellor (Reginald Maudling) and Northern Ireland secretary (Willie Whitelaw); the former Liberal leader Jo Grimond; the chairman of the Parliamentary Labour Party, Cledwyn Hughes, and the popular Labour minister Shirley Williams; the President of the National

Farmers' Union, Sir Henry Plumb; and the former general secretary of the Trades Union Congress, Lord (Vic) Feather. Other members of the Executive included the construction magnate Alistair McAlpine, the supermarket boss John Sainsbury and the future Liberal leader, David Steel.[5] The campaign had the backing of all three main party leaders, every living prime minister and all but one foreign secretary. (The sole exception, Selwyn Lloyd, was disbarred from campaigning as Speaker of the House of Commons.)

BIE's wealth, media backing and breadth of support made it one of the most formidable campaigns of the post-war era, dwarfing anything that could be mustered by its opponents. One Anti likened the contest to a race between a sports car and a bicycle; another compared his meagre forces to 'the Hungarians in Budapest resisting Russian tanks with their bare fists'.[6] Yet the support of businessmen, intellectuals and politicians offered no guarantee of success. Just three years earlier, an agile, anti-establishment campaign in Norway had won an unlikely victory over similar forces, and the spectre of the Norwegian defeat hung like a storm cloud over BIE. In the year before the vote, nothing was left to chance: media strategy, fundraising, celebrity endorsements and ground campaigns were meticulously organised. The result was one of the most professional campaigns of the modern era, but one that misled many of its participants on the direction of British politics.

FIGURE 3.1 'The most powerful all-party coalition since the War'. Jeremy Thorpe, Edward Heath and Roy Jenkins team up to 'Keep Britain in Europe'.
Source: Keystone, Hulton Archive: www.gettyimages.co.uk/license/451329613

PHONEY WAR

The campaign to keep Britain in Europe was born in the heart of London clubland, amidst the sumptuous surroundings of the National Liberal Club. Founded by the Victorian statesman William Gladstone, the club occupied a neo-Gothic palace in Whitehall Place, a short walk from Parliament and close to the Thames Embankment. It had served since 1973 as the headquarters of the European Movement (EM), the body that would mastermind the ground campaign during the referendum.

Like so many such bodies, the European Movement was born out of the ashes of the Second World War. Its first president, in 1948, was Winston Churchill's son-in-law, Duncan Sandys (whose daughter would lead its UK branch in 2016). Churchill himself was an honorary president, alongside Continental statesmen such as Léon Blum, Alcide De Gasperi and Paul-Henri Spaak, while the United States provided covert financial support. Since 1969, the European Movement in Britain had been under the energetic direction of Ernest Wistrich, a Polish émigré who had escaped his homeland before the Nazi invasion. Its chairman, Lord Harlech, was a former British ambassador to the United States, who counted the Kennedy family among his many influential friends.[7]

The European Movement first gained public notoriety in 1970, when Heath tasked it with building support for the accession negotiations. A fundraising drive (masterminded by the novelist Jeffrey Archer) raised more than £1.5 million, which paid for a massive advertising campaign and almost 4,000 public meetings. By the end of 1974 the European Movement in Britain had an annual turnover of £250,000, with twenty-five full-time staff, 1,500 individual subscribers and twenty-five regional branches.[8]

As soon as Labour returned to power in 1974, the organisation went onto a war footing. A Campaign Committee met weekly from May 1974, and over the summer the organisation distributed 6.5 million copies of a leaflet, *Out of Europe – Out of Work*. This included a response form for volunteers, which yielded a database of 7,000 potential recruits.[9]

To prepare for the campaign, Wistrich conducted a study of the accession referendums in Denmark, Norway and the Republic of Ireland. He drew the moral that pro-Marketeers should mobilise well-ahead of the vote, paving the way for the campaign with a rigorous programme of public education. He was particularly impressed by the 'Stem Nej!' ('Vote No!') campaign in Norway, which had multiplied campaign vehicles to cater for every conceivable interest group, generating a 'multiplicity of different arguments' that overwhelmed opposition.[10] With this model in mind, the movement dedicated £150,000 in 1974 to an 'early campaign', designed to recruit opinion formers, test messages and build the cell structure of the campaign. Wistrich recruited and trained 600 public speakers and 17 regional organisers, while a copy of the organisation's newsletter, *Facts*, was sent to every conceivable body. The victims of this largesse ranged from the British Lawnmower Manufacturers Association to the Water-Tube Boiler Makers, creating a network of useful contacts.[11]

Particular energy was directed towards 'opinion formers', who could act as nodes for professional support groups. The violinist Siegmund Nissel, who had escaped the Nazi regime in Austria before founding the Amadeus Quartet, was tasked with recruiting 'Musicians for Europe', while Thomas Arnold, son of the theatrical impresario, deployed his network of contacts in the acting profession. Max Beloff was asked to mobilise academics (though they spent so long debating methodology that they appear to have missed the campaign). Similar groups were created for accountants, artists, authors, bankers, doctors, farmers, town planners and creative writers. Appeals were placed in trade journals like the *Accountant*, while correspondence was sent out on an industrial scale: 30,000 to solicitors, 10,000 to clergy and many more to similar cohorts. The result was a thick file of contacts, all of which would be deployed in the referendum.[12]

By the winter of 1974, speakers had been recruited, regional organisers appointed and a flood of literature was in preparation, tailored to the needs of each distinct group. What was lacking was an attractive vehicle to take the lead. As Wistrich himself acknowledged, the European Movement was not well suited to this role. As self-confessed 'Euro-fanatics', Wistrich and his team were viewed with suspicion even by some pro-Marketeers, while the 1971–2 campaign had associated them too closely with Heath and the existing terms of membership. For this reason, Wistrich recommended that a new body be created, which would supersede the EM for the duration of the campaign.[13]

The same conclusion had been reached by a more clandestine organisation, which was meeting at roughly the same time. The European League for Economic Co-operation (ELEC) was a small and rather reclusive body, which existed to facilitate contact between politicians and industrialists across party lines. Early in 1974 the chief executive of Rank, Graham Dowson, convened a series of informal meetings. Roy Jenkins was represented by his close ally John Harris (said to be the man with 'the widest smile in British politics');[14] Douglas Hurd and Geoffrey Rippon reported to Heath; while other participants included the Liberal David Steel; Labour MPs Bill Rodgers and John Roper; and Geoffrey Tucker, the public relations guru who had run the Conservative election campaign in 1970. Over a series of breakfasts at the Dorchester Hotel, the European Movement and ELEC struck a tacit agreement. The former would provide the troops, the money and the strategic direction for the campaign, while ELEC supplied cross-party leadership and contacts with industry.[15]

BRITAIN IN EUROPE

The result was Britain in Europe, which went public in March 1975. The very name signalled a change in emphasis: if the European Movement existed to promote *Europe*, BIE was ostentatiously *British*. Press conferences were festooned with flags, while the organisation's logo was a dove painted in the colours of the Union Jack. Posters, leaflets and clothing were produced in the red, white and blue of the flag, and local organisations were advised to choose their name with care. A title like 'Acton for Europe' might provoke a rival body, called 'Acton for *Britain*'. 'Acton *in* Europe' would shut that option down, while better conveying the theme of patriotism in partnership.[16]

Britain in Europe could call on a galaxy of political talent, not just nationally but at local level. For example, 'Brighton and Hove in Europe' counted among its patrons the actor Laurence Olivier, the novelist Margaret Powell and the historian Asa Briggs. The chairman, Tom Jackson, was a local trade unionist, while employers were represented by a former president of the Chamber of Commerce. Religious authorities included the bishops of Chichester and Lewes; a Methodist superintendent; and a rabbi from the Brighton Hebrew Congregation. All major parties were represented, either by MPs, ministers, councillors or prospective candidates.[17]

It was not just its personnel that made BIE formidable. Unlike its rival, the National Referendum Campaign (NRC), BIE was rich beyond the dreams of avarice. It raised about £2 million in private donations – almost 200 times as much as the NRC and more than the entire spend at the previous general election.[18] Indeed, BIE had almost as much money left over at the end of the campaign as the total expenditure of the NRC.[19] By May 1975 there were 140 people on its payroll, contributing to a bill of £136,000 for salaries alone – more than forty-six times as much as for the NRC. The director, former diplomat Con O'Neill, was paid £7,000 for six months' work, while his opposite number in the NRC worked for free. T-shirts, bumper stickers and children's badges cascaded from the printing press, on a scale (and to a professional standard) of which their opponents could only dream. Bright, glossy and humorous – with slogans like 'Support your local Continent' – this contrasted starkly with the more staid material of the NRC. BIE spent £265,360 on printing, £587,507 on advertising and public relations, and £86,492 simply on office expenses. The comparable figures for the NRC – calculated as a percentage of BIE's expenditure – were £40,192 (15 per cent), £64,698 (11 per cent) and £2,271 (2.6 per cent).[20]

Such financial firepower made possible another expensive luxury: an innovative broadcasting strategy imported from the United States. On the recommendation of John Harris and Geoffrey Tucker, BIE hired the American film-maker Charles Guggenheim to produce their broadcasts. An Academy Award winner, Guggenheim had worked for the Kennedys and was considered 'one of the most effective propagandists in the United States'. At $3,000 a week, he charged accordingly. Deploying a form of *cinéma-vérité*, his films took politicians out of Westminster and into sometimes hostile crowds, allowing them to argue with passion and conviction. Guggenheim's technique of filming hours of footage, from which only a few minutes were broadcast, did not come cheap; the bill for the programmes totalled £105,000, compared to £2,500 for the NRC. Yet the results were worth paying for. Roy Jenkins, who could be condescending when speaking to camera, seemed passionate and authentic in conversation with shoppers, while the trade unionist Vic Feather provided one of the high points of the campaign when taking questions from steelworkers in South Wales. Commentators were impressed, judging the films a 'breakthrough in British political television'.[21]

The campaign's wealth also eased some of the difficulties that might have bedevilled so broad and decentralised a campaign. Following the Norwegian model, BIE chose to multiply campaign groups, each 'arguing their case from their different standpoints, but co-ordinating all their activities under the broad Britain in Europe umbrella'. The theme was to be unity in diversity, a 'strategy of many voices for Europe emerging both nationally and locally'. Business and trade were handed over to the Confederation of British Industry, while trade unions were handled by the Trade Union Alliance for Europe. There were campaign vehicles for Scotland, Wales and Northern Ireland, as well as offices focused on the churches, women voters, ethnic minorities and other groups. Local activists were drafted into bodies such as 'Pudsey in Europe', under the guidance of seventeen regional organisers. In this way, BIE operated not as a single, unified campaign but as the nerve centre of a wider network, knitting together an array of bespoke operations. BIE functioned as the co-ordinator, paymaster and central intelligence point, guiding and supporting rather than controlling their operations.[22]

As the NRC was to discover, holding together such divergent bodies was far from straightforward. By concentrating its finances at the centre, BIE was able to exert a centripetal force over the wider campaign. Regional organisers were employed by the European Movement and could be dismissed by Wistrich. Affiliates had to apply for funding, which could be withheld if their activities were not approved. The sums involved were considerable: Scotland in Europe, for example, received £20,500; Wales in Europe £8,330; and the Confederation of British Industry (CBI) £30,332. Smaller payments included £1,533 for Christians for Europe, £3,000 for the Youth Steering Group; and seed-funding for local bodies, drawn from a fund of more than £162,000. By contrast, the NRC could offer little more than exhortation.[23]

'PEOPLE FOR EUROPE'

Britain in Europe's superior resources were not a wholly unmixed blessing. To its critics, BIE reeked of privilege. It held press conferences in the Waldorf Hotel, was run by a career diplomat and was dominated by an array of plump and patrician politicians. As Roy Jenkins acknowledged, too many of his fellow campaigners looked like 'well-fed men who had done well out of the Common Agricultural Policy'.[24] To their critics, these were the 'guilty men' of British politics, who had presided over thirty years of national decline.[25] Questioned by pollsters in March, more than half of respondents agreed that 'only the politicians and people in big business gain from Britain's membership of the Common Market'. An even larger proportion agreed that 'I am fed up with politicians telling me what to think about the Common Market.'[26]

The shadow that hung over the campaign was the Norwegian referendum of 1972. In Norway, as in Britain, almost all senior politicians had backed membership; yet a bold anti-establishment campaign, run by the thirty-seven-year-old lawyer Arne Haugestad, had won a stunning victory for the Antis. The words 'remember Norway' were chanted like an incantation by pro-Marketeers as a protective charm against complacency. Not since 1940 had Norway loomed so large in British politics, ensuring that even substantial poll leads were viewed with suspicion.

To shake off the 'establishment' tag, Britain in Europe set out to foreground 'personalities' over politicians. The faces that beamed down from campaign posters were not the plump and sagging visages of Heath or Jenkins, but the clean-cut, athletic features of sports stars and celebrities. A series of glossy posters featured messages from the heavyweight boxing champion Henry Cooper ('Don't knock Britain out'); former England cricket captain Colin Cowdrey ('Don't hit Britain out'); and the Olympic gold medallist Mary Peters ('Don't run Britain out'). The *Daily Mirror*'s celebrated agony aunt, Marjorie Proops, was another who featured on posters, as did a range of actors and artists.

In one of the more innovative experiments of the campaign, the writer, broadcaster and international Monopoly champion Gyles Brandreth became director of 'People for Europe'. The goal was to build a campaign around 'young personalities ... ranging from pop-singers to actresses' and from 'D.J.s to footballers'. 'People for Europe', he assured journalists,

> won't be involving professional politicians at all. It won't involve heavyweight industrialists or earnest trade union officials either. It will involve all kinds of other people – many of them very famous, lots of them very young.

Celebrities were invited to donate £5, in return for which their names and pictures would appear on posters. Dirk Bogarde, Paul Eddington, Peter Ustinov and Michael York were just some of those who donated, while the novelist Frederick Forsyth lavished a full £20. The resulting posters brought together such unlikely bedfellows as the playwright J.B. Priestley; the sculptor Henry Moore; the photographer David Bailey; and Katie Boyle, the actress, game-show panellist and quondam agony aunt who had hosted the Eurovision Song Contest in 1974.[27]

Brandreth sometimes felt stifled by BIE, which vetoed his 'Wombles for Europe' idea and expressed horror at his more daring recruits. Its leaders were aghast when he tried to recruit Mike Yarwood, one of the most famous names in television, because he had made his reputation mimicking Heath and Wilson. Nonetheless, 'People for Europe' assembled an impressive array of talent. A press launch was held at the Cinderella Bar in the London Palladium, complete with punning pantomime stars ('Britain SHALL go to the European ball!') and a 'bemused' Andrew Lloyd Webber. (The latter, wrote Brandreth wistfully, 'was our "star attraction", but he lacks "star personality": he can barely string a sentence together'.)[28]

Sports personalities were especially sought after. The broadcaster David Coleman (the inspiration behind *Private Eye*'s 'Colemanballs' column) was put in charge of 'Sportsmen for Europe', with two full-time members of staff. Stars who backed membership included the captain of the British and Irish Lions, Willie John McBride; legendary Welsh scrum half, Gareth Edwards; the jockey Lester Piggott; tennis champion Virginia Wade; and three of the most successful football managers of all time: Jock Stein, Don Revie and Sir Matt Busby. Importantly, these were all Britons who had competed proudly and successfully in Europe. BIE circulated lists of the trophies won on the Continent, as proof that European competition could spur Britons to new heights.[29]

At the climactic campaign rally in Westminster Central Hall on 2 June, Roy Jenkins, Ted Heath and Jeremy Thorpe were joined on the platform by Colin Cowdrey, the racing driver Graham Hill and a host of other sporting names. Most rallies included an appearance by at least two sporting personalities, while others sent messages of support. At Nottingham, there was a good luck message from Brian Clough ('One of Nottingham's most avid supporters of the "Keep Britain in Europe" campaign'), while a rally at Manchester heard from both Sir Matt Busby, who had won the European Cup with Manchester United, and the manager of Manchester City, Tony Book. At Cardiff there were messages of support from the rugby internationals Gareth Edwards and Geraint Davies as well as from the Wales football manager, Mike Smith.[30] Young football bosses like Jimmy Armfield, Derek Dougan and Dave Sexton discussed the opportunities for British footballers to play and travel in Europe, while acknowledging that it would be 'a hell of a gamble' to sign a Continental player.[31]

For those of more rarefied tastes, 'Musicians for Europe' boasted the support of Benjamin Britten, Geraint Evans, Moura Lympany and Sir Charles Mackerras. 'Actors for Europe' assembled one of the great pantomime casts of modern times, with support from Richard Briers, Ronnie Corbett, Michael Hordern and Arthur Lowe. ('The only question', one satirist noted, was 'Why no Vanessa Redgrave?') More than 200 'Writers for Europe' signed an advert in *The Times*, including such unlikely shelf-fellows as Barbara Cartland, Agatha Christie, Karl Popper and Tom Stoppard.[32]

The strategy was replicated at a local level. Regional organisers were urged to recruit 'local bigwigs': 'footballers and others, to whom the public would look up'.[33] Most of these figures played no active role in the campaign, either from pressure of work or from a natural diffidence about speaking on politics. (One celebrated actor confessed to being 'useless to the point of embarrassment as a public speaker'.) Yet their utility lay in their names, rather than in their rhetorical gifts. The point was to show that 'Europe' was not simply the cause of 'politicians', who must, by definition, be out of touch with the lives of ordinary people. Recruiting national champions communicated the message that Britain could compete in Europe and win, while branding the European cause as modern, dynamic and optimistic. Even the most dedicated admirer of Miss Marple was unlikely to take her political cues from Agatha Christie, but this was not the purpose. The point was to demonstrate the sheer range of support, with membership the default position of sensible people from all walks of life.

'YOUNG EUROPEANS AFLOAT'

For any cause to be progressive, modern and idealistic, it must also have a youth wing. Older campaigners tended simply to assume that the young were pro-Market, on the rather vague grounds that 'so many youngsters go to Europe today'.[34] In fact, polling suggested that young people were among the least enthusiastic about integration, perhaps because they had no personal memory of war.[35] Student politics tended to ape the fashionable positions of the Left, which included hostility to 'Europe' as a capitalist enterprise: the National Union of Students, under the future home secretary Charles Clarke, voted by more than two-to-one against membership.[36] To counter this, BIE launched its own Youth Department, charged with delivering a campaign that would be 'radical, imaginative and above all interesting'. Its language crackled with youthful vigour: it would 'encourage, visit, bully and expand our 63 branches'; 'monitor, oppose, impede, thwart and publicize NUS policy on Europe'; organize 'flying minibus teams'; and 'monitor and infiltrate magazines read by young people'.[37]

That enthusiasm was not always well directed. The youth department devoted a surprising amount of energy to a military occupation of its own headquarters, in the hope that a 'good dose of youth revolt' would 'pep up' the campaign. Unfortunately, nobody noticed; 'our wise leaders', one activist complained, 'have decided on an admirable policy of repressive toleration ... I am assuming that they have read their Marcuse.'[38] A storm erupted over plans for a beauty contest called 'Miss Europa-Europe the Luscious', causing fury among female supporters, while posters that were intended to be hard-hitting were sometimes simply misjudged.[39] In Scotland, a poster issued by the Federation of Conservative Students had to be withdrawn following complaints from Jewish groups, who objected to its depiction of a concentration camp alongside the slogan 'Victims of a divided Europe'. Another drew protests for its portrayal of Vietnamese refugees, driven from their homes because 'They were too small' to stand alone.[40] Youth groups were not always mindful of electoral law or the prohibition against 'treating'. In Cambridge, organisers of a student drinks party promised to lubricate guests on such a magnificent scale as to convince them 'that prosperity does indeed lie with Europe!' Messages were hastily despatched, warning that such an event would fall foul of the courts.[41]

In a bid to channel their energies more effectively, a steering group was established with representatives from each of the main youth organisations. The chair was taken either by the Conservative MP Tom Spencer or by the Liberal press officer Chris Green. Another Liberal, Archie Kirkwood, was appointed to co-ordinate the youth campaign, while the future defence secretary, Michael Fallon, was variously described in documents as 'Youth Officer' and 'Head of Espionage'. Julian Priestley was seconded from Brussels, where he was working as secretary general of the Young European Left.[42] Broadcasters were provided with a list of young people who would be available for TV and radio, while eight 'Youth for Europe' seminars were held for 'non-political people'. The campaign particularly targeted 'young' magazines, while secretarial colleges were offered 'young speakers on Europe for their Current Affairs Courses'.[43]

Youth activists brought energy and humour to a campaign that could feel almost oppressively stage-managed. Piers Gardner, a student at Oxford, organised a series of minibus tours, sending shock teams of students as far afield as Devon, Cornwall, Strathclyde and York. In the final weeks of the campaign, the minibus parties were reported to be distributing '5,000 leaflets, 1,000 car stickers and 1,000 badges per day'. As a future barrister, Gardner impressed upon his drivers the importance of proper insurance. 'Kidding them [you're] not students', he warned, 'will lead to a very big claim by passengers when you go off the road singing "Tomorrow belongs to me".'[44]

Other activities included a 200-mile 'Keep Britain in Europe' relay race, which passed through Birkenhead, Blackburn, Blackpool, Bolton, Chester, Liverpool, Manchester, Preston and Southport.[45] In one of the more imaginative campaign stunts, a canal boat was hired to tour the Midlands, displaying the benefits of membership. Sponsored jointly by the Conservative Party and the European Movement, 'Young Europeans Afloat' served as an exhibition centre by day and showed films or hosted discussion groups by night. Eight female models were hired, dressed in the national costumes of the other member states, and the whole thing was to close with a disco at Stratford-upon-Avon.[46]

CONSERVATIVES FOR EUROPE

While celebrities added glamour and youth campaigners zest, the decisive contest was the ground war in the constituencies. BIE was worried about turnout, which it feared might either swing the vote to their opponents or discredit a decision to stay in. Getting out the vote would need the co-operation of party activists, with their squadrons of door-knockers, canvassing returns and electoral nous.

Of the two main parties, it was the Conservatives who were more enthusiastically pro-Market. It was a Conservative government, under Ted Heath, that had taken Britain into the Community, and even Margaret Thatcher hailed this as the 'outstanding achievement' of his premiership. During the leadership contest in February, Thatcher had acted quickly to snuff out rumours that she was sceptical about membership, insisting that the 'torch' lit by Heath 'must be picked up and carried' by his successor. Only eight Conservative MPs voted against the renegotiated terms on 9 April, and internal soundings found just thirty constituency parties where either the chairman, agent or candidate was

FIGURE 3.2 'It is with some temerity that the pupil speaks before the master.' Thatcher tries, unsuccessfully, to butter up her predecessor as they launch the Conservative Yes campaign, 17 May 1975.
Source: Central Press, Hulton Archive: www.gettyimages.co.uk/license/118582787

openly anti-Market. Just two subsequently took an anti-Market position in the referendum.[47]

Despite all this, it took time to coax the Tory machine into life. Local parties were exhausted and demoralised after two general election defeats the previous year; and the prospect of lining up behind a Labour prime minster, to rescue him from a crisis of his own making, was viewed with some distaste. Nor was there much enthusiasm for the renegotiated terms, which most Tories viewed as an attempt to save face for a Labour government by traducing the patriotism of the previous Conservative administration. It was important to insist, as Thatcher did, that voting Yes need have 'nothing to do with the re-negotiated terms – terms which did not alter one single clause of the treaty we signed'.[48]

In a column for the *Sunday Telegraph* in March, the right-wing commentator Peregrine Worsthorne urged Conservatives to vote No; not because he opposed membership, but because he saw it as the best way to remove a dangerously left-wing government from office.[49] That this view did not take deeper root owed something to the efforts of Conservative Central Office. Sir Christopher Soames ran a series of seminars for party activists, insisting that entry to the Common Market was a solidly Conservative achievement that must be protected from sabotage by the Left. The Conservative Group for Europe, run by Miles Hudson, arranged for each constituency party to nominate a European liaison representative, who could distribute literature, report on campaign activities and galvanise activists. While the party preferred to work through separate Britain in Europe groups in the localities (not least because they 'could raise funds without having to tap traditional sources of Conservative finance'), constituency parties were also asked to mobilise. By April seventy constituencies were reported to be 'well-organised' and a hundred more were 'doing something'. Thatcher met with constituency representatives to stress the need for activity, and in May she wrote to MPs urging their support.[50]

Thatcher herself kept a low profile during the campaign, for which she was excoriated by the right-wing press. The *Sun* printed a 'missing persons' notice, just a week before the vote:

> MISSING: One Tory leader. Answers to the name of Margaret Thatcher.
> MYSTERIOUSLY disappeared from the Market referendum campaign 11 days ago. Has not been seen since.
> WILL finder kindly wake her up and remind her she is failing the nation in her duty as Leader of the Opposition?[51]

Such criticism was not wholly fair. Thatcher penned a number of articles, intervened to pep up Tory activists and made several major speeches, including at a youth rally in Trafalgar Square. She even donned some European knitwear, appearing in a woolly jumper embroidered with the flags of the member states. It was true, however, that she felt uncomfortable in the clubbable atmosphere of BIE. She disliked its cross-party ethos and was suspicious of the Heathites and coalitionists by whom it was dominated. A visit to campaign headquarters quickly degenerated into farce. Taking an instant dislike to the Labour-supporting Wistrich, she talked incessantly, complained that there was too much socialist red in the posters and tore down a 'Communists for Europe' sticker. Her appearances on the campaign trail were similarly eccentric. Visiting a factory in Tamworth, she was displeased to find that workers had plastered the machinery with anti-Market posters. 'This won't do,' she announced, wagging a disapproving finger, before homing in on the solitary Yes voter on the production line.[52]

It did not help that the question was so closely associated with her predecessor. Heath blazed across the campaign trail like a meteor, displaying a charisma, vision and dynamism that had entirely eluded him as leader. A man who, as prime minister, had appeared almost pathologically uninspiring seemed suddenly to have acquired a magnetic personality, commanding the battlefield like 'the Achilles of the European cause'. 'Gone is the stiff, prickly Heath so criticized by his supporters and by the media,' journalists reported; in his place emerged a passionate, moving and often funny orator, delivering 'fighting' speeches packed with 'fervour, fire and fun'.[53] When he spoke at the Oxford Union, his arrival sparked 'a near pandemonium of enthusiasm' among the students. Barbara Castle was astonished. 'Heath was the hero of the hour,' she wrote, 'as he had never been as PM'.[54]

TACKLING THE BENN-MAN

While the Conservatives provided the backbone of the campaign, it was essential that Britain in Europe did not become a one-party operation. BIE also needed Labour voters, who could not be expected to enrol in a Tory crusade. For this reason, BIE recruited heavily from the Labour benches. In addition to Roy Jenkins, as president, the campaign appointed a Labour publicity director (Harold Hutchinson), research director (Peter Stephenson) and press officer (Norman Haseldine).[55] The government pamphlet setting out the renegotiated terms, delivered to every household in the country, was written by the political editor of the *Daily Mirror*, Sydney Jacobsen, who had long experience of writing for Labour supporters.[56]

The key task was to give those who had previously opposed membership – following what was then the official position of the party – permission to change their minds. Long-standing Europhiles like Heath, Thorpe and even Jenkins could not help here; what was needed were Labour 'switchers': men like Callaghan and Wilson, who could plausibly claim to have come round to membership from a position of scepticism. To make the case for a Labour Europe, brought about by the renegotiations, it was agreed that 'an alternative structure' would be needed, paid for by BIE but not visibly associated with it. This campaign would distance itself from Heath and the 'Tory terms', while urging socialist themes like solidarity, workers' rights and control of multinational finance.[57]

The Labour Campaign for Britain in Europe was launched in April, with Shirley Williams as president and the Scottish MP J. Dickson Mabon as chairman. Armed with a budget of around £92,000, the organisation signed up eighty-eight MPs, twenty-one Labour peers and twenty-five trade union officials behind an expressly left-wing vision.[58] 'The Europe that the Labour Party wants to join', it insisted

> is not the Europe that Edward Heath and Geoffrey Rippon seek to create. It is the social democratic Europe of Willy Brandt, the Common Market of millions of other socialists who, enjoying the benefits of membership and believing that socialism should be international, are anxious to welcome Britain (and the British Labour Party) into the Community.[59]

The strategy was devised by Jim Cattermole, the veteran party organiser who had become director of the Labour Committee for Europe in 1972. In a planning report circulated in February, Cattermole proposed a three-stage approach. In the first period, to mid-March, the campaign would focus on identifying and recruiting Labour pro-Marketeers, primarily through briefing conferences in Labour seats. In the second phase, until May, the campaign would focus on expanding its support, holding meetings and seminars for doubtful Labour voters. In the final three weeks, the emphasis would shift to rallies and public meetings, deploying the campaign's battery of Labour Cabinet ministers.[60]

Labour Pros deployed two main lines of argument. The first emphasised the rise of multinational finance, which risked outpacing the capacity of national governments to regulate it. 'By far the most significant development in capitalism over the last 25 years', claimed the Young European Left, 'has been that, while political units have remained national, economic units have become multinational.'[61] In such a world, socialism was only possible through co-operation across borders. David Basnett, the general secretary of the General and Municipal Workers' Union, warned that the days had passed when any single nation could be 'economically sovereign'; only 'multi-governmental agencies' could constrain the actions of 'world finance'. From this perspective, those who dismissed the Community as a 'rich man's club' were missing the point. As the Scottish MP John Mackintosh put it, Westminster had also been a 'rich man's club' at the start of the twentieth century, which was why the Labour Party had worked so hard to storm the gates. In Parliament, as elsewhere,

> We fought and we won. What did Nye Bevan say? Did he ever say to the Labour Party, 'If you see a lot of rich and powerful capitalists, ignore them. Leave them. Do not trouble them'? He said that we have to take over the commanding heights. If Europe is a centre of power and wealth, let us take it and use it for the good of the people.[62]

This was linked to a second line of argument, which stressed the progress Labour had already made in reforming the Community. The campaign's strongest card here was Harold Wilson. Like Mrs Thatcher, the prime minister had never claimed any emotional attachment to the European project. Mocking those who got 'dappy about the very concept of the thing', Wilson presented himself almost as an outside observer of the European debate, bemused by the 'exaggerated claims' and 'doctrinaire' views of those operating under 'pre-natal' influences. The rival campaigns, he complained, were 'screaming so hard at one another' that the 'cacophony' would 'deafen' and 'confuse' people.[63] He positioned himself as the ultimate floating voter, unimpressed by Heath's 'theological' commitment to membership, but basing his decision 'on practical, common-sense arguments'.[64]

Wilson claimed to be agnostic on the principle of integration, insisting that he would judge the Community on 'how it is in fact working now'.[65] What he found, he declared, was 'an essentially practical organization', in which member states came together in the pursuit of essential national interests. Membership was not a magic potion that could solve Britain's economic woes, but recovery would be 'immeasurably more difficult' in isolation.[66] In his speeches, Wilson was careful to press the benefits of membership without appearing to make exaggerated claims. The effect on jobs, he judged, had been 'marginally helpful' thus far, while on food prices 'there isn't 2½d in it either way'; but 'in the years ahead', the impact on both would be 'decisively in favour of staying in'. He hinted at large investment projects in the pipeline, which would not proceed if Britain voted to withdraw. Outside the Community, Britain might perhaps secure a free trading relationship through membership of EFTA, but it would be bound by the rules of the Market while losing any say in their formation.[67]

In this way, Wilson sought to present himself as 'the calm voice of reason', standing between those who viewed the Community as an invention either 'of the devil' or 'of the Almighty'. He pitched his appeal explicitly to 'that significant body of opinion, in my view almost certainly greater than either of the other two', who were 'neither whole-hearted Europeans or whole-hearted anti-Europeans'.[68] It was an astute political pitch, and one that Wilson was well placed to exploit. As the *Guardian* commented, 'it is Mr Wilson's very scepticism about what he calls Common Market theology which makes him such a Pole Star for the wandering voter'.[69]

The Labour campaign milked Wilson's support for all it was worth. His picture adorned the cover of 2 million copies of a pamphlet

FIGURE 3.3   Harold Wilson at an eve of poll rally in Sophia Gardens, Cardiff.
Source: Media Wales: www.walesonline.co.uk/news/politics/15-photos-show-how-life-11389370

headed 'Europe – Yes', alongside a quote endorsing membership as 'good for Britain, good for Europe, good for the Commonwealth, good for the developing world and good for the whole world'.[70] In the days before the vote, *Labour Weekly* – which urged a No vote – carried a picture of Wilson on its inside cover, above an advert backing membership.[71] After keeping a low profile early in the campaign, either Wilson or Callaghan spoke at a meeting every night in the final fortnight.

Wilson himself featured on the news or in an interview twenty-five times over the course of the campaign, a total exceeded only by Roy Jenkins for the Yes campaign.[72]

By mobilising the party leadership, it was possible to present Labour anti-Marketeers as rebels, acting in defiance of a Labour prime minister. In Bristol, where Tony Benn was an MP, pro-Marketeers issued a public letter warning that a No vote was a 'vote against the Prime Minister and the Labour Government'. It was signed by the Labour MP for Bristol North East, eight Labour councillors, workers from the co-operative movement, trade unionists and a former MP for Bristol South.[73] In the East Midlands, it was claimed that at least half the 'old hands at organization, including many of the constituency agents' were working for a Yes vote. The Labour majority on the Greater London Council also voted to stay in, 'to maintain and develop the industrial, commercial and social advantages already gained for London through our membership'.[74] Strikingly, a survey in June found that 49 per cent of those questioned thought that the Labour Party (as distinct from 'the Government') favoured staying in, while only 15 per cent thought that it favoured leaving.[75]

'LIBERALS PLAYED IT DIRTY'

Of all the major parties, the Liberals had been most consistently pro-Market. They had favoured entry since 1958 and their rhetoric had a federalist streak that was unusual in the wider campaign. In 1971 the Liberal Assembly had called for a 'political community in Europe which supersedes the existing sovereign nation states', with common foreign, monetary and financial policies, and an elected parliament that would 'supersede … national Parliaments'. The party's 1975 'Manifesto for Europe' proclaimed that 'For Liberals the pro-Europe campaign is a crusade!', adding unfashionably, 'The trouble is not that political integration has gone too far, but that it has not gone far enough.'[76]

For a party accustomed to shaking collecting tins at jumble sales, access to the riches of BIE was a giddying experience. As David Steel later recalled, 'cars, aeroplanes, helicopters, film units, stage equipment, photocopiers, typewriters' – all the 'basic materials which Liberals scratched hard to find or finance' – 'simply appeared at the flick of fingers'.[77] Britain in Europe allocated £95,000 to the Liberal campaign, and it responded enthusiastically. By the first week of April, it had recruited 360 'link men' in the constituencies, whose job it was to co-ordinate operations with BIE.[78] The Liberals commissioned half a million 'Vision of Europe' leaflets, 3 million 'Don't slam the door' leaflets, 20,000 posters and 250,000 car stickers, all of which struck an unambiguously idealistic tone.[79]

Liberal enthusiasm for the Community was very real, but the referendum was also 'a tremendous opportunity': a chance to fight a national election on what the party considered its natural terrain, with generous funding and an unusually high media profile.[80] After decades in the wilderness, the party had almost tripled its support in February 1974, winning more than 6 million votes and 19 per cent of the poll. Though it dipped a little in October – partly due to the expense of two elections in a year – the party still viewed itself as the coming force in British politics. With this in mind, an internal strategy document identified three goals for the campaign: 'to establish the Liberal Party as the forerunner on the European question'; 'to recruit a larger membership for the Party'; and to provide a platform for 'prominent Liberals'. Activists were urged to link the campaign to 'the Party's post-election drive for membership', while speakers were reminded 'not to lose their identity while working alongside colleagues of other political persuasions'.[81] In a list of objectives drawn up 'in order of importance' by the Liberal campaign director, Aza Pinney, securing a Yes vote ranked only third. The first was to 'maintain a distinct and different image for the Liberal Party', while the second was to 'ensure that as many people as possible know what the Liberal Party stands for and to reinforce Liberal voters' faith in the Party'. Other goals included to 'emphasize and exploit the divisions in other political parties', to 'strengthen the Party organization' and to 'put activists in good heart'.[82]

This had an influence on Liberal tactics. The party's support, as it cheerfully acknowledged, was 'largely a protest vote', so it was essential that supporters 'feel that a YES vote can still carry protest overtones'. For this reason, the party positioned itself deliberately on the fringes of the cross-party campaign, demanding *more* integration, lower tariffs and more democratisation of Community institutions. There was a particular emphasis on Third World aid and regional development. Speakers were urged to stress the 'dissatisfaction' of the Liberal Party, both 'with the present Community set-up and with the present British governmental set-up'. Activists should 'use the campaign to push Liberal regional policies', distinguishing themselves from the 'the two centralist parties in a way which could reap considerable electoral dividends'.[83]

This electioneering did not go unnoticed. There were mutterings throughout the campaign that the 'Liberals played it dirty', viewing the whole enterprise 'as a purely pro-Liberal exercise'. There were also rumours that money was being diverted to party organisation. While there was admiration for David Steel, Thorpe's determination to attack ministers at rallies made him as unpopular with Labour Europeans as he would later become with dog-owners.[84]

In general, however, there was strikingly little friction between the parties. There was much praise for the Britain in Europe Steering Committee and for the willingness of party representatives to respect one another's expertise.[85] At a local level, activists were often surprised by how much they enjoyed working across party lines. As one campaigner put it,

> I remember reading about the soldiers in the trenches playing football together on Christmas Day in the First World War. It was all rather like that at the Britain in Europe meetings in my constituency with Conservatives rather ostentatiously buying Liberal raffle tickets. I think a lot of us rather enjoyed working for a short time with our old opponents.[86]

'THOUGHTFUL THEMES'

Party organisations played a crucial role in the campaign, but the confusion of party allegiances meant that voters could not be relied upon to follow conventional patterns of support. For this reason, considerable energy was put into finding new ways to approach them. Con O'Neill was particularly keen to identity converts: 'sympathetic characters', in 'professions which the public respect', who had changed their minds since 1973. 'Policemen, milkmen, farmers or farm workers' would be 'ideal'; 'Any housewife could also be good', especially if they had 'strong regional speech'. The goal was to entrench 'the feeling that it is the reasonable, prudent, sensible and fashionable thing to vote Yes – to climb on the bandwagon of "everybody's doing it"'.[87]

In crafting its campaign messages, BIE deployed a sophisticated polling operation that drew on some of the biggest names in market research. Humphrey Taylor, who had founded the Opinion

Research Centre (ORC), was co-opted onto BIE's Steering Committee, and ORC was paid more than £33,000 over the course of the campaign. Bob Worcester, who had founded Market and Opinion Research International (MORI) in 1969, provided daily briefings to the Cabinet's steering committee, which were used to hone the government's message and the roles of Wilson and Callaghan.[88]

While newspaper polls focused on 'the state of the race', BIE's research was both more extensive and more sophisticated. Attitude surveys sought to reconstruct the public understanding of key issues, such as sovereignty or the price of food, so that messages could be crafted to address voter concerns. Polls were used to identify those cohorts who seemed likely to vote No; to draw up a comprehensive picture of their reasons; and to test campaign messages that might win them round. This was linked to the work of a Research and Information Unit, run by Peter Stephenson and Diana Villiers (later the distinguished academic Diana Villiers Negroponte). The Research Unit produced 129 files of reports and statistical analysis, covering everything from 'Consumer Prices' and 'Investment and Credit' to 'North Sea Oil' and 'the Queen'. Their findings were communicated directly to the relevant groups: Scotland in Europe, for example, was sent material on oil prices or devolved government, while the Women's Office was fed information on women's employment and social policy. Key figures and speaking notes were disseminated more widely, through a series of briefing papers sent out to 3,000 people each week.[89] A press agency, Charles Baker, provided comprehensive monitoring of the press (both national and regional), allowing immediate fact-checking against the research files.[90]

Many activists had little experience of electioneering, so BIE assisted with both the content of speeches and the structuring of messages over the campaign. Timing was as important as content. In a long campaign, fought on a single issue, it was important to pace both the delivery and tone so that voters did not switch off out of boredom. With this in mind, speakers were encouraged to think in terms of three approaches. The first, 'bread and butter themes', addressed material concerns such as jobs, food prices and social policy (the CBI was instructed not to 'rock the boat' on the latter). Speakers were urged to focus on unemployment ('Jobs at risk if we leave'), and should not be shy of 'arousing sensible worries about leaving'. The second category, 'Thoughtful themes', was more abstract, focusing on issues like sovereignty, the Commonwealth and peace. Speakers were reminded that '"Thoughtful Themes" can also be *passionate* themes', but were asked to 'avoid federalist commitment'. A third approach involved 'Knocking down anti-marketeers' nonsense', focusing on the alternatives to membership – seen as a particular weak point for the Antis – and on scare stories about the monarchy and the Church. The tone, it was suggested, should be one of weary resignation: 'if this rubbish is all they can produce, it shows how poverty-stricken are their arguments'.[91]

In the opening and closing weeks of the campaign, it was the 'thoughtful themes' that predominated. Posters played heavily on the memory of war and of the millions who had died in European conflicts. Events were designed to build a sense of cross-generational commemoration, binding in younger voters who had no personal memory of war. On 4 May – the weekend before VE Day – a youth rally in Trafalgar Square culminated in a spellbinding performance by Ted Heath, who told the crowd how he had returned from wartime service aflame with the vision of a united Europe. 'Those ideals', he declared, now rested in the hands of the young: 'you have ideals. You are not prepared to accept the injustices of the old world. You want to create a better Britain in a better Europe.'[92]

On the night before the vote, the youth campaign hosted a peace vigil under the statue of Churchill in Parliament Square. Organised by young voters, addressed by Margaret Thatcher and presided over by the almost Victorian figure of Harold Macmillan, the event was choreographed around the theme of unity across generations. Lighting a candle for peace, Thatcher reiterated the remarks she had made in an article for the *Daily Telegraph* earlier that day. The prevention of war, she argued,

> lies not only in the willingness of peoples to be vigilant in defence against tyranny; it consists of being prepared to live our lives together, in their becoming so enmeshed through trade and co-operation that to turn on one another would be unthinkable and impossible. ... The Community exists to do just that.[93]

Such appeals had an upbeat, even visionary flavour, part of a conscious attempt to maintain a balance of light and shade across the campaign. Roy Jenkins, in particular, was keen that membership be seen not simply as a grim necessity, but as a new adventure that could

FIGURE 3.4   Margaret Thatcher lights a torch for Europe at a youth rally in Parliament Square, beneath the statue of Churchill.

Source: P. Floyd, Hulton Archive: www.gettyimages.co.uk/license/641305205

supply 'an injection of national self-confidence'. A 'resounding' Yes vote, he argued, could 'mark the beginning of a real national revival'.[94] Membership was represented as a modernising project, which would enable the country to shake off the psychological debris of the Victorian age. Channelling the rebel spirit of the 1960s and '70s, Reg Prentice mocked the Antis as 'reactionary fuddy-duddies', while the *Guardian* accused the No campaign of trying 'to cling to a world that has passed'. The EEC, it told readers, 'forms an important part of contemporary reality', and this in itself was a 'primary reason' for staying in.[95]

'OUR ENEMIES … WILL REJOICE'

The tone was darker on what Stephenson called the 'bread and butter issues': jobs, prices and economic security. Stephenson urged speakers to '*avoid* trying to prove long-term economic growth benefits'; these were too abstract and speculative to sway voting intentions. Instead, the focus should be on the risk to jobs from leaving – an issue with particular resonance in the grim economic climate of the time.

The mood varied from the bleak to the apocalyptic. Ted Heath predicted the total collapse of the economy, with rationing and food shortages outside the EEC, while the Liberal Cyril Smith warned that 'If Britain withdraws now it will simply sink further into the mire.' MPs drew a dismal picture of Britain's prospects outside the Community. Prentice warned that no country could prosper alone, 'least of all Britain, the most vulnerable of all', while David Ennals, a Foreign Office minister, told voters that the 'truth is, we cannot live on our own in the world. We just cannot compete.'[96]

This led naturally into an argument that became increasingly prominent in the campaign: that withdrawal was favoured only by those, in Roy Jenkins' words, who 'desire to see our national morale undermined and our influence in the world destroyed'. Prentice – who would later defect to the Conservative Party – told a rally that the referendum posed a choice 'between the moderate centre in British politics, who are in favour of staying in, and the political extremists, who are not'. It did not go unnoticed that the Soviet Union was advocating a No vote, alongside the Communist Party, the IRA, the Powellites and the National Front. The minister of defence, Bill Rodgers, warned that 'our enemies' would 'rejoice' at a No vote, while the man with the most famous name in British politics, Winston Churchill Junior, told a rally that 'We are fighting for the survival of democracy itself.' Invoking the memory of his famous grandfather, Churchill drew a vivid portrait of communism on the march in Portugal, South Asia and the British Left. He accused anti-Marketeers of seeking 'to impose on the workers of Britain the living standards and liberties of the COMECON countries'.[97] Benn was furious when Heath compared him in a newspaper article to those who would have welcomed a Nazi invasion in 1940. 'Could anyone really be sure, if the Communists threatened Britain, whose side Anthony Wedgwood Benn would be on?'[98]

This played into perhaps the most powerful campaign theme of all: the question of 'which side are you on?' Cartoonists made hay with the motley collection of anti-Marketeers, imagining Benn and Powell at the head of a hairy collection of Trotskyites, Maoists, fascists and Scottish nationalists.[99] BIE simply lined up the names on its posters. For membership: 'The Labour Government. The Conservative Party. The Liberal Party. The National Farmers Union. Australia. Canada.

New Zealand.' Against membership: 'The IRA. The Communist Party. The National Front. International Marxists. The Rev. Ian Paisley.' The *Sun* told readers that the referendum was 'less and less about Europe' and more 'a battle between the sane, sensible, moderate majority' and 'lunatic fringe extremists'. 'You can tell a cause by the company it keeps,' warned BIE. 'On June 5th you have to decide who you stand beside.'[100]

Like so much of Britain in Europe's strategy, this was driven by market research. Polling by Louis Harris presented voters with twenty names that were involved in the campaign and asked for a positive or negative reaction. All thirteen pro-Marketeers had favourable ratings, some – Heath, Thorpe, Whitelaw, Jenkins, Callaghan and Williams – very substantially so. Of the seven Antis, only Powell, at +2, registered a favourable rating, and even he evoked a larger number of unfavourable responses than anyone except Benn or Paisley.[101] Not surprisingly, BIE lost no opportunity to identify its opponents as bigots and xenophobes. Heath accused the Antis of being 'frightened about the big wide world'. 'For people like Peter Shore,' he scoffed, 'international brotherhood stops at Margate.'[102]

PAPER ARMIES

In such a multi-vocal campaign, it was inevitable that the case assembled by BIE sometimes lacked coherence. While Labour Marketeers talked of social democracy and the taming of multinational finance, Soames was hailing the Community as a bulwark of 'the capitalist system'.[103] The charge that Antis lacked confidence in Britain sat uneasily with BIE's own warnings that the country could not survive outside the EEC. In such a diverse organisation, differences of this kind were probably inevitable; and so long as they were addressed to different audiences, could be a source of strength.

Such differences might have been more problematic had the media been less sympathetic. The NRC complained of systematic media bias, and it was true that almost all newspapers editorialised for a Yes vote.[104] Yet the problem lay as much with the respective output of the two campaigns as with any conspiracy on the part of reporters. BIE simply held more meetings, published more literature and generated more copy than its opponents. Its press office generated a steady stream of letters, articles and opinion pieces tailored to every conceivable outlet. Humphrey Taylor, of ORC, drummed into the campaign the importance of good press management. 'If it is not reported,' he insisted, 'it hasn't happened.' 'We have to make the media report us.'[105]

In consequence, even the most fair-minded reporters found it difficult to present a balance. The *Financial Times*, for example, was generally praised by anti-Marketeers, with the trade unionist Clive Jenkins hailing it as 'the best journal of record in this country'.[106] But even the *FT* struggled to balance the 'comprehensive pile of advance texts' coming from BIE against the smattering of poorly produced press releases that limped from the NRC offices. The problem, as the paper acknowledged, was partly one of resources. 'Britain in Europe's relations with the media are looked after by seven full-time and six part-time staff. "The National Referendum Campaign's Press machine", says a harassed man called John Allen, "is me".'[107]

Expertise was as important as manpower. As Uwe Kitzinger had written during a previous pro-Market campaign, a successful media operation had to understand 'cascades of opinion', learning 'which journalist is read by which other journalists'. Hierarchies could differ from one paper to another: in some cases, it was 'the lobby correspondent who really matters', while in others it was the editor or political correspondent who needed courting. It was no good organising media stunts unless one understood the technical requirements of camera crews and other 'nuts and bolts of the profession'.[108]

With this in mind, BIE recruited Christopher Serpell as its broadcasting officer. Serpell, who had recently retired as the BBC's Diplomatic Correspondent, understood the broadcasters in a way that most campaigners did not. The BBC's nine o'clock news programme, for example, could not cover distant rallies without hiring Outside Broadcasting units at prohibitive expense, so Serpell ensured that speeches were appropriately timed and in convenient locations.[109] He also understood the needs of different outlets; regional broadcasters, for example, often wanted 'basic literature' and advice on how to communicate the issue to the public. To this end, BIE hosted regular media breakfasts, the goal of which was not explicitly to influence coverage but to build connections and to match reporters with commentators in their field of interest. In this way, like the European Movement in 1971, they acted 'like a telephone exchange "plugging people into each other"'.[110]

Another priority was the ability to react swiftly to movements in the press: shooting down negative stories, spotting themes and encouraging or subverting particular media angles. Conservative Central Office produced a daily report on national radio, television and the London Broadcasting Company (LBC), as part of a comprehensive media monitoring system. A commercial organisation, Tellex Monitoring Service, was hired to cover local radio and TV, producing daily reports for BIE as well as for the regional organisers in Scotland and Wales. Local branches recruited volunteers to monitor coverage and gave them training in how to get their case across in phone-in programmes.[111]

This not only gave BIE the initiative in the media war; it also allowed it to pick up on the slightest flicker of perceived bias. It hounded the BBC in particular, filing complaints against *Woman's Hour*, for allowing a No campaigner to talk of 'going into Europe'; the *Radio Times*, for referring to 'administration from Brussels'; and *Midweek* for giving airtime to the former Fascist leader, Oswald Mosley, whose support for membership was entirely unwelcome. Some victories were registered: the anti-Marketeer George Gale was stood down by the Independent Broadcasting Association as an anchor for LBC's referendum phone-in, while the BBC apologised for a misleading account of the European 'beef mountain'. In general, however, the broadcasters provided a robust defence of their coverage, and BIE itself acknowledged after the vote that 'radio and TV kept a fair overall balance, with, if anything, a slight tilt in favour of Britain staying in Europe'.[112]

'POLICY NOT TO STRESS DIFFERENCES'

Throughout the referendum period, BIE had a rather paranoiac quality, scenting the possibility of defeat in the most mundane decisions. The first dilemma concerned when to go public. Convinced of the importance of the 'long' campaign, Wistrich had hoped to launch in January, which would have pre-empted the results of the renegotiation. That was acceptable to Liberal and Conservative activists, who had never put much faith in the exercise, but would have put Roy Jenkins in an impossible position. As a minister, he was bound to await the results of the renegotiation; yet as president of Britain in Europe, he would have been campaigning for a Yes vote regardless of the outcome. Whatever their private opinions, campaign directors acknowledged the strategic utility of the renegotiations, allowing Labour voters to opt for membership without endorsing the actions of the previous government. The decision to wait until March was almost certainly the right one, but it left the organisation rudderless for the early part of 1975.[113]

The choice of Con O'Neill as director also caused some unease. A career diplomat who had led the negotiating team that secured British entry, O'Neill had not been the first choice for the role. Names canvassed had included the historian Asa Briggs, the trade unionist Vic Feather, the farming leader Sir Henry Plumb and the former civil servant Baroness Sharp (described by Harold Macmillan as 'the ablest woman I have ever known').[114] O'Neill was respected for his integrity and, as a diplomat, had some experience of bringing together politicians from discordant backgrounds. Yet he had never run a campaigning organisation and had limited experience of domestic politics. Campaigners recalled him as a rather absent figure, and by the end of April it had become necessary to bring in a deputy, Peter Thring, to tighten up the management. Thring had worked at the chemical giant ICI, and was tasked with bringing order to the ever-expanding organisation. The publicity budget was widely viewed as having spun out of control, and while there was never any suggestion of corruption, there was unease at Geoffrey Tucker's double role as a member of the executive and as part of a company receiving large commissions for publicity. There was also some hostility to Wistrich, who narrowly survived an attempt to oust him from the leadership of the European Movement.[115]

There was grumbling, too, among campaign volunteers. Most had signed up because of an idealistic commitment to the cause of European unity, and some found the cautious tone of the campaign dispiriting. Three days before the vote, *The Times* reported 'simmering' anger over the role of professional consultants like Geoffrey Tucker and John Harris, whose 'slick advertising techniques' risked stifling 'honest enthusiasm and debate'. Key figures were suspected of 'jostling for position, in what might one day prove to have been the embryo of a new political party of the centre'. One staff member confided that 'political fighting and intrigue had made the campaign "absolute hell" to live through. "I would have left weeks or months ago if I did not actually care about staying in Europe".'[116]

Discontent was particularly severe in the youth wing. Student activists were unhappy with what they saw as the negative and uninspiring tone of the campaign. Some felt that the youth rally at Trafalgar Square had been 'overshadowed' by 'antique parliamentarians', and that the campaign had acquired an 'establishment-orientated grey image'.[117] Others grumbled that BIE wanted youthful vigour in principle, so long as it never attempted anything youthful or vigorous.

At a meeting with Jenkins in May, activists demanded representation on the steering group, more speakers, access to broadcasting time and three press conferences of their own. Jenkins was happy to concede more speakers, as well as one youth press conference, but the other demands were rejected. Even the press conference was scheduled on a bank holiday, when media interest would be at a low ebb. Pleas for a more idealistic campaign, stressing the appeal of a federal Europe, were batted away. As Lord Fraser delicately noted, Marketeers were divided on a federal Europe and 'it was policy not to stress differences'.[118]

IN VICTORY, DEFEAT

A degree of friction was probably inevitable in a campaign that had brought together so many unlikely allies. Most of those who worked in BIE remembered it with enthusiasm, and by comparison with the NRC, relations between the principals were positively kittenish. This was partly because they were winning, for even the most angst-ridden strategist could not ignore the evidence of the polls. But it was also because of the nature of the campaign and the peculiar character of its leaders.

For all its wealth and talent, BIE drew disproportionately on the dispossessed of British politics. Heath had been ejected from the Conservative leadership and would spend the next two decades smouldering ineffectually on the backbenches. Jenkins, once the heir apparent to the Labour leadership, had become so alienated from the party that he had considered declining office in 1974.[119] Thorpe had won 6 million votes for the Liberals in 1974, but a paltry fourteen seats in Parliament. Personal scandal was already engulfing his career: within a year he would be driven from the leadership, and in 1979 he would stand trial for conspiracy to murder.[120]

What Heath, Jenkins and Thorpe had in common – together with Shirley Williams, Bill Rodgers, Reg Prentice and David Steel – was not simply their commitment to Europe; it was also a disillusionment with the party system. Victory in 1975 suggested that a new politics of the centre was possible, a politics of great causes and missionary zeal, released from the pernicious extremes of Left and Right. Ironically, the effect was probably to deepen their alienation from conventional party politics. Rather than coming to terms with his defeat, Heath now dreamed of a 'national government', which he would lead from the centre. Rather than fighting to reclaim the Labour Party, Jenkins, David

Owen, Bill Rodgers and Shirley Williams would abandon it in 1981 for a new Social Democratic Party. Of the leading figures in BIE, only Whitelaw moved closer to the centre of power in the years that followed.

In this respect, the campaign for Britain in Europe misled its participants. The radical alliances on which it was built were possible precisely *because* the European question stood outside conventional politics. The referendum marked the suspension of party politics, not its supersession. For Heath, Jenkins and their allies, victory on 5 June contained the seeds of their own defeat; for by lifting the European question out of electoral controversy, it allowed the politics of Left and Right to reassert themselves with new vigour. As so often in the history of warfare, the soldiers of the European Movement returned victorious from the battlefield, only to find a world in which their hopes would be cruelly disappointed.

4 'BETTER OUT THAN IN': THE NATIONAL REFERENDUM CAMPAIGN

To be or not to be a Federal State – that is the question. To be or not to be an independent country.

Neil Marten, May 1975[1]

Don't be fooled by the press barons and the establishment politicians. They were wrong about Hitler and they're wrong again.

Get Britain Out[2]

Already one thing can be said with certainty about the first British referendum: if the antis win it, every known law of political campaigning will have to be re-written.

Hugo Young, 4 May 1975[3]

Like any really effective campaign, Britain in Europe was neurotic about its prospects. It fretted about turnout, bickered over tactics and lived in dread of some unexpected shock that might disrupt its carefully controlled campaign. When Leeds United lost to Bayern Munich in the European Cup final, just a week before the vote, the pandemonium in the stands was matched only by the horror at Europe House. Campaigners watched aghast as the French referee denied Leeds two first-half penalties, before chalking off an apparently legitimate goal. As the final whistle blew, a sepulchral voice was heard to intone, 'My God, there goes half a million votes.'[4]

Such jitters notwithstanding, Britain in Europe was a formidable campaign vehicle. It boasted a highly professional organisation, extensive media support and almost limitless financial resources.[5] It could draw on a galaxy of political talent, including the leaders of all three main parties and celebrities from across the worlds of sport and show business. Logistically, the biggest headache for the Yes campaign was how to find space on the platform for its array of high-profile supporters.

The National Referendum Campaign faced no such difficulty. Its big hitters were barely on speaking terms, while many of its activists were at least as hostile to one another as they were to Brussels. The campaign itself was run by enthusiastic amateurs, most of whom had no experience of a national election, and it was embarrassingly short of money. Such support as was forthcoming was often unwelcome: the NRC would cheerfully have dispensed with the backing of the IRA, the National Front and the Communist Party. Divided on tactics, chaotically managed and woefully under-resourced, the Antis played a poor hand badly. Having fought so hard for a referendum, they found the weapon splintering in their hands, in one of the most unequal battles in British electoral history.

'STRENGTH THROUGH DISUNITY'

In the early 1970s, the discerning anti-Marketeer could choose from a dizzying array of acronyms. Groups included the Anti-Common Market League (ACML), the Anti-Dear Food Campaign (ADFC), British Business for World Markets (BBFWM), the Common Market Safeguards Campaign (CMSC), Conservatives Against the Treaty of Rome (CANTOR), Get Britain Out (GBO) and the National Council of Anti-Common Market Organizations (NCACMO). These were supplemented by a range of semi-autonomous local bodies, such as the North Kent Anti-Common Market League, Yorkshire Get Britain Out and the West Country Anti-Common Market League, led by the splendidly monikered Sir Francis D'Aft. Most positioned themselves explicitly as 'outsiders', who took pride in their distance from a despised political 'establishment'.[6] The historian Paul Johnson invited readers to name a single major decision since the War on which 'the Establishment consensus' had been vindicated. The experts had been wrong on appeasement and they were wrong on the EEC.[7]

The two most prominent groups in the 1960s were the Anti-Common Market League and Keep Britain Out. ACML was founded in 1961 by a group of disaffected Tories led by John Paul, a Mobil executive and former Conservative candidate who had been a squadron leader in Bomber Command. Keep Britain Out, by contrast, was the creation of renegade Liberals, who saw the EEC as a protectionist entity that menaced global free trade. Its most prominent early figures were S.W. Alexander, a journalist who had worked for Lord Beaverbook during the First World War, and Oliver Smedley, a businessmen and pioneer of pirate radio who had won the Military Cross in the Second. The two organisations quickly shed their partisan character, but gravitated towards different styles of campaigning. While ACML was somewhat staid and respectable, KBO adopted a demotic campaigning style designed to gain attention in the press. It picketed the prime minister's official residence at Chequers, held informal referendums in ministers' constituencies and garnered considerable attention when an attractive young secretary claimed to have been strip-searched by the Rome police. One of its most successful stunts was a mock funeral procession held in Whitehall in 1967, complete with mourners in top hats and a coffin representing British democracy.[8]

From the late 1960s, the dominant figure in Keep Britain Out was a flamboyant solicitor called Christopher Frere-Smith. A self-proclaimed libertarian, Frere-Smith was a combative figure with a flair for publicity, who addressed journalists with a cigar clamped firmly between his teeth.[9] He was arrested three times while protesting on the Continent, enjoying his finest hour when he took 200 protestors on a ferry to Calais in 1972. When French police boarded the vessel, fighting broke out. Journalists watched in amazement as policemen traded blows with 'grey-haired middle-class English men and women', who retaliated with rolled umbrellas, Nazi salutes and choruses of 'Rule Britannia'. In what the press dubbed 'the Battle of Calais', a gendarme was knocked overboard and the Labour MP Anne Kerr had to be pulled away from the riot police, shouting 'let's have your gas'. On that day, Frere-Smith declared, the world had seen for itself 'what French democracy is all about'.[10]

In 1969, with an election approaching, KBO and ACML agreed to co-ordinate their activities under a new umbrella organisation: the Common Market Safeguards Campaign (CMSC), led by the Conservative Sir Robin Williams and the former Labour minister Douglas Jay. Yet CMSC was quickly engulfed in the factional disputes that characterised anti-Market politics. Meetings became increasingly chaotic, while the best that could be said of relations between the principals was that they no longer lived in an age when gentlemen shot

FIGURE 4.1   Protestors set sail for France, 17 April 1972. Police boarded the vessel, prompting the so-called 'Battle of Calais'.

Source: Keystone-France: www.gettyimages.co.uk/license/107421744

one another at dawn. By 1973 the body was so short of money that it was unable to pay its staff, and it was forced to deny reports that it had ceased to operate.[11] The final blow came when a row erupted over the funding of a bookshop during the party conference season. After a volcanic correspondence, Keep Britain Out – which renamed itself Get Britain Out after entry – broke off relations, vowing never to work with CMSC again.[12]

Relations were no less poisonous in the localities. In a contest worthy of Monty Python, the West Country Anti-Common Market League had to fight off a rival group called West Against the Common Market, in a struggle that absorbed considerable time and energy.[13] In 1973, a challenger to the CMSC emerged in the form of the National Council for Anti-Common Market Organisations (NCACMO), established by Air Vice-Marshal Don Bennett. A man of such unstinting patriotism that he even died on Battle of Britain Day, Bennett was an Australian-born pilot who had become the youngest air vice-marshal in the RAF during the Second World War. His military record guaranteed him a place at the top table, but NCACMO was widely believed to have been infiltrated by the National Front.[14]

It was no coincidence that anti-Market groups found it so hard to work together. Their leaders were rebels by temperament, who had rejected both the orthodoxies and the methods of the established parties. That rebel spirit was probably essential to the vitality of the anti-Market campaign, inoculating it against the pressure of the whips and insulating it from conventional wisdom; yet it made for difficult relations. Intellectually, too, the Antis encompassed an unusually wide spectrum. While BIE drew chiefly from the centre ground, the anti-Market campaign stretched from the Communist Party to the National Front. As one Anti put it, the Out campaign brought together people 'who would not want to be seen dead in the same coffin'.[15] Building a coherent movement out of such eclectic materials was a task of much greater difficulty than anything confronting BIE.

That task became more urgent as the referendum approached. The Referendum Act required that one organisation be designated as the lead campaign group, to liaise with government and the broadcasters and to disburse the grant of £125,000. By the end of 1974, CMSC had reluctantly acknowledged that it could not play this role without the co-operation of Get Britain Out, and that the chances of GBO reaffiliating were vanishingly small. GBO modestly suggested that *it* should be the lead organisation, arguing that its 12 regional organisers and 350 local branches dwarfed anything that could be mobilised by the Safeguards Campaign. Yet CMSC had the better contacts and the backing of the trade unions, which made clear that they would not work under Frere-Smith.[16]

After months of talks, which delayed the launch until January, it was agreed to form yet another new group: the National Referendum Campaign. The very title was a compromise, indicating both the limited role and ephemeral character of the organisation. CMSC and GBO would each contribute a vice-chairman (Douglas Jay and Frere-Smith), while the lead would be taken by the Conservative MP Neil Marten, a long-standing anti-Marketeer who had declined office under Heath. Marten had a distinguished war record, having served with the Special Operations Executive, but was neither a charismatic orator nor an experienced campaign manager. Barbara Castle thought him 'a pleasant chap', but doubted he would bring much 'drive'.[17] What he could bring was a reputation for decency and good humour, qualities that would be sorely tested over the coming months.[18]

FIGURE 4.2 'Out of Europe – and into the World'. Eric Deakins, Bob Harrison and Peter Shore at a press conference.

Source: J. Wilds, Hulton Archive: www.gettyimages.co.uk/license/3298518

'A DREADFUL RAG-BAG'

To call the NRC a skeleton operation would overstate its solidity and coherence. The campaign operated out of two rooms near the Strand and employed just three full-time staff. Marten himself took no payment, and the running of the office fell largely to his daughter, Mary-Louise. The entire wage bill came to the princely sum of £2,928, barely 2 per cent of the payroll for BIE. There was no full-time press officer until May, by which time a media strategy was more a regret than an aspiration.[19]

Money was in desperately short supply. The NRC raised around £11,734 over the course of the campaign, almost half of which came from the sale of literature. Together with the government grant of £125,000, that made a grand total of £136,734 – little more than half what BIE spent on printing alone. The trade union movement, which could have been a source of revenue, preferred to make donations in kind, either by seconding staff or providing office space. Only the Transport and General Workers' Union, which gave £3,250, made a significant cash donation.[20]

Get Britain Out had its own resources (which it refused to share with the NRC), but they were hopelessly inadequate for a national election. Over the four months of the campaign, GBO claimed to have spent more than £18,000, but the bulk of this had been exhausted a month before polling day. When a thief stole £310 from a cashbox in May, a spokesman for GBO showed reporters two fifty-pence pieces, which he claimed now constituted the organisation's entire cash reserves.[21]

In consequence, the campaign could barely afford basic office costs. Press releases were littered with errors; even Marten's name was routinely misspelled. Articles placed in trade journals were often embarrassingly mismatched; a farming journal, for example, noted sardonically that an article supplied by GBO made no reference to agriculture.[22] Speakers found themselves at the wrong meetings, while press releases were ignored because there were not enough copies. There was panic in February at reports that each side might be offered a free mailshot by the government. Jay was aghast: even if the postage was free, '[we] cannot afford to purchase the envelopes'.[23]

Frere-Smith tried to make a virtue out of scarcity, boasting to reporters that while the Yes campaign had the money, 'we have got the people'. He hounded BIE for its lavish expenditure, made lurid allegations about its donors and implied that it was taking funding from foreign companies anxious to exploit the British market.[24] Yet for all the talk of a people's army, mobilising against 'the well-heeled city-slickers' and 'expense-account businessmen', GBO had only the haziest notion of how many members it had or what they were getting up to.[25] 'We are a very devolved organization,' one official confessed. 'The groups spring up spontaneously.'[26]

The problem was not just money. While BIE could call on a range of senior party officials, who had run elections and managed complex organisations, the NRC lacked that anchoring in electoral politics. Its activists were mostly outsiders and there was little help from within Parliament. Labour Antis stood aloof, while only five of the forty-one Conservative MPs who had voted against membership in 1971 were active within the NRC. That left Enoch Powell as the most senior politician associated with the organisation, a man so alien to party discipline that he was now sitting with the Ulster Unionists. Frere-Smith, a free-trade Liberal, found the absence of Conservative and Liberal supporters 'patently distressing', and regretted the campaign's reliance on the Left. As he told *The Times*, 'greater terror is struck into Conservative hearts by trade unions and the Left than by anything else', and he rightly foresaw the use that would be made of this by Britain in Europe.[27]

A further dilemma for the Out campaign was that its biggest hitters all stirred strong negative emotions. Polling by Louis Harris found negative ratings of –15 for Tony Benn, –9 for Michael Foot, –7 for Clive Jenkins and –5 for Jack Jones. Ian Paisley nearly broke the scale, with a rating of –59, though he rarely featured outside Northern Ireland. Powell bucked the trend to some extent, returning a positive rating of +2, but he aroused strong emotions both for and against. Ironically, the very people who could most eloquently express the case for leaving were more likely to repel swing voters than to win them to the anti-Market cause.[28]

Unlike Britain in Europe, the NRC never mustered the kind of celebrity support that might have balanced its more contentious figures. Harry H. Corbett and Kenneth Tynan (famous, respectively, as Harold Steptoe and as the first man to say 'fuck' on British television) were the most prominent Antis from the world of showbusiness, though there was a flurry of excitement when the *Daily Mirror* published an interview with Paul McCartney. ('The Common Market', he was quoted as suggesting, was 'like the Beatles'. 'Now that the partnership has been dissolved, I'm much better off.')[29] Marten dreamed of recruiting Rod Stewart, but the organisation as a whole was wary of the celebrity politics of BIE. When a television company requested the names of celebrities for a feature programme, the NRC dismissed the idea out of hand.[30]

To make matters worse, the NRC was bedevilled by the activities of extremist groups over which it had little control. Marten had been determined from the outset that racist and revolutionary groups would be barred from membership. The National Front was refused affiliation, and responded by trashing the NRC's first major rally (though this public evidence of a rupture probably did more good than harm).[31] The British League of Rights, which was viewed by other groups as, at best, a 'cranky right-wing organization', and at worst, as 'anti-Semitic and white supremacist', was allowed only to send an observer.[32] NCACMO was admitted reluctantly, on Bennett's personal assurance that it had no connection with the National Front.[33] Yet the taint of extremism proved difficult to erase, and Marten spent much of his time putting out fires that were not of his making.

'A BOOZE-UP IN A BREWERY'

Despite all this, the image of the No campaign as a group of plucky underdogs, impossibly outgunned by the forces of the 'establishment', did not quite ring true. The anti-Marketeers had some significant assets of their own, which they failed to deploy to the full. In Tony Benn, Michael Foot, Neil Kinnock and Enoch Powell, they boasted some of the most formidable orators in British politics. They were backed by most of the major trade unions and two of the best-known union leaders in the country: Jack Jones of the Transport and General and Clive Jenkins of ASTMS. Senior economists like Nicholas Kaldor and Robert Neild supported the campaign, as did the author of the 'Lombard' column in the *Financial Times*, C. Gordon Tether. A majority of Labour MPs, seven Cabinet ministers and numerous constituency parties backed withdrawal, as did well-organised factions within the party such as the Tribune Group. In Scotland and Wales, the No campaign could call on Plaid Cymru and the Scottish National Party, both of whom had made substantial gains in recent years. In Northern Ireland, parties on both sides of the sectarian divide campaigned for withdrawal, as did para-military groups from the loyalist and republican communities. All this could be annexed to an array of highly motivated activist groups, many of whom had been organising for over a decade.

In this respect, the failure of the No campaign lay not in its stars but in itself. The splits which had characterised previous anti-Market campaigns cracked open again almost immediately. Frere-Smith was determined that GBO would take the lead in the campaign, and his organisation demanded that the NRC hand over the entirety of the government grant except what was necessary for basic office costs.[34] When the NRC decided instead to keep the money, producing its own campaign materials, GBO effectively walked out. Unlike the European Movement, which absorbed itself into BIE for the duration of the campaign, GBO kept its own funds and ran a largely autonomous campaign. Frere-Smith's attendance at NRC meetings became increasingly erratic and he never accepted Marten's leadership. Other groups were soon complaining that GBO was trespassing on their territory, and in April Marten was forced to publish a fruitless appeal for unity.[35]

It did not help that the NRC leaked like a rusty bathtub. Barbara Castle was convinced that 'we have a traitor in our midst', and some Labour operatives were almost certainly being squeezed by the leadership.[36] BIE usually knew what the NRC was doing before Marten did, enabling it to plan accordingly. Volunteers were infiltrated into local branches and NRC meetings, sometimes to rather comic effect. Irena Gutrowska, for example, had a history of infiltrating anti-Market groups; late in 1974 she joined the Safeguards campaign under the cunning pseudonym of Elena Pietrowska, reporting back on its meetings and literature.[37]

This was exacerbated by tension between senior campaigners. Tony Benn would not share a platform with anyone outside the Labour Party and had a particular abhorrence for Enoch Powell. Their enmity stretched back to 1968, when Powell delivered his famous 'Rivers of Blood' speech on the dangers of immigration. Benn had described Powell's remarks as 'evil, filthy and obscene', comparing 'the flag of racialism which has been hoisted in Wolverhampton' to 'the one that fluttered 25 years ago over Dachau and Belsen'. Powell had retaliated with a speech on 'the enemy within', identifying Benn with 'those who hate Britain and wish to destroy it'.[38]

In one of the more farcical moments of the campaign, the two were scheduled to appear together at a debate hosted by *Granada*. The studio was modelled on a committee room of the House of Commons, but Benn demanded to sit with his Labour colleagues on the pro-Market side, rather than share a bench with Powell and the Tory anti-Marketeers. Carpenters were brought in to find an arrangement of seats that Benn would accept, offering no fewer than seven variant designs; in the end, however, he pulled out just hours before the broadcast. Not until the final press conference of the campaign would Benn and Powell appear in public together.[39]

All this was meat and drink to the press, which mocked the Antis for their 'tantrums' and 'bad-tempered quarrelling'. Frere-Smith, joked the *Sun*, was 'unfit to organize a booze-up in a brewery'.[40] Part of the problem for the NRC was that it had no means of disciplining its constituent parts. Unlike Britain in Europe, it could not hold out the prospect of grants or funding as a means of exerting financial control. Marten could not, like Wistrich, threaten to remove difficult characters from their post, and he lacked the personal standing to assert his authority over GBO.

LABOUR AGAINST THE MARKET

Things might have been different had the Labour Party campaigned against membership. This was by no means implausible, even with a Labour prime minister on the other side. While they could not bind the hands of ministers, Labour's supreme policy-making bodies were the annual conference and the NEC, both of which had a strongly anti-Market inflection. Benn was determined to mobilise the party machine against the leadership, as he had done over the decision to hold a referendum. 'The first real target', he wrote privately, was to get more than 50 per cent of MPs on board. Then the NEC could pass a resolution against membership, which would be confirmed by a special party conference. Once opposition had become official policy, constituency parties and unions would commit themselves to the Out campaign. Then Benn could 'go back to the Cabinet and say, "Look, Cabinet is not representative of the Labour movement, change your recommendation"'.[41]

When the Cabinet met on 18 March, seven ministers voted against the renegotiated terms: Tony Benn, Barbara Castle, Michael Foot, Willie Ross, Peter Shore, John Silkin and Eric Varley. Judith Hart, the minister for overseas development, also registered her opposition, though she was not permitted to attend Cabinet.[42] As soon as collective responsibility lapsed, the so-called 'Dissenting Ministers' held a press conference in the Grand Committee Room of the House, where they were joined by more than eighty Labour MPs. A total of 129 MPs signed an Early Day Motion demanding withdrawal, which was followed by a motion to the NEC demanding that Labour campaign for a No vote.[43]

Had the motion succeeded, it would have transformed the referendum, placing at the disposal of the Out campaign all the resources of the Labour Party. Wilson was apoplectic; Castle wrote that he was 'angrier than I have ever heard him in my whole life ... The venom poured out of him.'[44] In a furious memorandum, he warned ministers that the agreement to differ was 'not a licence ... to invoke a coordinated and deliberate programme ... against the Government', and warned that he was 'ready to do whatever I think is necessary' to reassert his authority.[45] For only the second time in his premiership, Wilson put his leadership of the party on the line. By threatening resignation, he succeeded first in holding over the motion and then in substituting a milder version, which reaffirmed opposition to membership but explicitly recognised a 'right to dissent'.[46]

This took much of the steam out of the special conference in April. Speakers lined up to denounce the Common Market as 'a gigantic and overwhelmingly capitalist-oriented bureaucracy' and 'a dangerous attack on our fundamental belief in socialism'. Yet the most important declaration was the banner that hung behind each speaker: 'Conference will advise. The people will decide'.[47] As expected, the conference voted by more than two-to-one for withdrawal, but the motion did not require the party to take any further action. Benn therefore called a special meeting of the NEC, with the aim of committing the party to campaign for withdrawal.[48]

Had the NEC instructed the Labour Party to campaign against a Labour government, the very survival of the Wilson administration would have been in doubt. Following the contretemps in March, Wilson had circulated written instructions to ministers that expressly disbarred them from using the NEC to challenge government policy.[49] Defeat would have left his authority in ruins, and it was partly this that forced the Antis to back down. Even Antis like Foot and Shore were reluctant to bring down the government over the issue; as Foot had told an earlier meeting, 'If we knock Harold through the ropes, we also knock the referendum and the Labour Government.'[50] Just as importantly, two general elections the previous year had left the party's finances in dire straits. The general secretary, Ron Hayward – himself an anti-Marketeer – told the NEC that 'the party is broke', and the unions made clear that they would not fund a campaign that would set Labour against itself.[51] In a decisive victory for Wilson, it was agreed simply to circulate the conclusions of the special conference and to make publicity material available 'at cost price'. The publicity department would circulate speeches by both sides and no money would be made available from the centre.[52]

The failure to win the Labour Party for the 'Out' campaign was a severe blow. It deprived the anti-Marketeers not just of the money and manpower of a major party, but of the experience and campaigning knowledge that the Conservative and Liberal parties were supplying to BIE. Access to canvassing returns would also have been invaluable. Above all, it would have established Labour supporters of membership as rebels against party policy. Instead, it was the anti-Marketeers who became the 'Dissenting Ministers', despite expressing the majority view of the party.

At this point, it would probably have been wise for the Labour ministers to align themselves more firmly with the NRC. This was Barbara Castle's favoured policy; she was 'appalled by the prospect of Neil Marten, George Gale *et al.* cornering all the anti-Market money and the TV appearances', and 'pleaded' with the other Dissenting

Ministers to get involved.[53] But resistance to 'coalition' ran deep in the bloodstream of the Left, and the NRC itself was worried that such an infusion of Labour grandees might unbalance the organisation and undermine its 'populist element'.[54] Tony Benn, in particular, was hostile to any involvement. As the Brahmin of the Labour Left, Benn regarded contact with Tories almost as a form of ritual pollution. The NRC, he wrote privately, was 'an awful rag-bag'. 'The only thing I really want anything to do with is the Labour Party.'[55]

In consequence, the campaign's most experienced and charismatic figures spent the referendum talking to adoring crowds of their own supporters, at rallies organised by *Tribune* and the Labour Safeguards Committee. They enjoyed themselves tremendously. 'It's just like the old times', Castle told a *Tribune* rally in Manchester. 'The old fighting spirit of the Labour movement is back.'[56] Benn thought the Manchester rally 'one of the best meetings I have ever attended'. Mocking the failure of the media to cover their rallies, the confidence of the Left soared even as the polls marched ominously in the opposite direction. Benn wrote in his diary that the 'great tide of opinion' against membership 'cannot be held back now, of that I am sure'. Speaking to journalists just days before the vote, he was in buoyant mood; 'all the evidence', he announced, 'pointed to a massive "No" vote'.[57] It was not the last time that Benn would be cruelly disappointed by the electorate.

'BRITAIN'S INDEPENDENCE DAY'

In the absence of the Labour ministers, the burden of campaigning fell chiefly on the NRC and groups like Get Britain Out. What they lacked in money they made up for in enthusiasm, deploying an activist base that was accustomed to operating on a shoestring. Get Britain Out, in particular, specialised in stunts that cost little to stage but could be guaranteed to attract media attention, carried out by 'idealistic and very charming youngsters with no money and long hair'.[58] It held demonstrations outside storage units in Liverpool and Ealing, bringing pensioners to protest against the 'food mountains' allegedly concealed inside. There were classic car rallies to mark 'Empire Day', and in Coventry a modern-day Lady Godiva was persuaded to ride through the city dressed only in a body-stocking.[59] In Yorkshire, Arthur Scargill led miners on a door-to-door canvass, dressed in pit helmets and mining gear.[60] By the end of the campaign, the NRC claimed to have distributed 9 million leaflets, 100,000 posters and half a million badges: an impressive tally for a body that had been in existence for only a matter of months.[61]

The big themes of the No campaign – self-government, cheap food, 'a thousand years of history and imperishable freedoms' – lent themselves naturally to a populist campaigning style. As the *Sun* grumbled, the Antis 'have all the best tunes, if not the singers'.[62] Revelling in their outsider status, Antis sought to mobilise the British affection for the underdog against the 'city slickers' and 'tax-dodgers' who profited from membership: 'Don't listen to THEM. THEY have mismanaged our affairs.'[63] GBO claimed that it was only defensible to vote Yes 'if you are a politician seeking to strut on a bigger stage'; 'if you are big City operator'; 'if you are a big land-owner'; or 'if you are ashamed of being British'.[64] Broadcasts attacked the 'politicians and the press Lords' of BIE: the 'people who are telling you to vote Yes … are the people who have led the country into its present mess'.[65]

Antis presented the referendum as a national liberation struggle, in which the enemy was not just the Common Market but the corrupt assembly of plutocrats, politicians and 'faceless men' who had carried Britain in.[66] The *Morning Star* called it a 'battle for the liberation of Britain', while John Mills, who organised the NRC's meetings and publicity, urged campaigners to make 5 June 'Britain's Independence Day'.[67] 'The truth', claimed the Scottish politician Norman Buchan, 'is that the British establishment have been wrong on nearly all the great issues of the century, and the British people, whom they despise so much, have been usually right.'[68] Marten accused his opponents of 'the defeatism of exhausted men'.[69] 'Ever since Britain started flirting with the Common Market in 1961', he noted, 'things have gone consistently wrong for us. And it is just the people who were responsible for that state of affairs who are now urging you to vote Yes.'[70]

At the core of the No campaign was a warning about the survival of the UK. The 'true aim of the pro-Marketeers', Marten insisted, was 'the end of Britain as an independent country'. The federalists were determined, 'by stealth and by soothing words', to create a 'monster state'. 'Abandonment of democratic self-government has a long tradition on the continent – they have been ruled by dictators, defeated in war and occupied.' Yet Britain, surely, would not go gentle into that good night. This became the bedrock of Marten's speeches, stirring a positively Shakespearian strain of oratory. 'To be or not to be a Federal State – that is the question. To be or not to be an independent country.'[71]

Appeals to 'our right to rule ourselves' were at the heart of the anti-Market campaign, annexed to a distinctly romantic vision of constitutional history.[72] The Transport and General Workers' Union accused Marketeers of plotting 'the end of Britain', invoking a history of 'freedom-loving' Britons stretching back through the Magna Carta, the execution of Charles I and the achievement of women's suffrage. A cartoon in *Tribune* showed the country at a fork in the road; one path, pointing left, went to 'Runnymede (Magna Carta)', the other, pointing right, to 'Brussels (Treaty of Rome)'.[73] With the bicentenary of US Independence approaching, protestors invoked the mantra of 'No Taxation without Representation', while Benn drew comparisons with the Boston Tea Party.[74]

This linked the issue of sovereignty to that of food prices. GBO pushed especially hard on VAT, 'a Common Market tax' that was 'Vicious, Atrocious and Tiresome'.[75] Voters were warned that 'The Common Market authorities deliberately keep food prices high' and that increased prices were likely after the referendum.[76] Another recurring theme was unemployment. The Common Market was described as 'the graveyard of jobs', creating a trade deficit that was haemorrhaging capital to the Continent. 'Each pound from Britain invested overseas', GBO claimed, 'means a pound less invested in Britain and thus fewer jobs'.[77] Far from securing Britain's future, the EEC was 'a predator, taking jobs and savings from Britain and pumping them into the more prosperous continental centres'.[78]

The NRC's campaign broadcasts were designed to entrench its anti-establishment message. With its limited funds, the organisation could not hope to compete with the slick production values of BIE's broadcasts. Instead, it adopted a consciously low-budget, conversational style, which largely excluded politicians until the final stages of the campaign. Using figures such as Benn, Castle or Jack Jones, it feared, 'might savour of the old-fashioned "political programmes"', so the lead roles were taken instead by journalists like Patrick Cosgrave and Paul Johnson.[79]

Like their opponents, Antis had a taste for the lurid. Frere-Smith predicted the reintroduction of conscription, warning that young Britons would be forced to serve in a European army.[80] The *Morning*

Star went one better, suggesting that the Community might follow the example of General Pinochet by deploying the military against a left-wing British government. 'Common Market bureaucrats', it warned, 'see mass democratic action as a threat to their brand of "law and order".'[81] Only outside could British democracy be secure.

'OUT OF EUROPE – AND INTO THE WORLD'

As GBO warned campaigners in May, the challenge for the Antis was not simply to make the case for exit. Just as importantly, they had to 'demolish the aura of fear and panic which the pro-Marketeers are whipping up'.[82] If they were to win the referendum, they needed to ease voters' concerns about life outside, as well as dismantling claims that they were insular, bigoted and politically extreme.

Antis passionately denied that they were 'little Englanders', frightened of the world beyond their shores. As minister for overseas development and a former minister at the Commonwealth Office, Judith Hart had held international portfolios for much of her career. She had been vigorously engaged in debates about Rhodesia and international aid, and had written a well-regarded book in 1973 urging the cancellation of Third World debt.[83] Responding to attacks by Heath, she insisted that Antis were not just proud Europeans but 'Commonwealth people', 'United Nations people' and 'people whose vision of the world extends far beyond the tight and closed Community of the Nine'.[84] The slogan 'Out of Europe and into the World' was blazoned across press conferences, reinforcing the message that it was the EEC – a group of white, post-colonial states, huddled behind a common tariff barrier – that was insular and parochial. There was anger at talk of joining or leaving 'Europe', as if the Community was coterminous with the Continent. Filleting the government's official campaign pamphlet, *Britain's New Deal in Europe*, the *Morning Star* complained that 'Even the title contains a lie.' The EEC was not 'Europe', and government should not be complicit in a false elision of the two.[85] Marten, likewise, claimed to be 'a convinced "European" ... But my Europeanism is not limited to the Common Market.'[86]

Antis lavished special attention on Norway, which showed not only that 'the establishment' could be beaten, but that a European nation could flourish outside the Community. Marten had been parachuted into Norway during the War, serving behind enemy lines with the Resistance, and he had acted since 1960 as chairman of the Anglo-Norwegian Parliamentary Group. Norwegian delegates were invited to speak at rallies: Einar Førde, the Labour rebel who had masterminded the 'Stem Nei' campaign, spoke at *Tribune* rallies, while Scottish Antis recruited the No campaigner Bjørn Unneberg. The relevance of the Norwegian model was contested by pro-Marketeers, who pointed to its colossal reserves of oil; but references to the Norwegian case became a staple of Anti rhetoric.[87] As the *Scotsman* wryly observed, Norway became as 'tediously virtuous' as 'somebody else's little angel, paraded by parents to impress their own brats'.[88]

A more difficult challenge concerned the alternatives to membership. Some were reluctant to engage with this theme, arguing that the costs of staying in were so great that it was for the pro-Marketeers to make the case for membership. Others were wary of giving the Yes campaign a target on which to focus. As one strategist commented, 'The alternative to staying in is coming out'; it was for the people to decide, once self-government had been restored, what future they desired.[89] Marten's own emphasis on sovereignty was intended, in part, to make the same point: the question was not how *he* wished to manage the economy, but the right of voters to make that decision for themselves. NRC campaign broadcasts made a virtue out of diversity, bringing together men with as different economic visions as Michael Foot and Enoch Powell. As Marten told viewers, 'we all disagree, often violently, on policies', but they shared a belief in the right of the electorate to choose between them.[90]

Nonetheless, polls suggested that fear of the alternative loomed large in voters' minds. It was difficult for the Antis to give a coherent response, because of the sheer breadth of their support base. The Dissenting Ministers issued a paper on 'The Strategy of Withdrawal', which set out a procedure for disengagement by 1 January 1976. It promised to match EEC funding on agriculture, regional development and Commonwealth aid, but said little on trade relations beyond the need for discussions with EFTA and the Commonwealth. *Tribune* was more outspoken, envisaging a siege economy on socialist lines. The paper printed a handy checklist of policies to be introduced, which included petrol rationing, a freeze on incomes over £100 a week, import controls, restrictions on capital exports, lower foreign travel allowances and a government stake in all large foreign companies.[91]

Such a list could hardly appeal to Tory anti-Marketeers, who tended to favour a free trade agreement with the Community.[92] That

FIGURE 4.3   The *Sun* cartoonist Franklin declines to abandon ship with Tony Benn, Barbara Castle, Michael Foot, Enoch Powell and Peter Shore. 2 June 1975. The Sun/News Syndication.

would reduce the risks of withdrawal, but would do nothing to redress the balance of payments problem or the flight of capital to continental markets.[93] Confronted with such different visions of the future, the NRC tended to hedge on the issue, adopting policy positions so thick with caveats as to be meaningless. The NRC, it announced, would seek a free trade deal 'on terms which are satisfactory to the UK, but not otherwise'. It did 'not believe that tariff protection should be ruled out of consideration', but was 'prepared to give free trade a run', so long as it was 'free trade on *our* terms' (an inherently meaningless formula).[94] Commentators were not impressed. The *Manchester Evening News* concluded that the Antis had become desperate, 'not only because they sensed defeat but because they could not envisage what they would do with victory'.[95]

THE BENN EFFECT

While the NRC struggled to reach consensus, the 'Out' campaign's most charismatic performer was striking out on his own. Tony Benn dominated the campaign to an extent that not even Heath could match.

It was Benn, more than anyone, who had forced the referendum onto a reluctant government, and he quickly established himself as 'the storm centre of the referendum debate'. Castle, an often critical observer, thought him 'on the top of his oratorical form', drawing a reaction at rallies that 'fell only just short of idolatry'.[96] It was an open secret that Wilson, who mocked Benn as an 'Old Testament prophet without a beard', intended either to sack or demote him after the campaign, a fact which seemed to liberate him.[97] As the *Guardian* commented, Benn 'dominated the campaign single-handed, making the headlines day after day, the focus of attention even when ... silent himself'.[98]

Benn's oratory combined dizzying invocations of democracy and freedom with spine-chilling warnings about unemployment. No one in British politics conjured more vividly the long history of democratic struggle or the might and majesty of an emancipated people; listening to him in Cabinet, Barbara Castle confessed to sitting 'spellbound while the words flow out of him'.[99] Yet he also understood, as keenly as anyone in BIE, the power of fear when applied to jobs and wages. In this respect, Benn was one of the few politicians of the twentieth century who could climb cheerfully into the gutter while talking lyrically about the stars. His speeches focused remorselessly on Britain's burgeoning trade deficit with the Community, warning that every pound exported was a blow to investment at home. Continued membership, he warned, would 'put Britain on the dole', as unrestrained competition ripped through the steel, textile, engineering and motor industries. As national income contracted, 'the blight will spread through shops and offices and even into the public services'. With tax revenues collapsing, government would have no choice but 'to throw teachers, office workers, secretaries, local government officials and other public servants out of work'.[100]

Benn's most dramatic intervention came in May, when he announced that half a million jobs had been lost because of membership. That included 8,000 in the chemical industry, 43,000 in steel, 13,000 in textiles, 41,000 in the car industry and 28,000 in machinery. If Britain did not abandon its reckless experiment with the Common Market, he warned, it would face 'industrial disaster' and 'unemployment on the scale of the 1930s'.[101]

That statement – made with all the authority of the secretary of state for industry – caused a sensation. The shock value of the half a million figure provided a battering ram, behind which surged a wider argument about the nature of Britain's economic problems. What Britain was experiencing, Benn claimed, was not simply an economic crisis; more specifically, it was a crisis of capitalism, brought on by the contradictions of the market system. The Common Market was a doomed attempt to prop up that system by amalgamating the markets of western Europe, allowing British capital to find a safer haven abroad. To protect the interests of 'the rich and powerful', membership had delivered working people 'into a colonial relationship with the Common Market'. That was precisely why 'Big business, the multinational companies and the press Lords want us in.' For Benn, the referendum was a struggle 'between the "haves" and the "have nots"', in which 'the rich and powerful were in favour of staying in and the working people were against'.[102]

The NRC often complained that it was ignored by the press, but Benn's jobs claims swept the front pages. Yet the effect was not entirely helpful. Unemployment in May 1975 was approximately 830,000; deducting half a million from that total would have left Britain with its lowest unemployment rate since the 1940s. It was hard to believe that the underlying health of the economy was quite so robust, at a time of soaring inflation, turbulence in the Middle East and global recession. The *Sun* accused him of 'a Niagara of a nonsense', while industry bodies vigorously contested Benn's figures. The Chemical Industries Association, for example, claimed that, far from *shedding* 8,000 jobs, as Benn had asserted, 8,600 *new* jobs had been created as a result of membership.[103]

Benn found himself, as he had probably intended, at the centre of a storm of controversy. Conservative officials compared him to Josef Goebbels – the progenitor of the 'Big Lie' – while Roy Jenkins (still, remarkably, Benn's Cabinet colleague) told journalists acidly that he found it 'increasingly difficult to take Mr Benn seriously as an economic Minister'.[104] Even some on Benn's own side were embarrassed by his claims. Though critical of 'the almost hysterical anti-Wedgie campaign that is building up', Castle raged in her diary at Benn's exaggerations. After a *Tribune* rally in April, she noted that he had given 'a typically brilliant speech which contained a number of what I can only call distortions about the Community'; a few weeks later, after a speech in Sheffield, she complained that 'it is one thing to enthuse people, another to do it on a criminally over-simplified version of the facts'. She told her advisor, the future foreign secretary Jack Straw, that she was 'sick of Wedgie monopolizing everything'. 'He is losing us the referendum,' Straw replied gloomily.[105]

That view was shared by the Yes campaign, which deployed a conscious strategy 'to keep Benn talking'; for the more that he established himself as the voice of the No campaign, the harder it became for Conservative and even moderate Labour voters to back withdrawal.[106] When a *Guardian* journalist told 'Out' campaigners that he was off to hear Benn speak, there was a tone of weary resignation. 'Why does it

FIGURE 4.4   Tony Benn makes a pitch for the No vote at a rally in Cardiff.
Source: Media Wales.

always have to be Benn?', one asked gloomily. As the *Glasgow Herald* commented after the polls had closed, 'How many millions voted Yes in order to confound Mr Benn may never be known, but he will go down as the bogeyman of Britain's first national plebiscite.'[107]

CONCLUSION

The referendum campaign was a chastening experience for the anti-Marketeers. For almost a decade, they had worked for a referendum in the belief that it would prove the rock on which the European project would at last be shipwrecked. Instead, it endorsed membership by a margin that not even the Yes campaign had dared to think possible. The conviction of Benn, Frere-Smith and Powell that they represented 'the people' against 'the establishment' was rudely disabused. Benn was demoted within hours of the result being announced, to the jubilation of reporters gathered outside his house.

Looking back on the campaign, Antis tended to blame the superior resources available to their opponents. Douglas Jay called the referendum 'a travesty of free democratic choice', while the trade unionist Clive Jenkins described it as 'the worst election since Charles Dickens wrote about Eatenswill'. The *Morning Star* complained that voters had been 'lied to, swindled and blackmailed' by the combined forces of big business, the media and rich financiers.[108] Complaints about money, the media and the influence of the government and big business were ubiquitous.

There was no denying the superior firepower of the Yes campaign, but the anti-Marketeers were the authors of their own misfortune. Through a toxic combination of personality clashes, turf wars and the sectarian fastidiousness of the Left, they had failed to build anything resembling a coherent campaign. Their big guns had spent too much time feuding among themselves and preaching to the converted; where they clashed, they had barely attempted to sink their differences. The trade unions made grand declamations of principle on the Common Market, but proved reluctant to put their money where their mouths were. That left the campaign in the hands of enthusiastic amateurs, with little experience of electioneering and no conception of how to handle the media. In this context, the wonder was not that the Antis lost the referendum, or even that they were defeated by such a margin; it was that they managed to sustain a competitive campaign at all.

PART TWO

THEMES AND ISSUES

5 'THE BOARDROOM MUST LEAD!': EMPLOYERS, UNIONS AND THE ECONOMY

The economic problems facing Great Britain are so numerous and so urgent that Gladstone, Keynes, Adam Smith and St Francis rolled into one would find it hard to affect them'

The Director, April 1975[1]

Going to work I ran into Len Neal. I asked him how he was, to which he replied, 'Like everyone else, waiting for the collapse'.

Ronald McIntosh, 5 August 1975[2]

This is a battle for economic survival.

Shirley Williams, 29 May 1975[3]

Speaking at a rally at Musselburgh in May, the Labour MP for West Stirlingshire, Denis Canavan, launched a furious attack on the role of business organisations in the referendum. 'Workers', he complained, were being 'subjected to extreme pressure ... to vote Yes.' The 'intimidation tactics', he claimed, 'had already started': 'propaganda leaflets' were raining down upon the workforce, threatening job losses if they refused to toe the line. Such 'blackmail', he thundered, was reminiscent of Victorian times, 'when employers instructed their workers how to vote at elections'.[4]

Canavan was right about the scale of activism. Employers mobilised for the referendum on an unprecedented scale, canvassing not just their workforce but their shareholders, customers, employees' families and those on company pensions. Of Britain's top 200 companies, it was estimated that at least 150 played an active role in the campaign.[5] The CBI alone spent £50,000 on campaign literature, media training and a twenty-four-hour operations room. Giants like Barclays, ICI, Imperial Tobacco, Rolls-Royce, W.H. Smith and Rio Tinto–Zinc were joined on the front line by paint-makers, leather workers, shoemakers and the knitting industry, as well as by consumer organisations, trade associations and agricultural bodies. This was a *levée en masse* by Britain's commercial sector, of a kind never before seen at a national election.

Activism could take many forms. Supermarket chains, like Sainsbury's and Marks & Spencer, published articles in their customer magazines, showing how much of their meat, fruit, cheese and wine was sourced from the Continent. Companies set up workplace displays, distributed literature to employees and inserted material in the pay packet. The chairman of Guest, Nettlefold and Keen (GKN), Britain's largest engineering group, wrote 'a personal memorandum' to all employees and their families, warning that withdrawal 'would torpedo the company'. 'Membership', he wrote, 'is not a political issue, and what I have said about the danger of coming out is not a threat. It is hard commercial reality.'[6]

Business also wrote the cheques for the wider pro-Market campaign. Britain in Europe raised about £2 million from business – more than the total spent by the national parties in the two 1974 elections. British Petroleum gave £25,000; the shipping company P&O £20,000; and Allied Breweries £15,000. Other large donors included Chrysler, Debenhams, EMI, Shell, W.H. Smith and United Biscuits. The biggest gifts came from the City: £26,000 from the Stock Exchange, more than £100,000 from insurance companies and a colossal £200,000 from the clearing banks. Despite the efforts of an anti-Market organisation, 'British Business for World Markets', the NRC raised less than £9,000 *in total* during the campaign, with only a handful of donations above £100.[7]

For business to intervene so directly in a national election was unusual, and some employers were queasy about canvassing their workers. At a time of economic crisis, however, many felt a positive obligation to tell their workers what was at stake. The Institute of Directors told members that they had 'a clear duty' to 'be bold in expressing their views': 'The Boardroom must lead.' Addressing the Institute of Grocery Distribution in April, the supermarket tycoon John Sainsbury warned that the referendum would 'affect the whole future of our nation in a way that no General Election can ever do'. Retailers must put aside 'the natural instinct of the shopkeeper to shy away from political issues', for 'it is our livelihood which is involved'.[8]

In a decade marked by dire industrial relations, employers found themselves facing off once again against the trade union movement. Clive Jenkins, general secretary of ASTMS, described the referendum as 'a World War Three situation', and promised to fight membership with every weapon at his disposal. The TUC formally urged a No vote, while the Transport and General Workers' Union (TGWU) provided the backbone of the campaign to 'Get Britain Out'. Unusually, however, it was the employers who emerged triumphant – presaging, perhaps, the victories of the 1980s. This chapter explores why business fought so hard, the manner in which they sought to influence the vote, and why the response from organised labour proved so ineffective.

'CRISIS '75'

The referendum came at a grim moment for the economy. A stock market crash, the oil shock and surging inflation had fostered an apocalyptic mood in industry that was exploited by both sides in the campaign. Shirley Williams, the secretary of state for prices and consumer protection, warned that Britain was engaged in 'a battle for economic survival', while the Institute of Directors thought the economic situation 'uniquely grave in character'.[9] When Britain's biggest car manufacturer had to be rescued by the government, one commentator likened it to the war in Vietnam. The 'Leyland collapse', he wrote, 'hangs ominously over our industrial future like the fall of Saigon over the future of the free world.'[10]

That context, with politicians warning of a return to rationing, gave business both a licence and an imperative to intervene.[11] The National Association of Scottish Woollen Manufacturers, for example, displayed giant posters in the workplace, warning employees that 'your future is imperilled if Britain leaves the EEC'. A spokesman told journalists 'almost apologetically' that 'we don't normally dabble in politics'. 'We are only doing this because it's our bread and butter.'[12]

The weavers were not the only businesses to 'dabble in politics'. Companies like British Steel and the chemicals and textiles giant Courtaulds published articles in their staff newsletters, usually in the last issue before the vote so as to deny the unions a chance to reply. Employers organised seminars and meetings, where they could make the case for membership, and some broadcast messages over the tannoy. IBM displayed pro-Market material on company noticeboards, while the British Mechanical Engineering Confederation published a twenty-seven-point paper on the 'overwhelming case for staying in'.[13]

Businesses also provided rapid rebuttals of anti-Market claims. When Tony Benn alleged big job losses in the car industry, the Society of Motor Manufacturers and Traders insisted that *no* jobs had been lost from membership. Instead, it blamed Britain's poor strike record and import penetration from Japan, both of which it hoped would be ameliorated in the EEC.[14] The dairy company Unigate set up a 'Truth about Food Information Office', to respond to anti-Market attacks on food prices.[15]

Fundraising was organised on almost military lines. The supermarket boss John Sainsbury and the construction magnate Alistair McAlpine led a fundraising team that included the chairman of the National Coal Board, Derek Ezra; the financier Cyril Kleinwort; the chairman of Vickers, Alfred Robens; and the former Chancellor of the Exchequer, Peter Thorneycroft.[16] Donations ranged from the very large (£35,000 from Commercial Union, £25,000 from Debenhams, £20,000 from Cadbury Schweppes) to the relatively small (£1,000 from Penguin Books, £500 from Ladbrokes and £50 from Moss Bros). Money poured in from every sector of the economy: construction (Rugby Portland, Redland, Wimpey); oil and gas (Shell, Mobil, BP); the food and drink industry (Cadbury's, Hovis, Tate & Lyle, Rowntree Mackintosh, United Biscuits, Nestlé); motoring (Ford, Rolls-Royce, Chrysler, Datsun); the recording industry (Decca, EMI, Rank); breweries (Allied, Whitbread, Pilkington's); and engineering (Lucas, Vickers, Westland). Even the pet food company Spillers gave £10,000.[17]

Campaigning focused in particular on employment and the threat to jobs in the event of withdrawal. GKN, which employed 85,000 people in the UK, predicted a 20 per cent cut in output and the loss of 17,000 jobs. Lucas Industries, which made components for the automobile and aeronautical industries, anticipated 8–10,000 job losses, while Automatic Products, a motor components group based in Leamington, warned that 'job security will be at risk if we come out'.[18] As *The Economist* noted,

> The arguments are those of the breadbasket. If Britain pulls out, the employers say, it will find itself with a smaller market, less investment and consequently fewer jobs. Put at its crudest (and most employers try to avoid doing this) those who vote 'no' on June 5th may be voting themselves out of a job.[19]

Two days before the referendum, the Foreign Office released the names of six international companies, mostly in the chemicals sector, who proposed to cancel investment in the event of a No vote. BP Chemicals, for example, warned that a £100 million investment in Grangemouth was contingent on staying in, while the US company Monsanto declared that a nylon plant on Teesside would be cancelled if Britain withdrew.[20] Rowntree Mackintosh, the confectioners, made plans to move production to the Continent, so as to remain within the EEC's tariff wall, while the tobacco giant Rothmans International warned that it would close its main UK factory following a No vote.[21]

MEETING 'MR EUROPE'

Activity was co-ordinated by the Confederation of British Industry, which was celebrating its tenth anniversary. The Confederation had been pro-Market from the outset: at its inaugural meeting in 1965, the CBI Council had identified a closer relationship with Europe as 'a first task of the new organization'.[22] The director-general, Campbell Adamson, had spoken in 1971 of his 'unwavering dedication to the European ideal' (including 'some form of political confederation'), and described the work of integration as 'the prime task of this generation'.[23] When Heath signed the Treaty of Accession in January 1972, the CBI hailed 'the start of a new and revolutionary relationship'; and from April to June, it took to the country, criss-crossing the UK in a special 'Impact Europe' train. The train served as a mobile conference centre, educating businessmen and women on the new context for trade. 'The Community', visitors were told, would be 'an economic super-power', able to 'compete with the United States' and 'superior to the Soviet Union'.[24]

The CBI disapproved of the renegotiations and warned the government against 'any course of action that could lead to Britain leaving the Community'.[25] In January 1975, while the negotiations were still ongoing, its president, Ralph Bateman, wrote to members, asking them to provide funds for the campaign. He also asked that they nominate a single individual – a 'Mr Europe' – who could liaise with the central office. Companies were urged to ensure that 'the Europe dimension' was included in all reports, accounts and advertising, making clear to 'shareholders, employees and the general public … what the implications would be of our withdrawal'. Firms were encouraged

FIGURE 5.1   'Impact Europe'. The Confederation of British Industry's mobile conference centre, which criss-crossed the country in 1972 helping business prepare for entry to the Common Market.

Source: CBI Archive

to use workplace displays to communicate 'the advantages for exports and also for job availability in Britain and Europe'. There were regular meetings of 'Mr Europes', so that they could compare notes and report on the temperature of workplace debate.[26]

Electoral politics presented a complex set of challenges for the CBI. On the one hand, the future of Britain's trade relations was of legitimate interest to a commercial organisation, and there was little doubt of its mandate. When the CBI polled its 12,000 member organisations, only seven claimed that membership had been bad for business. An ORC poll for *The Economist*, which questioned 653 companies of varying sizes, found that 95 per cent favoured staying in, while just 2 per cent wished to withdraw. Chambers of Commerce produced similar results, with votes of 97 per cent for membership in Dundee and Tayside and 96 per cent in Birmingham.[27] When the Institute of Directors consulted its 'Chairman's Panel', it recorded 'one of the most enthusiastic [responses] that the editors of this magazine have ever seen'. Every single one of those who answered on the record (about two-thirds) argued for membership.[28]

Yet the CBI was wary of allegations that it was trying to 'buy' a national election. Mobilising the business sector risked antagonising the trade unions, while giving purchase to left-wing claims that Europe was a 'rich man's club'. *The Economist* thought that working-class figures like Vic Feather should take the lead, for fear that pressure from the boardroom might look like 'a businessmen's ramp'. Nothing was more likely to energise the unions than a campaign to enrich their bosses – particularly if it brought electoral pressure to bear on their members.[29]

For this reason, there was nothing so ostentatious in 1975 as a CBI train. Indeed, the CBI engaged in little overt campaigning of any kind, though senior figures did appear on BIE platforms. Instead, the organisation acted as a clearing house and information network, supplying the materials its members needed for their own activities. Companies were sent a steady stream of posters, leaflets and 'talking points'. Firms could commission letters and articles for company magazines, or hire TV cassettes for display in the workplace. Consultants were hired to monitor and respond to newspaper coverage, while telegenic CEOs were given media training. The CBI also circulated annotated critiques of anti-Market material, which could be used to rebut concerns on the shop floor.[30]

What businesses most needed was information, and this was the CBI's forte. Every 'Mr Europe' received a tasteful, lime-green folder, stuffed with booklets, posters and fact sheets. These were supplemented by weekly bulletins, constructed around a question-and-answer format that could be used as a prompt for workplace discussions: 'Will staying in Europe help safeguard jobs?' 'Will staying in the Community help our exports?' 'What has industry gained so far?' Briefing notes were distributed on everything from metrification to the arguments used by anti-Market speakers.[31]

The CBI also offered legal advice and guidance on how to avoid inflaming the workforce. Unlike the Institute of Directors, it warned against inserting material in pay packets – or, indeed, communicating with workers in any form outside the usual channels. It discouraged use of the tannoy to address workers, and offered guidance on the legal ramifications of giving staff time off to vote.[32]

An early problem for the CBI was the reluctance of large firms to get involved. Even companies that were enthusiastically pro-Market spoke of campaigning 'quietly' or 'sotto voce', for fear of angering the unions. ('Regrettably,' one chairman observed, 'there is a great tendency nowadays for people to believe that whatever the employers want cannot be in their interests.') In consequence, it was small and medium-sized businesses that took the lead in the early phase of the campaign. To the surprise of some, 'smaller non-unionised companies' seemed 'prepared to stick their necks out far further' than large ones, and were better placed to do so without stirring resistance on the shop floor.[33] When *The Economist* polled 653 firms in April and May, it found that 94 per cent of smaller companies favoured membership, compared to 97 per cent of larger ones.[34] The CBI Smaller Firms Council warned that withdrawal would 'damage living standards and jeopardize job security', and it worked hard to mobilise activity.[35]

WINNING IN EUROPE

The CBI spoke of the promise of Europe in almost chiliastic terms: 'a single integrated industrial and economic entity, free of tariffs and other barriers to trade, with its fiscal, legal and financial environment harmonized to facilitate the operations of industry and commerce of a fully continental magnitude'.[36] Yet it was surprisingly difficult to find solid evidence of these benefits. Of the 653 companies surveyed by *The Economist*, more than half reported that 'membership so far had had little effect on profits and sales'.[37] Writing in May 1975, the *Financial Times* could find 'little evidence that any of the main City institutions' had 'so far gained a significant direct benefit'. 'Immediate advantages' were 'not easy to find' and there seemed 'little prospect of a large upsurge in business'.[38]

By contrast, the costs were all too obvious. As tariff barriers came down, firms struggled to compete with more efficient Continental rivals, driving the UK balance of trade in manufactures with the Six' from a small surplus in 1971 to a deficit of over £1,000 million in 1974.[39] Import penetration was causing real pain, and there was concern about the level of investment flowing out of Britain to the Continent. The trade secretary Peter Shore claimed that, from 1971 to 1973, £1.4 billion of British capital had been invested in western Europe, while only £150 million had flowed back the other way.[40]

Enthusiasts argued that this was a temporary setback until domestic producers responded to competitive pressures. Even in 1971, when accession talks were still ongoing, the CBI had warned that the positive effects of membership would not be felt until the 1980s.[41] The benefits it anticipated thereafter focused on three areas: trade, investment and the defence of the free market.

The first centred on the sheer size of the Community. The EEC offered a 'highly developed home market of 260 million people' – five times the size of the UK – which was prosperous, technologically sophisticated and growing rapidly. Exports to the Community were worth £5.5 billion in 1974, roughly one-third of British sales overseas and an increase of 37 per cent on the previous year. Sales to the Community had increased by 134 per cent since 1970, more than double the increase to the Commonwealth over the same period and 50 per cent higher than the increase to all non-EEC countries.[42]

For the CBI, the Community was not just Britain's '*biggest* market', it was also her 'most *natural* market'. It was widely assumed that the world was coalescing into regional trading blocs, each with its own tariff walls. In such a world, 'countries of the size and economic strength of Britain' would 'have virtually no say'.[43] Echoing an argument that had been popular in the Edwardian period, Margaret Thatcher told a meeting of Conservative students that 'political and economic power in the world today is based much more on continents than on oceans – and on populations the size of America, Western

Europe, the Soviet Bloc, and now Japan. Where power resides, there must British influence be exerted.'[44]

The scale of the European market was also expected to facilitate modernisation. Membership, claimed the CBI, would 'give our industry the security to build up investments and to achieve economies of scale, leading to lower costs, stronger competitive power abroad and better job prospects at home'.[45] This, it was hoped, would facilitate the transition to those high skilled, high value and 'high-technology industries on which future living standards depend'. Companies exploiting 'advanced technologies', like aeronautics and the nuclear industry, could no longer function 'on a purely national basis'. To 'operate profitably', they needed 'a larger market' with 'uniform legal, fiscal and financial rules and regulations'.[46] Outside the EEC, Britain would become a low-skill, low-wage economy, reduced, in the words of the Labour MP Betty Boothroyd, to 'taking in the world's washing'.[47]

For Britain's struggling heavy industries, a second benefit was the possibility of European funding for new equipment or retraining. British Steel, for example, received £64 million of European money in the first two years of membership, while smaller, independent steel manufacturers got £28 million. The latter were so desperate to stay in that they requested a special treaty, allowing them to remain in the European Coal and Steel Community even if the national vote went the other way. Such payments also funded retraining programmes for workers made redundant by restructuring.[48] In Northern Ireland, 13,500 workers benefited from a training scheme paid for by £3.3 million from the European Social Fund.[49] £837,193 was spent on retraining 2,440 steelworkers made redundant in Lancashire and Cumberland. Other beneficiaries included 6,000 miners who had their homes modernised, courtesy of a twenty-five-year ECSC loan worth £1.7 million, at just 1 per cent interest. 'These', wrote the *Sun*, were 'just a few practical examples among hundreds.' In 'a world of rising unemployment, the Common Market is truly the best prospect open to beleaguered Britain'.[50]

A third benefit was the clout the Community could exert in international negotiations. The recent General Agreement on Tariffs and Trade (GATT) round had offered an uncomfortable reminder of how little weight Britain now carried in such forums. If British industry wished to shape the rules of world trade, it would need to do so in co-operation with others. This weighed heavily with sectors like shipping, which had little direct stake in the Continental market. In

1975, the UN Council on Trade and Development proposed new rules, which would have secured 80 per cent of the carriage trade to the two countries between whom goods were being traded. This threatened to wipe out carriers with no national base in either country, with devastating effect on British shipping. The General Council of British Shipping concluded that the proposal could only be stopped through concerted action at a European level.[51]

Alongside these direct benefits, two indirect considerations weighed heavily. The first was the need for a thriving UK market, whether or not a company traded with the EEC. Shell, for example, reminded shareholders that the UK was its largest market outside North America. Britain's prosperity was 'a matter of vital concern to us, and that prosperity in our view depends upon continuing membership of the European Community'.[52] Imperial Tobacco donated £25,000 to BIE on the basis that its sales relied on 'the more buoyant British economy that continued membership of the Community will ensure'. Sainsbury's, too, reminded employees that it could 'only sell what our customers can afford to buy'. High inflation, low productivity and a currency crisis would squeeze profits more than any regulation from Brussels.[53]

Secondly, though less commonly acknowledged, some firms saw the Community as the best guarantor of a liberal trading regime in Britain. Casting a jaundiced eye over the appointments of Benn and Foot, the *Director* warned readers that Britain was in the grip of the most left-wing government in its history, some of whose ministers 'wish to destroy utterly the free enterprise system'. Sir Marcus Sieff, chairman of Marks & Spencer, used his annual address to shareholders to defend the 'role of free enterprise', warning that ministers' preoccupation with redistributing wealth rather than creating it 'could both impoverish us and destroy our way of life'.[54]

For Sieff and his colleagues, the European Community provided some security for the survival of an open economy.[55] The chairman of Tarmac published an advertisement in the *Financial Times*, warning that the alternative to membership was 'a siege economy' of the kind found in eastern Europe, 'backed by powers of Government direction known only in wartime'. When the *Director* surveyed its members on the effects of withdrawal, one predicted 'a Left-wing dictatorship ... with a strong Right-wing reaction, with results the like of which the country has not seen since the days of Charles I and Oliver Cromwell'.[56]

From this perspective, the referendum was not simply a vote on the Common Market; it was a test of confidence in British industry and in the UK as a capitalist economy. The chairman of Lovell Holdings warned that withdrawal would trigger a collapse in international confidence, 'a run on the pound and an accelerating dip into depression'. 'My company will go down the slippery slope with everybody else.'[57]

The CBI did not deny the deteriorating trade deficit with the Continent or the imbalance between inward and outward investment. It insisted, however, that the deficit had 'NOTHING to do with membership of the EEC'. Rather, it blamed the surge in commodity prices, which had hit Britain especially hard as 'a major importing country'. That had been exacerbated by the so-called 'Barber boom' of 1972, which had stoked demand at a time when industry lacked the capacity to respond. Continental exporters had rushed to fill the gap, kneecapping the balance of payments with no benefit to home producers.[58] This was a view supported by the National Institute of Economic and Social Research, which was generally sceptical of the merits of membership.[59]

Business also acknowledged its own competitive weaknesses. No longer shielded by tariffs, British goods were being rejected by consumers in favour of cheaper and better imports from the Continent. For the CBI, the logic of this position was not to continue the deterioration of British industry behind tariff barriers, but to respond to the energising effects of competition. The hope was that competition would stimulate modernisation, investment and productivity, so that British goods could compete not just in Europe but across the world. In this sense, entry represented a cold turkey treatment, ripping out the tubes of subsidy and protection that had enervated home production. Short-term pain was inevitable if the patient was ever to recover.[60]

Pro-Marketeers denied that the flow of outward investment marked a flight of capital to safer havens. On the contrary, they presented it as part of a necessary process by which industry could equip itself for Continental markets. The long preoccupation with colonial and trans-Atlantic trade meant that many companies had little experience of trading in Europe. They responded with a wave of Continental acquisitions, buying companies with the supply chains and distribution networks that they themselves lacked. In 1972, the year before entry, investment in the 'Six' reached a colossal 30 per cent of total UK investment. This, it was argued, should be seen not as capital flight but as an investment in British export markets that would pay dividends in years to come.[61]

INDUSTRY VOICES

The experience of the textile industry illustrates the complex mix of costs and benefits involved in membership. Britain was home to four of the five biggest textile firms in Europe, employing more than 900,000 people, but the industry had been in headlong decline for much of the century. Low-cost producers in Asia had bitten deep into its markets, while the EEC had built up its own wool and cloth industries behind the protection of the external tariff barrier. The Wool Textile Delegation calculated that exclusion from the Community had cost the UK two-thirds of its trade in yarn and two-fifths of its trade in cloth with the Six. With full access to EEC markets, it hoped to claw back an additional £50 million in trade by 1977, enough to support more than 5,000 jobs.[62]

Few sectors campaigned harder than textiles. The chairman of Whitehead (Dyers) Ltd, a finishing company based in Shipley, told workers it was in their 'vital interest to vote Yes. The alternative could well be the closure of this company and the loss of your job.'[63] Outside the Community, adverts warned, '5,000 wage packets in West Yorkshire would become too expensive to fill. The chance of one being yours is just 1 in 14.'[64]

Yet the industry's enthusiasm for the EEC was in some respects surprising. This remained a global industry, which drew its raw materials from Australia, South America and India and sold the finished products to Europe, Japan, the US and the Middle East. Britain's balance of trade in textiles deteriorated significantly after entry, as Continental suppliers ate into vulnerable domestic markets. The catastrophic decline of the cotton industry in Lancashire was widely blamed by workers on the EEC, and was a central feature of the anti-Market campaign there.[65]

Two factors swung the industry behind membership. Firstly, manufacturers believed that they could win the competitive battle in the EEC, given the right framework for investment and modernisation. Britain still accounted for more than a fifth of turnover within the European textile market, and its trade in high-quality finished goods was growing. Trade journals like *Men's Wear* argued that exports of goods like Burberry or Aquascutum raincoats would offset the growth of French and Italian labels in British stores.[66] Most commentators felt that the future for the industry lay in the high-end, sophisticated products required by the Continental market, following changes in fashion to which local suppliers could respond most quickly. While new plant was sorely needed, it would be easier to finance in the expectation of a Continental 'home market'.[67]

Secondly, manufacturers in textiles – as in shipping – looked to the political influence of the Community for shelter in a hostile global environment. As the largest textile producers in Europe, British industrialists quickly came to dominate the major EEC bodies. By 1975, the three groups representing cottons, man-made fibres and wool were all headed by UK manufacturers, while the president of the British Textile Confederation, Alan Clough, also chaired the European umbrella group Comiltextil.[68] This amplified the UK's voice in world trade negotiations. For example, when the GATT agreed a 6 per cent increase in textile imports from the developing world to the EEC, a burden-sharing agreement was negotiated that limited Britain's share to a half of 1 per cent. Outside the EEC, manufacturers feared that they would be exposed to the full force of international competition. The Yorkshire industry expected 5,000 jobs to be lost outside the Community, while the Association of Jute Spinners and Manufacturers predicted 1,000 job losses in Scotland. Courtauld's, one of Britain's biggest textile manufacturers, warned that the effects of withdrawal on its operations would be 'nothing short of catastrophic'.[69]

Similar concerns animated the paper and board industry. The EEC was a key market for the sector, taking around 44 per cent of British exports. Sales had grown rapidly since 1973, with the volume of exports to the Community doubling in the first two years of membership. More important, however, were concerns about import penetration from cheap Scandinavian goods. Under previous EFTA agreements, Scandinavian paper could enter British markets free of duty. Within the EEC, imports could be spread more evenly across the Community, easing the strain on British suppliers.[70]

The motor industry, which donated handsomely to BIE, was another for whom the case for membership was not self-evident. From 1972 to 1975, Continental manufacturers had increased their share of the UK market from 17 per cent to almost 20 per cent. Companies like Renault saw the UK as a growth area, with aggressive plans for expansion. By contrast, imports from outside the EEC accounted for less than 13 per cent of market share, but were expanding faster. Japanese manufacturers like Datsun had tripled their sales in three years, and non-European imports had more than doubled over the same period. British manufacturers looked to the EEC both for protection against Japanese goods and for an enlarged export market for UK cars. In a series of remarkably sanguine projections, the Society of Motor Manufacturers and Traders predicted a market for more than 500,000 British cars and 80,000 commercial vehicles by 1985, almost tripling the value of UK exports. Datsun protested vigorously against the prospect of tariffs, but – like its American rival, Chrysler – still donated £5,000 to BIE. Even for non-European manufacturers, access to European markets and the ability to integrate their British and Continental activities outweighed the threat of tariffs.[71]

THERE IS NO ALTERNATIVE

Neither the CBI nor its members had much faith in the alternatives to the EEC. The hopes once vested in the Commonwealth had been disappointed long before the introduction of the external tariff barrier. As recently as 1954, the Commonwealth had taken 49 per cent of British exports and supplied 48 per cent of its imports; yet by 1972, the last year before British entry, those figures had dropped to 19 per cent each.[72] The EEC had overtaken the Commonwealth as a trade partner in 1962, and membership had accelerated the shift in trade patterns. By 1974, the Commonwealth accounted for just 15 per cent of British trade, less than half of the EEC's 33 per cent share.[73]

If the Commonwealth was a declining asset, nor was there much confidence in a deal with the United States. 'The decisive objection', for the CBI, was 'the lack of American interest'; but even had such a deal been on offer, the partnership would have been so unequal as to be overwhelmingly dominated by the US. Britain, it was argued, would have more control over its destiny – and so more 'sovereignty' – as an equal partner within the Community than as a supplicant at the American table.[74]

A third alternative, which was advocated vociferously by Antis like Douglas Jay, was for a European free-trade area that would dismantle tariff barriers while jettisoning political integration. The CBI made clear that it had no interest in such a deal. In its 1975 report on *British Industry and Europe*, the organisation openly applauded the ambition for 'political unification':

> In the longer term, whether the UK remains a member or not, the Community will move towards industrial, economic and monetary

union. This in itself will entail some form of political unification, and it is clearly in Britain's interest not only to welcome such a development but also to ensure that she can influence it.[75]

What the CBI wanted was not just 'a free trade arrangement' but 'a *true* common market where goods can be bought and sold freely across national boundaries'.[76] That meant setting common rules, which British business should play a part in writing. Glass producers, for example, feared that different industry standards in Britain and on the Continent would disadvantage British companies within complex international supply chains. Pilkington Brothers, for instance, produced parts for European car manufacturers, as well as the aerospace and railway industries. Outside the EEC, it feared, British firms would be unable to shape industry standards.[77] 'If we leave,' warned the CBI, 'British manufacturers will have to accept rules and standards they have had no part in framing. The result will be frustration, duplication of productive effort, and a reduction of our competitive ability.'[78]

FAITH IN THE CITY

No sector of the economy was more enthusiastically pro-Market than the City of London. The major banks, insurance houses and stockbrokers donated tens of thousands to BIE. The Stock Exchange alone gave almost £26,000, while firms like Sun Alliance, S.G. Warburg, Norwich Union, the Prudential, Morgan Grenfell and N.M. Rothschild also gave lavishly. The largest single contribution came from the high street clearing banks – Barclays, Lloyds, the Midland Bank and Natwest – which made a combined donation of £200,000. The Stock Exchange Council, the Committee on Invisible Exports and most of the major financial houses made public statements in support of membership, while the stock market rose and fell in line with the opinion polls.[79] Towards the end of May, when a freak poll suggested a surge in the No vote, the FTSE lost six points in half an hour. Two days before the vote, by contrast, when it was clear that membership would continue, the index reached its highest figure for eighteen months.[80]

In some respects, this enthusiasm was surprising. The City's financial networks had tended to be imperial and trans-Atlantic, rather than strictly European – a legacy of its history as the clearing house of empire. Continental financial markets were underdeveloped by international standards, and the London stock exchange had a turnover equivalent to the rest of Europe's bourses combined. The financial press found little evidence of short-term benefits from membership, though there was not yet much fear of regulation from Brussels.[81] On the contrary, there was some enthusiasm for the idea that financial regulation might be lifted out of the hands of the UK government. The stock market crash of 1974 had left the City in febrile mood, with confidence shaken further by the change of government. With the Labour Left on the rise and Harold Wilson talking menacingly of 'the weevils at work' in the City, optimism was a rare commodity on the trading floors of the Square Mile.[82]

At the same time, the Community offered an enticing opportunity for one of Britain's few globally competitive industries. After the US, Britain was the world's biggest exporter of 'invisible' services, with 20 per cent going to the EEC. Membership gave the City access to a large, but still inchoate, market for financial services, with the opportunity to shape the development of common financial policies. This was particularly appealing to the insurance industry, which viewed the Continent as its most important market outside the USA. Since 1970, insurers had engaged in a series of acquisitions and mergers, designed to strengthen their presence on the Continent. Eagle Star, for example, had merged with the Compagnie de Bruxelles to form the Groupe Eagle Star-C.B. The new Belgian entity ran a profit in 1974, as did the company's Dutch subsidiary, while a new French partner halved its operating loss. Commercial Union purchased the second largest Dutch insurance group, Delta-Lloyd, while Guardian Royal Exchange, Royal Insurance and Phoenix also made Continental acquisitions.[83]

The movement of capital was not all in one direction. Lloyd's of London changed its rules to permit foreign 'names', in a bid to draw in European finance. A number of Continental firms arranged listings on the London stock exchange, and several City firms began to make markets in Continental equities, even if they were not yet officially quoted in London.[84] Most promisingly, the Eurobonds market that had begun to emerge in the 1960s was located chiefly in the City; by the start of the twenty-first century, 70 per cent of all Eurobond issuance and secondary trading would take place in London.[85]

The big prize for British firms was the prospect of a Europe-wide capital market, shaped by British policymakers and dominated by the London houses. This required a political presence within

Community institutions, 'organising and influencing proposals for harmonisation'. Britain, it was argued, could play an important role in liberalising Continental markets, creating opportunities that UK firms would be well placed to exploit. As the *Financial Times* reported,

> it is in the committees and consultation groups where the City feels that much of the best and most fruitful work has been carried out in the past two years. These have been slow to produce results; but their effect on the ultimate aim of opening up the EEC to free competition could be substantial.

Progress had already been made on a directive opening up the market for non-life insurance, and work was ongoing on the lucrative market for life insurance. The danger of withdrawal was not simply that this work would go to waste; it was that a thriving European financial market might emerge outside British influence, which first closed off the Continent and then ate into British markets further afield.[86]

The banking sector also saw strong potential on the Continent, though progress had been slowed by the entrenched position of local banks. Barclays, which viewed the EEC as a refuge 'in a world beset by economic and political storms', warned that withdrawal would mean 'loss of official access to the EEC Institutions, loss of unofficial contact within the Community at all levels, abrogation of current EEC legislation and isolation from future developments'. Britain would lose its ability to 'influence ... the EEC's legal banking framework'; and rather than 'persuading the EEC to accept many of the UK's long established principles', the UK would become 'further estranged from European banking practices'.[87] Withdrawal, warned the Committee on Invisible Exports, would require an 'unscrambling of financial arrangements' that could set back penetration of the Continent for years.[88]

Any weakening of the wider British economy would also have consequences for financial services. As the *Financial Times* put it, the City 'would find it very hard to prosper as a major financial centre in a declining offshore economy, probably plagued by increasingly rigid controls on trade and capital flows'.[89] The chairman of Royal Insurance impressed this point upon shareholders at the annual general meeting in May.[90] The insurance industry's ability to raise capital depended partly on the wider buoyancy of the British economy; and if a vote for withdrawal triggered a sterling crisis, it risked further draining confidence in Britain's ability to meet its liabilities.[91] Denis Mountain, the chairman of Eagle Star, warned that withdrawal 'would do untold damage to Britain's trading position and to our industrial base', with serious consequences for insurers.[92]

'OUT OF EUROPE – AND INTO THE WORLD'

Even business opinion was not, of course, uniformly pro-Market. A small number of businessmen spoke out against membership, including the former chief executive of Jaguar, Geoffrey Robinson; others simply kept their heads down.[93] In Scotland, which was less reliant on Continental markets, a poll of 1,600 companies by the Scottish Council for Development and Industry found that almost one in five thought the issue unimportant. Some firms, like Kodak, refused to campaign despite endorsing membership, on the grounds that it was wrong to canvass workers on a political issue.[94]

Nonetheless, the overwhelming commercial support for membership was an obvious problem for the Antis. Christopher Frere-Smith accused business organisations of exerting 'immoral pressures', which made employers frightened to speak out and workers afraid to disobey their bosses. Barbara Castle wrote furiously of 'the employers' brainwashing in every factory', while C. Gordon Tether, who wrote the 'Lombard' column for the *Financial Times*, accused pro-Market bosses of breaching electoral law.[95] Enoch Powell went further, mocking the right of Britain's lazy, feather-bedded and hapless business class to advise on the economy at all. 'These are the people', he told a rally in Blackpool, 'who used to swear by all the gods there are that they would be ruined ... if ever the pound sterling were floated.' 'In their own businesses they couldn't see their hands in front of their faces ... What makes them so reliable in foretelling what is best for Britain?'[96]

Antis liked to imply that only the 'fat cats' of British industry (a term that took off in the late 1960s) favoured membership, while smaller and more agile companies looked to the wider world. Yet they struggled to find concrete examples. The only anti-Market body of any consequence was 'British Business for World Markets' (BBMW), founded in Yorkshire in 1971. Its leading spokesman was James Towler, chairman of the Shipley electronics firm Ultrasonics Ltd, who believed that Britain's trading future lay with the Middle East and the commodity-producers. BBWM commissioned a series of reports by Dr Brian

Burkitt, an academic at the University of Bradford, the most important of which was *Britain and the European Community: An Economic Re-Appraisal*. The report sold out almost immediately, but the group was unable to arrange a new print run. Instead, it was reduced to sending out a press release that merely described the report. BBWM made little impact outside Yorkshire, and even Towler's writing focused as much on constitutional as on economic questions.[97]

For some on the Left, the very fact that business favoured membership was enough to condemn the idea. Business, on this view, was drawn to the Common Market principally in the hope of 'protection' against 'the power of the British working class'. A truly socialist economics would have to repudiate the criteria by which capital measured success. As a trade unionist put it in May, a crisis of capitalism was something to be welcomed, and 'the days of capitalism would be infinitely shorter outside the Common Market than inside'.[98]

A more developed critique came from Douglas Jay and Peter Shore, both of whom had held economic portfolios in Labour administrations. Jay had been financial secretary during the Attlee government and was president of the Board of Trade in Harold Wilson's first administration, while Shore was the secretary of state for trade and a former head of the Labour Party Research Department. Both were gifted popularisers: Shore was one of the most effective public speakers in the Cabinet, while Jay had worked as an economics journalist before entering Parliament.

Shore attacked the Yes campaign at source, arguing that the growth rates enjoyed by the 'Six' had been misunderstood. It was not simply that these countries had been rebuilding from a low base, after the destruction wrought by the War. They had also been constrained by artificially high internal trade barriers after that conflict. Dismantling those barriers naturally provided a stimulus. Most also boasted large agricultural populations, providing a reserve army of labour that could bolster economic growth. Britain, by contrast, possessed no reserve army of labour and had well-established trade patterns outside Europe. Shore stressed that he was not an isolationist – a position he dismissed as 'great folly' – but he denied that the future lay with regional blocs. At a time when Europe was losing its pre-eminence, he argued, it made sense to be flexible in making trade arrangements, working where appropriate with oil producers in the Middle East or with new partners in Asia and Latin America.[99]

Jay, likewise, stressed the importance of global trade. Britain's prosperity, he argued, had always rested on its ability to source food and raw materials from the cheapest markets. That was especially important at a time when 'economic power has shifted from the European Continent to the Arab oil States'. Jay acknowledged that it was in Britain's interests to secure low tariffs for its manufactures, but not at the cost of food and commodities. The 'best solution for Britain', he argued, would be to withdraw from the EEC while rejoining EFTA, participating in 'a West European Industrial free trade area' while retaining the right 'to buy food and materials on whatever terms they wished'.[100]

That critique was developed in a document published by the Dissenting Ministers in May. Portentiously entitled 'The Economic Consequences of the Treaties', the document consciously evoked John Maynard Keynes' seminal work on *The Economic Consequences of the Peace* in 1919. Mostly written by Benn and his advisor Frances Morrell, it described Accession as 'an act of economic surrender'. Membership, it warned, would have three deleterious consequences. First, it would commit Britain to 'buy expensive Continental food', pushing up labour costs. ('That is why the French want us in.') Second, it would give West German industry unrestricted access to the British market, while denying Britain the policies of industrial development and state investment that would allow it to 'fight back'. ('That is why West Germany wants us in.') Thirdly, it would force the UK to share its oil reserves, rather than using them for domestic reconstruction. ('That is why all the EEC countries want us in.') Barbara Castle thought the document a 'mishmash' of 'exaggerated' claims, but all three featured prominently in the campaign.[101]

If Shore and Jay provided the intellectual firepower for the anti-Market campaign, its foot soldiers came largely from the trade union movement. The two most prominent unions in the No camp were the TGWU, led by the redoubtable Jack Jones, and the Association of Scientific, Technical and Managerial Staffs (ASTMS), under Clive Jenkins. Jones and Jenkins served as joint president and vice president respectively of the Get Britain Out Referendum Campaign, and both enjoyed a high public profile. The TUC also recommended a No vote, under the slogan 'Better out than in'. The National Union of Mineworkers (NUM) also backed the Out campaign, though miners in more prosperous coalfields were thought to favour staying in. The president of the South Wales NUM, the Communist Emlyn Williams, claimed that entry was a symptom of a wider crisis of capitalism. 'Capitalism', he declared, 'is moving inevitably and remorselessly into a deeper crisis that will lead us to greater authoritarian rule, to the vestiges of Fascism, unless we call a halt.'[102]

The most active union was the Transport and General, which boasted 1.75 million members. Its research officer, Bob Harrison, was seconded to the NRC, while the regional secretary in Wales, George Wright, was attached to GBO in Wales. The union's 170 regional and district offices doubled up as campaign headquarters, while officials lent their expertise in organising meetings and recruitment. The Transport and General also provided much of the campaign material for the anti-Marketeers. Its newspaper, the *Record*, usually had a print-run of around 300,000, but millions of copies were produced of its referendum specials and circulated to other unions and interested parties. Much 'Anti' material had a TGWU branding, contributing to an impression, as the *Financial Times* observed, 'that the Transport and General Workers' Union is single-handedly running the union campaign to vote Britain out of the Common Market'.[103]

Unlike the CBI, the unions painted a gloomy picture of Britain's prospects within the Community. Dennis Skinner, the celebrated 'Beast of Bolsover' and vice-president of the MPs' miners group, claimed that 'Free movement of capital and labour has put four million EEC workers in the dole queue.'[104] As the ASTMS pointed out, unemployment had been rising sharply in recent years across the Common Market, though unemployment rates of 3–3.5 per cent still compared favourably with the UK.[105] Unemployment across the Community was running at about 4.5 million, a fact which the unions attributed squarely to EEC policies.[106] A research paper produced by the ASTMS estimated that 250,000 jobs had been lost in Britain as a direct result of membership.[107] Tony Benn put the figure at 500,000, while Michael Meacher opted for 750,000.[108]

Such estimates assumed an explicit link between unemployment and the burgeoning trade deficit, on the principle that 'every product imported is one not produced in Britain'. The Oxford and District Trades Council accused employers of exporting 'capital, created by the workers of this country, to countries where it can find cheaper labour, weaker unions, and production closer to the European market'. 'Far from being the saviour of British trade', warned GBO, the EEC had 'revealed itself as a predator'.[109] Unions had little truck with claims that overseas investment would facilitate export growth. As the ASTMS put it, 'Every £1 invested in this way is £1 less invested in Britain.'[110]

While business saw Europe as the route to a high-skill, high-wage economy, the unions feared the opposite. Membership, they argued, would create a continental pool of reserve labour, with capital free to switch across borders in pursuit of the lowest wage costs. The Transport and General saw membership as part of larger package – also including the 1971 Industrial Relations Act – intended to drive down wages and employment rights. The goal, it believed, was to restore the authority of employers over their workforce, for 'there is no stronger argument in [the] hands of employers than the threat of cutting back, re-investment elsewhere or finally closure of the firm'.[111] Peter Shore warned of mass emigration, with 'British people in their thousands moving into Western Europe to find jobs they can no longer get in this country'.[112]

The unions also blamed Europe for inflation. This was politically convenient, as it absolved the unions themselves from responsibility; but it was true that prices were traditionally higher on the Continent and that food prices had risen steeply since entry. Since joining, they noted, inflation had risen by 31.8 per cent, almost double the 16.5 per cent rate in the two years previously. Worse would follow, as food prices continued to adjust upwards to the Community norm.[113]

In all these respects, the referendum brought into collision two visions of political economy. On the one hand, the CBI welcomed the competitive pressures of the EEC in the hope of stimulating modernisation and productivity. By contrast, the unions and the Left were suspicious of a model that forced workers to compete for free-floating international capital. Benn told a meeting in Bristol that it would be 'an act of lunacy', amidst a 'crisis of capitalism', to embrace an institution founded on 'the very principle that has led us to our present state'. Len Murray, the general secretary of the TUC, agreed: 'Britain should not be in a Market in which the guiding principle is competition.'[114]

This linked together two strands of trade union commentary, emphasising respectively the economic and political costs of membership. The unions, as we shall see, placed considerable emphasis on the sovereignty of Parliament, as the means by which capital could be subjected to democratic control. By liberating market forces from the oversight of national governments, membership would reduce the unions' ability to influence 'social, monetary, political or industrial policy inside Britain'.[115] Staying in, the TUC concluded, would mean 'business finding it easier to dodge its responsibilities to working people', while unions found it 'harder to win their programme of social reform'.[116]

Like Shore and Jay, trade unionists dismissed the charge of isolationism or 'little Englandism'. The slogan of the union campaign – 'Out of Europe and into the world' – was meant to signal a wider internationalism, turning the label of parochialism back against the Common Market. The ASTMS called the Community 'a closed, tariff-ridden, elitist grouping of countries, living an inward-looking existence'. Trade unionists, by contrast, were 'inherently internationalist in outlook', building links with unions abroad and pursuing 'closer ties between the peoples of *all* countries'.[117]

THE FORWARD MARCH OF LABOUR HALTED

The unions should have been a formidable ally for the NRC. The 1970s was probably the pinnacle of union influence, with roughly half the workforce enrolled in a union. Trade union activity had gutted the Industrial Relations Act of 1971, contributed to the fall of the Heath ministry in 1974 and secured a wide-ranging 'Social Contract' with the government. Offering a ready-made campaign machine, with a reach and membership that rivalled any of the pro-Market vehicles, the unions had been expected to be 'the most powerful organized force against the EEC in the referendum battle'.[118]

Yet union pressure proved remarkably ineffective. Even industrial heartlands like Glasgow, the Midlands and the North of England produced crushing majorities for staying in. Workers, it appeared, had followed the cues of their employers, rather than of their union representatives, in what might be seen as the first of the many defeats to be suffered by the movement over the following two decades.

This owed something to the strange mix of forces in the No campaign. Enoch Powell, the Tory Right and the nationalist parties in Scotland and Wales made awkward partners for the unions, making it hard to co-operate across party lines. Jimmy Milne, the secretary-general designate of the Scottish TUC, expressed incredulity at the idea that he might work with the SNP. 'Forgive the language,' he told the *Financial Times*, 'but they're bastards, they really are.'[119] A TGWU branch secretary, who stressed his own opposition to the Common

Market, condemned his union for aligning with 'racialists like Enoch Powell'. 'Businessmen and Tory MPs', he added, 'have always been the enemies of trade unionists and they always will be.'[120]

It was not only the personnel of the No campaign that made uneasy bedfellows. Intellectually, the unions tended to align themselves with the position drawn up by Douglas Jay, by which Britain would remain in a European customs union while eschewing political integration. Yet this would not have addressed the unions' concerns about import penetration or the flight of capital from the UK. Nor, given the rules necessary to regulate such a market, would it have resolved the constitutional problem that political control over economic policy would have been diminished.

Furthermore, the union movement itself was never as united against membership as TUC rhetoric might suggest. While miners in South Yorkshire campaigned for a No vote on the doorstep, miners in the East Midlands were openly pro-Market. So was the second biggest union in the region, the General and Municipal Workers' Union (GMWU). The Union of Shop, Distributive and Allied Workers was another powerful pro-Market union, while the Electrical, Electronic, Telecommunications and Plumbing Union (EETPU) remained formally neutral after a fighting performance by its pro-Market general secretary, Frank Chapple.[121]

Chapple was one of a number of senior trade unionists who openly campaigned for a Yes vote. Others included David Basnett of the GMWU, Roy Grantham of APEX and, most importantly, Vic Feather. Recently ennobled as Baron Feather of Bradford, Feather had been general secretary of the TUC until 1973, and he served in 1975 as president of the Trade Union Alliance for Europe (TUAFE). Having led the fight against Heath's Industrial Relations Act, Feather could hardly be dismissed as a Tory stooge, and his Yorkshire accent and bluff, genial manner made him a valuable asset to the Yes campaign. Britain in Europe dedicated an entire broadcast to an audience with the great man at a working men's club, in which he took questions from steelworkers and trade union representatives. An ORC poll shortly afterwards found that 84 per cent of viewers knew that Feather was in favour of British membership – up from just 12 per cent a few weeks before.[122] At a memorable press conference in London, he warned that Britain 'can't go it alone'. Outside, it would be 'knackered and I don't want to see us knackered'. Appeals to abstract notions like sovereignty were shot down in a hail of northern grit. 'The price of oil', he reminded voters, 'is not determined by the British Parliament. It is determined by some lads riding camels who don't even know how to spell national sovereignty.'[123]

TUAFE focused remorselessly on the prospects for jobs and wages. Roy Grantham, for example, predicted 'massive unemployment' if 'Britons foolishly vote No'.[124] If membership would protect levels of employment, then it stood squarely 'on the basis of trade union principles and interests'.[125] The organisation skilfully exploited the idea that the EEC, like a trade union, offered strength through solidarity. Vic Feather likened those who wanted to leave to 'a discontented trades unionist who threatened to tear up his [union] card'. Instead of retreating into isolation, trade unionists should 'remain in Europe, play our role and change those things which need improvement'.[126]

TUAFE also stressed the possibilities for international co-operation, building a European social democracy that could stand on an equal basis against the multinationals. George Thomson told a meeting in April that 'Private economic power has already gone multinational. Only concerted action on the part of the nine governments of the Community can match the power of the multinational company.'[127] The GMWU made a similar case. 'The fact is', wrote Basnett, 'that the world economic situation has so developed that it is not possible for the individual nation state to control its own destiny.' The European Community offered, for the first time, 'the possibility of a degree of control over these forces'. 'Alone we can do next to nothing.'[128]

TUAFE posed a problem for the unionist mainstream, but organisations like the TUC, the TGWU and the array of anti-Market unions should have had the firepower to respond. Yet the scale of union activity in 1975 rarely lived up to its rhetoric. Clive Jenkins may have likened the referendum to 'a World War Three situation', but officials seemed reluctant to press the nuclear button. There was little sign of the 'massive campaign in the streets and on the knocker' demanded by the AUEW.[129] Companies that mobilised in support of the Community reported 'a surprisingly low – even negligible – amount of adverse comment'. At a private meeting in May, the CBI's 'Mr Europes' reported 'an almost total absence of trade union activity' in the workplace.[130] Journalists visiting Mather and Platt in Manchester – where the Transport and General and the Amalgamated Union of Engineering Workers were both well represented – were surprised by the 'apparent lack of shop-floor impact'.[131]

In the East Midlands, too, reporters found that activists for the TGWU, AUEW and ASTMS, though nominally working for a No vote, 'have been inclined to get not too closely involved'.[132]

This lethargy was not restricted to the workplace. While the employers were donating handsomely to BIE, union coffers remained firmly closed. Staff were seconded and some premises made available, but the accounts of the National Referendum campaign record not a single significant donation from organised labour.[133]

For all the rhetoric of 'Magna Carta' and 'World War Three', Europe seems in practice to have been a low-salience issue for the unions. There was almost certainly a reluctance to embarrass the Labour government, and the No campaign itself was wary of being too closely associated with union influence. Richard Body later recalled 'trying to keep the trade unions quiet', while Clive Jenkins was 'very conscious that he might be losing support' for the campaign. When challenged on the lack of union funding, Jack Jones later claimed that he had feared a backlash in the anti-union press.[134]

Workers did not, in any case, necessarily take their political direction from the unions. Reporters commonly found that workers distinguished between the micro-economic opinions of their unions – regarding the management of their own industry and workplace – and their macro-economic prescriptions for the government. A convenor at the Hawker Siddeley works in Manchester told journalists that workers in the plant were two-to-one in favour of membership, 'because most of the men were ready to follow Mr Harold Wilson's lead rather than take great account of the political views of their shop stewards'. It was a similar story at the engineering firm Mather and Platt. 'What do the trade unions know about it?', asked a worker ('to a chorus of nods and grunts'). 'I am going to vote as the politicians say. Both Heath and Wilson are for staying in, and they ought to know.'[135]

When it came to jobs and investment, local evidence seems to have trumped the more abstract claims of the unions. While anti-Marketeers warned of import penetration, capital flight and the loss of sovereignty, their opponents identified specific examples of job creation and financing: £92 million for investment in steel; £34.3 million to retrain unemployed workers; £23 million for new equipment in the coal industry.[136] Literature gave specific instances of new plant and employment opportunities, or of investment from American or Japanese firms keen to export to the Continent. Examples included the

Concorde project and 140 foreign-owned factories in Bristol and the South West; a £1 million television factory funded by the Japanese electronics company Matsushita (later Panasonic) in Cardiff, as a bridgehead for sales to the Continent; and Sony's decision to use South Wales as its European base.[137] Yorkshire and Humberside were said to have received nearly £100 million in development grants, while projects funded in other parts of the country included £301,082 for a cheese and milk factory in County Tyrone, £184,000 for a meat-processing plant in Liverpool, £2.3 million to modernise a steel mill in Manchester and £208,422 for a slaughterhouse in Londonderry.[138] Antis raged at the 'pay-packet propaganda' of the employers; but with businesses threatening to cut jobs in the event of withdrawal, it was not surprising that workers voted with their payslips.[139]

Yet the resulting Yes vote was by no means a positive endorsement of integration. Reporters in Greater Manchester confidently predicted a vote to stay in, but concluded that 'fear is the spur' – 'fear of rising prices, fear of unemployment, and fear for the future [of] the country'. A woman working at Mather and Platt told journalists that Britain had no option but to stay in: 'This country is not much good on its own now, is it?' In nearby Altrincham, a Conservative stronghold, the mood was the same. 'We've got to stay in,' said one young man. 'This country will sink without trace if we don't.'[140] A poll for the NRC, a week before the vote, found that more than half of all voters expected an immediate political and economic crisis in the event of a No vote.[141] In such a climate, it was hardly surprising that voters chose to 'cling to nurse, for fear of finding something worse'. For the immediate purposes of the referendum, it was a highly effective strategy; but it would store up significant problems for the Europe debate in the years and decades to come.

6 'WOMEN AND CHILDREN FIRST!'

The wives may stage a revolt!

The Sun, 27 May 1975[1]

It isn't something we women can shrug off with a yawn and leave to the men. It's our life too. It's our children's lives and their children's lives.

Marjorie Proops, 2 June 1975[2]

Think of it as the Common Supermarket. Well-stocked shelves ... Plenty of choice ... And just around the corner.

Britain in Europe, May 1975[3]

On 20 November 1970, fifty-eight women in swimsuits stepped out onto the stage of the Royal Albert Hall. London was playing host to the annual 'Miss World' beauty contest, one of the iconic events of the television year, with an audience of 24 million in the UK alone. The contest was won by Jennifer Hosten from Grenada, the first black woman ever to wear the crown; but as contestants traded allegations of racism and corruption, it was a very different group of women who caught the attention of the cameras. As viewers watched in amazement, protestors from the Women's Liberation Movement rushed the stage, throwing flour bombs and unfurling banners. The historian and activist Sally Alexander, who was dragged from the stage by security guards, later described it as 'one of the most spectacular consciousness-raising episodes' in the history of the movement.[4]

If the 1970s was the decade of 'Women's Lib', the Miss World protest marked its coming-out party. The Women's Liberation

Movement had held its first national conference earlier that year, bringing together more than 600 delegates, and local groups were mushrooming across the country. A new generation of feminist newspapers, like *Spare Rib*, *Red Rag*, *Shrew* and *Socialist Woman*, was challenging the more conventional content of magazines like *Woman's Own* or *Honey*, and women's groups had begun to build alliances with movements for gay liberation and workers' rights. Britain had one of the highest levels in Europe of women's participation in the workforce, and the 1970s saw a wave of strikes by groups like auxiliary nurses and night cleaners.[5]

1975 found the women's movement in full force. Designated by the United Nations as the 'International Year of Women' – inaugurating the UN Decade for Women – it saw not only a surge of social activism but also a renewed attention to women's rights at the parliamentary level.[6] 1975 was the year in which the Equal Pay Act, passed five years earlier, was to come into full operation, drawing renewed attention to the differentials in pay between men and women. A Sex Discrimination Act outlawed discrimination in employment, education, housing and the provision of goods and services, while an Equal Opportunities Commission was established to police the Act. Less than four months before the referendum, Margaret Thatcher became the first woman to lead a major British party, an event that attracted considerable attention from the feminist press.[7]

Yet the 1970s was a paradoxical decade in the history of women's rights, and Thatcher herself encapsulated many of its ambiguities. On the one hand, she had smashed the glass ceiling of British politics and challenged assumptions about the roles appropriate to women. Yet she was contemptuous of feminism and cast herself chiefly as a wife and mother.[8] While the Equal Pay Act established the principle of fair treatment for men and women, it did little in practice to close the pay gap; for while it barred discrimination between a man and a woman doing the same job, it did not address the tendency for men and women to be recruited to different roles, at different levels of pay. Trade unions, which remained central to pay bargaining and the negotiation of working conditions, were overwhelmingly male-dominated and often slow to act on issues concerning women's employment.

As if to underline the precarious state of women's rights, a landmark legal decision in 1975 threatened to undo years of incremental progress on the treatment of sexual violence. In a brutal case of gang rape, four men – including the woman's husband – had taken turns to assault the victim, who fought back with sufficient force to require hospital treatment afterwards. The defence rested on a form of presumed consent: the husband had told the other three that his wife would *pretend* to resist, but that she was really a willing participant. In a case that went to the House of Lords, the courts ruled that a man could not be convicted of rape if he believed that the victim had consented – even if that belief was inherently 'unreasonable'. The judgement drew a storm of criticism from MPs and journalists, who called it a 'rapists' charter', but it was not fully overturned in statute until 2003.[9]

A referendum on the Common Market might seem an unlikely arena in which to debate the roles and responsibilities of men and women. Yet both sides paid close attention to women's votes and crafted material specifically with women in mind. Britain in Europe employed two full-time women's officers, who were among the highest paid officials in the organisation, while women like Barbara Castle, Judith Hart, Margaret Thatcher and Shirley Williams all took prominent roles in the campaign.[10] On one level, this marked a recognition of women's electoral power and of the need to craft appropriate campaign messages; yet the assumption that women formed a distinct electoral cohort also marked the continuing resonance of older ideas about 'the women's vote' and the issues that were thought to define it. While men were assumed to have multiple and sophisticated political identities, determined not by their sex but by occupation, political allegiance, religious belief and regional identity, appeals to women still leaned heavily on a set of well-worn feminine tropes: the housewife, the mother and the keeper of the household budget. At a time when feminists were struggling to recast political language, women who campaigned in the referendum found that their voices were most likely to be heard when they spoke in the tones of the wife and mother. Like the traditional cry of the shipwrecked sailor – 'women and children first' – the attention paid to women voters was indicative less of their political equality than of their continuing status as a 'special category', outside the perceived mainstream of electoral politics.

'A HIGH STREET REFERENDUM'

A week before the referendum, the *Sun* confronted readers with a terrible warning: 'the wives may stage a revolt'. Britain, it warned, faced a 'High Street Referendum', in which 'cost-conscious housewives could swing the decision about whether Britain stays a member of the Common Market'.[11] This echoed the findings of BIE's own polling, that women were significantly more likely than men to favour leaving the Community. 'Hard core anti-marketeers', it discovered, 'include a disproportionately high number of women,' while women appeared more likely to 'switch' to the anti-Market side over the course of the campaign. There was some evidence, too, that women were proving resistant to lines of argument tailored to male voters. In April, for example, a Scottish poll found that men had swung in favour of membership by 43 per cent to 37 per cent, while women continued to back withdrawal by 36 per cent to 32 per cent. If BIE was to win on 5 June, women would require 'special attention'.[12]

What troubled the pro-Marketeers was not so much the hard core of 'Antis' as the larger number of undecided voters. Women, a private poll concluded, were among the 'most volatile, the most weakly committed (and the most hostile)' groups, while a poll for the NRC found that 66 per cent of potential 'switchers' were women.[13] In a *Glasgow Herald* poll, 34 per cent of women described themselves as 'Don't Knows', compared to just 20 per cent of men. Likewise, a poll for the *Birmingham Post* found that 18 per cent of women were undecided just days before the vote, nearly twice the number of men.[14] That made women a crucial 'swing' vote, offering rich rewards to whoever could target them most effectively.

WOMEN FOR EUROPE

BIE began by establishing a dedicated Women's Section. It was run by Lady Kina Avebury, a federalist who had stood as the Liberal candidate at Orpington in October 1974, and the Conservative Ann Money-Coutts, who had worked in the European Commission at Brussels.[15] Like Avebury, Money-Coutts was from a political family: her mother, Lady Emmet of Amberley, had been a Conservative MP and a delegate to the United Nations Assembly in 1952, while her ex-husband, Hugo, was a scion of the banking dynasty. While Money-Coutts brought inside knowledge of the Commission and an extensive social and political network, Avebury was an experienced campaigner who spent much of her time on the road. At Newcastle City Hall, for example, she spoke alongside Ted Heath and Vic Feather, while she shared the platform

FIGURE 6.1   Lady Avebury, the Liberal who ran Britain in Europe's Women's Office with the Conservative Ann Money-Coutts.

Source: Frank Barratt, Hulton Archive: www.gettyimages.co.uk/license/3265968

at Bradford with Reginald Maudling and the former Labour minister Douglas Houghton.[16]

The first task for the new organisation was simply to ensure a proper representation of women's voices, in what threatened to be a very male-dominated operation. The National Liberal Club, which served as the headquarters for the European Movement, did not even admit women to full membership at this time, and it voted to uphold the ban just a month before the referendum.[17] At first, as Avebury and Money-Coutts later recalled, 'the whole tenor of advertising and publicity ... was consistently male-oriented'. Indeed, the first batch of posters 'had no women in them at all'. Such material as was designed for women was either crassly chauvinistic – women's T-shirts, for example, with the words 'Europe or Bust' blazoned across the bosom – or thoughtlessly so, like the posters of smiling children labelled 'Jobs for the Boys'. One voter was so nettled by such 'male chauvinist' material that she wrote to protest, wondering what such slogans said about 'the prospects for girls? Or do you accept that we women shall retain our second-class status in a European future?'[18]

If the campaign's own material was problematic, press coverage was even worse. Slogans like 'Europe or Bust' lent themselves readily to the increasingly pornographic culture of tabloid journalism in the seventies.[19] The *Mirror* had featured a series of 'Euro-dollies' during the accession negotiations in 1971, and in 1975 it hired a twenty-two-year-old model called Beverley Pilkington, who posed for the paper in her underwear and a 'Europe or Bust!' T-shirt that left little to the imagination. Pilkington had modelled for *Top of the Pops* and worked as an occasional Page Three girl for the *Sun*; she would later become famous as the face of 'Big D' peanuts. Under the headline 'Busting out for Europe', the *Mirror* sniggered that Pilkington would give voters 'a point or two to consider', adding lasciviously that readers 'could be forgiven for wishing that the exclamation on her T-shirt was a question mark'. The paper also employed a Swedish model called Siv, a former girlfriend of George Best, who was pictured in a bikini composed of the flags of the nine EEC member states. Siv, the paper drooled, was 'a curvy kind of flagpole', who 'always enjoys dressing up to the Nines'.[20]

Campaign events were strongly influenced by commercial advertising, which had also become increasingly sexualised. In Coventry, for example, a modern-day Lady Godiva – described by the organisers as 'an attractive woman, mature in her ideas and against the Common Market' – rode through the city wearing nothing but a body-stocking, waving a 'No to EEC Taxes' banner. (The event almost became a streak of a different kind, when her horse took exception to a protestor 'in full Punjabi dress, beating out rhythm on a Punjabi drum'.)[21] Britain in Europe hired models to pose in the national costumes of the member states, and a row broke out at a meeting of 'Students for a United Europe' over plans for a 'Miss Europe-Europa the Luscious' event. The idea followed a well-established pattern – there had been a beauty contest to mark the enlargement of the Community in 1973, won by the Dutch model and star of the *Emmanuelle* franchise, Sylvia Kristel – but it stirred strong opposition from female delegates, who complained that it was 'sexist' and 'inappropriate for a student organization'. In a misguided attempt to pour oil on troubled waters, a male delegate suggested that the event 'would go down well in Oxford', but might prove too racy for the provinces.[22]

One solution was for the Women's Section to produce its own campaign materials, bypassing the largely male publicity office. Avebury and Money-Coutts duly produced a stream of literature, including one and a quarter million copies of a leaflet covering such issues as jobs, benefits, pensions, the cost of living, peace and security. When they drafted a pamphlet on the status of women in the European Community, the Executive Committee refused to allocate funds; so the officers simply duplicated copies and distributed them as widely as possible to speakers.[23]

FIGURE 6.2   'I will always say YES to Europe.' Racing cars and racy slogans in South Glamorgan.
Source: Media Wales

As well as producing their own literature, Avebury and Money-Coutts fought to influence the wider tone of the campaign. They won the right to attend meetings of the Executive Committee and campaign breakfasts at the Waldorf, and to be consulted on all questions relating to broadcasting and publicity. They also fought to drive up the representation of women at press conferences. By the end of the campaign there was almost always a woman on the panel, with speakers including Betty Boothroyd, Linda Chalker, Lady Seear, Rita Stephen, Shirley Williams and Lady Young.[24]

This part of the job also involved co-ordinating and, where necessary, chivvying into action the regional organisers, to ensure that women were considered when devising their campaign strategies. Some needed more encouragement than others. Reporting on local groups at the end of May, Money-Coutts praised the work of activists in London, where meetings of the Townswomen's Guilds, Women's Institutes and Conservative women's organisations had been flooded with publicity material. In Berkshire, Buckinghamshire and Oxfordshire, where the regional organiser was a woman, things were better still: 'All women's groups approached and covered since Christmas – all councillors approached and most villages in all three counties have had meetings which have been very well attended. The impression is of great efficiency and hard work.' The West Midlands, by contrast, was 'thoroughly wet', while the campaign team in Northern Ireland was said to have '"No notion" of the situation regarding women', and 'a rather negative approach to women's votes'. Scotland, too, was 'badly organized as regards women'. The Welsh office, by contrast, had 'done a good deal', while Humberside and Yorkshire had run 'good meetings with women factory workers'.[25]

The Women's Section also undertook three more specific tasks. The first was to act as a point of contact for women's media outlets, ranging from the 'women's pages' in the press to sympathetic programmes on radio and television. Avebury herself appeared on *Woman's Hour* and stayed in touch with its producers.[26] In May, the office hosted a press conference exclusively for 'women journalists and editors of women's pages', as well as representatives of women's television and radio shows. Speakers included Janet Graham, who chaired the Housewives' Trust and was an advisory member of the Food Panel Price Committee; Kim McKinley, assistant secretary in the Union of Post Office Workers; Pat Turner, national women's officer for the General and Municipal Workers' Union; and Rachel Waterhouse, a consumer affairs activist and historian who served on the council of the Consumers' Association.[27] This media function also involved a rapid rebuttal operation, responding to negative reports focused on or addressed to women.[28]

The second main task of the organisation was the supply of information, providing material crafted specifically for women voters. This was thought particularly important, because of the low level of knowledge professed by women on the Market issue. Pollsters consistently reported that women simply knew less about the European question – or, more probably, were less reluctant to confess their ignorance. A poll at the end of April found that 26 per cent of women 'don't know for certain if we are in Europe at present although 12% think vaguely that we might be'.[29] One regional organiser told Avebury that 'what is of most interest to women in this particular area … [is] quite simply … just to be told something about what the European Community means'.

Even when addressing 'as political a group as a Co-operative Women's Guild, I found that it was quite simply best to assume that they knew absolutely nothing'. Simple information, he stressed, was more important than arguments about why the Community was a good thing; indeed, it was more likely to be effective if it came 'without excessive bias'.[30]

A third task was to plug into the extensive network of women's voluntary organisations. Avebury and Money-Coutts began by writing personally to 250 national women's organisations, ranging from the Association of Headmistresses and the Catholic Women's League to the Farm Women's Clubs and the Townswomen's Guilds. Those that were willing to campaign were given advice on how best to reach women voters; for example, by setting up 'stalls in major shopping precincts' or 'organizing small house meetings ... with a visiting speaker'. Others were consulted on the kind of information that might be useful to their members, so that literature could be produced accordingly.[31]

The scale and reach of these organisations remained impressive, despite anxieties about a shrinking and ageing base. The Women's Institutes (WI) recorded a membership in the early 1970s of 442,086; the Townswomen's Guilds boasted 275,700 members in 1969; while the Mothers' Unions had 380,000 members in the late 1960s. Though feminists were often critical of these bodies, lamenting their valorisation of housework and maternity, their 'Jam and Jerusalem' image belied a history of political activism. Organisations like the Women's Institutes and the National Council of Women placed considerable emphasis on political education, and had campaigned on such issues as the payment of family allowances to mothers, maternity services and the provision of social welfare. Indeed, it was precisely *because* they valorised their roles as 'housewives' and 'mothers' that they insisted upon an active and capacious citizenship for women. For such organisations, as Catriona Beaumont has noted, 'domesticity no longer demanded that women dedicate themselves exclusively to the demands of husband and children. On the contrary, domesticity was the means through which modern women could assert their right to participate in public life'.[32]

It helped that women's organisations already had extensive networks on the Continent. The 1970s had seen a conscious effort to build transnational networks, stretching not just across Europe and North America but into the Third World and the Soviet bloc.[33] Membership of the EEC gave a particular impetus to this movement, in a development that was cautiously promoted by government. In 1972, the Foreign Office had allocated £10,000 to help women's organisations in the UK to strengthen their contacts with similar organisations on the Continent. The grant, which was increased to £15,000 in 1973, was disbursed by a new Women's European Committee, with funds available for conferences, exchanges, visits and similar activities.[34] Organisations that benefited included the Women's Institutes, the Townswomen's Guilds, the British Federation of University Women and the Farm Women's Clubs. The amounts allocated were relatively small, but they helped to build networks between the voluntary sector and the European Movement.[35]

These proved invaluable during the referendum. Pamela Entwistle, for example, used an invitation to speak at the annual general meeting of the Wives' Fellowship to prepare an information pack for each branch, containing maps, leaflets, details of Britain in Europe's 'Speaker Service' and contact details for their local regional organiser. As she told Avebury, it helped that 'most of the secretaries are personally known to me'. A representative of the National Housewives Association corresponded with Avebury to discuss the kind of material that might suit its magazine, while the National Council of Women agreed to ask its membership what kind of information would be most useful. Similarly, the editor of the Women's Institute newsletter got in touch with Entwistle to advise on the kinds of information her members would most value, resulting in 'a couple of paragraphs in the News-Letter' and further contacts with local branches.[36]

Such organisations had, nonetheless, to be handled with care. Groups like the WI and the Mothers' Unions were fiercely protective of their non-partisan status and resented any attempt to co-opt them into activities that might divide their members. For this reason, most women's organisations took no formal position on the referendum. However, most agreed to communicate 'information', on the understanding that 'the whole question is non-party political'.[37] Some also communicated their views more obliquely. The National Federation of Women's Institutes, for example, resisted attempts to recruit it to the pro-Market campaign; yet it had a proud sense of itself as a European and internationally minded body, and gave considerable coverage to the European Year of Architecture in 1975 and to its growing links with bodies on the Continent. Regional federations had received £1,500 from the Women's European Committee in 1974, to pay for exchange schemes and visits to like-minded organisations in Europe.[38] During the campaign, the organisation ran a number of study groups and meetings, designed to increase women's understanding of the issues. The assumption of political neutrality allowed the organisation to operate as a clearing house for campaign information, the quality and quantity of which was always higher from the pro-Marketeers. An editorial after the result was announced gave a thinly veiled welcome to the verdict, advising its readers that 'we must now find ways to speak with one "European" voice'.[39]

The Townswomen's Guilds were more overtly pro-Market. The Guilds had opposed a referendum, complaining that 'Ninety per-cent of the electorate in Britain are completely uninformed,' and had voted to condemn the idea at their national assembly in 1974. While the organisation remained formally neutral, it was determined that 'the 200,000 Townswomen' would be 'the best informed people in the Country on the Common Market issue'.[40] Its magazine, the *Townswoman*, adopted an educative tone, but the balance of content leaned heavily towards membership. Opportunities were given to members of the Commission to explain their roles and to clear away 'myths' about the EEC, while no significant coverage was given to anti-Marketeers. At the National Union's special conference on Europe in 1975, the opening speaker was Valerie Williams, who worked in the Commission's London Office. The *Townswoman* also published articles by a Dutch economist for the Commission, Theo Hustinx, and by Inger Nielsen, chief advisor to the Directorate dealing with General External Relations.[41] Nielsen, in particular, was held up as an example of how women could succeed in Europe. Marjorie Rice, the national chairman, warned that a No vote would leave Britain in the 'wilderness'. 'I almost rate the loss of influence in world diplomacy more highly than the economic and trade repercussions, which would be considerable.'[42]

'THE HOUSEWIVES' CHAMPION OF EUROPE'

Appealing to female voters was not solely the responsibility of the Women's Section. The sheer voting power of women – and the fear that they would vote to leave – meant that all parts of Britain in Europe had to be sensitive to female voters. On taking up his post as director of publicity for BIE, Harold Hutchinson sought advice from Sheila Black, the first woman to write for the *Financial Times* and its Women's

Editor until 1972.[43] The Conservative MP for South Gloucestershire, John Cope, announced that he would hand over the writing of his referendum address to a housewife from his constituency. The short straw was drawn by Mrs Gillian Woolley, a thirty-nine-year-old with two children, whom Cope declared 'the constituency's typical housewife'. Woolley herself was more circumspect, telling journalists that 'I don't think anybody really regards themselves as the average housewife'; but her 750-word message made a good story for the local press.[44]

One publicity agency had more ambitious plans, offering to 'co-ordinate a force of intelligent and highly trained lady demonstrators'. This crack team would fan out across shopping centres and 'plazas', handing out leaflets and chatting to women as they shopped. The women would be selected to match 'the socio-economic profile' of their region, and the agency estimated the cost of a '100-girl operation' at £24,000, exclusive of fees. The proposal never got off the ground ('Not f__g likely', wrote an official), but the idea of deploying women in shopping precincts was widely used.[45]

Britain in Europe placed considerable emphasis on what would later be called the 'leadership effect': the tendency of voters to take their cues from those whose judgement they trusted on other matters.[46] For this reason, it lined up as many prominent women as possible, selected for their appeal to particular electoral cohorts. Campaign material in Northern Ireland, for example, deployed the Olympic gold medallist Mary Peters and the veteran peace activist Sadie Patterson. While Peters embodied youthful vigour, Patterson offered a more reassuring figure for older voters, expounding on the merits of the Community while pouring tea from a pot. Betty Boothroyd canvassed factory girls in the Midlands, while Lynda Chalker and Baroness Young addressed meetings of Conservative women. The campaign also mobilised columnists and broadcasters, such as the religious writer Barbara Ward Jackson and the *Daily Mirror*'s celebrated agony aunt, Marjorie Proops.

It was particularly important to appeal to working-class women, who were less susceptible to the middle-class sociability of the Townswomen's Guilds or Women's Institutes. Labour activists were crucial here, such as the MP for West Bromwich West and future Speaker of the House of Commons, Betty Boothroyd. Boothroyd's internationalism was not purely European: she had worked on John F. Kennedy's presidential campaign in 1960 and spent two years as an assistant to the Republican congressman Silvio Conte. Yet Europe had always been central to her politics. She was close to the Labour MP Geoffrey de Freitas, who had served as president of the Council of Europe, and she described Shirley Williams as her political 'heroine'. Outside the Community, she feared, Britain would decline into a low-skill, low-wage economy, reduced to 'taking in the world's washing'. She also looked to the Common Market to champion consumer rights, her other political passion and the subject of her maiden speech in Parliament. As a Member of the European Parliament, she would later gain a reputation as 'the housewives' champion of Europe'.[47]

Boothroyd focused her efforts on factory workers. In textile districts, in particular, working-class women were usually in paid employment, and Boothroyd had made a point of canvassing them in the workplace. Having driven to the factory gates before opening time, she would greet the women as they arrived before joining them for a discussion over their mid-morning tea-break. She also persuaded Chambers of Commerce to arrange lunchtime meetings in the canteen, at which she and other women could speak.[48] Boothroyd was particularly anxious that the campaign should address women as workers, not simply as wives and mothers. As she impressed upon Lady Avebury, this was especially vital in the Midlands, Yorkshire and Lancashire, where factory work was commonplace.[49]

Quick-witted and an impressive speaker, Boothroyd became a familiar figure at meetings, facing off against No campaigners such as John Prescott and Richard Body. Speaking at organisations like the Nottinghamshire Federation of Women's Guilds, she found the women 'interested in all matters, especially food, social services, jobs – *they* recognized the question of [the] third world – asked intelligent questions and were mainly pro-Europe needing only a push'. In particular, the women 'responded to the bit about *their responsibility* in deciding their children & *grandchildren's* future'.[50]

'MARKET MOTHERS'

The need to establish new campaign vehicles, outside the confines of the established parties, created new opportunities for women in regional and municipal organisations. Elizabeth Ward, for example, became a regional organiser for BIE, with responsibility for Berkshire, Buckinghamshire and Oxfordshire. In this role, she set up twelve local campaigning groups in provincial towns and co-ordinated a network of speakers, canvassers and activists. Politics was not a new arena for Ward – her husband, Christopher, had briefly been a Conservative MP – but the referendum established her as a political figure in her own right. In the words of the *Sunday Telegraph*: 'Having been hanging on to her husband's shirt tails for the past 10 years, she now … has a job of her own with a salary of £250 a month.' 'Letters come in and they're for *me*,' she told the paper, 'which is super.'

Likewise, Caroline Neill became an activist for the No campaign, organising meetings and writing a pamphlet on the judicial implications of entry. She, too, was from a political family: her father, Sir Piers Debenham, had fought a by-election in 1962 as an 'anti-EEC' candidate, while her husband, Patrick, chaired the Bar Council. Yet she now found herself for the first time at the centre of the action. Evicting her six children from the top floor of their Chelsea home, she set up her own 'think tank', with the floorboards groaning under the weight of pamphlets, leaflets and correspondence.[51]

Such women attracted a great deal of attention from the press, but their activities were narrated in distinctly conservative terms. A profile of Caroline Neill and Elizabeth Ward, for example, was headlined 'Market Mothers', and placed particular emphasis on the domestic sacrifices imposed by the referendum. Their campaigning activities were taken to be a temporary, and regrettable, suspension of their domestic duties. As the *Sunday Telegraph* told its readers, Ward had

> cut out dinner parties, coffee mornings, stopped short her plans to go to French classes, and put away her embroidery ('that was heartbreaking'). Now she gets up earlier, at seven, sees the children off to school, and has her immediate chores done by 9 a.m.

Neill, likewise, had been compelled to banish her children from the study, an observation that would not have been made of a male activist. In a trope that would become wearily familiar to Margaret Thatcher, journalists tended to explain these women's politics by reference to their husbands and fathers. The *Sunday Telegraph*, for example, simply took for granted that Neill's barrister husband had supplied 'her knowledge of the British constitution and the leaflet she has produced'.[52]

This media interest gave women a platform from which to speak on the referendum, but it also stereotyped them within a set of conventional gender roles. The *South Wales Echo*, for example, ran a feature on 'Women who have made up their minds', which focused on the pro-Marketeer, Carol Cobert, and the No campaigner, Margaret Leonard. The article was presented as an insight into how 'housewives' viewed the Common Market, though Leonard was a successful businesswoman, while Cobert had worked as a full-time trade union official and was now employed by her local housing authority. Questioned on her reasons for voting Yes, Cobert began by discussing the prospects for international relations, prosperity and job security; but she was pressed by the paper on the 'positive benefits to women'. She replied by noting the higher level of family allowances in France and Belgium, together with the Community's commitment to equal pay and improved facilities for married women at work. Leonard told the paper that 'I don't know much about the status of women in the EEC,' but speculated that higher VAT might particularly concern women.[53]

As such articles demonstrated, women were more likely to find an audience for their views if they spoke from the vantage point of the wife and mother. Not surprisingly, many did precisely that, representing their participation in the campaign as an extension of their maternal responsibilities. Elizabeth Ward claimed to have got involved because she didn't want her children 'peddling tourists' trinkets to visitors', while Caroline Neill stressed that her 'six children' gave her 'a large stake in the future'.[54] Even women with an established profile adopted a similar language. Marjorie Proops, the *Daily Mirror*'s popular agony aunt, was one of the most famous names in journalism, and her face was plastered across BIE's material. Yet she addressed her audience 'as a mother, a grandmother, a housewife and a woman'. In a feature for the *Mirror*, she posed with her grandsons under the headline 'These are the two main reasons why I shall vote YES'. She fronted a pamphlet listing the issues that 'We women care about', identified as 'our husbands' jobs', 'our children's future', 'our own jobs' and 'the cost of living'. It was an ordering of priorities that said much about the campaign.[55]

The same theme was evident in a pamphlet on *The Housewife and the Common Market*, by the barrister and former code-breaker, Diana Elles. Elles had served as British president of the European Union of Women and, after receiving a peerage in 1972, led for the Conservative Party in the House of Lords on foreign and European affairs. As the title indicated, however, her pamphlet focused on those questions 'which affect us ... as housewives and mothers': such as 'family allowances', 'our husbands' jobs', 'the cost of living' and, 'of course, … food prices'. She also emphasised the long years of peace since 1945, for which women, 'as wives and mothers', should be especially grateful.[56]

The extent to which this language was internalised was illustrated by the Newport Business and Professional Women's Club, which held an open meeting on the European question. Such meetings were commonplace in male business organisations, but the club president, Mrs Olive Shields, emphasised her members' status as *women* rather than as *business* people. It was women, she told journalists, 'on whose shoulders the job of balancing the weekly budget falls', and women were 'perhaps more directly affected by our Common Market ties than their husbands, brothers or fathers'. Significantly, the invited speakers were all men.[57]

This was characteristic of a tendency for men and women to be allocated different roles in the debate. Women were expected to focus chiefly on food prices, women's employment and peace, while the balance of trade, sovereignty and the operation of Community institutions were viewed as men's terrain. Even Margaret Thatcher focused mainly on issues like food prices and the cost of living. Strikingly, when the magazine *Woman's Own* turned to the referendum, it invited a man – the *Mirror* journalist Willy Wolff – to explain how the EEC worked. The article, which appeared in the political section edited by Deirdre Sanders, was written in almost embarrassingly condescending terms. The European question, wrote Wolff, was 'boring' but 'important'. 'It seems confusing only because those who keep on about it use words that play hide and seek with simple sense.'[58]

'THE COMMON SUPERMARKET'

Polling evidence encouraged the crafting of messages to women that privileged domestic themes. In February, 54 per cent of respondents thought that membership would be good for the next generation, while just 25 per cent thought it would be harmful. By April, the former figure had risen to 60 per cent.[59] Britain in Europe exploited this with a series of posters and newspaper adverts, depicting smiling children under the strapline: 'For their future – vote YES'.[60] An advert signed by Marjorie Proops, Katie Boyle and Eirlys Roberts was headlined 'What every mother in the country should know'. 'Think of your children,' it urged. 'Their future is more important than yours.'[61] An article in the *Mirror* portrayed a group of children from an international school in Brussels, playing together in the schoolyard. The British child, Dermott, 'stands slightly to one side, as if he's not sure whether to join in and play. Just like Britain in Europe, perhaps?' 'For the lad outside,' it urged readers, 'VOTE YES.' Anti-Market material also tapped into maternal themes. An advert in the *Labour News-sheet* portrayed a colossal child in a paddling pool, towering like Godzilla above the waters. 'He deserves the best life you can make for him,' said the paper, so 'Let's fight with *both* hands.'[62]

Polling also defined a second key battleground: the prospects for the housewife confronted with an increasingly strained household budget. In the inflationary climate of the 1970s, the cost of living was a serious concern for any family on a fixed income. Polling showed consistently that, of all the issues cited by opponents of membership, 'much the most important is prices, particularly food prices'.[63] Despite compelling evidence that men also ate and drank, the cost of food was presented almost exclusively as a *woman's* issue. Britain in Europe, for example, claimed that 'British housewives have been saved a total of £139m' in the Common Market, while Sir Henry Plumb of the National Farmers' Union insisted that membership 'had paid off "hands down" for the housewife'.[64] A broadcast for the National Referendum Campaign portrayed Eric Deakins, a junior minister at the Department of Trade, in conversation with a group of women out shopping (helpfully labelled '1st Housewife', '2nd Housewife' and so on).[65]

The housewife had been a focus of political campaign material ever since the enfranchisement of women in 1918, and canvassers were careful to flatter the canniness of the household manager.[66] Pro-Marketeers, in particular, presented the housewife as a shrewd and wise figure, too experienced in the ways of the world to fall prey to the distortions of the No campaign. Diana Elles, for example, was contemptuous of the various shopping trips organised by anti-Marketeers, designed to show how much higher prices were on the Continent. 'As the family's main shopper,' she commented,

> the housewife well knows that prices can and do vary enormously, for precisely the same article, let alone for two similar articles of different quality. She knows how the price of a packet of detergent can cost 3p or even 5p less in one store than in another down the road.

Adopting the brisk tones of the experienced housewife, she acknowledged that there would be costs to membership and that, in the short term, they would be significant. She likened this, however, to the expense incurred when a growing family moved to a larger house. Just as the wise housewife would budget for 'new curtains or hiring a van', so British business would have to absorb the short-term costs of preparing itself for more commodious living. In this way, Elles anticipated the household rhetoric later deployed by Margaret Thatcher, while simultaneously harking back to the 'Conservative feminism' of Tory electoral propaganda since the 1920s.[67]

Shopping baskets were central to one of the most audacious publicity stunts of the campaign, planned by the NRC a week before the vote. Barbara Castle, always one of the most colourful figures on the No campaign, went on a shopping trip to Brussels with Joan Marten (wife of Neil) and Castle's seven-year-old great niece, Rachel Hinton. The idea was to compare the price of goods in London and Brussels, to show how much more expensive life would become once transitional arrangements came to an end. To ensure a fair comparison,

FIGURE 6.3 Barbara Castle, her great-niece Rachel Hinton and Joan Marten show off the results of their shopping trip to Brussels.

Source: Keystone, Hulton Archive: www.gettyimages.co.uk/license/3260793

they visited the Marks & Spencer stores in London and Brussels, buying as nearly as possible the same items. At a press conference the next day, Castle showed off her two baskets, showing how goods costing £4.24 in London had come to £6.92½ in Brussels – a difference of 'more than 64 per cent'.[68]

Unfortunately for Castle, BIE got wind of the operation – possibly from an informer inside the NRC – and despatched an activist called Vicki Crankshaw, who spoke Norwegian, on her own trip to Oslo. By demonstrating that prices were even higher in a country outside the Community – and one that was often held up as the *desideratum* of the anti-Marketeers – they hoped to discredit the comparison with Brussels. Unaware that she was being gazumped, Castle waited a day before revealing her purchases, allowing BIE to hold its own press conference first. Under the visibly unenthusiastic eye of Roy Jenkins, who had probably never purchased such items in his life, Crankshaw unloaded tins of beans and instant coffee that had cost almost twice as much in Oslo as in London.[69]

FIGURE 6.4 The 'blond and vivacious' Vicki Crankshaw shows off the results of her own shopping trip to Oslo.

Source: Evening Standard, Hulton Archive: www.gettyimages.co.uk/license/2638474

FIGURE 6.5   Roy Jenkins radiates enthusiasm.
Source: Rolls Press/Popperfoto: www.gettyimages.co.uk/license/80751456

The message of the BIE event – that prices were just as high outside the Market – was less important than its success in stealing the initiative from Castle. What had been envisaged by the NRC as a striking media stunt, showing at a glance the threat to prices, lost its clarity when the story became about rival shopping expeditions delivering contradictory messages. It did not help that the blond and vivacious Vicki Crankshaw, described by *The Times* as 'an attractive secretary', proved rather more interesting to journalists than the secretary of state for health and social services.[70]

EQUAL PAY

The description of Crankshaw as 'an attractive secretary' spoke volumes about the assumptions of the press. Crankshaw had a long history of political activism: she had served as an advisor to the National Council of Social Services and was secretary of the Women's European Committee. She spoke at rallies during the campaign and had published on women's employment opportunities within the Common Market. Crankshaw was impatient with the political neutrality conventionally expected of women's organisations, warning that 'when women were pressing for equality in its broadest sense, they had no right, as citizens and electors, to opt out of the major areas of conflict'. Interestingly, she had been the first choice of the European Movement as its Women's Officer, but declined the post to continue her work with the WEC.[71]

Press reports, however, routinely described her as a 'housewife' and 'working mother' (two identities that might once have been thought contradictory) and Crankshaw herself made motherhood central to her campaign. 'Speaking as a mother,' she told the Townswomen's Guild, 'I want Britain to stay in the Common Market because I do not want any more wars. I want peace, trade and jobs for our children and this is how we will get it.'[72]

In private, however, Crankshaw was uneasy with the focus on domesticity. Writing to Money-Coutts in May, she warned that women were 'interested in a great many things other than food and it would do no harm to have their other points of concern given some attention'. 'Very little seems to have been said about the social fund and all that its provisions imply', nor 'the fact that the Commission is actually trying to DO something in International Women's Year'. She urged a greater focus on the employment protections available to women as workers. There was 'no need to go overboard on the Women's Lib front (which is any way boring), but the Commission is looking realistically at women's problems, both as members of the labour force and as equal partners in the social structure'.[73]

Crankshaw's concerns were shared by the Women's Officers. Lady Avebury, in particular, was determined that women should not be treated as if they only cared about food prices and the household economy. Though under orders to tone down her own federalist commitments, she had no intention of restricting herself to what men considered 'women's issues'.[74] This had been a subject of debate at an early strategy meeting among female MPs and peeresses. Lady Gaitskell, the widow of the former Labour leader, had argued that women should be treated as a 'special group', since they 'tend to think of the Community only in shopping basket terms'. By contrast, the Labour peer and former editor of *Nova*, Baroness Birk, was anxious to move beyond so-called 'women's issues' and 'the economics of the stomach'. Instead, she wanted a more pluralistic campaign, in which issues of interest to both sexes were made relevant to women. Concerns about sovereignty, she suggested, could be portrayed as 'as an expression of male chauvinist pride', while the campaign should play up Britain's capacity to lead in Europe. 'National pride is, after all, not the monopoly of men.'[75]

Avebury had hoped to interest the organised feminist movement in the campaign, but the response was distinctly frosty. 'Radical' feminists largely ignored the referendum, viewing it as a distraction from more pressing debates about marriage, patriarchy and the family. 'Socialist' feminists also paid little attention, though they tended to share the broader socialist critique of the Common Market. *Spare Rib* published only one substantial comment on the referendum, which was written by the left-wing economist Jean Gardiner. Taking a conventional left-wing position, Gardiner castigated the EEC as a vehicle for 'large multinational firms', which wanted to drive down wages and slow the advance of 'left labour policies'. If the oppression of women was rooted in the power structures of capitalism, the Community seemed to have little to offer but subordination on a continental scale.[76]

The indifference of the Women's Liberation Movement was in some respects surprising. Women's Liberation had always been conceived in transnational terms, for the struggle against unequal pay, discrimination in the workplace, oppressive marriage laws and patriarchal cultural systems clearly transcended national boundaries. As pro-Marketeers never tired of observing, the principle of 'equal pay for equal work' had been written into the founding documents of the EEC, forming Article 119 of the Treaty of Rome. Women's organisations on the Continent had played an important role, both in the drafting of Article 119 and in the struggle to enforce its application.

Pro-Marketeers made much of the Community's work in this field. In February 1975, after extensive and co-ordinated pressure, the Commission had issued a landmark directive clarifying that equal pay should be given not only for the *same* work but for work 'of equal value' – a way of tackling the tendency for men and women to do different kinds of work within a single organisation.[77] The directive required national governments to prepare legislation in accordance with that principle, an initiative that would lead – after a court case against the UK government – to the 1983 Equal Pay (Amendment) Regulations.[78] (In a curious twist of fate, the regulations were put before the House by the notorious womaniser Alan Clark, an unlikely champion of equal pay. Arriving in Parliament after a spectacularly boozy dinner, Clark made little secret either of his inebriation or of his contempt for the measure he was introducing. When challenged, he breezily informed MPs that 'a certain separation between expressed and implied beliefs is endemic among those who hold office'.)[79]

Article 119 and the 1975 Directive were hailed by pro-Marketeers, not only as a symbol of the Community's commitment to equality, but as a legally enforceable right that gave women a weapon in the courts. Campaigners assured women that 'The Common Market leads the way on equal pay for equal work, better training, and child care facilities for working mothers. Community funds already pay for women over 35 to train for new jobs, and to brush up their old skills.'[80] A pamphlet distributed to speakers reported that the Commission was already pursuing further initiatives, particularly with reference to the male-dominated professions. Over the coming year, wrote Ann Money-Coutts, the Commission would table proposals 'to eliminate all remaining discriminations still existing in the labour market, in training facilities and in promotion prospects in the professions'. The result would be 'a "Magna Carta" of women's demands', bringing new freedoms to women in the workplace.[81]

The campaign also emphasised the prospects for part-time workers, who made up roughly a third of the female workforce. Briefing notes issued by the Women's Section laid particular emphasis on the right to flexible working hours for women with young children. 'Objectives high on the Community's priority list', it was claimed, included greater freedom of choice for women in the labour market; recognition of 'the social dimension of maternity', so that women could 'reconcile their family responsibilities with their professional obligations'; better social security against illness, maternity and disability; and more robust mechanisms for challenging discrimination'.[82]

Like other distressed areas, women voters were also to be enticed by the riches of the European social fund. At the time of the referendum, the Commission reported, it had not received a single application to support women's employment, so governments were encouraged to submit formal proposals for 'integrated programmes ... where training and re-training for women workers can be co-ordinated with information campaigns, child care facilities and job improvement schemes'. The *Star*'s women's magazine reported that Europe would fund 'training schemes for women over the age of 35 who want to go back into employment: for young workers of both sexes below the age of 25; for special projects aimed specifically at increasing opportunities for women's employment'.[83]

One of the more curious publications of the period was *The How and Why Wonder Book of the Common Market*, part of a series of popular children's books whose other titles covered such topics as *Dogs*, *Dinosaurs* and *Primitive Man*. Written with no pretence at impartiality and a distinctly uneasy grasp of British history, it represented the Community as a defence against the shirking of parental responsibilities by men:

> One of the best results of the Market is that it is now no longer possible for people to run away from their responsibilities toward home and family simply by crossing a frontier. A poor Irish woman who was left with two children discovered that her husband had a good, well-paid job in Germany. In the old days she would still have been helpless. Under Common Market rules, her husband in Germany must contribute to her support; and if he does not, a German judge will see that the money is stopped from his pay cheque in Germany to do so. 'Thank God for the Common Market', she said when a British social worker told her the news.[84]

Appealing to a similar demographic, Avebury penned an article for Gingerbread, the charity for single-parent families, the vast majority of which were headed by women. Britain, she noted, was the only country in the EEC that did not pay family allowances for all first children. With its commitment to 'a common social policy', she argued, the EEC would bring the UK up to the level of other states and 'eradicate those pockets of real need still to be found in Britain'. Working parents would also benefit from the commitment to equal pay, flexible working hours and 'the reconciliation of women's dual role as contributors to economic life, and as potential wives and mothers'.[85]

CONCLUSION

By the time the campaign entered its final week, the gender gap identified by the polls had all but disappeared. A poll in the *Birmingham Post* found women in favour of membership by 54 per cent to 28 per cent, only slightly lower than the 60:30 split among men. A poll for the *Sun* found that women's support had risen from 53 per cent to 58 per cent in the last week of May alone. The number of 'Don't Knows' remained higher among women, but the prospect of a female No vote had ceased to be a political reality.[86]

There is no single explanation for the failure of the No campaign to capitalise on its early lead among women. Female voters made their decision for as many and as diverse reasons as men. Nonetheless, it is striking how little effort was made by the anti-Marketeers to speak directly to women voters. In an intelligence report on the anti-Market campaign, written at the end of March, Diana Villiers noted that neither the Common Market Safeguards Committee nor the Get Britain Out Referendum Campaign had produced a single pamphlet addressed specifically to women. Nor were there any significant women's groups associated with the No campaign. The most promising outlet, 'Women Against the Common Market' (WACM), had peaked in the years before entry and never recovered from the early death of its founder, Anne Kerr, in 1973. Kerr had won Rochester and Chatham for the Labour Party in 1964 and 1966, and was a well-known campaigner for racial equality. In the early seventies, she masterminded a series of eye-catching events, collecting money in shopping baskets and handing out bags labelled 'No Common Market' to shoppers, as well as lobbying MPs in the House of Commons.[87] Her loss deprived the No campaign of a charismatic figurehead, and there is no evidence that the organisation was still active by 1975. By the time of the referendum, the press officers for Get Britain Out were unable even to find a postal address.[88]

The Common Market Safeguards Campaign recognised the scale of Kerr's loss, but made little effort to compensate. The Labour MP Renée Short volunteered to write to women's organisations in 1973, but despite tempting readers with a copy of *Resistance News* and a pamphlet on *Why Meat is Dear*, received only four replies and no orders for literature. Rather than revise its approach, the committee decided that 'the formation of a new [women's] organization was not a practical proposition'.[89] In consequence, the No campaign lacked any institutional mechanism for targeting women voters.

The most vocal women's group to campaign against membership was the British League of Housewives, founded by Irene Lovelock in 1945. The League had been a significant force in the post-war era, but by the 1970s it had dwindled into a somewhat cranky entity preoccupied by solidarity with the white colonies, resistance to Marxism and an enthusiasm verging on mania for the white government in Rhodesia. The League's campaign focused on the inflationary consequences of entry, the threat to sovereignty and the loosening of ties with the Commonwealth. Its rhetoric was unapologetically inflammatory – describing the EEC as 'a totalitarian regime' and likening pro-Marketeers to Goebbels – but its impact was minimal.[90] Ward described it cheerfully as 'another nut's group!' while Boothroyd had seemed unaware a year earlier that the organisation still existed.[91]

By contrast, the Women's Section of BIE had been active, savvy and able to call on the services of a wide range of popular and respected women. It had produced well-targeted literature, distributed through a network of contacts with the voluntary sector, and had worked to moderate the tone of the wider organisation. In all these respects, the pro-Marketeers outperformed their opponents in their ability to target and mobilise women voters. Yet they struggled to move beyond conventional gender stereotypes, which privileged maternal and domestic expressions of women's political identity.

All this posed a challenge to the Women's Liberation Movement, with which this chapter began. The WLM demanded new ways of thinking about politics and sexual identity; yet what is most striking about the women's campaign in 1975 was the caution and conventionality of its gender politics. The appeal to women as mothers, housewives and consumers would not have been out of place between the two world wars; nor would the campaigning techniques on display, with their reliance on women's voluntary networks and public meetings, the production of dedicated leaflets and flyers, and the use of prominent women to address female audiences.[92] From this perspective, the novelty of the referendum inspired a campaign that was remarkably conservative. That trend was almost certainly exacerbated by the need to build campaign vehicles outside the established party system, relying on networks that privileged personal engagement above the 'new' media of television and radio.

Yet there had also been voices pushing beyond the conventional gender politics of the campaign. These did not come from the WLM, which largely ignored the vote, but from working women like Crankshaw and Boothroyd, who wanted a greater focus on women's employment. This reflected significant changes in the economy, as the proportion of women in the workforce increased, as well as a prescient sense of the EEC's potential to influence the labour market. Avebury's appeal to single mothers was also striking, identifying a cohort that would grow in importance during the 1980s.[93]

Reflecting on the campaign shortly after its end, Avebury and Money-Coutts hoped that 'there was some correlation between our activities and the final result on June 5th'. Given the unusually large swing among women voters, this was almost certainly the case. Yet they stressed, too, that the impact of the Women's Section should not be measured simply in terms of votes cast. 'In retrospect', they wrote, 'we feel that our main success was in getting more women involved in the Campaign, both at national and local level – in "humanizing" some of the issues, and broadening the scope beyond bread and butter arguments.'[94] Thanks in large part to their efforts, BIE had not simply approached women as an external voting bloc; it had created new opportunities for women's political participation and ensured that women's voices were heard at the highest levels of the campaign. At a time when women's roles were so dramatically in flux – when attitudes to the family and to paid work were evolving so rapidly, and when feminist movements were opening up such new and challenging forms of political discourse – it is no surprise that the messages generated by the campaign were sometimes mixed. In the 'International Year of Women', however, it was only fitting that a debate about Britain's place in the world should have provided such a vibrant forum for the discussion of women's politics.

7 'COME TO PRAY ON REFERENDUM DAY'

We pray thee, Father, that as our nation comes to make its great decision at the referendum, the minds of all may be enlightened to choose for Britain, for Europe, and for all mankind.

Prayer for use on 'Referendum Sunday', 1 June 1975[1]

What is God saying as we stand on the threshold of voting for or against a united Europe? Does He want division and isolationism, or is He beckoning us to take one more painful step toward a united world?

Methodist Recorder, 6 March 1975[2]

Except the Lord build the house, they labour in vain that build it.

Psalm 127[3]

Early in the morning on 5 June, as the polls opened for the referendum, worshippers from across Europe gathered in the small town of Crediton in Devon. They had come to mark the feast of St Boniface, the local saint martyred on that day in 754. For Christian pro-Marketeers, the timing was 'an auspicious coincidence'. Born Winfrid or Wynfryth, Boniface was an Anglo-Saxon monk who had carried the Gospel across the Frankish Empire, becoming Archbishop of Mainz and 'Apostle to the Germans'. As a Christian, an Anglo-Saxon and a European, Boniface was both 'one of the most European-minded Englishmen that has ever lived' and 'one of the main architects of the socio-political order in medieval Europe'. For the Catholic newspaper the *Tablet*, the life of Boniface drew a clear moral for the referendum: Christians must 'take their European citizenship no less seriously than their national citizenship'.[4]

It was not just the cult of St Boniface that was enthused by the cause of European unity. The mainstream churches threw themselves energetically into the referendum campaign, almost invariably in support of membership. An ecumenical alliance called 'Christians for Europe' claimed the active support of a quarter of all clergy, issuing prayers, Bible readings and study notes for the use of church reading groups. Parish magazines carried articles on the case for the Common Market, and it was estimated that a quarter of all churches held special services on or close to referendum day. The General Synod and the British Council of Churches both endorsed membership, while senior churchmen campaigned directly from the pulpit. In a breach of electoral protocol, a majority of bishops publicly backed the Yes campaign, with the Bishop of Manchester, Patrick Rodger, confessing himself at a loss to understand 'how any sane person could vote for Britain's withdrawal'.[5]

The 1970s was a difficult decade for all the mainstream Christian denominations, as congregations dwindled, the status of the clergy declined and inflation eroded the churches' financial resources. Yet this was also a decade of new promise, with a more socially active episcopate and radical initiatives in the missionary and industrial fields. There was a flourishing ecumenical movement, which strove for reunion between the churches, as well as a growing commitment to Third World aid. For a church dedicated to Christian reunion, peace and the redress of poverty, the promise of Europe went far beyond trade or political co-operation, offering an inspiriting new field for Christian mission.

Yet the work of 'Christians for Europe' is not simply an episode in church history. For all the talk of 'secularisation' – a word that was just entering common usage – the churches remained one of the largest networks of voluntary organisations in the country.[6] The Office for National Statistics calculated in 1970 that almost 9.3 million people were active in one of the mainstream Trinitarian churches. This was roughly equivalent to the combined populations of Scotland, Wales and Northern Ireland, and three times the aggregate membership of the main political parties.[7] The churches had a reach, an authority and a presence in local communities that few organisations could match. Clergy remained significant local figures, who were deliberately cultivated by the European Movement as opinion formers.[8] In a campaign dominated by apocalyptic prognostications, the churches provided one of the more idealistic contributions to the referendum debate. In so doing, they provided some defence against claims that the European movement was either excessively materialistic – lining the pockets of capitalists at the expense of ordinary workers – or that it lacked faith in Britain's future.

Britain in Europe had no monopoly on Christian support, and plenty of churchgoers voted No on 5 June. Yet the churches as institutions lined up overwhelmingly behind membership, while those Christians who took a different view rarely articulated their position in religious terms. Outside Northern Ireland, the subject of a separate chapter, only a handful of evangelical sects and Presbyterian churches came out openly against membership. Despite the efforts of the Christian Socialist Movement and groups like 'Catholics and Anglicans Against the Common Market', Christian commentary on the referendum campaign was overwhelmingly and noisily pro-Market.

This chapter seeks to write the churches back into the history of Britain and Europe, by exploring Christian commentary and activism during the referendum. It begins by outlining the activity of the churches and the formation of 'Christians for Europe'. It then explores the motives for Christian activism and the religious case for membership. The chapter concludes by looking briefly at the opposition to membership and at the religious legacy of the campaign.

'CHRISTIANS FOR EUROPE'

Christian Europeanism had a long pedigree. At the time of Britain's first application, in 1961, churchmen from all denominations had signed a declaration of support for membership. Signatories included J.C. Wand, former Bishop of London and Dean of St Paul's; the Catholic social reformer, Lord Longford; the former president of the Methodist Conference, Donald Soper; the Jesuit and popular theologian, Father Thomas Corbishley; and the president of the Church Missionary Society, Sir Kenneth Grubb. In 1967, the year of Britain's second application, the British Council of Churches published *Christians and the Common Market*, which hailed a 'congruence of Christian and federalist insights'. Its findings were reprinted in 1971, in a pamphlet by the chairman of the BCC's International Affairs Department, Kenneth Johnstone. (His work, he later boasted, 'lined the waste-paper baskets of the parish clergy of every major denomination in the British Isles'.) Membership was endorsed by both the General Synod of the Church of England and by the bishops in the House of Lords. When entry was finally achieved, on New Year's Day in 1973, a special service was held at Coventry Cathedral, at which the flags of the member states were dedicated on the altar.[9]

For the churches, entry was only the start of a new relationship with the Community, in which they sought to translate to the European arena their traditional 'witness at national level'.[10] To help their congregations to prepare for membership, the BCC issued a study kit in 1972 on *Going into Europe*, which included prayers and Bible readings to be used in discussion groups.[11] In 1974, an ecumenical conference at Roehampton brought together nearly 150 representatives of churches across western Europe. Hosted by Tom Corbishley and Noel Salter, the international secretary of the British Council of Churches, its report on *Christians and the European Community* ranged widely across the social, political and economic ramifications of membership.[12] It was agreed to establish a task force in Brussels to campaign on international aid and development (which became the European Ecumenical Commission for Overseas Development) and to create a permanent organisation in Britain, tasked with co-ordinating Christian activity within the Community.[13]

The decision to hold a referendum, with the possibility that Britain might leave the Community, required a sudden change of focus. For the first time since the early sixties, Christian pro-Marketeers were forced to evangelise for the *principle* of membership, rather than discussing how to exploit its opportunities. To this end, the Jesuit church at Farm Street, Mayfair, hosted a meeting in January 1975 between leading figures from the Roehampton conference and prominent pro-Marketeers. Lord Harlech, the chairman of the European Movement, called for a 'Churches' Committee for Europe', led by the Archbishop of Canterbury, the Catholic Archbishop of Westminster and the moderators of the Free Churches. The feeling of the meeting, however, was that the churches could not, as institutions, align themselves so openly with one side of the campaign, out of respect for those in their congregations who took a different view. Yet there was enthusiasm for the idea of an expressly Christian campaign vehicle, and, at the suggestion of Tom Corbishley, the reference to 'churches' was dropped in favour of 'Christians': not '*Churches* for Europe', but '*Christians* for Europe'. The new organisation, it was agreed, should be 'independent and lively', though Hugh Wilcox, secretary of the International Affairs Department of the British Council of Churches, promised to ensure that BCC pronouncements were 'as European as possible'.[14]

'Christians for Europe' went public on St George's Day, a date chosen to support the claim that, 'inside the European Community, our nation can play a vital part in building a better world'.[15] Its president was the Bishop of Leicester, Ronald Williams, but the driving force was the secretary and former Conservative MP, John Selwyn Gummer.[16] The two had worked together on the Church of England's Board of Social Responsibility and shared an explicitly Christian commitment to European integration. In 1972, Gummer had co-authored with Noel Salter a report on *Britain in Europe: The Social Responsibility of the Church*, which was signed by Williams and subsequently approved by Synod. For Gummer, membership of the European Community offered 'an exhilarating and spirit-stretching experience'; a 'spiritual adventure' that could redraw the religious map of Europe. Christians, he insisted, should play a full part in the work of political reconstruction; for 'Except the Lord build the house, they labour in vain that build it.'[17]

Like Harlech, Gummer had wanted to establish an interdenominational Churches Council on Europe, and he set up meetings with representatives of the Presbyterian, Roman Catholic, United Reform and Methodist churches. What he had in mind was 'a ginger group of Churchmen', 'for whom the growing unity of Europe is important religiously'. He was keen to shrink the space for 'those extreme Protestant groups' who viewed the Community 'as the work of the Pope!' The Free Presbyterian Church of Scotland, for example, warned of 'serious dangers' from 'the predominantly Roman Catholic nations of Europe'. In 1975, it reminded the Queen that she was bound by her coronation oath to the defence of Protestantism and rebuked the Church of Scotland for inviting a 'representative' of 'the anti-Christ' – the Catholic Archbishop Thomas Winning – to address its General Assembly.[18]

'No Popery' of this kind was a minority taste, but it had proven effective in the recent Norwegian referendum. Gummer was determined to shut that option down, by ensuring that the mainstream churches of all denominations were at the forefront of the Yes campaign. The evangelical churches of Scotland, Wales and Northern Ireland, he noted, would need particular work.[19]

As well as shrinking the space for ultra-Protestantism, Gummer identified three main functions for the group. First, it should 'alert the churches to the importance of Europe', persuading voters that the EEC was 'a fit concern for their prayers'. The churches 'should feel that just as they are concerned to pray for the Queen and her Government, so too ... we should commend the Community for God's blessing'. To this end, prayers and study packs should be commissioned and speakers organised. Gummer hoped to assemble 'a group of church people for whom the growing unity of Europe is important religiously', and he undertook to find MPs who could speak and recruit in their dioceses.[20]

Second, the churches should aim to raise the level of debate. Pro-Market churchmen, like Patrick Rodger, the Bishop of Manchester, feared that, without a strong lead from the churches, the 'great vision' of European brotherhood might 'be lost for fear of the price of sugar or of occasionally having to speak in a foreign language'.[21] By focusing on the spiritual dimensions of membership, the campaign should 'stimulate the Churches to put Europe on their agenda', elevating the discussion 'to a level more in keeping with the importance of the issue'.[22]

Third, the organisation should co-ordinate the churches' activities in the coming referendum. It aimed to insert material into every parish magazine and every Church publication, issuing fact sheets and newspaper articles to build a Christian momentum behind a Yes vote.[23] This would require active direction from the centre, helped by a grant of £1,500 from Britain in Europe.[24]

The decision to hold a referendum was not popular with the churches. The Bishop of London, Gerald Ellison, thought it 'deplorable', while the Bishop of Peterborough, Douglas Feaver, asked how a nation could be 'quietly and godly governed by mass opinion poll'.[25] Yet once the decision had been taken, churchmen threw themselves into the campaign with gusto. An official prayer was commissioned and published in the religious press: 'We pray thee, Father, that as our nation comes to make its great decision at the referendum, the minds of all may be enlightened to choose for Britain, for Europe, and for all mankind.'[26] A letter signed by Ronald Williams, Tom Corbishley and Alan Booth, the director of Christian Aid, was sent to all clergy, requesting their personal commitment and prayer for the European cause.[27] Cathedrals hosted seminars on the Christian approach to Europe, while the Evangelical Alliance urged Christians to set aside time on 'Referendum Sunday', to pray and prepare themselves spiritually.[28] 'Christians for Europe' sent out 25,000 mailshots, eliciting 4,000 mostly favourable replies. Voters in London were urged to 'come to pray on Referendum Day', at a special service at St Paul's Portman Square.[29] In Scotland, and possibly elsewhere, clergy acted as informants for Britain in Europe, reporting on anti-Market activity in their parishes.[30]

There was strong support from the Anglican episcopate. The bishops of Carlisle, Chichester, Leicester, London, Manchester, Monmouth, Peterborough, Truro and Worcester all spoke in favour of membership, either from the pulpit or in diocesan synods and newsletters. On 17 April, the Methodist Board of Social Responsibility unanimously approved a resolution endorsing membership, on the grounds of peace, development and the wider national interest.[31] Less than a week later, on 23 April, the General Assembly of the British Council of Churches passed *nem. con.* a resolution hailing membership 'as an opportunity for Christians to work for the ... reconciliation of Europe's enmities, the responsible stewardship of Europe's resources and the enrichment of Europe's contribution to the rest of mankind'. A further resolution, hoping that the referendum would produce 'a substantial majority' for membership, passed with just two dissentients.[32]

'WEEP FOR JERUSALEM'

This ecclesiastical activism did not go unchallenged. Neil Marten acknowledged the right of the churches to campaign, but deplored 'the unfortunate title "Christians for Europe"'. The implication that 'if you are against "Europe", you are not a Christian', he claimed, 'has caused distress to many', and he urged the Archbishop to find 'a more tactful title'.[33] Enoch Powell went further, dismissing the possibility of a Christian perspective. Had not Christ Himself urged the Apostles to 'render unto Caesar the things that are Caesar's; and unto God, the things that are God's'?[34] In one of the more unlikely counterfactuals of the campaign, he invited readers to imagine the disciples asking Jesus whether the United Kingdom should be part of the Common Market:

> Imagine the scorn with which Christ would have responded to such an inquiry! 'What', he would have asked, '*is* the United Kingdom, and what have I to do with it? My Kingdom is not of this world'.[35]

Powell's religious thought was complex and idiosyncratic. Having lost his faith as a young man, he had re-entered the Church of England after a mystical religious experience. He identified as a Christian for the rest of his life, but wrote a radical critique of Matthew's Gospel that disputed the crucifixion.[36] Powell's ecclesiology was national, rather than strictly theological; he treasured the established church chiefly as an

English institution, which served as a repository for the collective memory of its people. For Powell, the Church of England was defined less by its theology than by its constitutional position; it was 'that Church of which the supreme governor on earth is the Crown of the United Kingdom', and it served – like Parliament and the Common Law – as a 'refuge' against the claims of any authority 'extraneous to this realm'.[37]

If Powell's ecclesiology was national and constitutional, his theology was mystical and other-worldly, with little space for the concerns of secular politics. In this, however, he was at odds with the dominant tendencies of the post-war churches, which increasingly prized internationalism, social activism and political engagement over ceremonial or traditional forms of worship. At his enthronement as Archbishop of Canterbury in 1961, Michael Ramsey had commissioned the Church 'to penetrate the world of industry, of science, of art and literature'.[38] There could be no simple division between the sacred and the profane for a church of 'the Word made flesh'. Writing in the *Church Times* in 1971, Canon Barney Milligan declared that 'God is involved in how we spend our money and organize our trade, just as much as he is in how we teach our children or heal the sick.'[39] In similar vein, the Roman Catholic newsletter *Comment* told readers that 'To be concerned with politics is to be concerned with man', quoting Pope Paul VI's address to the diplomatic corps in 1967:

> The Church cannot remove herself from temporal affairs, because the temporal is the activity of men, and all that concerns men concerns the church. A disembodied church, separated from the world, would no longer be the church of Jesus Christ, the Church of the incarnate Word.[40]

The influential Methodist minister and principal of the Luton Industrial College, William Gowland, invoked the memory of Dietrich Bonhoeffer, the German theologian who was executed by the Nazis. Bonhoeffer had died, argued Gowland, precisely because he refused to accept 'that religion was to be confined to saying innocuous prayers, preaching smooth ineffective sermons, and confining its activity to its own parochial organization'. Christians should do no less in his memory.[41]

This conviction that the church should be engaged in the secular world ran like an electric current through Christian commentary on the referendum. The writer and clergyman David Edwards, a former general secretary of the Student Christian Movement and chaplain to the Speaker of the House of Commons, challenged Powell directly in the pages of the *Church Times*. The Church, he insisted, 'cannot be indifferent to the fate of a nation with which its own fortunes have been bound up so intimately for so long'. Powell, he wrote, could 'only imagine Christ as saying: "What is the United Kingdom?" – and presumably "What is Europe?" too. We know a Christ who weeps over Jerusalem: and that is why the Christian cares.'[42]

Edwards was a radical who wanted to collapse the divide between 'the Church' and 'the World', and was famous for having published John Robinson's controversial book *Honest to God* in 1963.[43] Yet his conviction that the church should be on the front line of the referendum debate was entirely orthodox. The Bishop of Monmouth, Derrick Childs, wrote in his diocesan newsletter that the European question was of 'deep spiritual significance', while the *Methodist Recorder* identified 'deep theological issues' in the relationship between Britain and Europe.[44] The British Council of Churches had urged its members in 1967 to view the European issue as a religious question, 'in obedience to our Lord's Prayer: "Thy will be *done on earth*, as it is in heaven"'.[45]

'GOD IS FOR EUROPE'[46]

The Christian case for integration rested on four principal foundations: Christian internationalism; ecumenism; peace-making; and anti-communism. Christian internationalism meant a commitment to the worldwide fellowship of the Church. Even those that catered, like the Church of England or the Kirk, to an explicitly national community saw themselves as part of a larger body that transcended the bounds of any one state. The Church, wrote William Gowland, was 'by nature ... supernatural', with a vocation 'to cross all barriers and to remove all obstacles which militate against the building of new communities'.[47]

For this reason, many churchmen were predisposed to the European Community from the outset, as an institution that could build bridges across borders. In a pamphlet on *Britain and Europe*, published in 1971, the Catholic Institute for International Relations insisted that 'Christians ... by definition believe in the breaking down of barriers between races'; they 'cannot but welcome the opportunities for contact with European peoples which the Common Market offers'.[48] The British Council of Churches, too, published a report on *Christians and the Common Market*, which set the European project within a larger Christian framework. 'English Christianity', it noted, was 'older than the English State'; 'it is a European, not an insular, thing'.[49]

There was particular admiration for the healing ministry of the Community, in closing the long enmity between France and Germany. As the *Church Times* put it, 'Peace between ancient adversaries, the making and development of European friendships – these are no small gains.'[50] Ronald Williams commented that an institution that 'brings to an end the threat of war' in western Europe had a Christian imperative at its heart, deserving the support of all who preached the gospel of peace.[51]

Barbara Ward Jackson, the popular Catholic writer and broadcaster, thought that the reconciliation of France and Germany might prove the first flowering of a new 'springtime of the peoples':

> if indeed it is the vocation of what was once called Christendom to carry forward this reconciliation to a wholly new kind of sharing and living in community, how can the Christians of Britain bear to be left out? We are offered another chance to build the City of Man on new foundations. Again, we must not 'pass by on the other side'.[52]

Just as the European Community had drawn together the old enemies of France and Germany, many hoped that it would act as a bridge between East and West. Gummer, in particular, hoped that a stable European Community might end the division of Germany and build stronger relations with the Eastern bloc. This had been a theme of the pamphlet he co-authored with Salter in 1972, and it recurred frequently in Christian commentary.[53]

Internationalism was also a theme in the Jewish press. The *Jewish Chronicle* claimed 'a specific Jewish interest' in reconciliation between peoples, for Jews were usually the 'scapegoats for national grievances'. From the Dreyfus case to the Holocaust, the Jewish people had paid a terrible price for the enmity between France and Germany. By working together, the peoples of Europe could shake off 'the inward-looking nationalism which has caused so much suffering in the past. How little in this scale of values does it matter whether we pay a few more or a few less pennies for our food!'[54]

'FOR COMMONWEALTH AND NATION'

Over the previous two centuries, even those churches most rooted in the nation had been globalised by the expansion of empire. The Anglican, Methodist and Baptist churches had established global communions across Africa, Asia and the Pacific, which were now being restructured in the wake of decolonisation. As a 'non-racial and trans-regional' organisation, the Commonwealth seemed to many churchmen to offer a new vision of Christian fellowship. Gummer and Salter thought that

> As Anglicans we have a special relationship with the Anglican Communion, so largely coterminous with what used to be coloured satisfactorily pink on older maps. As Christians we must set high store by the Commonwealth as an association which so successfully combines developed and developing nations in practical partnership, and bridges the racial chasm whose jaws gape wide to gobble up mankind.[55]

Enthusiasm for the Commonwealth was not at all incompatible with support for the European Community. On the contrary, with the problems of the 'Third World' moving rapidly up the churches' agenda, many Christians looked to the Community as a vehicle for aid and international development. Far from turning their backs on the former colonies, they saw the Common Market as a chance to build a continental aid effort that could do more for the developing world than an isolated and impoverished Britain. It is striking how many pro-Marketeers had Commonwealth or Third World links. Noel Salter had run the international department of the British Council of Churches, while Patrick Rodger, Bishop of Manchester, had been an executive secretary at the World Council of Churches and was nominated as its general secretary in 1966. Barney Milligan, who took part in the Roehampton Conference and worked for the European Ecumenical Commission in Strasburg, had links with Tanzania, Uganda and Rwanda, while Kenneth Johnstone had written reports for the British Council of Churches on South Africa and Rhodesia.[56] Such figures saw no contradiction between their commitment to the Commonwealth and their enthusiasm for European unity. In the view of the *Church of England Newspaper*, the simple 'fact that Commonwealth leaders [in] the Third World' favoured British membership was itself 'a strong reason' for voting Yes.[57]

The churches were not, of course, naive. They had worked extensively with governments and knew that the Community would not automatically play the generous, outward-looking role for which they had cast it. All institutions were susceptible to 'selfishness and sin', and an inward-looking, protectionist Europe might easily 'turn away from the Third World and its demands'.[58] It was for this reason that the churches were so keen to engage with the Community, establishing an institutional foothold from which to shape its development. As Kenneth Johnstone put it, in a document for Christian study groups:

[if] we want to prevent the Community from becoming a 'Rich Men's Club', concerned only with its own further enrichment, or if, positively, we want this wealthy Community to use its wealth to the advantage of the poorer nations, our best chance of doing so lies in having a voice in the policy-planning.[59]

With its 'world-wide contacts' and global interests, the UK seemed well placed to make the Community more outward-looking. Ronald Williams urged the government to keep 'the eyes of the whole Community lifted up to the wide horizons of the world', beating back 'any temptation to become purely a rich man's club'.[60] To mark accession, the churches had organised a 'Europe '73' campaign to demand more generous foreign aid. Patrons included Christian Aid, the Church of England Board for Social Responsibility, the United Reform Church, the Methodist Church, Oxfam, the Roman Catholic Justice and Peace Commission, the Quakers, Third World First, the Women's League for Peace and Freedom, the World Development Movement and War on Want.[61]

In a preliminary report for Britain in Europe, Gummer urged the churches to focus on Europe's trade and aid policies towards the Third World.[62] Campaigners took up the theme with alacrity. Preaching to his diocesan synod in 1975, the Bishop of Chichester, Eric Kemp, warned that the 'problems posed by global poverty and injustice could not be tackled by single nations'. Only the Community was 'in a position to make a meaningful response'.[63] Speaking at the General Synod, Williams again stressed the possibilities for aid, telling reporters that 'the EEC can make a bigger contribution to the welfare of the whole world than its nations could possibly do in their individual isolation'.[64]

The *Church Times* took up the theme in an editorial a week before the referendum. As a member of the EEC, it argued, Britain could impress on the Continent 'an outward-looking, compassionate concern for the poorer nations of the world'. Quoting the outgoing secretary-general of the Commonwealth, Arnold Smith, it predicted that continued British membership would secure 'a better economic relationship with the Third World', and reminded readers that 'most Commonwealth countries themselves are strongly in favour of a "Yes" vote'.[65] Robin Woods, Bishop of Worcester, wrote in his diocesan news-letter that Europe had brought 'benefits to our Commonwealth part-ners and others in Africa and Asia that would not have developed with us in isolation'.[66]

For this reason, the renegotiated terms of membership and the signing of the Lomé Convention in February 1975 featured prominently in the churches' campaign. The *Church Times* hailed the Convention as 'a godsend to some of the world's poorest countries' and a practical example of 'Christianity in action'.[67] Such arguments were especially prominent in Methodist commentary, which had a particular tradition of development work in Africa. Raymond Wright, a Methodist min-ister in the East Riding, sent out 500 newsletters to his congregation, reminding them 'that a "Yes" vote would not only benefit the people of England but also the underprivileged of the developing world'. As 'a member of the EEC', Britain 'would be in a better and stronger position to get EEC countries to increase their foreign aid bills'.[68]

As all this suggests, the churches aspired to a Europe that was outward-looking, not insular; a Europe that was united to serve. For this reason, they were rarely impressed by appeals to national 'sov-ereignty'. Barbara Ward Jackson thought the concept 'blasphemous' and 'sacrilegious'. The 'nation state', she insisted, was 'not a Christian concept. No group can arrogantly claim all rights, all demands, all loy-alties in the name of its sacred sovereignty.'[69] The Bishop of London, Gerald Ellison, called sovereignty a 'heresy' that was 'essentially self-ish and inward-looking'.[70] David Edwards was equally blunt. 'For readers of the Bible,' he insisted, 'sovereignty in an absolute sense can-not be said to reside in Westminster.' 'There is only one Lord; the earth is His.'[71]

At the urging of Eric Kemp, later Bishop of Chichester, the Convocation at Canterbury had voted in 1960 that the UK should make 'such sacrifices of independence and sovereignty' as might be nec-essary 'to secure justice, peace and mutual respect between the peoples of the world'. Reminding his synod of that vote in 1975, Kemp insisted that the erosion of national sovereignty was the central 'spiritual issue' of the campaign. Only by transferring authority from the nation state could governments end 'centuries of European rivalry and attempts at domination through armed conflict'.[72]

'THE SEAMLESS GARMENT OF CHRIST'

Just as Europe promised healing between the nations, so it was hoped that it might aid reconciliation between the churches. The movement for Christian reunion had been growing throughout the century, reaching a peak in the 1960s. Reforms inaugurated by the Second Vatican Council had seemed, for the first time in centuries, to open up the prospect of healing between Catholics and Protestants. In 1960 the Archbishop of Canterbury, Geoffrey Fisher, had paid a historic visit to Rome, becoming the first Archbishop since the Reformation to meet formally with the Pope. His successor, Michael Ramsey, returned to Rome in 1966, issuing a 'Common Statement' with Pope Paul VI that pledged the two churches to work to 're-establish unity'. The result was an Anglo-Roman Catholic International Commission (ARCIC), which issued agreed statements on the Eucharist in 1971 and ordination in 1973.[73] In Britain, the once hostile relations between the Anglican and Dissenting churches had been transformed. Though talks aimed at reunion between the Anglican and Methodist churches had failed in 1972, co-operation at a local level continued to flourish.[74] The movement for Christian union drew strength from the challenge of 'godless' ideologies, ranging from Marxism and Nazism to consumerism and atheism. In the face of communism, in particular, the doctrinal differences between churches came to seem less important than the things they held in common.

There was a clear overlap between support for the ecumenical movement and the campaign for European unity.[75] Bishop Kemp, for example, served as the Archbishop's special representative to the Old Catholics and Roman Catholics of Europe and had played a leading role in the discussions on Anglican–Methodist reunion. He organised a special service to celebrate British entry in 1973, and campaigned alongside Lord Hailsham during the referendum. Patrick Rodger, of Manchester, had worked at the World Council of Churches in the 1960s and was briefly nominated as its general secretary. After the failure of the Anglican–Methodist talks in 1972, he chaired the Churches'

Unity Commission, which sought closer relations between Anglicans, Methodists and the United Reform Church. He subsequently became president of the Conference of European Churches, combining his twin enthusiasms for European and Christian reunion. Noel Salter had moved throughout his career between the diplomatic service and the World Council of Churches, while Michael Marshall, vicar of All Saints Margaret Street and an active member of Christians for Europe, combined his Anglican orders with service as a Benedictine oblate. Marshall would later baptise Gummer's son, Benedict, whose namesake had recently been proclaimed by the Pope as patron saint of Europe.

Just as Heath and Jenkins saw in the Community an antidote to the 'Little Englander' mentality in politics, so Ronald Williams hoped that it would overturn the 'insularity in the British religious life which followed the Reformation'. Membership of the EEC, he believed, 'gives us a wonderful opportunity to refurbish our spiritual links with the Christianity which once very largely shaped our own traditions'. More than this, it was a chance 'for the Churches of the world to come closer to each other and thus to rekindle the light of Western Christendom, on which the culture and ideals of Europe have for so long been built'.[76] Gummer, too, looked to political integration to spur a new religious reconciliation. Just as 'events in the 16th Century tended towards dividing the Church', he hoped, so '20th Century political pressures may help to bring us together'.[77]

There was, of course, no inherent reason why co-operation between the churches required political or economic integration. Nonetheless, churchmen saw in the two movements a common commitment to healing and reconciliation. Like co-operation between states, ecumenism was seen to have gained in urgency from the devastation of the Second World War. At the first meeting of the World Council of Churches in Amsterdam in 1948 – just three months after the Hague Conference that founded the European Movement – participants had dwelt explicitly on the legacies of war:

> The Church carries a large share of responsibility for MAN's DISORDER ... If the churches had been faithful to their commission from Christ ... humanity might not have come to its present extremity. On the contrary, MAN's DISORDER finds its most pointed expression in the disorder of the Church itself.[78]

This was a theme developed in the 1967 BCC report on *Christians and the Common Market*:

> In the minds of the rest of the world, Europe is still identified as the home of Christianity. To Christians, therefore, secular disunity and strife in Europe must be particularly scandalous. ... It is precisely because we are committed to universal reconciliation, that reconciliation with our neighbours is our first duty.[79]

Bishop Rodger drew an express link between the reconciliation of nations in the European Community and the healing of sectarian divides between the churches. 'The isolationists', he wrote, 'have got it wrong. The future of these islands, like the future of our own Church, cannot lie in self-sufficiency, but in giving and receiving internationally and ecumenically.'[80]

For many churchmen, there was something chastening about the spectacle of politicians outstripping the church in the work of healing. As Gowland asked his readers, 'What a judgement will descend upon us if we permit the continuation of a disunited Church in a united Europe. In helping to unify Europe, the Church itself can become more united.'[81] The EEC, from this perspective, was less a political and economic project than a beating of swords into ploughshares, a vision of brotherhood that challenged the churches to respond. As the Bishop of Monmouth, Derrick Childs, told his diocese, it was 'surely inconceivable' that Christians could 'be blindly content to withdraw into an isolation which would be cultural and spiritual as well as economic and political'.[82]

COLD WAR CHRISTIANS

If ecumenical appeals were idealistic and visionary, the churches' thinking on Europe could also have a harder edge. Like many politicians, the churches hoped that membership would curb inflation, which was biting deep into their finances. Others saw the Community as a security against communism and as a bulwark against Soviet penetration. A parish priest in Swansea warned that Britain must become either 'a partner in Europe, or a satellite of Russia', in which case 'every effort will be made to stamp out Christianity in this country'.[83]

The association between communism and atheism, together with the persecution of Christians behind the Iron Curtain, encouraged a streak of anti-communism across all denominations.[84] The Bishop of Worcester, Robin Woods, and the Bishop of Truro, Graham Leonard, both identified 'resistance to Communism as a reason for Christian support for membership'. Writing in his diocesan newsletter, Woods concluded that the 'Communist World would be strengthened by any weakening of the Common Market countries', raising 'very serious issues ... for the Christian'. Leonard, in a call for prayers across Truro, insisted that communism was 'explicitly anti-religious and anti-Christian' and that 'resistance to Communism' would be 'seriously weakened if we vote "No"'.[85] The Catholic Church had a particular history of anti-communism, sharpened by the persecution of Catholics in eastern Europe. The *Tablet* accused anti-Marketeers of 'subservience to the extreme left', noting that the Soviet Union, the Communist Party and the Labour Left all favoured withdrawal.[86]

Anti-communism was also a concern for Jewish organisations, which saw the Soviet Union as an oppressor of its own Jewish population and as a menace to the state of Israel. As the *Jewish Chronicle* noted, 'a strong Europe' could form 'a counterweight to increasing Soviet influence', at a time when 'the Soviet Union ... has been recklessly arming the Arabs against Israel'. The *Chronicle* had previously been wary of the EEC, fearing that it would block imports from Israel and restrict the ritual slaughter of animals. That changed with the signing of a trade treaty between the EEC and Israel. As the *Chronicle* put it, Israel was now 'Europe's partner', for 'Israel becomes closely associated with the countries which have previously been under heavy Arab pressure to discriminate against Israel.'[87]

Conservative elements in the churches were as concerned by the direction of the Labour Party as with the Soviet Union. Hostility to communism did not make one a Conservative – Bishop Wood, for example, explicitly endorsed Labour's 'social contract' – but many churchmen were alarmed by the prominence of the Left. *Crockford's*, the clerical directory of the Anglican Communion, had begun the year with a call to arms against the Left, while the *Church of England Newspaper* warned that the Left hoped to use the referendum 'to promote an extreme left wing form of socialism'. It 'would be well if any hope of such electoral support is dashed'. If 'Christians are anti-Marxist', the paper concluded, 'they should support an alliance that is anti-Marxist. This is a significant political point.'[88]

AGAINST THE COMMON MARKET

Christian pro-Marketeers did not, of course, have the field entirely to themselves. The Free Presbyterian Church of Scotland called for withdrawal, while the Baptist chapels – which remained wary both of Rome and of ecumenism – took no formal position. The Catholic hierarchy was also less active than the Anglican episcopate, perhaps for fear of stoking Protestant neuroses. The Christian Socialist Movement campaigned against British membership, as did a Liverpool-based 'Committee of Catholics and Anglicans Against the Common Market'. Founded by a group of Catholics in 1963, the Committee claimed 'a large informal membership all over the country', and was 'anxious to show there is a religious case against continued Market membership'.[89]

In the case of the Free Presbyterian Church, opposition was driven by the same anti-Catholicism that inspired Paisleyite Unionism in Northern Ireland.[90] Suspicion of the Common Market as a Catholic entity was probably more widespread than was commonly acknowledged; but, outside the Presbyterian churches, it was not the principal driver behind religious opposition. Just as important was an anti-establishment ethic, which saw 'Christians for Europe' as the puppets of that 'privileged and elitist Establishment which put them in power and ensures their cosy existence'.[91] Underpinning that viewpoint was a wider critique of the European project, which focused on three concerns.

The first was a view of the Common Market as 'a rich man's club', whose 'primary purpose is pursuing and increasing our own wealth'. Where pro-Marketeers saw a vehicle for aid and development, critics viewed the EEC as an exploitative organisation that would suck wealth 'not merely from the pockets of others but from their very mouths'.[92] Frank Judd, a junior naval minister and 'committed Christian', reminded the bishops that 'You cannot serve God and mammon'. 'With its commitment to capitalism, the multinational companies, [and] selfish economic growth', he added, 'I cannot imagine a more blatant portrayal of mammon than the Common Market.'[93] The 'Catholic and Anglican Committee' was especially critical of the 'free movement of labour', which it feared would 'denud[e]' poor regions 'of their young folk', causing 'untold human misery and loneliness'.[94]

Anti-capitalist arguments were particularly important to the Christian Socialist Movement (CSM), chaired by Edward Charles.

The CSM warned that 'the influential banks and multinationals of the Market countries' had no interest in aid, seeking only the interests of capital. The Commission, it predicted, would shut down Benn's plans for workers' co-operatives and the relocation of industry; yet such ideas were 'more expressive of Christian values than their profit-seeking predecessors'.[95]

Criticism from the Left focused particularly on the Common Agricultural Policy, which was seen as supporting rich European farmers to the ruin of agriculture in the Third World. There was particular anger at the destruction of surpluses, at a time when millions were suffering from hunger. 'For those who see the abundance of nature as a gift from God,' wrote one critic, 'the destruction of food is a crime against the Creator for which we shall be answerable.'[96]

A second concern was that the Community would make war between East and West more likely. The Catholic and Anglican Committee insisted that 'the creation of a new power bloc' would heighten 'the danger of a pre-emptive strike by Russia'. Throughout history, it warned, wars had been generated by the attempt of one power to engorge those around it.[97] Creating 'a further political, economic and military power bloc' was 'not a step towards peace but a blow against it'.[98]

Thirdly, there were fears that Continental norms might corrupt the Christian culture of the UK. The CSM foresaw the introduction of Sunday trading and extended opening hours for pubs – ending what was still known as 'the English Sunday' – while the Catholic and Anglican Committee warned that 'the principles and practice of the EEC are contrary to Catholic Christian values'.[99] The free movement of labour, it feared, would break up the family, while the Community's monetary policies were 'an attempt to make workable the usurious system of debt creation'; 'a system completely contrary to Christian thinking'.[100] Anticipating concerns that would recur in 2016, it also feared the 'moral and social problems' associated with 'the infusion of Turkish labour'.[101] The Nationwide Festival of Light took no formal position on the referendum, but did not disguise its anxiety that 'continental standards of conduct will become more and more pervasive in Britain'. It was particularly concerned by Swedish and Danish pornography, and by the popularity of films like *Emmanuelle* and *Last Tango in Paris*; and it noted that Enid Wistrich, wife of the Polish-born director of the European Movement, had led the Greater London Council's campaign against film censorship.[102]

Despite the efforts of such groups, however, religious commentary on the referendum remained overwhelmingly pro-membership. The anti-Market organisations were small in number and hopelessly outgunned in the religious press; the 'Catholic and Anglican Committee' appeared only once in the pages of the *Catholic Herald* and received only a single passing reference in the *Church Times*. Though it claimed a large support, it was unable to produce membership figures and pro-Market organisations seem to have been unaware of its existence. The Committee was drawn from a somewhat eccentric group. Anthony Cooney, for example, who founded the organisation, had dedicated most of his life to a radical 'distributist' economics and to the patriotic cult of St George. The Christian Socialist Movement was larger in scale, but well to the left of the Anglican mainstream. In consequence, Christians who opposed membership tended to express their opposition in secular terms, focusing on the economic or political costs rather than on its religious bearings.

By contrast, the European movement within the churches was active, energised and stocked with senior churchmen. 'Christians for Europe' could call on an array of bishops, broadcasters and religious writers, which not only gave them a degree of authority within the church but also ensured that their words were widely reported. Despite allegations of bias in the religious press, the editor of the *Church Times* had intended to pay little attention to the referendum, on the basis that readers would not welcome 'an *excessive* amount on what is really a secular topic'.[103] Yet he found himself reporting a steady stream of interventions by senior churchmen, which could hardly be ignored by a religious paper of record. The effect was to give an overwhelming sense of church support, with hostile voices sounding only in the letters pages and on the margins of the news sections.

The Catholic hierarchy was less prominent than the Anglican, with Cardinal John Heenan, the Archbishop of Westminster, issuing a pastoral letter calling it 'an abuse of his position to tell Catholics how they should vote'.[104] The *Catholic Herald* also remained neutral, concluding that 'The Common Market has nothing to do with Christianity — whatever the Christians for Europe may piously suggest.' Yet its more outspoken rival, the *Tablet*, editorialised forcefully for membership, and Gummer reported strong support from Catholic clergy for 'Christians for Europe'.[105] Prominent Catholics like Tom Corbishley, Barbara Ward Jackson and Shirley Williams all played significant roles in the 'yes' campaign, whereas their opponents struggled to mobilise any senior Catholics.

CONCLUSION

The absence of the churches from most studies of the referendum says more about the preoccupations of modern historians than it does about the 1970s. For all the talk of secularisation and decline, the churches remained a powerful presence in British society, with a recorded membership only slightly smaller than that of the trade union movement. They contributed one of the more idealistic voices to the campaign, helping to counter some of the negativity and materialism of the wider referendum debate, and had a long history of advocating for European unity. The campaign also succeeded in shutting down any significant anti-Catholic movement beyond the boundaries of Northern Ireland. If this indicated, in part, the decline of Protestantism as a core element of national identity, it also marked the capacity of a looser, more 'diffuse Christianity' to transcend older sectarian divisions.

If the churches offered an important voice within the referendum debate, the campaign itself has a significant place in the history of the churches. It encapsulated many of the most important trends in post-war Christianity: in particular, the churches' increased social activism, ecumenism, anti-communism and commitment to Third World aid. With the party system no longer oriented around the confessional divide, the referendum campaign marked a rare intervention by the churches into mainstream electoral politics. Its success – and the clear enjoyment of many who participated in it – may have built the confidence of the churches for the collisions between church and state that would follow in the 1980s. To paraphrase Dean Acheson: the churches had lost an empire, but they were finding a role. For the churches, as for the country, the 1970s was a decade not just of endings but of beginnings; both in Britain and in the global communions of which they formed part.

8 'NO GOOD TALKING ABOUT SOVEREIGNTY'

We have not gone into Europe in order to lose our sovereignty but to regain and enhance it.

Winston Churchill (junior), 8 May 1975[1]

When Roy Jenkins tells us 'You don't need to cling to sovereignty', I say that we do need to cling to democracy, and we need to cling to the democratic institutions which we have fashioned to serve ourselves in this country.

Michael Foot, 26 April 1975[2]

Sovereignty is not like virginity. You can lose it more than once.

Manchester Evening News, 21 May 1975[3]

Introducing the EU Referendum Bill in June 2015, the foreign secretary Philip Hammond drew an explicit comparison with Britain's first referendum forty years earlier. As a young voter in 1975, Hammond had supported the campaign to keep Britain in Europe; but he now felt that he had done so on a false understanding of what was at stake:

> like millions of others I believed then that I was voting for an economic community that would bring significant economic benefits to Britain, but without undermining our national sovereignty. I do not remember anyone saying anything about ever-closer union or a single currency. But the institution that the clear majority of the British people voted to join has changed almost beyond recognition in the decades since then.[4]

Hammond's remarks drew an immediate riposte from Kenneth Clarke, whose robust support for the EU had thrice denied him the Tory leadership. Reminding MPs that he had played 'a very active part' in the 1975 campaign, Clarke insisted that most of 'the debates I took part in were about the pooling of sovereignty and the direct applicability of European legislation without parliamentary intervention'. The principle of 'ever-closer union', he noted, had hardly been smuggled through behind the backs of an unsuspecting public; it was set out in the first clause of 'the treaty to which we were acceding'. Hammond dismissed the intervention. 'Call me negligent', he told MPs drily, 'but as an 18-year-old voter in that election, I did not actually read the treaty before I cast my vote.'[5]

Hammond was articulating a conviction that has become deeply embedded in the memory of 1975: the idea that the erosion of sovereignty implicit in membership was, at best, not understood, or at worst, actively concealed. Nigel Farage, in a rare foray into contemporary history, called the referendum 'a majority obtained by fraud', while others allege that the Community was 'misrepresented as an economic union', its political purposes 'disguised' until after the vote.[6] The pro-Marketeers, it is claimed, 'made no mention of any restrictions on British sovereignty', or of 'the project of European integration as ... a fundamental transformation of the British state'.[7]

Such claims do not withstand much scrutiny. Clarke was right to say that sovereignty was a prominent issue in 1975, with both sides acknowledging the political implications of membership. Slogans like 'the right to rule ourselves' were blazoned across anti-Market literature, forming the core of the NRC campaign and the first item on its statement of principles. Sovereignty was the subject of a dedicated campaign broadcast and the theme of almost every speech by Tony Benn, Neil Marten and Enoch Powell. The decision before voters, Marten declared, was 'not a question of economics, of agriculture or of alternatives', but whether 'we want the power, independence and self-government of this country ultimately passed over to Brussels'.[8] Food prices and jobs were 'vitally important', but 'the real issue is whether we vote away our political birthright by staying in, or whether we retain our independence as a nation by coming out. There is no other issue.'[9]

Pro-Marketeers never denied either the political implications of membership or the limitations it would impose on formal sovereignty – though they argued that this would be balanced by an increase in *power*. Margaret Thatcher told a rally that 'the paramount motive' for entry was 'political', establishing peace in Europe and increasing Britain's clout.[10]

Winston Churchill (the grandson of the former prime minister) insisted that 'We have not gone into Europe in order to lose our sovereignty but to regain and enhance it.' Only through membership could the British 'regain the sovereignty that they have lost and regain control over their future destiny. That is why we are today in Europe.'[11]

At its best, the result was a sophisticated debate that brought different visions of sovereignty into collision. The problem (for both sides) was its failure to engage the public. Polls consistently reported that sovereignty was a low-salience issue for voters, even those most opposed to membership. As the Labour Anti Peter Shore later acknowledged, 'there was a political element, and quite a strong one, in the "Yes" campaign', but it was a message 'that, frankly, was not heard by many who are now very vociferously critical of the European Community'.[12]

Yet Clarke's recollection was also at fault, when he suggested that the direction of the Community had always been clear. For most of the 1970s, the commitment to 'ever-closer union' was disregarded by British policymakers, viewed more as a pious aspiration than as a practical blueprint. Vague aspirations to monetary and political union were rarely taken seriously, for the Commission seemed rudderless in the face of the political and economic headwinds of that turbulent decade. While pro-Marketeers broadly welcomed the prospect of integration, its pace, nature and direction were regarded as a question for future generations. As the Labour minister and pro-Marketeer Bill Rodgers later recalled, 'we thought that Europe was dynamic and that it was much too early to guess the direction in which it was going to move'. From this perspective, it was true to say that the referendum gave no mandate for the European Union as it later developed, for that was never its purpose. The question, as a civil servant observed, was simply whether Britain would 'be part of the argument'.[13]

SOVEREIGNTIES OLD AND NEW

'There has been much talk about "sovereignty"', observed a pamphleteer for the No campaign. 'Forget it. Politicians, political scientists and political philosophers quarrel about the meaning of the word, and to most people it has no meaning at all.'[14] Unlike the French, whose revolutionary history had bequeathed a dizzying array of constitutional systems, Britain had little recent tradition of abstract constitutional debate. The word 'sovereignty' was not widely used and had no precise definition; as one newspaper commented, it could denote 'anything from the Queen to British beer'.[15] Christopher Frere-Smith, who chaired the Get Britain Out campaign, told journalists that 'It's no good talking about sovereignty except to sophisticated audiences.' 'I dislike the word strongly and I hope people in this campaign won't use it.'[16]

Historically, the word had been used in at least three main senses. The most common was 'the sovereignty of Parliament': the doctrine that Parliament was both the supreme power in the state and the source of all other lawful authority. This idea was most famously expressed by the Victorian constitutionalist A.V. Dicey, as the doctrine that Parliament could 'make or unmake any law whatever', free from the constraints of a written constitution or set of fundamental laws. No 'person or body', either at home or abroad, could 'override or set aside the legislation of Parliament', or 'come into rivalry with the legislative sovereignty of Parliament'. In the words of the eighteenth-century jurist William Blackstone, Parliament could do 'everything that is not naturally impossible'; or as an earlier writer had put it, 'parliament could do anything but turn a man into a woman'.[17]

Even in its Victorian heyday, this vision of unlimited parliamentary sovereignty had never been universally accepted. Dicey himself had argued that Parliament was sovereign 'under the English constitution', which was conventionally understood as a set of customs and conventions, and the third section of his *Introduction to the Study of the Law of the Constitution* set out at length the conventions within which Parliament should operate. Others insisted that certain historic milestones, such as the Magna Carta, the Bill of Rights or the Act of Union, had at least the moral status of 'fundamental laws', which could not be overturned by a simple parliamentary majority.[18] When a Liberal government attempted to pass Home Rule for Ireland in 1912, Dicey insisted that a change of such magnitude required a direct mandate from the electorate. Without such a mandate, he decreed, the bill would 'be in form a law but will lack all constitutional authority'.[19]

Over the twentieth century, this model came under further pressure from the rise of economic interest groups claiming their own democratic legitimacy. In the post-war era, Britain operated increasingly as a 'corporate state', in which policy was negotiated between government, business and organised labour. The very language of industrial politics, with its trade union 'barons' and 'industrial democracy', borrowed freely from the lexicon of constitutional history. When the Conservatives, in an attempt to reassert the authority of government over the unions, fought an election on the question 'who governs Britain?', Labour accused them of an 'authoritarian and bureaucratic system'. It offered instead a 'Social Contract' between Parliament and people, a consultative politics that would 're-establish faith in the working of Britain's democracy'.[20]

A second way of thinking emphasised the sovereignty of the nation as a whole, rather than the authority of institutions within it. This focused less on the exercise of power by Parliament than on the right of a country to make its own decisions, free from external control. Historically, this tradition stressed Britain's island status, its resistance to entangling alliances and, above all, the repudiation of papal authority by Henry VIII. In Protestant historiography, the English Reformation was as much a constitutional as a religious milestone, marking a declaration of independence from the Continental church. The Act of Supremacy of 1558 was a favourite text for anti-Marketeers, with its insistence that 'no foreign prince, person, prelate, state or potentate' has 'jurisdiction' within the realm.[21]

This understanding of sovereignty was fortified by the experience of decolonisation. Colonial liberation movements placed special emphasis on national self-determination, an idea that transferred naturally to the European debate. Voters were urged to make the referendum 'Britain's independence day', while Tony Benn likened the Common Agricultural Policy to the tea duties that had sparked the American Revolution.[22] A statement issued by the Dissenting Ministers cast the No campaign explicitly in the language of colonial liberation:

> 25 years ago Britain dismantled a vast empire in the belief that no country has the right – or the wisdom – to govern another. Now we demand for ourselves what we freely conceded to the 32 members of the Commonwealth: the right of democratic self-government.[23]

The NRC deployed the same analogy in a guide for speakers. Sovereignty, it explained, 'means that our people and Parliament (and *no* external power) make the laws and impose the taxes … a right which the most recently liberated ex-Colonial state anywhere in the world takes for granted'.[24]

On one level, the conception of sovereignty as national self-determination was an easier formula to grasp than the sovereignty of parliament – and it tapped into the common perception of the British as an 'island race', doggedly resisting intrusion from without. Yet here, too, the case was less clear than at first appeared. The post-war era had generated a network of international agencies that were expressly designed to constrain the freedom of individual states. The United Nations, GATT, the International Monetary Fund and, most obviously, NATO imposed a mass of legal obligations to which all members were subject. The world order was conceived increasingly in terms of 'international law', a concept which by its nature challenged the ultimate authority of the state. As we shall see, it was possible to argue that the obligations imposed by the European Community were of a different order to those of NATO or the World Trade Organization. Nonetheless, the argument that membership involved a unique infringement of sovereignty was less compelling in the 1970s than would have been the case three decades earlier.

A third understanding of sovereignty was more demotic. Irene Ward, the longest-serving female MP of the twentieth century, told pro-Marketeers that 'ordinary people have never used the word sovereignty in relation to anything except the Monarchy'.[25] The Queen was still referred to as 'the sovereign', and prayers were said in churches and at public occasions for 'our sovereign lady, the Queen'. Here, as in so many other respects, the British constitution rested on a series of legal fictions, which it was hoped that no one would ever test too vigorously. The Royal Assent was required for all legislation (though it was administered on her behalf by a functionary); it was the monarch who invited a prime minister to form a government (though her choice was dictated by the electorate); and a variety of powers, ranging from the right to declare war to the power to make treaties, were vested in the 'royal prerogative' (to be exercised on the advice of her ministers). Antis tried sometimes to exploit concerns about the monarchy, warning of fearful dangers to the Queen, but this use of sovereignty generally worked to BIE's advantage. As one campaigner breezily put it, 'five of the member countries ... have monarchies, so the "loss of sovereignty" argument doesn't really follow'.[26]

All this rendered sovereignty a confused and confusing subject. Antis preached the sovereignty of Parliament, while denying the legitimacy of the European Communities Act. Geoffrey Rippon told MPs in 1972 that nothing in that Act would diminish 'the ultimate sovereignty of Parliament'; yet acknowledged that Community law would take precedence 'over future Acts of Parliament'.[27] While some pro-Marketeers celebrated the abridgement of national sovereignty, others claimed that membership would increase what they called the '*effective* sovereignty' of the nation.[28] If the 'Antis' failed to counter that message, it was not because their opponents were 'lying' or because the issue was concealed from sight. It was because they never clearly established what was meant by the term or how to deploy it as an issue in the campaign.

PARLIAMENTARY SOCIALISM

At the start of the campaign, most commentators expected sovereignty to be a major issue. Jon Akass, who covered the referendum for the *Sun*, predicted a strong emphasis on the topic from the anti-Marketeers, for 'there is a lot of mileage to be got out of sovereignty, rousing stuff about a thousand years of history and imperishable freedoms'.[29] From Lord Macaulay in the nineteenth century to Sir Arthur Bryant in the twentieth, popular histories of Britain had conventionally been built on two narrative devices: the rise of Parliament as the guardian of the people; and the defence of Britain's island fortress against intrusion from the Continent. Anti-Marketeers could deploy an array of resonant historical images, with a vote to leave the European Community standing alongside 'the signing of Magna Carta', 'the execution of King Charles', or 'the year when the British working man finally won the vote, when every woman finally got the vote'.[30]

Such images were as evocative for the Left as for the Right. Ralph Miliband, whose classic study of *Parliamentary Socialism* had been updated and reissued in 1972, thought the Labour Party 'one of the most dogmatic' of all socialist parties, though its dogmatism was reserved not for socialism but for 'the parliamentary system'.[31] From the Levellers, to the Chartists, to the campaign for women's suffrage, popular control of Parliament had established itself in Labour thought as the principal vehicle for social transformation. The idea that Parliament might surrender its powers to an unelected body, committed to the liberation of market forces from democratic control, struck many as a blow against the historic mission of social democracy. The ballot box, Benn declared, was a great leveller, for it constituted the sole means by which those without wealth and power could make themselves heard.[32] Inside the Community, democracy would be 'tethered' and the possibility of radical politics 'greatly weakened'; outside, governments could 'extend public ownership and advance towards socialism at a pace determined solely by the British people and their parliamentary democracy'.[33]

Similar ideas animated the trade union movement. Unions feared that it would become harder to influence 'social, monetary, political or industrial policy' if decision-making moved to Brussels. As a statement by the Transport and General noted, trade unions had never limited themselves to the 'day by day battles' of the workplace; instead, they had fought 'to influence the Government at Westminster to bring about social and industrial policies of assistance to all working people'.[34] Liberated from democratic control, capital would find it 'easier to dodge its responsibilities to working people', while unions would find it 'harder to win their programme of social reform'.[35]

In this respect, pro-Marketeers were wrong to accuse their opponents of subversive or revolutionary tendencies. The Left had its romantic histories, as did the Right, and they were dominated chiefly by the struggle for parliamentary representation. In a rousing speech to the party's special conference in 1975, Michael Foot invoked the Putney Debates, Cromwell's armies and the constitutional struggles of the seventeenth century in defence of parliamentary democracy.[36] Foot had made his reputation in 1940, as one of the authors of the pamphlet *Guilty Men*, and he reminded viewers in a television broadcast of how the country had 'been saved' in that year 'because the voters had a right to put out a government'.[37] Tony Benn told the Cabinet that membership of the European Community 'rolls back 120 years of parliamentary democracy', reversing 'hundreds of years of history which have progressively widened the power of the people over their governors'.[38]

That argument became central to the Labour No campaign. A statement by the Dissenting Ministers warned that 'the gravest disadvantages' of membership were not economic but 'political'. Judith Hart called the Community a 'contempt of British democracy', while Peter Shore viewed membership as

a weakening of the whole historical drive of the Labour Movement to win economic democracy alongside political democracy. This is the basic reason why the Tories want to keep us deep in the Market, so that it will weaken a Labour Government's ability to control the economy in the interests of the whole people.[39]

This was by no means an abstract concern. As industry secretary, Tony Benn was developing a new industrial policy based on state intervention that seemed almost certain to contravene EEC competition law. Fearing that membership would 'destroy the whole basis on which the labour movement was founded', he resolved to campaign for a No vote 'as though my life depended upon it'. The 'issue', he told the Cabinet, was 'all about sovereignty', for 'the European unity idea – whatever its idealistic objectives – is in fact part of a long retreat from parliamentary democracy'.[40]

None of this was incompatible with a suspicion of Parliament as it currently operated. Benn himself had come to believe that the conventions and flummeries of Westminster served rather to smother than to express the will of the people. His 1981 book, *Arguments for Democracy*, mocked 'the lace curtains hung by the Mother of Parliaments', and when he stepped down as an MP in 2001, he joked of leaving Parliament to spend more time on politics.[41] Benn put his faith in the principle of 'pressure from without', with external bodies such as the trade unions and the Labour Party conference 'dominating Parliament'. Yet it remained crucial to this model that decision-making be located in Westminster, where that pressure could be applied most effectively. Within the Market, he feared, decisions would be taken beyond the reach of voters, rendering Parliament 'an inferior assembly'.[42]

'OUR RIGHT TO RULE OURSELVES'

All this found a curious echo in the thought of Enoch Powell. Powell did not, like many on the Left, view the EEC as a capitalist enterprise that would impoverish the poor; nor, like some on the Right, did he regard it as a betrayal of the Empire. Instead, he focused squarely on the constitutional pretensions of the Community and the threat to British nationhood. What was at stake, he claimed, was more fundamental than economic prosperity or Britain's power in the world: it was 'the right to live under no laws but those made by our own representatives, to pay no taxes but those imposed by our own parliament, and to be governed by no government but that responsible to our own people'.[43]

In Powell's view, 'membership of the Common Market' was 'incompatible with democratic self-government'. The UK could not be a self-governing democracy, Powell argued, while accepting laws made elsewhere. 'It has to be one or the other: we can either be in the Common Market, or we can be governed and taxed and legislated for by a Parliament responsible to the British electorate.'[44]

For Powell, the fundamental principle of all politics was nationhood: that allegiance to a wider community that made all other forms of politics possible. A nation was the product of history and experience, and its defence rested not just on ships and armaments but on a fragile tissue of myths and collective memories.[45] In Powell's view, Parliament was so central to the story of British history that its erosion would constitute an act of psychological self-harm. 'So profoundly, so inherently, is Britain a Parliamentary nation', he argued, 'that she could not alter this without ceasing to be herself.' Speaking at a rally in Kent on the evening before the vote, Powell acknowledged that other countries, with different histories, might be able to give up their self-government while retaining a sense of nationhood. 'For a nation such as we are, our whole history dominated by the evolution of Parliament and our very existence inseparable from parliamentary self-government', the question was 'nothing less than whether we shall remain a nation at all'.[46]

In Powell's view, to subordinate Parliament to the will of foreign powers was to commit hara-kiri on a national scale. The willingness even to contemplate such an act could only be explained, he believed, by a catastrophic loss of national self-confidence. It was no coincidence, he mused, that Britain's ill-fated European adventure had coincided with violence in Northern Ireland, the promotion of 'Asiatic and negro immigration' and the rise of separatist parties in Scotland and Wales.[47] What all these things had in common, he believed, was a loss of faith in the nation as historically conceived; they 'no longer feel, unlike their forefathers, that there is anything to be proud about in being British'. For the SNP and Plaid Cymru, the solution was to 'cut [themselves] adrift from a show that has nothing to offer but the opportunity of going down the drain together'. For pro-Marketeers, it was to hand over the government to foreigners, in the conviction 'that nobody could make a worse hash of governing Britain than the British had made themselves'.[48]

Like Thomas Carlyle, the philosopher he in some respects resembled, Powell accused the governing class of a shameful repudiation of leadership. He was enraged by the argument, made by some Conservatives, that membership offered the best defence against socialism at home. Such an idea, he protested, was not simply anti-democratic: it revealed a shocking loss of faith in the electorate:

> These people say to their hearers: 'You can no longer rely upon yourselves, on the British electorate, to reject the politics which you abhor; you can no longer trust either the good sense of the British people or the democratic power of public argument inside and outside Parliament to make the right choice. Your only safety is that these matters be taken out of the hands of the British nation, and entrusted to those who are wiser, and incidentally more dedicated to capitalism, than the British'.[49]

For Powell, saying No to all this would involve more than a reclaiming of sovereignty. At a deeper level, it would be a reassertion of nationhood: a spiritual awakening that could rekindle Britain's sense of itself. 'Britain', Powell claimed, 'resembles a country that is not only asleep but is tossing and turning in the grip of bad dreams.' Yet 'nothing prevents us from getting up and walking away except the conviction that it is impossible'.[50]

The idea that Britain was in the grip of spiritual malaise was a staple of the anti-Market case. Frere-Smith told the *Sunday Telegraph* that 'it would be good for Britain's soul if she were forced to go it alone and battle harder for survival: "I believe in Mao to a certain extent – that people thrive on tension".'[51] Fliers produced by the NRC appealed to the spirit of the Blitz and the Spanish Armada: 'The British people have fought to remain free and independent for centuries. They will never accept alien rule.'[52] Such language viewed the Community explicitly as an invasion threat, which challenged the British to match the courage of former generations. Air Vice-Marshal Don Bennett claimed that a Yes vote would 'dishonour our dead who fought for our freedom', while the British League of Rights invoked the words of the unhappily named 'Philip the Bastard' in Shakespeare's *King John*:[53]

> This England never did, nor never shall,
> Lie at the proud foot of a conqueror,
> But when it first did help to wound itself.
> ... Nought shall make us rue,
> If England to itself do rest but true.[54]

'SOVEREIGNTY' OR 'POWER'?

For some pro-Marketeers, the restriction of national sovereignty was a consummation devoutly to be wished. The religious broadcaster Barbara Ward Jackson thought sovereignty a 'blasphemous' principle, which had 'wiped out the flower of Europe's youth after 1914'. The *Birmingham Post* took a similar view, invoking the 'dead of two World Wars' as a 'memorial to the unfettered sovereignty of the nation State'. Reflecting on his own experiences on the battlefields of northern Europe, Ted Heath told the Oxford Union that 'I am entirely prepared to make a contribution of national sovereignty to the building of peace in Europe.'[55]

Others questioned whether sovereignty had been impaired at all. The Lord Chancellor, Lord Elwyn-Jones, argued that the essence of sovereignty lay in the right of Parliament to make or repeal any law. On this reading, the European Communities Act was an *exercise* of sovereignty that could be reversed by Parliament in future. The fact that Parliament had chosen to 'delegate' certain powers to Brussels did not impair its 'ultimate sovereignty', for it could recall those powers at any time.[56]

What would happen if Parliament chose to legislate in defiance of Community law, while remaining a member, was less clear. The 1972 Act had acknowledged the precedence of EEC law, but the legal status of that Act remained uncertain. It was a principle of British law-making that one Parliament could not bind the hands of its successors, which meant that the 1972 Act itself had no formal superiority over legislation that came after it. If a subsequent Act contradicted Community law, it would be for the courts to adjudicate between rival parliaments.

There was a significant legal test in 1974, when Lord Denning ruled on the case of *Bulmer* v. *Bollinger*. The details, which pitted a UK cider manufacturer against a French champagne house, were less important than the principle, which was whether the question fell under the jurisdiction of the European Court of Justice. In a judgement that offered something to both sides, Denning ruled that the Treaty of Rome 'does not touch any of the matters which concern solely the mainland of England and the people in it. These are still governed by English law. They are not affected by the treaty.' On 'matters with a European element', however, Denning offered a memorable and even alarming image:

> the treaty is like an incoming tide. It flows into the estuaries and up the rivers. It cannot be held back. Parliament has decreed that the treaty is henceforward to be part of our law. It is equal in force to any statute.

On such questions, he concluded, 'English judges are no longer the final authority.' They were 'no longer in a position to give rulings which are of binding force. The supreme tribunal for interpreting the treaty is the European Court of Justice at Luxembourg. Our Parliament has so decreed.'[57]

The judgement could be read in two ways. On the one hand, Denning had confirmed a remarkable fact: that in a large and growing field of law, British courts were now subject to a higher authority outside the United Kingdom, which was not answerable to the electorate. At the same time, however, Denning rooted this judgement in the decision of Parliament. In so far as Community law took precedence, it did so at the will of Britain's own domestic institutions. 'Parliament has so decreed.'

If that argument was rather scholastic, pro-Marketeers also stressed the limited scope of Community law. It was true that civil servants in Brussels could make regulations that were binding in the UK, but these usually involved points of commercial and agricultural law that had rarely been subject to parliamentary scrutiny, even when governed from Westminster. Commercial regulations had, in any case, to take cognisance of the rules of other countries; even outside the EEC, British exporters would need to abide by the trade standards in operation there.[58] Meanwhile, those 'branches of law which most affect the citizen' – and were the subject of political controversy – would remain under the control of national governments. The 'law of the family, of landlord and tenant, of contract and tort, on health, housing, education', as well as 'our system of criminal justice', would all remain under British jurisdiction.[59]

How far the 'rising tide' of European law might flow into British politics in the future was difficult to foresee – and would depend on the decisions of British governments. As Roy Hattersley told the Association of Contemporary European Studies, there could be 'no question of creeping Federation without the consent of the national Parliaments. The Council cannot just seize new powers in new areas not laid down in the Treaty.' An editorial in the *Liverpool Daily Post* made a similar point: 'How much [sovereignty] we lose and how quickly will depend on us. We have the power of veto.'[60]

The veto was the strongest counter to fears of a power-grab by the Commission. Qualified majority voting did not become the norm until the Single European Act of 1986, meaning that governments could expect to block any important development of which they disapproved.[61] Ministers also vested great hopes in the new parliamentary Scrutiny Committee, a select committee designed to provide detailed assessment of European legislation. As the Conservative MP Peter Blaker wrote breezily, 'The Scrutiny Committee and a strengthened European Parliament between them can provide the two arms of a democratic nut-cracker sufficiently strong to deal with the sovereignty problem.'[62]

Yet these safeguards were unconvincing. The Scrutiny Committee was a paper tiger; *The Economist* called it a 'fig-leaf', with business rushed through late at night, on the basis of inadequate information. Its formal powers were almost non-existent: the House could 'take note' of Community law, but it had no power to amend or reject it.[63] The veto was a more powerful weapon, but cut both ways. Britain could veto legislation of which it disapproved, but other members could use the same mechanism to obstruct British interests or to prevent the repeal of measures already in place when Britain joined. In particular, the veto could be used to prevent the continuation of a temporary agreement, such as those reached during the renegotiations on steel or regional aid.

For this reason, most pro-Marketeers accepted that membership did indeed impose some restrictions on formal sovereignty. They tended to adopt one of two alternative positions: either that sovereignty itself had become an outmoded term, which required new ways of thinking and acting; or that 'sovereignty' could be traded for 'power', enlarging Britain's scope for independent action.

'A BOGUS ISSUE'

The two arguments were, of course, connected. When the Act of Supremacy was passed, in 1558, it was possible to declare by statute that 'no foreign prince, person, prelate, state or potentate' should have 'jurisdiction' within the realm. What the framers of that Act had in mind was the papacy and the hostile powers of France and Spain; so as long as the English Channel was fortified and the Protestant religion maintained, England was sovereign. The challenges of the twentieth century were different: two nuclear superpowers, capable of destroying all life on earth; colossal levels of public debt, built up in two world wars; an economy that was uniquely dependent on imported food; and giant, multinational companies that could move production at will from Dagenham to Detroit.

From this perspective, it was not Britain's membership of the European Community that had eroded the sovereignty of Parliament. It was the 'realities' of the modern world.[64] Parliament could not determine the price of fuel, the value of the pound or the terms of international trade.[65] It could not protect Britain from attack by the Soviet Union or shield it from the consequences of the nuclear bomb. A pamphlet issued by the Young European Movement concluded that

> Sovereignty in the second half of the twentieth century is an illusion. Trade liberalization, the activities of international financiers and companies and the nuclear bomb have all made the nation-state an inadequate framework for the exertion of democratic control.[66]

In such a world, talk of 'the sovereignty of Parliament' was like singing 'Britannia rule the waves': a quaint tradition that had long ceased to describe reality. The former prime minister, Lord Home, told a demonstration at Kelso that:

> I do not see much point in parading a banner called sovereignty,
> if at the same time trade, strength, authority and security slide away.
> We had full sovereignty in 1914 and in 1939, but it did not stop war,
> and victory only came when we shared with others in an alliance.
> We had sovereignty in 1931, but it did not prevent three million
> unemployed.[67]

This was exacerbated by Britain's economic and political weakness. Sovereignty, it was argued, had been draining away from Westminster for decades: not because of the EEC, but because governments could no longer translate policy into practice. In the 1960s, Labour's 'National Plan' for economic growth had been ripped up by the currency markets and the devaluation of sterling. Governments had made spending commitments to their voters, which were struck out of the budget by Britain's creditors at the IMF. Ted Heath had passed an Industrial Relations Act that he was unable to enforce, while parliamentary government had collapsed altogether in Northern Ireland. Debating entry in 1971, the Labour politician David Marquand reminded MPs how the 1964–70 governments had been shipwrecked on the rocks of economic crisis. They had failed, not from malice, but

> because economic power was not under their control. They were blown off course because no nation of 50 million people in the modern world can be wholly the master of its own economic destiny, wholly master in its own economic house. That is a fact of life whether we like it or not.[68]

Roy Hattersley, likewise, recalled his enthusiasm for the Housing Finance Act a decade earlier, which promised a major programme of slum clearance and subsidies for municipal housing. Yet economic crisis had made it impossible to provide the money, rendering the Act a dead letter. 'We passed the Bill', he recalled drily, 'but we did not clear the slums.' As Hattersley put it, the 'privilege of passing theoretical resolutions, which our economic and political state make it impossible to carry out in practice', was analogous to that 'concept of liberty which the founding fathers of the Labour Party so rightly derided – the freedom of any man to dine at the Ritz so long as he can pay the bill'.[69]

The *Western Mail* concluded that sovereignty was 'a bogus issue', because 'we have already lost much of our sovereignty in so far as we are a society in a state of steep industrial decline'.[70] On this reading, what mattered was not *sovereignty* but *power*: the capacity to make – and implement – effective decisions over one's own destiny. Ted Heath provided the most famous exposition of this argument in the House of Commons in 1975. Sovereignty, he told MPs,

> is not something to be hoarded, sterile and barren, carefully protected by the right hon. Member for Down South [Enoch Powell] in a greatcoat with its collar turned up. Nor is sovereignty something which has to be kept in the crypt to be inspected by my hon. Friend the Member for Banbury [Neil Marten] on the eve of the opening of Parliament.
> Sovereignty is something for us as custodians to use in the interests of our own country. ... [T]he sacrifice of sovereignty, if it be put in that extreme form, or the sharing of sovereignty, the transfer of sovereignty or the offering of sovereignty is fully justified. Indeed were we not to do so in the modern world, I believe that as a Parliament, as a party and as a Government we should be culpable in the eyes of history. I believe, therefore, that sovereignty is for this House to use in the way it thinks best.[71]

On this interpretation, sovereignty was best understood as a *currency*; something that could be *spent* in order to purchase power. As a member of the European Community, Britain might sacrifice some rights over its formal decision-making; but it would gain more control over its destiny. As *The Times* had noted in 1970, the public finances had for years been 'strongly influenced and almost at times controlled by the International Monetary Fund and by official foreign creditors. We may have been sovereign, but we were not our own masters.' If membership allowed Britain to rebuild its economic strength, it would 'increase rather than reduce' its power of self-government.[72]

In this respect, Britain's European membership could be seen simply as the latest in a long series of international engagements that traded *sovereignty* for *power*. The Bretton Woods agreement, the International Energy Agency, GATT and the United Nations were all called in evidence of a new world order, in which countries pooled their sovereignty to tackle problems that were too big to deal with in isolation.[73] Geoffrey Rippon, who had negotiated British entry, wrote in 1974 that the whole history of political progress was 'a history of the gradual abandonment of national sovereignty ... The question is not whether sovereignty remains absolute or not, but in what way one is prepared to sacrifice sovereignty, to whom and for what purpose.'[74] In an interconnected world, it made sense for Britain to seek a voice within this network of international organisations. Margaret Thatcher told Conservative voters that

> If Britain were to withdraw, we might imagine that we could regain complete national sovereignty. But it would, in fact, be an illusion. Our lives would be increasingly influenced by the EEC, yet we would have no say in decisions which would vitally affect us.[75]

For pro-Marketeers, the most potent example of pooling sovereignty was not the EEC but the North Atlantic Treaty Organization. As a NATO member state, the UK had given up what the German thinker Max Weber had defined as the essential element of statehood: 'the monopoly of the legitimate use of physical force within a given territory'.[76] Signatories agreed not only to regard 'an attack on one' as 'an attack on all' but, under some circumstances, to put their military forces under foreign command. Britain had accepted the presence of American military bases on its soil since the Second World War and was dependent on the United States for its nuclear deterrent. Sovereignty, as traditionally understood, had been traded for security: Britain could not defend itself alone against the Soviet threat, but it could pool its power with other countries in order to deter a potential attack. For Christopher Soames, NATO was just one example of a political order that had rendered old-fashioned notions of sovereignty irrelevant: 'every Treaty we have signed since the War has shown ... that we can improve the lot of the people by pooling ... sovereignty'.[77]

SOVEREIGNTY AND DEMOCRACY

Some Antis tacitly accepted the comparison between the European Community and Britain's other international entanglements. Foot and Benn, for example, were strongly critical of US military bases, not just because they abhorred nuclear weapons but because they saw them as embodying a neo-colonial relationship between Britain and the USA. More commonly, however, it was argued that entanglements of this kind were fundamentally different to those involved in the European Community. As a member of NATO, Britain had agreed a military relationship whose parameters were clear from the outset. NATO did not, like the EEC, have the power 'to enact laws which are directly binding in Britain' or 'which affect relations between different individuals in this country'.[78] Neither the UN, nor GATT, nor NATO had the power to 'change our law and taxes'; by contrast, 'membership of the EEC creates a new centre of power outside this country, with an open-ended authority to enact laws which are *directly binding in the U.K*'.[79] Powell insisted that a contractual relationship of this kind was wholly different to the creation of a new political authority:

> A man who has made a contract to deliver a sack of coals is still a freeman and not a slave ... A nation which, in its own discretion, promises not to impose tariffs on the goods of another nation remains independent. Not so the nation which relinquishes permanently to another authority the power to take all decisions, whatever they may be, respecting its trade.[80]

Foot, likewise, dismissed the idea that sovereignty was a relic of a bygone age. In a battling performance at the Labour special conference, Roy Jenkins had mocked those who viewed 'the preservation of sovereignty as the ark of the covenant of socialism', arguing that it was neither 'Socialist or realistic to think that you can cling to sovereignty in the world of today'. Delivering an impassioned response, Foot issued a challenge to his Cabinet colleague:

> supposing you change for the word 'sovereignty' – nobody knows quite what it means – the word 'democracy', which all of us should understand. If we said that you cannot regard the preservation of democracy as the ark of the Socialist covenant, I would not agree with that proposition, because I do regard the preservation of democracy as the ark of the Socialist covenant. When Roy Jenkins tells us 'You don't need to cling to sovereignty', I say that we do need to cling to democracy, and we need to cling to the democratic institutions which we have fashioned to serve ourselves in this country.[81]

The argument that pooling *sovereignty* had increased *power* was not so easily rebuffed. The comparison with France and West Germany was telling; both, it seemed, had gained more power over their own destinies through the prosperity achieved within the EEC. Speaking at the launch of Britain in Europe in March, Roy Jenkins told journalists that 'the legalistic definition of sovereignty' mattered less than 'our capacity to control our own destiny'. Over recent decades, 'the control over their own destiny of the major nations of the original Community ... has increased, while ours has diminished. I want to reverse that movement of relative decline, and not see it greatly accelerated.'[82]

Nor did the Antis deal effectively with the question of safeguards. They found it difficult to agree on whether the European Parliament was a step towards federalism, which would drain effective power from national legislatures, or a paper tiger that would exercise no meaningful control. GBO mocked it as a 'farce' and a 'talking shop', wielding 'none of the essential powers and functions which we normally associate with a Parliament'. Yet the NRC warned that an elected Assembly would become a direct rival to national legislatures, reducing Westminster to the status of 'a provincial institution'.[83]

'AN OLD-FASHIONED, IMPERIALISTIC SORT OF SOUND'

Pro-Marketeers had entered the campaign confident that they could win the argument on sovereignty. To their surprise, they found that they didn't need to. As polls for both sides persistently demonstrated, the issue simply failed to connect with voters, who were more concerned with food prices, job security and inflation. An analysis of polling data for the NRC concluded that warnings about 'British independence, or sovereignty' had made 'very little impact', even among confirmed No voters.[84] Of those who were certain to vote for withdrawal, only one in seven raised sovereignty as an issue.[85] Analysis by Bob Worcester, for Britain in Europe, told a similar story. Worcester asked voters what issues they thought would motivate *others* in the campaign – often considered a more reliable gauge of issue-salience, because respondents felt no obligation to parade their own lofty motivations. Fewer than one in ten chose 'sovereignty and independence', compared with 58 per cent who mentioned prices, 37 per cent who identified food prices specifically, and 15 per cent who raised unemployment. Given that respondents could pick multiple issues, this was a strikingly low score. Worcester urged BIE to focus on the issues that people cared about and 'let the opposition talk about sovereignty [and] independence'. 'If they spend two days on this and three days on that between now and the 5 June, this is the best thing that could happen to us.'[86]

Worcester's advice went against the grain for some on the Yes campaign. Many were openly enthusiastic about the political dimensions of the Market, and they found a receptive audience for their views at rallies of the Euro-faithful. But as Worcester pointed out, the votes they had to win were those of the uncommitted, '99 per cent of whom never went to a public meeting'.[87] Focusing on sovereignty seemed a poor use of resources, when the public apparently did not want to hear about it. In a strategy document written for the final week of the campaign, Jim Callaghan noted that 'the question of sovereignty ... seems to have evoked very little interest compared with the other priority issues'.[88] Newspapers commented with surprise that 'the sovereignty debate seemed to fade out early ... The main battlegrounds day after day have been jobs and prices.'[89]

The No campaign had recognised from the start that the issue would be a difficult sell. Abstract terms like 'sovereignty' were always likely to resonate less with voters than the day-to-day concerns of work, food and prices, especially in a period of economic crisis. An advisor to the NRC on media strategy warned that sovereignty would have to be linked directly to questions about 'food prices/taxation, regional policy, [and] trading agreements'. 'We must *not* treat the subject in the abstract.'[90] Reflecting on the referendum shortly after it had ended, Powell accepted that 'the word "sovereignty" has an old-fashioned, imperialistic sort of sound which for many people is repellent and to most is not conducive to clear thinking. It would probably be more enlightening if words such as "independent" or "self-governing" were used instead.'[91]

It did not help that the Antis themselves insisted on talking of the 'Common Market'. This was a conscious tactical decision, which was intended to rally left-wing opposition. Portraying the European project as a capitalist enterprise that was incompatible with socialism was useful in mobilising the Left, but made it harder to argue that what was truly at stake was the distribution of power. The idea that the public had been sold a lie in 1975 – that they had voted for a 'Common Market', not a political project – would become central to Euroscepticism in the 1990s; but it was the 'Antis' themselves who had framed the issue in this way.

The challenge for the No campaign was to prove that sovereignty meant something more than an imaginary threat to the Royal Family. As Tony Benn reminded his audiences, sovereignty was what made possible a generous regional policy, controls on exports and imports, or state intervention in industry. His claim that 500,000 jobs had been lost because a British government could no longer set the terms of trade – whether accurate or not – was a striking illustration of how the question 'who governs Britain?' had practical consequences. In this respect, the Antis were right to claim that sovereignty was the *fundamental* question, not just of European politics but of *all* politics. Whether one wished to intervene in industry or float the pound; to shut down immigration or build an enhanced welfare system; it was necessary first to establish the instruments through which power was exercised.

Yet this exposed a strategic dilemma within the campaign. Sovereignty, it appeared, could only be made meaningful by translating it into everyday terms, which meant talking about tax, employment and the role of government. Yet this risked shifting the debate from the *principle* of self-government to the uses which Benn, Foot and Powell proposed to make of it. This was an issue that bedevilled the campaign and the use of 'sovereignty' in its campaign broadcasts.[92] Once food prices had been neutralised as an issue, Benn's plans to intervene in industry were the most resonant example of the kind of independent policymaking that would become more difficult as a member of the European Community.[93] Yet Benn's plans were controversial, and were probably least popular with those swing voters who would decide the outcome of the referendum. The issue of principle involved – that it was for the British people to choose whether to implement Benn's prescriptions – risked being lost in the fear that a No vote would mean 'Bennery' or 'Powellism' run wild.

In this respect, figures like Benn, Foot and Powell were problematic salesmen for the defence of Parliament. Powell was widely viewed as a demagogue, whose rhetoric on race and immigration positioned him uncomfortably close to the National Front. Benn had championed the Clay Cross councillors, who had been disbarred by the courts for refusing to implement an Act of Parliament, and was convinced that 'parliamentary democracy' had been 'something of a fraud'.[94] Pro-Marketeers argued that the referendum was a more significant blow to Parliament than anything the Commission might have in store. Was it not ironic, a bishop asked, that 'those who are always howling about "the sovereignty of Parliament"' should have sought to bypass it in this way?[95]

It did not help that Britain's governing institutions had seemed so inadequate to the challenge of economic and political crisis. In the two general elections of 1974, the parties had competed with one another in their portrayals of national apocalypse. The Conservatives' February manifesto included fourteen references to the 'crisis' confronting the nation, while the Labour manifesto – subtitled *Labour's Way out of the Crisis* – warned of 'the most serious political and economic crisis since 1945'. Not to be left out, the Liberal manifesto also included sections headed 'The Crisis of Government'; 'A Crisis of Confidence'; 'The Long Term Crisis'; and 'Inflation – the Present Crisis'. In this context, as the *Sun* observed, complaints that MPs might lose their influence could prove a double-edged sword. A poll of Scottish voters in May found that 78 per cent of respondents thought that 'the present system of governing Britain' needed either 'quite a lot' or 'a great deal of improvement', making it difficult to rally a defence of the constitutional status quo.[96] 'No' campaigners repeatedly invited the public to vote against the whole gang of politicians who had misgoverned Britain since the War; but this sat uneasily with their impassioned defence of the institutions which had brought them to power.

All this gave resonance to the argument of the Yes campaign, not that sovereignty was irrelevant, but that the old forms of sovereignty were no longer adequate. In a world of food shortages, where oil supplies were under the control of a Middle Eastern cartel and Britain's finances were dependent on the goodwill of international creditors, the NRC's appeals to the sovereignty of Parliament struck many observers as quaintly Ruritanian. In the words of a leaflet issued by the Young Conservatives, membership might involve a theoretical loss of sovereignty; 'but if it is the sort of loss experienced by the oil producing countries when they formed OPEC then the sooner we pool our sovereignty with Europe the better. We then gain in real power.'[97]

The Antis argued in vain that international co-operation was still possible as an independent and sovereign country – and that the contrary argument was never applied to colonial liberation movements. As Enoch Powell wrote, shortly after the referendum:

> When a score of independent nations in Africa were being carved out
> of the European colonial empires, nobody got up and said that this was
> nonsense and would have to stop, because the new states would have
> to depend on world trade, international investment and maybe mutual
> defence. It was taken for granted that they would have the wish and
> the right to govern themselves and to live under their own laws and
> policies, as separate and independent nations: it occurred to no one
> to argue that this would be inconsistent with the satisfaction of their
> needs for trade, investment and defence.[98]

Like so many of Powell's arguments, this had both intellectual force and debating power; yet it was a risky analogy on which to base a campaign. The British public could admire the liberation struggles of their former territories, but they did not wish Britain to become a European equivalent of Ghana or St Vincent. The assumption that Britain should make its mark on the world survived the end of Empire, which meant finding new forms for the exercise of power. In this respect, the case for Europe drew on the continuing salience of an imperial mindset, as much as on the consequences of its decline. It is to the imperial dimensions of the campaign that we now turn.

9 'THE NEW BRITISH EMPIRE'

After years of drift and failure, the Common Market offers an unrepeatable opportunity for a nation that lost an empire to gain a continent.

The Sun, 10 March 1975[1]

Britain would get a far better deal in Europe if ... the Foreign and Commonwealth Office would stop dreaming of the EEC as a substitute for the British Empire.

Anonymous Home Office official, 1975[2]

I don't relish the thought that England might lapse into the position of Spain – looking to a mighty empire in the past and a peripheral influence for the future.

Gough Whitlam, 4 May 1975[3]

In 1972, as the European Communities Act was working its way through Parliament, the *Journal of Imperial and Commonwealth History* published its inaugural issue. The new journal was an ambitious undertaking, which sought to challenge the marginalisation of the Empire in British historical scholarship. Yet in retrospect, what was most striking was the assumption that both empire and Commonwealth were already the stuff of 'history'. Writing in the first issue, Max Beloff suggested two areas for the attention of researchers: the 'disappearance of the British Empire as a major factor in world affairs' and '*the short-lived attempt* to replace it by a Commonwealth'. The Commonwealth, he wrote elegiacally, had been 'a noble ideal'; 'a pity it failed'.[4]

For some, it was only fitting that empire should recede into the history books just as Britain embarked on a new adventure in Europe. Ever since the first application in 1961, negotiations had been bedevilled by the legacies of empire. The colonial era had left behind it a network of trade preferences, military responsibilities and currency arrangements that could not easily be unpicked, together with a less tangible – but no less potent – web of emotional ties, moral obligations and understandings of British history. Addressing the House of Commons in 1961, Harold Macmillan assured MPs that Commonwealth interests would be paramount at all times: 'if a closer relationship between the United Kingdom and the countries of the European Economic Community were to disrupt the long-standing and historic ties between the United Kingdom and the other nations of the Commonwealth, the loss would be greater than the gain'.[5]

From this perspective, the decision to join the Community in 1973 – ending colonial trade preferences and asserting a new European identity – could be seen as part of that long imperial recessional that marked Britain's post-war history. For some, like the Labour politician Peter Shore, membership signalled a tragic parting of the ways. 'The sense', he told a rally in 1975, 'is not one of gain but of loss; of an abrupt severance from the more broadly based English-speaking world.'[6] The NRC warned that Britain's links with the Commonwealth would be 'weakened much further if we stay in the Common Market', and that, after a few years of membership, the UK would 'cease, in practice, to be a member of the Commonwealth'.[7] Conversely, pro-Marketeers accused their opponents of an absurd nostalgia for empire. The *Sun* mocked Tony Benn ('the former Lord Stansgate') as 'the last British imperialist rampant, still inhabiting a world in which the poor countries sell us their food and raw materials on the cheap and gratefully purchase our manufactured goods in return'.[8] Erskine Holmes, who ran the Yes campaign in Northern Ireland, accused his opponents of hankering after 'a world where vital raw materials can be obtained by sending explorers with gifts of glass beads, to ignorant native chiefs'.[9] Claims that hostility to the EU fed off a reactionary imperial mindset were also present in the 2016 referendum and in the commentary that followed.[10]

Yet the idea that Britain had to 'choose' between Commonwealth and Common Market – or that imperial nostalgia held it back from participation – oversimplifies the complex relationship between the two. Supporters of membership in 1975 included such enthusiasts for empire as Margaret Thatcher and the *Sun*; conversely, the 'Out' campaign drew heavily on the anti-colonial left, which ranged from Tony Benn and Judith Hart to Plaid Cymru and the Communist Party. Enoch Powell, who thought the Commonwealth a 'farce' and wanted the Tory Party to be 'cured of the British Empire', was another who opposed membership.[11] The Commonwealth served as a receptacle for hopes and ideals of many complexions, some of which were actively hostile to Britain's 'imperial' past. Taking a particular view of imperial history did not commit one to a particular stance in the European debate; rather, the two questions acted and reacted upon one another in a dynamic chemical relationship.

IMPERIAL NOSTALGIA?

The disintegration of the Empire took place with remarkable speed. Between 1947 and 1968, countries regaining their independence included India, Pakistan, Sri Lanka, Burma, Malaya, the Gold Coast, Libya, Somalia, Nigeria, Tanzania, Jamaica, Trinidad, Sierra Leone, the Southern Cameroons, Uganda, Kenya, Zanzibar, Nyasaland, Zambia, Barbados, Bechuanaland, Basutoland and Swaziland. South Africa left the Commonwealth in 1960 and the white minority government of Ian Smith declared unilateral independence in Rhodesia in 1965. Australia, Canada and New Zealand never formally declared independence – 'de-dominionisation' was as much a cultural process as a set of political events – but none could plausibly be regarded as a 'colony' by 1975.[12] As John Darwin has suggested, the 1970s might be seen as 'the first real post-imperial decade', following the imperial 'scuttle' of the previous twenty years. The challenge – for Britain, as for its former territories – was to carve out a new identity and a new sense of its role in the world. In this respect, as Darwin puts it, the UK was as much 'a successor-state of the old imperial system' as any of its former colonies.[13]

Anyone who was old enough to vote in 1975 had witnessed an extraordinary contraction of British power. As Enoch Powell reflected in 1965, the effects of that change were difficult to measure, even – or perhaps especially – for those who had lived through it:

> One can never resolve in the span of a human lifetime that kind of a revolution without the marks being left of a struggle. I confess

> to you that for all that I write, for all that I think, for all that I try
> to demonstrate to myself and others I shall go to the grave with a
> conviction at the back of my mind that Her Majesty's ships still
> sweep the oceans of the world.[14]

That the psychological effects were not more visible owed something to the range of comforting myths that could be invoked, either to valorise or to minimise what had happened.[15] The first was the idea that Britain had always favoured independence, and that the purpose of empire had been the nurturing of stable, self-governing institutions. On this view, what decolonisation represented was not the collapse of British statecraft but its vindication. As Clement Attlee put it in 1960,

> There have been many great Empires in the history of the world that
> have risen, flourished for a time, and then fallen ... There is only one
> Empire where, without external pressure or weariness at the burden
> of ruling, the ruling people has voluntarily surrendered its hegemony
> over subject peoples and has given them their freedom.[16]

Attending the Independence Day celebrations in Delhi, the BBC journalist Robert Stimson told listeners that he had 'never felt happier or prouder to be an Englishman in India'.[17] The lowering of the flag, it appeared, could stand alongside Waterloo, El Alamein and the abolition of slavery as a triumph of imperial statecraft, as part of 'a unique record of service by one nation to another'.[18]

A second myth emphasised the sacrifice of imperial power in the Second World War. In this narrative, Britain had nobly exhausted its imperial resources in the struggle against Nazi tyranny. As Camilla Schofield has written, this rendered British decline 'a heroic sacrifice to the world'; an act of self-immolation that marked the apotheosis of Britain's benevolent empire.[19] Such narratives tapped into an older idea of empire as an obligation undertaken for the benefit of mankind. Rudyard Kipling, the archetypal poet of empire, had written of the 'white man's burden', while Matthew Arnold likened his country to a 'weary titan', struggling under 'the too vast orb of his fate'.[20] On this reading, the Empire had died that others might live; nothing, it appeared, so became Britain's imperial life as the leaving of it.

Both these accounts cast the end of empire as the fulfilment, rather than the failure, of Britain's imperial destiny. A third reading took a different approach, which marginalised the Empire altogether as a factor in British history. There had always been a strand of thought that viewed the colonies more as an *expression* of British power than as its *source*. Enoch Powell, for example, was contemptuous of the 'myth ... that Britain was rich, as well as powerful, *because* of her Empire'.[21] Heroic readings of British history were as likely to emphasise its 'island story' as its global expansion, valorising above all Britain's long resistance to Continental tyranny. In such narratives, the Empire featured as something that Britain had done in the world, rather than as something that was constitutive of its own identity. As Bill Schwarz has written of G.M. Trevelyan, perhaps the most influential popular historian of the twentieth century, 'it is as if the empire is a screen on which faraway images flicker and then disappear, never really connecting to the lives of those in the metropole. Essentially, England is where history happens. The rest appears as just a dream.'[22]

More radical versions of this myth stressed the transitory and episodic nature of the imperial connection. As the *Spectator* – an anti-Market paper – commented in 1975:

> The experience of worldwide Empire was, in the context of the thousand years, a brief one. For most of the time since the Norman conquest ours has been a vulnerable country, earning its living and its glory with wit, courage, cunning and a deep sense of herself and her own identity. Perhaps the greatest period of British history ... was the Elizabethan; and it was then that Britain confronted the massed might of a Europe bent on her extinction and threw it back from her shores.[23]

The memory of the Second World War as a conflict in which Britain had stood 'alone' both exemplified and reinforced that tendency. The role of the Empire tended to be underplayed in the popular memory of the War, for which the exemplary conflict was the Battle of Britain and the bravery of 'the few', not the 'desert war' in North Africa or the recovery of the Pacific empire.[24] From this perspective, the loss of the colonies could be understood less as a sacrifice of power than as the laying down of a burden, which Britain had borne heroically for perhaps too long.

The loss of formal empire was also cushioned by the existence of the Commonwealth, which was intended to secure into the post-imperial age some of the more tangible benefits of empire: military bases around the world, a currency system that gave special preference to sterling, and a trading network that secured food and raw materials in exchange for British manufactures. Its significance to the metropolis arguably increased after 1945, when Britain was desperately short of dollars and anxious to trade in its own currency.[25] With the economies of western Europe devastated by war, it made sense to base the recovery of British trade on the more buoyant markets of the Commonwealth. By 1954, the Commonwealth was taking 49 per cent of British exports and supplying 48 per cent of British imports, making it comfortably Britain's biggest trading partner.[26]

Yet the hopes vested in the Commonwealth were not simply economic. In an age of superpowers, Britain's ability to exert influence on the world stage seemed to rest more than ever on the belief, set out by Clement Attlee in 1948, that Britain was 'not solely a European power but a member of a great Commonwealth and Empire'.[27] The Right saw in the Commonwealth a bulwark against communism in Africa, Asia and the Pacific, which established Britain as America's most important Cold War ally. For the Left, it offered the prospect of a 'Third Force' in an otherwise bipolar world, able to balance the superpowers and to act as a bridge between them. A paper issued by the Tribune Group in 1967 looked to Britain as the 'proud leader of a united Commonwealth', in which the African and Asian states would 'gladly follow our lead'.[28]

There was also an ethical case for the Commonwealth. In an attack on the Common Market in 1962, Hugh Gaitskell implored the Labour Party to remember the sacrifices made by colonial troops at 'Vimy Ridge and Gallipoli', and 'the help they gave us after this last war'. Entry, he suggested, would mark a betrayal of those countries that had stood by Britain in its darkest hour, and would bring to an end a remarkable experiment in international cooperation. For Gaitskell, the Commonwealth stood as a model of a new world order, based on the same progressive impulses as Oxfam, the United Nations or War on Want. '[T]he existence of this remarkable multi-racial association, of independent nations, stretching across five continents, covering every race' was 'of immense value to the world'. Conservatives might measure the Commonwealth purely by its transactional value, but Labour should cherish its ethical purpose, in contrast to the merely economistic appeal of the 'Common Market'.[29]

It is no coincidence that it was a Labour leader who took up this cry, for the emergence of the Commonwealth as a focal point for opposition to apartheid and to the UDI regime in Rhodesia gave it 'a sense of moral purpose' that appealed strongly to the Left.[30] That governments found themselves so frequently at odds with the Commonwealth diminished the enthusiasm of the Right for the organisation (one paper likened Britain to the 'old convenient milk cow', wielding 'the ever-open wallet on which the sun never sets').[31] Yet it increased the prestige of the organisation for the Left, especially for Christian socialists and 'New Left' intellectuals.

The Commonwealth also retained a presence in British cultural institutions. From the BBC World Service (launched in 1932 as the Empire Service) and the Rhodes Scholarships at Oxford to the Boy Scouts and the Commonwealth Legal Bureau, colonial networks continued to thrive among the broadcasters, the universities, the judiciary and the banking system. The diplomatic and intelligence services both retained strong ex-colonial networks, as did many of the churches. Above all, the monarchy had found a new role as the focal point of the Commonwealth, to which the Queen felt a special personal commitment.[32] In consequence, Commonwealth sensibilities had to be treated with care, even as the material benefits of the organisation receded.

IMPERIAL RECESSIONAL

The idea that the Commonwealth might form a platform for British military and economic power, however, was increasingly hard to sustain. The sterling area never recovered from the shock of devaluation in 1967, and would lose much of its utility with the collapse of the Bretton Woods system. Commonwealth trade fell steeply from the early 1950s: by 1972 (even before the common external tariff) its share of British imports had fallen from 48 per cent to just 19 per cent, while the proportion of British exports going to Commonwealth markets had dropped from 49 per cent to 19 per cent.[33] Harold Wilson, who boasted that he was 'born – and I remain fundamentally – a Commonwealth man', told his party in 1975 that: 'We cannot now ignore the fact that politically as well as economically so many of our Commonwealth friends are reorienting their policies in terms of the region in which they live or the oceans that wash their shores.'[34]

Just as importantly, the illusion that the Commonwealth would meekly follow British leadership had fallen prey to its own internal contradictions. Commonwealth summits were no longer cosy meetings of like-minded statesmen from the white settler colonies; instead, they were unruly assemblages of leaders representing wildly divergent political viewpoints.[35] British diplomats came to view these meetings 'as an ordeal to be endured' rather than as 'an opportunity to advance UK interests'.[36] The 'New' Commonwealth was increasingly left of centre, while the 'Old' Commonwealth was pulling apart under the strain of apartheid and minority rule in Rhodesia. There were such furious exchanges at the Prime Ministers' Meetings of January and September 1966, following the declaration of unilateral independence by Ian Smith's all-white regime in Rhodesia, that the very survival of the Commonwealth seemed in question; Harold Wilson described the latter meeting as 'the worst ever held up to that time'.[37] In 1971 hostility over arms sales to South Africa 'came fairly close to wrecking the Commonwealth', and the issue of apartheid would bedevil the organisation until the release of Nelson Mandela in 1990.[38]

All this made it increasingly difficult to see the Commonwealth as a vehicle for British influence. Indeed, for some on the Right, the Commonwealth came to seem part of the problem: responsible both for high levels of non-white immigration and for the assault on Ian Smith's white regime in Rhodesia.[39] The election of a Labour government in 1964 only briefly changed the mood. As early as 1966, George Brown and Michael Stewart had warned ministers that 'developments in the Commonwealth' would make it 'more difficult for us to exercise world influence as ... [its] central nation'. Far from balancing the 'Six', there were fears that the former colonies might themselves be drawn away from British influence by the gravitational pull of the Common Market. The best way to secure British influence in Africa, Stewart concluded, was to make Britain a leading force in Europe.[40]

By the 1970s, policymakers had largely given up on the Commonwealth as a platform for British military power or economic regeneration. Lord Gladwyn, who had briefly been Acting Secretary-General of the United Nations, concluded as early as 1964 that the Commonwealth amounted to little more than 'playing cricket with fuzzy-wuzzies'.[41] The Conservative government's 1971 White Paper, making the case for entry to the Community, concluded that the Commonwealth could not offer – and did not wish to offer –

> alternative and comparable opportunities to membership of the European Community. The member countries of the Commonwealth

are widely scattered in different regions of the world and differ widely in their political ideas and economic development. With the attainment of independence, their political and economic relations with the United Kingdom in particular have greatly changed and are still changing.[42]

In 1972 the former Labour foreign secretary, George Brown, dismissed as 'make-believe' the idea 'that Britain's role in the world is to be the leader of the Commonwealth'. Most of the newly independent states had 'no tie with Britain except that they were once colonized from here', while the older Dominions looked increasingly to the United States for leadership. 'If we tell the absolute honest truth,' he concluded, 'there is no such thing as a united British Commonwealth.'[43]

None of this diminished the ethical case for the Commonwealth. Yet the argument that Britain had to choose between Commonwealth and Common Market was becoming harder to sustain. At the time of the first application in 1961, there had been vocal opposition from Britain's former colonies, who feared economic disaster from being locked out of membership.[44] The offer of Associate Status – a category created with France's colonies in mind – was itself the subject of controversy, with some viewing it as a form of neo-colonialism. By the 1970s, however, the EEC had reworked Associate Status in a way that was more attractive for African states, first through the Yaoundé Convention and then through the negotiations that led to the Lomé Convention. The new terms were not only more generous in the provision of aid, development and access to European markets; they were also framed more explicitly as an association of equals. As early as 1966, the Commonwealth Office discovered that Ghana, Sierra Leone, Zambia, Malawi and the Gambia were considering applying for Associate Status, regardless of Britain's decision.[45] Aid agencies and the churches looked increasingly to the EEC as a vehicle for Third World development. From this perspective, it seemed that Commonwealth interests might better be served by Britain joining the Community – where it could act as a representative of Commonwealth interests – than by maintaining an isolated position on the outside.

'QUEEN VICTORIA'S UMBILICAL CORD'

For many pro-Marketeers, the reluctance to embrace the European cause could only be explained by an 'empire complex' that blinded opponents to the modern world.[46] Tony Benn, during his period as a pro-Marketeer in the late 1960s, hoped that membership would cut 'Queen Victoria's umbilical cord', while the *Guardian* blamed imperial nostalgia for a wider national malaise:

> Much of our sense of national discontent and failure derives from indecision about where we ought to have gone in the past fifteen years, a period when it became clear to all but the most self-deceiving that the ties of Commonwealth were sentimental and diminishing rather than practical and dynamic.[47]

The *Scottish Daily Express* put it more bluntly. 'The argument that the Commonwealth is any longer an alternative to Europe is dead. It should be given a decent burial.'[48]

Yet this set up a false opposition between those who accepted the logic of decolonisation and those who did not. As Roy Jenkins once noted, anti-Marketeers had no monopoly on nostalgia for empire: on the contrary, pro-Marketeers like George Brown and George Thomson displayed 'an attachment to imperial commitments worthy of ... Joseph Chamberlain, Kitchener of Khartoum and George Nathaniel Curzon'.[49] The idea that Britain had a vocation to leadership – to 'imperium' – comfortably survived the end of empire, with the Community taking the role for which the Commonwealth had once been cast. Brown wrote in 1971 of Britain's destiny to become 'the leader of ... a new European bloc which would have the same power and influence in the world as the old British Commonwealth'. He dismissed the idea that Britain had 'lost an empire' but not 'found a role':

> We *have* a role: our role is to lead Europe. We are, and have been for eleven centuries since the reign of King Alfred, one of the leaders of Europe. It may be that Britain is destined to become *the* leader of Europe, of Western Europe in the first place, and of as much of Europe as will come later on.[50]

Such attitudes were widely ventilated during the referendum campaign. The *Sun*, which bowed to no one in either its patriotic ardour or its enthusiasm for the European Community, proclaimed that 'After years of drift and failure, the Common Market offers an unrepeatable opportunity for a nation that lost an empire to gain a continent.'[51] The government's official Referendum Information Unit, established to provide impartial analysis to voters, told callers that 'Britain needs new ways of exerting influence in a world where trading and political relationships have radically changed'; 'we have to find a role to replace the one we played up to and immediately after the last war.'[52]

Far from recalibrating Britain's role in the world, this assumed a continuum between empire and Britain's new destiny in the Common Market. Julian Amery, son of a former colonial secretary, urged Heath in 1974 to make Europe

> the central theme of our policy, in much the same way as the Conservative Party made Commonwealth and Empire its central theme from Joe Chamberlain's time to the 1950s. We have to present Europe as the condition of national security, economic growth, political freedom and international influence.[53]

Patrick Ground, later a Conservative MP, told a rally that 'it was natural for our country – with its record as a colonial power and exporter of democracy – to want to exercise some influence on the future development of Asian and African countries'. 'The Common Market, far from reducing British influence in Asia and Africa, had actually enhanced it.'[54] David Owen, a future foreign secretary, predicted 'that historians will see the transition from Empire to a member of the Community as a logical and inevitable trend'.[55] A letter published in the *Daily Mail* put the case more bluntly. 'Since it is no longer possible to win empires with arms, the matter has to be dealt with more cleverly. The EEC must become the new British Empire.'[56]

This was also a theme of Margaret Thatcher's rhetoric. Addressing the London University Conservative Association in 1975, she set British membership explicitly within the imperial tradition:

> As we look at our island history we see that our people have always been at their best when they have been outward-looking. A century ago we had the jewel of India, while enterprising Britons carried our flags, our trade, our culture, and our justice to the corners of the earth. Our Empire in turn grew into the British Commonwealth – a unique partnership of nations with us at its centre ... And so it is, in this decade, that the pursuit of this traditional outward-looking role has brought us to exert our influence within the growing European Community of nations.[57]

This conviction that Britain could only exert influence through some larger grouping had its own imperial ancestry. In the early twentieth century, it had underpinned campaigns for imperial preference and the federation of the Empire. Joseph Chamberlain had warned in 1902 that 'the days are for great Empires and not little states', identifying the challenge of great continental landmasses like Russia and the United States, while Alfred Milner had urged imperial unity on the grounds that 'the United Kingdom alone will be hard put to retain its place amongst the foremost powers of the world'.[58] By 1975, it was almost a cliché that the power blocs of the future would be regional and continental in orientation. Harold Wilson noted that 'nearly all the nations with whom we deal every day are themselves members of regional groupings, and they glory in it'.[59] Thatcher insisted that 'political and economic power in the world today is based much more on continents than on oceans'. Shirley Williams put it more crisply: 'Once upon a time the Commonwealth, now Europe.'[60]

In this respect, there was some truth in the allegation made by Powell and others, that it was the *pro*-Marketeers who were gripped by the fantasies of Empire. For pro-Marketeers, wrote Benn crisply, the 'myth of Empire had been replaced by the myth of Europe'.[61] Brian Wilson, of the Labour Committee Against the Common Market, joked that for Euro-enthusiasts, the 'old imperialist dream remains', 'but now we would have Common Market gunboats sent up the Zambesi to teach the fuzzy-wuzzies a lesson'.[62] The *Spectator* dismissed the European project as merely the latest manifestation of a long-standing pathology: the determination that Britain must cut a dash in the world. Only post-imperial nostalgia, it suggested, could explain the 'clamouring for Britain to abandon an identity that seems no longer lustrous for part of the identity of something bigger'.[63] It was Powell who put this case most strongly, arguing that the case for membership rested on a failure to come to terms with the imperial legacy. As a critic of Europe and Empire alike, his thought is worth considering in detail.

POWELLISM, EUROPE AND EMPIRE

'I BELIEVE IN THE BRITISH EMPIRE,' Powell told his constituents in 1951. 'Without the Empire, Britain would be like a head without a body.' Powell's youthful commitment to the Empire ran deep, carrying him to Australia in his twenties and then to Egypt and India during the War. By his own admission, he had fallen 'hopelessly and helplessly in love with India', and its loss in 1947 was a shattering emotional blow. When news of independence was announced, he remembered 'spending the whole of one night walking the streets of London trying to come to terms with it'. 'One's whole world', he later recalled, 'had been altered.'[64]

Powell's enthusiasm for Empire never extended to the institution designed to take its place. The Commonwealth, he believed, was a 'humbug' and a 'farce', 'invented' as a 'bluff' to disguise the reality of decolonisation. The 'Tory Party', he wrote in 1957, 'must be cured of the British Empire, of the pitiful yearning to cling to the relics of a bygone system.'[65] For Powell, it was absurd to think that a body which acknowledged no formal allegiance to Britain – whose members did not even have to accept the monarch as head of state – could be more than a fig leaf for the loss of power. He was equally contemptuous of the Commonwealth aid agenda, which he attributed to a preposterous affectation of colonial guilt. In a speech in 1970, he mocked the idea 'that the economic achievement of the Western countries has been at the expense of the rest of the world and has impoverished them':

> It is nonsense – manifest, arrant nonsense, but it is nonsense with which the people of the Western countries, clergy and laity – but clergy especially – have been so deluged and saturated that in the end they feel ashamed of what the brain and energy of Western mankind have done, and sink on their knees to apologize for being civilised.[66]

That same mix of colonial guilt and post-imperial posturing, he believed, was at the core of Britain's immigration policy. Powell's hostility to non-white immigration was rooted not solely in the connection he drew between race and nationhood, though he thought the instinct of race the 'deepest and strongest' instinct of mankind. Just as importantly, he saw the liberal immigration policy of the immediate post-war era as another manifestation of Britain's refusal to accept that its obligations to the Empire were over.[67] 'To have our laws so far out of relation with realities', he wrote in 1964, had 'inflicted social and political damage that will take decades to obliterate'.[68]

Powell's fundamental charge against the Commonwealth was the psychological grip he believed it to have exerted, of which he viewed Britain's European adventure as another malign result. Addressing an academic audience in 1964, Powell began with the striking claim that 'The life of nations, no less than that of men, is lived largely in the imagination.' There could be nothing 'more important to the well-being of a nation, than what ... it thinks about itself: the picture of its own nature, its past and future, its place among other nations in the world, which it carries in its imagination'. That picture, he believed, was usually historical, composed of stories and common understandings about the past, but it was also inherently mythological. In an argument that would enter the academic mainstream in the 1990s, Powell claimed that 'all history is myth'; not in the sense that it was untrue, but in so far as it wove together stories about the past in a way that gave them meaning. Crucially, that meaning was 'the creation of the human mind and not otherwise present in nature'.

For Powell, Britain was in the grip of an especially pernicious myth, which underpinned the wider crisis of the post-war era. At its core was the idea that 'Britain was once a great imperial power, which built up a mighty empire over generations and then, in the lifetime of most of us, lost or gave it up.' This myth, that Britain had exercised power through its empire before shrivelling into impotence after 1945, had caused 'grave psychological damage'. Its legacy could be seen both in the pervasive sense of 'decline' gripping the country and in the desperate search for new instruments of power – whether the Commonwealth, the 'special relationship' or the European Community.[69]

In response to the question, 'What has happened to the British Empire on which the sun never sets?', Powell eschewed the 'conventional answer': that it 'has changed into something better and nobler still, which we would like to call the British Commonwealth'. Instead, he concluded, it had 'never existed'.[70] For Powell, the idea of the British as an imperial race, wielding power through an integrated imperial system, was a myth created in the 1890s for domestic political purposes.[71] This was not, of course, to deny the existence of the Empire; simply to repudiate its centrality to British history. As early as 1961, Powell had argued in a speech to the Royal Society of St George that 'There was this deep, this providential difference between our empire and others, that the nationhood of the mother country remained unaltered through it all.' 'England', he insisted, 'underwent no organic change as the mistress of a world empire', and need not surrender its pride in nationhood at the Empire's close.[72] If the British were to recover their mental balance, they would need a new understanding of their past; not quite 'Britain without Empire', but 'Britain with the imperial episode in parenthesis'. They must re-learn the history of their country, as a story to which the actions of colonial governors were largely peripheral.[73]

Whether Powell believed his own analysis is a moot point. In a sense, it hardly mattered; for in Powell's view, the 'greatest task of the statesman' was 'to offer his people good myths and to save them from harmful myths'.[74] It did, however, inoculate him from the common allegation that hostility to the European Community was the result of post-imperial nostalgia. For Powell, it was the *pro*-Marketeers who were stuck in an imperial mindset. Enthusiasts for entry, he claimed, were 'crypto-imperialists who read nothing later than Kipling'; fantasists for whom 'membership of the European Community is seen as a compensation for the real or believed loss of Empire'. If Britain was to escape its 'post-imperial neurosis', it would have to surrender not only its colonies but its aspiration to lead a new power bloc on the Continent.[75]

It was no surprise to Powell that the United States wished Britain to submerge its identity in that of Europe. Powell's 'deep anti-Americanism' dated back to the Second World War, when he had suspected the US of exploiting the conflict to dismantle the Empire.[76] He disliked what he saw as the ahistorical universalism of the United States, a nation founded not on common history but on a set of abstract ideas, presumed to be of universal application and ready for export to less favoured nations.[77] Powell disliked the United Nations for the same reason, viewing it as part of a mania for 'sinking national sovereignty in organizations for uniting the world'. In 1970, when others were celebrating the UN's twenty-fifth anniversary, he dismissed it as 'an absurdity and a monstrosity', whose dream of abolishing war would render meaningless those very 'nations' on which it was built.[78]

For all these reasons, Powell's hostility to the Common Market cannot be dismissed as a regression to empire. On the contrary, he saw the European project as an expression of Britain's *failure* to come to terms with the end of empire. It was rooted in a false idea of British history, which saw the nation as broken by its loss of imperial power. Rather than submerging their nationhood in a new cosmopolitan project, Powell urged voters to 'come home again from years of distant wandering'.[79] Britain must find 'a new patriotism ... to replace the old, imperial patriotism of the past'. Commonwealth and Common Market alike were siren calls, luring Britain from a nationhood that could be truly its own.[80]

'BEFORE THEY DOUBTED. NOW THEY WANT US IN'

On one level, Powell's attacks on the Commonwealth were somewhat perverse, for Commonwealth sentiment formed one of the strongest cards in the anti-Market pack. A poll in 1961 found that unsatisfactory arrangements would be an 'important' or 'very important' obstacle to membership for 78 per cent of respondents. When asked, the following year, to identify any difficulties that might be so significant as to disbar entry to the Community, 39 per cent again named 'the Commonwealth'.[81] At the time of the first application, in 1961, a number of Commonwealth leaders had been vocal in their opposition. Kwame Nkrumah of Ghana warned that association with the Common Market would 'doom the economy of Africa to a state of perpetual subjection to the economy of Western Europe'.[82] The Australian trade minister, 'Black' Jack McEwen, was no less outspoken, anticipating 'a fight' with London 'for stakes which for us are very, very high'. If Britain intended 'to treat the Australian Government as opponents', he added, 'well and good, but [we] would like to know'.[83]

Even in 1975, when Commonwealth governments were more supportive of British membership, the emotional pull of the Commonwealth remained strong. BIE warned activists to treat this sentiment with respect, and advised speakers that they would have to address two constituencies: 'one interested in Australia/New Zealand, one interested in [the] developing world'. The theme, in both cases, would be the same – 'Before they doubted. Now they want us in' – but would need different presentation.[84]

It was the white Commonwealth that loomed largest in the public imagination. A report by the Social Policy Centre in 1974 found that, of the 59 per cent who thought that Britain should join up with other countries if it left the EEC, the vast majority mentioned either Australia (36 per cent), Canada (27 per cent), New Zealand (34 per cent) or the United States (17 per cent). Only 2 per cent mentioned any other Commonwealth country.[85] For the Right, in particular, the 'Old' Commonwealth evoked both an ideal of Anglo-Saxon kinship and a memory of wartime service from which non-white troops were all too often erased.[86] By 1975, however, the mood even of the 'Old' Commonwealth was changing. Australia and Canada had reduced their dependence on the British market, while the New Zealand government had transferred its attention to reciprocal arrangements with the EEC. Pierre Trudeau, of Canada, and Wallace Rowling, of New Zealand, both opened trade talks with the Common Market in 1974–5, and made clear that they had little interest in British withdrawal. Gough Whitlam, of Australia, went further, warning the UK not to 'lapse into the position of Spain – looking to a mighty empire in the past and a peripheral influence for the future'.[87] The official Yes pamphlet, distributed to every home in the country, declared that membership 'makes good sense for the Commonwealth' and that the 'Commonwealth wants us to stay in'. Like the government pamphlet, it brandished quotes from Whitlam and Rowling, and emphasised the benefits to the Commonwealth of the renegotiated terms.[88]

Anti-Marketeers retaliated by commissioning opinion polls, designed to bypass the relevant governments by appealing to public opinion in the Dominions. Yet the results were distinctly underwhelming. In New Zealand, the country most dependent on British markets, polls found that 49.4 per cent of respondents wanted Britain to vote No: the largest single group once 'don't knows' were accounted for, but less than half of the total. Significantly, only 3 per cent more thought that New Zealand trade would benefit if Britain withdrew.[89] Strikingly, the official No pamphlet dedicated just five sentences to the Commonwealth angle, limiting itself to a vague warning that Commonwealth links were 'bound to be weakened' if Britain remained in the Common Market.[90]

Discussion of the 'new' Commonwealth focused chiefly on international aid and on trade in primary goods. For those who saw the Community as the best vehicle for international development, the signing of the Lomé Treaty in February 1975 was a major advance. An agreement between the European Community and seventy-one countries from Africa, the Pacific and the Caribbean, Lomé offered three main benefits: tariff-free access for most agricultural products and raw materials; preferential access for commodities, like sugar and beef, which were in competition with the Community's own production; and a commitment to 3 billion Ecus in aid. Unlike previous agreements, it also dropped demands for reverse preferences for European goods, and offered a formula designed to protect the signatories' export earnings against fluctuations in world prices.[91]

Pro-Marketeers seized on the deal, which could hardly have been better timed.[92] It was a standing rebuke to claims that the Community was a protectionist entity that would impoverish poorer countries; it gave the Community the appearance of a higher ethical purpose than self-enrichment; and, although the agreement had been in preparation since the problematic Yaoundé negotiations of the 1960s, it could be called as evidence that British leadership was making the Community more outward-looking and benevolent. Announcing his conversion to the pro-Market camp, the education secretary, Reg Prentice, claimed that it was Lomé that had persuaded him. This may have been disingenuous: Prentice had been moving rightwards for some time, and Lomé may simply have provided the necessary cover. Yet that, in itself, would testify to the importance of what had been achieved at Lomé, and its resonance for public opinion and the party faithful.[93]

Even Judith Hart, the anti-Market minister for overseas development, hailed the Convention as 'an historic agreement' and 'a dramatic and highly significant step forward in the relationship between industrialised and developing countries'.[94] Her complaint was that the Convention did not go far enough, covering only one-sixth of the population of the developing countries and fewer than half the countries of the Commonwealth, while excluding states like India, Bangladesh and Sri Lanka. These were all countries in receipt of substantial British aid, drawing on funds that might now be depleted to support European aid programmes. The Convention, she argued, took a 'paternalistic and colonial approach to the developing countries', turning 'a smiling face only to those countries' with which it retained a colonial relationship. Labour, she concluded, had 'failed' to achieve its renegotiation objectives in this field, and 'it is the poorest Commonwealth countries which are the losers'.[95]

Barbara Castle took a similar view, dismissing the agreement as 'neo-colonial paternalism'. 'The whole EEC concept of "association"', she insisted, 'visualized lesser mortals rotating in the orbit of a superior power bloc.'[96] Such arguments had force, and discontent with Lomé would grow as its implementation became bogged down in detail.[97] Yet they lacked the clarity of a treaty that seemed to dismantle protectionist concerns and offered billions in aid to the Third World. A common view was that expressed by the *Guardian*, which of all the pro-Market papers was the most sceptical of the EEC. The Convention, it acknowledged, was 'not perfect', particularly in its neglect of 'the poverty-stricken millions of the Indian sub-continent'; but it was in treaties of this kind 'that the battle for a sane world prices structure will be fought, and Britain ought to be active in them'.[98]

Lomé also fed into a larger argument that was popular on the pro-Market side: the idea that the relationship between Britain and its former colonies was evolving into a new form, which rendered the old trading preferences unsustainable. Those who spoke of 'going back' to the Commonwealth, it was argued, were hankering after a neo-colonial relationship in which the former colonies themselves had no interest. Dickson Mabon, who chaired the Scotland in Europe campaign, told a rally in Eldershire that the cry of 'cheap food' was 'unabashed neo-colonialism, which the Third and Fourth World countries deeply resented'. As maturing economies, they expected decent prices for their goods, and the 260 million consumers of the European Community offered a more attractive market than Britain alone. For Mabon, the best service that Britain could render the Commonwealth was to work for its interests within the Common Market: 'A "No" to Europe was a "No" to the Commonwealth and a "No" to mankind.'[99] Roy Jenkins exploited that idea in a broadcast at the end of May. The Commonwealth, he declared, had 'grown up'. Britain should not behave 'like a parent ... complaining about his children getting married'.[100]

'COMMON MARKET REGGAE'

There was one group for which the Commonwealth remained of particular importance. BIE calculated that more than 2 million voters were either Commonwealth immigrants or of 'one time immigrant' families, and it feared that they would lean towards withdrawal. A number of Black or Asian organisations campaigned against membership, as did some of the most prominent immigrant newspapers. The Indian Workers' Association (IWA), which claimed to represent 150,000 people of Indian descent, called for 'a massive "No" vote' and distributed 10,000 leaflets in the Midlands written in Hindi, Gujarati and Punjabi. In Coventry, members of the Association went door-to-door in support of the No campaign, while the Pakistani Workers' Association also recommended pulling out.[101] *West Indian World*, a newspaper catering to immigrants from the Caribbean, ran a series of vox pops in which community leaders and opinion formers urged readers to vote No. Contributors included Rudy Narayan, the barrister and civil rights activist who founded the Society of Black Lawyers; Len Dyke, founder of the first million-pound Black British business, Dyke and Dryden; Peter Tucker, a civil rights campaigner who would later run the Commission for Racial Equality; and the businessman and member of the Institute for Race Relations, David Udo.[102]

This owed something to a socialist critique, in keeping with the broader left-wing character of many immigrant organisations. As the secretary of the Coventry IWA, Bachittar Singh, told reporters, 'We are working people and it is against the interests of the working classes for Britain to remain in the Common Market.'[103] Claims that membership would boost unemployment hit hard, for it was usually immigrant workers – concentrated in low-paid, low-skilled occupations – who were the first to be let go.[104] Loyalty to 'the Commonwealth ideal' also remained strong, as a 'monument to inter-racial co-operation and partnership', which it was feared might be 'diluted' within Europe.[105] As a contributor to *West Indian World* put it, there remained a powerful feeling 'that we should stay out of the Common Market and that Britain should continue to trade with the black countries'.[106]

This fed into a suspicion of the EEC as a colonial and inherently racist body. Some feared that the EEC would roll back the citizenship rights of non-white immigrants, reducing them to second-class status as 'guest workers'. 'In the Common Market', papers warned, European governments could 'systematically deny blacks employment, educational and commercial opportunity'. Blond, blue-eyed workers from northern Europe, it was rumoured, were already being preferred to Black Britons, depressing still further the wages and opportunities of non-whites.[107]

Such anxieties were not solely the preserve of poorer migrants.[108] Roughly one-third of doctors had qualified overseas, mostly in the Commonwealth, and a storm erupted in 1975 over their right to work elsewhere in the EEC. Under an agreement on free movement, practitioners who had qualified in the Commonwealth would be ineligible to work elsewhere unless they requalified in a member state. Furious doctors complained of being treated as 'second or even third-class citizens', while the president of the IWA hailed the directive as 'clear proof that even the highly qualified professionals among the Asian immigrants in Britain stand no chance in the European Community'.[109]

Britain in Europe was acutely aware of these concerns and worked hard to assuage them. A full-time officer, Rana Ashraf, was put in charge of 'Asians for Europe' and 'Commonwealth for Europe', with a budget of £9,000. Articles were translated into Bengali, Gujarati, Punjabi and Urdu and placed in immigrant newspapers, together with a statement by Callaghan on the benefits of membership for the Commonwealth. There was even an ill-judged attempt at a song, 'Common Market Reggae', which it was hoped would appeal to voters from the Caribbean. At Leicester, the newly elected pro-Market MP, Nigel Lawson, addressed a Commonwealth for Europe rally, alongside local dignitaries such as Councillor K.M. Shah, Dr A.F. Asayeed and Mr T.K. Mukherjee. Sympathetic organisations, such as the Federation of Bangladesh Associations and the West Indian Standing Conference, were supplied with literature, as were bodies that took no formal position, such as the Standing Conference of Asian Organizations and the Pakistani Cultural Institute.[110]

BIE's strategy was to isolate its opponents' arguments and neutralise them one by one. For those who feared unemployment, there were warnings of higher job losses outside the EEC, with Black workers the first to suffer.[111] Commonwealth enthusiasts were reminded of the Lomé Convention and of the support given to membership by Commonwealth leaders.[112] The government pamphlet stressed that the renegotiated terms of membership meant 'a better deal for our Commonwealth partners', and included a supportive quote from the Jamaican ambassador to the United Nations.[113]

Special emphasis was placed on the export opportunities for India and South Asia. Ramniklal Solanki, who edited the Gujurati weekly *Garavi Gujarat* (circulation 27,500), stressed that 'Indian trade with the EEC is increasing', and predicted that the UK would be able, as a member, 'to press for better terms for India'.[114] The EEC had already established a commercial co-operation agreement with India, while negotiations were ongoing with Bangladesh and Pakistan. Shortly before the referendum, the EEC agreed a 6 per cent increase in textile imports from India, which BIE took as evidence that the UK was opening up the Community to Commonwealth trade. The Home Office minister, Alex Lyon, told a meeting in Bradford that 'If the UK were to leave the Common Market these agreements would be dropped and there would be a decline in the export opportunities of Asian suppliers.'[115]

BIE had two further weapons in its arsenal. One was access to the resources of the European Commission. The editors of all the major immigrant newspapers – especially those in languages other than English – were invited to Brussels on fact-finding tours, at which officials could explain 'the enhanced job opportunities for immigrants in the Market' and 'the benefits … from the Common Market's growing relationship with developing countries'. Papers written in Bengali, Gujarati, Hindi, Punjabi and Urdu were already thought to be pro-Market, but the Commission supplied them with facts and figures to enforce their case.[116] There was a particular emphasis on financial assistance. In January 1975, the Commission had announced £2.5 million in funding for UK immigrant groups, paying for language classes, employment programmes, reception schemes and advice services.[117]

A second asset was the prominence within the No campaign of Enoch Powell and the National Front. Powell attracted special venom for his 1968 'Rivers of Blood' speech, in which he had spoken of 'the black man' having 'the whip hand over the white man', and of white women driven from their homes by 'grinning piccaninnies'.[118] At a time when the National Front seemed to be in the ascendant, Powell was seen as giving political and intellectual cover to the advocates of racial violence and forced repatriation. The *West Indian World* (which accused him of 'a fanaticism more native to the less sophisticated Welsh') warned that Powell was stirring up 'ancient tribal and blood instincts', in a manner that recalled 'the brute Teutonic flavour of Third Reich demagoguery'.[119]

The association with the far Right troubled even anti-Market papers. Such were the arguments within its editorial board that *West Indian World* accidentally published an editorial headed 'NO to the Market' that concluded with a recommendation that 'the Black Community should vote YES'.[120] When the West Indian Standing Conference came out for membership, it confessed that Powell's support for voluntary repatriation had influenced its decision. If Britain voted to withdraw, it feared, the kind of 'nationalistic feeling' embodied by Powell and the National Front would be 'island locked', with 'nowhere to look for its outlet and remedies but inward'.[121] By contrast, BIE could call upon Roy Jenkins, the home secretary who had championed race relations legislation, and Shirley Williams, who had made a point of challenging Powell on immigration. Both had strong followings among immigrant communities and were treated with respect even in anti-Market papers.[122]

Better still, BIE could call upon the support of Commonwealth governments. In something of a coup for Harold Wilson – and in defiance of an appeal from the anti-Marketeers – thirty-two Commonwealth heads of government signed a note in May 1975 endorsing the renegotiated terms.[123] The note insisted that 'Commonwealth interests were in no – repeat no – way threatened' by British membership, adding that 'Many Heads of Government' saw 'positive advantage to their countries' from a British voice in the EEC. The 'strong view' was also expressed that Britain could make the Community 'more outward looking towards the rest of the world'.[124] Returning in triumph from the meeting, Wilson told the public that the 'best judges' of Commonwealth interests were 'the Governments of those countries. And, spontaneously, on their own initiative, they went on record in expressing the strong hope that Britain would remain in the Common Market.'[125]

For the anti-Marketeers, the Kingston declaration was the final blow to a campaign that had persistently struggled to mobilise Commonwealth sentiment. Callaghan's insistence that 'the issue of the Commonwealth could no longer be a matter of controversy' overstated the case, but it is striking how quickly the Commonwealth angle faded from the debate.[126] In the official pamphlet delivered to households across the country, the NRC dedicated just five sentences to the Commonwealth – a remarkable abdication of what had once been its strongest card. Campaigners still spoke hopefully of new trade relationships with the Commonwealth, but there was little pretence that the preferences enjoyed in previous decades were still on offer. By the time of the referendum, polls suggested that only 10 per cent of voters believed that the Commonwealth wanted Britain to leave the EEC.[127] Anti-Marketeers found themselves forced onto the defensive, promising to make up any *losses* to the Commonwealth should the Lomé Convention break down as a consequence of withdrawal.[128]

CONCLUSION

In March 1975, just as the referendum campaign was beginning, the government published the findings of a major Defence Review. Like the European question, the defence budget forced governments to reassess Britain's place in the world, its global commitments and the instruments of international influence. Commissioned by the defence secretary, Roy Mason, the review marked a decisive retreat from the idea that Britain should play a permanent military role outside the confines of Europe and the Atlantic. Britain's naval presence in the Mediterranean was wound up, troops were withdrawn from Malaysia and Brunei, and military commitments at Gan and Mauritius were liquidated. The Simonstown Agreement with South Africa was terminated (just ten days after the referendum result) and two frigates were withdrawn from the West Indies.[129]

Pressure on the public finances had done what several decades of strategic thinking had failed to achieve: the abandonment of that worldwide network of military commitments built up over centuries of imperial rule. Commending his proposals to the House, Mason made no secret of the financial pressures driving the review, or of 'the need to tailor our defence commitments and capabilities to our economic and political position as a middle-rank European Power'.[130]

From this perspective, the Defence Review and the decision to enter the European Community might be viewed together, as part of the painful process of post-imperial readjustment. What they represented, however, was not so much a retreat from Britain's global ambitions as a shift to new instruments of power. As Clement Attlee had recognised, as long ago as 1945, the atomic bomb and the long-range bomber had made redundant the old model of 'a string of possessions scattered over five continents', protected 'by means of a fleet based on island fortresses'.[131] In a clash of Cold War ideologies, each of which self-identified as anti-imperial, 'empire' itself was an increasingly unhelpful word, and its commitments had left British forces overstretched and ineffective. As Mason made clear, the Defence Review was intended not just to cut costs, but to ensure that Britain could continue to play its role as the second power in the alliance against the Warsaw Pact.

The conclusion was neatly summarised by the imperial scholar John Darwin: 'Colonial rule must die that influence might live: empire must be sacrificed to world power.'[132] By participating in the European Community, it was hoped, Britain could regain the global influence it had once exerted through Empire. *The Economist* claimed that British governments would only carry weight with the superpowers if they spoke 'as a member of a powerful European club – a fully established member, not just a new recruit still havering in the doorway and haggling about the subscription'. The *Sun* put it more bluntly: the Community was 'a fledgling superpower', and 'Britain, as the nation most experienced in international affairs, would naturally have a hand on the steering wheel'. Why throw away 'the chance of a lifetime'?[133] This was the imperial spirit reborn and redirected, not a nation coming to terms with a more bounded future. As the historian Ashley Jackson has written, Britain 'never lost the appetite and capacity to perform a world role', despite the loss of formal empire. As it embarked on its new European adventure, 'Britain's global interests never vanished, and, even though the Cheshire cat of empire slowly faded, the grin remained.'[134]

10 'THINK OF IT AS THE COMMON SUPERMARKET'

The first priority of any nation is to feed its people. If it fails to do this then there can be no worthwhile sovereignty.

James Goldsmith, February 1975[1]

Like the day of the red-coated soldier beating the living hell out of fuzzy-wuzzies, the day of cheap food has now gone.

Marjorie Proops, *Daily Mirror*[2]

I believe that most housewives would rather pay a little more than risk a bare cupboard. In the Common Market we can be sure of having something in the larder.

Margaret Thatcher, 4 June 1975[3]

In the summer of 1974, British shops began to run dangerously short of sugar. Imports from the Caribbean had dropped by more than a third, as Britain's traditional suppliers abandoned Commonwealth trade agreements for more lucrative markets in the United States. As panic buying began to spread, the supermarket chain Sainsbury's and the Conservative MP Norman Tebbit called on the government to reintroduce rationing.[4] Some shopkeepers refused to wait, operating informal limits of their own. Amidst reports of empty shelves, the National Consumer Protection Council appealed to consumers to stop buying sugar altogether, at least until the immediate crisis had passed.[5]

The 'sugar crisis' brought home Britain's extraordinary dependence on imported food. No developed country in the world bought so much of its food from overseas, or was so vulnerable to changes in global supply. As one anti-Market organisation put it, 'Only the British have to import or die.'[6] As sterling declined in value, as global population increased and as a series of poor harvests drove up prices, Britain's ability to feed itself became a topic of serious political controversy.

The politics of food had always had a special resonance in British politics. The repeal of the Corn Laws in 1846 had shattered the government of Sir Robert Peel and dislocated the Conservative Party for a generation. Tariff policy had split the Conservatives again in the first decade of the twentieth century, while the rump Liberal Party had splintered over the introduction of imperial preference in the 1930s. The failure to end rationing had dealt a serious blow to the Attlee governments after 1945, and the inflationary climate of the 1970s made prices once again a major political issue. Margaret Thatcher never shook off the mantra of 'Thatcher the milk-snatcher', and she was forced, in the midst of the Tory leadership contest, to deny that she was hoarding food in anticipation of shortages.[7]

Debates about food and farming inevitably loomed large in the referendum debate. The Treaty of Rome had specified only two areas for common policy development: agriculture and transport; and only the first of these had been implemented by 1975. The Common Agricultural Policy (CAP) was the flagship of the European project, and by 1972 it was absorbing a colossal two-thirds of the Community's budget.[8] In no other area did decisions made in Brussels touch so directly the lives of ordinary voters, for the CAP influenced how much consumers paid for their food, who they could trade with and how much farmers received in return. Critics of the CAP accused it of betraying Commonwealth producers, driving up food prices and storing up 'butter mountains' and 'wine lakes' at a time when millions were starving across the world. At stake was not simply the price of food but Britain's ability to feed itself at all, as a declining economy in a world of scarcity.

THE CAP DOESN'T FIT

The Common Agricultural Policy predated British membership and had been designed with the needs of Continental agriculture in mind. Unlike Britain, the six founder members still had large agricultural populations: in 1958, the Six employed about 75 million people in agriculture, most on low incomes and working in small farms. The effects of wartime dislocation were still very tangible and the continent remained a net importer of food. In this context, the CAP was designed to do four things: to drive up food production, so as to ensure security of supply; to achieve stable prices for consumers; to increase agricultural wages (just 38 per cent of the average income in Italy, and 50 per cent across the Community); and to facilitate a gradual reduction of agricultural employment, releasing much-needed labour for work in the towns. The policy also sought to bridge the gulf in living standards between urban and rural workers, which had fuelled the authoritarian politics of the interwar years.

To achieve all this, the CAP set target prices for agricultural goods. A common external tariff barrier, with variable import duties, was designed to prevent undercutting from foreign imports; if prices fell more than 5–10 per cent below the target level, an intervention board would buy up surplus produce, removing it from sale until the price had recovered. It was these 'intervention' stocks that constituted the 'food mountains' of which critics complained. In theory, surpluses were stored until they could be released back onto the market without breaching the target price. In practice, surpluses were either sold at a loss outside the Community (a form of export subsidy), released as food aid to poorer countries, or rendered unfit for human consumption and used for animal feed.[9]

The CAP was problematic for Britain in three main respects. First, the UK's agricultural sector was smaller than in most other member states. In 1972, just 2.6 per cent of the UK workforce was employed in agriculture, compared (on 1968 figures) to more than a quarter in West Germany, 14.9 per cent in Italy and 8.9 per cent in France.[10] Under a formula agreed before British entry, the UK would pay more into the CAP than it could ever get out, creating a budgetary problem since the CAP was easily the biggest item of Community expenditure. A second problem was that Britain imported an unusual proportion of its food from outside the Community, which was why its own proposals for a Free Trade Area in the 1950s had expressly excluded agriculture.[11] The National Farmers' Union calculated in 1970 that just 11 per cent of food imports came from the original 'Six'. That rose to 30 per cent if one included the other applicant states – Denmark, Ireland and Norway – while associated territories brought the figure to 36 per cent. Of the remainder, some would not be taxed at all, either because of special arrangements or because it was tropical produce that did not compete with Continental suppliers. Nonetheless, it was clear that taxing non-EEC produce would affect Britain more than most.[12]

Third, while Britain had long subsidised its own agriculture, the CAP both shifted the incidence of taxation and made it more visible to consumers. Since the 1950s, governments had made 'deficiency payments' directly to the farmer, funded out of general taxation. The CAP shifted the subsidy from the tax system to the price mechanism, which made its effects more tangible. Shoppers would feel the effects in their weekly grocery bill, with those on lower incomes hit hardest.[13]

The CAP also made tangible the otherwise rather abstract question of Britain's Commonwealth loyalties, for goods like mutton, lamb, butter and cheese from New Zealand and sugar from the Caribbean, Mauritius and Fiji would all face higher duties.[14] It gave substance to the issue of sovereignty, restricting the right of a free country to buy food wherever it chose. Above all, it drew a direct link between decisions made in Brussels and the rising cost of food at home; and that, in turn, linked it to the wider question of inflation and its destructive effect on household budgets. Debates about the CAP were also shielded, to some extent, from the fatalistic argument that 'we're in now so might as well stay'. With Britain still operating under transitional arrangements, the full effects of the CAP would not be felt until later in the decade, while bridging arrangements with the Commonwealth would continue into the 1980s. Hence, it was possible to argue both that things would get *worse* if Britain stayed in and that it was not too late to unravel the effects of membership.

For all these reasons, the CAP promised to be fertile soil for the anti-Marketeers. The Labour manifesto in February 1974 had promised 'Major changes in the Common Agricultural Policy, so that it ceases to be a threat to world trade in food products, and so that low-cost producers outside Europe can continue to have access to the British food market.' The October manifesto had reinforced that theme, insisting that the 'intervention' scheme must be abandoned. It promised to 'renegotiate the Common Agricultural Policy ... to make sure shoppers get secure supplies of food at fair prices'.[15]

Yet when Wilson presented the results of the renegotiation in 1975, he was candid that not all these goals had been achieved. Member states had agreed a more flexible regime of sugar pricing and a new beef regime that released more meat for domestic consumption, while home producers were partially compensated by deficiency payments. It was agreed that, so far as possible, intervention surpluses would be released to domestic consumers rather than sold abroad, for example by a beef subsidy paid to pensioners. More generous quotas were agreed for New Zealand dairy produce and Caribbean sugar cane, partly because of poor sugar beet harvests in Europe. Nonetheless, as Wilson acknowledged, 'We have not changed the fundamental character of the CAP.' The common external tariff barrier, the intervention regime and target pricing all remained in place, while the most significant changes arguably came outside the renegotiations, in the form of the Lomé Convention.[16]

'FOOD COSTS MORE IN THE COMMON MARKET'

Anti-Marketeers seized on Wilson's admission that the 'theology or doctrine of the CAP' remained unaltered. What that meant, they argued, was the institutionalisation of high prices, for as Clive Jenkins put it, 'the prime purpose of the Common Agricultural Policy is to keep food prices high'.[17] The very first pamphlet issued by the NRC was written by the former permanent secretary at the Ministry of Agriculture, Fisheries and Food (MAFF), Sir John Winnifrith, and proclaimed its message in the title: Food Costs More in the Common Market. Winnifrith offered voters a choice: 'Vote "Yes" in the referendum and your food will cost you more'; 'Vote "No" and you'll get cheaper food again.' The very structure of the CAP, he insisted, meant that 'food is and must be dearer in the Common Market'; for if there was no alternative supply of cheap food outside the Community, there would have been no need for the whole structure of import duties and intervention stocks in the first place.[18]

Polling found that voters who were unmoved by concerns about 'sovereignty' made a strong association between membership and price rises. Of those questioned a week after the renegotiations were completed, 50 per cent mentioned prices as a concern, while 40 per cent thought that the effects of the CAP had been worse than anticipated. Women and poorer voters both saw membership as 'the main cause of price inflation', and there was a general view that leaving would slow down the rise in costs.[19] Polling for the NRC identified 'prices' as one of the few issues that might sway voters in the final month of the campaign, while almost a third expected prices to get higher inside the Community.[20]

This became one of the central messages of the Out campaign. Adverts in the press, on which the NRC concentrated most of its slender resources, displayed portions of butter, meat and cheese at eye-wateringly high Common Market prices. Consumers were urged to 'Keep Food Prices Down. Vote No!'[21] Food was also a theme of the NRC's broadcasts, with one sketch imagining 'Mrs Britain' going to the shops to buy butter. 'She passed by the world market, where traders competed to bring her butter at the lowest price, and she came to the rival Common Market shop.' She had naively believed that her 'club subscription' would entitle her to lower prices, but had instead to pay much more to fund a 'cheese mountain' and the 'personal helicopter' of the store manager.[22]

By stressing the impact on food prices, Antis gave concrete expression to more abstract arguments about sovereignty and national identity. Get Britain Out stressed that an EEC ban on beef imports would be 'legally enforceable in Britain, although it was never discussed by Parliament'. There was nothing more redolent of Englishness than roast beef, prompting GBO to warn, in the creaking humour characteristic of the campaign, that 'your joint is worth beefing about'.[23] Invoking 'the classic link between food and self-government', Tony Benn conjured the memory of the Boston Tea Party, when popular fury had overturned not just the taxes on food and drink but a whole colonial system.[24]

For its critics, nothing summed up the CAP better than the 'beef mountains' and 'wine lakes' locked away in storage facilities.[25] According to government figures, intervention stocks in 1975 amounted to 266,000 tons of beef, 1.7 million tons of wheat, 253,800 tons of barley, 66,000 tons of butter and 60,000 tons of cheese. For Neil Marten, it was 'repulsive' to think that taxpayers' money could be spent on *destroying* food – or exporting it at knock-down prices to the Soviet bloc – with the goal of driving up prices at home. GBO held protests outside storage units in Liverpool and Ealing, mobilising pensioners to demand that stocks be released.[26] Powell suggested mischievously that Britain, *outside* the Community, could benefit from the sale of intervention stocks. 'It will be nice', he commented, 'to enjoy the largesse now restricted to Eastern Europe.' Britain, he speculated, might even have 'to take precautions to ensure, when we are outside the Market that they do not unload their beef mountains or butter mountains on to us at knock-down prices, or drop us in a wine ocean'.[27]

A theme of the No campaign was that things would become worse rather than better over time. As they frequently pointed out, transitional arrangements meant that Britain would not come fully under the CAP regime until the late 1970s. In 1975 butter and cheese were still generously subsidised, under arrangements that were likely to be phased out over the decade.[28] If prices rose to Continental levels after the referendum, one of two consequences would have to follow: either wages would rise to keep pace, fuelling inflation and making exports uncompetitive, or they would remain stagnant, forcing families to cut their standard of living.[29] Christopher Frere-Smith predicted that VAT would be extended to food, an argument endorsed by the financial secretary to the Treasury, John Gilbert.[30] *Tribune* joined in the chorus, warning that new European food taxes would be tabled within weeks of a vote to stay in.[31]

FARMERS FOR EUROPE

Such fears were bolstered by the enthusiasm of so many in the farming community for the CAP. Ahead of the referendum, the English and Welsh Council of the National Farmers' Union voted almost unanimously to stay in, as did the NFU in Scotland, Wales and Northern Ireland.[32] The union's president, Sir Henry Plumb, was a vice-president of Britain in Europe and canvassed energetically for a Yes vote, while the General Purposes Committee (led by the felicitously named Mr Cattell) instructed union officials to 'take every opportunity of promoting the agricultural advantages attached to our continued membership'.[33] The National Federation of Young Farmers' Clubs volunteered to distribute literature to its 1,300 constituent branches, while the Farm Women's Clubs hosted BIE discussion groups.[34] In Scotland, where eight of the SNP's eleven Members represented rural areas, farmers formed a solidly pro-Market constituency. When the Norwegian prime minister visited the East Midlands, the branch secretary of the Nottinghamshire NFU was apparently hard put to find a single anti-Market farmer for him to meet. The local NFU cricket team even broke off its summer tour, so that members could get back in time to vote.[35]

This owed something to the febrile mood of British agriculture. The *British Farmer and Stockbreeder*, the official journal of the National Farmers' Union, calculated that the industry had seen a

12 per cent fall in income over the previous financial year, 'by far the largest drop in real income UK farmers have ever suffered'. Inflation, rising oil prices and the declining value of the pound had pushed up costs by more than £700 million, while global shortages of meal hit livestock herds especially hard. Real incomes were suffering a severe squeeze, leaving many farmers with severe cash-flow problems.[36]

The result was a significant hardening of the NFU's position. In the decade after the first application in 1961, the NFU had taken no formal position on membership. The issue, it acknowledged, raised questions that went far beyond the interests of agriculture, so it limited itself to advising on the terms that farmers would wish to see in the event of a successful application. In reality, the union was in 'direct and continuous contact' with the team negotiating entry, and later boasted that there had been no need for 'any special public or press campaigns' as 'We were already at the table.' While the union retained a formal neutrality until entry, its pronouncements were clearly favourable to the terms agreed and there was general optimism about the prospects for agriculture.[37]

For many farmers, it was precisely the Common Agricultural Policy that made the Community so appealing. The purpose of the CAP, as the *Financial Times* observed, was not 'to ensure cheap food for the consumer' but to maintain decent prices for 'the farmers of the Community', bringing 'their standard of living up to that of industrial workers'. While ministers tended to deny that the CAP would mean higher prices, farmers welcomed it on precisely this basis.[38] As NFU spokesmen pointed out, food prices had been falling for decades, both relative to other goods and as a proportion of household expenditure. In 1962, the average household in Britain had spent nearly 28 per cent of family income on food; by 1972, that had dropped to 22 per cent. While prices had risen markedly after the oil shock in 1973, little of that increase had made its way to the farmer. It was not the CAP that had driven up prices, it was argued, but the increased cost of feed, fertiliser and transportation.[39]

Part of the attraction of the CAP was that it countered the political pressure on governments to hold down food prices at times of economic difficulty. Farmers were as much the victims of inflation as any other part of the community, and many were tired of having their incomes squeezed for the benefit of others. For this reason, the NFU was alarmed at the 'fundamental' reform of the CAP promised in the manifesto. Ministers were urged not to 'undermine its basic principles', on the grounds that 'any tampering with the basic structure and intention of the CAP ... could have the gravest consequences'.[40] Rather than extending transitional arrangements, which kept food prices below the level set by the CAP, the NFU was keen to bring harmonisation forward. Farmers noted with dismay that the government's renegotiation demands were all directed to 'the benefit of the consumer', and they suspected the minister of agriculture, Fred Peart, of focusing exclusively on 'the political implications' of agricultural pricing. With few MPs from farming constituencies, a Labour government seemed particularly likely to sacrifice farming interests to the needs of consumers, either through opt-outs or by extending the transitional arrangements for the CAP.[41]

There was, of course, some criticism of the CAP, even from within the farming community. Poultry farmers were facing severe competition from French producers, whom they accused of dumping cheap eggs on the British market, while small farmers were often suspicious of the centralising tendencies of the Community. The National Union of Agricultural and Allied Workers urged members to vote No, though its opposition was notably lukewarm and had little to do with specific conditions in agriculture.[42] Christopher Harrington, the former chairman of the Egg Marketing Board, warned that a policy that deliberately created surpluses, only to withhold them from domestic consumption, was likely to prove politically unsustainable. Consumer pressure, he argued, would ultimately force those surpluses onto the market, exerting a severe downward effect on prices.[43]

Others feared that membership would strip agriculture of its influence over government. This was a particular concern for John Cherrington, a respected columnist for the *British Farmer* and the *Financial Times*. For an industry employing such a small proportion of the workforce, he noted, agriculture enjoyed an unusually privileged place in government. It was the only industry to have a dedicated department of state, and the NFU had built especially close relations with ministers and civil servants through the Annual Review of agricultural prices.[44] Once agricultural policy passed into the remit of the Community, British farmers would be dependent on their ability to build alliances on the Continent. 'Whitehall', Cherrington warned, 'will lose its power to help us,' and British farmers would carry less weight in the corridors of the European Commission.[45]

For most farmers, however, the chances of a fair hearing for agriculture seemed brighter in Brussels than at Westminster. In a country that imported so much of its food, and so few of whose workers were employed on the land, both parties were always likely to privilege consumer over producer interests. The political power of the consumer had been bolstered by the emergence of powerful organisations like the Consumers' Association, and by the appointment in 1974 of a Cabinet minister for prices and consumer protection. As secretary of state, Shirley Williams provided an institutional counterweight to the minister of agriculture, Fred Peart, and enjoyed a significantly higher profile.

The clearest indication that the NFU was losing its political clout came in the dispute over the 'Green Pound'. This was the artificial currency unit used for agricultural trade within the EEC, and was intended to protect agriculture from fluctuations in the currency market. In 1973, it was set roughly at parity with the pound; but, as sterling depreciated, ministers resisted calls to devalue the Green Pound accordingly. Keeping the Green Pound artificially high helped to hold down food prices, which was crucial to the success of the Labour government's 'Social Contract'; but farmers were furious to find themselves trading in a uniquely overvalued currency. Senior figures in the NFU called for full monetary union, in order to free agricultural exchange rates from manipulation by ministers.[46]

By contrast, the NFU was bullish about its ability to influence agricultural policy within the Community. The larger agricultural population of the 'Nine' could be harnessed, it was hoped, to the NFU's own experience of working closely with government in the formulation of policy. Plumb, who would later become an MEP and president of the European Parliament, had already built up strong networks in Continental agriculture. In January 1975 he became president of the Comité des Organisations Professionelles Agricoles, which represented farming organisations from across the nine member states. The *British Farmer* argued that the sector had already benefited from its ability to shape agricultural policy across the Continent, not least in securing the resumption of the live export trade, which had been banned by Parliament in 1973. British farming, it was argued, could exert *more* influence at Brussels than in Westminster. By contrast, 'the sovereignty we'd retain by going it alone would be the sovereignty to go bankrupt in our own way'.[47]

'A COMMON FOOD POLICY'

Agricultural support for the Community made itself felt on referendum day: the ten counties with the highest level of agricultural employment recorded an average vote of 72 per cent for staying in, compared to a UK average of 67 per cent.[48] Yet the enthusiasm of the farming community was not an unmixed blessing for BIE, for it was precisely those aspects of the Common Agricultural Policy that were attractive to farmers – the likelihood of higher prices, secure from political interference by national governments – that made it a difficult sell on the doorstep. A BIE strategy document identified food prices and sovereignty as 'our most difficult themes', and research by the CBI at the start of May found that 'a high proportion of people still believe that food costs more because we are in the Community'.[49] Just three weeks before polling day, Roy Jenkins warned that the Yes campaign seemed to be making no progress on the issue; 'there is a wall,' he complained, 'which we have not yet succeeded in penetrating, of understandable but misplaced incomprehension'.[50] BIE's own polling presented a bleak picture, with voters blaming the Community for rising prices and for shutting off cheap supplies from the Commonwealth.[51]

Despite all this, BIE did have three significant assets. Firstly, it could deploy a remarkable number of speakers who were trusted on issues of pricing and household economy. The most important of these were representatives of consumer organisations, like Janet Graham of the Housewives' Trust and Eirlys Roberts, the former editor of the consumer magazine *Which?* Unlike the NRC, Britain in Europe also had a flourishing Women's Office, which put out detailed guidance for speakers on the issue of food prices.[52] The pro-Marketeers could call on two of the most senior female politicians of the day, Margaret Thatcher and Shirley Williams. As secretary of state for prices and consumer protection, Williams spoke for the government on prices and was widely respected by voters. Thatcher was a more polarising figure, but spoke with authority on household economy.[53]

Secondly, Britain in Europe could draw on the resources of almost the entire food and drink industry. Supermarkets like Sainsbury's and Marks & Spencer campaigned vigorously for membership, publishing pro-Market material in their magazines.[54] Jimmy Goldsmith acted both as a fundraiser and as the brains behind BIE's Food Advisory Council, which brought together such well-known suppliers as Hovis,

Unigate, Sainsbury's and Goldsmith's own company, Cavenham Foods.[55] The Food and Drink Industry Council (FDIC), the umbrella group for British suppliers, funded a 'Truth About Food' office, which promised voters an 'unbiased picture so that they can make up their own minds'. While it presented itself as occupying a middle position, shielding voters from 'wild statements from either side', the office was in fact unequivocally pro-Market.[56] It spent £15,000 on its own campaign in the final weeks before the referendum, and made more than £6,000 of market research freely available to BIE.[57]

Thirdly, and most importantly, the eighteen months before the referendum had seen prices rise faster *outside* the Community than within. Thanks in part to the oil crisis, which pushed up transport costs, world food prices had risen significantly, and in some cases were now higher than within the EEC. That allowed BIE to challenge at source the argument that membership had driven up prices. A study by the Consumers' Association concluded that the overall effect of membership had 'probably been neutral', while another, by a group of academic economists, calculated that prices had been 1 per cent *lower* as a result of membership.[58] Harold Wilson, characteristically, chose to split the difference, concluding that 'there isn't 2d in it either way'.[59]

Shirley Williams went further, warning that withdrawal could spark a *rise* in food prices. This was partly because of the weakness of sterling, which had lost a fifth of its value over the previous four years. Under the EEC's monetary compensation scheme, subsidies cushioned the impact of currency depreciation, shielding Britain from what would otherwise have been even greater increases in its import bill.[60] If withdrawal was followed by a currency crisis, the food situation would get worse, rather than better. As *The Times* asked its readers, 'Could we afford to eat if we left the EEC?'[61]

Antis responded, as we have seen, by insisting on the *structural* tendency of the CAP to produce higher prices. They did not deny that, at rare moments, prices in Europe might drop below the world average; but they argued that a system designed to shield farmers from international competition must, in the long run, have an inflationary tendency. Pro-Marketeers argued that this was only true if one assumed continuing access to cheap Commonwealth supplies, which could no longer be taken for granted in an age of population growth and shifting economic power. In a paper for Labour's National Executive Committee, Callaghan predicted that EEC prices would be similar to world prices in the future, and that the CAP would 'provide a useful cushion when world prices peak'.

> Our experience in recent months has borne this out. British consumers have been protected against the effects of rocketing sugar and cereal prices: on balance food would have cost us much the same whether we were inside or outside the Community. The prospect is therefore that membership of the Community, a major food producing area, will offer us greater stability of prices at reasonable levels, and security of supply in times of shortage.[62]

This was annexed to a moral argument about the nature of Britain's trade flows. Cheap food, it was argued, was a relic of the old colonial system, by which prosperous industrial nations exploited their market power to buy food at starvation wages.[63] Speakers for the Women's Office accused anti-Marketeers of confusing 'food that is cheap to produce with food that is cheap to buy. Do they really *want* continued exploitation of tea workers in Ceylon or sugar growers in the Caribbean?' A columnist for the *New Scientist* warned that the No campaign had been left behind by a shift in power to agricultural producers: 'urban man is about to learn that unless he is prepared to pay an economic price for his food, he will not be fed'.[64]

The argument that, in the modern world, there was no such thing as cheap food seems to have struck a chord with voters. Polling by the FDIC found that, although voters blamed the Community for raising prices in the past, they had little expectation of savings were Britain to leave. Indeed, they feared that the alienation of Commonwealth suppliers might leave Britain dangerously exposed if it also abandoned the Common Market. The memory of the sugar crisis played an important role here. Britain's Commonwealth allegiances had not protected it when others were prepared to pay a higher price; had it not been for European subsidies, sugar would have cost more for the remainder of 1974. 'Anxiety about changes', the FDIC concluded, and the 'loss of what must now be seen as a reliable source of food, seems to be a major factor in making people feel that Britain should stay in. Availability of food appears to override the somewhat wishful feeling that price rises could be slowed down by our leaving the Community.'[65]

Polling by ORC suggested a clear 'win' for the pro-Marketeers on the issue of pricing. Asked in June 1975 to name those forces which were 'mainly to blame' for price increases over the previous three years, just 19 per cent suggested the Common Market, down from 51 per cent in July 1973. 'Worldwide increases' were blamed by 64 per cent of respondents, up from 49 per cent two years earlier. (In a shift that would have significant consequences later in the decade, the proportion blaming trade unions rose from 25 per cent to 47 per cent.)[66] SPRC (Social and Community Planning Research) produced a similar result in a panel study conducted just after the referendum, which showed a striking difference between Yes and No voters. Of those who had voted to stay in, 41 per cent identified world food prices as the main cause of domestic price increases, while just 21 per cent blamed the Community. Of those who had voted to leave, 42 per cent blamed the EEC and 30 per cent world prices.[67]

This allowed the Yes campaign to change the conversation, refocusing attention onto the issue 'of food *availability* rather than cheaper food *prices*'.[68] The seventies was a decade of severe anxiety about food security: a series of poor harvests had shrunk world food reserves, while population growth and the shift of economic power was increasing competition for supplies. The sugar crisis in 1974 had been followed, over the winter, by anxieties about grain stocks, with concerns that Canada might seek alternative markets because of the unreliability of sterling.[69] The question, it seemed, was not *how much* food would cost, but whether it would be available at any price.

In this context, BIE sought to repackage the CAP as a 'Common *Food* Policy'. Voters were encouraged to think of the Community as 'the Common Supermarket': 'Well stocked shelves'; 'Plenty of choice'; and 'just around the corner'.[70] Speakers were urged to 'Take the offensive' on food prices, by focusing on 'concern about availability'. In a Community that supplied more than 80 per cent of its own food, membership gave Britain 'secure and preferential access to reliable supplies'.[71] Janet Graham of the Housewives' Trust told journalists that 'It is no good talking about prices ... if there is no food to buy. The key to the whole debate is not prices, but supply.'[72] Sir Henry Plumb reinforced the message that shoppers 'would face a clear threat to continued regular food supplies if Britain left the Market', while Ted Heath told the 'housewife' in Scotland that 'The referendum is not about the price of her shopping basket, but about whether she will be able to fill it or go short.'[73]

The tone of this material was positively apocalyptic. Geoffrey Lean, the respected environmental columnist, warned that the world was entering 'a period of unstable and unpredictable climatic change', in which Britain, without preferential access to European stocks, would be 'one of the most vulnerable countries to the effects of famine'.[74] A pamphlet issued by Britain in Europe warned voters – in capital letters – that 'YOU CAN'T TAKE YOUR FOOD FOR GRANTED ANY LONGER!' The world was growing by more than the entire population of Great Britain every year, and food production was not keeping pace. With 'millions of people in the world on the brink of starvation', the vote on 5 June 'could decide whether you and your children continue to get all the food you need. Not ten years from now. But any year.'[75] Britain's dependence on imports, it was argued, left it peculiarly vulnerable to producer power. As the FDIC put it, 'Withdrawal would involve us each year in a continuous uncertainty as to our ability to feed ourselves properly at a price we could afford.'[76]

This helped pro-Marketeers to fight back on the sovereignty argument. The OPEC countries had provided definitive evidence of how scarcity could shift the balance of power between producers and consumers, and the prospect of a three-day week in food sent shivers down the spine. In 'a scarce food situation', wrote Lean, there could be 'few illusions that food will not be used as a political weapon'. 'Through lack of food we would in the end be likely to have less sovereignty outside the EEC than inside it.'[77] James Goldsmith reminded voters that 'there can be no worthwhile sovereignty' for a nation unable to feed itself, while Roy Jenkins warned that Britain could 'end up looking like an impoverished old country gentleman who keeps telephoning the village shop, only to be told they don't deliver groceries any more'.[78]

Talk of 'food mountains' was dismissed with contempt. The much-vaunted 'beef mountain' was estimated to constitute about seventeen days' worth of supplies, two days more than the 'butter mountain'.[79] As Lord George-Brown put it, 'One damned good outbreak of foot-and-mouth disease or one good action by Jack Jones and his lot and that is gone.'[80] Sainsbury's told customers that 'World food supplies are as low now as they have ever been in modern times,' while the CBI thought that the prospect of food shortages was greater than at any point in peacetime for the last 150 years.[81] Food might, perhaps, be more expensive within the Common Market, but, as Margaret Thatcher insisted, 'most housewives would rather pay a little more than risk a bare cupboard. In the Common Market we can be sure of having something in the larder.'[82]

FIGURE 10.1   People queue for bread in London, during a bakers' strike in 1974.
Source: Evening Standard, Hulton Archive: www.gettyimages.co.uk/license/3273301

Anti-Marketeers never got to grips with the argument about supply. With polls suggesting that voters no longer believed in cheap food from outside the Market, it was imperative that they find at least some response to the issue of food security. Yet their efforts were strangely unpersuasive. Neil Marten speculated ominously about the dangers of bad weather in Europe, while Get Britain Out suggested that climate change might reduce the growing season on the Continent. Neither argument seems to have gained much traction.[83] Partly for this reason, the pro-Marketeers did not need a conclusive 'win' on the issue of prices; they just had to generate enough uncertainty to neutralise the issue for the No campaign. Pollsters reported 'Extensive feelings that leaving the EEC will make food harder to get for the UK', and a reluctant conviction that staying was now 'less risky than leaving'. 'Availability of food', the FDIC reported, 'appears to override the somewhat wishful feeling that price rises could be slowed down by our leaving the Community.' In consequence, the food issue could now be regarded as an asset to the 'In' campaign, rather than as a compelling argument to leave.[84]

FISH AND SHIPS

The enthusiasm of the farming community for membership was not shared across the entirety of the food industry. Fishing enjoyed neither the political clout of the agricultural sector nor its importance to the rural economy. Even in 1970, before accession, fishing accounted for just 0.1 per cent of GDP, but it had a political, historical and emotional significance that dwarfed its purely economic contribution. In towns like Fraserburgh, Grimsby, Hull, Lerwick and Peterhead, fishing was a mainstay of the local economy. Even long-distance trawlermen, who fished thousands of miles away in the North Atlantic, were deeply entrenched in their local communities, while the names of pubs, clubs, restaurants and churches bore witness to the long relationship of these places with the sea.[85] Further inland, fishing evoked vague but romantic associations of men with craggy faces, blue knitted sweaters and far-fetched tales, while the prospect of foreign vessels intruding on British waters played to those folk memories of invasion that suffused the European debate, invoking images of 1588, the Armada and the small flotillas that saved the British army at Dunkirk. The result, as Con O'Neill wrote privately, was an industry that constituted 'economic peanuts but political dynamite'.[86]

Fishing also offered a case study for those who saw in the Community a malevolent cartel, looking to asset-strip the United Kingdom. The Common Fisheries Policy (CFP) had been hastily agreed in 1970, just hours before accession negotiations began with the UK, Denmark, Norway and the Republic of Ireland. The effect of this manoeuvre, which a leading British diplomat condemned as 'irresponsible in the extreme', was to deny these countries any say in a policy that would affect each of them profoundly, for their rich coastal waters produced a catch more than double that of the Six.[87] At the core of the CFP was the principle that all member states should enjoy equal access to European waters, an approach that posed an obvious menace to the inshore fleets of the applicant states. During the accession negotiations, the UK successfully demanded control over most waters within a 12-mile limit, but this was a temporary derogation and would be subject to review after a decade.[88]

Given its limited importance to the economy, fishing barely featured in the renegotiations. Wilson failed even to mention the subject when he reported to the Commons in March, to the fury of Scottish MPs in particular.[89] Fishing, as an industry, had traditionally found it difficult to exert pressure on government, because of its limited size, scattered distribution and the existence of long-standing tensions between (for example) long-distance trawlermen and the inshore fleet and between Scottish and English co-ordinating groups.[90] Yet anger in the industry was rising, and towards the end of the month it exploded in a blockade of British ports. Nearly 2,000 vessels from forty-three ports imposed a cordon along the coast, running from Fleetwood in Lancashire, via Lerwick in Shetland, to Bridlington in the East Riding. The fishermen's demands included a ban on imports of frozen fish and shellfish, a 50- or 100-mile exclusion zone for foreign fleets, and the total renegotiation of the Common Fisheries Policy. A spokesman for the strikers told reporters that 'The Government must decide whether it wants a British fishing industry or not, and if it does it will have to pay for it.'[91]

The blockade constituted a major embarrassment for the government; yet its implications for the European debate were not straightforward. The full force of the CFP would not be felt until at least 1982, which rendered it a prospective, rather than immediate threat. As even the blockade's leaders acknowledged, it was not practical to renegotiate the CFP until the UN Convention on the Law of the Sea, currently meeting in Geneva, had completed its work, which meant that the issue could be parked for the present with the promise of future action.[92] In the meantime, the major threat to UK fisheries came from states *outside* the EEC, such as Norway and Iceland. Both countries were dumping large stocks of frozen fish on the UK market, caught in subsidised fleets, which was driving down prices for domestic suppliers (while also providing much-needed work for the processing industry). At the same time, they were excluding British trawlers from traditional waters in the North Atlantic, a process that would trigger the third of the so-called 'Cod Wars' just weeks after the referendum.[93]

In this context, the Community could prove a useful ally. The EEC already set minimum import prices for wet fish, but under British pressure it extended the scheme to frozen produce. Minimum prices for Norwegian stocks came into force within days of the blockade, which proved decisive in calling off the action. Soon, newspapers were running headlines promising a 'new deal for fishing' by the summer, so long (and *only* so long) as Britain remained in the EEC. Hugh Brown, the minister responsible for ending the strike, told *The Times* that fishing was now a leading priority for the Community, which was working to recast the CFP, provide more support for domestic fleets and, crucially, reduce import penetration from non-member states. 'But a "no" vote in the referendum', he warned, would throw all this into jeopardy, requiring 'a total review' of ministers' efforts.[94]

Such hopes were largely disappointed. Subsequent reforms of the fisheries policy did not extend exclusive fishing rights to anything like the extent that domestic fleets had hoped, and the long decline of the industry accelerated in the years that followed. The number of fishermen regularly employed in Scottish-based vessels halved in the thirty years from 1970, while the Scottish Government would describe the CFP in 2009 as 'the EU's most discredited and unpopular policy'.[95] Jim Sillars later accused ministers of viewing fishing as a 'throw-away card' in the negotiations, because of its limited importance to the UK economy.[96] Yet the argument that membership posed a peculiar danger to British fishing was more difficult to make in 1975 than it would later become, and the preoccupation with imports from Norway – the country often held up by anti-Marketeers as an ideal – complicated the argument that withdrawal from the EEC would benefit British fishermen. On the contrary, pro-Marketeers could parade the grants and subsidies coming to fishermen from the Community, at the very moment when 'a non-EEC country, Norway, is dumping subsidised cod in Scottish ports'.[97]

CONCLUSION

Looking back on the campaign, Douglas Jay felt that the NRC had failed to play to its strengths. Food, he argued, should have been 'the central if not the only, theme of the whole campaign'. Warnings of higher prices were 'true'; they were 'overwhelmingly important for the whole nation'; and 'the public both understood and believed' what was being said. Jay blamed the heterogeneous nature of the campaign for starting too many hares; he also complained that its leaders 'had not the propaganda sense to see that in public sentiment the cost of food was the dominant and decisive issue'.[98]

Yet the problem for the No campaign was not simply a lack of 'message discipline'. Just as importantly, it had failed to adapt a message that had worked in the past to the changed conditions of 1975. With global prices rising, a shortage of key commodities and a reaction in the Commonwealth against quasi-colonial preferences, the cry of 'cheap food' lost much of its purchase. That allowed pro-Marketeers to change the focus from *price* to *supply*, and the Antis never responded effectively to concerns about food security. In the 1980s and '90s, as consumers came again to take food supplies for granted, anger at the CAP would become politically potent once more. But at the key moment, the Antis had been decisively outmanoeuvred – as much by events as by their political opponents.

PART THREE

THE UNRAVELLING OF BRITAIN?

11 'ULSTER SAYS YES!'

A vote for the Common Market is a vote for 1. Ecumenism 2. Rome 3. Dictatorship 4. Anti-Christ.

Free Presbyterian Church of Ulster, 4 June 1975[1]

it is the effects of Dr Mansholt's Common Market agricultural policies, and not the colour of the Pope's socks, towards which the attention of the electorate should be directed.

Brian Brennan, 29 May 1975[2]

Hardly a day goes by without the Common Market lobby telling us about so many million pounds from the EEC for some Ulster firm and so many million pounds for that. We almost start dabbing our eyes with emotion to think of those kind French and Germans, sending us their hard-earned cash out of pure affection and compassion for their bosom chums in Northern Ireland.

Enoch Powell, 29 May 1975[3]

On 5 June 1975, twenty-two-year-old Brendan McNamee was gunned down near his home in West Belfast. He had gone out to buy fish and chips with his girlfriend, but was shot dead by an IRA assassin as he walked down the Stewartstown Road. A member of the Irish Republican Socialist Party and an officer in the Irish National Liberation Army, McNamee was the latest casualty of a turf war between Republican organisations, a feud which had claimed at least five lives since February. His younger brother, Henry, would later be killed by the Irish People's Liberation Organisation, under suspicion of being an informer.[4]

McNamee was not the only fatality on referendum day. Later that evening, a young farmer called Francis Jordan threw an explosive device into a Protestant pub in Bessbrook, County Armagh. He was shot by security forces while trying to escape and died of his injuries in hospital. A staff captain in the South Armagh IRA, Jordan was described in Republican death notices as 'killed in action'. According to the official funeral oration, Jordan had 'died defending the people'.[5]

1975 was one of the bloodiest years of the 'Troubles'. At least 247 people were killed by paramilitary groups or the security forces, while hundreds more were injured or driven from their homes. Voters cast their ballots in June under the watchful eye of soldiers and armed police, and they did so at a time when the whole future of the province had been thrown into uncertainty. It was only three years since the Northern Ireland Parliament at Stormont, which had governed the province since 1921, had disintegrated under the pressure of communal violence, prompting a bizarre offer of mediation from the Ugandan despot Idi Amin.[6] Attempts to replace it with a power-sharing assembly, under the terms of the Sunningdale agreement, had collapsed in 1974, following a general strike orchestrated by Loyalist paramilitaries. With Harold Wilson privately considering a 'doomsday' option to cut off the province as an independent Dominion, 1975 saw yet another doomed attempt at a settlement, with elections to a Constitutional Convention at the beginning of May.[7]

The referendum campaign in Northern Ireland cannot be understood in isolation from the wider history of the 'Troubles'. Organisations like the Orange Lodges, the IRA, the Ulster Volunteer Force and Sinn Féin all campaigned actively in the referendum. For the Reverend Dr Ian Paisley, founder of the Free Presbyterian Church of Ulster and leader of the Democratic Unionist Party (DUP), the European project ranked with sodomy and ecumenism as a menace to the survival of Protestant Ulster. Sinn Féin and the IRA, who portrayed the armed struggle as a colonial liberation movement, viewed the EEC as a new imperial project that would entrench the border between North and South. In Ulster, more than in any other part of the United Kingdom, the significance of the European debate went far beyond trade relations or diplomatic policy. It was a debate about the sanctity of borders, the relationship between Catholics and Protestants and the very survival of the Northern Irish state.

All this gave the referendum a sectarian character that was quite alien to the debate in England, Scotland and Wales. Yet the referendum would also expose the limits of sectarianism, reminding us that Ulster has a politics – and a political history – beyond the bitter experience of the 'Troubles'. In Ulster, as in other parts of the UK, the European issue fired a missile through conventional party alignments, leaving traditional allies scattered haphazardly across the battlefield. Those campaigning to leave the European Community included Sinn Féin, the Democratic Unionist Party, the IRA, the Ulster Volunteer Force, the Orange Lodges and the National Front. Those fighting to 'Keep Northern Ireland in Europe' ranged from the Social Democratic and Labour Party (SDLP) and the Unionist Party of Northern Ireland to the British and Irish governments and the mainstream churches. In this respect, the campaign anticipated the alliances from which the Good Friday Agreement would emerge two decades later. For John Hume, of the SDLP, the capacity of the EEC to disrupt sectarian allegiances was part of its attraction; and this was to become a central plank of his party's campaign.

By complicating sectarian allegiances, the referendum opened up a space for groups that conventionally stood apart from the electoral politics of Northern Ireland. Organisations like the Confederation of British Industry in Northern Ireland, the Institute of Directors, the Farmers' Unions and the Townswomen's Guilds all played prominent roles, chiefly though not exclusively for the Yes campaign. As in other parts of the UK, both sides mobilised actors, celebrities and sports personalities, including the Olympic pentathlete Mary Peters, the rugby player Willie John McBride and the footballer George Best.

The sectarian dimensions of the campaign in Northern Ireland were not its only distinctive feature. Plebiscitary politics were less alien to Ulster than to other parts of the UK. There had been a Border Poll in March 1973 and referendums were mandatory in the Republic of Ireland for all changes to the constitution. There had been five such referendums since 1968, including a vote on European membership in 1972, all of which had been closely followed north of the border.

This gave campaigners in the North considerable experience on which to draw, but also posed peculiar difficulties. When voters went to the polls in June, many were doing so for the seventh time in two years.[8] Voter fatigue was inevitable, and only Shetland recorded a lower turnout.[9] Elections to the Constitutional Convention on 1 May monopolised the attention of the press and politicians alike, making it hard to campaign effectively on Europe until the final weeks before the vote.

Nonetheless, the fluidity of the party system in the North was in some respects well suited to the referendum. Within the broad categories of 'Unionist' and 'Nationalist', party alignment was more liquid than elsewhere in the UK. The five years before 1975 had seen a radical restructuring of the party system, with the emergence of the Alliance Party (1970), the Social Democratic and Labour Party (1970), the Democratic Unionist Party (1971), Ulster Vanguard (1972), the Unionist Party of Northern Ireland (1974) and the United Ulster Unionist Party (1975). Together with the United Ulster Unionist Council and the Ulster Workers' Council, founded in 1974, this constituted an unusually fluid environment in which ad hoc alliances were the norm. There was also more experience of managing dissent on second-order issues, because of the totemic significance of the border. Perhaps for this reason, the Unionist and Nationalist parties in Northern Ireland proved more successful than either Labour in the 1970s or the Conservatives in the 1990s at containing disagreements on Europe.

With its sectarian rhetoric and lurid anti-Catholicism, the debate in Northern Ireland could strike observers in Britain as mystifying or even risible. Yet the intellectual level of the debate was in some respects unusually high. Arguments about sovereignty, national identity and institution-building across borders were the common currency of Ulster politics, whereas other parts of the UK had little recent tradition of abstract constitutional debate. In Northern Ireland, the idea of 'pooling sovereignty' was not a vague abstraction but a question of practical politics, central to ongoing debates about power-sharing, Sunningdale and the Council of Ireland.

'ULSTER SAYS NO!' UNIONISTS AGAINST EUROPE

The most vehement opposition to membership came from the Unionist parties, especially the more evangelical wing represented by Ian Paisley and Ulster Loyalism. The Democratic Unionist Party, the Orange Lodges, the Ulster Volunteer Force and the Ulster Defence Association all campaigned against membership, with Paisley and Enoch Powell taking the leading roles. Unionists were not, of course, unanimous

FIGURE 11.1 An armed soldier on patrol passes anti-Market graffiti in Northern Ireland.

Source: With permission of Victor Patterson

on the question: the Unionist Party of Northern Ireland argued for a Yes vote, while the Ulster Unionist Council and the Official Unionist Party took no formal position. Ulster Vanguard was usually counted in the No camp, but its leader William Craig and rising star David Trimble were thought to favour membership.[10] An organisation called 'Unionists for Europe' placed adverts in the major newspapers, though its provenance was somewhat murky.[11] Nonetheless, the majority of Unionist politicians and the major Loyalist paramilitary organisations campaigned to leave the Community, mobilising a wide range of legal, confessional and economic arguments.

Unionists approached the referendum in febrile mood. Over the previous three years they had been deprived of their parliament, subjected to direct rule from Westminster and confronted with demands for 'power-sharing' with the Catholic minority. The abolition of Stormont was not simply a blow to Unionist pride; worse still, it placed the government of Ulster in the hands of politicians in London, whose commitment to the Union was distinctly suspect. Only a year earlier, in 1974, the Ulster Workers Council had beaten off a power-sharing Assembly established as part of the Sunningdale Agreement, prompting a furious riposte from the Labour government. The prime minister, Harold Wilson, was known to favour a united Ireland, and in 1974 he had launched a memorable assault on those Unionists 'who spend their lives sponging on Westminster and British democracy and then systematically assault democratic methods'.[12]

Wilson's Northern Ireland secretary, Merlyn Rees, had legalised Sinn Féin in 1974 and was known to be in contact with the IRA during the 1975 truce.

With an economic crisis in Britain and spiralling security costs in Northern Ireland, the prospect that the British might simply 'scuttle' – leaving the two sides to fight out their own future – was taken seriously by Unionists and Nationalists alike. It was a policy with an inglorious pedigree across the British Empire, and Garret FitzGerald, foreign minister in Dublin, was so alarmed at the prospect of a sudden withdrawal that he asked Henry Kissinger to intervene with the UK government.[13] Such fears, however ill-founded, encouraged two convictions that were always latent within Unionist thought: that the survival of the border depended solely on their own courage and determination; and that UK politicians were never far from betraying Ulster into the hands of the Republic.

Unionist thinking on the EEC focused heavily on the location of sovereignty, an issue with particular resonance in the North. The UK and the Republic of Ireland both claimed sovereignty over the six counties, while a strand of Loyalist thought identified Ulster itself as a sovereign territory.[14] The concept of 'pooling sovereignty' had formed part of numerous peace proposals, and many Unionists saw the EEC as another vehicle for the kind of cross-border interference they had fought off in Sunningdale. The Official Unionist Neil Oliver, who chaired the Northern Ireland 'Get Britain Out' campaign, urged voters to 'reject power-sharing and a Council of Europe', just as they had 'rejected power-sharing and a Council of Ireland'. It did not help that the presidency of the Council of Ministers in 1975 was held by the Republic, making Dublin a particular focus of Community activity. Nor was it reassuring that the European Court of Human Rights was hearing a case, brought by the Republic, concerning the treatment of detainees in the North.[15]

Some in the Republic undoubtedly hoped that membership would advance a united Ireland, by making partition a matter of common European concern.[16] Anticipating interference in the province, constitutionalists in Ulster were quicker than their British counterparts to identify the potential of Qualified Majority Voting, over the longer term, to erode the national veto. Such concerns were given special emphasis in *Combat*, the newsletter of the Ulster Volunteer Force,

which warned readers that the 'most serious objection' to the Common
Market was 'the erosion of our national sovereignty':

> The sovereignty, freedom, rights and liberties of the British people
> and their Parliament took hundreds of years and much blood to build
> up. By staying in the Common Market we are throwing away our
> birthright, our right to exist as a free self-governing people. We must
> get out of Europe.[17]

Sovereignty was a particular lodestone for Enoch Powell, the former
Conservative who had sat since October 1974 as the Unionist MP for
South Down. Powell's emphasis on sovereignty found a warmer reception in Ulster than it did elsewhere in Britain; indeed, the stubborn
determination of Unionists to govern themselves was partly what drew
Powell to Ulster politics.[18] Powell's speeches flattered the historical
sensibility of Ulster Protestantism, likening resistance to the EEC to the
muster of the Ulster Volunteers in 1912.[19] Deploying a word with special resonance in a context of terrorist violence, he accused the Heath
government of 'hijacking' the United Kingdom, claiming that Heath's
hatred of Ulster 'and his impatience to find some way, any way, of
getting rid of it altogether' was a principal reason 'why he forced the
United Kingdom into the EEC'.[20] Powell pledged to fight 'shoulder to
shoulder with the Ulster Unionists against the betrayal of Britain to the
Common Market', just as he had fought 'against the betrayal of Ulster
to Republican terror'.[21]

Powell was drawn to Ulster Unionism by its proud historical sense, its commitment to the defence of historic liberties and its
determination to uphold the right to independent self-government. He
was less comfortable with its confessional politics, refusing to join the
Orange Order and insisting that Unionism had no necessary connection with Protestantism.[22] This set him at odds with the highly charged
evangelicalism of Ian Paisley and the Orange Lodges. Paisley ran an
overtly sectarian campaign, warning that there was 'no future for traditional British Protestantism' or 'our Reformation heritage' in the
Community. For Paisley, the EEC was a Catholic organisation run by
and for its Catholic majority. To submit to Popish rule from Brussels,
he believed, made no more sense than to submit to Catholic rule from
Dublin.[23]

Paisley was a charismatic orator who revelled in the street politics of the referendum. He held news conferences, preached sermons and led a rumbustious motor cavalcade through Belfast.[24] As one of the few men to have founded a newspaper, a political party and a church, he commanded the loyalties of an unusual range of campaign vehicles. Through the *Protestant Telegraph*, the Democratic Unionist Party and the Free Presbyterian Church, he waged holy war on the European project, which he represented in nakedly anti-Catholic terms.[25] Had not the Pope set aside a feast day for 'the Madonna of the Common Market', the 'greatest Catholic Super State the world has ever known'? Posters warned that 'A vote for the Common Market is a vote for 1. Rome 2. Ecumenism 3. Dictatorship 4. Anti-Christ.' As 'a predominantly Roman Catholic community', Paisley insisted, the Common Market owed 'its first allegiance to the Pope and recognizes the ultimate authority of the Vatican'.[26]

In Paisley's view, everything from Heath's defeat in 1974 to rising inflation could be attributed to 'the Papist Super State'.[27] Headlines in the *Protestant Telegraph* became increasingly lurid: 'Communism is "Deeply Christian" – says Roman Catholic Priest'; 'Pope Defends Mass Murderer' (a reference to Pope Pius XII, 'the greatest war criminal unhung'). 'The very mention of … the "Treaty of Rome"', the paper grumbled, should have been 'sufficient to arouse most Ulstermen'.[28] Cartoons portrayed the Community as an extension of the Pope himself, his talons spelling out the letters EEC.[29]

The rhetoric of 'No Popery' was not confined to the Paisleyite press. Papers like *Loyalist News* also saw in the EEC a 'religious union' that would undermine the culture of Protestant Ulster.[30] Vanguard warned that Catholicism would be 'the dominant faith' in Europe and that 'Roman Catholic social doctrine' would infect every area of 'political and economic life'; 'all will come under the dictatorship of the Roman Catholic dominated beast.'[31] There were also concerns for the purity of the Sabbath, given lax Continental customs.[32]

Elsewhere in the UK, the potential for interdenominational exchange was part of the EEC's appeal. By contrast, Paisleyism, like many Calvinist sects, remained intensely suspicious of ecumenism, viewing it as an attempt to bring 'into one filthy cage all the unclean birds of Christendom'. For Paisley and his associates, the Catholic Church was not a misguided branch of Christianity but a 'disreputable, dishonest and deceitful suitor', bent on corrupting the bride of Christ.[33]

The visceral anti-Catholicism of Paisley and his allies was a minority taste, even among Unionists. For No campaigners seeking to win Catholic votes for their cause, Paisley was a positive embarrassment; as Brian Brennan, of the Antrim Republican Clubs, complained, it was the Common Agricultural Policy 'and not the colour of the Pope's socks towards which the attention of the electorate should be directed'.[34] Yet it was possible to construct a Protestant case against membership that did not rest on Paisleyite principles. Ulster Protestantism retained a strong historical sense, which viewed the Reformation as a constitutional milestone, not simply as a theological event. The Act of Supremacy of 1534 could be seen as a declaration of independence by the English state, which shook off the authority of a foreign court and made the secular authorities in London the highest court of appeal. From this perspective, the Treaty of Rome unpicked one of the great political achievements of the Reformation: it placed Britain once again under the instruction of 'a mainly foreign court'. *Loyalist News*, the organ of the Ulster Workers' Council, warned that

> Unless Britain fulfils her obligations under the Treaty of Rome, she must suffer the penalties imposed by a court outside of the land. This was just the situation before the Reformation. At that time this land was under the bondage of a foreign power, the Roman Church, but those chains were broken. To be forced to submit to the decrees of these articles would only be to return again to that bondage from which we have been liberated.[35]

The idea that British liberties had been carved out through resistance to foreign and clerical interference ran deep in Ulster Protestantism, and made the allegedly Catholic character of the Community especially disturbing. In the words of the *Protestant Telegraph*,

> Britain, under Henry VIII, broke the power of the Pope and rejected the Vatican's claim to jurisdiction over these islands. The Common Market concept aims to restore this power ... You have been warned.[36]

From this perspective, the challenge of the Common Market was analogous to that of the Catholic Pretender, James II, at the Battle of the Boyne. 'The No Surrender of 1690', urged the *Protestant Telegraph*, 'must still be our watchword when we record our NO TO EUROPE!'[37]

All this gave the Unionist case a character that was rooted as much in a form of constitutional politics as in sectarianism. In the politics of Northern Ireland, the word 'Nationalist' – with a capital 'N' – is conventionally applied to the supporters of a united Ireland; but the politics of the Province might equally be understood as a collision between rival nationalisms. For Unionists, as much as for Republicans, politics was structured around the defence of an authentic national community against alien intrusions, which were thought to endanger both the integrity and the democratic legitimacy of the nation. Paisley, in particular, was never slow to invoke suspicion of the foreigner or to mobilise jingoistic sentiments against the European project. Voters were urged to choose between 'British democracy and Brussels dictatorship', while Paisley complained that the 'terms of the Treaty of Rome are like those imposed by a conqueror on a defeated enemy – unconditional surrender'. Douglas Hutchinson, a DUP Convention Member from Armagh, noted that the EEC was controlled 'by Germany and France, the enemies of the British nation for centuries', and 'thanked God that in the past 1,000 years Britain had never bowed at the proud foot of a conqueror'.[38]

If Protestantism was a core part of Unionist identity, so too was a brand of colonial spirit. As a plantation people, operating on the margins of the British government's attention, Unionists felt an affinity with settler populations elsewhere. For this reason, the idea that membership was a betrayal of Commonwealth interests resonated more powerfully in Ulster than in other parts of the UK. Alleging a plot to separate the British people from their 'children in the Commonwealth', *Loyalist News* complained that entry to the Community, with its tariff barrier and protectionist trade arrangements, had 'made a devastating impact on the British World'.[39] This was also a theme of the National Front's campaign, which alleged that the 'Empire has disintegrated, not through a single defeat in battle, but because of total loss of political will'. With its hyper-charged nationalism and overwrought persecution complex, the Front saw Ulster as a key battleground, and its literature urged voters to get 'OUT of the Common Market' and 'back together with the White Commonwealth'.[40]

As a shipbuilding centre, Belfast had strong historic links with the Empire; and its declining economic significance boosted suspicion of the imperial metropole. Just as Britain stood accused of 'selling out' the colonies, once they had lost their economic value, so it was feared that Britain would abandon Ulster under the financial burden of the 'Troubles'. Here, as so often in Northern Ireland, imperial, constitutional and religious arguments intersected, pitting what a DUP official called 'the materialistic ethic which would sacrifice anything for economic gain' against 'the Christian ethic which cherished the British tradition of parliamentary democracy and sought to preserve our national identity, distinct and separate, from the latent forces of darkness and tyranny in Continental Europe'.[41] By disrupting the Commonwealth, it was claimed, the EEC would cut Britain off from 'those countries on other continents with whom we have the closest of traditional ties'.[42]

The emphasis on sovereignty, nationalism and the colonial spirit operated alongside a more hard-nosed economic campaign, focused on jobs, investment and the supply of cheap labour. In the 1970s, about 60 per cent of Ulster's exports went to the British market, which made the prospect of competition from the Continent extremely alarming.[43] Like the Left in Britain, the No campaign stressed the capitalist, free market credentials of the Community and the constraints it placed on state intervention. 'Rights denied' to members included the 'right to curb the activities of big monopolies and help the nationalized industries' as well as the 'right to stop British firms and financial institutions investing abroad instead of in Britain'.[44] The Ulster Workers Council, which oriented its campaign specifically towards the Ulster working class, condemned the EEC as 'an economic millstone around the necks of the British people', which would 'turn Britain and Ulster into an industrial backwater'.[45]

Northern Ireland was one of the few parts of the UK where immigration was a major issue in the campaign. This was partly an economic concern, based around competition for jobs. *Loyalist News* warned that Article 48 of the Treaty of Rome, guaranteeing free movement, could facilitate strike-breaking, allowing 'foreign labour ... to take over the jobs of the strikers'.[46] Immigration would increase competition for jobs, putting pressure on public housing and draining the social security budget. A Yes vote, the paper warned, would be 'a victory for the giant business concerns, the big investors and speculators and a defeat for the small businessmen and the ordinary worker'.[47]

Yet the real concern focused on Catholic immigration from the South, with its potential to recast the balance of population north of the border. There was particular anxiety about the Safeguarding of Employment Act, which reserved jobs in protected industries to workers from the North. On entry to the EEC, the UK had negotiated an extension of the Safeguarding Act for five years, but it was widely predicted that the legislation would fall foul of European law.[48] Thereafter, warned *Loyalist News*, 'we can expect the inhabitants of Eire to flock here in their thousands'.[49]

This allowed the No campaign to annex an economic critique of membership to anxieties about the border. The Ulster Workers Council warned that free movement would bring large numbers of Catholics into the North, swelling the electoral strength of the Nationalist parties with 'implications ... too obvious to spell out'. 'After the initial invasion' – a characteristic choice of words – 'consolidation would take place in the border counties and there would be a gradual thinning out of the Loyalist communities'. 'This newly acquired hinterland ... could be the terrorist launching ground for the final Republican armed onslaught on what was left of Northern Ireland.' It was futile to expect Britain to resist such an incursion: impoverished by the effects of European integration, it would be only too glad to be rid of an expensive burden. In short, integration into the European Community would 'achieve what an IRA terrorist campaign could never do – a 32 county Republic'.[50]

From this perspective, membership of the EEC was not simply a policy error; it represented an existential threat to the Ulster state. Thomas Passmore, Grand Master of the Belfast Orange Lodge, warned that membership would deliver Ulster 'lock, stock and barrel' into the hands of the Republic. In voting against the Market, voters 'would also be saying "No" to an eventual United Ireland'.[51] The Ulster Workers Council urged voters to 'treat the forthcoming referendum as yet another border poll', while the ultra-Protestant organisation TARA warned that 'if Britain says "Yes" Common Market troops will march through Belfast leading the Eire Army to hoist the tricolour over Stormont'.[52]

All this constituted a distinctly Unionist case against the European Community, a supranational entity whose *raison d'être* was the erosion of national borders. Yet organisations like the DUP, the Ulster Volunteer Force and the Orange Lodges found themselves in an uneasy alliance on the European question with Nationalist and Republican parties. These groups began from strikingly different premises, but forged similar warnings about employment, sovereignty and investment. In this respect, they demonstrated how the sectarian divide distorted political allegiances in Northern Ireland, while disguising the extent of common ground between the parties on issues other than the border.

'VOTE NO TO THE NEW ACT OF UNION'

With the SDLP campaigning for a Yes vote, the most prominent Nationalist voice for the Out campaign was Sinn Féin. For Sinn Féin to take part in the referendum at all was in some respects surprising, for Republicans did not recognise the validity of elections in what they regarded as occupied territory. The civil rights organisation People's Democracy, for example, boycotted the referendum, despite its 'long-standing opposition to the EEC as an imperialist and monopoly capitalist super power', because it denied 'that the 6-County area has any right to decide on its own future or its international links. The Six Counties are part of Ireland and all decisions about their future must be taken by the Irish people as a whole.'[53] The *Irish Catholic* demanded that Dublin make a formal protest against the claim of a foreign power to organise an election on Irish soil. Surely the EEC could not permit 'this violation of the sovereignty of one of its member-states by another'?[54]

Sinn Féin, by contrast, took an active part in the referendum. It urged its supporters to vote on 5 June and promised 'a full scale anti-EEC campaign'. Malachy Foots, the party's Ulster press officer, told journalists that 'Posters and leaflets would be circulated, there would be door to door canvassing and Sinn Féin members would be placed outside polling stations. There would also be public meetings.' Like People's Democracy, Sinn Féin denied the legitimacy of UK elections on Irish soil, but it reserved the right to participate where, as in 1918, doing so might advance the national struggle.[55]

For Sinn Féin, there were two obvious benefits to participation. First, the referendum provided a golden opportunity for the party, which had only been legalised a year earlier, to broaden its appeal. With the SDLP campaigning to stay in, the referendum allowed Sinn Féin to position itself as the leading Nationalist voice for a No vote, colonising what it believed to be the centre ground of Nationalist politics. The SDLP was experiencing its own tensions over the question; Gerry Fitt and Paddy Devlin both opposed the Common Market, as did many branches and activists. By fighting for a No vote, Sinn Féin hoped to peel away support from the SDLP while stoking its internal tensions. The party newspaper, *An Phoblacht*, predicted optimistically that 'The Referendum ... might see the end of the SDLP.'[56] A strong performance in the referendum might also break the perception that the party stood only for the removal of British troops. As Sinn Féin president Ruairí Ó Brádaigh told a press conference, the referendum campaign provided an opportunity to campaign on a wider prospectus and to engage the party with a broader range of social and economic concerns.[57]

The second great prize on offer was the possibility of driving a wedge between the politics of Northern Ireland and those of the wider UK. Like the nationalist parties in Scotland and Wales, Sinn Féin recognised that a No vote in Northern Ireland, which was subsequently overruled by a Yes vote in England, would strengthen the argument that the United Kingdom stripped its smaller nations of democratic self-government.[58] 'Massive NO votes in these countries', it argued, might even 'lead to a break-up of the UK'.[59]

Sinn Féin's opposition to the EEC, however, was not merely tactical. The party had campaigned for a No vote in the Republic in 1972, and it hoped that a No vote in the North would reanimate the anti-Market cause on both sides of the border.[60] Like the DUP, Sinn Féin was fiercely critical of what it called 'the dictatorship of the Catholic hierarchy in the ecclesiastical sphere', which it blamed for upholding conservative economic and social policies and interfering in the affairs of the Irish people. It accused the Papacy of conniving in British rule, and its newspaper, *An Phoblacht*, published a series of essays on this theme in the summer of 1975.[61] Like the DUP and the Labour Left, it also viewed the Common Market as an instrument of international finance, 'opposed to the interests of ordinary workers'.[62] Sinn Féin saw itself as a revolutionary socialist party, and warned that the Common Market 'stands for merciless competition and for driving smaller, weaker firms to the wall'. Membership would drive up unemployment, decimate small farms and move heavy industry away from 'peripheral' regions like Northern Ireland to the 'golden triangle' of France, Germany and the Benelux. Like Plaid Cymru and parts of the SNP, Sinn Féin preferred to align itself with anti-imperial, anti-NATO elements among the smaller countries of Europe. The EEC, it believed, was both 'an economic conspiracy', uniting 'the owners of wealth against those who work for a living', and 'a political conspiracy against the poor countries of the developing world'.[63]

That economic case resonated with Republicans of all stripes. The Irish Republican Socialist Party, which had broken from the Official IRA in 1974, pledged 'an intensive campaign of opposition to EEC membership', describing the EEC as 'a rich man's club where the European working class will be the victims'.[64] Writing for the Republican Clubs' Committee for Women's Rights, Philomena Donnelly urged voters to 'view the Common Market in class terms'. A Yes vote would blight 'the future of the working class', producing spiralling unemployment and rapid deindustrialisation.[65]

All this, however, was subordinate to the larger question of sovereignty. As a movement that existed to wrest back self-government, Republicanism was inherently suspicious of calls to 'pool' sovereignty. For *An Phoblacht*, the Common Market simply recreated in a new form the European empires of old, and was designed, like them, to bring peripheral economic zones under the control of their larger neighbours. The EEC, it declared, had perpetrated 'exploitation and robbery' on a scale

> experienced previously only under imperial regimes. The comparison is no accident: the Common Market and the Comecon both *are* empires, are acting like the empires we know from history and are having the same effects on the nations they have swallowed.[66]

This vision of economic imperialism was fundamental to the political thought of Sinn Féin.[67] In the words of *Republican News*, the EEC was simply 'an attempt to resurrect the old European empires, to make them viable in the modern world'. Republicans should 'VOTE NO TO THE NEW ACT OF UNION.' 'DON'T BE ENSLAVED BY THE NEW EMPIRE.'[68]

While Unionists saw the EEC as a threat to the constitutional status of the North, Republicans took precisely the opposite view. The Treaty of Rome, they warned, 'puts a seal on partition and accords formal recognition to existing frontiers'. Members were required to respect one another's territorial integrity, raising concerns that membership would embed Partition in international law. Was it a coincidence that 'the Dublin Government' (Sinn Féin did not accept the legitimacy of the Irish Republic) was 'preparing to draft a new Constitution ... in which partition will be fully recognized'?[69]

Underpinning all this was a more atavistic nationalism, which was suspicious of the very principle of foreign interference. *Republican*

News warned that membership would mean 'foreigners buying up our land' and Irish children 'digging sewers in Munich'. Europeans would 'grow rich by making Ireland poorer'. Continental states, it was feared, did not share the values of the Irish people, or their commitment to neutrality in world affairs. The newspaper of the Irish Republican Socialist Party, the *Starry Plough*, reminded readers that Ireland was already under occupation by '20,000 British Troops'. As a part of the Community, with Ireland's commitment to neutralism overturned, might they soon be joined by '20,000 French or Dutch troops in Ireland defending their interests?'[70]

'YES! YES! YES!' NORTHERN IRELAND FOR EUROPE

For the advocates of a Yes vote, the situation in Northern Ireland could hardly have seemed less propitious. Most of the leading parties were campaigning to leave the EEC, as were many of its most charismatic figures, and they had assembled a powerful, cross-community case for withdrawal. Britain in Europe seemed scarcely interested in the region: though its director, Con O'Neill, was himself from a prominent Ulster family and a cousin of the former prime minister, Terence O'Neill, BIE allocated only £2,000 of the £125,000 government grant to Northern Ireland.[71] Nationalists and Unionists seemed to be marching in step on the issue, while voter fatigue made it harder to change minds or to achieve the kind of positive mood for which the campaign was striving in Britain.

To make matters worse, the slightest misstep could inflame sectarian grievances. At Queen's University, stickers circulated by the Yes campaign had to be withdrawn after protests: intentionally or not, slogans like 'Don't Withdraw', 'Don't Pull Out', 'Stay Right in' and 'Yes! Yes! Yes!' looked more like a commentary on Catholic birth control than an intervention in the European debate.[72]

Yet the situation was less dire than at first appeared. On the one hand, both Unionists and Nationalists were in practice deeply divided. The Official Unionist Party and the SDLP both favoured membership, while the 'Northern Ireland in Europe' campaign included representatives from both sides of the confessional divide. The United Ulster Unionist Council was unable to agree a position on the referendum, disabling the campaigning vehicle that had been so effective in 1974.

At the same time, for all the sound and fury it generated, the European question was generally considered a second-order issue. Conscious of the need to maintain a united front on the border, Unionists and Nationalists alike took steps to contain their divisions on Europe. Magazines like *Combat* and the *UWC Journal* argued vehemently for a No vote, but also provided space for divergent viewpoints; a courtesy that they did not extend on many other subjects.[73] Even Paisley was careful to stress that he would accept a Yes vote, while letting it be known that he would welcome a seat in the European Parliament.[74]

Furthermore, the backing of the London and Dublin governments played to the advantage of the Yes campaign. It was difficult to argue that a No vote would strengthen the Union, when the rest of the UK seemed likely to approve membership. The idea that withdrawal would advance the cause of a united Ireland seemed equally perverse, when the Republic had made clear its own determination to remain in. For Nationalists who did not, like Sinn Féin, deny the legitimacy of the Southern state, the fact that 83 per cent had voted for membership in the 1972 referendum was a significant fact.[75]

The Yes campaign in Northern Ireland was run by Erskine Holmes, a lecturer and Belfast councillor who later founded and served as first chief executive of the Northern Ireland Federation of Housing Associations. Holmes was a member of the Northern Ireland Labour Party (NILP), like many of those working to 'Keep Northern Ireland in Europe'; yet the campaign was genuinely cross-party, bringing together activists from the Alliance Party, Labour, Ulster Vanguard, the SDLP and the Unionist Party of Northern Ireland.[76]

Outside the NILP, the main support for the campaign came from the SDLP, the Alliance Party and members of the Official Unionist Party. It was no coincidence that these were also the parties most sympathetic to power-sharing. The SDLP, in particular, had a long-standing strategy of reorientating political debate away from sectarianism towards more class-based issues of social and economic opportunity. Though individuals were permitted to dissent – and figures of the stature of Gerry Fitt and Paddy Devlin did so – the bulk of the SDLP saw in the EEC an opportunity for the kind of cross-border co-operation they had hoped to achieve through the Council of Ireland.[77] John Hume campaigned hard on the economic benefits of membership, warning that the choice lay between membership of 'a massive market and fast growing economy' or a state of 'permanent isolation pretending proudly that we are masters of our own affairs when we will have, in fact, very few affairs to master'.[78] Others, such as Seamus Mallon, Frank Feely, Michael Canavan and Hugh Logue, focused on issues like climate change, environmental degradation and the European Social Fund.[79]

For many of those involved in the referendum, the chance to work with people from diverse political backgrounds was among the most exciting opportunities of the campaign. It was also a microcosm of something larger: a chance to soften national rivalries and promote a more outward-looking spirit. As Hugh Logue, SDLP Convention member for Londonderry, put it:

> A 'yes' vote was an opportunity ... to assert that for this generation and its children the world did not end at Portavogie, Fairhead, or Larne Harbour, nor even in Dublin or London. Overseas did not mean just Rathlin Island, he said. 'There is a big wide world outside which we have shied away from for many centuries because of our own self inflicted complex'.[80]

For John Hume, the movement of peoples across borders offered a chance to break down 'the real border in Ireland, which is in the hearts and minds of our people'. Hume saw in the Community both a 'challenge' and an 'inspiration', showing how old enemies who 'in this century alone have killed each other by the million' could find peace through the building of common institutions that respected their national interests and identity. 'If bitter enemies like France and Germany can build new relationships, can we not do the same?'[81]

That view was not restricted to the SDLP. Berrie O'Neill, the treasurer of Northern Ireland in Europe, was just one of those who looked to membership to 'soften' the division between North and South, so that their 'political problems might be discussed in a wider regional context'. The violence of the Troubles, he believed, gave a special resonance to what he called 'the noble ideals of the German and French founders', with old antagonists working in partnership to prevent 'the horrors of war being repeated'.[82]

In this respect, the Yes campaign in Northern Ireland, as in the rest of the UK, pitched its appeal explicitly to the political centre, reaching out to those who disliked the atavistic nationalisms of both the Unionist and Republican extremes. This partly explains the appeal of the EEC to the Northern Ireland Labour Party, which hailed membership as a way of 'promoting internationalism and defeating nationalism'.[83] As Erskine Holmes later recalled, 'I opposed nationalism. I had absolutely no time for any form of nationalism.'[84] This anti-nationalist dimension also contributed to one of the more distinctive features of the referendum debate in Northern Ireland, which was the willingness of sections of the radical left to back membership. While the Communist Party of Ireland, under its chairman Andy Barr, favoured leaving, the Workers Association (WA) campaigned vigorously the other way. For the WA, nationalism was as much the enemy of class solidarity as international finance, and it found in the EEC 'a very welcome change from the sterile world of cul-de-sac nationalism'. The WA was keen to build links with trade unionists in Europe, on the principle that 'if the bourgeoisie can organize and develop on a European basis the working class can do the same'.[85]

There was also support from many churchmen, sick of sectarian violence and keen to distance themselves from the aggressive evangelicalism of Ian Paisley. Echoing the 'Christians for Europe' campaign in the rest of the UK, pro-Marketeers stressed the historic links between Irish Christianity (whether Catholic or Protestant) and a larger, European Christendom. As the Methodist minister R.G. Livingstone reminded his congregation on the Shankhill Road, the 'first carriers of the Christian Gospel to these shores came from Europe. In return we in Ireland sent Columba to Iona, Columbanus to France, Gall to Switzerland.' The idea that Protestantism was 'in danger of being swamped by the Roman Catholic population and priesthood of the EEC' seemed, to Livingstone, 'a frightening confession of weakness'. Preaching the following evening at Grosvenor Hall, the Rev Eric Gallagher accused the No campaign of 'unChristian' political values. 'An insistence on national sovereignty', he claimed, was 'almost a blasphemy ... The only sovereign rights were the rights of God.'[86]

Like the Yes campaign in London, pro-Marketeers in Northern Ireland worked to mobilise celebrities, sports personalities and other figures from outside the political mainstream. Posters gave pride of place to those men and women who had gone outside Northern Ireland to compete successfully in the world: the pentathlete Mary Peters, who had won gold in the 1972 Olympics; Derek Dougan, the record-breaking striker for Wolverhampton Wanderers; and Willie John McBride, who had captained the British and Irish Lions to victory in South Africa in 1974.[87] Voters were urged, like them, to 'give Europe a sporting chance' and to 'join their team' in the referendum fight.[88]

As well as mobilising celebrities and non-partisan public figures, the Yes campaign sought to align itself with trade unions, employers' organisations and representatives of Northern Ireland's leading industries. The Institute of Chartered Accountants, the Confederation of British Industry (Northern Ireland), the Northern Ireland Chamber of Commerce, the Bank of Ireland, the Northern Ireland Council and the Ulster Farmers' Union all campaigned strongly for membership. Key figures in the Yes campaign included Henry McLaughlin, director of the construction firm McLaughlin and Harvey; Berry O'Neill, of the Bank of Ireland; James O'Brien, chief executive of the Meat Marketing Board; William J. Black, managing director of Blaxnit Hosiery; and P. I. Foreman, managing director of Harland and Wolff. The campaign also recruited prominent trade unionists such as Billy Blease, regional secretary of the Irish Congress of Trade Unions, and Sandy Scott, the senior shop steward in the Belfast shipyards. Together, they sought to construct an economic case for membership that could bypass confessional loyalties.[89]

The core of their argument was a warning that Ulster could not survive economically outside the EEC. The economy of Northern Ireland depended on small farming and traditional heavy industries, both of which were increasingly reliant on European grants and loans. Voters in Belfast were warned that, if Northern Ireland left the Community, all existing loans would have to be repaid, while a £15 million application to the European Investment Bank from Harland and Wolff would become defunct. The result would be the loss of 'thousands of shipyard jobs'.[90] Foreign investors would relocate to the Continent, while exporters would face new barriers to their products. Industries such as 'shipbuilding, agriculture and man-made fibres', it was argued, 'can no longer be efficiently developed in a national market. These industries require a continental market.'[91]

This was a particular theme for the Labour Committee for Europe. Erskine Holmes warned that a No vote could cost Ulster 'up to £60 million of additional investment over the next three years'.[92] The vice-chairman, Alan MacLeod, mocked those who denied that Ulster benefited from membership: 'say so to the 24,000 unemployed who have been retrained under a scheme financed by the Social Fund, or the six thousand employed in various firms who have also been trained with funds from the EEC Social Fund'.[93]

To counter allegations that the EEC was in the pockets of great multinationals, advertisements for 'Northern Ireland in Europe' prominently displayed the names of local firms. Small and medium-sized companies like Raceview Woollen Mills, A. Warnock (bagpipe makers), Barlow Threads, Wright Industries (carpet and rug manufacturers), John Dowling & Sons Ltd (heating, plumbing and electrical contractors), Alexander Reid & Frazer & McCleary all lent their names to pro-Market material. Reports on pro-Market events stressed the business credentials of those who took part. A launch event in Belfast, for example, included representatives of the construction industry, Northern Ireland Railways, the Belfast Chamber of Commerce and the Bank of Ireland.[94]

Farming remained a crucial industry, with divergent views on Europe. Small farmers and pig farmers tended to be hostile, fearing that the EEC would consolidate holdings and expose small producers to unsustainable competition. This was the view of the Pigs Marketing Board and the Farmers' Defence Association, both of which canvassed for a No vote.[95] The prestigious Ulster Farmers' Association, however, which represented large and medium-sized holdings, worked actively to stay in. Farming subsidies, it noted, were traditionally higher on the Continent, and Ulster was already benefiting from the Common Agricultural Policy. There was some evidence that farming in the Republic had benefited from membership, with per capita incomes in agriculture more than doubling in real terms between 1970 and 1978.[96] Large-scale farming depended on imports of meal and fertiliser from the Continent, which would become more costly outside the Community. Just as importantly, the prosperity of the agricultural sector was clearly linked to that of the UK economy as a whole. If withdrawal led to a decline in British prosperity, agricultural prices and demand would all fall.[97]

As in Britain, the Yes campaign worked to reach out to women voters, for whom food prices were a particular concern. A conference at the Russell Court Hotel in Belfast brought together 150 representatives of women's groups and Townswomen's Guilds, where successive speakers sought to explode the 'myth' that food prices had risen as a consequence of membership. Particular emphasis was placed on the prospect of food shortages, and the protection provided by membership of the CAP.[98] Pro-Marketeers sought to woo organisations like the Townswomen's Guilds and the Women's Institutes, as bodies which could reach large numbers of voters without going through the established parties. Mrs D. McMurray, vice-president of the National Federation of Business and Professional Women's Clubs, featured prominently in literature, as did Sadie Patterson, who won international peace awards for her work in the organisation 'Women Together'. Posters showed Patterson pouring tea while reflecting on the benefits of membership, a reassuringly domestic image to set alongside younger figures like Mary Peters.[99]

In all these ways, 'Keep Northern Ireland in Europe' sought to lift the debate above the preoccupation with the border – a necessary strategy if it was to hold together Unionists and Nationalists. Yet it also proved skilful at annexing economic and social concerns to the sectarian allegiances of particular audiences. Colonel James Sleator, secretary of the Northern Ireland CBI, warned Protestants that withdrawal would see firms that traded with the Continent switch their operations south of the border, carrying jobs and investment from Northern Ireland to the Republic. For the first time, 'Eire would become more prosperous than Ulster'; 'the whole "economic balance" between Northern Ireland and Eire would be altered in favour of the South'.[100] Speaking for the Labour Committee for Europe, Brian Garrett warned that the 'real long-term threat to Northern Ireland' came not from the EEC, which would never tolerate changes against the will of the majority, but 'from the anti-Marketeers who will make this the poorer half of Ireland tied to a bankrupt Britain, under the control of elements so hostile to Northern Ireland, that we will be cut off without a penny in a hostile world'.[101]

The warning that, 'If Britain becomes poorer, it becomes more and more likely to eject Northern Ireland from the United Kingdom' certainly resonated with some Unionists. Outside the Common Market, it was feared,

> New investment will flow South and in a few years the Irish Republic will be very much more prosperous than the North. Bang will go much of the basis of unionism. Irish nationalism will be rekindled and for the first time in history the nationalists will have economics on their side.[102]

In this way, pro-Marketeers tried to link the case for union at both a British and European level. Douglas McIldoon, of the Labour Committee for Europe, told voters that the UK faced the same decision that had confronted Northern Ireland in 1921:

> Then Ulster had to decide whether or not to remain within the British common market with which its economic life was totally bound up or to leave and become a backward offshore island totally at the mercy of economic forces over which it could exercise no control.

'For voters in Northern Ireland', he concluded, only a decision to stay in the EEC was compatible with the 'overwhelming vote' in the recent Border Poll 'for staying within the United Kingdom'.[103]

In the same fashion, Yes campaigners sought to ground membership in the historic traditions of Ulster Unionism, contrasting it with the 'ourselves alone' approach of Sinn Féin:

> Ulstermen have always been shrewd enough to sacrifice part of their nominal sovereignty for the sake of being part of a bigger and richer country in which they would have real influence ... Ulstermen have valiantly resisted Irish Sinn Feinism for sixty years. It would be sad to see Ulster being conned by the English Sinn Feinism of Wedgwood Benn and Enoch Powell.[104]

'A NOBLE ENTERPRISE'

When the results were announced on 6 June, Northern Ireland defied pundits and pollsters alike. On a turnout of 47.4 per cent – the second lowest in the UK – it voted by 52.1 per cent to 47.9 per cent to remain in the Community. It was not an enthusiastic endorsement: only Shetland and the Western Isles, which voted to leave, showed lower levels of support; yet it was an endorsement nonetheless. Despite a late scare, when it wrongly appeared that 10,000 service votes had not been counted, voters had defied the paramilitaries and many of their politicians to produce the most unexpected result in the UK.[105]

The disorganisation of sectarian forces clearly played a role in that result. With the IRA and the UVF campaigning on one side, while the UPNI and SDLP co-operated on the other, the vote could not, like the Convention elections or Sunningdale, plausibly be represented as a test of strength between the two communities. Paisley could not, as in 1974, claim to speak for 'Ulster' or even for 'Unionism', when so many Unionists took an opposite view. Nor could Republican Antis speak unproblematically for nationalists, when the SDLP was backing membership and the Republic had pledged to stay in regardless. All this diminished the pressure that could be exerted on the electorate, for voting or campaigning against the party line was less obviously a betrayal of one's community.

It helped, of course, that this was not an issue on which Northern Ireland had any kind of veto. Unlike the Constitutional Convention, the Sunningdale Agreement or the Council of Ireland, membership of the EEC did not require the active co-operation of the people or politicians of Ulster. Given its tiny population, the vote in Ulster was unlikely to influence the overall result – a fact which encouraged a degree of posturing, but which also gave a fatalistic cast to the debate.

This made it easier for third parties to campaign, without appearing to take sides on a confessional question or on the constitutional status of the North. Organisations like the CBI, the Ulster Farmers' Association and the Women's Institutes all played an active role, deploying the campaigning techniques they had long brought to elections elsewhere in the United Kingdom. In so doing, they switched the debate to subjects like jobs, food prices and the prospects for the economy: precisely the issues that were dominating discussion across the Irish Sea.[106] In this respect, the referendum was the most 'normal' campaign of the 1970s; the one that most closely replicated British politics. Released from the obligation to align themselves with a particular confessional or sectarian bloc, Northern Ireland's voters responded in much the same way as voters elsewhere in the UK, privileging economic and material concerns over sovereignty and confessional loyalties.

With the Constitutional Convention sitting in the summer, there was less time for soul-searching after the result than among the defeated parties in Scotland and Wales. Powell told the electors bluntly that they were wrong, likening them to the crowds that had cheered the Munich Agreement in 1938.[107] The *Protestant Telegraph* wrote bitterly of 'A Nation's Folly', while the Orange Lodges made a virtue out of necessity by accepting the result as a mark of their commitment to democracy. Would Nationalists follow suit, they inquired, by accepting the democratic verdict of the Border Poll?[108]

The *Newsletter* struck a more optimistic note. Isolation, it acknowledged, was no longer an option in 'the era of superpowers', but membership of the European Community could be more than a pragmatic accommodation to necessity. It offered, instead, a new future for a nation disoriented by the end of empire, and a rebuke to Dean Acheson's famous dictum that Britain had 'lost an Empire, but not yet found a role':

> That role has now been discovered – the completion of centuries
> of defence of Western Europe by helping to organize its previously
> warring nation States into a new and prosperous Commonwealth of
> 250 million people. This is an opportunity to make permanent the
> liberation of Europe for which many Ulstermen fought and died.

The 'political unification of Europe on democratic lines', it argued, was 'a noble enterprise' which took on a special resonance as the bicentenary of the United States of America approached in 1976:

> Currently we are in the period of celebration of the joining-up in
> independence of 13 bickering and individually weak British States
> on the far side of the Atlantic, 200 years ago, to form 'a more perfect
> union' – the United States of America. Now, on this side of the Atlantic,
> the various States, including Britain, have the opportunity to fulfil their
> own centuries' old dream, and form 'a more perfect union' – the United
> States of Europe.[109]

For those who dreamed of a politics of moderation and co-operation across communities, the politics of Northern Ireland would rarely appear so hopeful again.

12 CYMRU YN EWROP: WALES IN EUROPE

Warily, without much enthusiasm and with some foreboding, more and more people in South Wales appear to be deciding to vote 'Yes' next Thursday.

Financial Times, 2 June 1975[1]

Our Treaty of Rome was the Act of Union in 1536 and some of my countrymen have still not got over it.

John Morris, 3 June 1975[2]

A 'yes' vote on Thursday could bring the biggest voluntary redundancy in history.

Neil Kinnock, 3 June 1975[3]

In the small hours of the night of 5 June, just hours before the polls opened for the referendum, a twenty-year-old woman from Brynglas in Newport went into labour. To the dismay of her family, she made clear that she had no intention of giving birth until she had cast her vote; and she insisted on being driven to the polling station before going on to the maternity unit at Pontypool. A few hours later, at the opposite end of the age scale, Mrs Anna Williams of Swansea, aged 102, was shocked to discover that she had mislaid her polling card. Donning her most intimidating hat, she descended on the Guildhall and refused to leave until a new paper had been issued. As she told reporters outside, she had voted in every election since the enfranchisement of women in 1918 and had no intention of stopping now.[4]

With determination like this, it is little wonder that Wales recorded the highest turnout of the four nations of the United Kingdom.

FIGURE 12.1   Mrs Anna Williams, aged 102, delivers her ballot to the Swansea Guildhall.

Source: Media Wales

A total of 66.7 per cent of Welsh voters cast their ballots, with 66.5 per cent opting to stay in the Community. Support rose as high as 74.3 per cent in Powys, and in only one county, Mid Glamorgan, did it fall below 60 per cent.[5] The *Western Mail*, the self-styled 'national newspaper of Wales', thought it 'the most exhilarating political event in Britain since the war'. The *Liverpool Daily Post*, in its Wales edition, hailed 'a new era of greatness' and 'a new upsurge of British influence' in the world.[6]

Yet conditions for the European movement in Wales had been far from propitious. Economically, Wales was dominated by declining heavy industries and inefficient, small-scale farming, neither of which had traditionally favoured membership. Politically, Wales was a stronghold of the Labour Party, which had won twenty-three of its thirty-six constituencies in October 1974. The two most charismatic orators in Welsh politics, Michael Foot and Neil Kinnock, were anti-Marketeers, as were the two most powerful trade unions, the National Union of

Mineworkers and the Transport and General Workers' Union. Plaid Cymru, which had established itself over the previous decade as the rising force in Welsh politics, was also committed to a No vote. In 1974 Plaid had campaigned on an explicitly anti-Market platform, securing more than 10 per cent of the vote and three Members of Parliament.[7]

The referendum came upon Wales at a time of cultural revival and economic decay. The coal and steel industries, once the mainstay of Welsh manufacturing, were in headlong decline. Between 1959 and 1969, the National Coal Board had closed 86 of its 141 collieries in South Wales, reducing its workforce from 93,000 to 40,000 in a decade. Over the same period, the North Wales coalfields had lost half their workforce, leaving just two pits still operating. In 1973 the British Steel Corporation, which employed 65,981 people in Wales, had announced plans to end production in Wales outside Port Talbot and Llanwern. The steelworks in Ebbw Vale closed in 1975, and by the early 1980s the company would employ fewer than 20,000 people across the principality. The result was a sustained fall in living standards, as entire communities lost their economic purpose. Household income in Wales dropped to 15 per cent below the UK average, the lowest of any region outside Northern Ireland. The number of men in paid employment had fallen by 100,000 in a decade, and public spending per capita on sickness and invalidity benefit was 71 per cent above the UK norm.[8]

This ran alongside a resurgence of national consciousness, to which successive governments responded with promises of devolution and localised decision-making. The Labour manifesto promised an elected assembly in Wales, the latest in a series of distinctively Welsh institutions that included the Welsh Trades Union Congress (1974), a Welsh Consumer Council and Land Authority (1975) and a Welsh Development Agency that would commence operations in 1976. Newspapers followed suit: *The Times* appointed its first Welsh affairs correspondent in 1968 and the BBC hired a Welsh political correspondent in 1970. Two years later the Conservative Party began holding an annual conference in Wales, and two years after that, when Wales played England at Twickenham, the Rugby Football Union accepted that 'Hen wlad fy nhadau' should replace 'God save the Queen' as the anthem of the Welsh team.[9]

As a Labour stronghold, with a decaying industrial base and a resurgent sense of its own national identity, Wales posed significant problems for pro-Marketeers. Ernest Wistrich had identified Wales from the outset as 'the main problem area' in setting up local organisations, and just six weeks before the vote there were effective campaign groups in only twenty of the thirty-six constituencies. Wistrich was on bad terms with Wil Edwards, the former Labour MP who ran the 'Wales in Europe' campaign, and repeatedly threatened to suspend him from his post. Edwards complained that Labour pro-Marketeers preferred to keep their heads below the parapet, and even the Conservative and Liberal parties seemed less enthusiastically pro-Market in Wales. Of the Liberals' two Welsh MPs, Geraint Howells (Cardigan) called himself a 'reluctant Marketeer', while Emlyn Hooson (Montgomery) had opposed membership in 1971. The Conservative MP for Denbigh, Geraint Morgan, had voted against joining and abstained in the vote on the renegotiated terms. At a time when Conservative associations were forming the backbone of the Yes campaign in England, Morgan's constituency party in Flint and Denbighshire voted not to be 'over-involved' in the campaign.[10] A week before the referendum, a national liaison officer found the Yes campaign at Rhyl 'a complete shambles', mainly because of a 'cynical and obstructive' Conservative agent.[11]

Yet the No campaign had problems of its own. Labour's internal divisions made it impossible to mobilise the party machine, not least as it was the MP for Cardiff South East, Jim Callaghan, who led the renegotiations. The NUM and the TGWU offered stronger support, but the unions were weak outside their industrial heartlands and were reluctant to work with Plaid. Wil Edwards reported that a meeting organised by the NUM in Merthyr, for which Plaid provided the speakers, was a 'disaster'. 'Its immediate effect was the setting up of a very strong Labour Group for Europe in Merthyr,' such was the anger at seeing 'Nationalists appearing on the same platform as Labour speakers'.[12]

In consequence, the No campaign splintered along regional and party lines. In the industrial south, meetings were well attended and Michael Foot was 'the main attraction'.[13] In the north, and especially in rural areas, Plaid took the lead, in a campaign that was often explicitly anti-Labour. Where the two crossed over there were serious tensions, which 'Wales in Europe' was quick to exploit.

PLAID CYMRU: 'DYWEDED CYMRA NA'

Plaid Genedlaethol Cymru, or 'The National Party of Wales', was founded in 1925. It brought together two older organisations, *Byddin Ymreolwyr Cymru* (the Home Rule Army of Wales) and *Y Mudiad Cymreig* (the Welsh Movement), and combined a commitment to self-government with a passionate defence of Welsh culture. Its most influential early figure was Saunders Lewis, the poet, dramatist and scholar who served as party president from 1926 to 1939. His leadership privileged cultural over political nationalism, focusing more on the revival of the Welsh language than on institutional reform. In so far as his goals were political, they focused not on 'independence' (which he thought 'anti-Christian') but on 'freedom', perhaps as a Dominion within the British Empire.[14]

For Saunders Lewis, there was no contradiction between a Welsh and European identity. Wales, he believed, was intrinsically European, steeped in the heritage of Greece, Rome and the medieval Church. His vision of the good society was shaped by Aristotle and Thomas Aquinas, and drew on French Catholic thinkers like Maurice Barrès and Charles Maurras. A Catholic convert, he looked back to a pre-Reformation Europe, when regional and national identities enjoyed free rein within the common life of the Church. It was the rise of the modern state, he believed, that had smothered and disrupted smaller nationalities, through centralising and homogenising state institutions.[15]

As a Catholic, Lewis was an oddity in a party that was steeped in the Welsh chapel tradition. Yet his commitment to multiple identities, which could be Welsh, British *and* European, found a wider resonance within the party. Two other key figures in the early history of Plaid were the economist David James Davies and the educationalist and scholar Noëlle French, who had met (and subsequently married) at the International People's College in Denmark. Their enthusiasm for Scandinavian social democracy became an important influence between the wars, particularly for those nationalists who distrusted Lewis's Catholic predilections.[16]

Following Lewis's resignation in 1939, the most important figure of the post-war period was Gwynfor Evans, who led the party from 1945 to 1981. Despite their differences, Evans agreed with Lewis that 'Wales is a European nation', whose people should 'think of themselves not as British but as Welsh Europeans'.[17] In the early 1960s he looked favourably on the EEC, viewing it as a model for a reconstituted British confederation in which Wales would be a free and equal partner. He set the campaign for Welsh nationhood within a European framework, noting that Wales was one of a 'number of small European nations which have long been submerged in imperialist states'. 'The Welsh and Scots', he wrote in 1975, should stand with 'Bretons, Catalans,

Corsicans and Basques', all of whom were 'striving to move from colonialist to national status'.[18]

That instinctive Europeanism made Plaid an unlikely bastion for the anti-Market cause. It could be accused neither of 'little Englandism', nor of imperial nostalgia, nor of an obsession with 'sovereignty'. Plaid had long been comfortable with the idea of overlapping political identities, and its emphasis on 'freedom' rather than 'independence' was entirely compatible with membership of a larger group. Yet Plaid's enthusiasm for 'Europe' in the abstract did not long survive contact with the institutions actually taking shape among the Six. Romantic appeals to European cultural heritage had not equipped the party for the emergence of a supranational customs union, with aspirations to 'ever closer union'. It was not until the 1970s, when membership became an imminent prospect, that Plaid engaged seriously with the European project, and the result was a rapid change of tone. The October 1974 manifesto told supporters that 'Plaid Cymru is, and always has been, opposed to membership of the EEC', and it campaigned firmly for a No vote in 1975.[19]

Plaid's critique had three dimensions. The first was anti-colonial, for the implosion of the British Empire across Africa and South Asia had encouraged Plaid to frame its own national struggle in colonial terms. The British state, Evans argued, was an imperial construct – 'the name given to England plus her internal colonies' – which was now itself in the final stages of decay. The same process, he suggested, was at work among minority communities in France and Spain, as nations 'long … submerged in imperialist states' recovered 'their will to live'. The EEC threatened to lock these emergent nationalities into a new imperial union, designed to secure power, wealth and influence in the hands of the old composite states. Such a union, Evans warned, was destructive of the very idea of Europe, the greatness of which lay in its myriad 'national cultures'. Far from liberating subject nationalities, Plaid warned, the goal was 'to create a common Western European Man – as the ideal in Britain has been to create a common Britisher'. He might no longer 'be an Englishman in disguise', but 'there will be precious little Welsh about him!'[20]

It was telling, in Evans' view, that Wales had been permitted 'no voice in designing the conditions of membership' and that it remained 'without any kind of direct and permanent representation in Brussels'. Luxembourg, with a population roughly the size of Cardiff, had its own Commissioner and six members of the European Parliament; yet Wales, as a subject nationality, had no direct representation at all. Wales, Plaid argued, could not exist as a colony within a colony. As Plaid's English-language newspaper, the *Welsh Nation*, pithily concluded: 'No say – say no.'[21]

This was annexed to an economic critique, which owed a considerable debt to the Left. Plaid largely shared the view of Labour critics, that the purpose of the Common Market was to liberate capital from democratic control. Unlike the US Constitution, with its commitment to the rights of man, the Treaty of Rome was 'solely concerned with the rights of capital' and the interests of 'Europe's privileged rich elite groups'. Robert Griffiths, a Plaid research officer who later became general secretary of the British Communist Party, warned that membership would strengthen monopoly power and enrich a new generation of multinationals, beyond the reach of any government.[22]

Where Plaid distinguished itself from the Labour Left was in its conviction that international finance threatened the distinctive national culture of Wales. Emrys Roberts, a former party chairman, warned that the brand of capitalism espoused by the Common Market had 'no social conscience whatsoever. It is a naked market and profit-oriented capitalism that rejects any attempt to influence its development in the interests of the community at large.'[23] The Welsh people were 'conceived of as raw material, not Welshmen', while Welsh coal and steel were simply peripheral branches of an industry that could more profitably be concentrated in the Ruhr.[24]

These cultural and economic critiques intersected over the free movement of labour. This subject drew little attention elsewhere in the UK, for the parlous state of the economy made it an unlikely magnet for European immigration. Yet the movement of populations – whether from England into Wales or from Wales to cities like Liverpool – had long been a concern for Plaid, because of its effect on the Welsh language. The party was especially concerned about rural depopulation, for the Welsh countryside had a special importance for Plaid as 'the bastion of the Welsh language, culture and way of life'.[25] For the pro-Marketeers, Roberts complained, 'local communities [and] national identity count for nothing. The only concern is to provide the capitalist with enough workers just where he wants them.'[26] Appearing on a regional broadcast for the NRC, Dafydd Elis Thomas warned that 'the philosophy of the Common Market' was 'to drag people away and to destroy their community'. 'If ... we want to protect our rural life, then we must come out.'[27]

All this was linked to a profound anxiety about Europe's great power aspirations. This was especially important for Gwynfor Evans, who had been a conscientious objector during the Second World War. Evans placed pacifism at the core of Plaid's identity, and he saw the emergence of a European superpower as a 'recipe for the third world war'.[28] The *Welsh Nation* predicted that NATO and the EEC would merge after the referendum, securing 'the death of Wales as a national entity as well as constituting the greatest possible threat to the peace of the world'.[29]

For all these reasons, the party conference in 1975 voted resoundingly for a Welsh 'No'. A co-ordinating group was established under the leadership of Dafydd Elis Thomas, the MP for Merioneth: an appointment rich with symbolism, as he had won his seat by defeating the co-ordinator of 'Wales in Europe', Wil Edwards. The group, which affiliated to the 'Wales Get Britain Out' campaign, developed a six-teen-point programme under the slogan 'Europe – Yes, EEC – No'.[30] The party's two newspapers – *Welsh Nation* and the Welsh-language *Yr Ddraig Goch* – pressed home the message, while the party issued thousands of bumper stickers pairing the Welsh dragon and 'triban' with the slogan '*Dyweded Cymra NA*' ('*Wales Says NO*').[31] Its research group issued papers on everything from agriculture and industry to regional policy and international development, while Elis Thomas led a busy programme of meetings.[32] Addressing as many as four meetings each evening, he focused principally on three issues: the menace to Welsh agriculture; the threat to jobs and industry; and the lack of representation on European institutions.[33]

With the Labour Party internally divided, the referendum provided a rare opportunity for Plaid to take the lead on a national issue – one that could cut across the Welsh language divide that was holding back its fortunes in industrial districts. Owen James, who wrote research papers for the party, told activists that the referendum was 'a magnificent opportunity for Plaid Cymru'. It would be fought, he believed, on issues that favoured Plaid, such as the defence of national culture, self-government and the dangers of remote power. The fact that these principles would also be articulated by English unionists, like Tony Benn or Enoch Powell, could only strengthen the case for the break-up of the UK. James hoped to use the referendum to expose the crisis at the heart of the British state, which he believed had lost its purpose and prosperity with the end of Empire. Joining the EEC, Plaid argued, marked a tacit admission of the failure of the British state. Whatever the result of the referendum, James believed, 'the concept of Britain will not outlast the Century.'[34]

Yet Plaid was more divided than such rhetoric suggested. A significant number of activists openly repudiated the party's position, cleaving instead to an older vision of Wales as part of a larger Europe. Saunders Lewis, still active at the age of 81, accused his successors of campaigning 'against Europe' and in defence of 'Westminster sovereignty'. Defying the leadership – with whom he was on poor terms – he urged voters to destroy their ballot papers rather than side with 'English nationalists' like Enoch Powell and Jack Jones, and he talked privately of ending his association with the party.[35] Dafydd Wigley, a future leader whose star was already in the ascendant, openly repudiated the party line and refused to take any role in the campaign. Other rebels included Eurfyl ap Gwilym, the party's senior economics advisor, and Robin Reeves, who had worked for the *Financial Times* in Brussels during the British accession negotiations.[36] As one of the few senior figures in Plaid with working experience of Brussels, Reeves accused the leadership of 'a stupid betrayal of Wales' best interests'. The Common Market, he believed, offered Plaid Cymru 'the chance of a lifetime to achieve its political aspirations for Wales on the best possible terms open to a small country in a world dominated by bigness'. Reeves was one of a number of nationalists (not all within Plaid) who had been impressed by the Republic of Ireland's success in building an international profile from within the European Community. As Reeves observed, Ireland had struggled for decades after 1922 to escape the magnetic pull of its larger British neighbour. 'But it is Common Market membership which has provided the real opportunity for Ireland to break away from Britain's apron strings.'[37]

Attitudes towards the Community broadly mirrored the party's Left/Right divide; yet even the party's newly acquired socialist intellectuals were divided on Europe. Raymond Williams, the novelist, cultural theorist and pioneer of the New Left, warned that no single nation could resist the power of the multinationals. Only through international co-operation could the Left reimpose democratic control over global finance. As a nationalist, Williams warned against an insular Welsh identity that turned its back on the wider world. 'Culturally,' he observed, 'I find more sense in a Welsh European identity than in the dominating English versions of sovereignty and tradition.'[38]

In consequence, Europe was no less disruptive an issue for Plaid than it was for the Labour Party. The idea that Wales was part of a common European heritage remained central to Plaid's self-image, and this disabled the party from running a more populist anti-Market campaign. Its rather lumbering slogan ('Europe – Yes, EEC – No') was indicative of these difficulties. Plaid's official position was to rejoin EFTA and to seek a special trading agreement with the EEC, and it hinted that Wales might rejoin the Community as a self-governing nation. Yet commentary in *Welsh Nation* insisted that 'Plaid Cymru fundamentally opposes the EEC aim of a Western European political union.' The Common Market, the paper insisted, was a 'life and death' question for Wales; rather than submerge its identity in a Europe dominated by large nations, Wales should seek allies within a looser Celtic League.[39] Even with its own representation, warned Phil Richards, a small nation like Wales would never have much say. 'Neither the UK state nor a Welsh state could ... cope with the flood of centrally-determined Common Market legislation affecting life at every level in society.'[40]

Relations between Plaid's leading figures were also strained. The two Dafydds (Wigley and Elis Thomas) were pulling in different policy directions, while relations between Evans and the party chairman, Phil Williams, were deteriorating badly. Insiders warned that 'the state of the organization is appalling', and its electoral machine was in disarray.[41] As a result, Plaid struggled to gain traction, even in its electoral heartlands. Liaison officers for Britain in Europe found little evidence of anti-Market activity, aside from graffiti and the occasional bumper sticker. (These were of such low quality, one activist reported, that he 'had to nearly ram' the car in front in order to read it.)[42] David Peter, who chaired the Yes campaign in Gwynedd, later recalled that he 'was not really aware of the No campaign', even though two of Plaid's three MPs sat for constituencies in the county. Gwynedd would go on to record the second highest 'yes' vote in Wales – exceeded only by Powys, where the Yes campaign was chaired by Peter's father.[43]

With Plaid unable to deliver its heartlands, the prospects for a No vote were reliant on the industrial South. This was Labour territory, yet relations with Labour were so poisonous as to render co-operation almost impossible. At the first meeting of the Wales branch of 'Get Britain Out', Plaid moved to rename it 'Get Wales Out', forcing a vote which it inevitably lost.[44] As the campaign developed, Plaid's leaders took pains to distance themselves from what they loftily dismissed as the 'narrow British chauvinism' of the Labour Antis.[45] Phil Williams, for example, contrasted the internationalism of Plaid's appeal, with its 'vision of a loose confederation of many European nations', with the insular aspirations of 'the English Left' for a 'siege economy in an island fortress'. For Plaid, he claimed, the ideal was a Europe of the nations, more truly international than the Community. For Labour, there was simply 'fog in the Channel and the Continent was cut off'.[46]

'THE BIGGEST VOLUNTARY REDUNDANCY IN HISTORY'

For the No campaign to gain traction in the south, it would have to operate through the Labour Party and the trade unions. The 'Wales Get Britain Out' campaign, created in February 1975, was dominated by Labour politicians and trade unionists. Its chairman, Jack Brooks, was leader of South Glamorgan County Council and Jim Callaghan's constituency secretary, while George Wright, the general secretary of the Wales TUC, served as secretary. Don Hayward, of the NUM, acted as treasurer, while the committee also included representatives of the TGWU, the Welsh Communist Party and the Amalgamated Union of Engineering Workers. The campaign operated under the auspices of the Wales TUC (WTUC), and staff members were seconded from the WTUC and TGWU.[47]

Welsh Labour should have been fertile territory for the Out campaign. Of the party's twenty-three Welsh MPs, ten had voted against the renegotiated terms in April. In Michael Foot and Neil Kinnock, the No campaign possessed two future leaders of the party, while other prominent Antis included Denzil Davies, Caerwyn Roderick and Roy Hughes. At its annual conference in April, the Welsh Labour Party voted by almost two to one in favour of withdrawal, and it could count on the organisational backing of the TGWU, the NUM and the WTUC.

With Foot sidelined by surgery at the end of April, it was Kinnock who emerged as the more prominent figure at public meetings and demonstrations. At the party conference in Llandudno, he warned that the 'whole purpose of the EEC' was 'to restrain and chain all the instincts for the advance of socialism in our people'. The European Community, he insisted, was an inherently capitalist organisation, which existed to disable the democratic control of ordinary people.

The idea that entry might prove an 'adventure', or administer a useful 'shock' to industry, constituted, for Kinnock, a form of 'kamikaze politics' that would make the pursuit of socialism 'immeasurably harder'.[48]

This view of the EEC as a capitalist conspiracy, designed to lift international finance beyond the control of democratic governments, struck deep roots in Welsh Labour. Roy Hughes, the Labour MP for Newport and president of the Newport Anti-Common Market League, warned that the 'guiding principle' of the Community was 'the free movement of market forces', and referred pointedly to 'the Heath–Jenkins European adventure'.[49] There was particular concern for Welsh industry, which was unusually dependent on state intervention and subsidy. Of the 200,000 manufacturing jobs in South Wales in 1970, it was estimated that two-thirds had been created with state assistance. By the end of the decade, about 40 per cent of all employment in Wales would come from the public sector, including 15 per cent in the nationalised industries.[50] In this context, any limits on state intervention carried grave risks. Kinnock warned that a Yes vote in Wales would constitute 'the biggest voluntary redundancy in history'. On polling day, adverts urged a No vote to 'Keep Your Children Off The Dole!'[51]

With South Wales home to so many declining industries, the Labour case was at times openly protectionist. Writing in the *Western Mail*, Roy Hughes focused on the danger to the Welsh steel industry from foreign imports, 3 million tonnes coming from the Common Market. The same quantity produced at home, he noted, would have created 30,000 additional jobs. George Wright accused the EEC of 'flagrant dumping'. Staying in, he claimed, would cost Wales between 50,000 and 65,000 jobs, most of them in the coal, steel and car industries.[52]

Yet Labour was no more united in Wales than in any other part of the country. A number of Welsh MPs were prominent pro-Marketeers: Tom Ellis (Wrexham), Ifor Davies (Gower) and Leo Abse (Pontypool) had all defied the party whips and voted for membership in 1971, while Cledwyn Hughes (Anglesey) had abstained.[53] Other pro-Marketeers included the Welsh secretary, John Morris (a recent convert), and Jim Callaghan. To campaign against the renegotiated terms was to speak out against the Labour government at Westminster, a problem that caused considerable soul-searching at the party conference in Llandudno.[54] Only about seven Labour MPs played prominent roles in the Welsh No campaign, probably from a reluctance to go into battle against Callaghan and Wilson. Yet in the absence of solidarity from their own ranks, Labour's anti-Marketeers proved no more enthusiastic than Plaid about cross-party co-operation. Tony Benn, for example, addressed a demonstration at Sophia Gardens in Cardiff, but refused to share a stage with Plaid.[55]

Nonetheless, the combination of a part of the Labour machine with the trade union networks of the NUM and TGWU presented a formidable challenge to the Yes campaign. With only limited support from the Conservative and Liberal parties, 'Wales in Europe' had to construct a different kind of campaign to the one it was fighting elsewhere in the United Kingdom: one that could counter both the economic and cultural critiques that were fuelling the Out campaign.

'CYMRU YN EWROP'/WALES IN EUROPE

The regional organiser for the European Movement in Wales was Wil Edwards, a former Labour MP who had lost his seat to Plaid in 1974. An energetic man with a shock of dark hair, Edwards combined

FIGURE 12.2   Women in traditional Welsh costume rally for Europe in Cardiff.
Source: Media Wales

considerable personal charm with a tendency to cause accidental offence. When first selected for Merioneth in the 1960s, the Welsh language newspaper Y Cymro observed wryly that his 'personal appeal' was both 'the big plus' in Labour's campaign and its most significant obstacle. 'The big problem is his tendency to put his foot in it, and lose friends as easily as making them.'[56]

Almost from the beginning, Edwards found himself on poor terms with Ernest Wistrich and the central campaign in London. Wistrich was concerned about the failure to build local organisations in Wales; just six weeks before the vote, nearly half of the thirty-six Welsh constituencies still lacked a functioning 'Wales in Europe' group.[57] Edwards blamed a lack of speakers and the reluctance of the Conservative Party to pull its weight, but Wistrich suspected the problem lay closer to home. In April, he intervened directly to restructure the Welsh organisation, with Phyllis Reeve and John Meredith taking over as joint co-ordinators, while Edwards was restricted to addressing meetings. There were rumblings throughout the campaign that things were going badly, and Wistrich threatened to dismiss Edwards if he did not co-operate with the new campaign team.[58]

Nonetheless, by the end of May a 'Wales for Europe' group had been established in every constituency and the campaign was beginning to take shape. Its Cardiff headquarters were decorated in emerald green, chosen as a happy medium between socialist red and Tory blue. The central organisation was a genuinely cross-party affair. Reeve was a Conservative national agent, while Meredith was an investment banker who was active in Conservative politics. On the Labour side, Edwards was joined by Cliff Prothero, a 'sprightly 76-year-old' who had been the chief Labour organiser in Wales a decade earlier.[59] The Welsh Liberal Party was well represented at a local level, including by the Peter family who ran the Yes campaign in Powys and Gwynedd.[60] It was, as Edwards put it, 'a skeleton staff earning little and surviving on enthusiasm', but it combined considerable campaigning experience with decades of accumulated local knowledge.[61]

Despite allegations of lavish expenditure, financial support was in practice fairly limited. Local groups were given £30 towards a first meeting and an initial print run; thereafter, they had to raise their own funds. The remaining cash was spent on shop frontages in city centres, with two in Cardiff and others in Swansea, Wrexham and Bangor. Edwards carried the main burden of public speaking, travelling across Wales with Aneurin Rhys Hughes, an official on secondment from the Commission. Together, they sought to carry the message outside the established parties, addressing meetings of the farming unions, Women's Institutes, Townswomen's Guilds and the Rotary Club.[62]

As in other parts of the UK, pro-Marketeers often chose military men to chair their local organisations. Like the use of the Welsh dragon, this was intended to disable allegations that the European cause was unpatriotic. Edwards' own branch, at Merioneth, was chaired by Group Captain R.B. Dowling, who had commanded balloon barrages during the Second World War. The Gwent group was led by Sir William Crawshay, who had parachuted into France before D-Day to work with the Resistance. Raiding Gestapo headquarters, Crawshay had been pleased to discover his own photograph in a filing cabinet, advertising a bounty on his head worth £10,000.[63]

Callaghan and Wilson spoke in Cardiff towards the end of the campaign, but the biggest hitter in the earlier stages was John Morris, the secretary of state for Wales. A Welsh-speaker and devolutionist, Morris had previously opposed membership. Born into a farming community and representing one of the major steel constituencies, he feared that EEC rules would undermine home investment, disable a socialist industrial policy and expose Welsh industry to the full force of Continental competition.[64] By 1975, however, he had undergone a dramatic conversion. He was now convinced that the most pressing requirement for Welsh industry was investment, 'from whatever part of the world it will come'. With the economy in such a parlous state, Wales would only be an attractive location if it could guarantee access to European markets. At press conferences and meetings, Morris hammered home the message that Welsh jobs and Welsh industry depended on membership. Withdrawal, he warned, would 'divert overseas investment away from Wales' and constitute 'an unacceptable risk' to its prosperity. 'I cannot and will not gamble with the livelihood of the people of Wales.'[65]

As a former opponent of entry, Morris could not be dismissed as a misty-eyed romantic, sacrificing Welsh prosperity to some visionary European ideal. Like Harold Wilson, he could present himself instead as a pragmatist, who had accepted membership out of necessity. In a joint statement with his three predecessors as Labour Welsh secretary, he warned that the Welsh economy had no future outside the EEC. The statement was also signed by Graham Saunders, secretary of the Labour Trade Union Committee for Europe and a union official in APEX.[66]

The Yes campaign in Wales focused heavily on the economy. Campaign literature majored on jobs and investment, a potent theme at a time when unemployment was running at 4.5 per cent in South Wales and the steel industry was on short hours. On the one hand, campaigners stressed the investment opportunities within a larger Common Market. Pro-Market newspapers painted an optimistic picture of a resurgent Welsh economy, with new investment flooding in. The *South Wales Argus* reported that major capital operations were already in the pipeline, waiting only for the security of a Yes vote. 'If Britain votes to stay in Europe, then these companies will immediately have to expand home production capacity. They will need the cash to build new factories.' As the *Western Mail* reminded readers, the Japanese company Sony was already using Wales as its European base, while Matsushita (later Panasonic) was building a £1 million television set factory in Cardiff.[67]

This emphasis on 'jobs for the boyos' was accompanied by dire warnings of the consequences of withdrawal. Henry Koch, whose company AB Electronics employed 2,200 people in the Abercynon and Porth area, told the press that his firm sent more than 77 per cent of its exports to the Common Market. An external tariff barrier to the Continent would be ruinous.[68] Harold Williams, chairman of the manufacturing conglomerate John Williams of Cardiff, warned voters that 'If Britain comes out ... we would not invest a penny piece in this country.' Leo Abse told workers at Girling, which made car brakes, that a No vote could cost a third of the workforce their jobs, while 'every ICI Fibres worker should know that a "No" vote ... would be a gamble with his future job security'.[69] 'Wales in Europe' adopted an unashamedly apocalyptic tone, making the 'DANGERS OF LEAVING' the first point in campaign literature. If Welsh industry was to avoid 'heavy redundancies', it insisted, 'we desperately need to be under the umbrella of the Community'.[70]

The campaign also focused on the benefits of the Common Agricultural Policy. Farming had an importance in Welsh politics beyond its economic contribution, because of the special place of the land in Welsh culture. 'Wales in Europe' took pains to woo rural voters, speaking at agricultural dinners and canvassing the agricultural unions. The predominantly Welsh-speaking Farmers' Union of Wales (of which John Morris was a founder-member) was neutral, though sympathetic to membership, but the mainly English-speaking National Union of

Farmers came out strongly for the EEC.[71] Plaid had been fiercely critical of the CAP, which it feared would eliminate the small farms in which the Welsh language and culture were so deeply rooted.[72] Yet the higher prices guaranteed by the CAP had many attractions for struggling farmers. Inflation had wrought havoc in the agricultural sector over the previous two years. Research by the Agricultural Economics Department at Aberystwyth calculated that Welsh farm incomes fell by 60 per cent in 1974, rising to 75 per cent for livestock farmers. The president of the Farmers' Union of Wales, Thomas Myrrdin Evans, claimed that 1974 would be remembered 'as one of the blackest years in the memory of most Welsh farmers'.[73] In this context, the main complaint of Welsh farmers was that the five-year transitional period was unnecessarily long. Some also took advantage of European funding to invest in new equipment, or to switch to more profitable forms of agriculture.[74] Such was the situation in Dyfed that one of the party's organisers, Peter Hughes Griffiths, wrote to Elis Thomas urging him to 'soft pedal' on the referendum, because the farmers were 'stupid sods' and not receptive to Plaid's message.[75]

A third theme of the Yes campaign was the potential for European loans and development money. George Thomson, the European Commissioner with responsibility for regional policy, came to Cardiff in May to announce a £15.5 million loan to protect jobs in the steel industry.[76] This was £1.5 million more than had been expected, and drew furious allegations of bribery. Pointing out that the timing of these loans was suspect to say the least, Kinnock accused the EEC of trying 'to rig the referendum'. European loans, he argued, were trivial by comparison with the regional aid on offer from the UK government, and could in any case be seen as a recycling of the British budgetary contribution.[77] Plaid was equally critical, complaining that reliance on European aid would simply confirm Wales' position as a dependency. A Plaid research paper described regional aid as 'a tool of the centralist state', intended 'to placate the peripheral regions and reconcile them to their subordinate position'.[78] It served principally 'to defuse political protest' and to open up Wales to foreign capital.[79]

Yet the loans were popular in hard-pressed industrial regions. The *Sun*, probably the best-selling newspaper in Wales, went to Michael Foot's constituency, Ebbw Vale, to show how 'the Market is paying off' for workers in declining industries. The British Steel Corporation was closing all its steelworks in Wales outside Port Talbot and Llanwern, putting more than 60,000 jobs at risk. Gerry Baxter, a sixty-four-year-old 'pipe-smoking, ex-maintenance fitter', told the paper that European money had allowed him to take early retirement. 'I've changed my mind about the Common Market,' he reported. 'It's given me a very fair deal.' Thomas Lewis, a fifty-four-year-old former steelworker who had recently been made redundant, agreed: 'It's a very good scheme, the Common Market one. It means I can retrain as a carpenter on my old wages.'[80] According to one paper, steelworkers at Ebbw Vale were so excited by the 'golden handshake' on offer that they were actively demanding to be made redundant.[81]

If the focus of the Yes campaign was on jobs and investment, it did not neglect the cultural dimensions of the campaign. 'Wales in Europe' was a consciously Welsh, not British, campaign, which worked hard to counter the nationalist appeal of the sceptics. It produced extensive campaign literature in Welsh, under the impress of 'Cymru yn Ewrop', and deployed the red dragon ('Yr Ddraig Goch') as its logo. It worked hard to mobilise Welsh sports stars, such as the Cardiff fly half Gareth Davies and the legendary scrum half Gareth Edwards.[82] More than twenty leading 'Welsh personalities' signed a public letter in support of a Yes vote, including the Bishop of Llandaff; the former British ambassador to the United States, Lord Harlech; and other figures from business, education and local government. Banner adverts in the newspapers listed Welsh supporters of membership, pairing Labour politicians like Callaghan and Morris with trade unionists from the Iron & Steel Trades Confederation, National Union of Railwaymen, AUEW, General and Municipal Workers' Union and APEX.[83]

The Community itself was growing more adept at appealing to national and regional identities. In May 1975, the Commission published its first official document in Welsh, illustrated by the cartoonist 'Gren' from the *South Wales Echo*. It was written by Aneurin Rhys Hughes, who had worked for Thomson in the Commission and who campaigned for membership in the referendum. Hughes argued that Wales would be better able to maintain its identity inside the Community than out, because the EEC would counter the gravitational pull of London. Wales, he argued, could forge alliances with similar regions across the Continent, forming 'a large and powerful regional lobby'. Membership of the EEC, he stressed, was entirely compatible with devolution. Indeed, 'With regional assemblies in Wales and Scotland, Britain would be moving towards a European pattern of democracy.'[84]

Though the No campaign took advice from Einar Førde, one of the architects of the No vote in Norway, it never mobilised Welsh civil society on a comparable scale. Almost all the major Welsh business organisations campaigned for a Yes vote, including the Welsh CBI, the South Wales Exporters Club and the Welsh Institute of Export. So did the major employers, such as British Steel and the National Coal Board. The latter, in particular, stressed the importance of its exports to the Continent and the receipt of loans worth £105 million by 1975.[85]

'THE VALLEYS OF RESIGNATION'

'Few parts of Britain', claimed the *Western Mail*, 'have been wooed more assiduously than Wales in this referendum campaign.' Harold Wilson, Jim Callaghan and Tony Benn all addressed rallies in Cardiff, and journalists reported that the question was 'being argued about in pubs, clubs and shops' in Wales 'as it never has been before'.[86] Turnout was the highest in the UK, though observers reported significant local discrepancies. In the South Wales coastal strip, turnout was said to be high in Conservative strongholds but 'exceptionally low' in Labour areas. In Cardiff, reports suggested that northern, more prosperous areas were polling heavily, while poorer districts saw lower turnouts. Interest was strong in Gwent, Pembrokeshire and Anglesey, but there was less enthusiasm in the Mid-Glamorgan valleys, where voters faced conflicting signals from the NUM and the Coal Board.[87]

The importance of the Welsh vote went beyond its numerical significance. As an editorial commented on the day of the poll, the result would indicate not only how voters felt about the Community, but 'how strongly Wales identifies with the rest of Britain'. This had obvious implications for the Union, for 'if Wales votes strongly "No", while England votes "Yes", Plaid Cymru will interpret this as evidence of the Welsh desire to split off from England'.[88] From this perspective, what was most striking about the result in Wales was how little it deviated from the pattern elsewhere in the UK.

Hopes of a different result in Wales had focused on two powerful forces that were redrawing Welsh politics: a growing anxiety about the economy, and a reassertion of Welsh cultural identity. Yet neither played to the advantage of the Out campaign. In Wales, as in other parts of the UK, economic concerns seem to have favoured membership, as voters opted for the security of the Community over the uncertainty of withdrawal. In Plaid and Welsh Labour alike, it is striking how many of those who rebelled against their party had a background in industry. Dafydd Wigley, for example, had trained as an accountant and worked for Hoover: the largest employer in Merthyr and a company that was rumoured to be considering relocation in the event of a No vote.[89] Robin Reeves had been commodities editor of the *Financial Times*, while Eurfyl ap Gwilym was Plaid's leading economist. Of the Labour Marketeers, Ifor Davies had worked for the Ministry of Labour and the Aluminium Wire and Cable Company, while Tom Ellis had worked in the mining industry and managed a colliery. John Morris's background lay in farming, but his constituency included a major steelworks.

The cultural nationalism espoused by Plaid was neither strong enough to overcome those concerns nor unambiguously the property of the Out campaign. The highest Yes votes in Wales came in Plaid's electoral strongholds, where the Welsh language was widespread and the defence of Welsh culture might have resonated most powerfully. As the *Liverpool Daily Post* commented, Wales had defied the expectations of pundits because it 'did not vote along linguistic lines. Pro-Europe voting was as strong in Welsh-speaking areas of the North West- and South West as it was in the English-speaking North East, Middle- and South East.'[90]

Plaid had been trimming its sails to the wind in the final weeks of the campaign, conscious that a vote for withdrawal had become all but impossible. The party's general secretary, Dafydd Williams, told a rally that a close vote in Wales would serve as a wake-up call to the European establishment. Claiming, rather improbably, that Community officials would be paying special attention to the Welsh result, he urged voters to 'show Brussels and London that the Welsh people will not be satisfied with a remote government which does not take account of their needs'. Even before the result, the party was preparing a policy document on devolution and direct representation in European institutions.[91]

Despite the high level of public interest in the campaign, there was little evidence of enthusiasm for the cause. Journalists wrote of 'the valleys of resignation', with voters casting their ballots 'warily, without much enthusiasm and with some foreboding'. Interviews with the public found a 'palpable sense of resignation', in which fear of withdrawal trumped any more positive vision of membership: 'We should never have joined the Market, but now that we're in …'; 'It has cost us so much that we can't give up all that money now'; 'It won't be any worse if we stay in than it is now'; 'If you're weak you need others to support you'. 'Only rarely', reporters found, 'did anyone evince enthusiasm for the market or any conviction that things will be much improved if we stay in.'[92]

Nonetheless, pro-Marketeers were overjoyed with the result. 'Properly utilized', thought the *Western Mail*, it could mark an epoch in British history, 'an era of exciting development, positive planning and, above all, optimism in our national and collective destiny'.[93] Neil Kinnock accepted the result on behalf of the Labour Antis, while Plaid announced that it would open an office in Brussels, working along-side sister parties from the Basque and Breton regions.[94] Indeed, Plaid would come, over time, to view European membership as the essential framework for Welsh nationhood, pivoting back to the position first advocated by Saunders Lewis. It was a political journey that would be matched by the Scottish National Party; and it is with the Scottish campaign that we now conclude.

13 'THE SCOTTISH TIME-BOMB'

Scotland knows from bitter experience what treatment is in store for a powerless region of a common market.

Alex Salmond, 10 May 1975[1]

I for my part am praying that you will get a good result, which in the case of Scotland seems to be almost more important than anywhere else.

Sir Con O'Neill, 3 June 1975[2]

If the rest of us are not careful, Scotland will blow up in our faces. ... For it is in Scotland that the unravelling of British politics might begin.

Financial Times, 13 May 1975[3]

In February 2014, during the run-up to the Scottish independence referendum, the president of the European Commission tossed a grenade into what had previously been a rather tepid campaign. Speaking to the BBC, José Manuel Barroso announced that an independent Scotland would have to reapply for membership of the European Union, and that admission would be 'extremely difficult, if not impossible'. His remarks drew a thunderous response from the Scottish National Party. The deputy first minister, Nicola Sturgeon, called it 'a preposterous assertion', while Angus MacNeil, who shadowed the deputy prime minister at Westminster, accused Barroso of 'playing politics' with Scotland's internal affairs.[4]

Barroso's intervention infuriated the SNP, because it challenged the foundations of the party's strategy for independence. Since 1988, the SNP had been committed to a policy of 'Independence in Europe', a slogan designed to reconcile the benefits of national self-determination with the security of a larger political union. As an independent state within the EU, Scotland would enjoy preferential access to continental markets while taking its rightful place among a larger family of nations. At a time when England seemed increasingly hostile to membership, Scotland's commitment to the EU could be called in evidence of a wider political divergence between the two countries. For the SNP, membership of the EU thus served a dual purpose, providing both the case for independence and the framework within which it could be achieved.[5]

That strategy paid dividends in the chaotic days that followed the 2016 EU referendum, in which Scottish voters backed membership by 62 per cent to 38 per cent.[6] Speaking on the morning of the result, Sturgeon deftly interpreted what had happened both as a vote of no confidence in 'the Westminster establishment' and as a mark of the 'divergence between Scotland and large parts of the rest of the UK in how we see our place in the world'. Following a campaign 'characterized in the rest of the UK by fear and hate', she concluded, Scots had chosen 'to renew our reputation as an outward-looking, open and inclusive country'. For Scotland to be torn from the bosom of the EU, against the will of its voters, would be 'democratically unacceptable', constituting a 'significant and material change' in the conditions on which independence had been rejected in 2014.[7]

Yet the SNP's enthusiasm for the EU was of comparatively recent vintage. In 1975 the party had campaigned enthusiastically to leave, echoing a wider mood of hostility to the Community. In the run-up to the earlier vote, polls had suggested that Scotland was significantly more hostile to membership than England, prompting fears that the European debate might prove the rock on which the UK would finally be shipwrecked. Con O'Neill, the director of BIE, wrote privately that 'a good result' in Scotland was 'almost more important than anywhere else', while a journalist for the *Financial Times* wrote of a 'Scottish time-bomb' ticking away as referendum day neared. Returning to London, he found himself 'plucking sleeves and interrupting conversations', anxious 'to warn as many people as possible of the momentous events that seem to be on the way'. 'For it is in Scotland that the unravelling of British politics might begin.'[8]

For the SNP, which campaigned to 'Get Scotland Out', the 1975 referendum offered a significant opportunity. With the Labour Party divided on the subject – and its parliamentary leadership committed to staying in – the SNP was able to seize the leadership of the Scottish No campaign, mobilising traditional Labour voters in parts of the country that had previously been resistant to its charms. Intellectually, the European debate played to issues on which the SNP was well equipped to fight, revolving as it did around questions of self-government, sovereignty and national identity. Above all, the decision to count votes on a regional basis meant that any divergence between England and Scotland would be laid bare for all to see. If, as was widely expected, Scotland voted to leave while England chose to stay in, the strain on the United Kingdom might become intolerable.

Yet the referendum also exposed divisions within Scottish Nationalism. The SNP's official position was to reject membership 'on London's terms', but its pronouncements suggested hostility to membership on principle, a position with which many of its MPs were visibly uncomfortable.[9] Defeat in the referendum would not only be a setback in electoral terms, interrupting several years of success at the polls; just as importantly, it would challenge the core claim of the SNP that Scotland had diverged politically from the rest of the UK. The campaign also risked exposing the party to some uncomfortable alliances, from Tony Benn on the Left to Enoch Powell on the Right.

It was not only the nationalist dimension that distinguished the debate in Scotland from that of England. The economic context and media landscape were also different. Farming and fisheries loomed larger in the Scottish economy, while exports to western Europe carried less weight. The industrial situation was in some respects gloomier than that of England, but in others more hopeful, for the discovery of North Sea oil offered some hope of reversing Scotland's dramatic deindustrialisation.[10] All this was reported in a distinctive national press, for as late as 1978, only about 6 per cent of Scottish adults regularly read one of the Fleet Street dailies.[11] To cater to the Scottish media, both sides created Scottish campaign vehicles that operated largely autonomously from London.

Despite all this, the result on 5 June followed the pattern of the UK as a whole, though with somewhat less enthusiasm. On a turnout of 61.4 per cent, Scottish voters chose by 58.4 per cent to 41.6 per cent to remain in the Community. The result was celebrated not only by pro-Marketeers but also by Unionists, who had feared that a Scottish 'No' might shatter the United Kingdom. For the SNP it was the first significant reverse in a decade of remarkable progress, and one that presaged the party's defeats in the devolution referendum and election of 1979.

A SCOTTISH 'NO'

In Scotland, as in Wales, the context for the 1975 referendum was one of accelerating industrial decline and insurgent nationalist politics. Before 1970, the SNP had never won a seat at a general election; by October 1974 it was the rising force in Scottish politics, winning a third of the vote and eleven seats. It had pushed the Conservatives into third place on votes cast, establishing a power-base in their former rural heartlands, and had come second in thirty-five of the forty-one Labour seats. With both parties pledging some form of devolution and the British state apparently mired in a crisis of governability, the political and intellectual tides seemed both to be flowing in favour of Scottish nationalism.

From this perspective, Scotland looked like fertile soil for the No campaign. Its economy was more dependent than that of England on declining heavy industries, which tended to be hostile to European integration. The dominant party in Scotland, the Labour Party, was broadly anti-Market – and slightly more so in Scotland than in England – and the Scottish TUC threw itself enthusiastically into the No campaign.[12] Even the Conservative Party was less devoutly pro-Market in Scotland, while the Liberal vote drew heavily on fishing constituencies that were wary of European fleets. The decline of Scottish industry had weakened the moral authority of the 'London Establishment', while the approaching oil boom made it possible to envisage a successful future outside the Community.

A poll for the *Glasgow Herald* in February found that just 29 per cent of Scots favoured membership while 45 per cent wanted to leave.[13] This coolness was reflected in the Commons on 9 April, when Scottish MPs voted by 35 to 32 against the renegotiated terms.[14] There was also opposition within the Scottish Office. Willie Ross, the secretary of state, was an Anti who thought that Britain had been 'conned into membership' by Heath, while Harry Ewing, the Scottish Office minister responsible for devolution, warned that membership would wreck the prospects for a devolved Assembly.[15]

The difficulty lay in mobilising the various fragments of a Scottish 'No' campaign into a single, cohesive movement. Labour and the

SNP were at daggers drawn, and there was little scope for co-operation when the SNP was handing out membership forms with its campaign literature. The Scottish TUC, under the leadership of 'genial Communist' Jimmy Milne, viewed the nationalists as 'bastards' and refused to co-operate with them.[16] Tory Antis tended to be both proudly Unionist and fiercely anti-Socialist, while the Labour Out campaign was beset by factional rivalries.

Money, which might have exerted a centripetal force, became a further bone of contention. Of the £125,000 in government funding given to the NRC, only £5,000 was allocated to the Scottish organisation.[17] This was not because the NRC was insensitive to Scotland: rather, it marked a decision to spend its limited funds on its own literature and advertising, rather than disbursing it, like Britain in Europe, to subsidiary organisations. The result, however, was to remove any incentive for Scottish 'No' campaigners to unite under a central umbrella. The consequence was a fractured No campaign, with a variety of splinter groups running their own discrete operations.

For Conservative Antis, the most important campaign vehicle was SCATOR: Scottish Conservatives Against the Treaty of Rome. SCATOR had a distinctly Powellite flavour; it was Powell, at Arbroath, who drew the largest single audience of the Scottish campaign, and SCATOR's campaign materials shared his sense of injured nationhood. Its secretary, David McLure, accused pro-Marketeers of an 'effete and torpid' view of their country, fomenting a 'mood of British defeatism and self-debasement' that posed a greater risk to the Union than any Nationalist.[18]

The most prominent Tory Anti was Teddy Taylor, the colourful MP for Glasgow Cathcart, who had resigned from the Heath government over Europe and would later campaign against the Maastricht Treaty. In 1975 he was particularly exercised by what he saw as the Communist threat in France, Italy and other Continental states. Taylor also appealed to the so-called 'Orange' vote, mobilising that Protestant, anti-Catholic feeling that remained especially potent in the west of the country. As one paper commented wryly, when Taylor excoriated the 'Treaty of *Rome*', 'every Protestant who wears a Glasgow Rangers scarf knows what he means'.[19]

Taylor had a strong personal following, and the Conservative Party remained the second largest party in Scotland in terms of seats. Yet it was already embarking on its long political decline: having won a majority of votes and seats as recently as 1955, it secured just 25 per cent of the vote in October 1974. For the No campaign to make headway in Scotland, the crucial constituency would be the 40 per cent of voters who backed Labour. A majority of Scottish Labour MPs had voted against the renegotiated terms, but the party found it difficult to mobilise on the issue. With Labour's NEC recommending a No vote, while a Labour prime minister argued for a 'Yes', the central party organisation largely shut down for the duration of the campaign, while constituency parties quietly went into suspended animation. Anti-Marketeers in Scotland lacked leaders of national stature, like Tony Benn, Barbara Castle or Peter Shore in England. Willie Ross, who might have played such a role, gave only one major speech, preferring not to jeopardise his alliance with Harold Wilson.[20]

The burden of campaigning fell instead on younger figures in the party, of whom the most prominent were Jim Sillars and Norman Buchan. Both had a certain public profile – Alex Salmond once called Sillars 'the most talented politician of his generation' – but they lacked the authority of Cabinet ministers or senior office holders. As Sillars later put it, they were 'factional leaders, not national leaders'.[21] They also found it difficult to work together. Buchan, the MP for West Renfrewshire and founder of Scottish Labour Against the Market (SLAM), was a former Scottish Office minister from the Left of the party, who was hostile to devolution. By contrast, Sillars, who represented South Ayrshire and served on the Executive of 'Get Scotland Out', was a 'maximalist' on devolution who would later create a separate Scottish Labour Party before joining the SNP in 1980. Sillars largely ignored Buchan and SLAM, setting out instead on a bus tour of the west of Scotland with Teddy Taylor and the deputy leader of the SNP, Margo MacDonald. The three struck up an unlikely friendship: Sillars and MacDonald would marry in 1981, and they were entertained rather than irritated by Taylor's platform orations against nationalism and socialism.[22]

With its network of shop stewards, activists and trade councils, the Scottish TUC should have been a major asset to the No campaign. It campaigned with gusto, distributing half a million pamphlets on the threat to democracy, 250,000 on food prices and a further half a million on the malign economic consequences of the Common Market. As in the rest of the UK, however, it proved reluctant to fund campaign activities by anyone else, while trade unionists in Scotland proved no more willing than in England to take their political cues from the unions. Meetings were sparsely attended, and the STUC proved powerless to prevent the swing to the Market among Labour's traditional voters.[23]

THE SNP AND EUROPE

That left the SNP as the main vehicle for the anti-Market campaign. A report for 'Britain in Europe' concluded that the SNP were 'the only anti-Marketeers of consequence' in Scotland, a view that the SNP itself was keen to foster. Like Plaid Cymru and the Ulster Unionists, it affiliated to the National Referendum Campaign, and it plunged into the referendum with all the fervour of a general election.[24]

Like Plaid Cymru, the SNP had never been isolationist.[25] Its leaders had always sought to locate Scotland within a wider international framework, whether as a 'Dominion' within the British Empire, a member of the League of Nations or a participant in the UN. At the start of the referendum campaign, SNP chairman William Wolfe embarked on a twenty-five-day tour of North America, designed to showcase the party's campaign theme of 'Scotland International'.[26] Throughout the campaign, the party insisted that Scotland should play a full role in the international order, through bodies such as the IMF, GATT, the OECD and the International Labour Organization.[27]

In the immediate post-war years, the SNP had taken a broadly positive view of the European project. The party had tried, unsuccessfully, to gain representation at the Hague Conference of the United Europe Movement in 1948, and it had participated in the Congress of European Communities and Regions. The SNP had urged membership of the European Coal and Steel Community in 1951 and looked sympathetically on the early moves towards a Common Market.[28]

The idea that Scotland was being held back from its rightful place in Europe by an insular British state had obvious attractions for the SNP. Over the 1960s, however, the party's enthusiasm fell markedly – just as UK governments were becoming more eager to participate. This owed something to the classic 'mirroring' of insurgent parties, taking positions at odds with Westminster; but there were also political and intellectual forces behind the party's changing attitude. The SNP's electoral success in 1974 had come chiefly in farming and fishing constituencies, which were wary of common agricultural and fisheries policies. Intellectually, the rhetoric of supranationalism was problematic for a party dedicated to Scottish nationhood; Wolfe compared the EEC in 1975 to the rise of Bismarck's Germany, and the emergence of a full-blown customs union with aspirations to economic and monetary union looked suspiciously like the United Kingdom on a continental scale.[29] In consequence, idealistic appeals to Scotland's place in Europe came to be tempered by anxieties about centralisation and the subjugation of national identities.

By 1975, the SNP was scarcely more united on the issue than the Labour Party, though it was more successful at concealing its divisions. Within the parliamentary party, there remained considerable support for membership; the deputy leader, Gordon Wilson, later recalled that 'a significant portion of the party was pro-European', while Donald Hardie, who ran Scotland in Europe, claimed that at least five SNP MPs favoured staying in. It was widely assumed that an SNP government would seek Scottish membership in its own right, once independence had been achieved.[30] Yet influential figures, like the press officer, Stephen Maxwell, the vice-chair, Isobel Lindsay, and the parliamentary leader, Donald Stewart, were pushing for a more robust line that ruled out membership on principle.[31]

The result, as Gordon Wilson put it, was a 'flimsily clad' compromise, ruling out entry 'on anyone else's terms'.[32] Scotland, it was agreed, could only decide on membership once it had negotiated its own terms as an independent country. At the very least, Scotland should have its own Commissioners, MEPs and independent representation at all levels of European government. Until that happened, the policy would be one of 'No Voice, No Entry'. By this means, the party hoped to refocus attention away from the merits of the Community and onto the right of Scotland to make its own decisions.

In consequence, policy documents constituted a tortuous balancing act, designed to appease both sides of the debate. The SNP, voters were assured, was 'not out of sympathy with the ideals behind the EEC'; but Europe had 'strayed from those ideals', building 'a cumbersome and centralised bureaucracy which is the antithesis of what Scotland looks for from a truly democratic and responsive Government'. These 'aberrations' might be 'corrected' – in which case 'a self-governing Scotland would be interested in becoming a full and equal member' – but it was impossible to 'conceive of any modifications being negotiated by the Labour Government which will appreciably help'. Pending future negotiations, Scotland would refuse membership ('or subordination') 'on London's terms'.[33]

The logic of this position was that Scotland should give a 'tactical No', a stance which Stephen Maxwell hoped would appeal both to 'the gut anti-EEC vote in Scotland' and to those voters who, while 'broadly sympathetic to the "European" idea', were 'sensitive to Scotland's lack of political status in European affairs'.[34] This allowed even some pro-Marketeers to back a No vote, by treating it not as a repudiation of the European project but as a protest against the form in which the decision would be taken. George Reid, for example, dismissed the referendum as 'a gigantic charade', which 'does not, of course, allow Scotland to choose'. A Scottish 'No', he argued, would not affect the overall result; and even if it did – securing a small UK 'No' vote against a narrow 'Yes' in England – he doubted whether Parliament would accept the result. Scottish voters, Reid claimed, were 'effectively disfranchised', presenting 'a unique opportunity for tactical voting'.[35]

Right from the start, however, there was pressure to rule out membership on principle. Donald Stewart, who led the SNP group at Westminster, insisted that the EEC 'represented everything the party was fighting against – centralization, undemocratic procedures, power politics and the fetish to abolish all the cultural differences that give life and variety to nations'. Stewart had been active since the 1960s in 'Get Britain Out', working with figures such as Christopher Frere-Smith and the Conservative Richard Body. 'Why', he asked, 'should the position of Nationalists be other than an uncomplicated "No"?'[36] The party's influential press officer and theorist Stephen Maxwell published a 10,000-word paper, arguing that Scotland's economic future lay with North America and the Scandinavian countries, rather than with western Europe.[37] The monthly newspaper of the SNP, the *Scots Independent*, largely ignored the case for a 'tactical no', instead making a robust argument against the very existence of the EEC. 'Scots', it declared,

> should have no part in the homogenising (the Marketeers call it 'harmonising') of man's work and spirit; which is the EEC's purpose.
>
> Scots should have no part in super-power political and military pretension; which is the EEC's purpose.
>
> Scots should develop their own potential, their own laws … which is what the EEC was formed to oppose.
>
> Scots of all people should abhor the idea of empire; which is at the heart of the EEC.
>
> Scots should abhor the division of the world into monolithic blocs; which is the chosen way of the EEC.

Scots, it concluded, should ignore the views of 'political strategists and economic tacticians' and return an unambiguous 'No'.[38]

Although the compromise held, it was inevitably the hostile voices within the party that spoke loudest. Winifred Ewing described a vote for membership as 'a death warrant' for Scotland. 'The EEC was one of the most undemocratic bodies in the world. It was a political superpower and was unacceptable to the SNP.'[39] Stewart warned that membership would propel Scotland back into 'a "dark age" of bureaucracy and remote control', imperilling the very survival of Scottish democracy.[40] The EEC was consistently presented as an imperial entity, founded on 'absurd dreams of renewed English imperial greatness'.[41] In a glorious parody of the Superman comics, a cartoon published by the Federation of Student Nationalists told the story of 'Super-Briton', an umbrella-wielding toff sent to Earth from the doomed planet 'Imperius'. With his mission 'to promote imperialism, to root out parochialism, to stamp out inferior cultures and impose a glorious uniformity', Super-Briton is commissioned by a copulating Harold Wilson and Margaret Thatcher to secure a Scottish 'Yes' vote in the referendum.[42]

At times, SNP commentary could take on a markedly anti-English inflection. Winnie Ewing accused pro-Marketeers of 'flooding Scotland with English cash in an attempt to brain-wash the Scottish voter', alleging that 'Scotland in Europe' (a 'front' organisation for the London campaign) was spending £250,000 in a bid to 'buy Scottish votes with English gold'. Scottish Antis, she claimed, had 'proved their loyalty and commitment to Scotland over years', whereas 'Yes' campaigners were tools of 'the London Establishment and multi-national companies who have exploited Scotland for decades'.[43]

References to 'the British propaganda machine' and 'the discredited London establishment' peppered SNP rhetoric, as did the idea that Scotland had been dragged into the Community as a 'province of the United Kingdom'. As Wolfe pointed out, a majority of Scottish MPs had voted against the European Communities Act in 1972, but had been overridden by English votes.[44] In an argument that would have been familiar to Powell, the very fact of Britain's application was presented as a mark of the bankruptcy of the British state, an acknowledgement that the UK was 'no longer viable' as a collective entity. The idea that prosperity was only possible with European assistance was dismissed as 'an English argument, which has no place in the Scottish debate'.[45]

FIGURE 13.1   An SNP view: Scotland as the reluctant bridegroom in a marriage of English convenience. *Scots Independent*, May 1975, p. 6.
Source: © Scots Independent Newspapers Ltd.

Not surprisingly, the analogy was often drawn between the Common Market and the United Kingdom. 'Scotland joined a Common Market in 1707,' Iain Murray reminded a rally in Banchory, and 'Scotland has been bled white by the effects of that Common Market.' David Rollo, a vice-chairman of the party who had launched 'Radio Free Scotland' in 1956, alleged that 'the common market of Britain' had turned Scotland into 'the industrial slum of Europe'. 'Why should we expect a better deal from another common market, which is even more remote than the present one?'[46]

None of this, the party insisted, was incompatible with the SNP's commitment to an outward-looking, internationalist Scotland.

In deference to the theme of 'Scotland International', the party stressed that an independent Scotland, far from cutting itself off from the rest of the world, would be able to play a more open and outward-looking role. Winnie Ewing mocked pro-Marketeers as 'political flat-earthers ... so obsessed with a narrow European "regionalism" that the rest of the world does not exist for them'. Distancing itself from what it claimed was the more insular campaign south of the border, the SNP insisted upon the peculiarly Scottish character of its internationalism, founded on a long history of trade and migration.[47]

THE SOUTHERN STRATEGY

Despite its suspicion of the EEC, the object of the SNP campaign was not principally to win the referendum. Comprising less than 10 per cent of the UK electorate, Scotland was unlikely to determine the result. For the SNP, the real importance of the vote lay in the opportunity to build support in areas traditionally dominated by Labour. A report on 'Enemy Action' by BIE concluded that the SNP was 'treating the Referendum as an election issue to strengthen their case', printing the SNP logo on campaign material and distributing it alongside membership forms and details of SNP events.[48]

Activity focused particularly on fishing constituencies, where the SNP already had a power-base, and on those industrial regions where Labour had traditionally dominated. Margo MacDonald, the former MP for Glasgow Govan and the party's deputy leader, had been arguing for some time for a 'southern strategy', designed to penetrate Labour's industrial heartlands in the major cities. By displacing Labour as the main voice of the No campaign, MacDonald hoped to mobilise industrial workers who feared for their jobs within an expanded Common Market. Referendum activity was folded into an existing 'Save Scottish Steel' campaign, warning of the threat to heavy industry from European centralisation.[49] There was a particular push in Strathclyde, easily the largest of the Scottish voting regions and home to many of Labour's urban strongholds. The SNP claimed to have delivered at least 800,000 leaflets during the campaign and planned to canvass every household in the region, in what activists claimed was the party's 'biggest campaign on any one issue'.[50]

With some of the EEC's most extensive coastline, fisheries were also a key concern. The SNP had been wooing the fishing industry for years, and even pro-Marketeers acknowledged that fishermen would face increased competition from European fleets. The party presented petitions at Westminster from fishermen in Shetland, where the issue helped to secure one of only two No votes in the UK. Douglas Henderson, whose East Aberdeenshire constituency included major fishing ports such as Fraserburgh and Peterhead, warned that a Yes vote would be 'one of the last nails in the coffin which the London Government has been building for Scotland's fishing industry'.[51]

A bigger potential constituency was affected by the recent oil discoveries in the North Sea. The slogan 'it's Scotland's oil' had brought dividends for the SNP in its struggle against Westminster, and the hope was that it would prove equally potent against the Common Market. Despite the insistence of the UK government, the Commission and the oil industry itself that the Community had no more designs on North Sea oil than it did on German coal or French vineyards, the SNP persistently alleged that a Common Energy Policy would seek to exploit the resource for the benefit of Continental, rather than Scottish, consumers. Membership, it was alleged, would prevent the kind of planned, state-led exploitation of the oil industry that was necessary to secure its maximum benefit to Scotland – a charge levied by Labour and SNP Antis alike.[52] Control of the industry, and in particular the pace of development and extraction, was at this time a bigger issue than revenues, and was more vulnerable to the charge of European interference. Anti-Marketeers argued that Scotland should follow the path taken by Norway, which had grown rich on oil revenues while retaining its independence. Bjørn Unneberg, who had taken a prominent role in the Norwegian 'No' campaign in 1972, was invited to SNP rallies, and references to the Norwegian model became a staple of SNP rhetoric.[53] As the *Scotsman* grumbled, the SNP 'mounted this steed at the outset, saddled it with oil predictions and Norwegian comparisons, and rode it grimly all the way through' the campaign.[54]

While pro-Marketeers emphasised the scale of European investment in Scotland, the SNP warned that membership would undermine the new Scottish Development Agency. The SDA, which was due to start work in 1976, was already the subject of a political auction, with the SNP demanding increased funds and investment of up to 50 per cent of the costs of new industrial ventures. That figure was deliberately chosen to exceed the 30 per cent cap set by European competition rules, for by challenging pro-Marketeers to deny that the 50 per cent figure would be illegal, the SNP hoped not only to draw attention to the constraints on national sovereignty imposed by the Community, but also to wrest political ownership of the Agency from the Labour government that had set it up.[55]

Yet for all the optimism of the SNP, anti-Marketeers fought a chaotic and ill-conceived campaign that struggled to engage the public. Underfunded, out-generalled and confused over its strategic direction, the Scottish 'No' campaign was divided both along and between party lines. The SNP's strength lay chiefly in rural areas – eight of its eleven seats were predominantly rural – but its campaign was focused mainly on industrial Scotland, where Labour was pre-eminent. Nationalist campaigning was targeted as much against the Labour Party as it was against 'Brussels', while Labour Antis were divided on devolution and on the whole future direction of the Left.

The result was a traumatic experience for anti-Marketeers of all stripes. Gordon Wilson likened it to 'blitzkrieg'; the No campaign, he recalled, 'was bulldozed out of the way by weight of numbers, money and … resources'. Sillars called it 'a nightmare', in which anti-Marketeers were 'washed away' by the tidal force of the Yes campaign. No campaigners, he recalled, 'might as well have been talking into the wind'.[56] For the SNP, in particular, it was traumatic to discover not only how badly they had misread the public mood but how little they had been able to shape it.

'SCOTLAND IN EUROPE'

Pro-Marketeers had problems of their own, though they were lubricated by more extensive financial resources.[57] Relations between the Conservative and Labour parties were no more cordial in Scotland than in England, and the Conservative Party itself was less wholeheartedly pro-Market. Donald Hardie, regional organiser for 'Scotland in Europe', was himself a Conservative, but he complained that only thirty-seven of the seventy-one Scottish Conservative Associations offered to help on polling day.[58] Turnout at meetings could be dire. Tam Dalyell, speaking in a town of 11,000 people, drew an audience of just four people, which included his wife, the headmaster of the school at which he was speaking, and the janitor who had to open and close the hall. The only authentic member of the public was a retired miner, who asked tartly what MPs were paid for if they expected the public to take all the decisions.[59] Even Harold Wilson, speaking at Glasgow, drew an audience of barely 100.[60] A diarist for the *Scotsman* reported that 'you can cross from East to West across Scotland's ample waist ... without seeing a sign or hearing a word about what we are told is the greatest issue the people of Britain have ever been called upon to resolve'.[61]

Co-ordination with the English campaign was also sometimes deficient. Despite claims of 'English gold' flooding into Scotland, the organisation was allocated only £25,000 by Britain in Europe. That left it reliant on campaign material produced in London, which was not always sensitive to Scottish needs.[62] In February, when the campaign took delivery of literature from BIE, officials were 'horrified' to find the words 'published by Conservative Central Office' blazoned on the back. As they protested to Con O'Neill, any suggestion that Scotland in Europe was a Conservative front organisation would 'kill all the progress we have made'. Activists from the Labour and Liberal parties would 'certainly not deliver any literature' bearing 'the Conservative imprint'.[63]

Nonetheless, the pro-Marketeers worked much more happily across party lines than the Antis, in part because they tended to agree on the question of the Union. There was even an official necktie, combining the blue and red colours of the two main parties. The Conservative Donald Hardie was given a Liberal, Ronnie Fraser, as his deputy, while Dr J. Dickson Mabon represented Labour as chairman of the campaign committee. Mabon, the 'cheerful and chubby-faced' MP for Greenock and Port Glasgow, was one of the few serving Labour MPs to put his head decisively above the parapet. In general, Labour Members preferred to keep their heads down, leaving the bulk of the campaigning to former MPs like George Lawson, Peggy Herbison, William Hannan and Dick Douglas.[64] A leading role was played by George Thomson, former Labour MP for Dundee East and now a European Commissioner. Despite complaints that a 'civil servant' was interfering in a UK election, Thomson played a major role as the architect of the new Regional Aid policy, which he hinted had been devised with Scotland in mind.[65]

For Scottish pro-Marketeers, the first priority was to rebut the charge that Scotland had been pulled into Europe on 'England's terms'. To this end, the Scottish operation was given almost complete autonomy to construct its own campaign.[66] 'Scotland in Europe' took as its symbol the linked hands of the nine member states, which had appeared on the 50 pence piece since 1973. Reworked as a thistle motif, this appeared on posters and literature alongside slogans like 'Scotland says YES to Europe'. Local committees as far afield as Aberdeen, Dundee, Edinburgh, Fife, Inverness, Orkney, Shetland and Stranraer hosted more than 300 meetings across Scotland, which sought to marry the idealistic case for membership with an appeal to material interests.[67] Thomson, in particular, stressed both the visionary aspirations of the Community – 'the prevention of war in Europe, in which so much Scottish blood has been spilt' – and the opportunities for regional aid. This was set alongside a rosy picture of Scotland's economic future as an *entrepôt* between Europe and the Atlantic. A series of leaflets headed '*Europe cares...*' set out the benefits for the fishing industry (£800,000 for new boats in Buckie, Eyemouth, Fraserburgh, Peterhead and Whalsay); farming (£732,000 for creameries in Inverness, Sorbie and Stranraer, £374,000 for improvements to farms in North Argyll); and heavy industry (£15 million for Ravenscraig steelworks, £10 million for a power station at Peterhead, £4 million for an oil rig at Stornoway).[68] More fancifully, the newly elected Conservative MP for Edinburgh Pentlands, Malcolm Rifkind, suggested that the European Court might relocate to Edinburgh, or that the new European Regional Fund could be administered from Scotland.[69]

As in Wales, it was argued that Scotland would enjoy more autonomy – and more scope for its identity – within a multinational entity that diluted English dominance. Pro-Marketeers drew attention to the 'international leverage that Ireland has acquired through its membership'. As Donald Hardie insisted, 'the Irish say that, for the first time in hundreds of years, they are away from the shadow of London and they enjoy it'.[70] Within the EEC, Scotland could exert influence through its MEPs, judges and civil servants; already, the eminent Scottish advocate Alexander ('Jack') Mackenzie Stuart had become the UK's first representative on the European Court of Justice. Outside, Scotland risked becoming peripheral to decisions affecting the world. Posters and fliers urged Scots to 'Be involved or be ignored,' while insisting that '*real* sovereignty' meant participation 'in the big league'.[71]

Despite these positive messages, however, Scotland in Europe fought a largely negative campaign. Willie Ross accused the pro-Marketeers of 'an avalanche of fear', and the economic prognostications of the Yes campaign were gloomy even by Scottish standards. Nicholas Fairbairn, the Conservative MP for Kinross and West Perthshire, warned that a No vote would mean 'the closing of schools and hospitals and the stopping of roads, railways and mines'.[72] Speaking at Edinburgh University, Ted Heath warned of rationing and food shortages outside the Community, while almost all commentators stressed the prospect of mass redundancies. The *Glasgow Herald* took up the grisly theme, arguing that withdrawal from the Common Market 'would be tantamount to national suicide'.[73]

As in the rest of the UK, the Yes campaign focused relentlessly on jobs and employment. A review of campaign material undertaken by the *Scotsman* found that the most common single argument was that 'Scottish jobs were in danger if Britain left the Market.'[74] Posters and fliers insisted that 'a YES for Europe is a YES for jobs'. If Scotland left the Community, voters were warned, 'companies will build their new factories inside the Common Market, instead of in Scotland'.[75] Lord George-Brown put the case with characteristic bluntness: inside the Community, 'we have a chance to achieve all the things we want to achieve; stay out and we don't have one bloody chance at all'.[76]

In making this argument, pro-Marketeers leaned heavily on the authority of business. Hardie himself would later run the Institute of Directors in Scotland, and the campaign understood the importance of mobilising support from employers. The Scottish Council (Development and Industry) sent questionnaires to 1,600 companies of various sizes. Of the 926 who replied, almost three-quarters said that withdrawal would be 'damaging' or 'very disadvantageous', while less than 6 per cent favoured withdrawal. The Council predicted that 30,000 jobs would be lost in the event of a No vote. Regional Chambers of Commerce told a similar story: in Dundee and Tayside, for example, 97 per cent of respondents favoured staying in.[77]

Large companies were particularly wary of the costs of exit. The Board of Grampian Holdings, for example, called for a Yes vote at their annual general meeting, and there was particular concern that American firms might reduce investment if Scotland no longer had free access to Continental markets.[78] But there were also efforts to mobilise smaller businesses, especially those with a Scottish flavour. Speakers were encouraged to give specifics on local industries: fishermen were reminded that 30 per cent of Scotland's herring catch went to the Community; textile workers that 28 per cent of woven cloth was bought by the EEC. On referendum day, the *Scottish Daily Express* published a picture of four bagpipe makers, who had found 'a booming market in Europe for this most traditional of Scottish products'. As proud Scots, they would be voting to keep Scotland in Europe.[79]

For the economic argument to stick, it was important to disable the analogy with Norway. As a small, oil-producing country that had broken free of its neighbour, Norway had obvious attractions for Nationalists; but David Steel, the rising star of Scottish Liberalism, dismissed the comparison as 'totally bogus'. Norway's mineral resources, he noted, far exceeded those of Scotland, and Norway did not compete with the EEC in its manufactures. In consequence, there was no guarantee that Britain would be offered the same free trade arrangement that had been constructed for Norway.[80] Even were it on offer, such an arrangement would not release the UK from European trade rules; it would simply disbar it from influence over their construction. In this respect, withdrawal might impair British sovereignty 'more cruelly than membership'.[81] Scotland in Europe warned that Norway was unable to develop her mineral wealth at Spitsbergen because of Soviet pressure; was powerless to uphold its 50-mile fishing limit, because the EEC would not recognise it; and had been forced to accept EEC prices for steel and aluminium. 'Norway, out', it concluded, 'is ignored.'[82]

SCOTLAND SAYS YES

The result on 5 June matched almost perfectly the result of the *Glasgow Herald*'s final poll. Discounting the undecided, the paper had anticipated a vote to stay of 58 per cent to 42 per cent; the actual result was 59 per cent to 41 per cent. This was a remarkable reversal of the situation in February, when the paper had found just 29 per cent in favour of membership and 45 per cent who wanted to leave. Scotland had experienced one of the biggest swings in the UK, a change that was particularly marked among Labour voters. As recently as April, Labour supporters had polled against membership by 44 per cent to 37 per cent; by June, they were polling 46 per cent to 32 per cent in favour. Not surprisingly, support was strongest among Conservative voters (71 per cent at the end of May, up from 63 per cent in April), and weakest in the SNP (20 per cent). Active support for membership was slightly higher among men than women (47 per cent to 45 per cent) but women were less likely to back leaving (29 per cent to 36 per cent). As in other parts of the UK, women were more likely to describe themselves as

'Don't Knows', with 26 per cent of Scottish women undecided in June to just 17 per cent of men.[83]

Support for a Yes vote was highest in the Borders, where almost three-quarters of voters backed membership. This may have reflected stronger economic links with England, and support was weaker further north. Nonetheless, every part of Scotland except Shetland and the Western Isles voted to stay in, defying predictions by the SNP that seven of Scotland's twelve regions would vote No.[84]

Despite the scale of the defeat, the SNP insisted that its campaign had been 'a success'.[85] Speaking to the press on 9 June, Donald Stewart claimed that the SNP had never expected to win the vote. Instead, the object had been twofold: 'to demonstrate the divergence between Scottish and English opinion'; and to secure 'wide-ranging guarantees of Scottish interests' within the Community. 'Both of these objectives', he claimed implausibly, 'have been secured.' Scotland's Yes, he insisted, had been given 'reluctantly' and on six specific conditions: 'Separate Scottish membership of the EEC, with Scotland represented on community institutions as a separate nation'; 'Total non-interference with Scottish ownership of Scottish oil'; 'No restrictions on the Scottish Development Agency'; the right for 'Scottish housewives' to buy food as cheaply inside the Community as out ('through EEC subsidies if necessary'); 'No interference with the Scottish steel industry'; and 'Renegotiation of the Common Fisheries Policy ... to reaffirm the prior claims to these stocks of the Scottish fishing industry'. The result, the party insisted, was only binding if those conditions were fulfilled. If they were not – in particular, if Scots were denied equal representation with countries like Denmark and Ireland – 'then the whole question of Scottish membership will be revived'.[86]

It was a valiant, but ludicrous, effort. Gordon Wilson described the campaign more accurately as 'a shambles', with the SNP's intellectual confusion on the issue resulting in 'a failure to have any line for or against the Common Market other than "No Voice, No Entry"'. The result, he noted, 'came as a great shock', marking the first serious reverse for the party after a period of almost continuous success. In 'a campaign that was run from London', it appeared, 'Scots were quite prepared to be steered to vote on a British basis.'[87] In this respect, the result marked a rebuff not only for the SNP campaign, but for its analysis of Scottish political culture.

While Stewart continued to insist that an independent Scotland would revisit the issue in future, it was the pro-Marketeers in the SNP who were emboldened. George Reid told journalists that 'Scotland's future obviously lies in Europe' and that he would cheerfully accept the vote. Despite a public rebuke from the leadership, Reid's preference for a policy of engagement with the Community would become the mainstream position in the party from the mid-1980s.[88]

With this in mind, the SNP quietly shifted focus. It began by accepting a motion tabled by Gordon Wilson at the NEC, which accepted the verdict of the referendum but committed the party to seek independent representation at all levels of the organisation. A series of more hostile resolutions were beaten off – one by just 148 votes to 80.[89] Sillars issued a similar statement on behalf of Labour anti-Marketeers, though it attracted little attention in the press. After joining the SNP in 1980, he would become one of the leading architects of the SNP's 'Independence in Europe' policy.

The Scottish result had a symbolic importance that went beyond its numerical significance. Had Scotland voted No, it would have strengthened the perception that Scotland and England were set irretrievably on different paths. The result would have dealt a further blow to the Union, while bolstering the claim of the SNP to have displaced the Labour Party as the voice of Scottish opinion. Victory for the Yes campaign avoided what many had regarded as a constitutional doomsday scenario, by which divergent results in Scotland and England tore open the fabric of the Union. That scenario would have to wait until 2016, by which time the position of the SNP, of Scottish Labour and of the English and Welsh vote would all have changed dramatically.

EPILOGUE: 'WE ARE ALL EUROPEANS NOW'

We are all Europeans now. Let us make sure that we are good Europeans.

The Sun, 7 June 1975[1]

This tiresome con-job has debased and ridiculed us all; they might as well ask us to vote on the Quantum Theory or the Communion of Saints.

The Guardian, 2 June 1975[2]

May I say how pleased we are to have some Europeans here, now that we are on the Continent? I didn't vote for it myself, quite honestly, but now that we're in, I'm determined to make it work.

Basil Fawlty, 24 October 1975[3]

As polling day approached in June, even the weather succumbed to the apocalyptic mood. A summer of glorious sunshine gave way to a freak weather system from the Arctic, bringing snow, sleet and freezing conditions across much of the country. At a shoe factory in Norwich, workers downed tools and walked out because the equipment had frozen. In the county championship, play was suspended between Derbyshire and Lancashire because of snow, allowing the West Indian cricket captain, Clive Lloyd, to enjoy his first-ever snowball fight on the playing surface. When play resumed the next day, conditions were so treacherous that one batsman removed his false teeth, wrapped them in a handkerchief and handed them to the umpire, Dickie Bird, for safe-keeping.[4]

    It was not just the weather, with its capacity to depress turnout, that alarmed pro-Marketeers. A week before the vote, Leeds United lost to Bayern Munich in the European Cup final. In a sign that the Franco-German axis was alive and well, a French referee denied Leeds two penalties and disallowed an apparently legitimate goal. English fans responded by rioting in Paris, prompting the slightly wistful headline in the *Scotsman*, 'Britain apologizes for Leeds'. A furious trade union official told reporters that the result was proof of 'Europe's envy' and its 'anger and jealousy towards Britain'.[5]

As the moment of decision drew near, a campaign to boycott the referendum gained some attention. The 'Don't Know' campaign was founded by Frank Bradbury, a design engineer from Ross-on-Wye, and claimed to have offices in London, Monmouth, Stockport and Bude. It encouraged voters to 'pass the buck back to Westminster – where it belongs' and accused MPs of 'cowardly' behaviour in shuffling responsibility onto the public.[6] More worryingly for ministers, local government workers threatened to strike during the count, in a pay dispute that was resolved only days before the vote.[7]

Yet despite the weather, the football and all the other neuroses that convulsed the Yes campaign, the result on 5 June was rarely in doubt. Turnout, at 64.5 per cent, was higher than some had feared and probably better than the headline figure suggests; given the outdated register and the holiday season, a contemporary study estimated that three-quarters of those who could have voted did so.[8] With 67.2 per cent opting to stay in, victory was as emphatic as any Marketeer could have hoped. Margaret Thatcher thought the result 'thrilling', while the *Sunday Times* called it 'the most exhilarating event in British politics since the war'.[9] Papers that had once condemned the referendum now hailed it as a masterstroke. 'Whatever its squalid origins', thought the *Evening Standard*, 'the referendum has turned out to be the best thing that has happened to British democracy for decades.'[10]

In the days that followed, newspapers dedicated acres of print to analysis of the result, exploring how it had come about and what it might mean for the future. This commentary is as much a part of the history of the referendum as the campaign itself; yet what is most striking in retrospect is how few of its conclusions stood the test of time. The vote did not, as predicted, bring an end to controversy over membership. It did not sideline the extremes in British politics, nor launch a new era of centrist government. The referendum was not banished from constitutional practice, nationalism was not extinguished and conventional party warfare was swiftly reignited. That the political runes were so comprehensively misread may serve as a warning for commentators on the 2016 vote. It can also tell us much about the hopes and fears that were vested in the referendum, and may help to explain why the decision did not, as Harold Wilson had anticipated, end 'fourteen years of national argument'.[11]

A NEW HOPE

In the immediate aftermath of the vote, what struck commentators most forcibly was the scale of the majority. Most took for granted that it had 'settled once and for all the European question'; the task now, as the *Sun* told its readers, was to 'make sure that we are good Europeans' by exploiting 'the massive opportunities Europe offers'.[12] Neil Kinnock, who had campaigned for a No vote, told journalists that 'Only an idiot would ignore or resent a majority like this.' 'We're in for ever'.[13]

"I'm not getting dressed till I know the result!"

FIGURE E.1 Harold Wilson waits to discover the results of the referendum. *The Sun*, 6 June 1975. The Sun/News Syndication

The Labour Party and the trade union movement ended their boycott of Community institutions, and even Tony Benn put a positive spin on the result. The campaign, he declared, had been 'the best debate the country has ever had. We did not really join the Market until today.'[14]

For Harold Wilson, the result was a rare bright spot in the most difficult period of his premiership. A cartoon in the *Daily Express* portrayed him as a Roman Emperor, parading in triumph through crowds of cheering subjects. His chariot was drawn by Heath, Jenkins and Thorpe; Mrs Thatcher threw flowers from the sidelines, while the Labour Antis and a hairy array of trade union leaders were dragged in chains behind him.[15] Speaking to President Ford, Wilson boasted that he had 'played it cool, acted as though we had to be convinced and only pulled out the stops at the end'; but the truth, as the *Daily Telegraph* commented, was that the referendum had been 'a great' – and successful – 'political gamble'.[16] Success had not been assured: as the head of the government's Referendum Unit later recalled, 'There was throughout the sensation of living in dangerous times and success seemed very far away.'[17] As the *Sunday Times* commented, 'if politicians are to be judged by their ability in the end to get what they want, Harold Wilson is a great politician'.[18]

Wilson shared the laurels with his former nemesis, Ted Heath. Heath had been deposed as leader of the Opposition only months before the vote, yet his performances on the campaign trail wholly eclipsed the lacklustre efforts of his successor. Journalists struggled to reconcile the inspirational, almost evangelical campaigner they saw on the referendum trail, whose speeches fizzed with 'fervour, fire and fun', with the

FIGURE E.2 'Caesar's Triumph', *Daily Express*, 7 June 1975. Cummings/ Express Newspapers/N&S Syndication

'stiff, prickly' figure who had lost the leadership 'because he seemed so remote from the heartbeat of ordinary people'.[19] Heath's 'star', it appeared, was once more 'in the ascendant', spelling danger to Mrs Thatcher. 'Mr Heath', thought the *Sun*, 'has looked more like a party leader than he ever did when he was one. And Mrs Margaret Thatcher has looked much less like a leader than she did when she was not.'[20]

By contrast, Tony Benn was thought to have suffered an almost terminal blow to his ambitions. Anthony King, whose history of the referendum was published in 1977, thought that it had 'brought to an abrupt end, at least for the time being, the brief "Benn era" in British political history'.[21] It was Benn who had demanded a referendum, Benn who had dominated the campaign and Benn who was most tarnished by defeat. Within days of the result, he was demoted from the Department of Industry to the Department of Energy. When his wife, Caroline, was called out of a meeting to be given the news, her first thought was that he had been assassinated. 'In a way,' Benn reflected, 'I had.'[22]

This was rooted in a conclusion that was almost universal in the press: that the referendum had dealt a lasting blow to the Left. It was a commonplace that the result had been 'a thrashing for the Left', 'a resounding anti-Benn vote', which had 'damaged, if not destroyed' the credibility of Labour's Bennite wing.[23] In Bernard Donoughue's colourful image,

> Tony Benn's army of the left was diverted from the dangerous fields of British industry onto the deceptively inviting marshes of the EEC. Once committed and trapped there, Mr Benn was blown up by a referendum of the British people.[24]

The *Sunday Times* concluded that the 'claim of Mr Benn and the trade union Left to speak for the Labour Party and working people has been exposed as a fraud'.[25] The block votes wielded by union leaders had proven 'quite unrepresentative of the millions whose views they pretend to convey', with implications that stretched beyond the European issue.[26]

For the *Daily Express*, the 'most encouraging lesson of the referendum is that the centre held'.[27] Released from party loyalties, voters had followed the judgement of the moderate voices in Parliament, whether Conservative, Labour or Liberal. The disabling of the Bennite

Left and the Powellite Right might, it was hoped, allow centrists on both sides of the aisle to reassert their political weight. If the pro-Marketeers could seize the moment, thought the *Sun*, they could 'light the touchpaper for a much-needed revolution of the moderates'.[28]

A revolution of this kind might also involve a reassertion of parliamentary government. The decision to hold a referendum had been widely condemned in the press, and the fact that voters had endorsed the actions of their elected representatives – and had done so by a similar margin – was hailed as a vindication of Parliament.[29] MPs, it transpired, 'spoke for us better than we knew'. The result, thought Tony Benn's local paper, 'should put an end to the referendum business for ever'.[30]

If Parliament was enhanced by the result, the opposite seemed true of the party system. The spectacle of Heath, Thorpe, Thatcher and Wilson lining up on one side of the battlefield, while Benn, Powell and the SNP took up arms on the other, raised questions about the relevance of party lines drawn up at the start of the twentieth century. Local activists, who had spent years pulling one another's leaflets out of letter boxes, were astonished to discover how much they had in common. Ben Dixon, the Liberal chairman of Havering in Europe, confessed to journalists that 'One wonders now why we're all in different political parties', or 'whether we're all going to break up after the referendum'.[31]

At a time of political and economic crisis, the spirit of cross-party solidarity embodied by Britain in Europe was widely applauded. There was considerable enthusiasm for the education secretary, Reg Prentice, when he appeared to call for a government of national unity at the end of May. Though Prentice himself rowed back from the claim, suggesting that he had simply appealed for 'a spirit of unity', his remarks were echoed by Tories such as Peter Walker, who had been sacked from the Shadow Cabinet by Mrs Thatcher, and Maurice Macmillan, son of the former prime minister.[32] Two elections in 1974 had failed to produce a decisive majority for either party, a situation that had the paradoxical effect of increasing the influence of determined minorities on the backbenches. The experience of Britain in Europe suggested that another way was possible, moving beyond 'the dreary old party game' that had brought the country to its current predicament. The *Sun* referred persistently to 'the Heath, Jenkins, Thorpe "coalition"', an array that 'excites the eye and delights the heart'.[33] The *Financial Times* hoped that BIE might prove 'a training ground in coalition'. For the first time since 1945, 'major politicians have been working closely together on a joint enterprise'. Both 'they and the public have been reminded that it is not as difficult as they thought'.[34]

DISAPPOINTED EXPECTATIONS

For many commentators, the significance of the referendum lay as much in what had *not* happened as in what had. In one of the most intriguing passages of his book on the referendum, Anthony King speculated on what might have happened to Labour in the event of a No vote. Defeat, he argued, would have undermined Wilson and Callaghan while strengthening the Labour Left. Benn or Foot might have become leader, opening a fissure between 'the moderate centre' and the 'extreme left'. Roy Jenkins and Shirley Williams might have left to form a new party, carrying many of their most popular colleagues with them, all of which could have had the cumulative effect of banishing Labour from power 'for at least a generation'.[35]

This, of course, was almost exactly what happened a few years later, the first of several indications that the referendum would disappoint the hopes vested in it. The Labour Party did not, as Wilson had predicted, return to 'a state of euphonious harmony' after the vote.[36] It was true, as Callaghan proudly noted, that the party conference in 1975 heard 'not a single reference to the bitter dispute that had split and divided the Party for fifteen years'; but this was a truce, not a settlement.[37] As the economy deteriorated over the years that followed, predictions that the EEC would accelerate rather than reverse Britain's industrial decline took on increased plausibility. The referendum came to be seen by the Left as one of the more egregious examples of the treachery of the 1974–9 governments, under a leadership that aped the positions of their Tory opponents.[38] On the principle that 'the blood of the martyrs is the seed of the Church', Benn and Foot actively gained in prestige by their defeat. Strikingly, it was those who had campaigned to leave in 1975, such as Benn, Foot and Kinnock, who would battle for control of the party in the 1980s, while pro-Marketeers such as Roy Jenkins, David Owen, Bill Rodgers and Shirley Williams left en masse for the SDP. In this respect, the referendum was to prove a pyrrhic victory for the Labour Right. It won the vote, but, as George Bernstein notes, it lost 'the struggle for the soul of the party'.[39]

Of those who had played a leading role in the Yes campaign, it is striking how few enjoyed much domestic success in the years that followed. Wilson retired through ill-health in 1976; Jenkins abandoned Westminster for the presidency of the European Commission; while Thorpe stood trial for conspiracy to murder. Buoyed by his performances in the referendum, Heath began to dream once again of leading a government of national unity. Instead, he spent a quarter of a century curdling on the backbenches, firing barbed but ineffectual darts at his Tory successor.

It is striking, too, how quickly the authority of party reasserted itself. For all the enthusiasm engendered by Britain in Europe, the experiment of cross-party co-operation was never likely to endure. The party machines, which had gone into suspended animation for the campaign, were eager to reactivate. For those who regretted that fact, stepping outside the party system meant entering a wilderness with no constituency, administrative support or realistic prospect of office. Things might have been different had a new party emerged, yet BIE lacked the infrastructure or the intellectual cohesion to form the basis of such a party. Its organisation was on loan from the Conservatives, while its leaders were held together chiefly by a question that no longer seemed to be at issue.[40] Victory in the referendum stripped BIE of its *raison d'être*, and reopened disagreements that had been muted during the campaign. Was the EEC a federal project or a partnership between nation states? Was it a bulwark of capitalism or a platform for socialism on a continental scale? Should Britain accept a more parochial, regional identity within Europe, or use the Community as a foundation for world power?

Partly for this reason, the referendum did not, as Wilson had hoped, end 'fourteen years of national argument'. With some exceptions, Antis did not run up the white flag and proclaim their allegiance to Brussels. Instead, they responded in one of three ways, each of which had a lasting impact.

The first was simply to reject the result as illegitimate, given the financial advantage enjoyed by the Yes campaign and its overwhelming support in the media. Clive Jenkins, general secretary of ASTMS, called the referendum 'the worst election since Charles Dickens wrote about Eatenswill'. The *Morning Star* claimed that voters had been 'deceived' by big business, the media and those 'with a private profit axe to grind': once they realised that they had been 'lied to, swindled and blackmailed', millions would rise up against 'the brainwashing battering'.[41] For Enoch Powell, voters had been misled as surely in 1975 as by the men of Munich in 1938. Once the public awoke to the deception, they would 'tear apart' those responsible.[42]

A second response was to reinterpret the result, for while it was obvious that 'the people' had spoken in 1975, it was not entirely clear what they had said. Neil Marten, addressing the Commonwealth Industries Association in July, insisted that the public had voted solely for 'the Community as it is'; they had given no mandate for federalism or for further integration of any kind. Immediately after the result, the National Referendum Campaign issued a press statement reminding ministers that the nation 'had not committed itself to economic and political union with Europe', and that they 'should beware the consequences' of outpacing the consent of the electorate.[43]

If the campaign had been fraudulent and the result contingent, there was no reason to believe that defeat could not be reversed. Antis consoled themselves with the reflection that 'peace in our time' had been as popular in the 1930s as the cause of Britain in Europe in the 1970s; yet 'the men of Munich are now dishonoured, and Winston Churchill ... has been abundantly vindicated'. The conviction that, one day, 'the men of Brussels' would be exposed as 'the betrayers of our highest national interests' burned through the embers of the anti-Market campaign, ensuring that the flame of resistance would shine on in the darkness of defeat.[44]

This encouraged a third response, which was to begin the campaign to overturn the result. Powell had made clear from the outset that only a vote to leave could be regarded as binding; any other verdict was merely 'provisional', until the electorate came to its senses.[45] Christopher Frere-Smith, likewise, had long believed that the only question to be decided on 5 June was 'whether we come out now ... or later'.[46] Tony Benn, whose conviction that he spoke for the people was impervious to the evidence of the electorate, concluded that the campaign had been too short to get the message across. Anticipating his verdict on the 1983 election, he embraced the result as a *moral* victory: to win 32.8 per cent was itself an achievement, 'considering we had absolutely no real organisation, no newspapers, nothing'. Six years later, Labour would commit itself to withdrawal, this time without a referendum.[47]

Preparations began within days of the result. While the NRC itself was wound up, it was agreed to found a successor, the

Safeguard Britain Campaign, which would work to expose, oppose and roll back all moves towards a federal Europe. Formally, this involved a shift in focus, away from the principle of membership towards the menace of federalism. The new organisation would be 'anti-federalist' rather than 'strictly anti-Market'; critics would become known as 'Euro-*sceptics*', rather than 'anti-Marketeers'. In practice, however, since the Antis assumed the EEC to be intrinsically federalist, the goal was to build opposition among those who had voted Yes in 1975.[48]

While the Antis armed themselves for a renewal of hostilities, their opponents largely withdrew from the battlefield. BIE was swiftly dismantled and there was little attempt either to create a successor organisation or to maintain the engagement with public opinion. For the next thirty years all the energy in the European debate would come from critics of the Community, while its supporters were reluctant to expend capital in its defence.

This mattered, because the argument made in 1975 was so deeply rooted in its time. BIE had largely eschewed a more visionary, idealistic case for membership, in favour of an appeal that stressed its transactional benefits. That case was rooted in a perception of economic crisis, political instability and geopolitical danger, at a time when Britain was falling behind the economies of western Europe. BIE's campaign was saturated in the language and apprehensions of the Cold War, of political extremism and of rising food prices across the world. Economically, it assumed that manufacturing was the engine of the British economy; that the world was fragmenting into regional trade blocs; and that the most plausible alternative to membership was a siege economy based on socialist controls.

That was a potent brew in 1975, for it spoke very precisely to the anxieties of its time. By the 1990s, however, little of that package remained intact. The Cold War was over, socialism was in retreat and the UK economy was beginning to outpace its Continental rivals. The City of London, rather than traditional manufacturing, was emerging as the beating heart of the economy, while inflation was at a sustained and historic low. The 'Washington consensus' was cutting tariff barriers around the world, opening up the possibility of global, rather than regional, free trade.

It was no accident that it was in the nineties that serious opposition to membership re-entered the mainstream of British politics; nor that it was on the Right, rather than the Left, that it gained traction. Margaret Thatcher, for example, had supported membership throughout her time as leader, despite never feeling the slightest enthusiasm for the Continent on social or cultural grounds. She had done so on impeccably Thatcherite principles, in the belief that membership secured solidarity against the Soviet Union, restrictions on the power of socialist governments at home and guaranteed access to food supplies. By 1990, however, the picture was very different. With the Soviet Union disintegrating and Germany reunited, 'Europe' began to look less like a bulwark against communism and more like a vehicle for German influence. The Delors Plan suggested that the Community might become an *agent* of socialism, rather than its antidote, while food supplies were cheaper and more abundant than at any time since rationing. The memory of war, which had loomed so large in 1975, was also receding; after 1990, for the first time since the early twentieth century, a political generation was coming to power with no personal memory of conflict. In all these respects, the intellectual foundations of the case constructed in the 1970s were crumbling; yet supporters of membership were slow to adapt, because they assumed that the argument no longer needed making.

From this perspective, it was the renegotiations, rather than the referendum, that set the pattern for the future. For Wilson, the purpose of the renegotiations had been chiefly domestic: to show that Labour, unlike the Conservatives, would defend the national interest in Europe. The temptation to adopt the role of St George, battling for Britain against the European dragon, was one that few subsequent administrations could resist. When a Conservative government was elected in 1979, some hoped for a more 'constructive' engagement with the Community.[49] Yet Thatcher quickly embarked on her own renegotiation, this time over Britain's budget contribution. The budgetary problem was real and serious, but the subsequent deal followed a familiar pattern, being represented as a victory *over* the Community, not as an agreement reached *within* it. Despite the achievement of the Single European Act in 1986 (hailed by ministers as 'Thatcherism on a European scale'), it was Thatcher's 'hand-bagging' of 'Europe' over the budget that was celebrated by her supporters, just as it was David Cameron's decision to veto a new treaty in 2011, not his role in the creation of a digital single market or of an Energy Union, that was trumpeted to the press. From John Major's opt-outs at Maastricht to David

Cameron's 'special status' in 2016, prime ministers tended to measure the success of their policy in Europe by their capacity to protect the UK from its ill effects and malign intentions.[50]

WINDS OF CHANGE

All this prompts a further question, which is perhaps inevitable in the wake of the vote to leave in 2016: why did the two referendums produce such divergent results? Questions like this should be approached with caution, for what happened in 2016 remains poorly understood. If the crystal ball proved so erratic in 1975, following a referendum that endorsed the status quo, we are unlikely to see more clearly when the plaster is still falling from the ceiling.

It is also fair to say that the question at issue in the two campaigns was not the same. It is not necessary to believe that the public was lied to in 1975 – an assertion that holds very little water – to accept that voters were being asked to assess a very different proposition in 2016. Over a forty-year period, a 'Community' of nine had morphed into a 'Union' of twenty-eight, with a currency zone, an active judiciary and competencies stretching far beyond those of the 1970s. The movement of peoples had swollen from a trickle to a flood; net migration from the EEC was roughly 3,000 in 1975, less than the figure each week from the enlarged EU in 2016.[51] Like the sky at night, whose stars adorned its banner, 'Europe' looked different at different points in time; and we should not be surprised that voters reacted in divergent ways.

Furthermore, the shift from a 'Yes' vote in 1975 to a 'Leave' vote in 2016 masks a more complex, multidirectional movement of opinion. In Scotland and Northern Ireland, support for membership has *risen* since the seventies: the two countries that were least enthusiastic in 1975 backed membership in 2016 by 62 per cent and 55.8 per cent respectively (up from 58.4 per cent and 52.1 per cent). Conversely, the two countries that voted most strongly for membership forty years ago, England and Wales, formed the bedrock of the Leave vote in 2016. Nationalist parties such as Plaid Cymru, Sinn Féin and the SNP have all moved from the 'Leave' column to 'Remain', whereas those who identify as 'English' rather than 'British' have grown more hostile to membership.[52] In this sense, there has been no single path from one vote to the next. Rather, there has been a recasting of the geology of

British politics, which has thrown up new formations of opinion and new alignments of class, culture and geography.

Nonetheless, the comparison remains useful, as much for what it reveals about the changing character of British politics and society as for the protean character of the European project. Two obvious areas of difference centre on the conduct of the campaigns and the context within which they took place.

RENEGOTIATIONS

Wilson had entered the renegotiations with a clear sense of what he wanted to achieve. The object was not to transform the Community, but to give critics of membership within his own party permission to change their minds. For this reason, Wilson left untouched what he contemptuously called the 'theology' of the EEC, in favour of practical changes that targeted the concerns of Labour sceptics. Left-wing suspicion of the Market centred on four concerns: that it was a capitalist club; that it was a betrayal of the Commonwealth; that it was bad for poorer countries; and that it was draining money from Britain. The first group was offered a new regional development fund, together with assurances on industrial policy. For Commonwealth enthusiasts, there were improved terms of trade for New Zealand and other importers. Though not formally part of the negotiations, the Lomé Convention also suggested a new direction for the Community, offering to developing countries a massive aid package and improved terms of trade. A new funding mechanism provided a refund on Britain's contribution to the Community budget, though it would later prove hopelessly inadequate.

At the same time, the direction of travel for the EEC seemed relatively benign. Under the ill-fated Ortoli Commission, the movement towards 'ever closer union' appeared to have ground to a halt. Wilson assured MPs that there was 'not a hope in hell' of economic or monetary union in the near future, while Helmut Schmidt dismissed such ideas as 'European cloud cuckoo land'.[53] It was during the renegotiation period that the European Council was put on a secure footing, making heads of government, rather than the Commission, the central decision-makers of the Community. The future of the EEC looked to be intergovernmental, not supranational, diminishing fears of a 'superstate'.

David Cameron shared neither the good fortune nor the strategic vision of his predecessor. Having promised a renegotiation, he appeared to have little idea what he wanted to achieve.[54] In consequence, where Wilson sought practical improvements that targeted specific grievances, Cameron was driven back onto the 'theology' of the EU, negotiating an opt-out from a commitment to 'ever-closer union' that governments had always insisted was meaningless. The final package was not insubstantial. One legal scholar concludes that it was 'more wide-reaching and substantive' than anything Wilson had achieved; but it never gained any traction with the public.[55] Meanwhile, the integrationist pressures unleashed by the crisis within the Eurozone and the ongoing migrant emergency provided a less benign environment for public debate. While Cameron could parade his various opt-outs, this risked confirming a perception that Europe was moving down a road that Britain did not wish to travel.

'DRACULA V. FRANKENSTEIN'

As a result, the renegotiations proved largely irrelevant in 2016. Whereas the package brought back by Wilson had triggered an immediate and enduring movement in the polls, the Remain campaign in 2016 decided simply to 'ditch' Cameron's new deal and to focus on the core case for membership.[56] Stripped of the 'change' mantle, Cameron was driven back onto a mostly negative message, which emphasised the risks to the economy from a Leave vote. It was the strategy that had brought victory in the Scottish referendum of 2014 and in the general election a year later, and rested on a conviction that had the status almost of an iron law for Cameron's circle: that in 'a straight fight between immigration and the economy, the economy wins'. As one of his strategists put it, 'there has been no election in the last hundred years where people have voted against their direct financial interest'.[57]

What came to be known as 'Project Fear' had its antecedents forty years earlier, in Heath's bloodcurdling warnings about Soviet penetration and economic collapse. There were, however, two key differences. The first is that, in 1975, such warnings formed only one part of a richly multi-vocal campaign. BIE crafted specific messages for every possible cohort, which paired the risks of leaving with the opportunities to be expected from membership. That strategy was assisted not only by a supportive national media, but by the existence of a vigorous regional press – now much less potent – that was more interested in the implications of membership for their localities than in the battles fought out at Westminster.[58] Different messages were tailored to farmers, fishermen, factory workers, single parents, Ulster Unionists, churchgoers, Scottish or Welsh Nationalists and members of ethnic minorities. The costs and benefits were translated into terms that spoke to the lived experience of individual voters, whether as employees whose factories formed part of European supply chains, or as shoppers buying food for their families. In 2016, the campaign was more mono-tonal, which made it difficult to sustain interest over a six-month period. The risk message was also less personal, focusing on rather abstract warnings that GDP would grow more slowly over the coming decade.

Secondly, warnings of economic risk resonated to a greater extent in 1975 because they connected with recent experience. For a generation that had lived through rationing, seen oil prices quadruple in 1973 and queued for sugar in 1974, the idea of economic collapse was not at all abstract. Polling for the Out campaign, at a time when inflation was nearing 25 per cent, found that more than half of voters expected 'an immediate economic and political crisis' in the event of withdrawal.[59] By contrast, warnings from the Treasury and the IMF in 2016 seem not to have hit home with voters who had no lived experience of shortages or power cuts.

That was partly because they were not believed. Despite the anti-establishment mood of the seventies, polling in 1975 suggested high levels of trust in those politicians most associated with the Yes campaign.[60] By contrast, the 2016 vote took place amidst a collapse of trust not just in politicians but in almost all forms of public authority. Ten days before the vote, a YouGov poll found that only 19 per cent of respondents believed the statements and claims made about the EU by David Cameron; a colossal 70 per cent did not. Even among those who had voted Conservative in 2015, 60 per cent did not regard him as trustworthy. Economists, businesspeople and the Bank of England also recorded high levels of distrust, while only 13 per cent trusted politicians as a class.[61] In consequence, despite a torrent of grim prognostications by economists, ministers and business organisations, polling suggested that only 30 per cent of voters believed that their personal finances would deteriorate outside the EU. A much larger share, 58 per cent, thought that withdrawal would make no difference or were unsure of its impact.[62]

In any case, anxieties about the economy no longer worked automatically to the advantage of the Remain campaign. In 1975 it had been a truism that Britain was the 'sick man of Europe', outpaced by the dynamic economies of the Continent. Cartoons represented the UK as a sinking ship, its sailors paddling desperately towards the sanctuary of the Common Market.[63] In 2016, by contrast, it was the Eurozone that seemed mired in debt, stagnation and soaring unemployment. Leave campaigners made much of claims that only Antarctica had a slower rate of growth than the EU. For many voters, it was now the European ship that appeared holed beneath the waterline.[64]

This had implications for the discussion of 'sovereignty'. As we have seen, there was an extensive and sophisticated discussion of sovereignty in 1975. The problem for Leave campaigners was that it barely registered with the public. 'Sovereignty' was an unfamiliar and abstract term, of low salience for voters more concerned with jobs and prices. In 2016, by contrast, sovereignty acquired a hook in the issue of immigration and the demand that Britain 'take back control' of its borders. The debate about immigration spoke not only, or even principally, to concerns about race. Just as importantly, it invoked a wider sense of disempowerment: a conviction that voters were no longer permitted a say on who could live or work in their communities. Conversely, the argument that had been so potent in 1975, that sovereignty could only be exercised in partnership, had lost some of its resonance, for Britain had no recent experience, comparable to the three-day week, of the incapacity of national governments in the face of global economic forces.[65]

That might have been countered had there been more evidence of the 'power' that had been promised in exchange for sovereignty. In 1975 BIE could trade on the prospective benefits of membership. Forty years later, voters naturally expected something more concrete; yet the UK was one of the few member states never to develop a compelling story about its achievements within the Community. For the Six, membership was associated with the extraordinary growth rates of the post-war decades, known variously as the *'trentes glorieuses'*, the *'Wirtschaftswunder'* and the *'miracolo economico'*. For states like Spain, Greece and Portugal, membership was associated with the transition from military rule and fascism. For the former Eastern bloc, the EU had eased the transition to democracy and a market economy after the collapse of the Soviet Union. Had the UK developed such a story, it would presumably have centred on the economic transformation of the late twentieth century, as the struggling economy of the 1970s reinvented itself as one of the most dynamic participants in the global market. That this never happened owed more to the domestic politics of the 1980s than to the inherent viability of such a narrative. The Right preferred to credit the government of Margaret Thatcher and an 'Anglo-Saxon' economic model that seemed at odds with the culture of western Europe; while the Left viewed the Thatcher era as a time of economic failure, scarred by deindustrialisation, mass unemployment and inequality. In consequence, Remainers had few positive stories to tell to counter the history of interference and regulation alleged by their opponents.

THE MAN IN THE MIDDLE

These contextual forces also shaped the tone of the campaign and the conduct of central government. In 1975, as in 2016, Wilson suspended collective responsibility and allowed ministers to campaign for or against the government position. That produced occasional moments of friction, as when Roy Jenkins primly declared that he found it 'difficult to take Mr Benn seriously as an economic Minister'.[66] In 2016, by contrast, it produced such spectacular 'blue-on-blue' bloodshed that the media talked of little else.

This cannot be explained solely by the coarsening of political debate or by the echo chambers of abuse constructed on social media. Nor can it be blamed entirely on a journalistic culture that privileges the theatre of politics over substantive policy debate. Just as important was a shift in the role of the prime minister. In 1975 Wilson took a back seat in the campaign. With Roy Jenkins, Ted Heath, Shirley Williams and Jeremy Thorpe leading the charge to stay in, while Tony Benn, Barbara Castle and Enoch Powell fought to get out, Wilson could present himself almost as a spectator, bemused by the 'exaggerated claims' and 'doctrinaire' views of both sides.[67] That position of baffled scepticism   dismissive of the 'theology' of the Marketeers, but reluctantly persuaded of their economic case – located him very close to the swing voters who would decide the result. As the *Guardian* commented, 'it is Mr Wilson's very scepticism about what he calls Common Market theology which makes him such a Pole Star for the wandering voter'.[68]

David Cameron did not have that luxury. With the Labour Party convulsed by its own internal divisions, under a leader whose enthusiasm for the EU burned less than bright, and with no one else in his party willing to take a lead, Cameron had little choice but to run the Remain campaign himself. That disabled him as a mediator between the two sides, making it almost impossible for him to moderate the behaviour of his own cabinet. From the moment that Cameron returned from the negotiations and mocked Boris Johnson in Parliament, his authority to temper the debate was gravely diminished.[69] The ensuing rancour would probably have ended his premiership, even if the result had been different.

THE FINAL COUNTDOWN

The vote to leave the EU marks the end of a distinct period in British history, which began in 1973 and was confirmed in 1975. For good or for ill, governments must now unpick four decades of political integration, peeling apart two economies and legal systems that have grown together like the roots of ancient trees. For those who support withdrawal, the task is akin to eliminating a computer virus. For those who regret it, the experience is closer to amputation. What is not in doubt is the scale of the task, or how much will change as a result of that vote.

In this respect, Cameron's defeat has put into fresh perspective the significance of Wilson's victory. Where Wilson had won the referendum, reimposed his authority and secured Britain's place in the EEC, Cameron had presided over the disintegration of his government, the ruin of his career and the most significant policy reverse since decolonisation. The journalist Stephen Bush once suggested that the theme of Cameron's premiership was 'doing what Wilson did, only a little bit worse'.[70] As Britain begins to unravel forty years of membership, the scale of Wilson's achievement is only now becoming apparent. 'Doing what Harold Wilson did' has proven harder than anyone had believed.

Appendix 1: The Referendum Result, 5 June 1975

The Government have announced the results of the renegotiation of the United Kingdom's terms of membership of the European Community. Do you think that the United Kingdom should stay in the European Community (the Common Market)? YES/NO

	% Turnout	Yes Votes	No Votes	% Yes	% No
United Kingdom	64.5	17,378,581	8,470,073	67.2	32.8
England	64.6	14,918,009	6,812,052	68.7	31.3
Avon	68.7	310,145	147,024	67.8	32.2
Bedfordshire	67.9	154,338	67,969	69.4	30.6
Berkshire	66.4	215,184	81,221	66.4	33.6
Buckinghamshire	69.5	180,512	62,578	74.3	25.7
Cambridgeshire	62.2	177,789	62,143	74.1	25.9
Cheshire	65.5	290,714	123,839	70.1	29.9
Cleveland	60.2	158,982	77,079	67.3	32.7
Cornwall	66.8	137,828	63,478	68.5	31.5
Cumbria	64.8	162,545	63,564	71.9	28.1
Derbyshire	64.1	286,614	131,452	68.6	31.4
Devon	68	334,244	129,179	72.1	27.9
Dorset	68.3	217,432	78,239	73.5	26.5
Durham	61.5	175,284	97,724	64.2	35.8
Essex	67.7	463,505	222,085	67.6	32.4
Gloucestershire	68.4	170,931	67,465	71.7	28.3
Greater London	60.8	2,201,031	1,100,185	66.7	33.3
Greater Manchester	64.1	797,316	439,191	64.5	35.5

(*Continued*)

	% Turnout	Yes Votes	No Votes	% Yes	% No
Hampshire	68	484,302	197,761	71	29
Hereford and Worcester	66.4	203,128	75,779	72.8	27.2
Hertfordshire	70.2	326,943	137,266	70.4	29.6
Humberside	62.4	257,826	122,199	67.8	32.2
Isles of Scilly	75	802	275	74.5	25.5
Isle of Wight	67.5	40,837	17,375	70.2	29.8
Kent	67.4	493,407	207,358	70.4	29.6
Lancashire	66.4	455,170	208,821	68.6	31.4
Leicestershire	67.2	291,500	106,004	73.3	26.7
Lincolnshire	63.7	180,603	61,011	74.7	25.3
Merseyside	62.7	465,625	252,712	64.8	35.2
Norfolk	63.8	218,883	93,198	70.1	29.9
Northamptonshire	66.7	162,803	71,322	69.5	30.5
Northumberland	65	95,980	42,645	69.2	30.8
Nottinghamshire	63.1	297,191	147,461	66.8	33.2
Oxfordshire	67.7	179,938	64,643	73.6	26.4
Shropshire (Salop)	62	113,044	43,329	72.3	27.7
Somerset	67.7	138,830	60,631	69.6	30.4
Staffordshire	64.3	306,518	148,252	67.4	32.6
Suffolk	64.9	187,484	72,251	72.2	27.8
Sussex (East)	65.8	249,780	86,198	74.3	25.7
Sussex (West)	68.6	242,890	75,928	76.2	23.8
Tyne and Wear	62.7	344,069	202,511	62.9	37.1
Warwickshire	68	156,303	67,221	69.9	30.1
West Midlands	62.5	801,913	429,207	65.1	34.9
Wiltshire	67.8	172,791	68,113	71.7	28.3
Yorkshire (North)	64.3	234,040	72,805	76.3	23.7
Yorkshire (South)	62.4	377,916	217,792	63.4	36.6
Yorkshire (West)	63.6	616,731	326,993	65.4	34.6
Wales	66.7	869,135	472,071	64.8	35.2
Clwyd	65.8	123,980	55,424	69.1	30.9
Dyfed	67.5	109,184	52,264	67.6	32.4
Glamorgan (Mid)	66.6	147,348	111,672	56.9	43.1
Glamorgan (South)	66.7	127,932	56,224	69.5	30.5
Glamorgan (West)	67.4	112,989	70,316	61.6	38.4
Gwent	68.2	132,557	80,992	62.1	37.9

(Continued)

	% Turnout	Yes Votes	No Votes	% Yes	% No
Gwynedd	64.3	76,421	31,807	70.6	29.4
Powys	67.9	38,724	13,372	74.3	25.7
Scotland	61.7	1,332,186	948,039	58.4	41.6
Borders	63.2	34,092	13,053	72.3	27.7
Central Scotland	64.1	71,986	48,568	59.7	40.3
Dumfries and Galloway	61.5	42,608	19,856	68.2	31.8
Fife	63.3	84,239	65,260	56.3	43.7
Grampian	57.4	108,520	78,071	58.2	41.8
Highland	58.7	40,802	33,979	54.6	45.4
Lothian	63.6	208,133	141,456	59.5	40.5
Orkney	48.2	3,911	2,419	61.8	38.2
Shetland	47.1	2,815	3,631	43.7	56.3
Strathclyde	61.7	625,959	459,073	57.7	42.3
Tayside	63.8	105,728	74,567	58.6	41.4
Western Isles	50.1	3,393	8,106	29.5	70.5
Northern Ireland	47.4	259,251	237,911	52.1	47.9

Appendix 2: Note on Prices

All costs and prices in the text are given at their contemporary (or 'nominal') value. No attempt has been made to update them to 2018 prices: first, because such figures would themselves quickly become outdated; and second, because changes in *relative* prices make such comparisons of doubtful utility. Prices do not move up and down in lockstep: the cost of 200 cigarettes, for example, increased by 1,150 per cent between 1975 and 2005, while the price of twelve bottles of sherry rose by just 227 per cent. In 1975, it was more expensive to buy a video recorder (£500) than a week's holiday for four in a British holiday camp (£20). Nonetheless, it may help readers to orient the figures in the text to know that the average house price in the first quarter of 1975 was £10,388. The average annual wage was £2,291, though a male manual labourer over the age of twenty-one averaged £2,529. A secondary school teacher could expect to earn £3,550; a nursery or primary school teacher £3,220; and a miner £3,800. It cost £40 to tax a car for twelve months, £18 to buy a colour TV licence and 7p for a first-class stamp. Ten pints of bitter cost £2, which would barely cover the peanuts today.[1]

Notes

Introduction

1. John Le Carré, *Tinker, Tailor, Soldier, Spy* (London: Hodder and Stoughton, 1974), p. 241.
2. Tony Benn, *Against the Tide: Diaries 1973–76*, ed. Ruth Winstone (London: Century Hutchinson, 1989), p. 279 (5 December 1974).
3. Peter Jenkins, 'Power to the People?', *The Guardian*, 21 May 1975, p. 13.
4. 'Brexit panic wipes $2 trillion off world markets', *The Guardian*, 24 June 2016, www.theguardian.com/business/live/2016/jun/24/global-markets-ftse-pound-uk-leave-eu-brexit-live-updates [all web links accessed 26 June 2017].
5. Catherine Baker, 'Brexit has echoes of the breakup of Yugoslavia', *Europp: European Politics and Policy*, 5 July 2017, http://blogs.lse.ac.uk/europpblog/2016/07/05/brexit-echoes-yugoslavia/; Timothy Garton Ash, 'As an English European, this is the biggest defeat of my political life', *The Guardian*, 24 June 2016, www.theguardian.com/politics/commentisfree/2016/jun/24/lifelong-english-european-the-biggest-defeat-of-my-political-life-timothy-garton-ash-brexit; BBC News, 25 June 2016, www.bbc.co.uk/news/uk-politics-eu-referendum-36625209; *The Observer*, 26 June 2016, p. 48.
6. BBC News, 24 June 2016, www.bbc.co.uk/news/uk-politics-eu-referendum-36613295.
7. Politics Home, 3 July 2016, www.politicshome.com/news/europe/eu-policy-agenda/brexit/news/76869/poll-finds-young-remain-voters-reduced-tears-brexit.
8. Statement by the Prime Minister, 6 June 1975, Harold Wilson Papers, Bodleian Library, Oxford, MS Wilson [hereafter: MS Wilson] c.1267, f. 300. The 1931 National Government could be said to have achieved a slightly larger vote share, if one includes all the parties that at some stage participated.
9. 'EU Speech at Bloomberg', 23 June 2013, www.gov.uk/government/speeches/eu-speech-at-bloomberg.

10. *Britain Says Yes: The 1975 Referendum on the Common Market* (Washington DC: American Institute for Public Policy Research, 1977), p. 129.

11. Dominic Sandbrook, *Seasons in the Sun: The Battle for Britain, 1974–1979* (London: Allen Lane,2012), pp. 315–39; Stephen Wall, *The Official History of Britain and the European Community: Volume II: From Rejection to Referendum, 1963–1975* (London: Routledge, 2013) [hereafter: *From Rejection to Referendum*], pp. 578–90.

12. *Daily Express*, 7 June 1975, p. 10.

13. Anthony Smith, 'Broadcasting', in David Butler and Uwe Kitzinger (eds.), *The 1975 Referendum* (Basingstoke: Macmillan, 1976), p. 212.

14. *Daily Express*, 7 June 1975, pp. 1, 10.

15. David Reynolds, *Britannia Overruled: British Policy and World Power in the 20th Century*, second edition (Harlow: Pearson, 2000), p. 224.

16. *The Times*, 1 January 1973, p. 10.

17. Edward Heath, Speech to the Conservative Party Conference, Blackpool 1970: www.britishpoliticalspeech.org/speech-archive.htm?speech=117. See also Iain Dale (ed.), *Conservative Party General Election Manifestos, 1900–1997* (London: Routledge, 2000), pp. 175–98.

18. P. Ziegler, *Edward Heath: The Authorized Biography* (London: HarperCollins, 2010), p. 48; John Young, *Britain and European Unity, 1945–1999*, second edition (Basingstoke: Macmillan, 2000), p. 72.

19. *The Times*, 25 September 1972, p. 4; 4 January 1973, p. 10.

20. *The Times*, 4 January 1973, p. 8. For a programme of events, see *The Times*, 1 January 1973, p. 7. For an overview of the Fanfare, see R. Weight, *Patriots: National Identity in Britain, 1940–2000* (Basingstoke: Macmillan, 2002), pp. 498–503.

21. Edward Heath, *The Course of My Life: My Autobiography* (London: Hodder and Stoughton, 1998), p. 394.

22. Benjamin Grob-Fitzgibbon, *Continental Drift: Britain and Europe from the End of Empire to the Rise of Euroscepticism* (Cambridge: Cambridge University Press, 2016), pp. 368, 382; King, *Britain Says Yes*, p. 20.

23. Grob-Fitzgibbon, *Continental Drift*, p. 371.

24. Ibid., p. 373.

25. Iain Dale (ed.), *Labour Party General Election Manifestos, 1900–1997* (London: Routledge, 2000), pp. 186–7.

26. *The Sun*, 5 June 1975, p. 2; 19 March 1975, p. 2; 10 April 1975, p. 2; 26 April 1975, p. 2.

27. *Hansard* 888, 11 March 1975, 314. She was quoting the former Labour premier, Clement Attlee. See Chapter 2.

28. *The Times*, 27 May 1968, p. 2; Tony Benn, *Office without Power: Diaries, 1968–72* (London: Hutchinson, 1988), pp. 72–3 (25 and 29 May 1968); see also Philip Goodhart, *Referendum* (London: Tom Stacey, 1971), p. 64.

29. Philip Goodhart, *Full-Hearted Consent: The Story of the Referendum Campaign – and the Campaign for the Referendum* (London: Davis-Poynter, 1976), p. 149.

30. Ibid., p. 168.

31. Margaret Thatcher, speech at Hendon, 19 May 1975, http://margaretthatcher.org/document/102692.

32. In 2016, the highest Leave votes were recorded in Boston (75.6 per cent), South Holland (73.6 per cent), Castle Point (72.7 per cent) and Thurrock (72.3 per cent). For full results, see www.electoralcommission.org.uk/__data/assets/file/0014/212135/EU-referendum-result-data.csv.

33. For a map showing levels of support in 1975, see Butler and Kitzinger, *1975 Referendum*, p. 270.

34. David Torrance, *Salmond: Against the Odds*, third edition (Edinburgh: Birlinn, 2015), p. 20.

35. According to figures released by the Commission, the number 'accepted for settlement' in the UK from West Germany fell from 1,236 in 1971 to 631 in 1973, and stood at just 318 for the first nine months of 1974. The number of residence permits issued to EEC nationals fell by 5 per cent in the first nine months of 1974, following a drop of 53 per cent in 1973, 12 per cent in 1972 and 23 per cent in 1971. Written question No. 609/74, Britain In Europe Papers, Parliamentary Archives, Westminster, BIE [hereafter: BIE] 22/147.

36. 'The Economic Consequences of the Treaties', statement issued by Peter Shore, Barbara Castle, Tony Benn, John Silkin and Judith Hart, 4 May 1975, Barbara Castle Papers, Bodleian Library, Oxford, MS Castle [hereafter: MS Castle] 306 f. 317.

37. For the sad curtailing of the Wombles' activities, see Gyles Brandreth, *Something Sensational to Read in the Train: The Diary of a Lifetime* (London: John Murray, 2009), p. 318 (27 March 1975). There were, however, sightings of a 'Womble into Europe' bumper sticker in Highgate: *The Guardian*, 30 May 1975, p. 8.

38. Harriet Wistrich, 'Ernest Wistrich Obituary', *The Guardian*, 12 June 2015, www.theguardian.com/world/2015/jun/12/ernest-wistrich-obituary.

39. G. Eley, 'Finding the People's War: Film, British Collective Memories and World War II', *American Historical Review*, 106:3 (2001), pp. 818–19. There is now a voluminous literature on the contested memory of World War II. For a good introduction, see Lucy Noakes and Juliette Pattinson (eds.), *British Cultural Memory and the Second World War* (London: Bloomsbury, 2014). For the place of the war and of Germany in the construction of national identity, see Weight, *Patriots*, pp. 452–64.

40. Predictably, Basil confesses that he voted to leave. 'The Germans', *Fawlty Towers*, series 1 episode 6, script by John Cleese and Connie Booth, directed by John Howard Davies. First broadcast on BBC1, 24 October 1975.

41. *South Wales Argus*, 4 June 1975, p. 12.

42. These quotations are all taken from letters to Barbara Castle, written by (mostly older) women in the first week of June 1975. MS Castle 307. For hostility to Germany in popular culture and its roots in a memory of war, see Mark Connelly, *We Can Take It! Britain and the Memory of the Second World War* (Harlow: Pearson, 2004), pp. 284–94. A poll for the *Sun* three days before the referendum found that West Germany was the European country Britons most admired ('The French are the most disliked, by a mile') – though admiration is not the same as affection, and Germany was more popular with men than with women. *The Sun*, 2 June 1975, p. 2.

43. *Bristol Evening Post*, 31 May 1975, p. 2.

44. *Financial Times*, 20 May 1975, p. 12; *Daily Telegraph*, 7 June 1975, p. 30.

45. 'Common Market Vote No', Papers of the Campaign for an Independent Britain, London School of Economics, [hereafter: CIB] 10/2 GBO.

46. Posters can be found in BIE/18.

47. Victor Montagu and Anthony Meyer, *Europe – Should Britain Join?* (London: Monday Club, 1966), p. 3.

48. Prime Ministerial broadcast, 8 July 1971, in Uwe Kitzinger, *Diplomacy and Persuasion: How Britain Joined the Common Market* (London: Thames and Hudson, 1973), p. 149.

49. Speech in Manchester, 10 May 1975, Roy Jenkins Papers, Bodleian Library, Oxford, MS Jenkins [hereafter: MS Jenkins] 304/213. With the kind permission of Roy Harris Jenkins' executors.

50. *The Sun*, 23 May 1975, p. 6. The long-expected Communist coup took place in Portugal on 25 November 1975, but failed.

51. *Belfast Newsletter*, 8 April 1975, p. 6; *The Spectator*, 10 May 1975, p. 568.

52. *The Guardian*, 2 June 1975, p. 12.

53. Benn, *Against the Tide*, p. 265 (17 November 1974); Roy Jenkins, Speech in Manchester, 10 May 1975, MS Jenkins 304/213. In an interview for *Newsday* on 6 May 1975, Robin Day asked Wilson whether a 'wise' defence policy should no longer 'assume the American help which we have assumed in the last twenty years'; MS Wilson c. 1266, f. 41.

54. *South Wales Argus*, 25 April 1975, p. 1; *The Scotsman*, 3 May 1975, p. 8.

55. Speech to the NATO Council at Brussels, 30 May 1975, MS Wilson c.1267, f. 4.

56. *The Scotsman*, 30 May 1975, p. 7.

57. *The Sun*, 2 June 1975, p. 2; *The Scotsman*, 2 June 1975, p. 9; *South Wales Argus*, 25 April 1975, p. 5.

58. *Scottish Daily Express*, 3 May 1975, p. 8.

59. Shirley Williams, speech to the National Council of Women, 7 May 1975, BIE 19/49(b).

60. Speech in Manchester, 10 May 1975, MS Jenkins 304/213.

61. *The Sun*, 2 June 1975, p. 2; *The Scotsman*, 2 June 1975, p. 9; *South Wales Argus*, 25 April 1975, p. 5.

62. See, for example, 'Who do they think we are?', *The Spectator*, 31 May 1975, p. 649.

63. Conservative Central Office, Quick Brief No. 76: 'Britain in Europe', BIE 14/2.

64. Benn, *Against the Tide*, 27 April 1975, pp. 369–70. Benn was furious and considered legal action.

65. *The Scotsman*, 10 May 1975, p. 5.

66. 'EEC or Red Britain – Cordle', newspaper cutting, source unknown, Neil Marten Papers, Bodleian Library, Oxford [hereafter: Marten Papers] c.1132, f. 153.

67. George Brown, *In My Way: The Political Memoirs of Lord George-Brown* (Harmondsworth: Penguin, 1972), p. 203.

68. Speech by Neil Marten at the Tottenham Chamber of Commerce, 30 April 1975, Marten Papers c.1132, f. 351; Speech by Neil Marten at Annerley Town Hall, 5 May 1975, Marten Papers c.1132, f. 356.

69. Speech at Annerley Town Hall, 5 May 1975, Marten Papers c.1132, f. 356.

70. 'Market result of cold war – Mrs Hart', *Middlesex Chronicle*, 25 April 1975, in Judith Hart Papers, People's History Museum, HART/10/11.

71. Michael Foot, draft article for *Der Spiegel*, no date, Foot Papers, People's History Museum, Manchester, MF/L28/4.

72. Some also feared that the EEC would stoke tensions by creating a new military power (perhaps with nuclear aspirations) in Europe. See, for example, 'Peace or War – the Defence Argument', *Labour Weekly*, 5 June 1975, p. 4.

73. NOP, 'Report on E.E.C.', 29 May 1975, NOP/8580/03, Marten Papers c.1133, ff. 34–68.

74. Reynolds, *Britannia Overruled*, p. 214.

75. Dean Acheson, Speech at the United States Military Academy, West Point, 5 December 1962, in *Vital Speeches of the Day*, 29:6 (1 January 1963), pp. 162–6.

76. Freda Harcourt, 'Disraeli's Imperialism, 1866–1868: A Matter of Timing?' *Historical Journal*, 23:1 (1980), p. 96.

77. A.J.P. Taylor, in 'Going into Europe – Again? A Symposium', *Encounter*, 36:6 (June 1971), p. 4.

78. P. Ludlow, 'Us or Them? The Meaning of Europe in British Political Discourse', in M. Malmborg and B. Stråth (eds.), *The Meaning of Europe: Variety and Contention within and among Nations* (Oxford: Berg, 2002), 101–24. See also K. Robbins, *History, Religion and Identity in Modern Britain* (London: Hambledon Press, 1993), pp. 45–57; M. Spiering, *A Cultural History of British Euroscepticism* (Basingstoke: Palgrave, 2015).

79. Kitzinger, *Diplomacy and Persuasion*, p. 415.

80. Featured on the album *Adge Cutler & the Wurzels: Live at the Royal Oak* (Columbia Records, 1967).

81. 'Advantages of staying in the Common Market', May 1975, BIE 15/72.

82. *The Sun*, 10 March 1975, p. 9.

83. *Western Mail*, 4 June 1975, p. 6; Piers Ludlow, *Roy Jenkins and the European Commission Presidency, 1976–1980: At the Heart of Europe* (Basingstoke: Palgrave Macmillan, 2016), p. 46.

84. Speech by Winifred Ewing, 12 April 1975, SNP Press Release, Scottish National Party Papers, National Library of Scotland, [hereafter: SNP Papers] NLS Acc. 10754/26: 154; *Sunday Times*, 27 April 1975, p. 32.

85. David Butler and Gareth Butler, *Twentieth Century British Political Facts, 1900–2000* (Basingstoke: Palgrave Macmillan, 2000), p. 418.

86. *The Director*, 27:7 (January 1975), p. 108; 27:8 (February 1975), p. 148.

87. Cabinet Conclusions, 14 March 1974, The National Archives, Kew, [hereafter: TNA] CAB 128/54.

88. Harold Wilson interviewed by Peter Jay for *Weekend World*, Sunday 11 May 1975, MS Wilson c. 1266, f. 66.

89. *The Times*, 1 July 1974, p. 14; S. Brittan, 'The Economic Contradictions of Democracy', *British Journal of Political Science*, 5 (1975), pp. 129, 132.

90. For 'Doomwatch', see Richard Vinen, *Thatcher's Britain: The Politics and Social Upheaval of the Thatcher Era* (London: Simon & Schuster, 2009), p. 77.

91. Benn, *Against the Tide*, p. 266 (17 November 1974). Callaghan gives a rather different account of this 'joke' in James Callaghan, *Time and Chance* (Collins: London, 1987), p. 326.

92. John Davan Sainsbury, 'The Challenge of Confidence', speech to Institute of Grocery Distribution Convention, 28 April 1975, Sainsbury Archive, Museum of London Docklands, SA/PR/1/1/5; *St Michael News* 1 (February 1975), p. 1.

93. Arthur Seldon (ed.), *Crisis '75...?* (London: Institute of Economic Affairs, 1975), p. 6. Contributors included Samuel Brittan, Alec Cairncross, Ralph Harris, James Meade, Peter Oppenheimer and Alan Walters. Meade warned that 'there is now every prospect of a major economic crisis in the near future', the results of which 'will be catastrophic', p. 28.

94. For an excellent series of essays on the politics of declinism, see L. Black, H. Pemberton and P. Thane (eds.), *Reassessing 1970s Britain* (Manchester: Manchester University Press, 2013).

95. *The Scotsman*, 4 June 1975, p. 8; *The Times*, 19 May 1975, p. 2.

96. *The Scotsman*, 5 June 1975, p. 1.

97. *Liverpool Daily Post*, 12 May 1975, p. 6.

98. 'Report on E.E.C.', 29 May 1975, NOP/8580/03, Marten Papers, c.1133, ff. 34–68.

99. Benn, *Against the Tide*, p. 279 (5 December 1974).
100. Barry Hedges, 'The Final Four Years: From Opposition to Endorsement', in R. Jowell and G. Hoinville (eds.), *Britain into Europe: Public Opinion and the EEC, 1961–75* (London: Croom Helm, 1976), pp. 41, 49, 68–9.
101. David Butler and Uwe Kitzinger, *The 1975 Referendum* (Basingstoke: Macmillan, 1976); Philip Goodhart, *Full-Hearted Consent: The Story of the Referendum Campaign – and the Campaign for the Referendum* (London: Davis-Poynter, 1976); Anthony King, *Britain Says Yes: The 1975 Referendum on the Common Market* (Washington DC: American Institute for Public Policy Research, 1977).
102. Douglas Evans, *While Britain Slept: The Selling of the Common Market* (London: Victor Gollancz, 1975), p. 6.
103. The Brussels Treaty, which merged the three sets of institutions, was signed in April 1965 and came into force in July 1967. The full text is available at http://eur-lex.europa.eu/legal-content/EN/ALL/?uri=CELEX:11965F/TXT.
104. *Hansard* 736, 17 November 196, 652–3.
105. *Hansard* 888, 11 March 1975, 296 (Ted Short). As late as 1984, the distinguished Anglo-German historian Agatha Ramm disclaimed the 'modern usage' of 'the United Kingdom', preferring 'a consistent use of "Britain"'; *Europe in the Twentieth Century, 1905–1970* (London: Longman, 1984), p. xv.

1 Opportunity and Illusion: The Road to 1975

1. Speech to the Conservative Party Conference, Brighton, 16 October 1971, www.britishpoliticalspeech.org/speech-archive.htm?speech=118.
2. 'The Prime Minister Says "Yes"'. Interview with Llew Gardner for *This Week*, 15 May 1975, MS Wilson c.1266, f. 133.
3. *Hansard* 323, 27 July 1971, 278.
4. *Western Mail*, 5 June 1975, p. 4; *Liverpool Daily Post*, 5 June 1975, p. 3; *Yorkshire Post*, 5 June 1975, p. 1; *Daily Express*, 5 June 1975, p. 1; *The Times*, 5 June 1975, p. 5.
5. Hedges, 'The Final Four Years', in Jowell and Hoinville (eds.), *Britain into Europe*, p. 49.
6. Anthony Nutting, *Europe Will Not Wait: A Warning and a Way Out* (New York: Hollis & Carter, 1960), p. 103; George Ball, quoted in Elisabeth Barker, *Britain in a Divided Europe, 1945–1970* (London: Weidenfeld & Nicolson, 1971), p. 3.
7. Konrad Adenauer, *Memoirs, 1945–53*, translated by Beate Ruhm von Oppen (London: Weidenfeld & Nicolson, 1966), p. 382; Derek W. Urwin, *The Community of Europe: A History of European Integration since 1945*, second edition (Harlow: Longman, 1995), pp. 31, 37; Michael Charlton, *The Price of Victory* (London: BBC, 1983), p. 9.

8. Sir Michael Palliser', 'Foreword', in S. Dokrill, *Britain's Retreat from East of Suez: The Choice between Europe and the World?* (Basingstoke: Palgrave Macmillan, 2002), p. x.

9. Oliver J. Daddow, *Britain and Europe since 1945: Historiographical Perspectives on Integration* (Manchester: Manchester University Press, 2004), pp. 5–6.

10. Charlton, *Price of Victory*, p. 11.

11. Hugo Young, *This Blessed Plot: Britain and Europe from Churchill to Blair* (Basingstoke: Macmillan, 1999), p. 1.

12. Ibid., p. 3.

13. King, *Britain Says Yes*, p. 38.

14. Sean Greenwood, *Britain and European Cooperation since 1945* (Oxford: Blackwell, 1992), p. 2.

15. Charlton, *Price of Victory*, p. 307.

16. Roger Broad, 'Cross-Channel or Transatlantic?', in R. Broad and V. Preston (eds.), *Moored to the Continent? Britain and European Integration* (London: IHR, 2001), p. 1; Brian Brivati, 'A Problem of Synchronicity: The Labour Party, European Integration and the Search for Modernization' and I. Davidson, 'Missing the Bus, Missing the Point: Britain's Place in the World since 1945' in *idem*, pp. 193, 239.

17. Stephen George, *An Awkward Partner: Britain in the European Community*, third edition (Oxford: Oxford University Press, 1998); Stephen Wall, *A Stranger in Europe: Britain and the EU from Thatcher to Blair* (Oxford: Oxford University Press, 2008); David Gowland and Arthur Turner, *Reluctant Europeans: Britain and European Integration, 1945–1998* (Harlow: Longman, 2000).

18. Alan S. Milward, *The Rise and Fall of a National Strategy, 1945–1963: The United Kingdom and the Common Market, Volume 1* (London: Routledge, 2005), pp. 7–8, 13. For a critical engagement with Milward's argument (and its evolution over time), see James Ellison, 'The European Rescue of Britain', in F. Guirao, F. Lynch and S. Ramírez Pérez (eds.), *Alan S. Milward and a Century of European Change* (Abingdon: Routledge, 2012), pp. 444–58.

19. Bernard Porter, *Britain, Europe and the World, 1850–1982: Delusions of Grandeur* (London: George Allen & Unwin, 1983), pp. 123–4.

20. P. Speiser, *The British Army of the Rhine: Turning Nazi Enemies into Cold War Partners* (Chicago: University of Illinois Press, 2016), p. 1. The figure remained above 50,000 in 1975: 'The Alliances and Europe', *The Military Balance*, 75:1 (1975), p. 19.

21. For the pursuit of a Free Trade Area (FTA) that could encompass the Six, see James Ellison, *Threatening Europe: Britain and the Creation of the European Community, 1955–58* (Basingstoke: Macmillan, 2000), who sees the FTA

'developing from negative origins before eventually becoming an attempt to complement the Common Market' (p. 222). Miriam Camps argued that the FTA, though 'ineptly presented and badly negotiated', marked a 'real and substantial shift in the British Government's attitude towards Europe'; Miriam Camps, *Britain and the European Community, 1955–1963* (Oxford: Oxford University Press, 1964), pp. 509–10. For the argument that 'EFTA was not a means to "sabotage" the Common Market' but a 'holding or balancing operation', see Roland Maurhofer, 'Revisiting the Creation of EFTA: The British and the Swiss Case', *Journal of European Integration History*, 7:2 (2001), p. 82.

22. Adenauer, *Memoirs*, p. 388 (19 May 1951).
23. Barker, *Britain in a Divided Europe*, p. 15.
24. Ibid., p. 6.
25. 21 March 1943, quoted in Charlton, *Price of Victory*, p. 19.
26. For the Schuman Declaration of 9 May 1950, see http://europa.eu/about-eu/ basic-information/symbols/europe-day/schuman-declaration/index_en.htm.
27. For biographies of each of these figures, which emphasise their post-national credentials, see 'The Founding Fathers of the EU', http://europa.eu/about-eu/ eu-history/founding-fathers/index_en.htm.
28. Charlton, *Price of Victory*, p. 34. For federalist movements, see M. Dedman, *The Origins and Development of the European Union, 1945–95: A History of European Integration* (London: Routledge, 1996), pp. 16–33.
29. Alan S. Milward, *The European Rescue of the Nation-State*, second edition (London: Routledge, 2000), p. 18. Martin Dedman agrees that 'National interest, not Euro-federal idealism, propelled the schemes for economic integration'; Dedman, *Origins and Development of the European Union*, p. 31. For a series of case studies, see Alan S. Milward, Frances M.B. Lynch, Federico Romero, Ruggiero Ranieri and Vibeke Sørensen, *The Frontier of National Sovereignty: History and Theory, 1945–1992* (London: Routledge, 1993).
30. See Piers Ludlow, 'Challenging French Leadership in Europe: Germany, Italy, the Netherlands and the Outbreak of the Empty Chair Crisis of 1965–1966', *Contemporary European History*, 8:2 (July 1999), pp. 231–48; Jean-Marie Palayret, Helen Wallace and Pascaline Winand (eds.), *Visions, Votes and Vetoes: The Empty Chair Crisis and the Luxembourg Compromise Forty Years On* (Brussels: Peter Lang, 2006). For the debate in France, see Frances B. Lynch, 'Restoring France: The Road to Integration', in Milward et al., *The Frontier of National Sovereignty*, pp. 72–87.
31. Milward, *European Rescue of the Nation-State*, p. 3.
32. Adenauer, *Memoirs*, pp. 387, 395–7.
33. Richard Toye, 'Churchill and Britain's "Financial Dunkirk"', *20th Century British History*, 15:4 (2004), p. 329.

34. David Russell, '"The Jolly Old Empire": Labour, the Commonwealth and Europe, 1945–51', in Alex May (ed.), *Britain, the Commonwealth and Europe: The Commonwealth and Britain's Application to Join the European Communities* (Basingstoke: Palgrave, 2001), p. 22.

35. Porter, *Britain, Europe and the World*, p. 112.

36. Dedman, *Origins and Development of the European Union*, pp. 19–20.

37. Speech at the University of Zurich, 19 September 1946, www.churchill-society-london.org.uk/astonish.html.

38. Charlton, *Price of Victory*, p. 20.

39. Young, *Britain and European Unity*, p. 7.

40. For Bevin's position, see ibid., pp. 13–16.

41. Barker, *Britain in a Divided Europe*, p. 5.

42. Adenauer, *Memoirs*, p. 388 (19 May 1951).

43. Barker, *Britain in a Divided Europe*, p. 5.

44. Gowland and Turner, *Reluctant Europeans*, p. 84.

45. Milward, *Rise and Fall of a National Strategy*, p. 3; Young, *Britain and European Unity*, pp. 49–50.

46. Porter, *Britain, Europe and the World*, p. 118.

47. Milward, *European Rescue of the Nation-State*, p. 353; Gowland and Turner, *Reluctant Europeans*, p. 94.

48. Porter, *Britain, Europe and the World*, p. 113.

49. Greenwood, *Britain and European Cooperation*, p. 15.

50. Gowland and Turner, *Reluctant Europeans*, p. 75.

51. King, *Britain Says Yes*, p. 4.

52. K.O. Morgan, *Labour in Power* (Oxford: Oxford University Press, 1985), p. 420.

53. Porter, *Britain, Europe and the World*, p. 128.

54. Gowland and Turner, *Reluctant Europeans*, p. 5.

55. Reynolds, *Britannia Overruled*, p. 204.

56. Gowland and Turner, *Reluctant Europeans*, p. 116.

57. Harold Macmillan, *Pointing the Way, 1959–1961* (London: Macmillan, 1972), p. 258. For the stormy debate in Parliament, see *Hansard*, 13 April 1960, 621: 1265–75, 1279–81.

58. Macmillan, *Pointing the Way*, p. 300; Ronald Hyam, 'The Parting of the Ways: Britain and South Africa's Departure from the Commonwealth, 1951–61', *Journal of Imperial and Commonwealth History*, 26:2 (1998), p. 172.

59. Dean Acheson, Speech at the United States Military Academy, West Point, 5 December 1962, *Vital Speeches of the Day*, 29:6 (1 January 1963), pp. 162–6.

60. Reynolds, *Britannia Overruled*, p. 214; Edward Longinotti, 'Britain's Withdrawal from East of Suez: From Economic Determinism to Political Choice', *Contemporary British History*, 29:3 (2015), p. 323.

61. *Hansard*, 16 January 1968, 756: 1577, 1580–1. For the twin debates about 'Europe' and 'East of Suez', see Dockrill, *Britain's Retreat from East of Suez*.

62. Helen Parr, 'Britain, America, East of Suez and the EEC: Finding a Role in British Foreign Policy, 1964–67', *Contemporary British History*, 20:3 (2006), pp. 403–21, argues that withdrawal from 'East of Suez' accelerated the British embrace of the European Community; Longinotti, 'Britain's Withdrawal from East of Suez', pp. 318–40, reverses the story, arguing that the choice to withdraw was itself a product of the reordering of priorities around Europe.

63. James Ellison, *The United States, Britain and the Transatlantic Crisis: Rising to the Gaullist Challenge* (Basingstoke: Palgrave Macmillan, 2007), p. 118.

64. The British ambassador to the United States, Patrick Dean, warned in 1967 that 'The continuing value of our relationship to [the US] will depend largely on the degree to which we can act as a force for stability, reason and responsibility, within … Europe'; ibid., pp. 126–7.

65. Ibid., p. 13.

66. Young, *Britain and European Unity*, p. 67.

67. Porter, *Britain, Europe and the World*, p. 116.

68. *The Times*, 9 October 1954, p. 9; 22 July 1957, p. 4.

69. Jim Tomlinson, *The Politics of Decline: Understanding Post-War Britain* (Pearson: Harlow, 2000). See also George L. Bernstein, *The Myth of Decline: The Rise of Britain since 1945* (London: Pimlico, 2004).

70. Wall, *From Rejection to Referendum*, pp. 588–9.

71. Reynolds, *Britannia Overruled*, p. 195.

72. Report of the Productivity and Conditional Aid Committee, in Tomlinson, *Politics of Decline*, p. 19.

73. Kitzinger, *Diplomacy and Persuasion*, p. 58.

74. Reynolds, *Britannia Overruled*, p. 218.

75. See Douglas Jay, 'The Free Trade Alternative to the EC: A Witness Account', in Brian Brivati and Harriet Jones (eds.), *From Reconstruction to Integration: Britain and Europe since 1945* (Leicester: Leicester University Press, 1993), pp. 125–7.

76. See Tomlinson, *Politics of Decline*, p. 23.

77. John Campbell, *Edward Heath: A Biography* (London: Pimlico, 1994), p. 398.

78. *Evening Standard*, 11 July 1967, quoted in Gowland and Turner, *Reluctant Europeans*, p. 158.

79. Kitzinger, *Diplomacy and Persuasion*, pp. 184–5.

80. Command Paper 4715, *The United Kingdom and the European Communities* (London: HMSO, 1971), p. 17.

81. Young, *Britain and European Unity*, p. 63.

82. George Thomson in 'The Labour Committee for Europe' [witness seminar, 12 June 1990], *Contemporary Record*, 7:2 (Autumn 1993), p. 393. The 'folly'

remark was used by Richard Crosland and Denis Healey; Helen Parr, *Britain's Policy towards the European Community: Harold Wilson and Britain's World Role, 1964–67* (London: Routledge, 2006), p. 121; Helen Parr, 'Anglo-French Relations, Détente and Britain's Second Application for Membership of the EEC, 1964 to 1967', in Piers Ludlow (ed.), *European Integration and the Cold War: Ostpolitik–Weltpolitik, 1965–1973* (Abingdon: Routledge, 2007), p. 81.

83. Heath, *Course of My Life*, p. 372.

84. Kitzinger, *Diplomacy and Persuasion*, p. 147.

85. Heath, *Course of My Life*, p. 390.

86. Kitzinger, *Diplomacy and Persuasion*, p. 150.

87. Pompidou once told Heath that it was pointless to call on the telephone, as 'I do not speak English and your French is awful.' The most generous praise that Heath's French friends could offer was that 'you were certainly trying'. Heath, *Course of My Life*, pp. 368, 389. David Croft subsequently claimed to have based Officer Crabtree's French on Heath: *The Return of 'Allo 'Allo*, BBC1, 28 April 2007.

88. Kitzinger, *Diplomacy and Persuasion*, p. 150; Heath, *Course of My Life*, p. 381. The reference was to Psalm 122.

89. Campbell, *Edward Heath*, p. 344.

90. *Washington Post*, 5 February 1973, p. 12.

91. Campbell, *Edward Heath*, pp. 334–5.

92. For Heath's faith in the economic stimulus to be expected from membership, see George, *Awkward Partner*, p. 61; Greenwood, *Britain and European Cooperation*, p. 95.

93. Simon Heffer, *Like the Roman: The Life of Enoch Powell* (London: Phoenix, 1998), pp. 580, 585, 622–23, 669.

94. *Hansard* 809, 21 January 1971, 1376.

95. Enoch Powell, 'Speech to the Lyon's Club of Brussels', 24 January 1972, The Papers of Enoch Powell, Churchill Archives Centre, Cambridge, GBR/0014/POLL [hereafter Powell Papers] 4/1/8 file 4.

96. Heffer, *Like the Roman*, p. 672.

97. *The Times*, 4 June 1975, p. 14.

98. *European Communities Act, 1972*, Part I, clause 2(1).

99. Dale (ed.), *Conservative Party General Election Manifestos*, p. 196.

100. David Butler and Michael Pinto-Duschinsky, *The British General Election of 1970* (Basingstoke: Macmillan, 1999), p. 440.

101. Kitzinger, *Diplomacy and Persuasion*, p. 153.

102. Heath, *Course of My Life*, pp. 359, 362.

103. Heffer, *Like the Roman*, p. 598.

104. Melissa Pine, *Harold Wilson and Europe: Pursuing Britain's Membership of the European Community*, revised edition (London: I.B.Tauris, 2012), p. 173.

105. Dale (ed.), *Labour Party General Election Manifestos*, pp. 156, 179.

106. B. Pimlott, *Harold Wilson* (London: Harper Collins, 1992), pp. 580–1; Kitzinger, *Diplomacy and Persuasion*, p. 271.

107. *Hansard*, 823, 25 October 1971, 1362 (Robert Carr).

108. Alf Lomas, *The Common Market: Why We Should Keep OUT* (London Co-operative Political Committee, 1970), pp. 5–6.

109. *Hansard*, 823, 21 October 1971, 936 (Healey), 955–65 (Lestor), 1010 (King Murray), 1057 (Pavitt); 25 October 1971, 1275 (Spearing).

110. Heffer, *Like the Roman*, pp. 639–40. In a further example of cross-bench bonhomie, the anti-Market Tory Alan Clark told Labour's Dennis Skinner that 'I'd rather live in a socialist Britain than one ruled by a lot of fucking foreigners'; A. Clark, *Diaries: Into Politics, 1972–1982*, ed. I. Trewin (London: Weidenfeld & Nicolson, 2000) (10 April 1975), p. 64.

111. *Hansard* 823, 25 October 1971, 1261.

112. Ibid., 1381 (Fernyhough).

113. Ibid., 1259 (Foot).

114. *Labour and the Common Market: Report of a Special Conference of the Labour Party* [26 April 1975] (London: Transport House, 1975) p. 7.

115. Bernard Donoughue, *Downing Street Diary: With Harold Wilson in No. 10* (London: Pimlico, 2006), p. 402 (6 June 1975); see also Donoughue, 'The Inside View from No. Ten', in Mark Baimbridge (ed.), *The 1975 Referendum on Europe: Volume 1: Reflections of the Participants* (Exeter: Imprint-Academic, 2006), p. 132.

116. King, *Britain Says Yes*, p. 49.

117. For two studies that peer bravely into the gloom, see Parr, *Britain's Policy towards the European Community*; Pine, *Harold Wilson and Europe*.

118. Wilson's speech at the Guildhall, 13 November 1967, in favour of 'a Technological Community', is reprinted in U. Kitzinger, *The Second Try: Labour and the EEC* (Oxford: Pergamon Press, 1968), pp. 307–10. See also S. Holland, 'Alternative European and Economic Strategies', in Black, Pemberton and Thane (eds.), *Reassessing 1970s Britain*, pp. 96–122. The possibilities for technological co-operation also inspired Tony Benn's support for membership in the 1960s; see Tony Benn, *Speeches by Tony Benn*, ed. J. Bodington [1974] (Nottingham: Spokesman, 2012), pp. 94–5.

119. Donoughue, 'Inside View', p. 128.

120. *James Callaghan on the Common Market* (London: Labour Committee for Safeguards on the Common Market, 1971), pp. 3–4.

121. Kitzinger, *Diplomacy and Persuasion*, p. 386.

122. *The Guardian*, 11 May 1971, p. 7.

123. For the division list, see *Hansard* 823, 28 October 1971, 2212–17.

124. Benn, *Against the Tide*, p. 305 (21 January 1975).

125. A. Brown, 'A Ghost of Ramsay MacDonald', *Labour Monthly: A Magazine of Left Unity*, 57:5 (May 1975), p. 193.

126. See, for example, Benn, *Against the Tides*, p. 351 (20 March 1975); Pimlott, *Harold Wilson*, p. 654.

127. P. Hennessy, *The Prime Minister: The Office and its Holders since 1945* (London: Allen Lane, 2000), p. 365.

128. Barbara Castle, *The Castle Diaries, 1974–76* (London: Weidenfeld & Nicolson, 1980), p. 302 (4 February 1975).

129. He made similar remarks at a press conference in January 1970; Pine, *Harold Wilson and Europe*, pp. 17, 157.

130. 'The Prime Minister Says "Yes"': interview with Llew Gardner for *This Week*, 15 May 1975, MS Wilson c.1266, f. 135.

2 'A Device of Dictators and Demagogues': Renegotiation to Referendum

1. *The Sun*, 5 June 1975, p. 2.
2. *Hansard* 835, 18 April 1972, 258.
3. *Daily Mail*, 20 March 1975, p. 6.
4. *Castle Diaries*, p. 248 (12 December 1974).
5. Goodhart, *Full-Hearted Consent*, p. 45.
6. *Hansard* 792, 25 November 1969, 199–200.
7. Butler and Kitzinger, *1975 Referendum*, p. 11; *Hansard* 820, 8 July 1971, 1515.
8. *The Times*, 22 May 1945, p. 4.
9. *New Statesman*, 7 August 1970, p. 137.
10. *Hansard* 888, 11 March 1975, 314. She later claimed that a referendum on rearmament in 1936 would have produced a No vote; *The Guardian*, 24 April 1975, p. 5.
11. *The Sun*, 5 June 1975, p. 2; see also 19 March 1975, p. 2; 10 April 1975, p. 2; 26 April 1975, p. 2; *Daily Mirror*, 13 March 1975, p. 2.
12. *Church Times*, 4 April 1975, p. 3; *The Tablet*, 1 February 1975, p. 97.
13. *Daily Mirror*, 28 February 1975, p. 7.
14. Harold Wilson, *Final Term: The Labour Government, 1974–1976* (London: Weidenfeld & Nicolson, 1979), pp. 51, 85–6; Donoughue, *Downing Street Diary*, p. 263 (12 December 1974).
15. Greenwood, *Britain and European Cooperation*, p. 100; King, *Britain Says Yes*; David Sanders, *Losing an Empire, Finding a Role: British Foreign Policy since 1945* (Basingstoke: Macmillan, 1990), p. 158.
16. For the history of the referendum in British politics, see Vernon Bogdanor, *The People and the Party System: The Referendum and Electoral Reform in British Politics* (Cambridge: Cambridge University Press, 1981). See also Goodhart, *Referendum*.

17. For an overview, see Robert Saunders, 'Democracy', in David Craig and James Thompson (eds.), *The Languages of Politics in Modern British History* (London: Palgrave, 2013).

18. For the democratic argument against Home Rule, see Robert Saunders, 'Tory Rebels and Tory Democracy: The Ulster Crisis, 1900–1914', in R. Carr and B. Hart (eds.), *The Foundations of Modern British Conservatism* (London: Continuum, 2013).

19. *Hansard* 793, 10 December 1969, 442–50. A 'Ten Minute Bill' is a procedure by which backbenchers can table legislation and speak for ten minutes in its support. Such bills serve chiefly as a way to force debate on a subject.

20. For the debate and division list, see *Hansard* 835, 18 April 1972, 246–363, 367–407

21. Goodhart, *Full-Hearted Consent*, p. 19.

22. *The Times*, 1 August 1970, p. 13.

23. David Powell, *Tony Benn: A Political Life* (London: Continuum, 2001), p. 151.

24. *Legal and Constitutional Implications of United Kingdom Membership of the European Communities*, Cmnd 3301 (London: HMSO, 1967), p. 8 [paragraph 23]. My emphasis.

25. *Hansard* 888, 11 March 1975, 362–3 (Marten), 368 (MacFarquhar).

26. *Hansard* 823, 27 October 1971, 1762 (Benn).

27. *Speeches by Tony Benn*, pp. 202–5.

28. *The Guardian*, 21 May 1975, p. 13.

29. *Hansard* 835, 18 April 1972, 257–8.

30. Kitzinger, *Diplomacy and Persuasion*, pp. 248–50.

31. Max Weber, 'Politics as a Vocation' (1918), in H. H. Gerth and C. Wright Mills (eds.), *From Max Weber: Essays in Sociology* (Abingdon: Routledge, 2009), p. 78.

32. *The Times*, 1 August 1970, p. 13.

33. Goodhart, *Full-Hearted Consent*, pp. 32–3.

34. *Hansard* 888, 11 March 1975, 311.

35. Enoch Powell, Speech at Tamworth, 15 June 1970, Powell Papers POLL 4/1/6 file 2.

36. 'Minutes of the Meeting of the Party', 12 April 1972, *British Archives Online* (Microform Academic Publishers, 2006–2016), www.britishonlinearchives.co.uk/.

37. Kitzinger, *Diplomacy and Persuasion*, p. 392.

38. Goodhart, *Full-Hearted Consent*, p. 32; *New Statesman*, 7 August 1970, pp. 137–8.

39. John Pinder, *Danger: Referendum at Work* (PEP/New Europe, n.d.), BIE 16/3.

40. Powell, *Tony Benn*, p. 152.

41. Tony Benn, 'European Communities Bill: New Clause calling for a referendum', 13 March 1972, minutes of the Shadow Cabinet, 15 March 1972, *British Archives Online*.

42. Speech to the annual meeting of the Christian Socialist Movement, 17 March 1972, Benn, *Speeches*, p. 113. www.cvce.eu/content/publication/1999/1/1/a3d116ff-3ebe-44ee-99b8-e2b038253def/publishable_en.pdf.

43. *The Times*, 24 March 1972, p. 15.

44. Benn, *Speeches*, p. 114.

45. Minutes of the Shadow Cabinet, 29 March 1972; 'Minutes of the Meeting of the Party', 12 April 1972, *British Archives Online*.

46. 'Minutes of the Meeting of the Party', 12 April 1972, *British Archives Online*.

47. 'The Labour Committee for Europe' [Witness Seminar], *Contemporary Record*, 7:2 (Autumn 1993), p. 397.

48. Tony Benn, 'European Communities Bill: New Clause calling for a referendum', 13 March 1972, minutes of the Shadow Cabinet, 15 March 1972, *British Archives Online*.

49. Dale (ed.), *Labour Party General Election Manifestos*, pp. 186–7.

50. *Hansard* 323, 27 July 1971, 278.

51. Speech to the Conservative Party Conference, 13 October 1973, www.britishpoliticalspeech.org/speech-archive.htm?speech=120.

52. Con O'Neill, *Britain's Entry into the European Community: Report by Sir Con O'Neill on the Negotiations of 1970–1972* [1972], ed. with a Foreword by Sir David Hannay (London: Frank Cass, 2000), pp. 355–6.

53. Dale (ed.), *Labour Party General Election Manifestos*, pp. 186–7.

54. Grob-Fitzgibbon, *Continental Drift*, p. 388.

55. Aoife Collins, 'The Cabinet Office, Tony Benn and the Renegotiation of Britain's Terms of Entry into the European Community, 1974–1975', *Contemporary British History*, 24:4 (2010), p. 477.

56. 'The EEC Renegotiations: A Note on the Commitments' (TUC–Labour Party Liaison Committee, March/April 1975), Labour History Archive and Study Centre, People's History Museum, Manchester (hereafter LHASC) 7/1974/75 f. 81.

57. Benn recognised the danger but failed to reverse the position: see Collins, 'Cabinet Office', pp. 477–8.

58. Grob-Fitzgibbon, *Continental Drift*, p. 381; Speech to the Labour Party Conference, 17 July 1971, www.britishpoliticalspeech.org/speech-archive.htm?speech=169.

59. Wall, *From Rejection to Referendum*, pp. 511–12.

60. Ibid., pp. 558–9.

61. Ibid., p. 522.

62. Mathias Haeussler, 'A "Cold War European"? Helmut Schmidt and European Integration, c.1945–1982', *Cold War History*, 15:4 (2015), p. 437.

63. Ibid.; Wall, *From Rejection to Referendum*, p. 527.

64. Gowland and Turner, *Reluctant Europeans*, p. 191.

65. M. Haeussler, 'A Pyrrhic Victory: Harold Wilson, Helmut Schmidt, and the British Renegotiation of EC Membership, 1974–5', *International History Review*, 37:4 (2015), p. 774.

66. Wilson, *Final Term*, p. 94.

67. Wall, *From Rejection to Referendum*, pp. 524–5. The text of the Paris communiqué can be found at www.cvce.eu/content/publication/1999/1/1/b1dd3d57-5f31-4796-85c3-cfd2210d6901/publishable_en.pdf.

68. Wall, *From Rejection to Referendum*, p. 546.

69. Wilson, *Final Term*, pp. 94–5; Castle, *Castle Diaries*, p. 249 (12 December 1974); see also Benn, *Against the Tide*, p. 341 (17 March 1975).

70. *Hansard* 883, 16 November 1974, 1128, 1139. Wilson attributed the 'quick geographical correction' to 'the fact that hell is not a Parliamentary expression, outside strictly germane theological debates'; Wilson, *Final Term*, p. 97.

71. See Chapter 10. Paper by Callaghan on the progress of the renegotiations, 21 March 1975, NEC Papers, LHASC NEC 7/1974/75.

72. Paper by Callaghan on the progress of the renegotiations, 21 March 1975, LHASC NEC 7/1974/75, f. 59; Wall, *From Rejection to Referendum*, p. 545.

73. Minutes of a meeting between Roy Hattersley and Hans-Jürgen Wischnewski, 17 February 1975 (with Castle's annotations); Benn to Wilson, 24 February 1975; Callaghan to Wilson, 26 February 1975; MS Castle 306, ff. 59–61, 63–4. *The Economist*, 1 March 1975, p. 34. For the Cabinet discussion, see Castle, *Castle Diaries*, p. 323 (1 March 1975); Benn, *Against the Tide*, p. 321 (21 February 1975).

74. Wall, *From Rejection to Referendum*, pp. 520, 537.

75. Donoughue, *Downing Street Diary*, p. 257 (6 December 1974).

76. One hopes that he had washed his hands. Wilson *Final Term*, p. 102; Donoughue, *Downing Street Diary*, pp. 329–30 (10–11 March 1975).

77. Wall, *From Rejection to Referendum*, p. 3. See also *Membership of the European Community: Report on Renegotiations*, Command Paper 6003 (HMSO: London, 1975). For a detailed insider account, written by the head of the Foreign and Commonwealth Office Referendum Unit in 1975, see Nigel Spreckley, *The Common Market Renegotiation and Referendum: 1974–1975* [1975], with a Foreword by Stephen Wall (FCO: London, 2014), https://issuu.com/fcohistorians/docs/1_spreckley_report_-_part_1, https://issuu.com/fcohistorians/docs/2_spreckley_report_-_part_2, https://issuu.com/fcohistorians/docs/3_spreckley_report_-_part_3_appendi.

78. Wall, *From Rejection to Referendum*, p. 553.

79. Paper by Callaghan on the progress of the renegotiations, 21 March 1975, LHASC, NEC 7/1974/75, f. 41.

80. Cabinet, 2 July 1974, TNA, CAB 128/54 CC(74) 22nd Conclusions, point 3.

81. Wall, *From Rejection to Referendum*, p. 544.

82. Wilson, *Final Term*, p. 102; Callaghan paper, 21 March 1975, f. 37; Fred Peart to Harold Wilson, 20 November 1974, MS Castle 306, ff. 30–3; Press statement by J.A. Walding, 19 November 1974, MS Castle 306, ff. 35–6; Wall, *From Rejection to Referendum*, pp. 569–71, 576.

83. Callaghan Paper, 21 March 1975, f. 39.

84. Harold Wilson, 'Speech at the Commonwealth Heads of Government Meeting, Kingston, Jamaica', 1 May 1975, MS Wilson c. 1266, f. 20.

85. '"New economic order" is endorsed', *Financial Times*, 7 May 1975, p. 4. For the text of the statement, see 'Text of Commonwealth Heads of Government Statement on the European Community', May 1975, MS Castle 306, f. 324.

86. Wilson, *Final Term*, p. 96.

87. King, *Britain Says Yes*, pp. 76–7.

88. George, *An Awkward Partner*, p. 53.

89. Wall, *From Rejection to Referendum*, p. 513.

90. Wilson, *Final Term*, p. 93.

91. Callaghan, *Time and Chance*, p. 314.

92. Labour Committee for Europe, 'Summary of the Renegotiations', 12 March 1975, MS Castle 306, f. 86.

93. Wall, *From Rejection to Referendum*, pp. 564–5.

94. *Hansard* 888, 18 March 1975, 1465.

95. Speech at Bedworth, 31 May 1975, MS Wilson c.1267, f. 40.

96. See *Labour's Programme 1973* (London: Transport House, 1973); King, *Britain Says Yes*, p. 82.

97. 'The Common Market: Why we object. Statement by Dissenting Ministers', 26 March 1975, MS Castle 306, f. 216.

98. *New Statesman*, 17 January 1975, p. 64.

99. Speech at the Confederation of British Industry Dinner, 20 May 1975, MS Wilson c. 1266, f. 187.

100. Philip Lynch, 'The Conservatives and the Wilson Application', in Oliver J. Daddow (ed.), *Harold Wilson and European Integration: Britain's Second Application to Join the EEC* (London: Routledge, 2003), p. 60.

101. Speech at Manchester, 1 June 1975, MS Wilson, c. 1267, f. 102.

102. Speech at Dewsbury, 27 May 1975, MS Wilson c.1266, ff. 255–6.

103. *Labour and the Common Market*, p. 6.

104. *Daily Mail*, 12 March 1975, p. 1. Its political editor was more cynical, writing that the 'unacceptable "Tory terms" now modified by the Community's natural progress, have been refurbished with a coat of the famed Harold Wilson patent political gloss'. A cartoon showed a box of soap powder, with the label 'Wilson's EEC Re-negotiation' pasted over the words 'Ted Heath's EEC'; *Daily Mail*, 13 March 1975, p. 6.

105. *Daily Mirror*, 12 March 1975, pp. 1–2.

106. *New Statesman*, 14 March 1975, p. 327.
107. Labour Committee for Europe, 'Summary of the Renegotiations', 12 March 1975, MS Castle 306, f. 90.
108. *The Guardian*, 18 March 1975, p. 14.
109. *The Economist*, 15 March 1975, p. 11.
110. James Spence, 'Movements in the Public Mood: 1961–75', in Jowell and Hoinville (eds.), *Britain into Europe*, p. 33.
111. Robert Worcester, 'Public Opinion and the 1975 Referendum', in Baimbridge (ed.), *The 1975 Referendum*, vol. 1, pp. 77–8.
112. Butler and Kitzinger, *1975 Referendum*, p. 250.
113. See, for example, Speech at Bedworth, 31 May 1975, MS Wilson c.1267, ff. 18–64.
114. King, *Britain Says Yes*, p. 92.
115. *Labour and the Common Market*.
116. Hansard 888, 11 March 1975, 326–7 (Thorpe) and 337–8 (Rose).
117. Ibid., 311.
118. Ibid., 296.
119. Ibid., 296.
120. Ibid., 329 (Hughes), 343 (Molyneaux), 348 (Hurd).
121. Ibid., 343.
122. Alan Watkins, 'A Whiter than White Paper', *New Statesman*, 28 February 1975, p. 262.
123. 'Record of a meeting between the Foreign and Commonwealth Secretary and members of the International Committee of the Trades Union Congress', 4 February 1975, MS Castle 306, ff. 56–7.
124. Hansard 888, 11 March 1975, 300 (Short), 301 (Powell), 365 (Marten), 373 (Ewing), 388 (Thomas).

3 'Support Your Local Continent!' Britain in Europe

1. Irene Fekete, *The How and Why Wonder Book of the Common Market* (London: Transworld Publishers, 1974), p. 2.
2. *Labour and the Common Market*, p. 16.
3. Speech at the Winter Gardens, Blackpool, 31 May 1975, Powell Papers POLL 4/1/11/5.
4. *The Sun*, 27 March 1975, p. 2.
5. For a full list, see Butler and Kitzinger, *1975 Referendum*, p. 88.
6. Butler and Kitzinger, *1975 Referendum*, p. 102; Douglas Jay, *Change and Fortune: A Political Record* (London: Hutchinson, 1980), p. 484.
7. Ernest Wistrich, *Recollections of a Federalist: My Life* (London: Bettany Press, 2013); Harriet Wistrich, 'Ernest Wistrich Obituary', *The Guardian*, 12 June 2015; Roy Jenkins, 'Gore, (William) David Ormsby, fifth Baron Harlech

(1918–1985)', *Oxford Dictionary of National Biography* (Oxford: Oxford University Press, 2004), www.oxforddnb.com.

8. Wistrich, *Recollections*, pp. 110–19. For the campaign before accession, see Kitzinger, *Diplomacy and Persuasion*.

9. For the 'early campaign', see BIE 17/1–4, from which the following paragraphs are chiefly drawn.

10. Ernest Wistrich, 'The Irish, Norwegian and Danish Referenda: The Lessons for Britain', *New Europe*, 3:1 (Winter 1974/75), pp. 7–32; Wistrich, *Recollections*, pp. 124–5.

11. Wistrich, *Recollections*, pp. 122–8; list of correspondents, BIE 17/2.

12. See correspondence in BIE 17/11.

13. Wistrich, *Recollections*, p. 126.

14. *The Scotsman*, 14 May 1975, p. 6.

15. Butler and Kitzinger, *1975 Referendum*, pp. 70–2.

16. Ibid., p. 120.

17. BIE press release, 'Brighton and Hove in Europe Group', 2 May 1975, BIE 19/49(b).

18. The precise sum raised by BIE is unclear. The formal accounts, published after the referendum, list contributions totalling £996,508. However, only donations received after 27 March had to be declared. Donations *not* recorded in this list include £200,000 from the clearing banks, and numerous donations in the tens of thousands. A list of contributions *actually received* totals £1,789,645, but runs only to 2 May. With a month still to go, it seems safe to assume that contributions totalled more than £2 million. *Referendum on United Kingdom Membership of the European Community. Accounts of Campaigning Organisations*, Command Paper 6251 (London: HMSO, 1975), pp. 3–18, 18–20; 'Actual Cash Contributions Paid', 2 May 1975, BIE 11/2.

19. In October 1975, BIE reported a surplus of £100,000: Minutes of BIE Executive Committee, 15 Oct 1975, BIE 28/1. For business contributions, see below, Chapter 5.

20. *Referendum on United Kingdom Membership of the European Community*; Harlech to O'Neill, 31 January 1975, BIE 1/4.

21. Anthony Smith, 'Broadcasting', in Butler and Kitzinger (eds.), *1975 Referendum*, pp. 198–9; *The Guardian*, 2 June 1975, p. 13.

22. 'Strategy for the Campaign', February 1975, BIE 1/9.

23. *Referendum on United Kingdom Membership of the European Community*; Cecil Dawson [secretary to the Budget Committee], 'Budget Control', 17 July 1975, BIE 28/2.

24. John Campbell, *Roy Jenkins: A Well-Rounded Life* (London: Jonathan Cape, 2014), p. 444.

25. 'Running Scared into the Market', *The Spectator*, 24 May 1975, p. 625.

26. Louis Harris, 'British Attitudes to EEC Membership', LHI 47502, March 1975, p. 9, BIE 26/1.

27. Brandreth, *Something Sensational*, p. 318 (27 March 1975). For the posters, see BIE 18/23.

28. Brandreth, *Something Sensational*, pp. 319–20 (20 May 1975); interview with Gyles Brandreth, 2 February 2016.

29. 'Britain's European Successes', BIE 17/30; 'Sport for Europe: Statement of the Case', BIE 17/24.

30. 'List of supporters in Sport attending the London meeting', 2 June 1975, BIE 17/27; for messages, see BIE 17/27.

31. *Evening Standard*, 3 June 1975, p. 41.

32. *Glasgow Herald*, 27 May 1975, p. 6; *The Times*, 2 June 1975, p. 24. See also BIE 17/14 (actors) and 17/23 (musicians).

33. 'Strategy for the Campaign', February 1975, BIE 1/9.

34. Baroness Birk to Baroness Emmet of Amberley, 24 April 1975, BIE 26/2.

35. 'Britain in Europe/Public Opinion Summary 20th May 1975', BIE 26/1.

36. *Tribune*, 18 April 1975, p. 6; 30 May 1975, p. 5; *Yorkshire Post*, 3 June 1975, p. 9. Clarke was technically president-elect at this time, but featured prominently in coverage.

37. 'Youth Department: Campaign Responsibilities', BIE 14/1.

38. 'Youth Revolt: The Next Stages' and 'The Occupation of Britain in Europe', n.d. [mid-May], BIE 27/2.

39. Students for a United Europe (SUE) National Committee minutes, 1 March 1975, BIE 27/1.

40. *Glasgow Herald*, 30 May 1975, p. 2.

41. Students for a United Europe (Cambridge) to Archie Kirkwood, 6 May 1975, and reply, 14 May 1975, BIE 27/4/2.

42. Memorandum from Con O'Neill: 'Organization of the Youth Campaigns', 1 April 1975, BIE 27/1.

43. Students for a United Europe (SUE) National Committee minutes, 1 March 1975, BIE 27/1.

44. Piers Gardner memorandum, 9 April 1975, BIE 27/2; see also memo by Anthony Speaight, 27 May 1975, BIE 27/2.

45. *Liverpool Daily Post*, 28 May 1975, p. 5.

46. 'Boat will Blazon EEC Benefits', *Express & Star*, 17 April 1975, BIE 27/4/2; 'Young Europeans Afloat: Narrow Boat Scheme', 9 April 1975, BIE 27/4/2; 10.4.75: Memo on 'Manpower', n.d., BIE 27/4/2.

47. *The Times*, 8 February 1975, p. 1; Butler and Kitzinger, *1975 Referendum*, pp. 76, 78.

48. Minutes of the Shadow Cabinet, 2 December 1974, discussing a paper on 'Problems of Public Decision on Britain's EEC membership', Conservative Party Archive, LSC (74) 19; Margaret Thatcher, 'Europe: The Choice

Before Us', *Daily Telegraph*, 4 June 1975, www.margaretthatcher.org/document/102701.

49. 30 March 1975, quoted in Butler and Kitzinger, *1975 Referendum*, p. 78.

50. Conservative Campaign Committee minutes, 21 April 1975, BIE 14/1; Butler and Kitzinger, *1975 Referendum*, pp 77–8.

51. *The Sun*, 30 May 1975, p. 2.

52. Wistrich, *Recollections*, pp. 131–2; *Birmingham Post*, 7 June 1975, p. 3.

53. *The Times*, 5 June 1975, p. 15; *Financial Times*, 31 May 1975, p. 11; *The Sun*, 6 May 1975, p. 2.

54. *Castle Diaries*, p. 405 (1–6 June 1975).

55. Butler and Kitzinger, *1975 Referendum*, p. 75.

56. Wall, *From Rejection to Referendum*, p. 584.

57. 'Labour Campaign for Europe 1975', 10 February 1975, BIE 15/50.

58. 'Budget for Labour Committee for Europe Referendum Campaign, March–June 1975', Colin Beever Papers, LHASC 3/2/2; Butler and Kitzinger, *1975 Referendum*, p. 79.

59. 'The Socialist Case for Joining Europe: A Statement by the Labour Committee for Europe' (no date, c. 1971), Colin Beever Papers, LHASC 3/2/2.

60. Jim Cattermole, 'The Labour Committee for Europe: Planning Report', 12 February 1975, BIE 14/1.

61. Young European Left, *Labour's Programme and Europe* (London: YEL, 1974), pp. 4–5.

62. *Labour and the Common Market*, pp. 15, 20.

63. Interview with John Timpson, BBC *Today* programme, 29 May 1975, MS Wilson c.1266, f. 340; 'The Prime Minister Says "Yes"': interview with Llew Gardner for *This Week*, 15 May 1975, MS Wilson c.1266, f. 137.

64. *Labour and the Common Market*, p. 5.

65. Speech at Dewsbury, 27 May 1975, MS Wilson c. 1266, f. 281.

66. Speech at the Confederation of British Industry Dinner, 20 May 1975, MS Wilson c.1266, ff. 183, 189.

67. Speech at Dewsbury, 27 May 1975, MS Wilson c.1266, ff. 242, 247, 253; Speech at Manchester, 1 June 1975, MS Wilson c.1267, f. 85.

68. 'The Prime Minister Says "Yes"', 15 May 1975, MS Wilson c.1266, ff. 136–7; Speech at the Confederation of British Industry Dinner, 20 May 1975, MS Wilson c.1266, f. 182.

69. *The Guardian*, 13 March 1975, p. 12.

70. *Financial Times*, 14 May 1975, p. 12.

71. 'HAROLD WILSON Says…', *Labour Weekly*, 5 June 1975, p. 2.

72. Wall, *From Rejection to Referendum*, p. 588.

73. *Bristol Evening Post*, 3 June 1975, p. 3.

74. *Financial Times*, 22 May 1975, p. 12; 15 May 1975, p. 11.

75. Hedges, 'The Final Four Years', in Jowell and Hoinville (eds.), *Britain into Europe*, p. 66.

76. *The Liberal Manifesto for Europe, 1975* (London: Liberal Europe Campaign, 1975), pp. 3–4, 11–14, BIE 16/3.

77. David Torrance, *David Steel: Rising Hope to Elder Statesman* (London: Biteback, 2012), p. 71.

78. 'Report From Campaign Director', 8 April 1975, BIE 16/5.

79. 'Report From the Director of Policy Promotion', 25 April 1975, BIE 16/5.

80. 'European Referendum Campaign in the North of England', *c.* 12 December 1974, BIE 16/4.

81. 'Liberal Party Europe Campaign, 1975' [briefing for Lord Banks], 6 February 1975; 'Notes for a speech to be made by Richard Wainwright, M.P. in Leeds on 24th January, 1975', BIE 16/4; Press release, 'Eastern Region Liberal Seminar for Europe at Churchill College', 22 April 1975, BIE 16/3.

82. March 1975; quoted in Butler and Kitzinger, *1975 Referendum*, p. 130.

83. 'European Referendum Campaign in the North of England', *c.* 12 December 1974, BIE 16/4.

84. Butler and Kitzinger, *1975 Referendum*, p. 130; *The Guardian*, 10 May 1975, p. 5.

85. Butler and Kitzinger, *1975 Referendum*, p. 87.

86. Goodhart, *Full-Hearted Consent*, p. 149.

87. O'Neill to Hutchinson, 26 March 1975, BIE 18/1; O'Neill to local campaign groups, 4 April 1975, BIE 18/2.

88. *Referendum on United Kingdom Membership*, pp. 3–18; Worcester, 'Public Opinion and the 1975 Referendum'.

89. For the Research and Information Department, see BIE 22/1-151. For the weekly briefing, see Minutes of the Campaign Committee, 17 April 1975, BIE 14/1.

90. See BIE 19/71-87 ('Daily sequence files') and BIE 19/88-142 ('Subject files').

91. 'Policy Guidance Document for Publications and Speaker Briefing', 5 March 1975, BIE 15/49.

92. Heath, 'Speech for Trafalgar Square Rally', Sunday 4 May 1975, BIE 19/49(b).

93. Thatcher, 'Europe: The choice before us', *Daily Telegraph*, 4 June 1975, www.margaretthatcher.org/document/102701.

94. *Western Mail*, 4 June 1975, p. 6.

95. Prentice, Speech at Ealing, 13 May 1975, BIE 19/49(b); *The Guardian*, 2 June 1975, p. 12. Wilson dismissed his remarks as 'balderdash': 'The Prime Minister Says "Yes"': interview for *This Week*, 15 May 1975, MS Wilson c. 1266, f. 137.

96. *Scottish Daily News*, 23 May 1975, p. 5; speech by Smith at Clapham County School, 29 April 1975, BIE 19/49(b); speech by Prentice at Trafalgar

Square, 4 June 1975, BIE 19/49(b); speech by Ennals at Dover (no date), BIE 19/49(b).

97. Speech by Jenkins in Manchester, 10 May 1975, MS Jenkins 304/213; speech by Prentice at Ealing, 13 May 1975, BIE 19/49(b); speech by Bill Rodgers at Wigan, 2 June 1975, BIE 19/49(a); speech by Winston Churchill at Withington, Manchester, 8 May 1975, BIE 19/49(b).

98. Benn, *Against the Tide*, pp. 369–70 (27 April 1975).

99. *Evening Standard*, 24 March 1975, p. 12.

100. *The Sun*, 2 May 1975, p. 2; BIE 18/23.

101. Harris Poll, 1–6 April 1975, reproduced in Butler and Kitzinger, *1975 Referendum*, p. 256.

102. Reg Prentice, Speech at Ealing, 13 May 1975, BIE 19/49(b); *Western Mail*, 4 June 1975, p. 6; Heath, 'Speech for Trafalgar Square Rally', Sunday 4 May 1975, BIE 19/49(b).

103. Butler and Kitzinger, *1975 Referendum*, p. 76.

104. See British Business For World Markets (Yorkshire Group), 'The Press and the Common Market', 15 May 1975, Marten Papers, MS 1132, ff. 24–5.

105. Butler and Kitzinger, *1975 Referendum*, p. 82.

106. *Scottish Daily News*, 13 May 1975, p. 5.

107. *Financial Times*, 30 May 1975, p. 12.

108. Kitzinger, *Diplomacy and Persuasion*, pp. 204–5.

109. Christopher Serpell to Con O'Neill, Memorandum: 'Uses of a Broadcasting Officer', 10 June 1975, BIE 1/5.

110. Kitzinger, *Diplomacy and Persuasion*, p. 205.

111. '"Britain in Europe" Broadcasting Department (Monitoring)', 10 June 1975, BIE 1/5.

112. Ibid.; Campaign Committee Minutes, 10 April 1975, BIE 1/9.

113. Butler and Kitzinger, *1975 Referendum*, pp. 74–5.

114. D.R. Thorpe, *Supermac: The Life of Harold Macmillan* (London: Pimlico, 2010), p. 281.

115. Butler and Kitzinger, *1975 Referendum*, pp. 90–2; Wistrich, *Recollections*, p. 130.

116. *The Times*, 2 June 1975, p. 2.

117. Colin S. Deans, Campaign Organiser, Radical Youth for Europe, 5 May 1975, BIE 27/4/2; 'Youth Revolt: The Next Stages', n.d. [mid May 1975], BIE 27/2.

118. Minutes of a meeting at the Waldorf Hotel, 21 May 1975, BIE 27/2; Butler and Kitzinger, *1975 Referendum*, p. 172.

119. McIntosh, *Challenge to Democracy*, p. 120 (30 June 1974).

120. Thorpe's biographer speculates that he suffered a breakdown in the summer of 1975. Michael Bloch, *Jeremy Thorpe* (London: Abacus, 2016), pp. 425–6.

4 'Better Out Than In': The National Referendum Campaign

1. Speech at Banbury, no date (*c.* 30 May 1975), Marten Papers c.1132, f. 363.
2. 'Common Market: Vote NO', no date, CIB 10/2 GBO.
3. *Sunday Times*, 4 May 1975, p. 17.
4. Goodhart, *Full-Hearted Consent*, pp. 168–9.
5. The surviving archives of BIE fill 869 boxes; those of the National Referendum Campaign fill just two.
6. For an excellent study, see David Richardson, 'Non-Party Organizations and Campaigns on European Integration in Britain, 1945–1986: Political and Public Activism', unpublished Ph.D. thesis (Birmingham, 2013).
7. *Sunday Times*, 11 May 1975, p. 32.
8. Kitzinger, *Diplomacy and Persuasion*, p. 247; *The Times*, 31 May 1976, p. 3.
9. *Sunday Telegraph*, 16 March 1975, p. 19.
10. *The Guardian*, 17 April 1972, pp. 1–2; *Daily Express*, 17 April 1972, p. 9; *Daily Mirror*, 17 April 1972, p. 2; Kitzinger, *Diplomacy and Persuasion*, pp. 246–8. For KBO and the ACML, see Robert F. Dewey Jr., *British National Identity and Opposition to Membership of Europe, 1961–63: The Anti-Marketeers* (Manchester: Manchester University Press, 2009), pp. 118–30.
11. Ron Leighton to Don Martin, 23 February 1973, CIB 1/3, folder 1.
12. The correspondence can be found in CIB 1/3, folder 2.
13. See correspondence from Francis D'Aft to Robin Williams and Margaret Conybeare, CIB 7/17.
14. CMSC Executive Committee, Minutes, 16 December 1974, CIB 1/3, folder 3.
15. Kitzinger, *Diplomacy and Persuasion*, p. 242.
16. Williams to Jay, 15 July 1974, CIB 9/2; *Financial Times*, 23 May 1975, p. 29; Butler and Kitzinger, *1975 Referendum*, pp. 102–3.
17. *Castle Diaries, 1974–76*, p. 374 (21 April 1975).
18. CMSC Executive Committee, Minutes, 16 December 1974, CIB 1/3, folder 3.
19. *Referendum on United Kingdom Membership*, pp. 18–20; Butler and Kitzinger, *1975 Referendum*, p. 102. This owed something to disdain for the media. As Ron Leighton cheerfully acknowledged in 1971, 'it never occurred to us to tell the press what we were doing'. Kitzinger, *Diplomacy and Persuasion*, p. 237.
20. 'National Referendum Campaign Financial Summary', Marten Papers c.1132, f. 156. This includes contributions made before the official accounting period, so is higher than in the published accounts. Bob Harrison, head of the TGWU Research Department, worked full time from mid-April, while ASTMS loaned GBO its head of research, Barry Sherman, the pollster Sally Kellner and the future minister Hilary Benn. Butler and Kitzinger, *1975 Referendum*, p. 102.

21. Typed accounts for GBO, 31 July 1975, Marten Papers c.1132, ff. 157–8; *Guardian*, 15 May 1975, p. 8.

22. Ron Leighton, 'Why you should vote "No" to the Common Market', *Land Worker*, April 1975, p. 83.

23. Douglas Jay to Neil Marten, 4 February 1975, CIB 9/2(2).

24. *Sunday Telegraph*, 16 March 1975, p. 19. For the correspondence between Frere-Smith and Con O'Neill, see BIE 1/18. O'Neill replied icily that 'your continual harping on the question of the funds available to Britain in Europe' suggests 'that you lack confidence in the strength of your other arguments'; 18 April 1975, BIE 1/18.

25. Shaun Stewart, 'Television Programmes', 6 May 1975, Marten Papers c. 1132, f. 5.

26. *Sunday Times*, 4 May 1975, p. 17.

27. *The Times*, 24 April 1975, p. 4.

28. Louis Harris poll, 1–6 April 1975, quoted in Butler and Kitzinger, *1975 Referendum*, p. 256.

29. *Daily Mirror*, 23 May 1974, p. 7. Tynan called the EEC 'the greatest historical vulgarity since Hitler's 1,000-year Reich'; John Lahr (ed.), *The Diaries of Kenneth Tynan* (Bloomsbury: London, 2002), p. 49 (13 May 1971).

30. 'Referendum Campaign', Marten Papers c.1132, f. 174; Butler and Kitzinger, *1975 Referendum*, p. 110.

31. *Sunday Times*, 13 April 1975, p. 1.

32. [Robin Williams?] to Douglas Jay, 15 July 1974, CIB 9/2(2); Richardson, 'Non-Party Organizations', p. 197.

33. CMSC Executive, Minutes, 16 December 1974, CIB 1/3 folder 3.

34. 'Referendum Campaign', no date, Marten Papers c.1132, ff. 171–6.

35. Victor Montagu to Christopher Frere-Smith, no date, CIB 9/2; *Daily Telegraph*, 15 April 1975, p. 8.

36. *Castle Diaries*, pp. 402–3 (30–31 May 1975).

37. See the cache of letters in BIE/22, and BIE 1/18: 'Enemy Action'.

38. Camilla Schofield, *Enoch Powell and the Making of Postcolonial Britain* (Cambridge: Cambridge University Press, 2013), p. 284; J. Enoch Powell, Speech at Northfield, Birmingham, 13 June 1970, p. 16, Powell Paper POLL 4/1/6 file 2.

39. Goodhart, *Full-Hearted Consent*, pp. 132, 177–8.

40. *Sunday Times*, 4 May 1975, p. 17; *The Sun*, 17 April 1975, p. 6.

41. Benn, *Against the Tide*, p. 340 (15 March 1975).

42. Judith Hart to Harold Wilson and the Cabinet, 14 March 1975, MS Castle 306 ff. 100–1.

43. For the Dissenting Ministers' declaration, see 'Labour united against the Common Market!' *Tribune*, 21 March 1975, p. 1. A fuller statement was issued on 26 March 1975: 'The Common Market: Why we object. Statement

by Dissenting Ministers', MS Castle 306, ff. 216–18. For the Early Day Motion and signatories, see MS Castle 306, ff. 111–12.

44. *Castle Diaries, 1974–76*, p. 345 (19 March 1975).

45. Wilson, 'To Ministers who are members of the NEC', 24 March 1975, MS Castle 306, ff. 182–3.

46. NEC Agenda and Minutes, 26 March 1975, LHASC, NEC 5/1975/75; *The Observer*, 23 March 1975, p. 1.

47. *Labour and the Common Market*, pp. 14 (Lawrence Daly, Jack Jones), 15 (Roy Hughes).

48. The battle for control of the NEC is best traced through the diaries of Tony Benn and Barbara Castle.

49. Wilson, 'To Ministers who are members of the NEC', 24 March 1975, enclosing a minute circulated on 14 May 1974, MS Castle 306, ff. 182–6.

50. *Castle Diaries, 1974–76*, p. 349 (20 March 1975).

51. Ibid., pp. 381, 395 (29 April and 21 May 1975).

52. Minutes of the special meeting of the NEC, 30 April 1975, LHASC, NEC 8/1974/75.

53. *Castle Diaries, 1974–76*, p. 383 (1 May 1975).

54. 'Referendum Campaign', Marten Papers c.1132, f. 174.

55. Benn, *Against the Tide*, pp. 285–6 (17 December 1974).

56. *Tribune*, 18 April 1975, p. 1.

57. Benn, *Against the Tide*, p. 362 (11 April 1975); *Glasgow Herald*, 3 June 1975, p. 1.

58. *Castle Diaries, 1974–76*, p. 403 (1–6 June 1975).

59. 'Anti-Common Market Activities', No. 76, 10 May 1975, Marten Papers c.1132, f. 2h–i; *Coventry Telegraph*, 24 May 1975, p. 8. The stunt bore a curious similarity to an episode of *Dad's Army*, broadcast five months earlier: 'The Godiva Affair', *Dad's Army*, series 7 episode 4, written by Jimmy Perry and David Croft, first broadcast 6 December 1974.

60. For a photo, see *Sunday Times*, 1 June 1975, p. 1. *The Guardian*, 20 May 1975, p. 8; *Daily Telegraph*, 27 May 1975, p. 6.

61. John Mills to local organisers, 29 May 1975, Marten Papers, c.1132, f. 67.

62. *The Sun*, 11 April 1975, p. 6.

63. 'Television Programmes', 6 May 1975, Marten Papers c.1132, fs 7, 9.

64. 'Common Market Vote No', CIB 10/2 GBO.

65. Transcript of NRC Referendum Broadcast, BBC1, 23 May 1975, National Referendum Campaign Archive, Parliamentary Archive, NRC [hereafter: NRC]/1.

66. The 'faceless man' featured prominently in GBO posters.

67. 'On the Doorstep' in GBO/ NRC, *Talking Points* no. 16 (4 June 1975), CIB 9/2; *Morning Star*, 1 May 1975, p. 3; John Mills to activists, 29 May 1975, Marten Papers c.1132, f. 67. For the 'Independence Day' theme, see also

Marten Papers c.1132, ff. 341–4; 'An eve of poll statement by the dissenting Ministers', 4 June 1975, MS Castle 307, f. 52.

68. *Scottish Daily News*, 26 May 1975, p. 4.

69. Speech at Devizes, 'Saturday night', Marten Papers c.1132, f. 366.

70. Marten, 'Article for NATSOPA' [draft], 12 May 1975, Marten Papers c.1132, f.13b.

71. Marten, Speech at Conway Hall, London, 12 April 1975; speech at Oxford, 16 May 1975; speech at Banbury, 'Friday night', Marten Papers c.1132, ff. 341–2, 359, 363.

72. Stickers and fliers, Marten Papers c.1132, f. 215.

73. TGWU *Record* (February 1975), pp. 8–9; *Tribune*, 30 May 1975, p. 6.

74. GBO memo, 'possible discussion points', CIB 10/2 GBO; *The Guardian*, 2 June 1975, p. 13.

75. GBO *Talking Points*, No. 12 (23 May 1975), Marten Papers c.1132, f. 57.

76. 'Europe's Food Mountains', in GBORC, *Talking Points*, no. 10 (20 May 1975), Marten Papers c.1132, f. 34.

77. GBORC, 'A Vote YES to the Common Market is a Vote NO to Jobs', Feb. 1975, Marten Papers c.1132, fs 183–5.

78. GBO *Talking Points*, No. 12 (23 May 1975), Marten Papers c.1132, f. 56.

79. Jay, *Change and Fortune*, p. 485.

80. *Glasgow Herald*, 3 June 1975, p 1; *Liverpool Daily Post*, 3 June 1975, p. 4.

81. *Morning Star*, 4 June 1975, p. 1.

82. 'The Points to Punch Home', GBO *Talking Points*, No. 9 (May 1975), Marten Papers c.1132, f. 69.

83. Judith Hart, *Aid and Liberation: A Socialist Study of Aid Politics* (Gollancz: London, 1973); Duncan Sutherland, 'Hart, Judith, Baroness Hart of South Lanark (1924–1991)', *Oxford Dictionary of National Biography* (Oxford University Press: Oxford, 2004); online edition, May 2008.

84. Hart, Speech to the Fire Brigades Union, Bridlington, 7 May 1975, Hart Papers, HART/10/11.

85. *Morning Star*, 1 May 1975, p. 3.

86. Neil Marten, 'Out of Europe and into the World', proof of article, c. 30 May 1975, Marten Papers c.1132, f. 72.

87. *Tribune*, 28 February 1975, p. 1; 18 April 1975, p. 5; Marten, 'Unite to Fight', n.d., Marten Papers c.1132 f. 149; 'Scotland and the EEC. Province or Nation?', 6 March 1975, SNP Papers, National Library of Scotland, Acc. 7295/24.

88. *The Scotsman*, 13 May 1975, p. 8.

89. 'Television Programmes', 6 May 1975, Marten Papers c.1132, f. 7.

90. Transcript of NRC Referendum Campaign Broadcast, BBC1, 3 June 1975, NRC/1.

91. *Tribune*, 7 March 1975, p. 7.

92. Marten, 'Out – and into the World', proof of article, c. 30 May 1975, Marten Papers c.1132, f. 72.

93. *Financial Times*, 20 May 1975, p. 2.

94. S. Stewart to Marten and the NRC 'O' Group, Marten Papers c.1132, 'Statement of Policy', May 1975, f. 90; 'Trade and the Alternative', no date, Marten Papers c.1132, f. 329.

95. *Manchester Evening News*, 4 June 1975, p. 8.

96. *Daily Mail*, 27 May 1975, p. 6; *Castle Diaries, 1974–76*, p. 392 (18 May 1975).

97. Harold Wilson interviewed by Peter Jay for *Weekend World*, 11 May 1975, MS Wilson, c. 1266, f. 86.

98. *The Guardian*, 2 June 1975, p. 13.

99. *Castle Diaries, 1974–76*, p. 302 (4 February 1975).

100. *Glasgow Herald*, 27 May 1975, p. 1.

101. *Financial Times*, 19 May 1975, p. 7; *Bristol Evening Post*, 10 May 1975, p. 2.

102. *Bristol Evening Post*, 10 May 1975, p. 2; *The Guardian*, 2 June 1975, p. 13; *Bristol Evening Post*, 30 May 1975, p. 2.

103. *The Sun*, 28 May 1975, p. 2; *Glasgow Herald*, 27 May 1975, p. 1.

104. *Bristol Evening Post*, 29 May 1975, p. 1; *The Guardian*, 2 June 1975, p. 13.

105. *Castle Diaries, 1974–76*, pp. 378 (25 April 1975), 391 (16 May 1975), 392 (18 May 1975).

106. Jowell and Hoinville, *Britain into Europe*, p. 88.

107. *The Guardian*, 2 June 1975, p. 13; *Glasgow Herald*, 7 June 1975, p. 1. For the Benn effect, see NOP, 'A Summary Report Prepared for the National Referendum Campaign: The E.E.C.', 16 May 1975, NOP/8580, MS Castle 306, f. 349.

108. Jay, *Change and Fortune*, pp. 484, 490; *Daily Telegraph*, 7 June 1975, p. 30; *Morning Star*, 7 June 1975, p. 1.

5 'The Boardroom Must Lead!' Employers, Unions and the Economy

1. *The Director*, 27:10 (April 1975), p. 3.

2. R. McIntosh, *Challenge to Democracy: Politics, Trade Union Power and Economic Failure in the 1970s* (London: Politico's, 2008), p. 226.

3. *Financial Times*, 29 May 1975, p. 1.

4. *The Scotsman*, 24 May 1975, p. 5.

5. *The Economist*, 3 May 1975, p. 41.

6. 'Barrie Heath, GKN Group Chairman, to all GKN employees and their families', 30 May 1975, NRC/1.

7. *Referendum on United Kingdom Membership*, pp. 3–18; 'Actual Cash Contributions Paid', 2 May 1975, BIE 11/2.

8. *The Director*, 27:8 (February 1975), p. 147; 27:11 (May 1975), p. 135; John Davan Sainsbury, 'The Challenge of Confidence: Speech to the Institute of Grocery Distribution Convention, 28 April 1975', Sainsbury Archive, Museum of London Docklands, SA/PR/1/1/5.

9. *Financial Times*, 12 May 1975, p. 18; 29 May 1975, p. 1.

10. *The Spectator*, 10 May 1975, p. 595.

11. See, for example, *Scottish Daily News*, 23 May 1975, p. 5.

12. *Financial Times*, 22 May 1975, p. 12.

13. *Scottish Daily News*, 15 May 1975, p. 6; *Financial Times*, 16 May 1975, p. 16.

14. *Financial Times*, 30 May 1975, p. 10.

15. Press release by Food and Drink Industry Council, 14 April 1975, BIE 12/1.

16. 'Members of the Fund-Raising Committee', BIE 11/1.

17. *Referendum on United Kingdom Membership*; 'Actual Cash Contributions Paid', 2 May 1975, BIE 11/2.

18. *Financial Times*, 13 May 1975, p. 14; *Daily Telegraph*, 13 March 1975, p. 19; *Coventry Telegraph*, 30 May 1975, p. 24.

19. *The Economist*, 3 May 1975, p. 41.

20. *Financial Times*, 4 June 1975, p. 12.

21. CBI, 'Talking Points No. 8. Industry Speaks Out', CBI Archive, Modern Records Centre, University of Warwick [hereafter: CBI] MSS.200/C/3/INT/3/50/6; *The Director*, 27:11 (May 1975), pp. 208–11.

22. *British Industry and Europe: A Report by the CBI Europe Committee, March 1975* (London: CBI, 1975), p. 1.

23. Kitzinger, *Diplomacy and Persuasion*, p. 260.

24. *British Industry and Europe*, p. 1; 'Correspondence relating to CBI Impact Europe train', CBI MSS.200/C/3/INT/3/24; *CBI Impact Europe: Annotated Transcript* (London: CBI, 1972), pp. 1, 4, CBI MSS.200/C/3/INT/3/50/5.

25. *British Industry and Europe*, p. 3.

26. Gary Waller [Campaign Organiser], 'CBI Europe Campaign', 19 February 1975, BIE 1/9; Gary Waller to 'Mr Europe's, February 1975; 'Meeting of "Mr Europes" of Larger Companies Supporting the CBI Campaign', 20 February 1975; Waller, 'Analysis of 104 Replies to First Letter to "Mr Europes"', 4 March 1975; Waller to 'Mr Europe', 10 April 1975, CBI MSS.200/C/4/1975/12.

27. *The Economist*, 17 May 1975, p. 44; *Scottish Daily Express*, 4 June 1975, p. 2; *Birmingham Post*, 3 June 1975, p. 3; 'Midlands firms say: "Stay in Community"', *Birmingham Express and Star*, 17 April 1975, BIE 27/4/2; S.G. Sperryn to Aza Pinney, 28 May 1975, BIE 16/3; *Bristol Evening Post*, 3 June 1975, p. 3 and 4 June 1975, p. 7.

28. *The Director*, 27:11 (May 1975), pp. 208–11.

29. *The Economist*, 1 March 1975, p. 11.

30. Waller, 'CBI Europe Campaign'.

31. 'Metrication and the EEC'; 'Some Comments on the National Referendum Campaign's "No" Leaflet', 8 May 1975; 'Quit the Market, May 1975'; CBI MSS.200/C/4/1975/12.

32. 'Europe Campaign Bulletin No. 1', 14 March 1975; 'Europe Campaign Bulletin No. 4', 19 May 1975; 'Europe Campaign Bulletin No. 6', 30 May 1975, CBI MSS.200/C/4/1975/12.

33. 'Meeting of "Mr Europe"s'; Waller, 'Extracts From Letters Received Up to 22nd February 1975 From Companies Supporting the Campaign'; 'Analysis of 104 Replies'. Christopher Frere-Smith warned that 'The EEC may be good for big business – but for small traders it will be slow torture, and then death'; *Financial Times*, 23 May 1975, p. 13.

34. *The Economist*, 17 May 1975, pp. 44–5.

35. *Financial Times*, 9 May 1975, p. 13.

36. *British Industry and Europe*, p. 2.

37. *Financial Times*, 17 May 1975, p. 9.

38. Ibid., 27 May 1975, p. 29.

39. Get Britain Out/National Referendum Campaign, *Talking Points* No. 13 (29 May 1975), p. 3.

40. *Financial Times*, 2 June 1975, p. 7.

41. *British Industry and Europe*, p. 31.

42. CBI leaflet, 'Europe – what it means to British industry', CBI MSS.200/C/3/INT/3/50/6.

43. *British Industry and Europe*, pp. iii, 6; 'Europe: Questions & Answers', CBI MSS.200/C/3/INT/3/50/6.

44. Margaret Thatcher, Speech to the London University Conservative Association, 7 March 1975, http://margaretthatcher.org/document/102647.

45. CBI, 'Europe – what it means to British industry'; *British Industry and Europe*, p. ii.

46. 'Why should Britain vote to stay as a member of the European Economic Community?', CBI MSS.200/C/3/INT/3/50/6; *British Industry and Europe*, pp. ii, 9.

47. Interview with Betty Boothroyd, 18 June 2014.

48. *The Economist*, 24 May 1975, p. 34; *The Scotsman*, 16 May 1975, p. 9; 23 May 1975, p. 4; *Financial Times*, 16 May 1975, p. 16; *The Sun*, 1 April 1975, p. 6; 28 May 1975, p. 2.

49. CBI, 'Europe – what it means to British industry'.

50. *The Sun*, 28 May 1975, p. 2.

51. *Financial Times*, 12 May 1975, p. 22.

52. Ibid., 16 May 1975, p. 21.

53. *The Director*, 27:11 (May 1975), p. 156 ; 'Why Sainsbury's says Yes to the Common Market', *JS Journal*, April 1975.

54. *The Director*, 27:7 (January 1975), p. 4; *St Michael News*, 3 (June 1975), p. 1.

55. *Financial Times*, 12 May 1975, p. 18.
56. Ibid., 27 May 1975, p. 6; *The Director*, 27:11 (May 1975), pp. 208–11.
57. *The Director*, 27:11 (May 1975), pp. 208–11.
58. CBI 'Talking Points No. 3: Trade', CBI MSS.200/C/3/INT/3/50/6. See also *The Economist*, 31 May 1975, p. 8.
59. *The Economist*, 24 May 1975, p. 34.
60. *Financial Times*, 12 May 1975, p. 19; *British Industry and Europe*, p. 25.
61. *Financial Times*, 12 May 1975, p. 19; *British Industry and Europe*, pp. 7, 27–8.
62. *British Industry and Europe*, p. 8.
63. *Yorkshire Post*, 2 June 1975, p. 3.
64. *Yorkshire Post*, 4 June 1975, p. 5. See also *Yorkshire Post*, 23 May 1975, p. 8; 3 June 1975, p. 8.
65. *Financial Times*, 21 May 1975, p. 11.
66. *Men's Wear*, 29 May 1975, p. 12; *Evening Standard*, 4 June 1975, p. 20.
67. *Financial Times*, 21 May 1975, p. 11;, 2 June 1975, p. 14. See also Advertisement placed by P.J.D. Marshall, managing director of Wilkinson Warburton Ltd, Pudsey, *Yorkshire Post*, 2 June 1975, p. 9.
68. *Financial Times*, 1 May 1975, p. 18; 2 June 1975, p. 14.
69. Ibid., 2 June 1975, p. 14; *The Scotsman*, 23 May 1975, p. 6; *The Economist*, 3 May 1975, p. 41.
70. *Financial Times*, 10 May 1975, p. 23.
71. *Financial Times*, 30 May 1975, p. 10; 'Actual Cash Contributions Paid'.
72. *Industry in Europe*, p. 6.
73. CBI, 'Europe – what it means to British industry'.
74. *Industry in Europe*, p. 6.
75. *British Industry and Europe*, p. 6.
76. CBI, 'Europe – what it means to British industry'.
77. *Financial Times*, 3 June 1975, p. 13.
78. CBI, 'Why should Britain vote to stay as a member of the European Economic Community?', CBI MSS.200/C/3/INT/3/50/6.
79. *Financial Times*, 1 May 1975, p. 16; 20 May 1975, p. 12; 'Europe: Why it must be Yes', *Barclays Bank Briefing – 29: A Quarterly Information Service on Money Matters*, 11 April 1975, pp. 1, 4, BIE 16/3; *The Economist*, 19 April 1975, pp. 26, 140; 26 April 1975, p. 84.
80. *The Scotsman*, 21 May 1975, p. 4; *Financial Times*, 3 June 1975, p. 1.
81. *Financial Times*, 27 May 1975, p. 29.
82. *The Director*, 27:7 (January 1975), p. 108; 27:8 (February 1975), p. 148.
83. *Financial Times*, 7 May 1975, p. 23;, 12 May 1975, p. 18.
84. Ibid., 12 May 1975, p. 18.
85. For the emergence of the Eurobond market and the hope that financial integration would promote political unity, see N. Ferguson, *High Financier: The Life and Times of Siegmund Warburg* (London: Allen Lane, 2010), pp. 201–32.

86. *Financial Times*, 27 May 1975, p. 29.

87. 'Europe: Why it must be Yes', *Barclays Bank Briefing* – 29, 11 April 1975, p. 4; *The Times*, 15 March 1975, p. 21; CBI, 'Talking Points No. 8. Industry Speaks Out', CBI MSS.200/C/3/INT/3/50/6.

88. *Financial Times*, 20 May 1975, p. 12.

89. Ibid., 12 May 1975, p. 18.

90. Ibid., 15 May 1975, p. 10.

91. Ibid., 27 May 1975, p. 29.

92. Ibid., 7 May 1975, p. 23.

93. *The Sun*, 29 May 1975, p. 7.

94. *The Scotsman*, 14 May 1975, p. 11; 'Extracts from letters received up to 22nd February 1975 from companies supporting the campaign', CBI MSS.200/C/4/1975/12. Even in Scotland, however, 73.4 per cent of companies polled thought withdrawal either damaging or disadvantageous. Only 5.6 per cent favoured leaving.

95. *Castle Diaries*, p. 388 (8 May 1975); *Financial Times*, 9 May 1975, p. 13; 19 May 1975, p. 2.

96. Speech at the Winter Gardens, Blackpool, 31 May 1975, Powell Papers, POLL 4/1/11/5.

97. *Resistance News*, 14 (January–February 1975), p. 2; TGWU *Record*, February 1975, p. 10. *Yorkshire Post*, 2 June 1975, p. 8.

98. *Tribune*, 7 March 1975, p. 5; *Morning Star*, 2 May 1975, p. 1.

99. *The Director*, May 1975, p. 202.

100. Douglas Jay, *The Better Alternative for Britain* (London: CMSC, 1975), pp. 1–2; *The Spectator*, 7 June 1975, p. 681.

101. 'The Economic Consequences of the Treaties', 4 May 1975, MS Castle 306, ff. 316–19; *Castle Diaries*, p. 383 (1 May 1975).

102. *The Miner*, May–June 1975, p. 3. The Nottinghamshire county executive took a neutral line, anticipating its later break with the NUM leadership; *The Guardian*, 2 June 1975, p. 6.

103. *Financial Times*, 29 May 1975, p. 11.

104. *The Miner*, May–June 1975, pp. 4–5.

105. *ASTMS Journal*, March–April 1975, p. 6.

106. *The Economist*, 7 June 1975, p. 23.

107. *Financial Times*, 16 May 1975, p. 16. See also *Morning Star*, 3 June 1975, p. 1.

108. *Financial Times*, 29 May 1975, p. 10; 'Statement by Michael Meacher MP at the National Referendum Campaign Press Conference', 28 May 1975, Marten Papers c.1132, ff. 62–4.

109. GBO/NRC, *Talking Points* no. 12, 23 May 1975, CIB 9/2; 'Defeat the Common Market – Vote No! Statement by Oxford and District Trades Council', NRC/1.

110. *ASTMS Journal* (March–April 1975), p. 6. See also TGWU *Record*, February 1975, p. 7.

111. TGWU *Record* (April 1975), p. 10.

112. *Financial Times*, 2 June 1975, p. 7.

113. TGWU *Record*, February 1975, p. 7; *ASTMS Journal*, January–February 1975, p. 5; *ASTMS Journal*, March–April 1975, p. 7.

114. *Bristol Evening Post*, 10 May 1975, p. 2; *The Sun*, 29 May 1975, p. 7.

115. Statement by the Get Britain Out Referendum Campaign, *ASTMS Journal*, January–February 1975, p. 5.

116. 'The Scales are Weighted Against Us', *Special Edition of the TUC's Information Broadsheet*, May 1975, Marten Papers c.1155/21.

117. *ASTMS Journal*, January–February 1975, p. 5; March–April 1975, p. 5.

118. *The Economist*, 15 March 1975, p. 13.

119. *Financial Times*, 13 May 1975, p. 17.

120. TGWU *Record*, March 1975, p. 11.

121. *Financial Times*, 22 May 1975, p. 12.

122. King, *Britain Says Yes*, p. 115; Goodhart, *Full-Hearted Consent*, p. 128.

123. *The Scotsman*, 2 May 1975, p. 7.

124. *The Sun*, 29 May 1975, p. 7.

125. *GMW Herald*, 5 (June 1975), p. 2.

126. *Workers' Voice* [published by TUAFE], p. 1, BIE 15/2.

127. 'First speech by George Thomson, as President of the Young European Left, at launch of YEL manifesto', 18 April 1975, BIE 15/1.

128. *GMW Herald*, 5 (June 1975), p. 2.

129. *The Scotsman*, 24 May 1975, p. 5; *Morning Star*, 2 May 1975, p. 3.

130. CBI Talking Points: 'Feedback from the Shopfloor'.

131. *Financial Times*, 3 June 1975, p. 13.

132. Ibid., 4 June 1975, p. 13.

133. The only union donation of more than £100 during the campaign seems to have been £1,377.30 from the TGWU; *Referendum on United Kingdom Membership*, p. 19. The TGWU had also given £1,000 before the start of the campaign: handwritten accounts, LSE CIB 9/2/2; see also unsigned letter to Jack Jones, 3 January 1975, CIB 9/1.

134. R. Broad and T. Geiger (eds.), 'Witness Seminar: The 1975 British Referendum on Europe', *Contemporary British History*, 10:3 (Autumn 1996), pp. 101–2. When IPSOS-MORI began polling on the subject in October 1975, they found that 75 per cent of respondents (including 65 per cent of union members) agreed that 'Trade Unions have too much power in Britain today', while 64 per cent (including 56 per cent of unionists) agreed that 'Most trade unions are controlled by extremists and militants'. www.ipsos.com/ipsos-mori/en-uk/attitudes-trade-unions-1975-2014.

135. *Financial Times*, 3 June 1975, p. 13. The Labour Campaign for Britain in Europe saw the support of Wilson and Callaghan as crucial in winning 'manual workers and trade unionists'; 'Notes on state of public opinion, 28 May 1975', BIE 15/49.

136. *Financial Times*, 16 May 1975, p. 16; *The Sun*, 28 May 1975, p. 2; *The Miner*, May–June 1975, p. 5.

137. *Bristol Evening Post*, 3 June 1975, p. 4; 4 June 1975, p. 7; *Western Mail*, 27 May 1975, p. 5.

138. *Yorkshire Post*, 21 May 1975, p. 7; 'European Community Financial Aid' leaflets, BIE 26/7.

139. *Yorkshire Post*, 2 June 1975, p. 3.

140. *Financial Times*, 3 June 1975, p. 13.

141. 'Report on E.E.C., 29th May 1975', NOP/8580/03, Marten Papers, c.1133, f. 46.

6 'Women and Children First!'

1. *The Sun*, 27 May 1975, p. 7.

2. *Daily Mirror*, 2 June 1975, pp. 14–15.

3. 'Shoppers – How you answer these questions is how you should vote', BIE 18/26.

4. 'Miss World: My Protest at 1970 Beauty Pageant', BBC Witness, 5 March 2014, www.bbc.co.uk/news/magazine-26437815.

5. Women's trade union membership increased by 73 per cent from 1966 to 1979; see Tara Martin López, *The Winter of Discontent: Myth, Memory and History* (Liverpool: Liverpool University Press, 2014), pp. 30–3 and *passim*. In 1975, women constituted 38.8 per cent of the civilian workforce in Britain, higher than in Belgium (34.4 per cent), France (37.2 per cent), Germany (37.7 per cent), Ireland (27.4 per cent) or Italy (28.1 per cent). See Catherine Hoskyns, *Integrating Gender: Women, Law and Politics in the European Union* (London: Verso, 1996), p. 31.

6. For International Women's Year, see Helen McCarthy, 'The Diplomatic History of Global Women's Rights: The British Foreign Office and International Women's Year, 1975', *Journal of Contemporary History*, 50:4 (2015), pp. 833–53.

7. See, for example, Elizabeth Wilson, 'An Opposing Image', *Socialist Woman*, Winter 1974/5, pp. 24–5.

8. See Laura Beers, 'Thatcher and the Women's Vote', in Ben Jackson and Robert Saunders (eds.), *Making Thatcher's Britain* (Cambridge: Cambridge University Press, 2012), pp. 113–31. See also R. Saunders, 'The Many Lives of Margaret Thatcher', *English Historical Review*, forthcoming (2017).

9. Regina v. Morgan, HL 30 April 1975. See, for example, 'MP raps "crazy charter for rapists"', *The Sun*, 2 May 1975, p. 2.

10. The two women's officers were paid £985 and £795, significantly more than the £750 paid to the regional organisers for Scotland and Northern Ireland. *Referendum on United Kingdom Membership*, pp. 3–18.

11. *The Sun*, 27 May 1975, p. 7.

12. Louis Harris International, *British Attitudes to the EEC/Panel Survey* (April 1975), BIE 26/1; 'Britain in Europe/Public Opinion Summary 20th May 1975', BIE 26/1; 'Table drawn from Glasgow Herald', BIE 26/1.

13. 'Britain in Europe/Public Opinion Summary 20th May 1975', p. 4, BIE 26/1; NOP Market Research, 'A Summary Report Prepared for The National Referendum Campaign' (NOP/8580: 16 May 1975), p. 6, Marten Papers, c.1133.

14. 'Table drawn from Glasgow Herald', BIE 26/1; *Birmingham Post*, 4 June 1975, p. 1.

15. Avebury's husband, Eric Lubbock, was a Liberal peer who had won a sensational by-election in Orpington in 1962.

16. The following paragraphs draw extensively on 'Draft Outline of Campaign Geared to Women' [no date/ author], BIE 26/6 and Kina Avebury and Ann Money-Coutts, 'Resumé of Women's Officers' Activities: 3 April–5 June 1975', BIE 29/11. I am grateful to Lady Avebury for sharing her memories of the Women's Section in an interview, 10 July 2015.

17. *The Guardian*, 8 May 1975, p. 5.

18. Letter, 18 May 1975, BIE 26/8. The same picture subsequently appeared with the words 'and the girls!' added. *Our Europe*, no date [but probably May 1975], Marten Papers c.1155/1.

19. For the sexualisation of the newspaper industry, see Adrian Bingham, *Family Newspapers? Sex, Private Life and the British Popular Press, 1918–1978* (Oxford: Oxford University Press, 2009).

20. *Daily Mirror*, 20 May 1975, p. 3; 7 June 1975, p. 3. See also Kitzinger, *Diplomacy and Persuasion*, p. 346.

21. *Coventry Telegraph*, 24 May 1975, p. 8; *Coventry Telegraph*, 31 May 1975, p. 1.

22. For the national costumes, see 'Girls to Wear European Costumes', 10 April 1975, BIE 27/4/2; see also press cutting from *Chelmsford Weekly News*, 29 May 1975, BIE 27/1. For 'Miss Europe', see Students for a United Europe (SUE) National Committee minutes, 1 March 1975, BIE 27/1.

23. Kina Avebury and Ann Money-Coutts, 'Resumé of Women's Officers' Activities: 3 April–5 June 1975', BIE 29/11.

24. For press releases, see BIE 26/10.

25. 'Confidential report from the Women's Section', 22 May 1975, 23 May 1975, BIE 26/4.

26. For media correspondence, see BIE 26/5.

27. 'Press conference for women journalists and editors of women's pages as well as representatives from radio and television programmes', 14 May 1975, BIE 26/10.

28. See, for example, Kina Avebury and Ann Money-Coutts to *Western Morning News*, 6 May 1975, BIE 26/10.

29. Single printed sheet, no date, reporting ORC/Harris poll, BIE 26/1.

30. To Avebury, 18 April 1975, BIE 26/4.

31. See, for example, Avebury to the Chairmen of Women's Liberal Associations, 23 April 1975, BIE 26/8; Ann Money-Coutts to all Branch Secretaries and Chairmen, European Union of Women, 7 May 1975, BIE 26/8.

32. Caitriona Beaumont, *Housewives and Citizens: Domesticity and the Women's Movement in England, 1928–64* (Manchester: Manchester University Press, 2013), pp. 3–4, 8, 40, 216.

33. More than 6,000 women attended a forum of non-governmental organisations organised alongside the UN conference on the status of women at Mexico City in 1975. See McCarthy, 'Diplomatic History of Global Women's Rights', p. 834.

34. Minutes of the Women's European Committee, 19 April 1972, p. 2, LSE Women's Library, LSE 5/WFM/C21. For correspondence relating to the organisation, see LSE Women's Library, LSE 5FWI/D/2/2/47. The committee went through a variety of names, but was known colloquially as the Women's European Committee. It played no part in the referendum, as its grant expired at the end of the 1974/5 financial year. It was formally wound up on 3 June 1975.

35. For examples of the sums disbursed, see WEC Minute Book, LSE Women's Library, LSE 5/WFM/C21.

36. Avebury to Mrs Sandra Brooks (Chairman of the National Housewives Association), 15 April 1975, BIE 26/8; Entwistle to Avebury, 9 April 1975, BIE 26/7.

37. Entwistle to Avebury, 9 April 1975, BIE 26/7.

38. See 'NFWI Accounts for Block Grant by Women's European Committee, 1974/75', LSE Women's Library, LSE 5FWI/D/2/2/47.

39. *Home and County: Journal of the National Federation of Women's Institutes*, July 1975, p. 253.

40. *Townswoman*, 42:4 (April 1975), p. 128; Birmingham Federation of Townswomen's Guilds to Ann Money-Coutts, 16 May 1975, BIE 26/8.

41. *Townswoman*, 42:4 (April 1975).

42. Ibid., pp. 127, 128.

43. Black, who was now working in public relations for Debenham's, advised him 'that the strongest factor for women was the stability that remaining in the Common Market could represent and the upheaval involved in withdrawal'.

Harold Hutchinson, 'Report on Britain in Europe Campaign Publicity, Feb–June 1975', 11 June 1975, BIE 18/3.

44. *Bristol Evening Post*, 31 May 1975, p. 5.

45. Christopher Morgan to Tom Spencer, 14 April 1975, BIE 18/1; Kina Avebury to the Chairmen of Women's Liberal Associations, 23 April 1975, BIE 26/8; Ann Money-Coutts to all Branch Secretaries/Chairmen, European Union of Women, 7 May 1975, BIE 26/8.

46. 'Britain in Europe/Public Opinion Summary, 20th May 1975', BIE 26/1.

47. Betty Boothroyd, *The Autobiography* (London: Century, 2001), esp. pp. 109, 126–9; Paul Routledge, *Madam Speaker: A Biography* (London: Harper Collins, 1995), pp. 121–3, 30; interview with Lady Boothroyd, 18 June 2014.

48. Interview with Lady Boothroyd, 18 June 2014; minutes of meeting of female MPs and Peers in the House of Lords, 29 April 1975, BIE 26/2.

49. Betty Boothroyd to Kina Avebury, 7 May 1975, BIE 26/2.

50. Boothroyd to Avebury, 13 May 1975, BIE 26/2.

51. *Sunday Telegraph*, 2 March 1975, p. 8.

52. Ibid., 2 March 1975, p. 8.

53. *South Wales Echo*, 4 April 1975, p. 14.

54. *Sunday Telegraph*, 2 March 1975, p. 8.

55. *Daily Mirror*, 2 June 1975, pp. 14–15; 'We women care about ...', flier, BIE 18/25.

56. Diana Elles, *The Housewife and the Common Market* (London: CPC, 1971) [reissued in 1975], pp. 3, 6.

57. *South Wales Argus*, 30 April 1975, p. 6.

58. *Woman's Own*, 31 May 1975, p. 53.

59. Louis Harris International, 'British Attitudes to the EEC', BIE 26/1.

60. Advert in *The Federalist*, 1 May 1975, no. 3, BIE 26/13. See also 'For Their Future, As Well As Yours, Vote Yes on Thursday' [advert], *Daily Mirror*, 2 June 1975, p. 10.

61. *Sunday Mail* (Glasgow), 25 May 1975, p. 24.

62. *Daily Mirror*, 5 June 1975, pp. 16–17; 'Let's fight with *both* hands', *Labour Newssheet*, NRC/1.

63. 'Britain in Europe/Public Opinion Summary 20th May 1975', BIE 26/1. This was also the experience of activists; see, for example, Lynda Chalker to Kina Avebury, 23 April 1975, BIE 26/2.

64. *Financial Times*, 10 April 1975, p. 27; 'Community Saved British Housewives £139 million', BIE weekly briefing no. 12, 19 May 1975, p. 2, BIE 22/5.

65. 'Referendum Campaign Broadcast on Behalf of the National Referendum Campaign', 22 May 1975, Radio 2, NRC/1.

66. See, for example, David Jarvis, 'Mrs Maggs and Betty: The Conservative Appeal to Women Voters in the 1920s', *Twentieth Century British History*, 5:2 (1994), 129–52.

67. Elles, *Housewife and the Common Market*, pp. 6, 12–13.

68. 'Statement by Mrs Barbara Castle and Mrs Neil Marten' [29 May 1975], NRC/1.

69. *The Guardian*, 2 June 1975, p. 13.

70. *The Sun*, 30 May 1975, p. 7; *The Guardian*, 30 May 1975, p. 8; *The Times*, 30 May 1975, p. 4; *Financial Times*, 30 May 1975, p. 12.

71. 'Summary of the Talk Given by Mrs V. Crankshaw, Secretary of the Women's European Committee, to the Women's Forum AGM, 10 December 1974: "Women's European Committee: A Personal View"', LSE Women's Archive, 5FWI/D/2/2/47. The European Movement was so keen to secure her services that, when she declined the post, it wrote again asking her to reconsider. Minutes of the WEC, 3 July 1974, p. 6 and 23 July 1974, p. 1 ('European Movement Referendum Campaign Women's Officer'), LSE 5/WFM/C21.

72. 'Rallying cry from Vicki', *Liverpool Daily Post*, 31 May 1975, p. 3. The use of first names in journalism was also more common for women than for men.

73. Vicki Crankshaw to Ann Money-Coutts, 14 May 1975, BIE 26/8.

74. Interview with Kina Avebury, 10 July 2015.

75. Minutes of the meeting of female MPs and Peers in the House of Lords, 29 April 1975, BIE 26/2; Baroness Birk to Baroness Emmet of Amberley, 24 April 1975, BIE 26/2. Birk's letter was read aloud at the meeting.

76. *Spare Rib*, 35 (May 1975), pp. 26–7. The article, by Jean Gardiner, claimed to investigate 'the arguments on both sides', but – as a subsequent correspondent pointed out – was a straightforward assault on the principle of membership.

77. For the origins of Article 119, the struggle to enforce it and the drafting of the 1975 directive, see Hoskyns, *Integrating Gender*, chs. 3–5.

78. Beatrix Campbell, *The Iron Ladies: Why Do Women Vote Tory?* (London: Virago, 1987), p. 206.

79. Alan Clark, *Diaries: In Power, 1983–1992* (London: Phoenix, 2001 edition), pp. 28–32 (22 July 1983); *Hansard* 46, 20 July 1983, 481.

80. 'We Women Care About...', BIE 18/25.

81. 'The European Community', BIE 26/6.

82. 'Women's Briefings', BIE 26/3.

83. 'The European Community', BIE 26/6; 'What does the Common Market mean to women?', *The Star* Women's Magazine, 19 May 1975, BIE 26/9.

84. Irene Fekete, *The How and Why Wonder Book of the Common Market* (London: Transworld Publishers, 1974), p. 35.

85. Article by Avebury for 'Gingerbread', *c.* April 1975, BIE 26/8.

86. *Birmingham Post*, 4 June 1975, p. 1; *The Sun*, 2 June 1975, p. 1.

87. Richardson, 'Non-Party Organizations', pp. 132–5, 146.

88. Diana Villiers, 'Report on the Anti-Common Market Campaign', 27 March 1975, BIE 26/14. The minutes of the NRC executive for 21 January 1975

record that 'The affiliation of Women Against the Common Market was not accepted', which suggests that the organisation was still formally extant, but I have found no evidence of WACM activity in 1975. After the referendum, Uwe Kitzinger wrote to a large number of organisations in preparation for the book he co-wrote with David Butler. He received a choleric reply on 'Women Against the Common Market' notepaper, but the letter makes no reference to any campaigning activities of its own. NRC minutes, 21 January 1975, Marten Papers c.1131, f. 153; Barbara Fellowes, Betty Hunt and Mary Stanton to Uwe Kitzinger, 30 July 1975, NRC 1.

89. CMSC, minutes of the Executive Committee, 27 March 1973, 18 April 1973 and 16 May 1973, CIB 1/3, folder 1.

90. See, for example, *Housewives Today*, 27:3 (December 1974), p. 8; 27:4 (January 1975), pp. 3–4; 27:6 (March 1975), p. 6; 27:7 (April 1975), pp. 1–2; 27:7 (April 1975), pp. 3–5; 27:8 (May 1975), pp. 3–5; 27:9 (June 1975), p. 2.

91. Elizabeth Ward to Diana Villiers, 14 April 1975, BIE 22/1; *Hansard* 860, 18 July 1973, 538.

92. See, for example, Jarvis, 'Mrs Maggs and Betty'; David Thackeray, 'From Prudent Housewife to Empire Shopper: Party Appeals to the Female Voter, 1918–1928', in J. Gottlieb and R. Toye (eds.), *The Aftermath of Suffrage* (Basingstoke: Palgrave, 2013); H. McCarthy, *The British People and the League of Nations: Democracy, Citizenship and Internationalism, c.1918–48* (Manchester: Manchester University Press, 2011), esp. ch. 7.

93. For the politics of unmarried motherhood, see Pat Thane and Tanya Evans, *Saints, Sinners, Scroungers? Unmarried Motherhood in Twentieth-Century England* (Oxford: Oxford University Press, 2013), esp. chs. 7–8.

94. Kina Avebury and Ann Money-Coutts, 'Resumé of Women's Officer's Activities: 3 April–5 June 1975', BIE 29/11.

7 'Come to Pray on Referendum Day'

1. Prayer circulated by 'Christians for Europe' for use on Sunday 1 June 1975; *Church Times*, 30 May 1975, p. 11.

2. *Methodist Recorder*, 6 March 1975, pp. 6–7.

3. Quoted in Noel Salter and John Selwyn Gummer, *Britain in Europe: The Social Responsibilities of the Church* (London: Board of Social Responsibility, 1972), p. 5.

4. *The Tablet*, 31 May 1975, p. 15; *South Wales Argus*, 5 June 1975, p. 1. For Boniface, see I.N. Wood, 'Boniface [St Boniface]', *Oxford Dictionary of National Biography* (Oxford: Oxford University Press, 2004).

5. *Church Times*, 27 March 1975, pp. 1, 20.

6. Sam Brewitt-Taylor, 'The Invention of a "Secular Society"? Christianity and the Sudden Appearance of Secularization Discourses in the British National Media, 1961–4', *20th Century British History*, 24:3 (2013), pp. 327–50.

7. J. Matheson and C. Summerfield (eds.), *Social Trends 30* (London: Office of National Statistics, 2000 edition), p. 219.

8. Philip M. Coupland, *Britannia, Europa and Christendom: British Christians and European Integration* (Basingstoke: Palgrave Macmillan, 2006), p. 189.

9. Coupland, *Britannia, Europa*, pp. 172–3, 179, 183, 190–1. *Going into Europe: Implications of Britain's Membership of the Common Market. A Study Kit for British Christians* (London: British Council of Churches, 1972).

10. *Britain in Europe: The Social Responsibilities of the Church*, p. 3. As part of its preparations for entry, the Church of England also overhauled its arrangements for Anglicans in northern and central Europe, expanding the responsibilities of the Bishop of Gibraltar and reviewing its administrative and pastoral structures. 'Church Commissioners General Purposes Committee Working Party on Europe: Note by the Secretary', 2 May 1974, Church of England Record Centre, Bermondsey, [hereafter: CERC] GP (74) 27.

11. *Going into Europe*, 'Suggestions i: WORSHIP: Bible Readings, Prayer and Hymns' and 'Suggestions ii: WORSHIP: Sermon Outline' [not paginated].

12. *Christians and the European Community: Reports and Papers of Conference, 1974, 16–20 April, Roehampton, London* (London, 1974). For the Roehampton conference, see Lucian N. Leustean, *The Ecumenical Movement and the Making of the European Community* (Oxford: Oxford University Press, 2014), pp. 162–6.

13. B. Milligan, *The Bridge: Reflections of an Unreconstructed Ecumaniac* (London: Christians Aware, 2011), p. 42.

14. Hugh Hanning to Giles Ecclestone, 'Ecumenical Meeting at Farm Street', 30 January 1975, CERC BSR/IAC/EUR/2/2.

15. Press release: 'Bishop launches Europe Campaign on St George's Day', 23 April 1975, BIE 17/17.

16. Gummer was elected for Lewisham West in 1970, but lost his seat in 1974. He re-entered the Commons in 1979, later serving as Conservative Party chairman, minister of agriculture, fisheries and food, and environment secretary.

17. *Britain in Europe: The Social Responsibilities of the Church* (London: Board of Social Responsibility, 1972), pp. 5, 18. The report was signed by Bishop Ronald Williams, but he credits Gummer and Salter as authors, p. 19. It was subsequently referred to in correspondence as 'the John Gummer "Britain in Europe" document'; e.g. Hugh Hanning to Giles Ecclestone, 30 January 1975, CERC, BSR/IAC/EUR/2/2. The reference was to Psalm 127.

18. 'Synod calls for vote against the EEC', *The Scotsman*, 23 May 1975, p. 15.

19. Gummer, 'The Churches and the Referendum – a Preliminary Report' (no date, 1974), BIE 19/53'; 'Second Report on the Churches and the Referendum', 23 January 1975, BIE 1/10. Interview with Lord Deben (John Selwyn Gummer), 10 June 2014.

20. Gummer, 'The Churches and the Referendum; 'Second Report on the Churches and the Referendum'.

21. *Church of England Newspaper*, 21 March 1975, p. 1.

22. Gummer, 'The Churches and the Referendum'; 'Second Report on the Churches and the Referendum'.

23. Ibid.

24. *Referendum on United Kingdom Membership of the European Community*, pp. 3–18.

25. *Church Times*, 4 April 1975, p. 3; *Church of England Newspaper*, 9 May 1975, p. 4. See also *The Tablet*, 1 February 1975, p. 97.

26. *Church Times*, 30 May 1975, p. 11.

27. *Church of England Newspaper*, 2 May 1975, p. 1.

28. 'Vision of Europe': day seminar at Coventry Cathedral organised by the Coventry Council of Churches, 22 May 1975, BIE 1/10. Letter from Gordon Landreth, general secretary of the Evangelical Alliance, *Church of England Newspaper*, 30 May 1975, p. 9; *Church Times*, 30 May 1975, p. 12.

29. Advert, *Church of England Newspaper*, 30 May 1975, p. 1.

30. 'Anti-Marketeers in Scotland: Enemy Action', 22 April 1975, BIE 1/79.

31. *Methodist Recorder*, 24 April 1975, p. 7.

32. 'Resolution passed at meeting of the Assembly of the British Council of Churches', 23 April 1975', BIE 1/10.

33. The debate, he added, 'is about the Common Market and not Europe and I am surprised that Christians condone this misleading propaganda'. Neil Marten to Archbishop of Canterbury, no date, Marten Papers c.1132, f. 190.

34. Matthew 22:21; Mark 12:17; Luke 20:25.

35. J. Enoch Powell, *No Easy Answers* (Sheldon Press: London, 1973), pp. 56–7.

36. For Powell's account of his own religious history, see *No Easy Answers*, pp. 2–6; J. Enoch Powell, *The Evolution of the Gospel: A New Translation of the First Gospel, with Commentary and Introductory Essay* (London: Yale University Press, 1994), pp. 205–7. Powell thought it more likely that Jesus had been killed by stoning.

37. J. Enoch Powell, 'Crown and Canon: An Address to the Annual General Meeting of the Prayer Book Society' [26 June 1993], *The Churchman*, 107:3 (1993), p. 269.

38. Alan M. Suggate, 'The Christian Churches in England since 1945: Ecumenism and Social Concern', in S. Gilley and W.J. Sheils (eds.), *A History of Religion in Britain: Practice and Belief from pre-Roman Times to the Present* (Oxford: Blackwell, 1994), p. 478.

39. *Church Times*, 3 September 1971, p. 11. Milligan later became the Archbishop of Canterbury's special representative to the European Institutions in Strasburg. See Milligan, *The Bridge*.

40. [Catholic Institute for International Relations,] *Comment 5: Church and Politics* [no date].

41. *Methodist Recorder*, 6 March 1975, pp. 6–7.

42. *Church Times*, 30 May 1975, pp. 11, 13.

43. For Edwards and his milieu, see Sam Brewitt-Taylor, '"Christian Radicalism" in the Church of England, 1957–70', unpublished Oxford D.Phil. thesis (2012).

44. *Church Times*, 4 April 1975, p. 3; *Methodist Recorder*, 6 March 1975, pp. 6–7.

45. *Christians and the Common Market: A Report Presented to the British Council of Churches* (London, 1967), pp. 10–11.

46. 'God is for Europe', *The Economist*, 26 April 1975, p. 42.

47. *Methodist Recorder*, 6 March 1975, pp. 6–7.

48. *Comment 25: Britain & Europe* (1971).

49. *Christians and the Common Market*, p. 17.

50. *Church Times*, 30 May 1975, p. 10.

51. Ronald Williams, quoted in *Church of England Newspaper*, 2 May 1975, p. 1.

52. *The Tablet*, 31 May 1975, pp. 499–500.

53. *Britain in Europe: The Social Responsibility of the Church*, pp. 3–4.

54. *Jewish Chronicle*, 30 May 1975, p. 14. The rival *Jewish Telegraph* provided almost no coverage of the referendum.

55. *Britain in Europe: The Social Responsibility of the Church*, pp. 12, 17.

56. Milligan, *The Bridge*, pp. 57–61; *Church Times*, 1 December 1978, p. 2.

57. *Church of England Newspaper*, 30 May 1975, p. 5.

58. *Britain in Europe: The Social Responsibility of the Church*, pp. 3, 17.

59. 'Which Way Now?', enclosed with Kenneth Johnstone to Con O'Neill, 20 May 1975, BIE 1/10.

60. *Church Times*, 27 March 1975, pp. 1, 20.

61. *Going Into Europe*.

62. John Selwyn Gummer, 'The Churches and the Referendum – a Preliminary Report', 1974, BIE 19/53.

63. *Church of England Newspaper*, 7 March 1975, p. 1.

64. Ibid., 2 May 1975, p. 1.

65. *Church Times*, 30 May 1975, p. 10.

66. *Church of England Newspaper*, 23 May 1975, p. 1.

67. *Church Times*, 30 May 1975, p. 11.

68. 'Methodists Urged to Back EEC', *Hull Daily Mail*, 6 May 1975, in BIE 19/53.

69. Ward, 'Europe Preserved', pp. 499–500.

70. *Church Times*, 30 May 1975, p. 1.

71. Ibid., p. 11.

72. Ibid., 7 March 1975, p. 1; *Church of England Newspaper*, 7 March 1975, p. 1.

73. Christopher Hill and E.J. Yarnold (eds.), *Anglicans and Roman Catholics: The Search for Unity* (London: SPCK, 1994), pp. 3–11.

74. Methodists voted for unity in 1969 and 1972, but the proposals failed to achieve the necessary majority in the Anglican synod. See David Carter,

'Methodists and the Ecumenical Task', in J. Morris and N. Sagovsky, *The Unity We Have and the Unity We Seek: Prospects for the Third Millennium* (London: T & T. Clark, 2003), pp. 54–5.

75. For the long relationship between ecumenism and the European movement – and the hopes vested in European institutions as a focus for ecumenical activity – see Leustean, *Ecumenical Movement*.

76. *Church Times*, 27 March 1975, pp. 1, 20; *Church of England Newspaper*, 2 May 1975, p. 1.

77. John Selwyn Gummer: 'Second Report on the Churches and the Referendum', BIE 1/10, 23 January 1975.

78. H. van Dusen, 'General Introduction' to *The Universal Church in God's Design: an Ecumenical Study Prepared under the Auspices of the World Council of Churches* (London: WCC, 1948), pp. 9–10, quoted in Brewitt-Taylor, '"Christian Radicalism"', pp. 215–16.

79. *Christians and the Common Market*, p. 18.

80. *Church Times*, 27 March 1975, pp. 1, 20.

81. *Methodist Recorder*, 6 March 1975, pp. 6–7.

82. *Church Times*, 4 April 1975, p. 3.

83. Rev. Cyprian Dymoke-Marr, *Church Times*, 12 April 1975, p. 12.

84. The role of the churches in the later Cold War remains understudied; for the earlier period, see Ian Jones, 'The Clergy, the Cold War and the Mission of the Local Church; England, ca. 1940–60', in Dianne Kirby (ed.), *Religion and the Cold War* (Basingstoke: Palgrave Macmillan, 2002/2013); Dianne Kirby, 'Ecclesiastical McCarthyism: Cold War Repression in the Church of England', *Contemporary British History*, 19:2 (2005), 187–203.

85. *Church of England Newspaper*, 23 May 1975, p. 1.

86. *The Tablet*, 15 March 1975, p. 241. Cold War influences also weighed heavily with some evangelical groups, who might otherwise have been wary of the Community's Catholic populations. The Prophetic Witness Movement, for example, hailed the Community as a 'bulwark against Communism'. *Church of England Newspaper*, 30 May 1975, p. 3.

87. *Jewish Chronicle*, 3 January 1975, p. 5; 31 January 1975, p. 3; 16 May 1975, pp. 1, 16; 30 May 1975, p. 14. For Arab states' anger at the treaty, see *The Economist*, 24 May 1975, p. 33.

88. *Church of England Newspaper*, 30 May 1975, p. 5; 'Preface', *Crockford's Clerical Directory, 1973–74*, 85th issue (Oxford: Church Commissioners, 1975), pp. xvi–xvii. The (anonymous) authors claimed that Labour had abandoned 'the kind of socialism which was taught by Christian thinkers such as F.D. Maurice, Bishops Westcott and Gore, Scott Holland and Archbishop Temple', in favour of an emphasis 'on conflict and on restricting freedom of choice'. *Church of England Newspaper*, 2 May 1975, p. 5.

89. *Liverpool Daily Post*, 28 May 1975, p. 5.

90. *The Scotsman*, 23 May 1975, p. 15. For Paisleyism, see Chapter 11.

91. Barry Lynch, *Church Times*, 4 April 1975, p. 12.

92. Ibid.

93. *Resistance News*, no. 17 (May, 1975), p. 3.

94. *Catholic Herald*, 30 May 1975, p. 1.

95. Edward Charles, *Church Times*, 16 May 1975, p. 13.

96. *Church of England Newspaper*, 30 May 1975, p. 9.

97. *Catholic Herald*, 30 May 1975, p. 1.

98. Barry Lynch, *Church Times*, 4 April 1975, p. 12.

99. Canon Edward Charles, *Church Times*, 16 May 1975, p. 13; *Church of England Newspaper*, 30 May 1975, p. 3.

100. *Catholic Herald*, 30 May 1975, p. 1.

101. *Liverpool Daily Post*, 28 May 1975, p. 5.

102. Matthew Grimley, 'Anglican Evangelicals and Anti-Permissiveness: The Nationwide Festival of Light 1971–1983', in A. Atherstone and J. Maiden (eds.), *Evangelicalism and the Church of England in the Twentieth Century: Reform, Resistance and Renewal* (London: Boydell Press, 2014), pp. 192–3.

103. Bernard Palmer to Hugh Hanning, 6 February 1975, CERC, BSR/IAC/EUR/2/2. For claims of bias, see letter from Canon Edward Charles, *Church Times*, 16 May 1975, p. 13.

104. *Catholic Herald*, 23 May 1975, p. 1.

105. *The Tablet*, 15 February 1975, p. 147; 31 May 1975, p. 499; *Catholic Herald*, 23 May 1975, p. 1; 30 May 1975, p. 4.

8 'No Good Talking About Sovereignty'

1. Speech at Withington, Manchester, 8 May 1975, BIE 19/49(b).

2. *Labour and the Common Market*, p. 40.

3. *Manchester Evening News*, 21 May 1975, p. 10.

4. *Hansard* 596, 9 June 2015, 1047.

5. *Hansard* 596, 9 June 2015, 1047–8. (Hammond was actually nineteen at the time.) See also Ken Clarke, *Kind of Blue: A Political Memoir* (Basingstoke: Macmillan, 2016), pp. 86–8.

6. Nigel Farage, 'A Referendum Stitch-Up? How the EU and British Elites are Plotting to Fix the Result' (2012), p. 8, www.ukipmeps.org/uploads/file/ReferendumStichUp.pdf; Juliet Lodge, 'Britain and the EU: Exit, Voice and Loyalty Revisited – Public Diplomacy Failure?' in Baimbridge (ed.), *1975 Referendum*, vol. 1, p. 92.

7. Chris Gifford, *The Making of Eurosceptic Britain*, second edition (Farnham: Ashgate, 2014), p. 71.

8. *Hansard* 888, 11 March 1975, 366.

9. *Morning Star*, 5 June 1975, p. 1.

10. Speech in Hendon, 19 May 1975, http://margaretthatcher.org/document/102692.

11. Speech at Withington, Manchester, 8 May 1975, BIE 19/49(b).

12. Broad and Geiger, 'Witness Seminar', p. 99.

13. Ibid., p. 100 (quoting Patrick Nairne, who led the Cabinet Office European Unit).

14. William Pickles, *Where Do We Come In? Your Rights and the Common Market* (London: GBO, [1975?]), NRC/1. Pickles was a lecturer at the London School of Economics and the author of *Not with Europe: The Political Case for Staying Out* (Fabian Tract 336; London: Fabian International Bureau, 1962).

15. *Bristol Evening Post*, 4 June 1975, p. 4.

16. *Sunday Telegraph*, 16 March 1975, p. 19.

17. A.V. Dicey, *Introduction to the Study of the Law of the Constitution* [1885], eighth edition (London: Macmillan, 1915), p. 38. The latter quote was attributed to Lord Burleigh by Algernon Sidney; Angus Hawkins, *Victorian Political Culture: 'Habits of Heart and Mind'* (Oxford: Oxford University Press, 2015), p. 29. For a brief survey of Victorian constitutional thought, see Robert Saunders, 'Parliament and People: The British Constitution in the Long Nineteenth Century', *Journal of Modern European History*, 6 (2008); Hawkins, *Victorian Political Culture*; Pavlos Eleftheriadis, 'Parliamentary Sovereignty and the Constitution', Oxford Legal Studies Research Paper No. 45 (2009).

18. Saunders, 'Parliament and People'.

19. A.V. Dicey, *A Fool's Paradise: Being A Constitutionalist's Criticism on the Home Rule Bill of 1912* (London: Macmillan, 1913), p. 117. For the constitutional arguments against Home Rule, see Saunders, 'Tory Rebels and Tory Democracy'.

20. Dale (ed.), *Labour Party General Election Manifestos*, p. 199.

21. See, for example, *Housewives Today*, 27:4 (January 1975), pp. 4–5.

22. GBO, 'Possible discussion points', CIB 10/2 GBO; *The Guardian*, 2 June 1975, p. 13.

23. 'The Common Market: Why We Object. Statement by Dissenting Ministers', 17 March 1975, MS Castle 306, f. 217.

24. *Questions & Answers For Speakers* (London: NRC, 1975), p. 1 ('What does sovereignty mean?'), NRC/1.

25. Minutes of a meeting of female MPs and Peers, 29 April 1975, BIE 26/2.

26. *South Wales Echo*, 4 April 1975, p. 14.

27. *Hansard* 831, 15 February 1972, 278, cited in F.A. Trindade, 'Parliamentary Sovereignty and the Primacy of European Community Law', *Modern Law Review*, 35:4 (1972), p. 375.

28. 'What is Sovereignty?', BIE, *Weekly Briefing*, No. 1 (3 March 1975), BIE 22/5.

29. *The Sun*, 11 April 1975, p. 6.

30. TGWU *Record* (February 1975), pp. 8–9.

31. Ralph Miliband, *Parliamentary Socialism: A Study in the Politics of Labour* [1972] (Pontypool: Merlin, 2009), p. 13.

32. *Bristol Evening Post*, 30 May 1975, p. 2.

33. *1975 Referendum: The Common Market: IN or OUT* (Labour Research Department, March 1975), p. 30; 'The Common Market: Why We Object', MS Castle 306, ff. 216–17.

34. Statement by the Get Britain Out Referendum Campaign, *ASTMS Journal* (January–February 1975), p. 5.

35. 'The Scales are Weighted Against Us', *TUC Information Broadsheet*, May 1975, Marten Papers, c.1155/21.

36. *Labour and the Common Market*, p. 41.

37. Referendum campaign broadcast by the NRC, BBC1, 3 June 1975, NRC/1.

38. Benn, *Against the Tide*, 18 March 1975, pp. 329 (27 February 1975), 343 (18 March 1975).

39. Judith Hart, Speech to the Fire Brigades Union, Bridlington, 7 May 1975, Hart Papers, HART/10/11; TGWU *Record*, April 1975, p. 7. See also *Financial Times*, 2 June 1975, p. 7.

40. Benn, *Against the Tide*, pp. 253 (31 October 1974), 292 (31 December 1974), 343 (18 March 1975).

41. T. Benn, *Arguments for Democracy*, ed. Chris Mullin (London: Cape, 1981), p. 6; *The Independent*, 27 June 1999.

42. Benn, *Against the Tide*, pp. 253 (31 October 1974), 264 (15 November 1974), 270 (21 November 1974), 276 (28 November 1974).

43. Speech at West Bromwich, 17 May 1975, Powell Papers POLL/4/1/11/5.

44. Speech at Hornsey, 22 February 1975, Powell Papers POLL/4/1/11/6.

45. 'True history is concerned with the life of nations, with their birth, their fortunes, and their death. All else is chronicle': Enoch Powell and Angus Maude, *Biography of a Nation*, second edition (London: John Baker, 1970), p. 7.

46. Speech at Sidcup, 4 June 1975, Powell Papers, POLL/4/1/11/4.

47. Powell and Maude, *Biography of a Nation*, p. 238.

48. Speech at Iveagh, County Down, 25 January 1975, Powell Papers, POLL/4/1/11/6.

49. Speech at Bournemouth, 10 May 1975, Powell Papers, POLL/4/1/11/5.

50. Speech at the Reform Club, 31 January 1975, Powell Papers, POLL/4/1/11/6.

51. *Sunday Telegraph*, 16 March 1975, p. 19.

52. NRC, 'Concerned about your FREEDOM?', LSE CIB 9/2.

53. Air Vice-Marshal Don Bennett, '10 Points on the Common Market' [flier] NRC/1.

54. *On Target* [British League of Rights], 6:23, 10 May 1975, Marten Papers c.1132, f. 2a.

55. *The Tablet*, 31 May 1975, pp. 499–500; *Birmingham Post*, 5 June 1975, p. 8; *A Question of Europe*, BBC1, 3 June 1975.

56. Britain in Europe, *Weekly Briefing*, no. 14 (26 May 1975), p. 6.

57. Lord Denning, 'H.P. Bulmer Ltd and another v. J. Bollinger SA and others' (22 May 1974), *All England Law Reports* (1974), vol. 2, pp. 1231–2.

58. Roy Hattersley, speech in Bristol, 6 January 1975, BIE 18/1, p. 18.

59. Britain in Europe, *Weekly Briefing*, No. 14 (26 May 1975), p. 6 ('Lord Chancellor says Parliament's Sovereignty not Affected'), BIE 22/5.

60. *Liverpool Daily Post*, 4 June 1975, p. 6.

61. *Speaking Notes: Britain in Europe* (Conservative Central Office, 1975), BIE 14/2.

62. Peter Blaker, 'Labour's "Renegotiation" Policy: A Conservative View', 28 June 1974, Conservative Party Archive, Bodleian Library, Oxford, LCC/74/27, p. 7.

63. *The Economist*, 15 March 1975, p. 25.

64. 'Women's Section Briefing Notes', BIE 26/3.

65. 'George Thomson Says Scotland Says YES to Europe', BIE 1/79.

66. 'Young European Federalists' [flyer], BIE 15/1. YEF was an alliance made up of Students for a United Europe, Young European Left, Young European Democrats and Radical Youth for Europe.

67. *The Scotsman*, 31 May 1975, p. 5.

68. Quoted in P. Ludlow, 'Safeguarding British Identity or Betraying It? The Role of British "Tradition" in the Parliamentary Great Debate on EC Membership, October 1971', *Journal of Common Market Studies*, 53:1 (2015), p. 29.

69. Hattersley, 'Speech to the Annual Meeting of the Association of Contemporary European Studies', BIE 1/81, p. 4.

70. *Western Mail* (Wales edition), 4 June 1975, p. 6.

71. *Hansard* 889, 9 April 1975, 1282.

72. *The Times*, 1 August 1970, p. 13.

73. *The Economist*, 1 March 1975, pp. 11–12; 31 May 1975, p. 8; 'Labour's Case for Europe' [flyer], BIE 15/1; 'George Thomson Says Scotland Says YES to Europe', p. 6, BIE 1/79.

74. Geoffrey Rippon, *Our Future in Europe* (CPC: September 1974), quoted in Ben Patterson, *The Conservative Party and Europe* (London: John Harper, 2011), p. 88.

75. Margaret Thatcher, 'Our duty is to make it "Yes"', *Conservative Monthly News*, April 1975, p. 7.

76. Max Weber, 'Politics as a Vocation' (1918), in H.H. Gerth and C. Wright Mills (eds.), *From Max Weber: Essays in Sociology* (Abingdon: Routledge, 2009), p. 78.

77. Christopher Soames, *The Director*, January 1975, p. 102.

78. TUC–Labour Party Liaison Committee. 'The EEC Renegotiations. A Note on the Commitments' (Labour Party Research Department, 1975), f. 164. This paper was circulated to all delegates at Labour's Special Conference in April.

79. NRC, *Questions & Answers for Speakers* (NRC, 1975), NRC/1, p. 1; GBORC, *Talking Points No: 10*, 20 May 1975, Marten Papers, c.1132, ff. 34–41.

80. J. Enoch Powell, 'The Nature of Sovereignty', in Douglas Evans and Richard Body (eds.), *Freedom and Stability in the World Economy* (London: Croom Helm, 1976), p. 89.

81. *Labour and the Common Market*, pp. 16, 40–1.

82. *The Times*, 27 March 1975, p. 8.

83. GBORC, *Talking Points No. 10*, 20 May 1975, p. 8, Marten Papers 1132, 34–41; NRC, *Questions & Answers For Speakers*, NRC/1.

84. 'Poll Assessment, 25 May 1975', Marten Papers 1133, ff. 99–100.

85. 'Notes on NOP survey', Marten Papers 1133, ff. 97–8.

86. Broad and Geiger (eds.), 'Witness Seminar', p. 98, quoting a memorandum written by Worcester on 16 May 1975.

87. Broad and Geiger (eds.), 'Witness Seminar', pp. 98–100.

88. James Callaghan, 'EEC Referendum: The Campaign as we Move into the Last Week', 28 May 1975, BIE 15/49.

89. *Birmingham Post*, 2 June 1975, p. 6.

90. 'Television Programmes', 6 May 1975, Marten Papers, c.1132, f. 12.

91. Powell, 'Nature of Sovereignty', p. 88.

92. 'Draft for Discussion', NRC Memorandum [n.d. 1975], quoted in Richardson, 'Non-Party Organisations', p. 193.

93. For food prices, see Chapter 10.

94. Benn, *Against the Tide*, 5 November 1974, p. 259; 9 February 1975, p. 313; see also 17 November 1975, p. 265.

95. *Church Times*, 27 March 1975, p. 1.

96. *The Sun*, 11 April 1975, p. 6; ORC poll, conducted 24–27 May 1975, published in the *Scotsman*, 3 June 1975, p. 11.

97. Young Conservatives, 'Keep Britain in Europe – Don't Pull Out', BIE 26/13.

98. Powell, 'Nature of Sovereignty', p. 88.

9 'The New British Empire'

1. *The Sun*, 10 March 1975, p. 9.

2. *The Guardian*, 5 June 1975, p. 9.

3. 'Prime Minister's Press Conference, Kingston', 4 May 1975, Department of Foreign Affairs News Release, Transcript 3729, https://pmtranscripts.pmc .gov.au/release/transcript-3729.

4. Max Beloff, 'The Commonwealth as History', *Journal of Imperial and Commonwealth History*, 1:1 (1972), pp. 107, 111. My emphasis. S. Dubow,

'The Commonwealth and South Africa: From Smuts to Mandela', *Journal of Imperial and Commonwealth History*, 45:2 (2017), p. 285.

5. *Hansard* 645, 31 July 1961, 928.

6. Speech at Brighton, 19 January 1975, quoted in Grob-Fitzgibbon, *Continental Drift*, p. 390.

7. NRC, *Why You Should Vote No*, reproduced in Butler and Kitzinger, *1975 Referendum*, p. 303.

8. *The Sun*, 4 June 1975, p. 6.

9. *Belfast Newsletter*, 16 May 1975, p. 2.

10. See, for example, Nadine El-Enany, 'Brexit as Nostalgia for Empire', *Compass*, 21 June 2016, www.compassonline.org.uk/brexit-as-nostalgia-for-empire/; Evan Smith and Steven Gray, 'Brexit, Imperial Nostalgia and the "White Man's World"', *History & Policy*, 20 June 2016, www.historyandpolicy .org/opinion-articles/articles/brexit-imperial-nostalgia-and-the-white-mans-world; Shaj Matthew, 'Brexit exposes Britain's massive inferiority complex', *New Republic*, 22 June 2016, https://newrepublic.com/article/134513/ brexit-exposes-britains-massive-inferiority-complex.

11. Schofield, *Enoch Powell*, pp. 113, 172.

12. For 'de-dominionisation' (a term coined in the 1970s), see A.G. Hopkins, 'Rethinking Decolonization', *Past & Present*, 200 (2008), 211–47; Philip Murphy, *Monarchy and the End of Empire: The House of Windsor, the British Government, and the Postwar Commonwealth* (Oxford: Oxford University Press, 2013), ch. 9; J. Davidson, 'The De-Dominionisation of Australia', *Meanjin*, 38:2 (1979), 139–53.

13. John Darwin, *Britain and Decolonisation: The Retreat from Empire in the Post-War World* (Basingstoke: Macmillan, 1988), p. 324.

14. Quoted in Schofield, *Enoch Powell*, p. 76.

15. This is not to say that those effects were not real or profound. The impact of decolonisation is a fiercely contested topic that lies beyond the remit of this study, but notable contributions include: David Cannadine, *Ornamentalism: How the British Saw Their Empire* (London: Penguin, 2001); Catherine Hall and Sonya O. Rose (eds.), *At Home with the Empire: Metropolitan Culture and the Imperial World* (Cambridge: Cambridge University Press, 2006); Stephen Howe, 'Internal Decolonization? British Politics since Thatcher as Post-Colonial Trauma', *20th Century British History*, 14:3 (2003); John M. Mackenzie (ed.), *Imperialism and Popular Culture* (Manchester: Manchester University Press, 1989); Bernard Porter, *The Absent-Minded Imperialists: Empire, Society and Culture in Britain* (Oxford: Oxford University Press, 2004); Bill Schwarz, *The White Man's World* (Memories of Empire, volume 1) (Oxford University Press: Oxford, 2011); Andrew Thompson, *The Empire Strikes Back? The Impact of Imperialism on Britain from the Mid-Nineteenth Century* (London: Pearson, 2005); Andrew Thompson (ed.), *The*

British Experience of Empire in the Twentieth Century (Oxford: Oxford University Press, 2011).

16. Clement Attlee, *Empire into Commonwealth: The Chichele Lectures* (London: Oxford University Press, 1961), p. 1.

17. 'News Talk', BBC Radio, 15 August 1947, quoted in Wendy Webster, *Englishness and Empire, 1939–1965* (Oxford: Oxford University Press, 2005), p. 60.

18. *Yorkshire Post*, 12 March 1947; *Sunday Times*, 10 August 1947; quoted in Webster, *Englishness and Empire*, p. 60.

19. Schofield, *Enoch Powell*, pp. 15–16.

20. Rudyard Kipling, 'The White Man's Burden', was published in 1899; Arnold published 'Heine's Grave' in 1867.

21. 'The Myth of Empire', in J. Enoch Powell, *Reflections of a Statesman: The Writings and Speeches of Enoch Powell* (London: Bellew Publishing, 1991), p. 594.

22. Bill Schwarz, '"Englishry": The Histories of G.M. Trevelyan', in Catherine Hall and Keith McClelland (eds.), *Race, Nation and Empire: Making Histories, 1750 to the Present* (Manchester: Manchester University Press, 2010), p. 128.

23. *The Spectator*, 7 June 1975, p. 675.

24. Ashley Jackson, *The British Empire and the Second World War* (London: Hambledon, 2006), p. 1. For the forgetting of the war in the Far East, see Connelly, *We Can Take It!* pp. 248–55.

25. For the sterling area, see Catherine Schenk, *Britain and the Sterling Area: From Devaluation to Convertibility in the 1950s* (London: Routledge, 1994). For the role of the sterling area in the European debate, see S. Newton, 'Britain, the Sterling Area and European Integration, 1945–50', *Journal of Imperial and Commonwealth History*, 13:3 (1985), pp. 163–82.

26. CBI, *Industry in Europe* (May 1975), p. 6.

27. R.A.C. Parker, 'British Perceptions of Power: Europe between the Superpowers', in Josef Becker and Franz Knipping (eds.), *Power in Europe? Great Britain, France, Italy and Germany in a Postwar World, 1945–1950* (New York: De Gruyter, 1986), p. 456.

28. C. Cotton, 'The Labour Party and European Integration, 1961–1983', Ph.D. thesis, Cambridge University (2010), p. 40.

29. Gaitskell, speech to the Labour Party Conference, 3 October 1962, www.cvce.eu/content/publication/1999/1/1/05f2996b-000b-4576-8b42-8069033a16f9/publishable_en.pdf.

30. Dubow, 'Commonwealth and South Africa', p. 301.

31. *Sunday Mail* (Glasgow), 11 April 1975, p. 8.

32. See, for example, Murphy, *Monarchy and the End of Empire*; Simon Potter, *Broadcasting Empire: The BBC and the British World, 1922–1970*

(Oxford: Oxford University Press, 2012); J.F. Wilkinson, 'The BBC and Africa', *African Affairs*, 71:283 (1972), pp. 176–85; Allen Warren, 'Citizens of the Empire: Baden-Powell, Scouts and Guides, and an Imperial Ideal', in Mackenzie, *Imperialism and Popular Culture*. For the Church of England, see Chapter 7.

33. CBI, *Industry in Europe* (May 1975), p. 6. The decline was particularly marked in the Dominions: between 1950 and the early 1970s, the share of imports accounted for by Britain fell from 60 per cent to 28 per cent in New Zealand; from 50 per cent to 20 per cent in Australia; and from 41 per cent to 20 per cent in South Africa. Hopkins, 'Rethinking Decolonization', pp. 224, 237–8.

34. *Labour and the Common Market*, p. 7.

35. Clement Attlee had foreseen this problem in 1960: Attlee, *Empire into Commonwealth*, p. 50.

36. Murphy, *Monarchy and the End of Empire*, p. 108.

37. Phillip R. Alexander, 'The Labour Government, Commonwealth Policy and the Second Application to Join the EEC, 1964–67', in Alex May (ed.), *Britain, the Commonwealth and Europe: The Commonwealth and Britain's Applications to Join the European Communities* (Basingstoke: Palgrave, 2001), p. 141.

38. Dubow, 'Commonwealth and South Africa', p. 301.

39. Murphy, *Monarchy and the End of Empire*, pp. 10–11.

40. Cotton, 'Labour Party', p. 53.

41. Schofield, *Enoch Powell*, p. 158.

42. 1971 White Paper, 'The United Kingdom and the European Communities', in Darwin, *Britain and Decolonisation*, p. 324.

43. Brown, *In My Way*, p. 201.

44. For a case study, see Lindsay Aqui, 'Macmillan, Nkrumah and the 1961 Application for European Economic Community Membership', *International History Review*, 39:4 (2017), pp. 575–91. For earlier visions of 'Eurafrica', see Robert Heywood, 'West European Community and the Eurafrica Concept in the 1950s', *Journal of European Integration*, 4:2 (1981), pp. 199–210; P. Hansen and S. Jonsson, 'Bringing Africa as a "Dowry to Europe": European Integration and the Eurafrica Project, 1920–1960', *Interventions: International Journal of Postcolonial Studies*, 13:3 (2011), pp. 443–63; P. Hansen and S. Jonsson, *Eurafrica: The Untold History of European Integration and Colonialism* (London: Bloomsbury, 2014).

45. Alexander, 'The Labour Government', pp. 144–5. For the shift from Yaoundé to Lomé, see Obadiah Mailafia, *Europe and Economic Reform in Africa: Structural Adjustment and Economic Diplomacy* (London: Routledge, 1997), chs. 3–4.

46. Letter from Norman Hart, *Tribune*, 29 June 1961, quoted in Cotton, 'Labour Party', p. 48. Hart repeated the allegation in 1969, accusing anti-Marketeers

of 'latter day imperialism' (p. 103). See also Christopher Cotton, 'Labour, European Integration and the Post-Imperial Mind, 1960–75', in B. Frank, C. Horner and D. Stewart (eds.), *The British Labour Movement and Imperialism* (Newcastle upon Tyne: Cambridge Scholars Press, 2010).

47. Cotton, 'Labour Party', p. 49; *The Guardian*, 2 June 1975, p. 12.
48. *Scottish Daily Express*, 3 May 1975, p. 8.
49. Roy Jenkins, *A Life at the Centre* (Basingstoke: Macmillan, 1991), pp. 224–5.
50. Brown, *In My Way*, p. 209.
51. *The Sun*, 10 March 1975, p. 9.
52. Referendum Information Unit, 'Advantages of Staying in the Common Market', May 1975, BIE 15/72.
53. Quoted in Grob-Fitzgibbon, *Continental Drift*, p. 384.
54. Press cutting from [Slough] *Evening Mail*, 19 May 1975, BIE 26/9.
55. Speech at Sutton, Ashfield (Notts), 27 May 1975, BIE 19/49a. Owen did, however, acknowledge that in the shift from empire to Common Market, 'Britain has had to shatter some of her most precious illusions about herself.'
56. *Daily Mail*, 4 June 1975, p. 31.
57. Speech to London University Conservative Association, House of Commons, 7 March 1975, Conservative Central Office News Service, 206/75. Strikingly, when Thatcher gave the famous 'Bruges speech' in 1988, she chose Europe's colonial heritage as one of the few areas for praise: 'the story of how Europeans explored and colonised – and yes, without apology – civilised much of the world is an extraordinary tale of talent, skill and courage'; 'Speech to the College of Europe', 20 September 1988, www.margaret-thatcher.org/document/107332.
58. *The Ideals of Empire: Political and Economic Thought, 1903–1911* (6 volumes), edited and introduced by Ewen Green (London: Routledge, 1998), volume 1, p. x.
59. Speech in Glasgow, 2 June 1975, MS Wilson c.1267, ff. 134–5.
60. Margaret Thatcher, Speech to London University Conservative Association, 7 March 1975, Conservative Central Office News Service, 206/75; Shirley Williams, BBC *Midweek*, 10 April 1975, quoted in Cotton, 'Labour Party', p. 63.
61. Benn, *Against the Tide*, p. 143 (25 April 1974).
62. *Belfast Newsletter*, 13 May 1975, p. 4.
63. *The Spectator*, 7 June 1975, p. 675.
64. Webster, *Englishness and Empire*, p. 178; Schofield, *Enoch Powell*, pp. 55, 78.
65. *The Times*, 2 April 1964, p. 13; Schofield, *Enoch Powell*, pp. 101, 113, 172, 198.
66. Quoted in Schofield, *Enoch Powell*, p. 277.
67. Schofield, *Enoch Powell*, p. 288.

68. *The Times*, 2 April 1964, p. 13.
69. Speech to the 1964 Committee, Trinity College, Dublin, 13 November 1964, Powell Papers, POLL/4/1/1/3.
70. Schofield, *Enoch Powell*, p. 149.
71. Speech to the 1964 Committee, Trinity College, Dublin, 13 November 1964, Powell Papers, POLL/4/1/1/3.
72. Speech at the St George's Day Banquet, 22 April 1961, Powell Papers POLL/4/1/1/6.
73. Schofield, *Enoch Powell*, p. 162.
74. Speech to the 1964 Committee, Trinity College, Dublin, 13 November 1964, Powell Papers, POLL/4/1/1/3.
75. Speech at Blackpool, 31 May 1975; speech at Bournemouth; Powell Papers, POLL 4/1/11/5; Schofield, *Enoch Powell*, p. 161.
76. Schofield, *Enoch Powell*, p. 31.
77. Powell, 'The Great American Dilemma', *Sunday Telegraph*, 17 March 1968, in Schofield, *Enoch Powell*, p. 73.
78. Schofield, *Enoch Powell*, pp. 84, 294.
79. Speech at the St George's Day Banquet, 22 April 1961, Powell Papers POLL/4/1/1/6.
80. Schofield, *Enoch Powell*, p. 168. For the character of this nationhood – whether English, British or Ulster – see Paul Corthorn, 'Enoch Powell, Ulster Unionism and the British Nation', *Journal of British Studies*, 51:4 (2012), 967–97.
81. Webster, *Englishness and Empire*, p. 174.
82. Quoted in Aqui, 'Macmillan, Nkrumah', p. 579.
83. Stuart Ward, 'A Matter of Preference: The EEC and the Erosion of the Old Commonwealth Relationship', in May (ed.), *Britain, the Commonwealth and Europe*, pp. 162, 168.
84. 'Policy Guidance Document for Publications and Speaker Briefing', 5 March 1975, BIE 15/49.
85. Hedges, 'The Final Four Years', in Jowell and Hoinville (eds.), *Britain into Europe*, p. 59.
86. For the cinematic tendency to portray the imperial contribution in wartime as mainly white, see Webster, *Englishness and Empire*, esp. chs. 1–2.
87. For Trudeau, see the *Guardian*, 10 March 1975, p. 3; 12 March 1975, p. 3; for Rowling, see Chapter 2 above. For Whitlam, see 'Prime Minister's Press Conference, Kingston', 4 May 1975, Department of Foreign Affairs News Release, Transcript 3729, https://pmtranscripts.pmc.gov.au/release/transcript-3729.
88. The pamphlets are reprinted in Butler and Kitzinger, *1975 Referendum*, pp. 290–304.
89. NOP surveyed 500 people by phone, 20–22 May 1975; typescript, Marten Papers c.1132; see also 'ANZAC Appeal for Britain to come out of the

Common Market', *On Target*, 6:23 (10 May 1975), Marten Papers c.1132, ff. 2a–b.

90. Butler and Kitzinger, *1975 Referendum*, p. 303.

91. See Mailafia, *Europe and Economic Reform*, ch. 3.

92. See, for example, Shirley Williams, Speech to the National Council of Women, 7 May 1975, BIE 19/49(b); George Thomson, Speech at Bristol, 17 May 1975, BIE 19/49(b); *West Indian World*, 5–12 June 1975, p. 10.

93. Cotton, 'Labour Party', p. 51.

94. Judith Hart, *The New Realities of Development: The Fourth Annual Tom Mboya Lecture, Ruskin College, Oxford, February 1975* (Dorking: Ariel Foundation, 1975), p. 6.

95. Judith Hart Cabinet memorandum, 14 March 1975, MS Castle 306, ff. 100–1; Judith Hart, Speech to the Joint Students Union, Cardiff, 12 April 1975, Hart Papers, People's History Museum, Hart/10/11; Hart, *New Realities*, pp. 7–8; Judith Hart, 'Renegotiation: The Commonwealth and Developing Countries' (no date), Marten Papers, c.1132, ff. 294–9. Neil Marten underlined the reference to a 'paternalistic and colonial approach'.

96. *Castle Diaries, 1974–76*, p. 406 (1–6 June 1975).

97. Criticism remained fairly subdued until after the referendum, but for an example see *The Scotsman*, 5 June 1975, p. 5.

98. *The Guardian*, 2 June 1975, p. 12.

99. *The Scotsman*, 30 May 1975, p. 7.

100. Cotton, 'Labour Party', p. 63.

101. *India Weekly*, 5 June 1975, p. 8; *Morning Star*, 3 June 1975, p. 3; 4 June 1975, p. 3; *Coventry Telegraph*, 30 May 1975, p. 4.

102. *West Indian World*, 30 May–5 June 1975, p. 8.

103. *Coventry Telegraph*, 30 May 1975, p. 4.

104. *Morning Star*, 3 June 1975, p. 3.

105. *India Weekly*, 12 June 1975, p. 1; *West Indian World*, 25 April–1 May 1975, p. 2.

106. *West Indian World*, 30 May–5 June 1975, p. 8.

107. *West Indian World*, 30 May–5 June 1975, p. 8; for a Muslim view, see *West Indian World*, 5–12 June 1975, p. 6.

108. See 'Immigration to and from EEC countries', briefing note by Jack Straw, 15 May 1975, MS Castle 306, f. 335.

109. *Coventry Telegraph*, 30 May 1975, p. 4; *The Guardian*, 3 June 1975, p. 28.

110. 'EEC poll leaflets in Urdu', *Daily Telegraph*, 27 May 1975, p. 6; Ernest Wistrich to Con O'Neill, 15 April 1975, 'Asians for Europe', BIE 17/18; Caroline de Courcy-Ireland to Lord Harris and Geoffrey Tucker, 22 April 1975, 'Professional Groups', BIE 17/11; de Courcy-Ireland to Rana Ashraf and to Glyn Roberts, 17 April 1975, BIE 17/18; press release: 'Leicester in Europe Commonwealth Rally', 31 May 1975, BIE 22/147; *Coventry*

Telegraph, 30 May 1975, p. 4. For translations, see BIE 19/55. 'Common Market Reggae' was written by Rudy Otter and Roger Darvill, and can be found in BIE 20/18. For its genesis, see *Asian Voice*, 31 May 2016: www.asian-voice.com/Opinion/That%E2%80%99s-our-song-again.

111. Press release: 'Leicester in Europe Commonwealth Rally', 31 May 1975, BIE 22/147.

112. 'Commonwealth Heads of Government Statement on the European Community', May 1975, MS Castle 306, f. 324.

113. *Britain's New Deal in Europe*, reprinted in Butler and Kitzinger, *1975 Referendum*, p. 297.

114. *Daily Telegraph*, 16 April 1975, p. 6.

115. *West Indian World*, 5–12 June 1975, p. 10. The speech was delivered on 4 May 1975.

116. *Daily Telegraph*, 16 April 1975, p. 6. I lack the language skills to test this assertion.

117. European Communities Commission, press release: 'European Social Fund Gives £2½m aid to Commonwealth Immigrants', 15 January 1975, BIE 22/147.

118. Speech to the Annual General Meeting of the West Midlands Area Conservative Political Centre, 20 April 1968, Powell Papers, POLL 4/1/3 file 3.

119. *West Indian World*, 7–13 March 1975, p. 1.

120. Ibid., 30 May–5 June 1975, p. 2. An editorial the following week blamed 'an unfortunate printing error', while acknowledging that the mistake 'revealed the deep heart-searching among the editorial team on the coming referendum. There was a point where we almost decided for Europe'; *West Indian World*, 5–12 June 1975, p. 2.

121. *The Guardian*, 3 June 1975, p. 28.

122. See, for example, *West Indian World*, 12–27 February 1975, p. 1; 7–13 March 1975, p. 1. The former article noted that Jenkins 'knows something about class discrimination which was as bad as race discrimination' and praised his 'very civilised achievements in the race-relations field'.

123. Benn, *Against the Tide*, pp. 368–9 (24 and 25 April 1975).

124. 'Text of Commonwealth Heads of Government Statement on the European Community', 6 May 1975, MS Castle 306, f. 324.

125. 'The Prime Minister Says "Yes"': interview with Llew Gardner, ITV, 15 May 1975, MS Wilson c.1266, ff. 133–4; Speech at Bedworth, 31 May 1975, MS Wilson c.1267, ff. 37–9.

126. *Financial Times*, 7 May 1975, p. 4.

127. Hedges, 'The Final Four Years', in Jowell and Hoinville (eds.), *Britain into Europe*, p. 59.

128. 'The Strategy of Withdrawal', 20 April 1975, MS Castle 306, ff. 278–9.

129. Darwin, *Britain and Decolonisation*, pp. 325–6.

130. *Hansard* 891, 6 May 1975, 1227–8.

131. David Russell, '"The Jolly Old Empire": Labour, the Commonwealth and Europe, 1945–51', in May (ed.), *Britain, the Commonwealth and Europe*, p. 22.

132. Darwin, *Britain and Decolonisation*, p. 334.

133. *The Economist*, 8 February 1975, p. 12; *The Sun*, 29 May 1975, p. 7.

134. Ashley Jackson, 'Empire and Beyond: The Pursuit of Overseas National Interests in the Late Twentieth Century', *English Historical Review*, 123:499 (December 2007), p. 1366.

10 'Think of It as the Common Supermarket'

1. CBI, *Talking Points no. 6: Food*, CBI MSS. 200/C/3/INT/3/50/6. James Goldsmith, chairman of Cavenham Foods Ltd, was a major fundraiser for BIE in 1975. In the 1990s he founded the Referendum Party, which campaigned for a referendum to get Britain out of the European Union.

2. *Daily Mirror*, 2 June 1975, pp. 14–15.

3. Margaret Thatcher, 'Europe: The Choice Before Us', *Daily Telegraph*, 4 June 1975, www.margaretthatcher.org/document/102701.

4. *The Times*, 24 August 1974, p. 1; *Hansard* 880, 7 November 1974, 1230–1.

5. *The Times*, 27 August 1974, p. 1; *The Guardian*, 9 July 1974, p. 6. In theory, Britain enjoyed privileged access to Caribbean produce under the Commonwealth Sugar Agreement. By 1974, however, the agreed price had fallen to less than a third of the level being paid on world markets. Not surprisingly, suppliers chose – in Tebbit's words – to 'rat' on the agreement, selling their sugar for the best price available. *The Times*, 27 August 1974, p. 11; *Hansard* 880, 7 November 1974, 1230–1. Bernard Donoughue, head of the Number 10 Policy Unit, used a diplomatic visit to Paris to stock up on sugar in case of rationing; Donoughue, *Downing Street Diary*, p. 261 (10 December 1974).

6. Advert by the Anti-Dear Food League, *The Guardian*, 2 June 1975, p. 5.

7. Thatcher, 'Remarks about Hoarding', 28 November 1974, www.margaretthatcher.org/document/101832.

8. John Martin, *The Development of Modern Agriculture: British Farming since 1931* (Basingstoke: Macmillan, 2000), p. 139.

9. This account of the CAP is drawn chiefly from Martin, *Development*, pp. 134–6; NFU, *A Review of the Common Agricultural Policy* (London: NFU, September 1973), pp. 8–9.

10. Martin, *Development*, p. 139.

11. Greenwood, *Britain and European Cooperation*, p. 69.

12. NFU, *British Agriculture and the Common Market* (London: NFU, July 1971), p. 6.

13. Lorena Ruano, 'Elites, Public Opinion and Pressure Groups: The British Position in Agriculture during Negotiations for Accession to the EC, 1961–1975', *Journal of European Integration History*, 5:1 (1999), pp. 11–12.

14. Ibid., p. 13.

15. Dale (ed.), *Labour Party General Election Manifestos*, pp. 186, 200.

16. *Hansard* 889, 7 April 1975, 827; see also 18 March 1975, 1456–9.

17. *Hansard* 889, 7 April 1975, 827; *Yorkshire Post*, 2 June 1975, p. 9; see also *The Spectator*, 7 June 1975, p. 675.

18. Speech by Sir John Winnifrith, 12 April 1975, NRC/1; see also 'Notes on Food and Food Prices', Marten Papers c.1132, f. 326; GBO 'Talking Points No. 9, May 1975', Marten Papers c.1132, ff. 68–70.

19. 'Food and Drink Industry Council Attitude Survey to European Community', 23 April 1975, BIE 2/3.

20. NOP, 'The EEC: A Summary Report Prepared for the National Referendum Campaign', 16 May 1975, Marten Papers c.1133, ff. 7, 11, 41.

21. For example, *Daily Mirror*, 5 June 1975, p. 13.

22. 'Referendum Campaign Broadcast on Behalf of the National Referendum Campaign', 23 May 1975, BBC 1, NRC/1.

23. Get Britain Out Referendum Campaign, 'EEC Makes Many Foods Dearer', NRC/2; 'CAP: Your Joint is Worth Beefing About', in GBO, *Talking Points*, No. 12 (23 May 1975), p. 5, Marten Papers c.1132, f. 58.

24. *The Guardian*, 2 June 1975, p. 13.

25. See 'Europe's Food Mountains', in GBORC, *Talking Points*, no. 10 (20 May 1975), p. 1, Marten Papers c.1132 f. 34.

26. Written answer, *Hansard* 892, 20 May 1975, 395W; Marten, speech at Kensington Town Hall, 'Wednesday evening' (no date), Marten Papers c.1132, f. 364; *Tribune*, 23 May 1975, p. 8; 30 May 1975, p. 3.

27. Enoch Powell, speech at Hornsey, 22 February 1975, Powell Papers POLL 4/1/11/6. See also the NRC's claim that 'The Six will be among the first to sell us foodstuffs at far below the cost at which they can be bought inside the EEC'; 'Statement of Policy', Shaun Stewart to NRC 'O' Group, May 1975, Marten Papers c.1132, f. 91.

28. 'Notes on Food and Food Prices', Marten Papers c.1132, f. 325. See also Peter Shore, Barbara Castle, Tony Benn, John Silkin and Judith Hart, 'The Economic Consequences of the Treaties', 4 May 1975, MS Castle 306, f. 317.

29. *The Guardian*, 30 May 1975, p. 8.

30. *Financial Times*, 23 May 1975, p. 13; 2 June 1975, p. 7.

31. *Tribune*, 23 May 1975, p. 1.

32. *British Farmer and Stockbreeder*, 4:99 (29 March 1975), p. 10; *Liverpool Daily Post*, 7 May 1975, p. 7; *Liverpool Daily Post*, 5 May 1975, p. 7.

33. NFU press release: 'Presidential Message to the Annual General Meeting of the National Farmers' Union at the London Hilton Hotel, Tuesday 21 January 1975', BIE 1/3; G.H.B. Cattell to members, 17 April 1975, BIE 17/20.

34. Christine Johnson to Ernest Wistrich, 26 July 1974, BIE 17/2.

35. *Daily Mail*, 5 June 1975, p. 9; *Financial Times*, 22 May 1975, p. 12.

36. *British Farmer and Stockbreeder*, 4:97 (1 March 1975), pp. 9–10.

37. NFU, *British Agriculture and the Common Market* (London: NFU, July 1971), pp. 3, 5, 29; *British Farmer and Stockbreeder*, 4:96 (15 February 1975), p. 3.

38. *Financial Times*, 24 May 1975, p. 12.

39. NFU, *Review of the Common Agricultural Policy*, p. 14.

40. National Farmers' Union press release: 'Presidential Message to the Annual General Meeting of the National Farmers' Union at the London Hilton Hotel, Tuesday 21 January 1975', BIE 1/3.

41. 'We did better than the Six', *British Farmer and Stockbreeder*, 4:97 (1 March 1975), pp. 9–10. In fact, Peart became a 'prize convert' to British membership; 'Why Peart changed his mind to vote Yes', *The Sun*, 27 May 1975, p. 7.

42. For the strongest statement of NUAAW opposition, see *Land Worker*, June 1975, p. 122. Previous articles and editorials had rarely come to firm conclusions, with hostile pieces tending to rely on boilerplate left-wing arguments with little connection to agriculture. See, for example, *Land Worker*, March 1975, p. 62; May 1975, p. 99.

43. *Morning Star*, 3 May 1975, p. 3; John A. Montgomery, *British Farmer and Stockbreeder*, 4:100 (12 April 1975), p. 7.

44. It was claimed in 1978 that 'not a single day passes when someone from the Ministry is not in negotiation with someone from the NFU'; quoted in Alun Howkins, *The Death of Rural England: A Social History of the Countryside since 1900* (London: Routledge, 2003), p. 157.

45. *British Farmer and Stockbreeder*, 4:100 (12 April 1975), p. 37; Ruano, 'Elites', p. 19.

46. *Financial Times*, 24 May 1975, p. 12; *British Farmer and Stockbreeder*, 4:99 (29 March 1975), p. 10; Wynn Grant, 'The Politics of the Green Pound, 1974–79', *Journal of Common Market Studies*, 19:4 (June 1981), 313–29.

47. *British Farmer and Stockbreeder*, 4:102 (10 May 1975), p. 15.

48. Martin Collins, 'Who Voted What?', in Jowell and Hoinville (eds.), *Britain into Europe*, p. 102.

49. Minutes of the Executive Committee, 7 May 1975, BIE 28/1; 'Europe Campaign Bulletin No. 3', 8 May 1975, CBI MSS. 200/C/4/1975/12.

50. Weekly Briefing, no. 11, 14 May 1975, BIE 22/5.

51. 'Food and Drink Industry Council Attitude Survey to European Community', 23 April 1975, BIE 2/3.

52. For the work of the women's office, see Chapter 6.

53. See Beers, 'Thatcher and the Women's Vote', pp. 118–19.

54. See, for example, *JS Journal*, April 1975; *St Michael's News*, May 1975.

55. For the membership, see minutes in BIE 12/2.

56. FDIC Press Release: '"Truth About Food" to be Re-established', 14 April 1975, BIE 12/1.

57. *The Times*, 7 May 1975, p. 4; Con O'Neill to Roy Jenkins, 1 May 1975, 'BIE and the Food Campaign', BIE 2/3; Invoice for Mr T. Fortescue, Food and Drink Industries Council, 22 April 1975, for 'Beliefs about the effects of the Common Market on British food', BIE 2/3.

58. *Which?* (May 1975), p. 130. The academic study was conducted by a Federal Trust for Education and Research Study Group, led by Tim Josling, Professor of Agricultural Economics at Reading University; *Yorkshire Post*, 21 May 1975, p. 6. *The Economist*, likewise, calculated that Britain had paid £25 million *less* for its grain in 1974 than it would have done outside the Community. 'The pluses and minuses for Britain from the CAP', it concluded, 'just about cancel each other out'. Quoted in CBI, *Talking Points no. 6: Food*, CBI MSS.200/C/3/INT/3/50/6.

59. Harold Wilson, speech at Manchester, 1 June 1975, MS Wilson c.1267, f. 85.

60. *Financial Times*, 29 May 1975, p. 10.

61. *The Times*, 14 March 1975, p. 8.

62. James Callaghan, paper on the renegotiations, 21 March 1975, circulated with NEC Minutes, 23 April 1975, LHASC, NEC 7/1974/75, f. 41.

63. *The Scotsman*, 30 May 1975, p. 7.

64. Women's Section Briefing Notes, BIE 26/3; *New Scientist*, 12 June 1975, p. 621.

65. 'Food and Drink Industry Council Attitude Survey to European Community', 23 April 1975, BIE 2/3.

66. James Spence, 'Movements in the Public Mood: 1961–75', in Jowell and Hoinville (eds.), *Britain into Europe*, p. 34.

67. Hedges, 'The Final Four Years', in Jowell and Hoinville (eds.), *Britain into Europe*, pp. 54–5.

68. Con O'Neill to Roy Jenkins, 'BIE and the Food Campaign', 1 May 1975, BIE 2/3. My emphasis.

69. McIntosh, *Challenge to Democracy*, p. 184 (19 December 1974).

70. 'Think of it as the Common Supermarket', BIE 18/26. For a wider study of consumer politics, which shows just how deeply embedded such approaches were in British political advertising, see Frank Trentmann, *Free Trade Nation: Commerce, Consumption and Civil Society in Modern Britain* (Oxford: Oxford University Press, 2009).

71. 'Policy Guidance Document for Publications and Speaker Briefing', 5 March 1975, BIE 15/49; Con O'Neill, speech at Edinburgh, 17 March 1975, BIE 1/79.

72. *Liverpool Daily Post*, 5 June 1975, p. 4.

73. *The Sun*, 31 May 1975, p. 7; *The Scotsman*, 21 May 1975, p. 7.

74. *Yorkshire Post*, 2 June 1975, p. 10.

75. 'YOU CAN'T TAKE YOUR FOOD FOR GRANTED ANY LONGER!', BIE 18/25.

76. FDIC, 'The Referendum Debate. Brief for speakers on behalf of the Food Industry' (May 1975), BIE 26/13.

77. *Yorkshire Post*, 2 June 1975, p. 10.

78. CBI, *Talking Points no. 6: Food*, CBI MSS. 200/C/3/INT/3/50/6; Roy Jenkins, speech in Manchester, 10 May 1975, MS Jenkins 304/213.

79. *The Sun*, 31 May 1975, p. 7.

80. *The Scotsman*, 31 May 1975, p. 5.

81. *JS Journal*, April 1975; CBI, *Talking Points no.6: Food*, CBI MSS.200/C/3/INT/3/50/6.

82. Margaret Thatcher, 'Europe: The Choice Before Us', *Daily Telegraph*, 4 June 1975, www.margaretthatcher.org/document/102701.

83. Neil Marten, speech at Worcester, 3 May 1975, Marten Papers c.1132, f. 354; GBO/NRC, *Talking Points* no. 16, 4 June 1975, p. 3, LSE CIB 9/2.

84. 'FDIC Attitude Survey to European Community', 23 April 1975, BIE 2/3.

85. See, for example, Jo Byrne, 'After the Trawl: Memory and Afterlife in the Wake of Hull's Distant-Water Fishing Industry', *International Journal of Maritime History*, 27:4 (2015), pp. 816–22. I am enormously grateful to Jo Byrne and Martin Wilcox for generously sharing their expertise on post-war fisheries.

86. O'Neill, *Britain's Entry into the European Community*, p. 246. For the accession negotiations, see pp. 242–79.

87. Sir David Hannay, 'Foreword', in O'Neill, *Britain's Entry*, p. xiv.

88. Wall, *Rejection to Referendum*, pp. 410–11.

89. *Hansard* 888, 8 April 1975, 1111 (Winifred Ewing); *The Times*, 25 March 1975, p. 17.

90. As John Silkin later noted, fishing was 'a disparate industry, or perhaps a series of industries'; *Hansard* 967, 18 May 1979, 643.

91. *The Times*, 1 April 1975, p. 1.

92. *The Times*, 2 April 1975, p. 1. The Convention was expected to extend the right of states to declare an exclusive economic zone 200 nautical miles beyond their coastlines. This would inevitably require reform of the fisheries policy, *first*, because member states would lose some of their rights in more distant waters; *second*, as the territorial waters of member states would themselves change; and *third*, because third-parties fishing less than 200 miles out would require increased regulation. See K. Seidel, 'Creating a "Blue Europe": The Common Fisheries Policy', in *The European Commission, 1973–86: History and Memories of an Institution* (Brussels: European Commission, 2014), pp. 329–30.

93. For previous 'Cod Wars', see G. Jóhannesson, 'Troubled Waters. Cod War, Fishing Disputes, and Britain's Fight for the Freedom of the High Seas, 1948–1964', Ph.D. thesis, Queen Mary University of London (2004).

94. *The Times*, 4 April 1975, pp. 1, 4.
95. *Scottish Sea Fisheries Statistics 2007* (Edinburgh: Scottish Government, 2007), p. 9, www.gov.scot/Resource/Doc/237232/0065067.pdf; *The Scottish Government's Response to the European Commission's Green Paper on Reform of the Common Fisheries Policy* (Edinburgh: Scottish Government, 2009), p. 1, www.gov.scot/Publications/2009/12/21104310/10.
96. Interview with Jim Sillars, 10 November 2015.
97. *Hansard* 888, 8 April 1975, 1083 (Russell Fairgreave).
98. Jay, *Change and Fortune*, p. 485.

11 'Ulster Says Yes!'

1. Advert published by the Free Presbyterian Church of Ulster, printed in *Belfast Newsletter*, 4 June 1975, p. 2.
2. *Belfast Newsletter*, 29 May 1975, p. 8.
3. Speech at Newtownards, 29 May 1975, Powell Papers, POLL/4/1/11/5.
4. D. McKittrick, S. Kelters, B. Feeney, C. Thornton and D. McVea (eds.), *Lost Lives: The Stories of the Men, Women and Children Who Died as a Result of the Northern Ireland Troubles* (revised edition: Edinburgh: Mainstream Publishing, 2007), p. 545.
5. Ibid., pp. 545–6.
6. Telegram from Idi Amin to Harold Wilson and Arnold Smith, 28 May 1974, The National Archives, PREM 16/148.
7. Brendan O'Leary, 'Northern Ireland', in Kevin Hickson and Anthony Seldon (eds.), *New Labour, Old Labour: The Wilson and Callaghan Governments, 1974–79* (London: Routledge, 2004), p. 242.
8. Voters had been called on in 1973 for a Border Poll, Local Government elections and Assembly elections; for two general elections in 1974; and for elections to the Constitutional Convention in 1975.
9. Turnout in Northern Ireland was just 47.5 per cent, compared to a UK average of 64.5 per cent.
10. The Official Unionists reiterated the position set out in their 1974 manifesto, which objected to the existing terms of membership, but declined to campaign in order to avoid a split. *Belfast Newsletter*, 19 May 1975, p. 1.
11. 'Unionists for Europe' shared an address with a body called 'Socialists for Europe', whose adverts appeared in the Nationalist press. It was probably little more than a letterhead, or at best an office operating from within the 'Northern Ireland in Europe' campaign. An official for the latter told me that the advert was 'probably' funded by 'Keep Northern Ireland in Europe' (private information). 'No: "Rebels" ask for break', *Belfast Newsletter*, 5 June 1975, p. 8.
12. 'UWC Strike – Text of Broadcast Made by Harold Wilson, 25 May 1974', CAIN web service, http://cain.ulst.ac.uk/events/uwc/docs/hw25574.htm.

13. D. McKittrick and D. McVea, *Making Sense of the Troubles: A History of the Northern Ireland Conflict*, revised edition (London: Penguin, 2012), p. 131.

14. *Belfast Newsletter*, 26 May 1975, p. 4.

15. E. Moxon-Browne, 'Northern Ireland', in M. Kolinsky (ed.), *Divided Loyalties: British Regional Assertion and European Integration* (Manchester: Manchester University Press, 1978), pp. 30, 33.

16. D. Ferriter, *Ambiguous Republic: Ireland in the 1970s* (London: Profile, 2012), p. 389; Gary Murphy, '"A Measurement of the Extent of Our Sovereignty at the Moment": Sovereignty and the Question of Irish Entry to the EEC, New Evidence from the Archives', *Irish Studies in International Affairs*, 12 (2001), 191–202, p. 199.

17. 'Freedom or Bondage for Britain', *Combat: The Voice of the Ulster Volunteer Force* (May 1975), *Northern Ireland Political Literature: Periodicals, 1966–1989* (Belfast: Linen Hall Library, 1993) [hereafter: NIPL], fiche 7.

18. Speech to the AGM of the Iveagh Unionist Association, 25 January 1975, Powell Papers, POLL 4/1/11/6. For Powell's insistence on a *British*, rather than *Ulster*, identity, see Corthorn, 'Enoch Powell', 967–97.

19. See, for example, speech at Bambridge, 26 May 1975, Powell Papers, POLL 4/1/11/5.

20. Speech at Newtownards, 29 May 1975, Powell Papers, POLL 4/1/11/5; *Belfast Newsletter*, 27 May 1975, p. 7; 30 May 1975, p. 8.

21. Speech at Bambridge, 26 May 1975, Powell Papers, POLL 4/1/11/5; *Protestant Telegraph*, 7 June 1975, p. 5.

22. Corthorn, 'Enoch Powell', pp. 973–4. For Powell's constitutional, rather than theological, suspicion of Catholicism, see J. Enoch Powell, 'Crown and Canon: An Address to the Annual General Meeting of the Prayer Book Society' [26 June 1993], *Churchman*, 107:3 (1993).

23. *Belfast Newsletter*, 27 May 1975, p. 7.

24. Advertisement for day of prayer and fasting at Martyrs' Memorial Free Presbyterian Church, *Belfast Newsletter*, 31 May 1975, p. 9; 'TONIGHT: Massive car cavalcade', *Belfast Newsletter*, 3 June 1975, p. 5.

25. Paisley was a founder member of the Free Presbyterian Church in 1951 acting as Moderator for the next 57 years. He founded the *Protestant Telegraph* in 1966 (closing it in 1982) and the Democratic Unionist Party in 1971.

26. *Protestant Telegraph*, 4 January 1975, p. 7; Advert published by the Free Presbyterian Church of Ulster, printed in *Belfast Newsletter*, 4 June 1975, p. 2; *Protestant Telegraph*, 1 March 1975, p. 12.

27. *Protestant Telegraph*, 4 January 1975, p. 7.

28. Ibid., 29 March 1975, pp. 6–7; 24 May 1975, p. 2. In the British Library, the *Protestant Telegraph* is bound together with *Knitting News* and the *Golden Wonder Times*, which suggests an archivist with a sense of humour.

29. *Protestant Telegraph*, 8 June 1975, p. 8.

30. *Loyalist News*, 8 February 1975, NIPL fiche 8.

31. *Belfast Newsletter*, 21 May 1975, p. 5.

32. *Loyalist News*, 15 February 1975, NIPL fiche 8.

33. Patrick Mitchel, *Evangelicalism and National Identity in Ulster, 1921–1998* (Oxford: Oxford University Press, 2003), pp. 181, 197.

34. *Belfast Newsletter*, 29 May 1975, p. 8. Erskine Holmes, who ran the Northern Ireland in Europe campaign, recalls canvassing a major Catholic employer in Belfast, who engaged him for some time in discussion. When asked how Paisley would be voting. Holmes confessed that he favoured leaving. 'That's good enough for me,' came the reply; 'I'll vote to stay in.' A generous donation followed. Interview with Erskine Holmes, 27 February 2014.

35. *Loyalist News*, 15 February 1975, NIPR f. 8.

36. *Protestant Telegraph*, 1 March 1975, p. 12.

37. Ibid., 24 May 1975, p. 2.

38. *Belfast Newsletter*, 3 June 1975, pp. 5, 7.

39. *Loyalist News*, 24 May 1975, NIPL, fiche 9.

40. *National Front*, n.d. [February? 1975], NIPL fiche 5; *British Ulsterman*, no. 4, n.d. [April? 1975], NIPL fiche 5.

41. *Protestant Telegraph*, 1 February 1975, p. 2.

42. Ibid., 24 May 1975, p. 2.

43. Moxon-Browne, 'Northern Ireland', p. 27.

44. 'The Common Market – *Why we should come out!*', *UWC* 1:2 (n.d), NIPL fiche 16.

45. Statement by Ulster Workers' Council, *Belfast Newsletter*, 14 May 1975, p. 9.

46. *Loyalist News*, 15 February 1975, NIPL fiche 8.

47. *Loyalist News*, 14 June 1975, NIPL fiche 10.

48. 'Can Ulster Survive?', *UWC Journal*, n.d. issue 1, NIPL fiche 16. See also Moxon-Browne, 'Northern Ireland', p. 27.

49. *Loyalist News*, 14 June 1975, NIPL fiche 10.

50. Ibid.

51. *Belfast Newsletter*, 15 May 1975, p. 2; 2 June 1975, p. 3.

52. *Belfast Newsletter*, 14 May 1975, p. 9; 3 June 1975, p. 2. Named after the hill where the High Kings of Ireland had once been crowned, Tara was an ultra-Loyalist organisation led by the evangelical millenarian William McGrath.

53. 'EEC Referendum – Correction', *Unfree Citizen: The Newspaper of People's Democracy*, 4: 29, NIPL fiche 34.

54. *Irish Catholic*, 6 March 1975, p. 3.

55. 'Provisional Sinn Féin Anti-EEC Press Conference', *Irish Republican Information Service [IRIS]*, 23 May 1975, p. 5, NIPL fiche 29; *Republican News*, 7 June 1975, p. 1, NIPL fiche 21.

56. *An Phoblacht*, 23 May 1975, p. 1.

57. 'Provisional Sinn Féin Anti-EEC Press Conference', *IRIS*, 23 May 1975, p. 5; NIPL fiche 29. See also Martyn Frampton, 'Sinn Féin and the European Arena: "Ourselves Alone" or "Critical Engagement"?', *Irish Studies in International Affairs*, 16 (2005), pp. 236–7.

58. *Republican News*, 7 June 1975, p. 1, NIPL fiche 21. For Scotland and Wales, see chs. 12–13.

59. 'Why the Provisional Republican Movement Oppose the E.E.C.', *IRIS*, 23 May 1975, pp. 6–7, NIPL fiche 29. This also worried the Conservative leadership, which partly explains its resistance to a referendum. See Shadow Cabinet minutes 2 December 1974, Conservative Party Archive, Bodleian Library, Oxford, LSC (74) 19.

60. For Sinn Féin's European thought, see Frampton, 'Sinn Féin and the European Arena', pp. 235–53.

61. *An Phoblacht*, 2 May 1975, p. 6. The essays centred on the 'Laudabiliter' controversy, referencing the papal bull issued by Adrian IV in 1155, which gave Henry II of England the right to govern Ireland and to reform the Irish church.

62. 'Why the Provisional Republican Movement Oppose the E.E.C.', *IRIS*, 23 May 1975, pp. 6–7, NIPL fiche 29.

63. Statement of the Belfast Comhairle Ceantair (district executive) of Sinn Féin: 'Republicans to Vote "No" in North's E.E.C. Referendum: Antithesis of Proposed New Ireland', *IRIS*, 16 May 1975, pp. 5–7, NIPL fiche 28; *Republican News*, 31 May 1975, p. 1, NIPL fiche 21.

64. 'Irish Republican Socialist Party: Press Statement', 13 December 1974, NIPL fiche 40; *Starry Plough* [magazine of the IRSP], June 1975, p. 2, NIPL fiche 40.

65. Letter to the *Belfast Newsletter*, 29 May 1975, p. 4.

66. *An Phoblacht*, 30 May 1975, p. 2.

67. For the relationship between 'Republicanism and Imperialism', see Richard Bourke, *Peace in Ireland: The War of Ideas*, second edition (London: Pimlico, 2012), Part One.

68. *Republican News*, 7 June 1975, p. 4, NIPL fiche 21; 7 June 1975, p. 1; 7 June 1975, p. 8; NIPL fiche 21.

69. 'Republicans to vote "No" in North's E.E.C. Referendum', *IRIS*, 16 May 1975, pp. 5–7.

70. *Republican News*, 7 June 1975, p. 8, NIPL fiche 21; *Starry Plough*, vol. 1 no. 3 (June 1975), p. 2, NIPL fiche 40. For the willingness of some politicians in the South to reopen the commitment to neutrality, see Ferriter, *Ambiguous Republic*, p. 388. This was a key concern for Sinn Féin: see Frampton, 'Sinn Féin and the European Arena', p. 238.

71. This constituted nearly a quarter of the £8,500 spent by Northern Ireland in Europe: Butler and Kitzinger, *1975 Referendum*, p. 156.

72. *Belfast Newsletter*, 22 May 1975, p. 3. The stickers can be found in BIE 18/27.

73. For pro-Market opinion pieces, printed with a disclaimer, see 'The Case for Retaining Membership, by a pro-Euro, pro-British Loyalist', *Combat*, June 1975, NIPL fiche 7; 'Inside Europe – Prosperity. Outside Europe – Poverty', *UWC Journal*, 1:2, NIPL fiche 16.

74. *Protestant Telegraph*, 9:25, 7 June 1975, p. 5.

75. For the debate in the Republic, see Ferriter, *Ambiguous Republic*, ch. 34, and Murphy, 'Measurement'.

76. Interview with Erskine Holmes, 27 February 2014.

77. Moxon-Browne, 'Northern Ireland', pp. 31–2.

78. *Belfast Newsletter*, 21 May 1975, p. 5.

79. *Belfast Newsletter*, 21 May 1975, p. 5; 30 May 1975, p. 8; 31 May 1975, p. 6; 3 June 1975, p. 6; 4 June 1975, p. 9.

80. Ibid., 4 June 1975, p. 7.

81. John Hume, *Personal Views: Politics, Peace and Reconciliation in Ireland* (Dublin: Town House, 1996), pp. 47, 74, 114.

82. Email from Berrie O'Neill to the author, 25 June 2017. O'Neill was also a leading figure in the Irish Association for Cultural, Economic and Social Relations, an all-Ireland body that sought to promote 'reconciliation, mutual trust and respect', so that 'reason and goodwill' might 'take the place of passion and prejudice'. www.irish-association.org/

83. *Ulster, the Left and the Future of Europe: A Manifesto* (Belfast: Northern Ireland Labour Committee for Europe and Northern Ireland Young Europe League, 1975), p. 2; BIE 18/27.

84. Interview with Erskine Holmes, 27 February 2014.

85. 'The Officials and the EEC', *Workers' Weekly* (Workers' Association Bulletin), 22 March 1975, NIPL fiche 3; 'VOTE YES!' *Workers' Weekly*, 31 May 1975, p. 1, NIPL fiche 4. The Workers' Association had rejected Bolshevism after the Russian Revolution, so was less inclined than the Communist Party of Ireland to adopt Moscow's opposition to the EEC. Publications routinely attacked the 'Stalinism' of the CPI and its faith in 'socialism in one country'.

86. *Belfast Newsletter*, 2 June 1975, p. 6; 3 June 1975, p. 8.

87. Goodhart, *Full-Hearted Consent*, p. 168.

88. 'They are going to give Europe a sporting chance', *Northern Ireland in Europe* [promotional newspaper], pp. 4–5, BIE 18/27.

89. *Belfast Newsletter*, 13 May 1975, pp. 1–2; interview with Erskine Holmes.

90. Ibid., 8 May 1975, p. 1.

91. *Combat*, June 1975, NIPL fiche 7.

92. *Belfast Newsletter*, 17 May 1975, p. 2.

93. Ibid., 1 May 1975, p. 4.

94. Ibid., 23 May 1975, p. 13; 13 May 1975, p. 2.

95. Ibid., 15 May 1975, p. 1; 2 June 1975, p. 3. For concerns that the CAP would damage Ulster farming, see *Ulsterman*, February 1975, NIPL fiche 15.

96. According to Diarmaid Ferriter, the CAP 'resulted in increased output and incomes for one-third of Irish farms. It also gave some breathing space for those farms that were struggling to survive'; Ferriter, *Ambiguous Republic*, p. 388.

97. *Belfast Newsletter*, 3 June 1975, p. 7; 4 June 1975, p. 9; 5 June 1975, p. 8.

98. Ibid., 5 May 1975, p. 5.

99. 'Women in Europe Together', *Northern Ireland in Europe* [promotional newspaper], p. 8, BIE 18/27. Sadie Patterson was another veteran of the NIPL. She had been an active trade unionist before the Second World War and campaigned for Labour in 1945. Margaret Ward, *Celebrating Belfast Women* (Belfast: WRDA, 2012), p. 3.

100. *Belfast Newsletter*, 13 May 1975, p. 1.

101. Ibid., 17 May 1975, p. 2.

102. *Combat*, June 1975, NIPL fiche 7.

103. *Belfast Newsletter*, 26 May 1975, p. 6.

104. *Combat*, June 1975, NIPL fiche 7.

105. *Belfast Newsletter*, 7 June 1975, p. 1. A total of 259,251 people voted Yes while 237,911 voted No.

106. I differ here from Moxon-Browne, who writes that 'these groups ... probably carried less weight with the voters than did the political parties, since the latter were able, in some cases, to capitalise on the affective ties of religion'; Moxon-Browne, 'Northern Ireland', p. 29.

107. *Belfast Newsletter*, 7 June 1975, p. 6.

108. *Protestant Telegraph*, 21 June 1975, p. 8; *Orange Cross*, no. 78 (n.d.), NIPL fiche 13.

109. *Belfast Newsletter*, 9 June 1975, p. 1.

12 Cymru yn Ewrop: Wales in Europe

1. *Financial Times*, 2 June 1975, p. 7.

2. Press conference for the 'Labour Campaign for Britain in Europe', 3 June 1975, BIE 1/89.

3. *South Wales Argus*, 4 June 1975, p. 3.

4. Ibid., 5 June 1975, p. 1; *Western Mail*, 6 June 1975, p. 2.

5. Butler and Kitzinger, *1975 Referendum*, pp. 266–9.

6. *Western Mail*, 9 June 1975, p. 6; *Liverpool Daily Post (Wales)*, 4 June 1975, p. 6.

7. *Power for Wales: Plaid Cymru Election Manifesto* (Cardiff: Plaid Cymru, 1974).

8. M. Johnes, *Wales since 1939* (Manchester: Manchester University Press, 2012), pp. 247–8, 251, 255.

9. Ibid., pp. 283, 294. For rugby and the singing of the anthem, see also John Morris, *Fifty Years in Politics and the Law* (Cardiff: University of Wales Press, 2011), p. 104.

10. Wil Edwards to Diana Villiers, 24 April 1975, BIE 1/89; Denis Balsom and P. J. Madgwick, 'Wales, European Integration and Devolution', in Kolinsky (ed.), *Divided Loyalties*, p. 81.

11. [Signature illegible] to Jock Bruce-Gardyne, 29 May 1975, BIE 11/4.

12. Wil Edwards to Diana Villiers, 24 April 1975, BIE 1/89.

13. Ibid.

14. Anwen Elias, *Minority Nationalist Parties and European Integration: A Comparative Study* (Oxford: Routledge, 2009), p. 48.

15. Laura McAllister, *Plaid Cymru: The Emergence of a Political Party* (Bridgend: Seren, 2001), pp. 44–53; Elias, *Minority Nationalist Parties*, pp. 45–9.

16. McAllister, *Plaid Cymru*, p. 54.

17. Elias, *Minority Nationalist Parties*, p. 48; McAllister, *Plaid Cymru*, p. 145.

18. Gwynfor Evans, *A National Future for Wales* (Swansea: Plaid Cymru, 1975), p. 9. See also See Rhys Evans, *Gwynfor: Portrait of a Patriot* (Talybont: Y Lolfa, 2008).

19. *Power for Wales: Plaid Cymru Election Manifesto*.

20. Evans, *National Future*, p. 101; *Welsh Nation*, 28 March 1975, p. 4.

21. Evans, *National Future*, pp. 100–2; *Welsh Nation*, 4 April 1975, p. 2.

22. *Welsh Nation*, 25 April 1975, pp. 4–5; R. Griffith, 'Industry and Capital in the E.E.C.', in *Wales and the Common Market* (Cardiff: Plaid Cymru Research Group, 1975), p. 10.

23. *Welsh Nation*, 28 March 1975, p. 4.

24. *Welsh Nation*, 'Referendum Special: Part 1', 16 May 1975, p. 3; 'Referendum Special: Part 2', 23 May 1975, p. 3. Evans predicted a 50 per cent cut in Welsh coal production over the next decade: *Welsh Nation*, 28 February 1975, p. 1.

25. Ieuan Wyn Jones, 'Agriculture', in *Wales and the Common Market*, p. 5.

26. *Welsh Nation*, 28 March 1975, p. 4. See also O. James, 'The EEC and Migrant Development', in *Wales and the Common Market*, p. 6.

27. Transcript of a broadcast for the National Referendum Campaign, 31 May 1975, BBC Wales, NRC/1.

28. G. Evans, 'No Voice, No Entry', *Welsh Nation*, 4 April 1975, p. 9; Evans, *National Future*, p. 101.

29. *Welsh Nation*, 'Referendum Special: Part 1', 16 April 1975, p. 7; *Welsh Nation*, 'Referendum Special: Part 2', 23 May 1975, p. 3; Phil Williams, 'Defence Policy and the E.E.C.', in *Wales and the Common Market*.

30. McAllister, *Plaid Cymru*, p. 147.

31. *Welsh Nation*, 9 May 1975, p. 12.

32. *Wales and the Common Market*.

33. Balsom and Madgwick, 'Wales, European Integration and Devolution', p. 79.

34. *Welsh Nation*, 'Referendum Special: Part 1', 16 May 1975, pp. 1–2.

35. James, 'Now's the time', p. 1; Elias, *Minority Nationalist Parties*, p. 52.

36. McAllister, *Plaid Cymru*, p. 148.

37. Robin Reeves, 'Only way for small nation to get big voice', *Welsh Nation*, 4 April 1975, p. 4. See also Geraint Talfan Davies, *At Arm's Length: Recollections and Reflections on the Arts, Media and a Young Democracy* (Bridgend: Seren, 2008), pp. 60–1. Talfan Davies recalled a meeting with the Irish foreign minister and future taoiseach, Garret FitzGerald, who 'painted for us a sophisticated picture that interwove British membership of the EEC, Ireland's aspirations for its own economy and for European regional policy, devolution in the UK and a distant resolution of the troubles in the north' (p. 61).

38. McAllister, *Plaid Cymru*, p. 57.

39. *Welsh Nation*, 'Referendum Special: Part 2', 23 May 1975, pp. 1, 3.

40. Phil Richards, 'Bureaucracy and Democracy in the E.E.C.', in *Wales and the Common Market*, p. 12.

41. Evans, *Gwynfor*, pp. 342–5.

42. [Signature illegible] to Jock Bruce-Gardyne, 29 May and 2 June 1975, BIE 11/4.

43. Interview with David Peter, 22 May 2014. The Yes vote was 70.6 per cent in Gwynedd and 74.3 per cent in Powys. The average in Wales was 66.5 per cent; Butler and Kitzinger, *1975 Referendum*, pp. 268–9.

44. Balsom and Madgwick, 'Wales, European Integration and Devolution', p. 75.

45. Michael Geddes, 'Wales and Regional Development', in *Wales and the Common Market*, p. 8.

46. 'A Foreign Policy for Plaid Cymru', 31 July 1976, in Phil Williams, *Voice from the Valleys* (Aberystwyth: Plaid Cymru, 1981), pp. 80–1.

47. Balsom and Madgwick, 'Wales, European Integration and Devolution', p. 75. For the Wales TUC, see Joe England, *The Wales TUC: 1974–2004. Devolution and Industrial Politics* (Cardiff: University of Wales Press, 2004).

48. *Western Mail*, 12 May 1975, p. 7; 10 May 1975, p. 3.

49. Ibid., 30 May 1975, p. 6. See also 12 May 1975, p. 7.

50. Johnes, *Wales since 1939*, pp. 250–1.

51. *South Wales Argus*, 4 June 1975, p. 3; Johnes, *Wales since 1939*, p. 292.

52. *Western Mail*, 30 May 1975, p. 6; 20 May 1975, p. 7; 29 May 1975, p. 3.

53. Balsom and Madgwick, 'Wales, European Integration and Devolution', p. 81.

54. *Western Mail*, 1 May 1975, p. 7.

55. Balsom and Madgwick, 'Wales, European Integration and Devolution', p. 76.

56. Quoted in A. Edwards, *Labour's Crisis: Plaid Cymru, the Conservatives and the Decline of the Labour Party in North-West Wales, 1960–74* (Cardiff: Cardiff University Press, 2011), pp. 202–3.

57. Campaign Committee minutes, 3 April 1975, BIE 1/9.

58. Wistrich to Edwards, 28 April 1975 and 7 May 1975, BIE 1/89; see also H. M. Llewellyn to Con O'Neill, 19 May 1975, BIE 1/89.

59. C. Prothero, *Recount* (Ormskirk: Hesketh, 1982), pp. 109–10.

60. Interview with David Peter, 22 May 1975.

61. *Western Mail*, 27 May 1975, p. 4.

62. Edwards to Diana Villiers, 24 April 1975, BIE 1/89.

63. *Liverpool Daily Post* (Welsh edition), 5 May 1975, p. 7; 'The Balloon Barrage', *Sheffield at War, 1939–1945*, website: www.sfbhistory.org.uk/Pages/SheffieldatWar/Page03/page03g.html; *South Wales Argus*, 30 April 1975, p. 3; 'What the butler saw, by Lord Crawshay's servant', *WalesOnline*, 6 September 2012, www.walesonline.co.uk/news/local-news/what-butler-saw-lord-crawshays-2059222.

64. Morris, *Fifty Years in Politics and the Law*.

65. John Morris, transcript of Labour Campaign for Britain in Europe press conference, 3 June 1975, BIE 1/89.

66. *Liverpool Daily Post* (Welsh edition), 3 June 1975, p. 1; Johnes, *Wales since 1939*, p. 293.

67. *South Wales Argus*, 29 May 1975, p. 3; *Western Mail*, 27 May 1975, p. 5.

68. *Western Mail*, 27 May 1975, p. 5.

69. Ibid., 29 May 1975, p. 5; *South Wales Argus*, 28 May 1975, p. 3.

70. 'Referendum on Europe: A Special Message from your Local Wales in Europe Group', 5 June 1975, BIE 18/29.

71. Morris, *Fifty Years in Politics and the Law*, ch. 3.

72. *Welsh Nation*, 'Referendum Special: Part 2', 23 May 1975, p. 1.

73. *Welsh Nation*, 30 May 1975, p. 2.

74. *Liverpool Daily Post* (Welsh edition), 7 May 1975, p. 7; *Western Mail*, 29 May 1975, p. 4.

75. Evans, *Gwynfor*, p. 347.

76. *Western Mail*, 22 May 1975, p. 7; 23 May 1975, p. 9.

77. *South Wales Argus*, 4 June 1975, p. 3.

78. M. Geddes, 'Wales and Regional Development', in *Wales and the Common Market*, p. 7.

79. *Welsh Nation*, 'Referendum Special: Part 1', 16 May 1975, p. 6.

80. *The Sun*, 1 April 1975, p. 6; Johnes, *Wales since 1939*, p. 272.

81. *South Wales Argus*, 22 May 1975, p. 1.

82. *Western Mail*, 23 May 1975, p. 9.

83. E.g. *Liverpool Daily Post* (Welsh edition), 5 June 1975, p. 7. For the letter, see *Western Mail*, 4 June 1975, p. 7.

84. *Cymru yn Ewrop* (Comisiwn y Cymunedau Ewropeaidd, 1975); *Western Mail*, 20 May 1975, p. 7.

85. *South Wales Argus*, 9 April 1975, p. 7; 27 May 1975, p. 3; 28 May 1975, p. 3.

86. *Western Mail*, 3 June 1975, p. 6; *Financial Times*, 2 June 1975, p. 7.

87. *Western Mail*, 6 June 1975, p. 1; 9 June 1975, p. 1.

88. *Liverpool Daily Post* (Welsh edition), 5 June 1975, p. 1.

89. *Financial Times*, 20 May 1975, p. 12.

90. *Liverpool Daily Post* (Welsh edition), 7 June 1975, p. 1.

91. *Western Mail*, 22 May 1975, p. 4; 5 June 1975, p. 4.

92. *Financial Times*, 2 June 1975, p. 7.

93. *Western Mail*, 9 June 1975, p. 6.

94. Ibid., p. 5.

13 'The Scottish Time-Bomb'

1. *St Andrew's Citizen*, 10 May 1975: David Torrance, *Salmond: Against the Odds*, third edition (Edinburgh: Birlinn, 2015), p. 20.

2. Con O'Neill to Donald Hardie, 3 June 1975, BIE 1/79.

3. *Financial Times*, 13 May 1975, p. 17.

4. 'Scottish Independence: Barroso Says joining EU would be "difficult"', BBC News, 16 February 2014: www.bbc.co.uk/news/uk-scotland-scotland-politics-26215963; 'President of the EC: it will be extremely difficult for iScotland [*sic*] to join the EU', *Herald*, 16 February 2014: www.heraldscotland.com/news/home-news/president-of-the-ec-it-will-be-extremely-difficult-for-iscotland-to-join-the-eu.1392553775. See also David Torrance, *The Battle for Britain: Scotland and the Independence Referendum* (London: Biteback, 2013), pp. 124–38.

5. V. Tarditi, 'The Scottish National Party's Changing Attitude towards the European Union', *Sussex European Institute Working Paper* No. 112 (Sussex European Institute, 2010): www.sussex.ac.uk/webteam/gateway/file.php?name=epern-working-paper-22.pdf&site=266.

6. Turnout, however, was lower than in England or Wales at 67.2 per cent, falling to just 56.25 per cent in Glasgow.

7. Nicola Sturgeon, remarks at Bute House, Edinburgh, 24 June 2016; https://news.gov.scot/speeches-and-briefings/first-minister-eu-referendum-result.

8. Con O'Neill to Donald Hardie, 3 June 1975, BIE 1/79; *Financial Times*, 13 May 1975, p. 17.

9. Winnie Ewing, quoted in *Scottish Daily News*, 9 May 1975, p. 7.

10. An ORC poll carried out in May 1975 found that 50 per cent of respondents thought Scotland had 'much better economic prospects than the rest of Britain', rising to 69 per cent among SNP voters. 'ORC Poll', *The Scotsman*, 3 June 1975, p. 11.

11. Bryon Criddle, 'Scotland, the EEC and Devolution', in Martin Kolinsky (ed.), *Divided Loyalties: British Regional Assertion and European Integration* (Manchester: Manchester University Press, 1978), p. 45.

12. When the Commons voted on the renegotiated terms on 9 April 1975, the 35 Scottish Labour MPs who voted divided 20 (57 per cent) to 15 (43 per cent) against the government. The margin for UK Labour as a whole was 145 (51 per cent) to 137 (49 per cent). Criddle, 'Scotland, the EEC and Devolution', p. 53.

13. For a summary of the paper's polls, see 'Scotland swings to "Yes"', *Glasgow Herald*, 2 June 1975, p. 1.

14. *Scottish Daily Express*, 1 May 1975, p. 5.

15. *The Scotsman*, 5 May 1975, p. 1; *Scottish Daily Express*, 2 June 1975, p. 1; *Glasgow Herald*, 3 June 1975, p. 3; 4 June 1975, p. 4.

16. Criddle, 'Scotland, the EEC and Devolution', p. 55; *Financial Times*, 13 May 1975, p. 17.

17. *Sunday Times*, 4 May 1975, p. 17.

18. Letter from David McLure, 'Scots and the referendum', *Financial Times*, 20 May 1975, p. 25.

19. *Daily Mail*, 5 June 1975, p. 9.

20. Criddle, 'Scotland, the EEC and Devolution', pp. 53–4.

21. Gerry Hassan, 'Jim Sillars', in James Mitchell and Gerry Hassan (eds.), *Scottish National Party Leaders*, (London: Biteback, 2016), p. 409; interview with Jim Sillars, 10 November 2015.

22. According to MacDonald, Taylor was convinced that a car following their bus was packed with Communists. The driver was actually from the *Financial Times*. *Glasgow Herald*, 4 June 1975, p. 6; *The Scotsman*, 26 May 1975, p. 4.

23. *Financial Times*, 13 May 1975, p. 17; *Glasgow Herald*, 6 May 1975, p. 2.

24. 'Anti-Marketeers in Scotland', 22 April 1975, BIE 1/79.

25. Eve Hepburn, 'Degrees of Independence: SNP Thinking in an International Context', in Gerry Hassan, *The Modern SNP: From Protest to Power* (Edinburgh: Edinburgh University Press, 2009), pp. 190–203.

26. *Scots Independent*, May 1975, p. 5.

27. 'Appendix 2', circulated with the agenda for the National Assembly Meeting on 18 January 1975, SNP Papers, National Library of Scotland [NLS], Acc. 11987/58.

28. Peter Lynch, *Minority Nationalism and European Integration* (Cardiff: University of Wales Press, 1996), pp. 25–9.

29. Christopher Harvie, 'William Wolfe', in Mitchell and Hassan (eds.), *Scottish National Party Leaders*, p. 258.

30. Interview with Gordon Wilson, 25 September 2015; *The Scotsman*, 14 May 1975, p. 6; 20 May 1975, p. 7.

31. *The Scotsman*, 20 May 1975, p. 7; 2 June 1975, p. 5; see also Gordon Wilson, *SNP: The Turbulent Years, 1960–1990* (Stirling: Scots Independent, 2009), p. 101.

32. Wilson, *SNP*, p. 101.

33. *Scottish Daily News*, 9 May 1975, p. 7 (quoting Winnie Ewing); 'Appendix 1: The E.E.C. Referendum', agenda for the National Assembly Meeting on 18 January 1975, 8 January 1975, SNP Papers, NLS Acc. 11987/58.

34. 7 February 1975, NEC Minute E75/14, quoted in Wilson, *SNP*, p. 101.

35. *The Scotsman*, 2 June 1975, p. 6.

36. *Glasgow Herald*, 2 June 1975, p. 3; Butler and Kitzinger, *1975 Referendum*, p. 98.

37. 'Paper on Scots future outside the EEC', *The Scotsman*, 20 May 1975, p. 7. The SNP agreed to circulate the document to the National Council, with the proviso that it was written in a personal capacity and did not necessarily express the views of the party; SNP Papers, NLS Acc. 10754/26, no. 179.

38. *Scots Independent*, June 1975, p. 1.

39. SNP Press Release, 8 May 1975, SNP Papers, NLS Acc. 10754/26, no. 172; *The Scotsman*, 9 May 1975, p. 6.

40. SNP Press Release, 16 May 1975, SNP Papers, NLS Acc. 10754/26, no. 176.

41. 'COMMON MARKET: Stop the sell out', SNP Papers, NLS Acc. 7295/24, [no date: 1971?].

42. Graeme Purves, 'Super-Briton', SNP Papers, NLS Acc. 7295/30.

43. SNP press release, 25 May 1975, SNP Papers, NLS Acc. 10754/26, no. 187.

44. SNP press release, 22 May 1975, SNP Papers, NLS Acc. 10754/26, no. 184 (William Wolfe); *The Scotsman*, 27 May 1975, p. 7 (Gordon Murray); William Wolfe, speech at Usher Hall, 'Scotland – European Nation or EEC Province?', SNP press release, 6 March 1975, SNP Papers, NLS Acc. 10754/26, no. 136.

45. Speech by Douglas Henderson in Aberdeen, SNP press release, 28 May 1975, SNP Papers, NLS Acc. 10754/26, no. 193.

46. SNP press releases, 11 and 28 April 1975, SNP Papers, NLS Acc. 10754/26, nos. 153, 166.

47. Speech by Winifred Ewing, SNP press release, 12 April 1975, SNP Papers, NLS Acc. 10754/26, no. 154. See also *Scots Independent*, January 1975, p. 9.

48. 'Anti-Marketeers in Scotland', 22 April 1975, BIE 1/79; Criddle, 'Scotland, the EEC and Devolution', p. 55.

49. 'Anti-Marketeers in Scotland', 22 April 1975, BIE 1/79.

50. *The Scotsman*, 27 May 1975, p. 7. Strathclyde alone accounted for nearly 48 per cent of Scottish voters. It ultimately voted Yes by 57.7 per cent to 42.3 per cent.

51. *The Economist*, 5 April 1975, p. 72; *The Scotsman*, 2 June 1975, p. 5; speech by Douglas Henderson at Aberdeen, 28 May 1975, SNP press release, SNP Papers, NLS Acc. 10754/26, no document number. See also above, Chapter 10.

52. *Scottish Daily News*, 5 May 1975, p. 11.

53. Letter from Gordon Wilson, *The Scotsman*, 28 May 1975, p. 8. It was Wilson, a future leader, who coined the slogan 'It's Scotland's oil'. 'Scotland and the EEC. Province or Nation?', 6 March 1975, SNP Papers NSL Acc. 7295/24.

54. *The Scotsman*, 5 June 1975, p. 1.

55. Ibid., 28 May 1975, p. 8; speech by Douglas Crawford, 27 May 1975, SNP press release, SNP Papers, NLS Acc. 10754/26, no. 190.

56. Interview with Gordon Wilson, 25 September 2015; interview with Jim Sillars, 10 November 2015.

57. I am grateful to Donald Hardie for sharing his memories of the campaign in an interview on 28 June 2017.

58. Donald Hardie to Con O'Neill, 2 and 5 June 1975, BIE 1/79.

59. Tam Dalyell, 'No Regrets: Then, Now or for the Future', in Baimbridge (ed.), *1975 Referendum*, vol. 1, p. 148.

60. Butler and Kitzinger, *1975 Referendum*, pp. 148–9.

61. *The Scotsman*, 27 May 1975, p. 9.

62. *Referendum on United Kingdom Membership of the European Community*, pp. 3–18.

63. To Con O'Neill, 26 February 1975, BIE 1/79.

64. Criddle, 'Scotland, the EEC and Devolution', p. 54. Douglas was another who defected to the SNP, in 1990.

65. See, for example, 'George Thomson Says Scotland Says YES to Europe', BIE 1/79.

66. Hardie thanked O'Neill 'for giving me a free hand to get on with organizing the Scottish effort', adding that 'I really do think we have been much more effective for being a separate Scots effort.' O'Neill replied: 'We have indeed tried to keep out of your hair and leave you to run your own show in Scotland.' Donald Hardie to Con O'Neill, 2 June 1975; O'Neill to Hardie, 3 June 1975, BIE 1/79.

67. Hardie to O'Neill, 5 June 1975, BIE 1/79.

68. 'George Thomson Says Scotland Says YES to Europe', BIE 1/79; 'Scotland is in Europe', SIE flier, BIE 18/28.

69. *The Scotsman*, 2 June 1975, p. 9.

70. Ibid., 13 May 1975, p. 8; 14 May 1975, p. 6.

71. 'Be involved or be ignored. Scotland MUST say YES to Europe', SIE poster; 'Sovereignty: Scotland has her say in Europe', SIE flier, BIE 18/28.

72. *The Scotsman*, 2 June 1975, p. 9; 4 June 1975, p. 8.

73. *Scottish Daily News*, 23 May 1975, p. 5; *Glasgow Herald*, 24 January 1975, p. 6.

74. *The Scotsman*, 5 June 1975, p. 1.

75. Scotland in Europe fliers, BIE 18/28.

76. *The Scotsman*, 31 May 1975, p. 5.

77. *Glasgow Herald*, 14 May 1975, pp. 1, 6; *Scottish Daily Express*, 14 May 1975, p. 2; 4 June 1975, p. 2.

78. *The Scotsman*, 23 May 1975, p. 4.

79. 'Replies to Glasgow Herald Questionnaire 30th May 1975', BIE 22/6; *Scottish Daily Express*, 5 June 1975, p. 2.

80. *Scottish Daily News*, 15 May 1975, p. 3.

81. *The Scotsman*, 13 May 1975, p. 8.

82. 'Norway', Scotland in Europe flier, BIE 18/28.

83. 'Scotland swings to "Yes"', *Glasgow Herald*, 2 June 1975, p. 1.

84. *The Scotsman*, 7 June 1975, p. 6. The SNP had rashly predicted a No vote in Strathclyde, Tayside, Highlands, Western Isles, Fife, Central and Shetland; ibid., 5 June 1975, p. 11.

85. [Margo MacDonald], 'Minutes of Meeting of National Council', 14 June 1975, SNP Papers, NLS Acc. 11987/12.

86. Press conference in Glasgow, 9 June 1975, SNP press releases, SNP Papers, NLS Acc. 10754/26, no. 197.

87. Interview with Gordon Wilson, 25 September 2015.

88. *The Scotsman*, 7 June 1975, p. 1; *Scottish Daily Express*, 7 June 1975, p. 1.

89. Wilson, *SNP*, p. 102.

Epilogue: 'We Are All Europeans Now'

1. *The Sun*, 7 June 1975, p. 1.

2. *The Guardian*, 2 June 1975, p. 11.

3. 'The Germans', *Fawlty Towers*, series 1 episode 6, script by John Cleese and Connie Booth, directed by John Howard Davies. First broadcast on BBC1, 24 October 1975.

4. *The Scotsman*, 3 June 1975, p. 1; *Buxton Advertiser*, 17 June 2011; *Yorkshire Post*, 3 June 1975, p. 1.

5. *The Scotsman*, 30 May 1975, p. 13; *Yorkshire Post*, 2 June 1975, p. 3.

6. *The Scotsman*, 30 May 1975, p. 6; *The Times*, 25 January 1975, p. 13. See also Esther Webber, 'The 1975 "Don't Know" campaign', *BBC News*, 11 June 2016, www.bbc.co.uk/news/uk-politics-eu-referendum-36418605.

7. *Scotsman*, 31 May 1975, p. 1.

8. Martin Collins, 'Who Voted What?', in Jowell and Hoinville (eds.), *Britain into Europe*, p. 94.

9. *The Times*, 7 June 1975, p. 1; *Sunday Times*, 8 June 1975, p. 16.

10. *Evening Standard*, 4 June 1975, p. 15.

11. Statement by the Prime Minister, 10 Downing Street, 6 June 1975, MS Wilson c.1267, f. 300.

12. *Coventry Telegraph*, 7 June 1975, p. 4; *The Sun*, 7 June 1975, p. 1.

13. *Western Mail*, 9 June 1975, p. 1.

14. *Bristol Evening Post*, 7 June 1975, p. 2.

15. *Daily Express*, 7 June 1975, p. 10.

16. 'Memorandum of conversation', 30 July 1975, Gerald R. Ford Presidential Library, GRF-0314, available at https://catalog.archives.gov/id/1553188; *Daily Telegraph*, 7 June 1975, p. 14.

17. Spreckley, *Common Market Renegotiations*, Part 1, p. 6.

18. *Sunday Times*, 8 June 1975, p. 16.

19. *The Sun*, 6 May 1975, p. 2; *Financial Times*, 31 May 1975, p. 11.

20. *Belfast Newsletter*, 7 June 1975, p. 1; *The Sun*, 7 June 1975, p. 2.

21. King, *Britain Says Yes*, pp. 138–9.

22. Benn, *Against the Tide*, p. 390 (9 June 1975).

23. *Daily Express*, 7 June 1975, p. 1; *Glasgow Herald*, 2 June 1975, p. 6; *Coventry Telegraph*, 7 June 1975, p. 4.

24. Gowland and Turner, *Reluctant Europeans*, p. 193.

25. *Sunday Times*, 8 June 1975, p. 16.

26. *The Times*, 7 June 1975, p. 13.

27. *Daily Express*, 7 June 1975, p. 10.

28. *The Sun*, 2 June 1975, p. 2; see also *The Economist*, 31 May 1975, p. 7.

29. *Sunday Times*, 8 June 1975, p. 16.

30. *Bristol Evening Post*, 7 June 1975, p. 1.

31. *Financial Times*, 15 May 1975, p. 11.

32. *The Times*, 2 June 1975, p. 1; *Bristol Evening Post*, 2 June 1975, p. 1; *Sunday Times*, 1 June 1975, p. 1.

33. *The Sun*, 29 May 1975, p. 2.

34. *Financial Times*, 16 May 1975, p. 19.

35. King, *Britain Says Yes*, pp. 142–3.

36. Interview for *The World This Weekend*, 11 May 1975, MS Wilson c.1266, f. 59.

37. Callaghan, *Time and Chance*, p. 326.

38. See, for example, Ken Coates (ed.), *What Went Wrong? Explaining the Fall of the Labour Government* (Nottingham: Spokesman Books, 1979/2008).

39. Bernstein, *Myth of Decline*, p. 246.

40. *Financial Times*, 16 May 1975, p. 19.

41. *Daily Telegraph*, 7 June 1975, p. 30; *Morning Star*, 7 June 1975, p. 1.

42. *Belfast Newsletter*, 7 June 1975, p. 6; *Daily Mail*, 4 June 1975, p. 9; Patterson, *Conservative Party*, p. 60.

43. Neil Marten, 'After the Referendum', speech to the Commonwealth Industries Association, July 1975, Marten Papers c. 1132, ff. 160–2; *Daily Telegraph*, 7 June 1975, p. 30.

44. Sir Cyril Black to Neil Marten, 13 June 1975, Marten Papers c.1132, f. 135.

45. *Belfast Newsletter*, 7 June 1975, p. 6; *Daily Mail*, 4 June 1975, p. 9; Patterson, *Conservative Party*, p. 60.

46. *Morning Star*, 2 June 1975, p. 3.

47. Benn, *Against the Tide*, p. 387 (6 June 1975).

48. Typescript, 'June 1975'; John Mills [national agent] to NRC supporters, no date [July 1975?]; 'Rules and Constitution of the Safeguard Britain Campaign', no date, Marten Papers c.1132, ff. 131, 133, 179–82.

49. Reg Prentice, 'Right Turn', in P. Cormack (ed.), *Right Turn: Eight Men Who Changed Their Minds* (London: Leo Cooper, 1978), p. 12.

50. Geoffrey Howe, *Conflict of Loyalty* (London: Macmillan, 1994), p. 456. See also Daniel Korski (deputy director of the Policy Unit under Cameron), 'Why we lost the Brexit vote', *Politico*, 20 October 2016: www.politico.eu/article/why-we-lost-the-brexit-vote-former-uk-prime-minister-david-cameron/. The same tendency is noted for an earlier period in Wolfram Kaiser, *Using Europe: Abusing the Europeans. Britain and European Integration, 1945–63* (Basingstoke: Macmillan, 1996).

51. Office of National Statistics, *EU Migration to and from the UK* (17 June 2014), http://webarchive.nationalarchives.gov.uk/20160105160709/, www.ons.gov.uk/ons/rel/migration1/migration-statistics-quarterly-report/may-2014/sty-eu-migration.html; *Migration Statistics Quarterly Report: August 2016*, www.ons.gov.uk/peoplepopulationandcommunity/populationandmigration/internationalmigration/bulletins/migrationstatisticsquarterlyreport/august2016

52. A. Henderson et al., 'England, Englishness and Brexit', *Political Quarterly*, 87:2 (2016), pp. 196–7. For valuable studies of Englishness and the European question, see M. Kenny, *The Politics of English Nationhood* (Oxford: Oxford University Press, 2014); B. Wellings, *English Nationalism and Euroscepticism: Losing the Peace* (Oxford: Peter Lang, 2012).

53. *Hansard* 883, 16 November 1974, 1128, 1139; Wall, *From Rejection to Referendum*, p. 527.

54. For the 2015–16 renegotiations, see Korski, 'Why we lost'; Tim Shipman, *All Out War: The Full Story of How Brexit Sank Britain's Political Class* (London: William Collins, 2016); Craig Oliver, *Unleashing Demons: The Inside Story of Brexit* (London: Hodder & Stoughton, 2016).

55. Kenneth Armstrong, *Brexit Time: Leaving the EU – Why, When and How?* (Cambridge: Cambridge University Press, 2017), p. 35.

56. Shipman, *All Out War*, pp. 140–1. Strikingly, Oliver, *Unleashing Demons*, has no index entry for 'renegotiations'.

57. Oliver, *Unleashing Demons*, p. 114.

58. For rising hostility to membership in the national press, see P. Copeland and N. Copsey, 'Rethinking Britain and the European Union: Politicians, the Media and Public Opinion Reconsidered', *Journal of Common Market Studies*, 55:4 (July 2017), pp. 709–26; Oliver Daddow, 'The UK Media and "Europe": From Permissive Consensus to Destructive Dissent', *International Affairs*, 88:6 (2012), pp. 1219–36. For the impact of declining local media in 2016, see Jean Seaton, 'Brexit and the Media', *Political Quarterly*, 87:3

(July–September 2016), pp. 332–7. In 2016, over half of parliamentary constituencies and local authority districts had no significant local daily; see Gordon Ramsay and Martin Moore, *Monopolising Local News* (London: Centre for the Study of Media, Communication and Power, King's College London, 2016), www.kcl.ac.uk/sspp/policy-institute/CMCP/local-news.pdf

59. 'Report on E.E.C.', 29 May 1975, NOP/8580/03, Marten Papers, c.1133, ff. 34–68.

60. A poll by Louis Harris in April 1975 asked voters whether they 'respect and like' or 'dislike' a series of public figures. Particularly high scores were recorded by Thorpe (+29), Jenkins (+25), Whitelaw (+25), Heath (+21) and Wilson (+19). Butler and Kitzinger, *1975 Referendum*, p. 256.

61. 'YouGov/ Today Programme Survey Results', 13–14 June 2016, http://d25d2506sfb94s.cloudfront.net/cumulus_uploads/document/x4iyndimn7/TodayResults_160614_EUReferendum_W.pdf

62. H.D. Clarke, M. Goodwin and P. Whiteley, *Brexit: Why Britain Voted to Leave the European Union* (Cambridge: Cambridge University Press, 2017), p. 156.

63. For examples reproduced in the British Cartoon Archive, see Leslie Gibbard, *Guardian*, 27 February 1975, http://archives.cartoons.ac.uk/Record.aspx?src=CalmView.Catalog&id=27575&pos=3; Nicholas Garland, *New Statesman*, 21 March 1975, http://archives.cartoons.ac.uk/Record.aspx?src=CalmView.Catalog&id=NG1319&pos=42; Stanley Franklin, *The Sun*, 2 June 1975, http://archives.cartoons.ac.uk/Record.aspx?src=CalmView.Catalog&id=28026&pos=27

64. Boris Johnson, 'The only continent with weaker economic growth than Europe is Antarctica', *Daily Telegraph*, 29 May 2016, www.telegraph.co.uk/news/2016/05/29/the-only-continent-with-weaker-economic-growth-than-europe-is-an/

65. Attitudes to immigration also strongly influenced voters' perceptions of the economic costs and benefits of leaving; Clarke, Goodwin and Whiteley, *Brexit*, p. 168.

66. John Campbell, *Roy Jenkins: A Well-Rounded Life* (London: Vintage Books, 2014), p. 447.

67. *The Sun*, 30 May 1975.

68. *The Guardian*, 13 March 1975.

69. Shipman, *All Out War*, p. 178.

70. Stephen Bush, 'Why David Cameron's Harold Wilson Tribute Band Faces a Hostile Crowd', *New Statesman*, 9 June 2016, www.newstatesman.com/politics/uk/2016/06/why-david-cameron-s-harold-wilson-tribute-band-faces-hostile-crowd

Appendix 2: Note on Prices

1. Nationwide, 'UK House Prices since 1952' (2017), www.nationwide.co.uk/~/
media/MainSite/documents/about/house-price-index/downloads/uk-house-
price-since-1952.xls; G. Clark, 'What Were British Earnings and Prices Then?',
Measuring Worth (2017), www.measuringworth.com/ukearncpi/; P. Bolton,
'Teachers' Pay Statistics', *House of Commons Library* (2008), http://dera
.ioe.ac.uk/22821/1/SN01877.pdf; D. Butler and G. Butler, *Twentieth-Century
British Political Facts, 1900–2000*, eighth edition (Basingstoke: Macmillan,
2000), pp. 375, 547; Parliamentary Written Answer, *Hansard* 890, 18 April
1975, 176W. I am enormously grateful to Alwyn Turner for generously sharing
his work on the Littlewood's Archive.

Select Bibliography

Archives and Manuscripts

Bodleian Library, Oxford University
    Conservative Party Archive
    Papers of:
        Castle, Barbara
        Jenkins, Roy
        Marten, Neil
        Wilson, Harold
British Archives Online (www.britishonlinearchives.co.uk/)
    Parliamentary Labour Party Papers
Cardiff University
    Plaid Cymru Archive (microfilm)
Church of England Record Centre, London
    Papers of:
        Board of Social Responsibility
        General Synod
Churchill Archives Centre, Cambridge University
    Papers of:
        Powell, J. Enoch
        Thatcher, Margaret
Labour History Archive and Study Centre (LHASC), People's History
Museum, Manchester
    Papers of:
        Beever, Colin
        Foot, Michael
        Hart, Judith
        Heffer, Eric

London School of Economics
  Papers of:
    Campaign for an Independent Britain
    Shore, Peter
Modern Records Centre, University of Warwick
  Association of Scientific, Technical and Managerial Staff
  Confederation of British Industry
  Trades Union Congress
  Transport and General Workers' Union
Museum of London
  J. Sainsbury Archive
The National Archives, Kew
  CAB 128 (Cabinet Conclusions)
National Library of Scotland
  Scottish National Party Archive
Northern Ireland Political Literature: Periodicals, 1966–1989 (Belfast: Linen Hall, 1993)
Parliamentary Archive, London
  Britain in Europe (BIE)
  National Referendum Campaign (NRC)
The Women's Library, London School of Economics
  Women's Europe Committee Papers

Newspapers

An Phoblacht/Republican News
ASTMS Journal
Belfast Newsletter
Birmingham Post
Bristol Evening Post
British Farmer and Stockbreeder
British Ulsterman
Catholic Herald
Church of England Newspaper
Church Times
Combat: The Voice of the Ulster Volunteer Force
Comment
Coventry Evening Telegraph
Daily Express
Daily Mail
Daily Mirror
Daily Telegraph

Director
The Economist
Encounter
Evening Standard [London]
Federalist
Financial Times
Glasgow Herald
GMW Herald
Guardian
Home and County: Journal of the National Federation of Women's Institutes
Housewives Today
India Weekly
Irish Catholic
Jewish Chronicle
JS Journal [Sainsbury's]
Labour Monthly: A Magazine of Left Unity
Labour Newssheet
Labour Weekly
Land Worker
Liverpool Daily Post
Loyalist News
Manchester Evening News
Methodist Recorder
Miner
Morning Star
New Europe
New Scientist
New Statesman
Observer
On Target
Orange Cross
Protestant Telegraph
Red Rag
Resistance News
Scots Independent
Scotsman
Scottish Daily Express
Scottish Daily Mail
Scottish Daily News
Shrew
South Wales Argus
South Wales Echo

Spare Rib
Spectator
Starry Plough
St Michael News [M&S]
Sun
Sunday Express (Scotland)
Sunday Mail
Sunday Telegraph
Sunday Times
Tablet
TGWU Record
The Times
Townswoman
Tribune
Ulsterman
Ulster Workers' Council Journal
Unfree Citizen: The Newspaper of People's Democracy
Welsh Nation
Western Mail
West Indian World
Which?
Woman's Own
Workers' Voice
Workers' Weekly
Yorkshire Post

Diaries and Memoirs

Adenauer, K., *Memoirs, 1945–53*, translated by Beate Ruhm von Oppen (London: Weidenfeld & Nicolson, 1966)

Adeney, M., *Baggage of Empire: Reporting Politics and Industry in the Shadow of Imperial Decline* (London: Biteback, 2016)

Benn, Tony, *Office without Power: Diaries, 1968–72*, ed. Ruth Winstone (London: Century Hutchinson, 1988)
  Against the Tide: Diaries 1973–76, ed. Ruth Winstone (London: Century Hutchinson, 1989)

Boothroyd, B., *The Autobiography* (London: Century, 2001)

Brandreth, G., *Something Sensational to Read in the Train: The Diary of a Lifetime* (London: John Murray, 2009)

Brown, G., *In My Way: The Political Memoirs of Lord George-Brown* (Harmondsworth: Penguin, 1972)

Callaghan, J., *Time and Chance* (London: Collins, 1987)

Castle, B., *The Castle Diaries, 1974–76* (London: Weidenfeld & Nicolson, 1980)

Clark, A., *Diaries: Into Politics*, ed. I. Trewin (London: Weidenfeld & Nicolson, 2000)

Diaries: In Power, 1983–1992, ed. I. Trewin (London: Phoenix, 2001 edition)

Donoughue, B., *Downing Street Diary: With Harold Wilson in No. 10* (London: Jonathan Cape, 2005)

'The Inside View from No. Ten', in Mark Baimbridge (ed.), *The 1975 Referendum on Europe: Volume 1: Reflections of the Participants* (Exeter: Imprint-Academic, 2006)

Evans, G., *For the Sake of Wales: The Memoirs of Gwynfor Evans*, translated from the Welsh by Meic Stephens (Caernarfon: Welsh Academic Press, 1996)

Heath, E., *The Course of My Life: My Autobiography* (London: Hodder and Stoughton, 1998)

Hume, J., *Personal Views: Politics, Peace and Reconciliation in Ireland* (Dublin: Town House, 1996)

Jay, D., *Change and Fortune: A Political Record* (London: Hutchinson, 1980)

Macmillan, H., *Pointing the Way, 1959–1961* (London: Macmillan, 1972)

McIntosh, R., *Challenge to Democracy: Politics, Trade Union Power and Economic Failure in the 1970s* (London: Politico's, 2008)

Milligan, B., *The Bridge: Reflections of an Unreconstructed Ecumaniac* (London: Christians Aware, 2011)

Morris, J., *Fifty Years in Politics and the Law* (Cardiff: University of Wales Press, 2011)

Oliver, C., *Unleashing Demons: The Inside Story of Brexit* (London: Hodder & Stoughton, 2016)

O'Neill, C., *Britain's Entry into the European Community: Report by Sir Con O'Neill on the Negotiations of 1970–1972* [1972], ed. with a Foreword by Sir David Hannay (London: Whitehall History Publishing/Frank Cass, 2000)

Prothero, C., *Recount* (Ormskirk: Hesketh, 1982)

Shore, P., *Separate Ways: The Heart of Europe* (London: Duckworth, 2000)

Talfan Davies, G., *At Arm's Length: Recollections and Reflections on the Arts, Media and a Young Democracy* (Bridgend: Seren, 2008)

Tynan, K., *Diaries of Kenneth Tynan*, ed. J. Lahr (London: Bloomsbury, 2002)

Williams, P., *Voice From the Valleys* (Aberystwyth: Plaid Cymru, 1981)

Wilson, G., *SNP: The Turbulent Years, 1960–1990* (Stirling: Scots Independent, 2009)

Wilson, H., *Final Term: The Labour Government, 1974–1976* (London: Weidenfeld & Nicolson, 1979)

Wistrich, E., 'The Labour Committee for Europe' [witness seminar, 12 June 1990], *Contemporary Record*, 7:2 (Autumn 1993), 363–385

Recollections of a Federalist: My Life (London: Bettany Press, 2013)

Pamphlets and Contemporary Literature

Attlee, C., *Empire into Commonwealth: The Chichele Lectures* (London: Oxford University Press, 1961)

Benn, T., *Arguments for Democracy*, ed. C. Mullin (London: Cape, 1981)
  Speeches by Tony Benn, ed. J. Bodington [1974] (Nottingham: Spokesman, 2012)

BCC, *Going Into Europe: Implications of Britain's Membership of the Common Market. A Study Kit for British Christians* (London: British Council of Churches, 1972)

Britain in Europe: The Social Responsibilities of the Church (London: Board of Social Responsibility, 1972)

Christians and the European Community: Reports and Papers of Conference, 1974, 16–20 April, Roehampton, London (London, 1974)

Christians and the Common Market: A Report Presented to the British Council of Churches (London, 1967)

Blaker, P., *Labour's 'Renegotiation' Policy: A Conservative View* (London: CPC, 1974)

Brittan, S., 'The Economic Contradictions of Democracy', *British Journal of Political Science*, 5 (1975), pp. 129–59

Callaghan, J., *James Callaghan on the Common Market* (London: Labour Committee for Safeguards on the Common Market, 1971)

Coates, K. (ed.), *What Went Wrong? Explaining the Fall of the Labour Government* (Nottingham: Spokesman Books, 1979/2008)

Crockford's Clerical Directory, 1973–74, 85th issue (Oxford: Church Commissioners, 1975)

Dale, I. (ed.), *Conservative Party General Election Manifestos, 1900–1997* (London: Routledge, 2000)
  (ed.), *Labour Party General Election Manifestos, 1900–1997* (London: Routledge, 2000)

Dicey, A.V., *Introduction to the Study of the Law of the Constitution* [1885], eighth edition (London: Macmillan, 1915)

Elles, D., *Housewives and the Common Market* (London: CPC, 1971)

Evans, D., *While Britain Slept: The Selling of the Common Market* (London: Victor Gollancz, 1975)

Evans, G., *A National Future for Wales* (Swansea: Plaid Cymru, 1975)

Farage, N., 'A Referendum Stitch-Up? How the EU and British Elites are Plotting to Fix the Result' (UKIP, 2012): www.ukipmeps.org/uploads/file/ReferendumStichUp.pdf.

Fekete, I., *The How and Why Wonder Book of the Common Market* (London: Transworld Publishers, 1974)

Goodhart, P., *Referendum* (London: Tom Stacey, 1971)
  The People's Veto (London: Bow Group, 1975)

Grimond, J. and Neve, B., *The Referendum* (London: Rex Collings, 1975)

Hart, J., *Aid and Liberation: A Socialist Study of Aid Politics* (London: Gollancz, 1973)

The New Realities of Development: The Fourth Annual Tom Mboya Lecture, Ruskin College, Oxford, February 1975 (Dorking: Ariel Foundation, 1975)

Jay, D., *The Better Alternative for Britain* (London: CMSC, 1975)

Labour Research Department, *1975 Referendum: The Common Market: IN or OUT* (London: Labour Research Department, 1975)

Le Carré, John, *Tinker, Tailor, Soldier, Spy* (London: Hodder and Stoughton, 1974)

Lomas, A., *The Common Market: Why We Should Keep OUT* (London Co-operative Political Committee, 1970)

Miliband, R., *Parliamentary Socialism: A Study in the Politics of Labour* [1972 edition] (Pontypool: Merlin, 2009)

Montagu, V. and Meyer, A., *Europe – Should Britain Join?* (London: Monday Club, 1966)

National Farmers' Union (NFU), *British Agriculture and the Common Market* (London: NFU, July 1971)

A Review of the Common Agricultural Policy (London: NFU, September 1973)

Nutting, A., *Europe Will Not Wait: A Warning and a Way Out* (New York: Hollis & Carter, 1960)

Pickles, W., *Not with Europe: The Political Case for Staying Out* (London: Fabian International Bureau, 1962)

Where Do We Come In? Your Rights and the Common Market (London: GBO, [1975])

Pinder, J., *Danger: Referendum at Work* (PEP/New Europe, n.d.)

Plaid Cymru, *Power For Wales: Plaid Cymru Election Manifesto* (Cardiff: Plaid Cymru, 1974)

Wales and the Common Market (Cardiff: Plaid Cymru Research Group, 1975)

Powell, J. E. and Maude, A., *Biography of a Nation* [1955], revised second edition (London: John Baker, 1970)

Powell, J. E., *No Easy Answers* (London: Sheldon Press, 1973)

'The Nature of Sovereignty', in Douglas Evans and Richard Body (eds.), *Freedom and Stability in the World Economy* (London: Croom Helm, 1976)

Reflections of a Statesman: The Writings and Speeches of Enoch Powell (London: Bellew Publishing, 1991)

'Crown and Canon: An Address to the Annual General Meeting of the Prayer Book Society', *Churchman*, 107:3 (1993)

The Evolution of the Gospel: A New Translation of the First Gospel, with Commentary and Introductory Essay (London: Yale University Press, 1994)

Salter, N. and Gummer, J. S., *Britain in Europe: The Social Responsibilities of the Church* (London: Board of Social Responsibility, 1972)

Seldon, A. (ed.), *Crisis '75...?* (London: Institute of Economic Affairs, 1975)

Spreckley, N., *The Common Market Renegotiation and Referendum: 1974–75* (London: Foreign and Commonwealth Office, 2014): https://issuu.com/fcohistorians/docs/1_spreckley_report_-_part_1, https://issuu.com/fcohistorians/docs/2_spreckley_report_-_part_2, https://issuu.com/fcohistorians/docs/3_spreckley_report_-_part_3_appendi

Wistrich, E., 'The Irish, Norwegian and Danish Referenda: The Lessons for Britain', *New Europe*, 3:1 (Winter, 1974/75)

Young European Left, *Labour's Programme and Europe* (London: YEL, 1974)

Official and Party Papers

Labour and the Common Market: Report of a Special Conference of the Labour Party [26 April 1975] (Transport House, London: 1975)

Labour's Programme 1973 (Transport House, London: 1973)

Legal and Constitutional Implications of United Kingdom Membership of the European Communities, Cmnd 3301 (HMSO, London: 1967)

Membership of the European Community: Report on Renegotiations, Command Paper 6003 (HMSO, London: 1975)

Referendum on United Kingdom Membership of the European Community. Accounts of Campaigning Organisations, Command Paper 6251 (HMSO, London: 1975)

The Liberal Manifesto for Europe, 1975 (Liberal Europe Campaign, London: 1975)

The United Kingdom and the European Communities, Command Paper 4715 (HMSO, London: 1971)

Secondary Literature

Adams, J., *Tony Benn: A Biography* (London: Biteback, 1992)

Addison, P., *The Road to 1945: British Politics and the Second World War* (London: Jonathan Cape, 1975)

Alexander, P., 'The Labour Government, Commonwealth Policy and the Second Application to Join the EEC, 1964–67', in Alex May (ed.), *Britain, the Commonwealth and Europe: The Commonwealth and Britain's Applications to Join the European Communities* (Basingstoke: Palgrave, 2001)

Aqui, L., 'Macmillan, Nkrumah and the 1961 Application for European Economic Community Membership', *International History Review*, 39:4 (2017), pp. 575–91

Armstrong, K., *Brexit Time: Leaving the EU – Why, How and When?* (Cambridge: Cambridge University Press, 2017)

Baimbridge, M. (ed.), *The 1975 Referendum on Europe: Volume 1: Reflections of the Participants* (Exeter: Imprint-Academic, 2006)

Baimbridge, M., Whyman, P. and Mullen, A. (eds.), *The 1975 Referendum on Europe: Volume 2: Current Analysis and Lessons for the Future* (Exeter: Imprint-Academic, 2006)

Balsom, D. and P. J. Madgwick, 'Wales, European Integration and Devolution', in M. Kolinsky (ed.), *Divided Loyalties: British Regional Assertion and European Integration* (Manchester: Manchester University Press, 1978)

Barker, E., *Britain in a Divided Europe, 1945–1970* (London: Weidenfeld & Nicolson, 1971)

Beaumont, C., *Housewives and Citizens: Domesticity and the Women's Movement in England, 1928–64* (Manchester: Manchester University Press, 2013)

Beers, L., 'Thatcher and the Women's Vote', in Ben Jackson and Robert Saunders (eds.), *Making Thatcher's Britain* (Cambridge: Cambridge University Press, 2012)

Beloff, M., 'The Commonwealth as History', *Journal of Imperial and Commonwealth History*, 1:1 (1972), pp. 111–25

Bernstein, G. L., *The Myth of Decline: The Rise of Britain since 1945* (London: Pimlico, 2004)

Bingham, A., *Family Newspapers? Sex, Private Life and the British Popular Press, 1918–1978* (Oxford: Oxford University Press, 2009)

Black, J., *Convergence or Divergence? Britain and the Continent* (Basingstoke: Macmillan, 1994)

Black, L., Pemberton, H. and Thane, P. (eds.), *Reassessing 1970s Britain* (Manchester: Manchester University Press, 2013)

Bloch, M., *Jeremy Thorpe* (London: Abacus, 2016)

Bogdanor, V., *The People and the Party System: The Referendum and Electoral Reform in British Politics* (Cambridge: Cambridge University Press, 1981)

Bourke, R., *Peace in Ireland: The War of Ideas*, second edition (London: Pimlico, 2012)

Brewitt-Taylor, S., 'The Invention of a "Secular Society"? Christianity and the Sudden Appearance of Secularization Discourses in the British National Media, 1961–4', *20th Century British History*, 24:3 (2013), pp. 327–50

Brivati, B. and Jones, H. (eds.), *From Reconstruction to Integration: Britain and Europe since 1945* (Leicester: Leicester University Press, 1993)

Broad, R. and Geiger, T. (eds.), 'Witness Seminar: The 1975 British Referendum on Europe', *Contemporary British History*, 10:3 (Autumn 1996)

Broad, R. and Preston, V. (eds.), *Moored to the Continent? Britain and European Integration* (London: IHR, 2001)

Butler, D. and Kavanagh, D., *The British General Election of October 1974* (Basingstoke: Macmillan, 1975)

Butler, D. and Kitzinger, U., *The 1975 Referendum* (Basingstoke: Macmillan, 1976)

Butler, D. and Pinto-Duschinsky, M., *The British General Election of 1970* (Basingstoke: Macmillan, 1999)

Campbell, B., *The Iron Ladies: Why Do Women Vote Tory?* (London: Virago, 1987)

Campbell, J., *Roy Jenkins: A Well-Rounded Life* (London: Jonathan Cape, 2014)
Edward Heath: A Biography (London: Pimlico, 1994)

Camps, M., *Britain and the European Community, 1955–1963* (Oxford: Oxford University Press, 1964)

Cannadine, D., *Ornamentalism: How the British Saw Their Empire* (London: Penguin, 2001)

Carter, D., 'Methodists and the Ecumenical Task', in J. Morris and N. Sagovsky, *The Unity We Have and the Unity We Seek: Prospects for the Third Millennium* (London: T. & T. Clark, 2003)

Charlton, M., *The Price of Victory* (London: BBC, 1983)

Collins, A., 'The Cabinet Office, Tony Benn and the Renegotiation of Britain's Terms of Entry into the European Community, 1974–1975', *Contemporary British History*, 24:4 (2010), pp. 471–91

Connelly, M., *We Can Take It! Britain and the Memory of the Second World War* (Harlow: Pearson, 2004)

Corthorn, P., 'Enoch Powell, Ulster Unionism and the British Nation', *Journal of British Studies*, 51:4 (2012), pp. 967–97

Cotton, C., 'Labour, European Integration and the Post-Imperial Mind, 1960-75' in B. Frank, C. Horner and D. Stewart (eds.), *The British Labour Movement and Imperialism* (Newcastle upon Tyne: Cambridge Scholars Press, 2010)

Criddle, B., 'Scotland, the EEC and Devolution', in Martin Kolinsky (ed.), *Divided Loyalties: British Regional Assertion and European Integration* (Manchester: Manchester University Press, 1978)

Crowson, N., *The Conservative Party and European Integration since 1945: At the Heart of Europe?* (London: Routledge, 2006)

Coupland, P., *Britannia, Europa and Christendom: British Christians and European Integration* (Basingstoke: Palgrave Macmillan, 2006)

Daddow, O., *Britain and Europe since 1945: Historiographical Perspectives on Integration* (Manchester: Manchester University Press, 2004)

Darwin, J., *Britain and Decolonisation: The Retreat from Empire in the Post-War World* (Basingstoke: Macmillan, 1988)

Davidson, J., 'The De-Dominionisation of Australia', *Meanjin*, 38:2 (1979), pp. 139–53

Dedman, M. J., *The Origins and Development of the European Union, 1945–95: A History of European Integration* (London: Routledge, 1996)

Dewey Jr., R. F., *British National Identity and Opposition to Membership of Europe, 1961–63: The Anti-Marketeers* (Manchester: Manchester University Press, 2009)

Dockrill, S., *Britain's Retreat from East of Suez: The Choice between Europe and the World?* (Basingstoke: Palgrave Macmillan, 2002)

Dubow, S., 'The Commonwealth and South Africa: From Smuts to Mandela', *Journal of Imperial and Commonwealth History*, 45:2 (2017)

Edwards, A., *Labour's Crisis: Plaid Cymru, the Conservatives and the Decline of the Labour Party in North-West Wales, 1960–74* (Cardiff: University of Wales Press, 2011)

Eleftheriadis, P., 'Parliamentary Sovereignty and the Constitution', Oxford Legal Studies Research Paper No. 45 (2009)

Eley, G., 'Finding the People's War: Film, British Collective Memories and World War II', *American Historical Review*, 106:3 (2001), pp. 818–38

Elias, A., *Minority Nationalist Parties and European Integration: A Comparative Study* (Oxford: Routledge, 2009)

Ellison, J. E., *Threatening Europe: Britain and the Creation of the European Community, 1955–58* (Basingstoke: Macmillan, 2000)

    'Britain and Europe' in P. Addison and H. Jones (eds.), *A Companion to Contemporary British History, 1939–2000* (Oxford: Blackwell, 2005)

    The United States, Britain and the Transatlantic Crisis: Rising to the Gaullist Challenge (Basingstoke: Palgrave Macmillan, 2007)

    'The European Rescue of Britain', in F. Guirao, F. Lynch and S. Ramírez Pérez (eds.), *Alan S. Milward and a Century of European Change* (Abingdon: Routledge, 2012)

England, J., *The Wales TUC: 1974–2004. Devolution and Industrial Politics* (Cardiff: University of Wales Press, 2004)

Evans, R., *Gwnyfor: Portrait of a Patriot* (Talybont: Y Lolfa, 2008)

Ferguson, N., *High Financier: The Life and Times of Siegmund Warburg* (London: Allen Lane, 2010)

Ferriter, D., *Ambiguous Republic: Ireland in the 1970s* (London: Profile, 2012)

Frampton, M., 'Sinn Féin and the European Arena: "Ourselves Alone" or "Critical Engagement"?', *Irish Studies in International Affairs*, 16 (2005), pp. 235–53

George, S., *An Awkward Partner: Britain in the European Community*, third edition (Oxford: Oxford University Press, 1998)

Gifford, C., *The Making of Eurosceptic Britain*, second edition (Farnham: Ashgate, 2014)

Goodhart, Philip, *Full-Hearted Consent: The Story of the Referendum Campaign – and the Campaign for the Referendum* (London: Davis-Poynter, 1976)

Gowland, D. and Turner, A., *Reluctant Europeans: Britain and European Integration, 1945–1998* (Harlow: Longman, 2000)

Grant, W., 'The Politics of the Green Pound, 1974–79', *Journal of Common Market Studies*, 19:4 (June 1981), pp. 313–329

Green, E. H. H. (ed.), *The Ideals of Empire: Political and Economic Thought, 1903–1911*, 6 volumes (London: Routledge, 1998)

Greenwood, S., *Britain and European Cooperation since 1945* (Oxford: Blackwell, 1992)

Grimley, M., 'Anglican Evangelicals and Anti-Permissiveness: The Nationwide Festival of Light 1971–1983', in A. Atherstone and J. Maiden (eds.), *Evangelicalism and the Church of England in the Twentieth Century: Reform, Resistance and Renewal* (London: Boydell Press, 2014)

Grob-Fitzgibbon, B., *Continental Drift: Britain and Europe from the End of Empire to the Rise of Euroscepticism* (Cambridge: Cambridge University Press, 2016)

Haeussler, M., 'A "Cold War European"? Helmut Schmidt and European Integration, c.1945–1982', *Cold War History*, 15:4 (2015), pp. 427–47

'A Pyrrhic Victory: Harold Wilson, Helmut Schmidt, and the British Renegotiation of EC Membership, 1974–5', *International History Review*, 37:4 (2015), pp. 768–89

Hall, C. and Rose, S. O. (eds.), *At Home with the Empire: Metropolitan Culture and the Imperial World* (Cambridge: Cambridge University Press, 2006)

Hansen, P. and Jonsson, S., 'Bringing Africa as a "Dowry to Europe": European Integration and the Eurafrica Project, 1920–1960', *Interventions: International Journal of Postcolonial Studies*, 13:3 (2011), pp. 443–63.

Eurafrica: The Untold History of European Integration and Colonialism (London: Bloomsbury, 2014)

Hawkins, A., *Victorian Political Culture: 'Habits of Heart and Mind'* (Oxford: Oxford University Press, 2015)

Heffer, S., *Like the Roman: The Life of Enoch Powell* (London: Phoenix, 1998)

Henderson, A. et al., 'England, Englishness and Brexit', *Political Quarterly*, 87:2 (2016)

Hepburn, E., 'Degrees of Independence: SNP Thinking in an International Context', in Gerry Hassan, *The Modern SNP: From Protest to Power* (Edinburgh: Edinburgh University Press, 2009)

Heywood, R., 'West European Community and the Eurafrica Concept in the 1950s', *Journal of European Integration*, 4:2 (1981), pp. 199–210

Hickson, K. and Seldon, A. (eds.), *New Labour, Old Labour: The Wilson and Callaghan Governments, 1974–79* (London: Routledge, 2004)

Hill, C. and Yarnold, E. J. (eds.), *Anglicans and Roman Catholics: The Search for Unity* (London: SPCK, 1994)

Hopkins, A. G., 'Rethinking Decolonization', *Past & Present*, 200 (August 2008)

Hoskyns, C., *Integrating Gender: Women, Law and Politics in the European Union* (London: Verso, 1996)

Howe, S., 'Internal Decolonization? British Politics since Thatcher as Post-Colonial Trauma', *20th Century British History*, 14:3 (2003), pp. 286–304

Howkins, A., *The Death of Rural England: A Social History of the Countryside since 1900* (London: Routledge, 2003)

Hyam, R., 'The Parting of the Ways: Britain and South Africa's Departure from the Commonwealth, 1951–61', *Journal of Imperial and Commonwealth History*, 26:2 (1998), pp. 157–75

Jackson, A., *The British Empire and the Second World War* (London: Hambledon Press, 2006)

'Empire and Beyond: The Pursuit of Overseas National Interests in the Late Twentieth Century', *English Historical Review*, 123:499 (December 2007), pp. 1350–66

Jackson, B. and Saunders, R. (eds.), *Making Thatcher's Britain* (Cambridge: Cambridge University Press, 2012)

Jarvis, D., 'Mrs Maggs and Betty: The Conservative Appeal to Women Voters in the 1920s', *20th Century British History*, 5:2 (1994), pp. 129–52

Johnes, M., *Wales since 1939* (Manchester: Manchester University Press, 2012)

Jones, I., 'The Clergy, the Cold War and the Mission of the Local Church; England, ca. 1940–60', in Dianne Kirby (ed.), *Religion and the Cold War* (Basingstoke: Palgrave Macmillan, 2002/2013)

Jowell, R. and Hoinville, G. (eds.), *Britain into Europe: Public Opinion and the EEC, 1961–75* (London: Croom Helm, 1976)

Kaiser, W., *Using Europe: Abusing the Europeans. Britain and European Integration, 1945–63* (Basingstoke: Macmillan, 1996)

Kenny, M., *The Politics of English Nationhood* (Oxford: Oxford University Press, 2014)

King, A., *Britain Says Yes: The 1975 Referendum on the Common Market* (Washington DC: American Institute for Public Policy Research, 1977)

Kirby, D., *Religion and the Cold War* (Basingstoke: Palgrave Macmillan, 2002/2013)

'Ecclesiastical McCarthyism: Cold War Repression in the Church of England', *Contemporary British History*, 19:2 (2005), pp. 187–203

Kitzinger, U., *The Second Try: Labour and the EEC* (Oxford: Pergamon Press, 1968)

Diplomacy and Persuasion: How Britain Joined the Common Market (London: Thames and Hudson, 1973)

Kolinsky, M. (ed.), *Divided Loyalties: British Regional Assertion and European Integration* (Manchester: Manchester University Press, 1978)

Leustean, L., *The Ecumenical Movement and the Making of the European Community* (Oxford: Oxford University Press, 2014)

Longinotti, E., 'Britain's Withdrawal from East of Suez: From Economic Determinism to Political Choice', *Contemporary British History*, 29:3 (2015), pp. 318–40

Ludlow, N. P., 'Challenging French Leadership in Europe: Germany, Italy, the Netherlands and the Outbreak of the Empty Chair Crisis of 1965–1966', *Contemporary European History*, 8:2 (July 1999), pp. 231–48

'Us or Them? The Meaning of Europe in British Political Discourse', in M. Malmborg and B. Stråth (eds.), *The Meaning of Europe: Variety and Contention within and among Nations* (Oxford: Berg, 2002), 101–24

(ed.), *European Integration and the Cold War: Ostpolitik-Weltpolitik, 1965–1973* (Abingdon: Routledge, 2007)

'Safeguarding British Identity or Betraying It? The Role of British "Tradition" in the Parliamentary Great Debate on EC Membership, October 1971', *Journal of Common Market Studies*, 53:1 (2015), pp. 18–34

Roy Jenkins and the European Commission Presidency, 1976–1980: At the Heart of Europe (Basingstoke: Palgrave Macmillan, 2016)

Lynch, P., *Minority Nationalism and European Integration* (Cardiff: University of Wales Press, 1996)

'The Conservatives and the Wilson Application', in Oliver J. Daddow (ed.), *Harold Wilson and European Integration: Britain's Second Application to Join the EEC* (London: Routledge, 2003)

Mackenzie, J. M. (ed.), *Imperialism and Popular Culture* (Manchester: Manchester University Press, 1989)

Mailafia, O., *Europe and Economic Reform in Africa: Structural Adjustment and Economic Diplomacy* (London: Routledge, 1997)

Martin, J., *The Development of Modern Agriculture: British Farming since 1931* (Basingstoke: Macmillan, 2000)

Martin López, T., *The Winter of Discontent: Myth, Memory and History* (Liverpool: Liverpool University Press, 2014)

Maurhofer, R., 'Revisiting the Creation of EFTA: The British and the Swiss Case', *Journal of European Integration History*, 7:2 (2001), pp. 65–84

May, A. (ed.), *Britain, the Commonwealth and Europe: The Commonwealth and Britain's Application to Join the European Communities* (Basingstoke: Palgrave, 2001)

McAllister, L., *Plaid Cymru: The Emergence of a Political Party* (Bridgend: Seren, 2001)

McCarthy, H., *The British People and the League of Nations: Democracy, Citizenship and Internationalism, c.1918–48* (Manchester: Manchester University Press, 2011)

  'The Diplomatic History of Global Women's Rights: The British Foreign Office and International Women's Year, 1975', *Journal of Contemporary History*, 50:4 (2015), pp. 833–53

McKittrick, D., Kelters, S., Feeney, B., Thornton, C. and McVea, D. (eds.), *Lost Lives: The Stories of the Men, Women and Children Who Died as a Result of the Northern Ireland Troubles* (revised edition: Edinburgh: Mainstream Publishing, 2007)

McKittrick, D. and McVea, D., *Making Sense of the Troubles: A History of the Northern Ireland Conflict*, revised edition (London: Penguin, 2012)

Milward, A. S., *The European Rescue of the Nation-State*, second edition (London: Routledge, 2000)

  The Rise and Fall of a National Strategy, 1945–1963: The United Kingdom and the Common Market, Volume 1 (London: Routledge, 2005)

Milward, A. S., Lynch, F., Romero, R., Ranieri, R. and Sørensen, V., *The Frontier of National Sovereignty: History and Theory, 1945–1992* (London: Routledge, 1993)

Mitchel, P., *Evangelicalism and National Identity in Ulster, 1921–1998* (Oxford: Oxford University Press, 2003)

Mitchell, J. and Hassan, G., *Scottish National Party Leaders* (London: Biteback, 2016)

Moore, R. 'Bad Strategy and Bomber Dreams: A New View of the Blue Streak Cancellation', *Contemporary British History*, 27:2 (2013), pp. 145–66

Morgan, K. O., *Labour in Power* (Oxford: Oxford University Press, 1985)

  Callaghan: A Life (Oxford: Oxford University Press, 1997)

  Michael Foot: A Life (London: Harper, 2007)

Moxon-Browne, E., 'Northern Ireland', in M. Kolinsky (ed.), *Divided Loyalties: British Regional Assertion and European Integration* (Manchester: Manchester University Press, 1978)

Murphy, G., '"A Measurement of the Extent of Our Sovereignty at the Moment": Sovereignty and the Question of Irish Entry to the EEC, New Evidence from the Archives', *Irish Studies in International Affairs*, 12 (2001), pp. 191–202

Murphy, P., *Monarchy and the End of Empire: The House of Windsor, the British Government, and the Postwar Commonwealth* (Oxford: Oxford University Press, Oxford: 2013)

Newton, S., 'Britain, the Sterling Area and European Integration, 1945–50', *Journal of Imperial and Commonwealth History*, 13:3 (1985), pp. 163–82

Noakes, L. and Pattinson, J. (eds.), *British Cultural Memory and the Second World War* (London: Bloomsbury, 2014)

O'Hara, K., *The Referendum Roundabout* (Exeter: Societas, 2006)

O'Leary, B., 'Northern Ireland' in Kevin Hickson and Anthony Seldon (eds.), *New Labour, Old Labour: The Wilson and Callaghan Governments, 1974–79* (London: Routledge, 2004)

Palayret, J.-M., Wallace, H. and Winand, P. (eds.), *Visions, Votes and Vetoes: The Empty Chair Crisis and the Luxembourg Compromise Forty Years On* (Brussels: Peter Lang, 2006)

Parker, R. A. C., 'British Perceptions of Power. Europe between the Superpowers', in Josef Becker and Franz Knipping (eds.), *Power in Europe? Great Britain, France, Italy and Germany in a Postwar World, 1945–1950* (New York: De Gruyter, 1986)

Parr, H., 'Britain, America, East of Suez and the EEC: Finding a Role in British Foreign Policy, 1964–67', *Contemporary British History*, 20:3 (2006), pp. 403–21

Britain's Policy towards the European Community: Harold Wilson and Britain's World Role, 1964–67 (London: Routledge, 2006)

'Anglo-French Relations, Détente and Britain's Second Application for Membership of the EEC, 1964 to 1967', in N. Piers Ludlow (ed.), *European Integration and the Cold War: Ostpolitik–Weltpolitik, 1965–1973* (Abingdon: Routledge, 2007)

Patterson, B., *The Conservative Party and Europe* (London: John Harper, 2011)

Peele, G., 'European Integration' in Andrew S. Crines and Kevin Hickson (eds.), *Harold Wilson: The Unprincipled Prime Minister?* (London: Biteback, 2016)

Pimlott, B., *Harold Wilson* (London: Harper Collins, 1992)

Pine, M., *Harold Wilson and Europe: Pursuing Britain's Membership of the European Community*, revised edition (London: I. B.Tauris, 2012)

Pocock, J. G. A., 'British History: A Plea for a New Subject', *Journal of Modern History*, 47:4 (December 1975), pp. 601–21

'History and Sovereignty: The Historiographical Response to Europeanization in Two British Cultures', *Journal of British Studies*, 31:4 (1992), pp. 358–89

A Discovery of Islands: Essays in British History (Cambridge: Cambridge University Press, 2005)

Porter, B., *Britain, Europe and the World, 1850–1982: Delusions of Grandeur* (London: George Allen & Unwin, 1983)

The *Absent-Minded Imperialists: Empire, Society and Culture in Britain* (Oxford: Oxford University Press, 2004)

Potter, S., *Broadcasting Empire: The BBC and the British World, 1922–1970* (Oxford: Oxford University Press, 2012)

Powell, D., *Tony Benn: A Political Life* (London: Continuum, 2001)

Ramm, A., *Europe in the Twentieth Century, 1905–1970* (London: Longman, 1984)

Reynolds, D., *Britannia Overruled: British Policy and World Power in the 20th Century*, second edition (Harlow: Pearson, 2000)

Robbins, K., *History, Religion and Identity in Modern Britain* (London: Hambledon Press, 1993)

Roberts, A., *Eminent Churchillians* (London: Phoenix, 1995)

Routledge, P., *Madam Speaker: A Biography* (London: Harper Collins, 1995)

Ruano, L., 'Elites, Public Opinion and Pressure Groups: The British Position in Agriculture during Negotiations for Accession to the EC, 1961–1975', *Journal of European Integration History*, 5:1 (1999), pp. 7–22

Russell, D., '"The Jolly Old Empire": Labour, the Commonwealth and Europe, 1945–51', in A. May (ed.), *Britain, the Commonwealth and Europe: The Commonwealth and Britain's Application to Join the European Communities* (Basingstoke: Palgrave, 2001)

Sandbrook, D., *Seasons in the Sun: The Battle for Britain, 1974–1979* (London: Allen Lane, 2012)

Sanders, D., *Losing an Empire, Finding a Role: British Foreign Policy since 1945* (Basingstoke: Macmillan, 1990)

Saunders, R., 'Parliament and People: The British Constitution in the Long Nineteenth Century', *Journal of Modern European History*, 6 (2008), pp. 72–87

'Democracy' in David Craig and James Thompson (eds.), *The Languages of Politics in Modern British History* (London: Palgrave, 2013)

'Tory Rebels and Tory Democracy: The Ulster Crisis, 1900–1914' in R. Carr and B. Hart (eds.), *The Foundations of Modern British Conservatism* (London: Continuum, 2013)

'The Many Lives of Margaret Thatcher', *English Historical Review*, forthcoming (2017)

Schenk, C., *Britain and the Sterling Area: From Devaluation to Convertibility in the 1950s* (London: Routledge, 1994)

Schofield, C., *Enoch Powell and the Making of Postcolonial Britain* (Cambridge: Cambridge University Press, 2013)

Schwarz, B., '"Englishry": The Histories of G.M. Trevelyan', in Catherine Hall and Keith McClelland (eds.), *Race, Nation and Empire: Making Histories, 1750 to the Present* (Manchester: Manchester University Press, 2010)

The *White Man's World* (Memories of Empire, volume 1) (Oxford: Oxford University Press, 2011)

Shipman, T., *All Out War: The Full Story of How Brexit Sank Britain's Political Class* (London: William Collins, 2016)

Speiser, P., *The British Army of the Rhine: Turning Nazi Enemies into Cold War Partners* (Chicago: University of Illinois Press, 2016)

Spiering, M., *A Cultural History of British Euroscepticism* (Basingstoke: Palgrave, 2015)

Stapleton, J., *Sir Arthur Bryant and National History in Twentieth-Century Britain* (Oxford: Lexington Books, 2005)

Suggate, A., 'The Christian Churches in England since 1945: Ecumenism and Social Concern', in S. Gilley and W.J. Sheils (eds.), *A History of Religion in Britain: Practice and Belief from pre-Roman Times to the Present* (Oxford: Blackwell, 1994)

Tarditi, V., 'The Scottish National Party's Changing Attitude towards the European Union', *Sussex European Institute Working Paper No. 112* (Sussex European Institute, 2010)

Thackeray, D., 'From Prudent Housewife to Empire Shopper: Party Appeals to the Female Voter, 1918–1928', in J. Gottlieb and R. Toye (eds.), *The Aftermath of Suffrage* (Basingstoke: Palgrave, 2013)

Thane, P. and Evans, T., *Saints, Sinners, Scroungers? Unmarried Motherhood in Twentieth-Century England* (Oxford: Oxford University Press, 2013)

Thompson, A., *The Empire Strikes Back? The Impact of Imperialism on Britain from the Mid-Nineteenth Century* (London: Pearson 2005)

(ed.), *The British Experience of Empire in the Twentieth-Century* (Oxford: Oxford University Press, 2011)

Thorpe, D. R., *Supermac: The Life of Harold Macmillan* (London: Pimlico, 2010)

Tomlinson, J., *The Politics of Decline: Understanding Post-War Britain* (Harlow: Pearson, 2000)

Torrance, D., *David Steel: Rising Hope to Elder Statesman* (London: Biteback, 2012)

The Battle for Britain: Scotland and the Independence Referendum (London: Biteback, 2013)

Salmond: Against the Odds, third edition (Edinburgh: Birlinn, 2015)

Toye, R., 'Churchill and Britain's "Financial Dunkirk"', *20th Century British History*, 15:4 (2004), pp. 329–60

Trentmann, F., *Free Trade Nation: Commerce, Consumption and Civil Society in Modern Britain* (Oxford: Oxford University Press, 2009)

Trindade, F. A., 'Parliamentary Sovereignty and the Primacy of European Community Law', *Modern Law Review*, 35:4 (1972), pp. 375–402

Turner, A., *Crisis? What Crisis? Britain in the 1970s* (London: Aurum, 2008)

Urwin, D., *The Community of Europe: A History of European Integration since 1945*, second edition (Harlow: Longman, 1995)

Varouxakis, G., 'Mid-Atlantic Musings: The "Question of Europe" in British Intellectual Debates, 1961–2008', in J. Lacroix and K. Nicolaïdis (eds.),

European Stories: Intellectual Debates on Europe in National Contexts (Oxford: Oxford University Press, 2010)

Vinen, R., *Thatcher's Britain: The Politics and Social Upheaval of the Thatcher Era* (London: Simon & Schuster, 2009)

Wall, S., *A Stranger in Europe: Britain and the EU from Thatcher to Blair* (Oxford: Oxford University Press, 2008)

The Official History of Britain and the European Community: Volume II: From Rejection to Referendum, 1963–1975 (London: Routledge, 2013)

Ward, M., *Celebrating Belfast Women* (Belfast: WRDA, 2012)

Ward, S., 'A Matter of Preference: The EEC and the Erosion of the Old Commonwealth Relationship', in A. May (ed.), *Britain, the Commonwealth and Europe: The Commonwealth and Britain's Application to Join the European Communities* (Basingstoke: Palgrave, 2001)

Warren, A., 'Citizens of the Empire: Baden-Powell, Scouts and Guides, and an Imperial Ideal', in John M. Mackenzie, *Imperialism and Popular Culture* (Manchester: Manchester University Press, 1989)

Webster, W., *Englishness and Empire, 1939–1965* (Oxford: Oxford University Press, 2005)

Weight, R., *Patriots: National Identity in Britain, 1940–2000* (Basingstoke: Macmillan, 2002)

Wellings, B., *English Nationalism and Euroscepticism: Losing the Peace* (Oxford: Peter Lang, 2012)

Wilkinson, J. F., 'The BBC and Africa', *African Affairs*, 71:283 (1972), pp. 176–85

Young, H., *This Blessed Plot: Britain and Europe from Churchill to Blair* (Basingstoke: Macmillan, 1999)

Young, J. W., *Britain and European Unity, 1945–1999*, second edition (Basingstoke: Macmillan, 2000)

Ziegler, P., *Edward Heath: The Authorized Biography* (London: HarperCollins, 2010)

Unpublished Dissertations

Brewitt-Taylor, S. '"Christian Radicalism" in the Church of England, 1957–70', unpublished Oxford D.Phil. thesis (2012)

Cotton, C. 'The Labour Party and European Integration, 1961–1983', unpublished Cambridge Ph.D. thesis (2010)

Jóhannesson, G. 'Troubled Waters. Cod War, Fishing Disputes, and Britain's Fight for the Freedom of the High Seas, 1948–1964', unpublished Ph.D. thesis (Queen Mary University of London, 2004)

Richardson, D. 'Non-Party Organisations and Campaigns on European Integration in Britain, 1945–1986: Political and Public Activism', unpublished Ph.D. thesis (Birmingham, 2013)

Online Resources

British Cartoon Archive: www.cartoons.ac.uk
Conflict Archive on the Internet [CAIN]: http://cain.ulst.ac.uk/
Enoch Powell: The Official Speech Archive: http://enochpowell.info/
Hansard, 1803–2005: http://hansard.millbanksystems.com/
Margaret Thatcher Foundation Website: www.margaretthatcher.org
Oxford Dictionary of National Biography: www.oxforddnb.com

Index

Note: Page numbers in **bold** refer to figures.

'Allo 'Allo, 52
Abse, Leo, 335, 339
Acheson, Dean, 17, 44–45, 230, 323
Act of Supremacy (1534), 307
Act of Supremacy (1558), 235, 244
Adamson, (William Owen)
    Campbell, 159
Adenauer, Konrad, 31, 33, 37, 40, 50
Affluence, Post-War, 46–47
Akass, Jon, 237
Alexander, S.W., 132
Alexander, Sally, 183
Alliance Party of Northern Ireland,
    302, 315
Allied Breweries, 156, 158
Amadeus Quartet, 102
Amalgamated Union of Engineering
    Workers (AUEW), 180, 334, 341
Amin, Idi, 300
An Phoblacht, 312, 313
Anti-Common Market League (ACML),
    131, 132, 335
Anti-Dear Food Campaign (ADFC), 131
ap Gwilym, Eurfyl, 332, 343
Apartheid, 261
Arab-Israeli War (1973), 19
Archer, Jeffrey, 101
Armada, Spanish, 241, 294
Armfield, Jimmy, 107
Arnold, Matthew, 257
Arnold, Thomas, 102
Ashraf, Rana, 273
Association of Headmistresses, 191

Association of Jute Spinners and
    Manufacturers, 168
Association of Professional, Executive,
    Clerical and Computer Staff (APEX),
    179, 338, 341
Association of Scientific, Technical and
    Managerial Staffs (ASTMS), 138,
    157, 175, 176, 178, 372
Attlee, Clement, 38, 42, 257, 259,
    277, 279
  Condemns referendum, 64
Australia, iv, 41, 59, 82, 87, 123, 167,
    256, 265, 269, 438, 440, 478
Avebury, Kina, ix, xii, 186–87, **187**, 188,
    189, 190, 191, 192, 195, 203, 204,
    206, 208, 209, 424, 425, 426,
    427, 428

Bach, Johann Sebastian, 52
Bagehot, Walter, 75
Bailey, David, 106
Baker, Janet, 6
Balance of Payments, 19, 79, 80,
    147, 166
Balance of Trade, 80, 144, 148, 163, 166,
    167, 176, 198
Banks and Financial Institutions, 170
Barber, Anthony, 166
Barclays Bank, 156, 170, 172
Barker, Elisabeth, 33
Barr, Andy, 317
Barroso, José Manuel, 345
Basnett, David, 114, 179

Bateman, Ralph, 159
Battle of Britain, 12, 53, 55, 258
Battle of Calais (1972), 132, 133
Bayern Munich, 130, 366
Bayeux Tapestry, 6
Beauty Contests, 6, 109, 188
Beaverbook, Lord (William Maxwell
    Aitken), 132
Beckenbauer, Franz, 6
Belgium, 5, 33, 36, 84, 171, 197, 423
Beloff, Max, 102, 254
Benn, Caroline, 369
Benn, Tony, 30, 81, 117, 124, 138, 142,
    150, 151, 147–51, 151, 158, 165,
    177, 228, 232, 235, 248, 251, 256,
    283, 331, 336, 342, 347, 350, 370,
    371, 381
    Accused of Communism, 123
    Arguments for Democracy, 239
    Attacks on, 16, 148, 149–51, 255, 381
    Claims 500,000 jobs lost since entry,
      20, 148, 176, 251
    Debates with Roy Jenkins on
      Panorama, 30
    Demotion, 151, 369
    Impact of referendum defeat, 368–69
    Likened to Goebbels, 149
    Military service, 11
    Negative poll ratings, 137
    On Commonwealth and Empire,
      262, 265
    On industrial policy, 85
    On sovereignty, 237, 238–39, 251
    Oratory, 148
    Predicts 'a massive "No" vote', 142
    Predicts collapse of capitalism, 1
    Proposes referendum at NEC, 76
    Publishes 'The Economic Consequences
      of the Treaties', 175
    Refusal to co-operate with other
      parties, 139
    Relations with Powell, 139
    Reluctance to co-operate with
      NRC, 142
    Responds to referendum result,
      368, 373
    Speech at Llandudno (1968), 71
    Tries to commit Labour Party against
      membership, 139–40
    Urges a referendum on membership, 8,
      69, 71, 77
    Votes against renegotiated terms, 140
    Warns of unemployment within EC,
      148–49
Bennett, Air Vice-Marshall Don, 133,
    137, 241
Bernstein, George, 371
Best, George, 8, 188, 301
Bevan, Aneurin, 114
Bevin, Ernest, 39, 42
Bird, Dickie, 365
Birk, Alma, 203
Birmingham Post, 186, 206, 242
Black, Sheila, 193
Blackstone, William, 234
Blair, Tony, 31
Blaker, Peter, 244
Blitz, The, 6, 12, 241
Blue Streak, 44
Blum, Léon, 101
Body, Richard, 181, 195, 353
Bogarde, Dirk, 106
Bonhoeffer, Dietrich, 217
Boniface, Saint, 210
Book, Tony, 107
Booth, Alan, 215
Boothroyd, Betty, 3, 164, 189, 194–95,
    208
Boston Tea Party, 144, 283
Bowels, the Anti-Market, 52
Boyle, Katie, 106, 198
Bradbury, Frank, 366
Brandreth, Gyles, 106, 107
Brandt, Willy, 83, 114
Brennan, Brian, 299, 307
Bretton Woods system, 14, 247, 260
Briers, Richard, 108
Briggs, Asa, 103
Brighton and Hove in Europe, 103
Britain in Europe (BIE), 10, 103–10,
    130, 134, 136, 138, 141, 179, 183,
    198, 199, 212, 250, 284, 346, 349,
    351, 356, 359, 370, 372, 374, 378,
    380. *See also* Common Agricultural
    Policy (CAP); Northern Ireland in
    Europe; Scotland in Europe; Wales
    in Europe
Actors for Europe, 10, 108

Britain in Europe (BIE) (*cont.*)
  Appeals to wartime memory, 13, 121
  Asians for Europe, 273–76
  Broadcasting strategy, 104
  Campaign themes, 120–21
  Chauvinism, 187
  Church campaign. *See* Christians for
    Europe
  Commonwealth for Europe,
    273–76
  Conservative involvement, 110–13
  Cross-party co-operation, 119
  Danger of establishment image, 105
  Economic risk, 122–23
  Focus on Benn, 150
  Food Advisory Council, 288
  Funding, 103–4, 156
  Infiltrates NRC, 138–39
  Launch, March 1975, 99–100, 100
  Learns from Norwegian referendum,
    105–6
  Local campaign groups, 104–5
  Media strategy, 124–26
  Musicians for Europe, 108
  Neuroses, 130
  Northern Ireland in Europe,
    301, 314–21
  People for Europe, 106–7
  Research and Information Unit, 120
  Sportsmen for Europe, 107
  Unionists for Europe, 303
  Use of celebrities, 108
  Use of female models, 188
  Use of polling, 119–20
  Women's Office, 120
  Women's Section, 185, 186–87,
    188–93, 205, 208, 209, 288, 290,
    319–20
  Writers for Europe, 108
  Young Europeans Afloat, 110
  Youth wing, 105, 108–10, 127–28
British Army of the Rhine (BAOR),
  33, 45
British Broadcasting Corporation (BBC),
  3, 30, 125, 126, 260, 326, 345
British Business for World Markets,
  131, 156, 173–74
British Farmer and Stockbreeder, 284,
  286, 287

British Housewives' League, 207–8
British Lawnmower Manufacturers
  Association, 102
British League of Rights, 137, 241
British Leyland, 92, 157
British Petroleum (BP), 156, 159
British Steel Corporation, 157, 164,
  340, 342
British Textile Confederation, 168
Britten, Benjamin, 6, 108
Broad, Roger, 32
Brooks, Jack, 334
Brown, George, 16, 261, 262, 263,
  292, 361
Bryant, Arthur, 237
Buchan, Norman, 143, 350
Bulmer v Bollinger, 242
Burkitt, Brian, 174
Busby, Matt, 107
Bush, Stephen, 382
Butler, David, 22
Butler, Michael, 82

Cadbury Schweppes, 158
Callaghan, James, 76, 77, 81, 82, 113,
  116, 124, 276, 289, 327, 334, 335,
  338, 341, 342, 371
  'Agnostic' on European issue, 81
  Atlanticism, 81
  Attacks EC, 57, 60
  Emphasis on party management, 82
  Enjoys working with European
    governments, 85
  Gloom, 20
  On industrial policy, 85
  On sovereignty, 250
Cameron, David, 2, 375, 377–78, 378,
  379, 382
Campbell, John, 52
Canada, 41, 123, 256, 269, 291
Canavan, Denis, 155
Caribbean, The, 88, 92, 270, 272, 273,
  278, 281, 282, 290, 445
Cartland, Barbara, 108
Castle, Barbara, 12, 140, 142, 173, 185,
  200, 350, 381
  On Benn, 148, 149, 175
  On Callaghan, 61
  On Heath, 113

Castle, Barbara (*cont.*)
  On Lomé Convention, 271
  On Neil Marten, 134
  On NRC, 138, 141
  On Wilson, 63
  Shopping trip to Brussels,
    200–201, 202
Catholic Herald, 229
Catholic Women's League, 191
Cattermole, Jim, 114
Chalker, Lynda, 189, 194
Chamberlain, Joseph, 263
Chamberlain, Neville, 13, 74
Chambers of Commerce, 161, 319, 361
Chapple, Frank, 179
Charles I, King, 237
Charles, Edward, 227
Charlton, Bobby, 6
Charlton, Michael, 31
Chemical Industries Association, 149
Cherrington, John, 286
Childs, Derrick, 218, 225
Christian Socialist Movement,
    227, 228, 229
Christianity, 210–30, 305. *See also*
    Christians for Europe; Northern
    Ireland
  Anglo-Roman Catholic International
    Commission (ARCIC), 223
  Baptist Church, 220, 227
  British Council of Churches, 211, 212,
    213, 216, 218, 219, 220, 225, 429,
    430, 474
  Christian Aid, 215, 221
  Christian Socialist Movement, 212
  Church Missionary Society, 212
  Church of England, xi, 212, 214, 216,
    217, 218, 220, 221, 223, 226, 227,
    429, 430, 431, 432, 433, 440
  Church of Scotland, 214, 218
  Cold War, 225–26
  Committee of Catholics and Anglicans
    Against the Common Market, 212,
    227, 228, 229
  Ecumenism, 211, 213, 218, 220,
    223–25, 299, 300, 306
  Evangelical Alliance, 215
  Free Presbyterian Church of Scotland,
    214, 227

  Free Presbyterian Church of Ulster,
    299, 300, 306
  General Synod, 211, 212, 221
  Methodism, 103, 210, 212, 214, 216,
    217, 218, 220, 221, 222, 223, 317,
    428, 430, 431, 432
  Roman Catholic Church, 214, 217,
    218, 221, 223, 226, 227, 229,
    306, 317
  Second Vatican Council, 223
  Student Christian Movement, 218
  United Reform Church, 214, 221, 224
  World Council of Churches, 220, 223,
    224, 432
Christians for Europe, 10, 211, 216, 227,
    229, 317
  Commonwealth and Third World,
    220–22
  Ecumenism, 223–25
  Formation and goals, 212–16
  Funding, 105
  Internationalism, 218–19
  Official Prayer, 215
Christie, Agatha, 108
Chrysler, 156, 158, 169
Church of England Newspaper, 226
Church Times, 217, 218, 219, 221,
    222, 229
Churchill, Winston, 34, 37, 38, 39,
    40, 373
  Sponsorship of European
    Movement, 101
  Suggests referendum, 64
Churchill, Winston (Junior), 123,
    231, 233
City of London, 156, 374
  Insurance companies, 172
  Support for membership, 170–73
Clark, Alan, 204–5
Clarke, Charles, 108
Clarke, Kenneth, 231–32, 233
Cleese, John, 11
Climate Change, 292, 293
Clough, Alan, 168
Clough, Brian, 107
Coalitionism, 112, 142, 370
Cobert, Carol, 196–97
Cold War, 14–17, 22, 259, 277, 374
  Churches and the, 225–26

Coleman, David, 107
Collective Responsibility, Suspension of, 96
Combat, 304, 315
Comiltextil, 168
Commercial Union, 158, 171
Commission for Racial Equality (CRE), 272
Committee on Invisible Exports, 170, 172
Common Agricultural Policy (CAP), 10, 36, 79, 81, 105, 279, 299, 319
  Christan commentary on, 228
  Criticism, 282–84
  History, 279–82
  Renegotiation, 86–87
  Support for, 284–87, 288–93
  Wales, 339–40
Common Fisheries Policy, 10, 293–96, 363
Common Law, 217
Common Market. *See* European Community
Common Market Safeguards Campaign (CMSC), 12, 131, 132, 134, 207
  Finance, 133
  Language of Wartime Resistance, 12
Commonwealth, 41, 121, 208, 254–77, 278, 281
  And Northern Ireland, 308–9
  And the Churches, 220–22
  British trade with, 41, 43, 48, 49, 163, 169, 259, 260, 279, 289
  Endorses UK membership, 1975, 88
  Europe as substitute for, 263–65
  Gains in renegotiations, 87–88
  Immigrants, 272–76
  Support for UK Membership, 275–76
Commonwealth Industries Association, 373
Communism, Fear of, 15–17
Communist Party of Great Britain, 8, 123, 124, 131, 134, 226, 330
Communist Party of Ireland, 317
Communists for Europe, 10
Concentration Camps, 34, 139
Concorde, 182

Confederation of British Industry (CBI), 120, 155, 159–66, 180, 288, 292, 301, 318, 320, 322, 342
  Expenditure, 155
  Funding, 105
  'Impact Europe' campaign, 159, 160
  Mandate from membership, 161
  Preference for European over US trade deal, 169
  Smaller Firms Council, 162
  Support for entry, 159
  Supports 'political unification', 169
Conservative Party, 279
  Conservative Group for Europe, 111
  Conservatives for Europe, 110–13
  Early reluctance to campaign, 111
  Federation of Conservative Students, 109
  Manifesto (1970), 55
  Manifesto (February 1974), 252
  Opponents of membership, 111
  Wales, 327
  Young Conservatives, 253
Conservatives Against the Treaty of Rome (CANTOR), 131
Consumers' Association, 190, 287, 288, 289
Contraception, 314
Cooper, Henry, 8, 106
Co-operative Women's Guild, 191
Cope, John, 194
Corbett, Harry H., 137
Corbett, Ronnie, 108
Corbishley, Thomas, 212, 213, 215, 229
Corn Laws, Repeal of, 279
Cosgrave, Patrick, 144
Council of Europe, 33, 195, 304
Council of Ireland, 302, 304, 322
Council of Ministers, 36, 304
Courtaulds, 157, 168
Coventry Cathedral, 6, 213
Cowdrey, Colin, 106, 107
Craig, William, 303
Crankshaw, Vicki, 201–3, 208
  Declines post of BIE Women's Officer, 203
  Political activism, 202–3
  Press coverage, 202, 203
  Shopping trip to Oslo, 201

Crawshay, William, 338
Cricket, 284, 365
Crockford's Clerical Directory, 226
Cromwell, Oliver, 165
Crowther, Geoffrey, 79
Cummings, Michael, 67, 369

D'Aft, Francis, 131
Dad's Army, 11, 415
Daily Express, 9, 16, 368
  Celebrates result of referendum, 3, 4,
    369
Daily Mail, 9, 264
  Hails renegotiated terms, 92
  Opposes holding a referendum, 63
Daily Mirror, 106, 113, 137, 187, 188,
    194, 197, 198, 199, 278
  Hails renegotiated terms, 92
  Opposes holding a referendum, 64
Daily Telegraph, 19, 94, 121, 368
Dalton, Hugh, 38
Dalyell, Tam, 358, 462
Darwin, John, 256, 277
Datsun, 158, 168, 169
Davies, David James, 328
Davies, Denzil, 334
Davies, Gareth, 341
Davies, Geraint, 107
Davies, Ifor, 335, 343
de Freitas, Geoffrey, 195
De Gasperi, Alcide, 101
De Gaulle, Charles, 42, 51, 58
  Death (1970), 51
  Resignation (1969), 51
  Vetoes British entry to EC, 46
Deakins, Eric, 135
Debenhams, 156, 158
Decca, 158
Decolonisation, 256–60. See also Empire,
  British
Defence Review (1975), 276
Delors, Jacques, 375
Democracy, Threat to, 20
Democratic Unionist Party (DUP),
  9, 300, 301, 302, 306, 308, 309,
  310, 312
Denmark, 6, 76, 101, 280, 294,
  328, 363
Denning, Lord, 242, 243, 436

Devlin, Paddy, 311, 315
Devolution, 326, 338, 341, 343, 348,
  350, 358
Dicey, Albert Venn, 68, 234
Dickens, Charles, 151
Dimbleby, David, 30
Disraeli, Benjamin, 17
Dissenting Ministers, 85, 91, 140,
    141, 235
  On sovereignty, 238
Don't Know Campaign, 366
Donnelly, Philomena, 313
Donoughue, Bernard, 369
  On Harold Wilson, 59, 60, 86
Doomwatch, 20
Dougan, Derek, 107, 317
Douglas, Dick, 359
Douglas-Home, Alec, 245
Dowling, Group Captain R.B., 338
Dracula, Count, 21
Dunkirk, Treaty of (1947), 33
Dyke and Dryden, 272

Eagle Star, 171, 173
Economic and Monetary Union (EMU),
    80, 84, 170, 377
Economist, The, 93, 158, 244, 277
Eddington, Paul, 106
Eden, Anthony, 40
Edwards, David, 217, 218, 222
Edwards, Gareth, 107, 341
Edwards, Wil, 327, 331, 336,
    337, 456
Egg Marketing Board, 286
Eldon League, 29–30
Electrical, Electronic,
    Telecommunications and Plumbing
    Union (EETPU), 179
Eley, Geoff, 11
Elizabeth II, Queen, 6, 234, 236, 260
Elles, Diana, 197–98, 199–200
Ellis, Tom, 335, 343
Ellison, Gerald, 215, 222
EMI, 156, 158
Emmanuelle, 6, 228
Empire, British, 53, 239. See also
    Commonwealth
  Churches and, 220
  City of London and, 171

Empire, British (*cont.*)
  EC as substitute for, 18, 46, 254,
    263–65, 277, 323
  EC compared to, 235, 313,
    329–30, 353
  Empire Day, 142
  End of, 2, 22, 38, 254–58, 256–60, 308
  Enoch Powell and, 265–68
  Forgetting of, 39, 258
  Legacies, 255
  National Identity and, 17
  Northern Ireland and, 304, 308–9
  Plaid Cymru and, 328, 329–30, 351
  SNP and, 353
Empty Chair Crisis (1965-6), 36
Ennals, David, 123
Entwistle, Pamela, 192
Equal Opportunities Commission, 184
Equal Pay, 204, 205
Equal Pay (Amendment) Regulations
  (1983), 204
Equal Pay Act (1970), 184
Erised, Mirror of, 81
European Atomic Energy Community
  (Euratom), 25, 37
European Coal and Steel Community
  (ECSC), 25, 36, 37, 164, 351
European Commission, 205, 286, 330,
  341, 345, 372, 377
European Communities Act (1972), 55,
  62, 76, 236, 242, 254
  Implications for British Sovereignty, 55
  Narrowly survives scond reading, 56
European Convention on Human
  Rights, 33
European Council, 83, 92, 377
European Court of Human Rights
  (ECHR), 304
European Court of Justice, 242,
  243, 360
European Cup, 130, 366
European Defence Community, 36
European Economic Community (EEC)
  Creation, 35–37
  Nomenclature, 25
European Free Trade Association (EFTA),
  33, 115, 333
European League for Economic
  Co-operation, 102–3

European Movement (EM), 101, 129,
  138, 187, 211, 213, 224, 228
  Campaign in support of
    accession, 101
  Formation and history, 101
  Preparations for 1975 referendum,
    101–2
  Stands aside for referendum
    campaign, 102
European Parliament, 195, 244, 249,
  287, 330
European Political Community, 36
European Recovery Programme
  ('Marshall Plan'), 15, 33
European Regional Development Fund,
  80, 89, 92, 340, 359, 360, 377
European Social Fund, 164, 205, 318
European Union (EU), 1, 233, 345
European Union (proposal), 84
  Ambiguity of, 84
Euroscepticism, 24
Eurovision Song Contest, 106
Eurozone, 380
Evans, Geraint, 108
Evans, Gwynfor, 328–29, 329, 331
Evening Standard, 366
Ever Closer Union, 81, 84, 232, 233
Ewing, Harry, 348
Ewing, Winifred, 18, 98, 354, 394,
  449, 461
Ezra, Derek, 158

Fairbairn, Nicholas, 360
Fallon, Michael, 109
Fanfare for Europe, 5–7, 62
Farage, Nigel, 232
Farm Women's Clubs, 191, 192, 284
Farmers' Union of Wales, 339, 340
Farmers' Defence Association, 319
Farming. *See also* Common Agricultural
  Policy (CAP)
  Northern Ireland, 319
  Scotland, 347, 351, 360
  Wales, 331, 338, 339–40
Fawlty Towers, 11, 463
Feather, Vic, 100, 127, 161, 179–80, 186
  Campaign broadcast, 179–80
  On sovereignty, 180
  President of TUAFE, 179

Feaver, Douglas, 215
Federal Union, 39
Federation of Bangladesh
     Associations, 274
Federation of Student Nationalists, 354
Feminism, 184, 185, 191, 200, 209. *See
     also* Women's Liberation
     Movement (WLM)
   Lack of interest in referendum, 204
   Suspicion of EC, 204
Festival of European Art, 6
Financial Times, 285, 286, 332, 345,
     346, 370
   Praised by Anti-Marketeers, 125
Fisher, Geoffrey, 223
Fishing, 348, 361. *See also* Common
     Fisheries Policy
Fitt, Gerry, 311, 315
FitzGerald, Garret, 304, 457
Food and Drink Industry Council
     (FDIC), 289, 290, 292, 293
Food Mountains, 142, 280, 283
Food Prices, 175, 198, 199, 203, 219,
     232, 250, 278–93
   Rising world prices, 84
Foot, Michael, viii, 8, 17, 61, 137, 138,
     146, 147, 165, 248, 251, 325, 327,
     334, 340, 371, 393, 482
   Compares VAT to ship money, 59
   Dismisses Fear of Communism, 17
   On sovereignty, 59, 231, 238, 248–49
   Reluctant to endanger Wilson's
     leadership, 141
   Speeches against accession, 58
   Votes against renegotiated terms, 140
Foots, Malachy, 311
Ford Motor Company, 158
Ford, Gerald, 83, 368
Førde, Einar, 146, 342
Forsyth, Frederick, 106
France, 5, 12, 14, 16, 33, 36, 39, 42, 44,
     46, 48, 56, 77, 83, 89, 133, 197,
     219, 244, 249, 262, 280, 308, 312,
     316, 329, 338, 349
Frankenstein, Dr, 21
Franklin, Stanley, 147
Fraser, Ronnie, 359
Free Trade Area (FTA), 33, 280
French, Noëlle, 328

Frere-Smith, Christopher, 12, 96, 134,
     136, 138, 139, 151, 234, 241,
     284, 353
   Attacks business lobby, 173
   Becomes Vice-Chairman of NRC, 134
   Campaigning style, 132
   Poor relations with NRC, 138
   Predicts reintroduction of
     conscription, 144
   Responds to referendum result, 373

Gaitskell, Dora, 203
Gaitskell, Hugh, 259
Gale, George, 126, 141
Garavi Gujarat, 274
Gardiner, Jean, 204
Gardner, Piers, 110
Garrett, Brian, 320
Gasperi, Alcide de, 36
General Agreement on Tariffs and Trade
     (GATT), 164, 168, 236, 247,
     248, 351
General and Municipal Workers' Union
     (GMW), 114, 179, 190, 341
General Election (1970)
   Conservative Manifesto, 55–56
   Labour Manifesto, 57
   Lack of discussion of entry, 56
General Election (February 1974), 7
General Election (October 1974),
     325, 348
George, Stephen, 32
George-Brown, Lord. *See* Brown,
     George
Germany, 5, 12, 19, 33, 35, 36, 37, 39,
     42, 43, 45, 46, 47, 48, 80, 83, 85,
     89, 90, 175, 206, 219, 249, 280,
     308, 312, 316, 352, 357, 375, 391,
     392, 397, 423, 439, 481, 483
   Hostility to, 12
Get Britain Out (GBO), 12, 131, 132,
     134, 142, 144, 176, 234, 249, 293
   Battle of Calais (1972), 132
   Common Agricultural Policy and,
     282–84
   Flair for publicity, 132
   Funding, 135
   Inattention to women, 207
   Northern Ireland, 304

Get Britain Out (GBO) (*cont.*)
  Reluctance to co-operate with
    NRC, 138
  Withdraws from CMSC, 133
Get Scotland Out, 346
Gilbert, John, 284
Gingerbread, 206
Giscard d'Estaing, Valéry, 82
Gladstone, William Ewart, 67, 101, 155
Glasgow Herald, 348, 361, 362
Godiva, Lady, 142, 188
Goebbels, Josef, 149, 208
Goldsmith, James, 278, 288, 292, 445
Goodhart, Philip, 22, 23, 72
Gowland, William, 217, 218, 225
Graham, Janet, 190, 288, 291
Grampian Holdings, 361
Grantham, Roy, 179
Greater London Council (GLC), 117, 228
Green Pound, 287
Green, Chris, 109
Greenwood, Sean, 32, 66
Griffiths, Peter Hughes, 340
Grimond, Jo, 99
Grubb, Kenneth, 212
Guardian, The, 1, 14, 60, 71, 93, 115,
  122, 148, 263, 271, 365, 381
Guest, Keen and Nettlefolds (GKN),
  156, 158
Gummer, John Selwyn, 214, 213–15,
  220, 224, 229
Gutrowska, Irena, 138

Hailsham, Lord, 223
Haitink, Bernard, 6
Hamilton, Neil, 29
Hammond, Philip, 231–32
Hardie, Donald, xii, 352, 358, 359, 360,
  361, 459, 462
Harland and Wolff, 318
Harlech, Lord, 101, 213, 214, 341
Harrington, Christopher, 286
Harris, John, 103, 127
Harris, Louis, 124, 136
Harrison, Bob, 135, 176
Hart, Judith, 145, 185, 238, 256, 271,
  391, 393, 414, 416, 435, 443, 446
  Dismisses Fear of Communism, 17
  Opposes renegotiated terms, 140

Haseldine, Norman, 113
Hattersley, Roy, 12, 85, 243, 246,
  405, 436
Hayward, Don, 334
Hayward, Ron, 141
Healey, Denis, 11, 19
Heath, Edward, 4, 29, 100, 107, 110,
  113, 114, 124, 128, 178, 186, 224,
  242, 245, 291, 305, 306, 361, 368,
  370, 372, 381
  Admiration for European Culture, 52
  And terms of membership, 80
  Appeals to Memory of War,
    13, 51, 121
  Attacked by protestor, 1972, 4
  Disdains 'Special Relationship', 52
  Dislikes term 'Common Market', 25
  Dominates referendum campaign,
    112–13
  Formative influences, 5
  Hideous Attempts to Speak French,
    52, 400
  Hostility Towards, 52
  On dynamic effects of membership, 49
  On 'full-hearted consent', 56
  On sovereignty, 246
  Opposition to Communism, 15, 16, 52
  Patriotism, 52
  Praise for, 368
  Predicts food shortages and rationing,
    20, 123
  Resigns as Prime Minister, 62
  Role as Chief Negotiator in first
    application, 51
  Supports Schuman Plan, 51
  Vice-President of BIE, 99
Heathcoat-Amory, Derick, 46
Hederby, Siv, 188
Henry VIII, King, 235, 307
Herbison, Peggy, 359
Hill, Graham, 107
Hinton, Rachel, 200
Hitler, Adolf, 13, 130
Holmes, Erskine, xii, 255, 315, 317, 318,
  452, 454
Home Rule for Ireland, 67
Honest to God, 218
Hooson, Emlyn, 327
Hoover, 343

Hordern, Michael, 108
Hosten, Jennifer, 183
Houghton, Douglas, 187
Housewives' Trust, 190, 288, 291
Hovis, 158, 288
How and Why Wonder Book of the Common Market, 206
Howells, Geraint, 327
Hudson, Miles, 111
Hughes, Aneurin Rhys, 338, 341
Hughes, Cledwyn, 99, 335
Hughes, Roy, 334, 335
Hume, John, 301, 315, 316, 454
Hunt, John, 7
Hurd, Douglas, 97, 103
Hutchinson, Douglas, 308
Hutchinson, Harold, 113, 193

Immigration, 10, 240, 273, 309–10, 376, 378, 380
Imperial Chemical Industries (ICI), 156, 339
Imperial Tobacco, 156, 165
Indian Independence (1947), 38
Indian Workers' Association, 272, 273
Industrial Relations Act (1971), 177, 178, 179, 245
Inflation, 19, 22, 49, 87, 149, 157, 165, 177, 199, 207, 211, 225, 250, 252, 279, 281, 282, 284, 285, 289, 306, 340, 374, 379
Institute for Race Relations, 272
Institute of Chartered Accountants, 318
Institute of Directors, 156, 157, 161, 162, 165, 301, 361
Institute of Economic Affairs, 20
Institute of Grocery Distribution, 156
International Business Machines Corporation (IBM), 157
International Monetary Fund (IMF), 73, 236, 245, 247, 351, 379
Ireland, Bank of, 318, 319
Ireland, Republic of, 6, 294, 301, 313, 315, 320, 322, 332, 360, 363
   Accession Referendum (1972), 101, 301, 312, 315
Irish Catholic, 311
Irish Congress of Trade Unions, 318
Irish National Liberation Army, 299

Irish People's Liberation Organisation, 299
Irish Republican Army (IRA), 123, 124, 131, 299, 300, 301, 304, 310, 321
Irish Republican Socialist Party, 299, 313, 314, 453
Iron & Steel Trades Confederation, 341
It Ain't Half Hot Mum, 11

Jackson, Ashley, 277
Jackson, Barbara Ward, 194, 219, 222, 229, 242
Jackson, Tom, 103
Jacobsen, Sydney, 113
Japan, 48, 158, 164, 167
Jay, Douglas, 72, 132, 136, 151, 174, 179, 296
   Challenges economic case for membership, 174–75
   Favours European free trade area, 169
   Urges referendum on membership, 69, 296
   Vice-Chairman of NRC, 134
Jay, Peter, 19
Jebb, Gladwyn, 261
Jenkins, Clive, 125, 137, 138, 175, 180, 181, 282, 372
   Compares referendum to World War Three, 157
   Likens referendum to Eatenswill, 151
Jenkins, Peter, 71
Jenkins, Roy, 8, 18, 30, 60, 81, **95**, 99, 100, 105, 107, 113, 121, 123, 124, 126, 128, 201, 202, 224, 231, 275, 288, 292, 368, 371, 372, 381
   Appeals to Memory of War, 14
   Attacks Benn, 149, 381
   Debates with Tony Benn on *Panorama*, 30
   On American Power, 14
   On Commonwealth and Empire, 263, 272
   On Security of Western Europe, 15
   On sovereignty, 248–49
   President of BIE, 99
   Resigns Deputy Leadership of Labour Party, 78
   Warns against the referendum, 75
   Warns of Short-term Costs of Entry, 48

Jewish Chronicle, 219, 226, 431, 432
Jewish Telegraph, 431
Jobert, Michel, 84
Johnson, Boris, 382
Johnson, Paul, 131
Johnstone, Kenneth, 212, 220, 221, 431
Jones, (Frederick) Elwyn (Lord
    Elwyn-Jones), 242
Jones, Grenfell ('Gren'), 341
Jones, Jack, 137, 138, 144, 175, 181, 332
*Journal of Imperial and Commonwealth
    History*, 254
Judaism, 109, 219
    Anti-Communism, 226

Kaldor, Nicholas, 138
Karajan, Herbert von, 6
Keep Britain Out (KBO). *See* Get Britain
    Out (GBO)
Kemp, Eric, 221, 222, 223
Kennedy, John F., 194
Kerr, Anne, 132, 207
Keynes, John Maynard, 38, 155, 175
Khmer Rouge, 14
King, Anthony, 2, 22, 23, 32, 66,
    368, 371
Kinks, The, 6
Kinnock, Neil, 138, 324, 325, 334, 335,
    340, 344, 367, 371
Kipling, Rudyard, 257
Kirkwood, Archie, 109
Kissinger, Henry, 83, 304
Kitzinger, Uwe, 22, 23, 125
Kleinwort, Cyril, 158
Koch, Henry, 339
Kristel, Sylvia, 6, 188

Labour Campaign for Britain in
    Europe, 113–14
Labour Committee Against the Common
    Market, 265
Labour Committee for Europe, 60, 93,
    318, 320
Labour Party, 139, 226, 289, 346,
    371, 382
    69 MPs defy whip (1971), 60
    And sovereignty, 58
    Association of EC with capitalism, 58
    Backs referendum, 77

Conference, 1970, 57
    Decides not to campaign for
        withdrawal, 141
    Dissenting Ministers, 175
    Growing opposition to
        membership, 57
    Hostility to SNP, 348
    Labour Committee for Europe, 321
    Manifesto (1970), 57
    Manifesto (February 1974), 79, 80,
        252, 281
    Manifesto (October 1974), 281
    Opposition to renegotiated terms, 140
    Promises 'fundamental renegotiation',
        1974, 7
    Rebellion against 1967 application, 58
    Scotland, 349–51
    Special Conference (1975),
        140–41, 238
    Special Conference, (1975), 92, 94
    Support for Yes campaign, 113–17
    Wales, 327, 334–36
Labour Safeguards Committee, 142
Ladbrokes, 158
Last Tango in Paris, 228
Lawson, Nigel, 273
Le Carré, John, 1
Lean, Geoffrey, 291, 292
Leeds United, 130, 365
Leonard, Graham, 226
Leonard, Margaret, 196–97
Lever, Harold, 78
Lewis, Saunders, 328, 332, 344
Liberal Party, 117–19, 279
    Campaign activity, 118
    Campaign goals and electioneering,
        118–19
    Criticism of, 119
    Longstanding support for membership,
        117
    Manifesto (February 1974), 252
    Wales, 327, 337
Lindsay, Isobel, 352
Liverpool Daily Post, 243, 325, 342, 343
Lloyd Webber, Andrew, 107
Lloyd, Clive, 365
Lloyd, Selwyn, 100
Lloyds Bank, 170
Logue, Hugh, 316

'Lombard'. *See* Tether, C. Gordon
    ('Lombard')
Lomé Convention (1975), 88, 91, 92,
    222, 262, 270–71, 274, 276,
    282, 377
London Broadcasting Company
    (LBC), 126
Longford, Frank (Pakenham), 212
Lovelock, Irene, 207
Lowe, Arthur, 108
Loyalist News, 306, 307, 308, 309, 310
Lucas Industries, 158
Lympany, Moura, 108
Lyon, Alex, 274

Maastricht Treaty, 349, 375
Mabon, J. Dickson, 78, 113, 272, 359
MacDonald, James Ramsay, 61, 92
MacDonald, Margo, 350
MacFarquhar, Roderick, 70
Mackenzie Stuart, Alexander
    ('Jack'), 360
Mackerras, Charles, 108
Mackintosh, John, 114
Macmillan, Harold, 44
    And the Special Relationship, 46
    First Application for Membership,
        46, 50
    On the Commonwealth, 255
Macmillan, Maurice, 370
MacNeil, Angus, 345
Magna Carta, 144, 205, 234, 237
Major, John, 375
Mallon, Seamus, 316
Manchester City, 107
Manchester Evening News, 231
Manchester United, 107
Mandela, Nelson, 261
Mansholt, Sicco, 299
Market and Opinion Research
    International (MORI), 120
Marks & Spencer, 156, 165, 201, 288
    Warns of Shortages, 20
Marple, Miss, 108
Marquand, David, 245
Marshall Plan. *See* European Recovery
    Programme ('Marshall Plan')
Marshall, Michael, 224
Marten, Joan, 200

Marten, Mary-Louise, 135
Marten, Neil, 63, 96, 130, 136, 137, 138,
    139, 143, 146, 232, 246, 283, 293
    Claims to be 'a convinced
        European', 145
    Moves referendum amendment to
        European Communities Bill, 76
    Norwegian links, 145
    On 'Christians for Europe', 216
    Responds to referendum result, 373
    Warns of Communism in Europe, 17
    Wartime Service, 11, 134
Marxism, 223, 226
Mason, Roy, 276, 277
Mather and Platt, 180, 182
Matsushita (Panasonic), 182, 339
Maudling, Reginald, 99, 187
Maxwell, Stephen, 352, 353
Mayaguez, Seizure of, 14
McAlpine, Alistair, 100, 158
McBride, Willie John, 8, 107, 301, 317
McCartney, Paul, 137
McEwen, Jack, 269
McIldoon, Douglas, 320
McIntosh, Ronald, 155
McKinley, Kim, 190
McLaughlin, Henry, 318
McLure, David, 349
Meacher, Michael, 176
Mellish, Robert, 60
Men's Wear, 167
Meredith, John, 337
Methodist Recorder, 218
Meyer, Anthony, 13
Midland Bank, 170
Midweek, 126
Miliband, Ralph, 237
Milligan, Barney, 217, 220
Mills, John, 143, 465
Milne, Jimmy, 178, 349
Milward, Alan, 32, 36, 37
Ministry of Agriculture, Fisheries and
    Food (MAFF), 282, 286, 287
Miss World (1970), 183
Monarchy, 120, 251
Money-Coutts, Ann, ix, 186–87, 187,
    188, 189, 191, 203, 205, 209, 424,
    425, 426, 427, 428
Monnet, Jean, 32

Monsanto, 159
Moore, Bobby, 6
Moore, Henry, 106
Morgan Grenfell, 170
Morgan, Geraint, 327
Morning Star, 9, 143, 145, 151, 372
Morrell, Frances
  Publishes 'The Economic Consequences
  of the Treaties', 175
Morris, John, 324, 335, 338, 339, 341,
  343, 456, 458
Morrison, Herbert, 33, 40, 42
Moss Bros, 158
Mosley, Oswald, 126
Mothers' Union, 191, 192
Motor industry, 168–69. *See also* Society
  of Motor Manufacturers and
  Traders
Mountain, Denis, 173
Munich Agreement (1938), 12, 38, 55,
  74, 322, 373
Murray, Iain, 355
Murray, Len, 177

Nairne, Patrick, 434
Narayan, Rudy, 272
National Association of Scottish Woollen
  Manufacturers, 157
National Coal Board (NCB),
  158, 326, 342
National Council of Anti-Common
  Market Organisations (NCACMO),
  131, 133, 137
National Council of Social Services,
  202
National Council of Women,
  191, 192
National Farmers' Union (NFU), 8, 123,
  199, 280, 340
  And the Common Agricultural Policy,
  284–87
National Front, 8, 96, 123, 124, 131,
  134, 137, 252, 275, 301, 308
  Denied affiliation to NRC, 137
  Disrupts NRC meeting, 137
National Housewives Association, 192
National Institute of Economic and
  Social Research, 166
National Liberal Club, 187

National Referendum Campaign (NRC),
  105, 131, 136, 142, 143, 182, 199,
  232, 241, 249, 250, 296, 349, 351,
  373
  Admiration for Norway, 145–46
  Alternatives to membership, 146–47
  Broadcasts, 144, 146, 283
  Campaign activities, 142–43
  Campaign themes, 143–47
  Formation, 134
  Funding, 103–4, 135–36, 156
  Inattention to women voters, 207
  Internal divisions, 138
  Internationalism, 145
  Lack of Conservative support, 136
  Leaks, 138–39
  Media strategy (lack of), 125, 135, 413
  On Commonwealth and Empire,
  255, 276
  On sovereignty, 235
  On the Common Agricultural Policy,
  282–84
  Rejects celebrity politics, 137
  Responds to referendum result, 373
  Skeleton administration, 135
National Union of Agricultural and
  Allied Workers, 286
National Union of Mineworkers (NUM),
  142, 175, 326, 327, 334, 336, 342
  Votes against Accession, 57
National Union of Railwaymen, 341
National Union of Students (NUS), 108
Nationwide Festival of Light, 228
Nazism, 5, 12, 16, 38, 39, 42, 64, 102,
  123, 132, 217, 223
Neal, Len, 155
Neild, Robert, 138
Neill, Caroline, 196, 197
Nestlé, 158
New Scientist, 290
New Statesman, 93
  Argues for 'delegated democracy', 76
  Condemns referendum, 64
New Zealand, 41, 59, 82, 87, 88, 91, 92,
  124, 256, 269, 270, 281, 282,
  377, 440
  Renegotiations, 87–88
Newsletter (Belfast), 322
Nielsen, Inger, 193

Nissel, Siegmund, 102
Nixon, Richard, 14, 83
Nkrumah, Kwame, 269
North Atlantic Treaty Organisation
    (NATO), 15, 33, 38, 69, 236, 247,
    248, 312, 331, 393
Northern Ireland, 299–323
    Agriculture, 319
    Border Poll, 77, 301, 321, 322
    Commonwealth and, 308–9
    Constitutional Convention, 300, 301,
        321, 322
    Economy, 309
    Good Friday Agreement, 301
    Immigration, 309–10
    Nationalist Opposition to EC, 311–14
    Northern Ireland in Europe, 314–21
    Parliament, 300, 303
    Referendum result, 321–23
    Sunningdale Agreement, 300, 302, 303,
        304, 321, 322
    Turnout, 321
    Unionist Opposition to EC, 302–11
Northern Ireland Labour Party (NILP),
    315, 317
Norway, 284, 294, 342, 362
    Accession Referendum (1972), 100,
        101, 214
    BIE and, 105–6, 201
    European Movement and, 101
    NRC and, 145–46
Norwich Union, 170
Nuclear Weapons, 38, 44, 244, 245,
    248, 277

Ó Brádaigh, Ruairí, 312
Office of National Statistics, 211
Oil Crisis, 19, 21, 83, 84, 157, 285, 289,
    379
Oil, North Sea, 120, 146, 175, 347, 348,
    357, 362, 363
Oliver, Neil, 304
Olivier, Laurence, 6, 103
O'Neill, Berrie, 316, 318
O'Neill, Con, 80, 119, 294, 314, 345,
    346, 359, 462
    Appointed director of BIE, 127
    Payment of, 104
O'Neill, Terence, 314

Opinion Research Centre (ORC), 119,
    124, 161, 290
Opportunity Knocks, 6
Orange Order, 300, 301, 302, 305, 310,
    322, 349
Organisation for Economic Co-operation
    and Development (OECD), 351
Organisation for European Economic
    Co-operation (OEEC), 33
Organisation of Petroleum Exporting
    Countries (OPEC), 253, 292
Ormsby-Gore, (William) David. See
    Harlech, Lord
Ortoli Commission, 83, 377
Owen, David, 78, 129, 371
Oxfam, 221, 259
Oxford and District Trades Council, 176
Oxford Union, 3, 113, 242

P&O Group, 156
Paisley, Ian, 124, 300, 302, 306, 308,
    315, 317, 321
    Negative poll ratings, 137
Pakistani Cultural Institute, 274
Pakistani Workers' Association, 272
Panorama, 30
Paper and Board Industry, 168
Passmore, Thomas, 310
Patterson, Sadie, 194
Paul VI, Pope, 217
Paul, John, 131
Peart, Fred, 286, 287, 406
Peel, Sir Robert, 279
Penguin Books, 158
People's Democracy, 311
Peter, David, 333, 337
Peters, Mary, 8, 106, 194, 301, 317
Pickles, William, 434
Pietrowska, Elena. See Gutrowska, Irena
Piggott, Lester, 107
Pigs Marketing Board, 319
Pilkington, Beverley, 187
Pinder, John, 76
Pinochet, General Augusto, 145
Plaid Cymru, 9, 138, 240, 256, 312, 326,
    327–34, 340, 342, 343, 351, 376
    Anti-colonialism, 329
    Divisions over EC, 332–33
    Economic critique of EC, 330

Plaid Cymru (*cont.*)
  Hostility to EC, 329–31
  Manifesto (October 1974), 329
  On Freedom of Movement, 330–31
  On Regional Aid, 340
  Pacifism, 331
  Responds to Defeat, 343, 344
Plumb, Henry, 100, 127, 199, 284,
  287, 291
Pompidou, Georges, 77, 82, 83
  Supports UK accession, 51
Popper, Karl, 108
Porter, Bernard, 43
Portugal, Fear of Soviet Penetration, 14
Powell, J. Enoch, **54**, 53–55, 99, 124,
  136, 137, 138, 146, 151, 179, 232,
  246, 248, 251, 299, 302, 322, 331,
  332, 347, 349, 354, 370, 381
  And Commonwealth voters, 275
  Compared to De Gaulle, 55
  Compares European debate to Battle
    of Britain, 53
  Condemns business elite, 173
  Contempt for Heath, 53
  Criticises the referendum, 75
  Leaves Conservative Party, 62
  Likens Accession to the Munich
    Agreement, 55
  Northern Ireland, 305
  On British History, 54
  On Commonwealth and Empire, 256,
    258, 265–68
  On decolonisation, 256
  On European Communities Act
    (1972), 56
  On History, 267
  On Immigration, 240
  On referendum result, 373
  On sovereignty, 55, 239–41, 251, 253
  On the Common Agricultural
    Policy, 283
  On the United Nations Organisation
    (UNO), 268
  On the United States of America, 268
  Praise for Michael Foot, 58
  Relations with Benn, 139
  Religious Thought, 216–17, 218
  Resigns from Treasury (1958), 53
  Responds to referendum result, 373
  'Rivers of Blood' Speech (1968), 53,
    139, 275
  Urges supporters to vote Labour in
    1974, 62
  Wartime service, 11
Powell, Margaret, 103
Prentice, Reg, 122, 123, 128, 271, 370
Prescott, John, 195
Priestley, J.B., 106
Priestley, Julian, 109
Prior, James, 72
Proops, Marjorie, 106, 183, 194, 197,
  198, 278
Protestant Telegraph, 306, 307, 322
Prothero, Cliff, 337, 458, 473
Prudential, 170
Public Ownership of Industry, 42, 43, 58,
  75, 238
Purves, Graeme, 461

Qualified Majority Voting, 243, 304

Radio Free Scotland, 355
Radio Times, 126
Ramsey, Michael, 217, 223
Rationing, 16, 20, 21, 38, 47, 123, 146,
  157, 278, 279, 361, 375, 379, 445
Reagan, Ronald, 14
Reconstruction, Post-War, 34–35, 36,
  37, 41
Red Rag, 184
Redgrave, Vanessa, 108
Redland, 158
Rees, Merlyn, 304
Reeve, Phyllis, 337
Reeves, Robin, 332, 343
Referendum, 67–68
  Amendment to 1972 European
    Communities Bill, 68
  And responsible government, 74–75
  And sovereignty of Parliament, 74
  French enlargement referendum
    (1972), 77
  Opposition to, 65
  Precedents for, 71–72
  Ten Minute Bill (1969), 68
  Unofficial constituency referendums
    (1971), 72
  Victorian and Edwardian support for, 68

Referendum (1975)
  Result, 366
  Turnout, 366
Referendum (2016), 1–2, 367
  Comparison with 1975, 376–82
  Scotland, 346
Referendum Act (1975), 94–98, 134
  Advisory, 98
  Broadcasting, 95
  Collective responsibility, 96
  Counting Votes, 97–98
  Creation of umbrella groups, 94–96
  Provision of public funds, 95
  Question, wording of, 96–97
Referendum Information Unit, 18, 263
Reggae, 273
Reid, George, 353, 364
Renault, 168
Renegotiations, 79–90
  Budget, 88–90
  Comparison with 2016, 378
  Impact on public opinion, 94
  Labour manifesto demands, 80, 91
  Purpose of, 91
Republican News, 313, 314
Resistance News, 12, 207
Revie, Don, 107
Rhodesia, 60, 145, 207, 220, 256,
  260, 261
Rice, Marjorie, 193
Richards, Phil, 333
Rifkind, Malcolm, 360
Rio Tinto-Zinc Corporation, 156
Rippon, Geoffrey, 50, 72, 103, 114,
  236, 247
Robens, Alfred, 158
Roberts, Eirlys, 198, 288
Roberts, Emrys, 330
Robinson, Geoffrey, 173
Robinson, John, 218
Roderick, Caerwyn, 334
Rodger, Patrick, 211, 215, 220,
  223, 225
Rodgers, William, 103, 123, 128,
  233, 371
  Resignation, 78
Rollo, David, 355
Rolls Royce, 156, 158
Roper, John, 103

Ross, Willie, 348, 350, 360
  Votes against renegotiated terms, 140
Rotary Club, 338
Rothman's International, 159
Rothschild, N.M., 170
Rowling, Wallace, 87, 269
Rowntree Mackintosh, 158, 159
Royal Insurance, 172
Rugby Football Union, 326
Rugby Portland, 158

Safeguard Britain Campaign, 374
Sainsbury, John Davan, 20, 100, 156, 158
Sainsbury's, 156, 165, 278, 288, 289, 292
  Backs membership of the EC, 3
Salmond, Alex, 10, 345, 350
Salter, Noel, 213, 214, 219, 220, 224,
  428, 429
Sampson, Anthony, 56
Sanders, Deirdre, 198
Sandys, Duncan, 101
Sandys, Laura, 101
Sargent, Orme, 39
Saunders, Graham, 338
Scargill, Arthur, 142
Schmidt, Helmut, 80, 377
  Atlanticism and links to Labour
    Party, 83
  Dismisses EMU, 84
  Vision of intergovernmental Europe, 83
Schofield, Camilla, 257
Schuman Declaration (1950), 35, 40
Schuman, Robert, 36
Schumann, Maurice, 51
Schwarz, Bill, 258
Schwarzkopf, Elisabeth, 6
Scotland, 345–64
  Comparison with Norway, 362
  Economy, 347
  Oil revenue, 347, 348
  Opposition to EC, 348–58
  Referendum Result, 347–48, 362–63
  Support for EC, 358–62
  Turnout, 347
Scotland in Europe, 120, 272, 352, 354,
  358–62
  Autonomy from BIE, 359
  Business Support, 361–62
  Funding, 105, 359

Scotland in Europe (*cont.*)
  Logo, 359
  On oil, 362
Scots Independent, 353, 355
Scotsman, 15, 359, 361, 366
  Rejects Norwegian analogy, 146
Scott, Sandy, 318
Scottish Conservatives Against the Treaty
  of Rome (SCATOR), 349
Scottish Council for Development and
  Industry, 173, 361
Scottish Daily Express, 263, 361
Scottish Development Agency, 357, 363
Scottish Independence Referendum
  (2014), 345, 378
Scottish Labour Against the Market
  (SLAM), 350
Scottish Labour Party (1976-81), 350
Scottish National Party (SNP), 9, 138,
    178, 240, 284, 312, 345–46, 348,
    350, 351–58, 370, 376
  'Independence in Europe', 345, 364
  Campaign Activity, 356–58
  Divisions over EC, 347, 352
  Early support for EC, 351
  Internationalism, 351, 355–56
  Opposition to EC, 351–52, 352–56
  Response to Defeat, 363–64
Scottish Trades Union Congress (STUC),
    178, 348, 349, 350
Secularisation, 211
Seear, Nancy, 189
Serpell, Christopher, 125
Sex Discrimination Act (1975), 184
Sexton, Dave, 107
Sexual Violence, 184–85
Shakespeare, William, 241
Sharp, Evelyn, 127
Shell (Royal Dutch Shell Corporation),
  156, 158, 165
Shetland, 4, 295, 301, 321, 357, 360, 363
Shields, Olive, 198
Shipping, 164–65
Shore, Peter, 77, 124, 135, 141, 163,
    174, 350
  Challenges economic case for
    membership, 174
  On sovereignty, 233, 238
  On the Commonwealth, 87, 255

  Votes against renegotiated terms, 140
  Warns of mass emigration, 177
Short, Renée, 207
Shrew, 184
Shrewsbury Pickets, 60
Sieff, Marcus, 165
Silkin, John, 140, 449
Sillars, Jim, 296, 350, 358, 364
Singh, Bachittar, 272
Single European Act (1986), 243, 375
Sinn Féin, 9, 300, 301, 304, 311–14,
    315, 376
  Anti-colonialism, 313
  Revolutionary socialism, 312
Skinner, Dennis, 176
Slade, 6
Sleator, James, 320
Smedley, Oliver, 132
Smith, Arnold, 222
Smith, Cyril, 123
Smith, Ian, 261
Smith, W.H., 156
Soames, Christopher, 111, 124, 248
Social and Community Planning
  Research (SCPR), 291
Social Contract, 178, 235, 287
Social Democratic and Labour Party
  (SDLP), 301, 302, 311, 312, 314,
    315–16, 321
Social Democratic Party (SDP), 129, 371
Socialist Woman, 184
Society of Black Lawyers, 272
Society of Motor Manufacturers and
  Traders, 158, 169
Solanki, Ramniklal, 274
Sony, 339
Soper, Donald, 212
South Africa, 44, 220, 256, 261, 276, 317
South Wales Argus, 339
South Wales Echo, 196, 341
Sovereignty, 55, 59, 121, 146, 177, 179,
    181, 203, 208, 231–53, 282, 283,
    292, 302, 317, 380
  And the referendum, 74
  Implications of membership, 70
  Loss of outside the EC, 73
  Low salience for voters, 233
  Meaning of, 233–37
  Northern Ireland, 304–5, 313

Spaak, Paul-Henri, 36, 101
Spare Rib, 184, 204
Spectator, 9, 14, 258, 265
Spencer, Tom, 109
Spinelli, Altiero, 85
St. John-Stevas, Norman, 75
Starry Plough, 314
Steel, David, 100, 103, 117, 128
Steeleye Span, 6
Stein, Jock, 107
Stephen, Rita, 189
Stephenson, Peter, 113, 120, 122
Steptoe, Harold, 137
Sterling
    Area, 48
    Crises, 45, 48
    Devaluation (1967), 48
Stewart, Donald, 352, 353, 354, 363
Stewart, Michael, 261
Stewart, Rod, 137
Stock Exchange. See also City
    of London
    Council, 170
    Crash, 1974, 19, 157, 171
    Donations to BIE, 156, 170
    Fluctuations during referendum, 170
Stoppard, Tom, 108
Straw, Jack, 149
Sturgeon, Nicola, 345, 346
Suez
    Crisis (1956), 44
    East of, 45–46, 46
Sugar, 92
    Crisis, 278, 290, 291
Sun Alliance, 170
Sun, The, 9, 20, 64, 99, 143, 164, 183,
    185, 188, 206, 237, 252, 254, 255,
    256, 263, 277, 340, 365, 367, 368,
    370
    Accuses Thatcher of apathy, 112
    Attacks Benn, 149
    Mocks Frere-Smith, 139
    Opposes holding a referendum,
        7, 63
    Supports membership of
        the EC, 18
    Urges 'revolution of the
        moderates', 370
    Warns against extremists, 124

Sunday Telegraph, 74, 111, 196, 241
Sunday Times, 366, 368, 369
Super-Briton, 354
Superman, 354

Tablet, 210, 226, 229
Talfan Davies, Geraint, 457
Tara (Northern Ireland), 310, 452
Tarmac Group, 165
Tate & Lyle, 158
Taverne, Dick, 78
Taylor, A.J.P., 18
Taylor, Humphrey, 119, 124
Taylor, Teddy, 349, 350
Tebbit, Norman, 278
Tellex Monitoring Service, 126
Tether, C. Gordon ('Lombard'),
    138, 173
Textiles, 167–68
Thatcher, Margaret, 9, 111, 115, 122,
    163, 184, 185, 198, 232, 256, 278,
    279, 288, 292, 354, 368, 370,
    375, 381
    Accused of inactivity, 112
    Bootless attempts to woo
        Heath, 111
    Budget renegotiations, 375
    Denounces decision to hold a
        referendum, 7, 64
    Distaste for BIE and Wistrich, 112
    Hails accession to EC, 110
    Hails referendum result, 366
    Invokes memory of War, 121
    Leadership election (1975), 110
    Mobilises Conservative Party for
        referendum, 112
    On Empire, 264
    On sovereignty, 247
    Wears eye-catching jumper, 9, 112
Thomas, Dafydd Elis, 330, 331, 333, 340
Thompson, E.P., 18
Thomson, George, 180, 263, 340, 341,
    359, 360, 399, 422, 436, 443, 462
    Resigns from Shadow Cabinet, 78
Thorn, Gaston, 83
Thorneycroft, Peter, 158
Thorpe, Jeremy, 95, 100, 107, 113, 124,
    128, 368, 370, 372, 381
Thring, Peter, 127

Times, The, 19, 68, 72, 77, 108, 127,
   136, 202, 247, 289, 295, 326
   Opposes holding a referendum, 72–74
Tindemans, Leo, 84
Tomlinson, Jim, 47
Top of the Pops, 188
Towler, James, 173
Townswomen's Guild, 189, 191, 192,
   203, 301, 338
   Condemns referendum, 193
   Referendum activity, 193
Trade Union Alliance for Europe
   (TUAFE), 179, 180
Trade Unions, 114, 134, 135, 136, 138,
   151, 174, 175–78, 230, 318, 326, 336
   and sovereignty, 238
   and women's rights, 184
   Emphasis on sovereignty, 177
   Internationalism, 178
   Lack of influence, 181
   Muted campaign, 180
   Opposition to entry, 57
   Reluctance to fund NRC, 181
   Support for membership, 179–80
Trades Union Congress (TUC), 81, 175,
   177, 178, 179
   Urges a 'no' vote, 157
Transport and General Workers' Union
   (TGWU), 135, 138, 144, 157, 175,
   176, 177, 178, 180, 326, 327,
   334, 336
Treaty of Accession (1972), 159
Treaty of Paris (1951), 37
Treaty of Rome (1957), 4, 33, 35, 37, 56,
   131, 144, 232, 242, 279, 306, 307,
   308, 309, 313, 324, 330, 349
   Article 119 (Equal Pay), 204, 205
Trevelyan, George Macaulay, 258
Tribune, 142, 144, 146, 284
Tribune Group, 138, 259
Trimble, David, 303
Trudeau, Pierre, 269
Truth about Food Information Office.
   See Unigate
Tucker, Geoffrey, 103, 127
Tucker, Peter, 272
Turkey, 44, 228
Turner, Pat, 190
Tynan, Kenneth, 137

U-2 Incident (1960), 44
Udo, David, 272
Ulster. *See* Northern Ireland
Ulster Defence Association (UDA), 302
Ulster Farmers' Association, 319, 322
Ulster Farmers' Union, 318
Ulster Unionist Party, 136, 303, 314
Ulster Vanguard, 302, 303, 315
Ulster Volunteer Force (UVF), 300, 301,
   302, 304, 310, 321, 451
Ulster Workers' Council, 302, 303, 307,
   309, 310
Unigate, 158, 289
Union of Postal Workers, 190
Union of Shop, Distributive and Allied
   Workers (USDAW), 179
Union of Soviet Socialist Republics
   (USSR), 14, 16, 37, 39, 44, 52, 123,
   159, 225, 226, 245, 248, 283,
   375, 380
Unionist Party of Northern Ireland, 301,
   302, 303, 315, 321
United Biscuits, 156, 158
United Europe Movement, 351
United Nations Organisation (UNO),
   165, 236, 247, 248, 259, 261
   International Year of Women (1975),
   184, 209
United States of America (USA), 14, 33,
   37, 38, 39, 40, 41, 44, 45, 46, 47,
   48, 83, 101, 104, 159, 169, 248,
   262, 265, 268, 269, 323, 399
   Declaration of Independence, 144
   Fear of weakness/isolation, 15
   Revolution, 235
   'Special Relationship', 40, 52
United Ulster Unionist Council, 302,
   314
United Ulster Unionist Party, 302
Unneberg, Bjørn, 146
Ustinov, Peter, 106
UWC Journal, 315

Value Added Tax (VAT), 59, 80, 144,
   197, 284
Varley, Eric, 140
Vaughan Williams, Ralph, 6
Vickers, 158
Victory in Europe (VE) Day, 121

Vietnam War, 14, 157
Villiers, Diana, 120, 207

Wade, Virginia, 107
Walding, Joe, 88
Wales, 324–44
  Agriculture, 339–40
  Economy, 326, 335
  Referendum result, 325
  Regional Aid, 340–41
  Turnout, 324, 342
Wales Get Britain Out, 331, 333, 334
Wales in Europe, 327, 336–42
  Divisions, 337
  Funding, 105
Wales Trades Union Congress, 334,
  335
Walker, Peter, 370
Wall, Stephen, 32, 86
War on Want, 221, 259
War, Memory of, 11–14, 242
Warburg, S.G., 170
Ward, Barbara. See Jackson, Barbara
  Ward
Ward, Elizabeth, 195–96, 196, 197, 208
Ward, Irene, 236
Warsaw Pact, 277
Watergate Scandal, 14
Waterhouse, Rachel, 190
Water-Tube Boiler Makers, 102
Weber, Max, 73, 247
Welsh Development Agency, 326
Welsh Nation, 330, 331, 333
Welsh Trades Union Congress, 326
West Against the Common Market, 133
West Country Anti-Common Market
  League, 131, 133
West Indian Standing Conference, 274,
  275
West Indian World, 272, 273, 275
Western European Union, 33
Western Isles, 4, 321
Western Mail, 246, 325, 335, 339,
  342, 344
Westland Aerospace, 158
Which?, 288
Whitbread's, 158
White Papers, 50, 69, 261
Whitehead (Dyers) Ltd, 167

Whitelaw, William, 99, 124, 129
  Military Service, 11
Whitlam, (Edward) Gough, 254, 269
Wigg, George, 55
Wigley, Dafydd, 332, 333, 343
Williams, Anna, 324, 325
Williams, Dafydd, 343
Williams, Emlyn, 176
Williams, Phil, 333, 334
Williams, Raymond, 332
Williams, Robin, 132
Williams, Ronald, 214, 215, 219, 221,
  224, 429, 431
Williams, Shirley, 15, 60, 124, 128, 129,
  155, 157, 185, 189, 195, 229, 265,
  275, 287, 288, 289, 371, 381, 393,
  441, 443
  President of Labour Campaign for
    Britain in Europe, 113
  Vice-President of BIE, 99
Williams, Valerie, 193
Wilson, Gordon, xii, 352, 358, 363, 364,
  460, 461, 462, 463
Wilson, Harold, 19, 57, 81, 92, 113, 116,
  140, 181, 261, 275, 281, 282, 289,
  335, 338, 342, 350, 354, 359, 367,
  370, 371, 372, 375, 381
  Applies for Membership of EC, 50
  Attacks City of London, 171
  Britain's 'frontiers are in the
    Himalayas', 17, 45
  Declares European debate at an end, 2
  Dismisses EMU, 84
  Failure of Second Application
    to EC, 46
  Hopes to dominate EC, 46
  Ill health, 65
  Importance to the Yes campaign,
    115–16
  Longstanding hostility to
    referendum, 64
  Negotiating priorities, 82
  Northern Ireland and, 300
  Not 'emotionally European', 29
  Notes changed character of EC, 91
  On American power, 14
  On Benn, 148
  On NATO, 15
  On Northern Ireland, 303

Wilson, Harold (*cont.*)
  On sovereignty, 61
  On technological co-operation, 60
  On the Commonwealth, 59, 260
  Party Management, 60–62
  Performance during campaign, 115–17
  Preparing to renew application
    (1970), 57
  Renegotiations, 90–91, 377
  Special Relationship and, 46
  Talent for obfuscation, 63
  Threatens resignation, 140
  Victory in referendum, 368
  Wades through excrement, 61
  Withdrawal from 'East of Suez', 45
Wimpy, 158
Winnifrith, John, 282
Winning, Thomas, 214
Wistrich, Enid, 228
Wistrich, Ernest, 105, 126, 139, 326,
    337, 391, 407, 408, 443, 447
  Becomes director of EM, 101
  Conducts study of European
    referendums, 101
  Hostility towards, 127
  Military Service, 11
  Preparations for 1975 referendum, 102
  Recommends creation of BIE, 102
Wives' Fellowship, 192
Wolfe, William, 351, 352, 354
Wolff, Willy, 198
Woman's Hour, 126, 190
Woman's Own, 184, 198
Wombles for Europe, 10
Women
  Assumed to be anti-Market, 185–86
  Polling of, 185–86, 190, 198, 199,
    206–7
  Pornographic treatment of, 187–88

Women Against the Common Market
    (WACM), 207
Women's European Committee,
    192, 202
Women's Institute, 189, 191, 192,
    322, 338
  Funding from Women's European
    Committee, 192
  Tacit support for membership,
    192–93
Women's Liberation Movement (WLM),
    183, 184, 204, 208
Woods, Robin, 222, 226
Wool Textile Delegation, 167
Worcester, Robert, 120, 250
World At War (1973–74), 11
World Trade Organization (WTO),
    236
World War Two, 34, 224, 257, 258
  Britain stands 'alone', 39
  Economic Impact on UK, 38, 41
Worsthorne, Peregrine, 74
  Urges a 'No' vote in referendum,
    111
Wright, George, 176, 334, 335
Wurzels, The, 18

Y Cymro, 337
Yaoundé Convention, 262, 270
York, Michael, 106
Young European Left, 109, 114
Young European Movement, 245
Young Farmers' Clubs, 284
Young, Hugo, 31, 32, 130
Young, Janet, 189, 194
Younger, George, 15
Younger, Kenneth, 42
Yr Ddraig Goch, 331